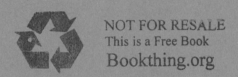

RICHARD
STRAUSS

Advisor in music to Northeastern University Press
GUNTHER SCHULLER

RICHARD STRAUSS

Matthew Boyden

Northeastern University Press
BOSTON

Northeastern University Press

Copyright 1999 by Matthew Boyden

Published in England by Weidenfeld & Nicolson, an imprint
of The Orion Publishing Group Ltd. Published in the United
States of America by Northeastern University Press, by
arrangement with Orion Publishing Group Ltd.

Library of Congress Cataloging-in-Publication Data

Boyden, Matthew.
    Richard Strauss / Matthew Boyden
        p.   cm.
    Includes bibliographical references and index.
    ISBN 1-55553-418-x (cloth)
        1. Strauss, Richard, 1864–1949. 2. Composers—Germany
    Biography. I. Title
    ML410.S93B66   1999
    780'.92—dc21
        [B]   99-21100

MANUFACTURED IN GREAT BRITAIN
03 02 01 00 99   5 4 3 2 1

CONTENTS

ILLUSTRATIONS

A section of photographs appears between pages 180 and 181

Pschorr Beer Hall at Altheimer Eck 2, Munich, where Strauss was born on
    June 11, 1864.[1]
Father and son in a portrait taken towards the end of Franz's life.[2]
Husband and wife in a portrait taken after their wedding in 1894.[2]
A publicity photograph of Strauss the conductor in 1888.[1]
Strauss and cast on stage in Dresden for the first production of *Salome* in
    1905.[3]
Strauss and the production team of the first *Der Rosenkavalier*, gathered in
    Dresden in 1911.[1]
In the gardens outside the family villa in Garmisch, c. 1912.[2]
Strauss, Pauline and grandson Richard, in Strauss's study at Jacquingasse,
    Vienna, c. 1929.[4]
Strauss and cast at rehearsals for the first production of *Intermezzo* in
    Dresden, in 1924.[1]
At Bayreuth in 1933 with Heinz Tietjen and Winifred Wagner.[5]
At Bayreuth in 1933 with Franz and Adolf Hitler.[6]
In Berlin on February 18, 1934 for a concert by the Berlin Philharmonic
    Orchestra.[7]
Conducting at the first *Reichsmusiktage* in Düsseldorf on May 28, 1938.[8]
In Dresden playing *Die Schweigsame Frau* to the conductor Karl Böhm in
    1935.[3]
In Vienna for the first performance of Gerhard Hauptmann's *Iphigenia* in
    1943.[2]
Edward Steichen's portrait of Strauss, taken in New York in 1904.[1]

Sources
[1] AKG Photo London
[2] Lebrecht Collection
[3] Sächsischer Staatsoper, Dresden

[4] Hulton Deutsch
[5] Berlin Bildarchiv
[6] Strauss Bild-Archive, Garmisch
[7] Ullstein Bilderdienst, Berlin
[8] Landschaftverband Rheinland, Düsseldorf

For Lorraine Bradshaw and David Summerfield

But the danger of being uncreative – what do you think? Is it perhaps
still only a danger, or is it already a fixed and settled fact?

Dr Faustus, Thomas Mann

Honour your German Masters,
then you will conjure up good spirits!
And if you favour their endeavours,
even should the Holy Roman Empire dissolve in mist
for us there would yet remain Holy German Art!

Die Meistersinger von Nürnberg, Richard Wagner

It rises up above the ruins of battle, a proud Phoenix – my opera!

Capriccio, Richard Strauss

It's a popular belief . . . that the lives of the extrordinary are
necessarily extraordinary. They are not. We – you and I and all
our humdrum coevals – live our lives down on the sea-level
plains, and we look up at the Andean plateau on which Tom and
his spiritual brethren conduct their lives, and are tempted to
believe that life up there must be an exalted business, full of
drama. But no, a flat horizon is a flat horizon, whether it is a mile
above the sea or is the sea itself. Most lives within our experience
are a landscape of little hills, little dips, more or less rocky paths
. . . The landscape of Tom's life was as mundane as yours or mine,
albeit, as it were, a landscape transposed to a different level.

The Biography of Thomas Lang, Jonathan Buckley

May you live in interesting times.

Chinese Curse

1   AND PARADISE WAS ALL AROUND US[1]

My heart swells with a father's joy as I do myself the honour of informing you, my dear father-in-law, that yesterday (Saturday), at 6 o'clock in the morning, my dear good little wife bestowed on me the happiness of a boy, healthy, pretty and as round as a ball, and at the same time it gives me the greatest pleasure to tell you that mother and son are both well ... I think my wife has already told you that Georg is to be godfather and that, according to her wishes, our small son is to receive the name Richard Georg – Your grateful son-in-law, Strauss.

Franz Strauss sent this letter to Georg Pschorr on June 12, 1864, the day after the birth of his son. Richard's arrival exorcised demons that had tormented him since the death of his first two children over a decade earlier. Three years later, on June 9, 1867, his second wife Josephine gave birth to Johanna, Richard's only sibling.

Franz was born in illegitimacy and poverty. As a child, he and his family wanted for much, particularly after his father, Johann Urban Strauss, deserted them in 1827. The five-year-old boy was then unofficially adopted by his uncle Michael Walter, a tower master in Nabburg, a small town some sixty miles south of Bayreuth. A strict authoritarian, Walter raised Franz in a Catholic-Bavarian tradition that involved an unenviable mixture of violent discipline and vigorous tuition. As the man in charge of local musical events, he introduced his adopted son to a wide range of music. Franz studied guitar, violin, trumpet, dulcimer and Waldhorn[2] – an instrument on which he was an obvious natural. As a child he divided his time between fire-watching from the tower, playing the horn at public ceremonies, and singing in the local choir. By the age of fifteen his future as a musician was assured.

In 1837 two of Franz's uncles left to join the private orchestra of Duke Max of Bavaria and Franz soon followed, enjoying a busy life that brought him before the elite of Munich society. He began composing, had some music published, and in 1847 joined the Court Orchestra – for whom he played the horn and viola for an amazing forty-two years. In 1851 he married Elise Seiff, the daughter of a military bandmaster by whom he had a son three years later. The boy contracted cholera after just ten months and died – followed almost immediately by his new-born baby sister and their mother. As a widower of thirty-two Franz held out little hope of finding another wife.

Two years later, however, he was introduced to Josephine (née Josepha) Pschorr, the eighteen-year-old daughter of a wealthy, middle-class brewery owner Georg Pschorr. It took him seven years to muster the courage (and the savings) to propose, but by the time Josephine married Franz Strauss in 1863, the Pschorr family wielded considerable regional influence (not least for their patronage of the arts), and Strauss – working class and illegitimate – looked to the Pschorrs for the middle-class probity lacking in his own parentless circumstances.

Although Josephine's father took a somewhat medieval attitude to discipline, once claiming that his children were 'beaten every Saturday, whether they've done anything or not – they always deserve it', she enjoyed a secure and privileged upbringing. For this reason, and perhaps because he was sixteen years older than his bride, Franz fell short as a model husband. In 1942 Richard jotted down some memories of his father: 'At home he was extremely temperamental, quick-tempered, and tyrannical, and my delicate mother required all her meekness and goodness to allow the relationship between my parents, sustained as it always was by genuine love and high esteem, to continue in undisturbed harmony ... He was what is called a man of principle. He would have considered it dishonest ever to revise a judgement on an artistic subject once he had arrived at it, and remained impervious to my theories even in his old age.'

In short, Franz was not an easy man to live with. From the outset Josephine looked upon him as something of a patriarch (increasingly so after her father's death in 1867), which helped him overcome some of his insecurities. The aggressive manner, his aversion to compromise and his arrogance were easily explained, but his confrontational disposition made family life a strain. Certainly, the sensitive Josephine (recalled by Richard's sister Johanna as a woman of 'a rare simplicity, modest and undemanding') felt it more than anyone else.

Few were surprised when she began to wither beneath her husband's stentorian personality. By the late 1870s she was suffering prolonged bouts of depression, brought on by a growing sense of inferiority (which Franz did little to dispel), and it was not long before her mind began to fail her. Long stretches in primitive psychiatric institutions made a bad situation worse, and by 1899 Josephine was threatening suicide.

Franz was rather more successful as a musician and the first quarter of the nineteenth century, when he was growing up, was an especially exciting time in the history of Munich's musical life. The 1787 ban on works by Italian composers was lifted in 1805 and The Residenztheater staged many important premières, including Weber's *Abu Hassan* in 1811 and Meyerbeer's first opera,

Jepthas Gelübde, in 1812. *Singspiels* and farces, by Röth, Weigl, Müller and others, were performed at the Theater am Isartor under the direction of Peter von Lindpainter, and when this theatre was closed in 1825 by Ludwig I, operatic life in Munich floundered until Franz Lachner was appointed to reorganise the repertoire, establish a full-time orchestra and create a methodical theatrical troupe. Lachner almost single-handedly defined musical life for middle-century Munichers, devoting courageous amounts of time and faith to living composers – regardless of their nationality. He staged premières of operas by Spohr, Lortzing, Marschner, Gounod and Verdi; and while by no means a natural Wagnerian, finding the composer almost as disagreeable as his music, he dutifully staged the city premières of *Lohengrin* and *Tannhäuser*.

The achievements of Ludwig I and Franz Lachner were fully appreciated by Ludwig II, born in 1845. But where the grandfather had taken a holistic approach to his city's administration, the son was prone to shortsightedness, especially after his discovery of Richard Wagner – whose arrival in Munich in 1864 – effectively squeezed Lachner, and his achievements, from living memory. With no talent for bureaucracy, politics or economics, the state lost considerable influence under Ludwig II, just as it lost a fortune to his passion for castle-building; and although Munich played its part in the wars of 1866 and 1870, the city's reputation was left irredeemably stained. He was murdered, not without reason, by drowning, in 1886.

As far as Franz Strauss was concerned, the young king was the very embodiment of decadence, and Franz was not alone in considering Ludwig's patronage of Wagner a unique marriage of insanity and depravity. The composer's arrival in Munich had coincided almost exactly with the birth of Franz's son Richard, and Strauss and Wagner were thrust together from 1864[3] until the final performances of *Parsifal* some eighteen years later. Although Wagner was swift to burn his bridges in Munich, being forced from the city within just eighteen months (having cheated and exploited both friends and acquaintances), his operas and their admirers (led by Hans von Bülow, who ousted Lachner from his official positions in 1867) continued to wield influence long after his departure. The premières of *Tristan und Isolde*, *Die Meistersinger von Nürnberg*, *Das Rheingold* and *Die Walküre* demanded regular visits by their composer, and the two men became close enemies. Wagner brought out the worst in natural conservatives such as Franz Strauss, which was doubly unfortunate since Wagner thought him one of the greatest horn players in Germany.

Honoured by the conductor Hans von Bülow as 'the Joachim of the horn', Franz was acclaimed for the smoothness of his tone and the security of his *embouchure*. On May 24, 1867 Hans Richter, Wagner's assistant and copyist, paid a visit to Franz in Munich (where the horn player's two-year-old son caught his attention). Although Richter was himself an outstanding horn

player, he considered Franz his superior and, although Richter disapproved
of Franz's hostility towards Wagner, he too was compelled to acknowledge
his talent. But within the orchestra, and throughout the 'good families' of
Munich, Franz had developed a reputation for trouble which was ascribed
to his rectitude and because so few were willing to stand their ground against
him his view of himself became somewhat inflated.

In 1854 Franz Strauss's status was officially recognised by the Munich
Academy, who elected him 'Controller'. He was engaged as professor at the
Royal School of Music in 1871, was appointed 'Kammermusiker' by the King
in 1873 and, in recognition of his services to the city, he was presented
with the Ludwig Medal for Learning and Art in May 1879. However, just as
marriage into money and respectability, when bestowed on a working-class
illegitimate, was unlikely to pass unnoticed, so the ever greater triumphs
that came his way became increasingly a measure of honour for Franz.
Contemporary accounts suggest that, as the years passed, he grew into something of a caricature of the society to which he had so long aspired.

Desperate for the Establishment's warm embrace, it was no less inevitable
that his musical taste should look back rather than forward; as with most
things in life, Franz considered a commitment to aesthetic order as unshakeable as the obligation to his wife and family. Probably the most conservative
musician in the Munich Court Orchestra, Franz, according to Richard, 'worshipped the trinity of Mozart (above the others), Haydn and Beethoven.
These were followed by the Lieder composer Schubert, by Weber, and, at
some distance, by Mendelssohn and Spohr. To him the later Beethoven works,
from the finale of the Seventh Symphony onward, were no longer "pure
music" ... Where music ceased to be a play of sounds and became, quite
consciously, music as expression, my father only followed with mental reservations ... he was incapable of appreciating the later Wagner, although no
one gave as spirited a rendering of the horn solo in *Tristan* and *Die Meistersinger* as he.'

Franz's lack of affection for Wagner's music was as nothing when compared
to his hatred for the man. Wagner violated Franz's uncompromising moral
and aesthetic principles, leaving little hope of reconciliation. On one occasion
he commented: 'You can have no conception of the idolatry that surrounds
this drunken ruffian. There is no ridding me now of my conviction that the
man is ill with immeasurable megalomania and delirium, because he drinks
so much, and strong liquor at that, that he is permanently intoxicated.
Recently he was so tight at a rehearsal that he almost fell into the pit.' When
news of Wagner's death reached the pit of the Munich Staatsoper in 1883,
Franz Strauss was alone in ignoring Hermann Levi's suggestion that the
orchestra rise to their feet as a mark of respect.

When not warring with Wagner, Franz Strauss directed his hostile attentions towards the composer's foremost champion, Hans von Bülow. As well

as conducting the Munich Court Orchestra in the first performances of *Tristan* and *Meistersinger*, Bülow also premièred Brahms's Fourth Symphony in 1885 and innumerable other works defined by their classical principles. Although Franz was by no means an advocate of Brahms's work, he sympathised with that composer's classical predilections. Wagner, on the other hand, represented a break with the long-established German tradition, and anything that disavowed its past was, by his thinking, inferior.

Franz's truculence stemmed, in part, from his assumed responsibilities as a self-appointed cultural (and when prompted, moral) guardian. It is easy to play down the anxiety engendered by works such as *Tristan*, but as a father as well as a musician he considered it his responsibility to protect the classical grail. When his first wife bore him children he had embarked on fatherhood with an academic belief in the significance of his heritage and his country's superiority. He intended to champion an aesthetic doctrine which he considered under threat from Wagner – 'the Mephistopheles of music' – and his disciples. By the time Richard was born, that urgency was amplified by the ever-quickening step of the Wagner cult.

It is worth remembering that the most significant works composed by Brahms and Wagner (*Tristan* and the D minor Symphony) were both premièred in 1865 – the year after Richard's birth – and although the debate would run until Brahms's death in 1897, Franz greeted *Tristan* almost as an affront to the classical spirit of Mozart and Haydn. It was a measure of Richard's character that he was able to distance himself from his father's reductive aesthetic credo and although Franz's influence is sometimes overstated, there is little doubt that the middle-class security of the Pschorr-Strauss household provided an unusually stable platform for the fostering of young Richard's talents.

'WACH AUF!'[1]

June 1864–January 1880

Little is recorded about the first three years of Richard Strauss's life but it is clear he was immersed in music from the start. Franz's long hours of practice and his amateur musical gatherings were the child's most consistent sounds. He is said to have reacted to the violin with tears and to the horn – an instrument with which he and his music were to become synonymous – with smiles. The only reliable recollections of his early childhood come from his sister Johanna, whose memoirs, while bland, are none the less unique. Three years younger than her brother, she remembered him as a 'remarkably beautiful child, curly headed, lively, with sparkling eyes, which could, however, take on a rapt, dreamy expression, as a photo of him as a small boy shows...'

As to his personality, Johanna remembered Richard as a 'lively child and so of course his urge to be always doing something led him into all kinds of mischief'. This mischief was relatively tame. In the 1860s, middle-class parents saw their children almost as infrequently as they wanted to hear them, and as Franz was so often away from the family home it was Josephine's task and responsibility to ensure that Richard and Johanna were brought up in a manner befitting the social refinement of the Pschorrs.

Johanna recalled their 'holy respect' for their father, and how they made him 'so proud and happy'; but Franz found his young son a source of frustration as well as pride. Writing to Josephine on July 25, 1867, he beseeched his wife 'to keep a close watch on Richard, so that he doesn't become so naughty and disobedient, for that might drive me to distraction. Take care not to let him have too much to do with bad children. He may be as lively and as merry as can be, but he shall not be naughty.'

Franz's menace frequently gave way to despair. On May 17, 1868, for example, he wrote to the long-suffering Josephine: 'I pray to God every day that He will not visit unhappiness upon us through our children. For the only thing that stands up to all the tests of life is a firm, wholesome upbringing based on a strict but loving foundation.' According to Johanna, her 'ever-kind' mother helped 'pour oil on the troubled waters'.

Nevertheless, Richard's emerging sympathy for music was an unexpectedly cathartic development and, whenever Franz had the time, father and son would walk to the Marienplatz to hear the band play at the Changing of the Guard: 'Richard takes great delight in the music,' he wrote to Josephine; 'when we were making our way home he whistled the tune of the whole march on the horn, but I couldn't, because I paid no attention to it.'

Six months later, when Richard was four and a half, Franz asked a colleague from the Munich Court Orchestra[2] to give him piano lessons. With Josephine's encouragement and enthusiasm the boy made swift progress, learning to play, from memory, a number of tunes from a book of operatic arrangements. Later that year he completed his first composition, a *Weihnachtslied* (Christmas carol), but as he was unable to manage the words as easily as the three-part music, these had to be written out by his mother. A few months later he composed his *Schneider* (Tailor) *Polka* – which has survived in Franz's hand. By the middle of 1870 he was enrolled at the Cathedral School where, according to Johanna, he quickly made 'a whole crowd of friends'.

There is little doubt that Richard was unusually gifted as a child; although he never shone as brightly as the wunderkinds Mozart, Mendelssohn and Saint-Saëns, he was far in advance of his peers, both in musical sympathy and intellectual capacity. His earliest studies took him no further than the rudiments of music, allowing for a sense of fun to enter what is frequently an arduous and painful process, but within just four years he was able to play Mozart sonatas to visitors and, as Johanna recalled, 'sight-reading presented him with no problems'.

Richard never studied music with his father. By the time he was old enough to hold his own in Franz's company there was nothing for the boy to learn that the man could teach. Consequently, Franz's influence on Richard was almost exclusively ideological. While others[3] instructed Richard in counter-point, harmony, melody and instrumentation, Franz remained a general guide as to what (and who) was to be considered central to a young boy's musical education. Under his guidance Richard decided that the gods of music were Bach and Haydn. Beethoven was too daring (according to Johanna 'the first time he heard a Beethoven symphony he did not understand it, remained unmoved and even said he didn't care for it') and Weber was downright radical – the appearance of Samiel in *Der Freischütz* causing the boy an indelible combination of awe and horror.

The young Richard was rarely exposed to the harsher realities of modern life; and although he was instructed in basic morality, manners and Bavarian codes of responsibility – receiving a constant barrage of opinion on the wisdom of thrift – he wanted for little and was protected from the harsher truths of existence. While contemporary philosophy encouraged an extreme of social pessimism, Richard was weaned on Goethe and Schiller. Conse-quently, the Franco-Prussian war of 1870–1 seems to have made little difference to the Strausses and their family life. But with soldiers parading about the streets it was impossible for Richard not to have known something of the absorption of his home city into a national union. The family may not have been politically motivated, and Franz cared little for politics outside the Munich Court Orchestra, but a certain degree of interest, particularly in educated circles, was taken for granted.

By 1873 Richard's talents were developing at a furious rate. Not long after his eighth birthday he completed a thirty-three-page overture to a *Singspiel*, *Hochlands Treue* (Highland Truth), which he orchestrated himself. He was writing dozens of songs, many for his aunt, the amateur mezzo-soprano Johanna (after whom his sister had been named), as well as piano pieces – one of which, the *Panzenburg Polka*,[4] was orchestrated and performed by his father. As Josephine was away at the time Franz delighted in informing her: 'They were all amazed and said they didn't believe that it was all his own work ... It really is very nice and sounds well. He asked me this morning if the gentlemen had liked it, and when I assured him that they had, his eyes shone.'

In spite of reservations about his piano technique (which he blamed on a failure to practise), and regardless of his weak left hand, he exhibited a superhuman capacity for sight-reading, so that he would eventually be able to sight-read any full orchestral or operatic score, no matter how complex. Later that year Richard and Johanna filled an exercise book with their compositions, including three piano sonatas, one of which, in B flat, was by Richard. Some private tuition followed and, shortly after the death of his great-grandmother Elizabeth Pschorr (whose legacy of 5,000 gulden enabled the Strausses to buy a Blüthner grand piano and take a holiday in Italy), Richard was sent to the Ludwig Grammar School in Munich.

He was a model student, working hard at every subject except mathematics, which he found impossible. Many years later it was a running joke that Richard no longer feared his innumeracy because he employed an army of bookkeepers to do his counting for him. Aware that music was but one of the humanities, Richard never allowed his preferred subject to interfere with his other studies, and he read voraciously, consuming huge amounts of classical and contemporary literature.

At the end of his first year Carl Welzhofer, Richard's form master, wrote the following report:

There can be few pupils in whom a sense of duty, talent and liveliness are united to the degree that they are in this boy. His enthusiasm is very great, he enjoys learning and finds it easy. He attends closely in class; nothing escapes him. And yet he is incapable of sitting still for a moment, he finds a bench a very tiresome object. Unclouded merriment and high spirits sparkle in his eyes day after day; candour and good nature are written on his face. His work is good, very good.

No teacher could help but take to a boy like this, indeed it is almost difficult to conceal one's preference. Strauss is a promising musical talent.

That Richard was considered merely a 'promising musical talent' might, in retrospect, seem odd; but in 1875 (the year he first began piano lessons with Carl Niest) he was no more remarkable than many another gifted child. Music in the 1870s was a luxury for the many, and the heart of most German domestic life. Nearly everyone with an education could read music, and elemental skill with an instrument was taken for granted. Typically for a prominent middle-class family, the Strausses considered music the hearth-stone of respectable family life. In their apartment in the Pschorr house, surrounded by spacious windows, cherry-wood Biedermeier furniture and austere family portraits, the Blüthner enjoyed pride of place in the main room and it was from there that the evening's entertainment grew. Everyone played an instrument and family concerts were regular events. One such gathering, for which a lavishly designed programme was produced, is documented in a letter written by Richard to Franz on July 31, 1878:

> The Pschorrs came back on Saturday evening and I at once threw myself into organising a concert at which the following were performed: Enghausen's C major Sonata, played by Robert, then the Tirolean folk song *Hans und Lise*, sung very prettily by Johanna, who was given a very pretty bouquet by Aunt Johanna, just like a proper singer, and very well accompanied by Robert; they both reaped great success. Then August played one of Mendelssohn-Bartholdy's 'Songs without Words' with – I am sorry to have to say – very little style or finesse; then August and I played *Ich wollt', meine Liebe ergösse sich*, also by M.B., in which we both pleased greatly. Then I played Weber's E flat Rondo to loud applause. The 'Toy Symphony' was given a most successful performance conducted and directed by me alone, but with everyone contributing their mites to its good conclusion and performing their parts very well.

In June 1876 his father joined the orchestra at Bayreuth for the first complete performance of Wagner's *Ring* cycle. After the festival the Strauss family left for the Italian Alps and a much-needed holiday for Franz, who had begun to suffer from mild asthma. As usual, the family stayed at the Black Eagle Inn in Sillian, on the border of Italy and the East Tyrol. Richard persuaded the innkeeper to allow him access to a piano and divided his time between private thought, composition and lengthy walks. It was during such periods that he developed his affection for the outdoors. As his sister later recalled: 'He had a great love for everything, mountains and forests, meadows and flowers, for all animals … On excursions and mountain walks, fishing, playing in the open air, we children were able to live without restrictions. Sillian was the quintessence of bliss for us …'

In 1878 Richard was trapped on a mountain by a particularly vicious burst of weather. As he recalled to a friend: 'On the way there a terrible storm had overtaken us, which uprooted trees and threw stones in our faces ... we arrived – tired, soaked to the skin ... The hike was interesting, unusual and original in the highest degree.' The next day he 'described the whole hike on the piano. Naturally huge paintings and smarminess à la Wagner.' Thirty-seven years later, in 1915, that youthful musical response was transformed into the mammoth tone poem *Eine Alpensinfonie*.

Back in Munich Richard revised a number of earlier works, mostly songs and piano pieces, and he completed his first official opus – the *Festmarsch* for orchestra. Most of this music imitates Strauss's models, chiefly Mendelssohn and Schumann (although he was critical of the latter's 'inevitable tendency to ride his figures to death'), and by 1877 he had come no closer to his own time in musical aesthetics than Bach, Czerny, Viotti, Kreutzer, Mendelssohn and Schumann. With the exception of the première of his own G major Serenade, performances by Franz's amateur orchestra, the Wilde Gung'l,[5] did little to challenge the young Richard's increasingly fixed preconceptions.

Later that year, however, he began a correspondence with Ludwig Thuille,[6] a talented young contemporary. Josephine Strauss had heard of the young orphan's musical talent and, in 1872, she had introduced him to her son. Before long he was a regular visitor to the Strauss household, and by the time the children began writing to each other in 1877 (after Thuille left to study at the Innsbruck Gymnasium) Richard's best friend had also become his first and most significant guide to the world of music beyond his father's influence.

Their letters, which span some thirty years, are of immense value, not least for the detail they bring to Richard's poorly documented childhood. They trace the evolution of Strauss's attitude to contemporary music and provide concrete evidence for his wildly precocious intelligence. There is a tendency towards blind criticism, but this naïvety can easily be forgiven in someone yet to reach puberty. In later years Richard was irritated whenever excerpts from his correspondence with Thuille were published, but the letters underline the extent of Franz's influence over his son, just as they illustrate the speed with which Richard matured. Sadly, many of Thuille's replies have been lost.

Richard's first letter (like most of the others, on monogrammed paper) was sent on October 5, 1877, two weeks after he first visited Thuille at Innsbruck. He talks of lessons in harmony, violin and piano, of Czerny's *Schule der Fingerfertigkeit*, Field's nocturnes, J. S. Bach's *Well-Tempered Keyboard* and Mendelssohn's D minor Concerto for Piano. In the three letters that followed he tells his 'loyal friend' that he is 'already far advanced in double counterpoint', that he has completed his Serenade in G major and is busily composing songs. His concerts have brought him into contact with the music of Haydn, Mozart and Beethoven and he mentions that the Strauss Christmas holidays will begin on December 22 and end on January 2. He is rude about Wagner's *Faust* Overture, condemns Berlioz as a 'scribbler and hack' and, in challenging Thuille's suggestion that Schubert is better recognised than Mozart, he informs his friend that 'in his own time Mozart was more recognised than now' and that he is 'no longer understood by most people'.

Although Richard's prose is enlivened by conviction and opinion, it tends to sag beneath the endless detailed reports of his own progress and achievement. From his comments it is evident that Thuille, though three years older, recognised his friend's superior intellect. Richard did his best not to let him forget it. His letters are littered with Latin quotations and references to literature that Thuille, who struggled at school, must have found intimidating. In a letter dated February 6, 1878, for example, he wrote: 'I am sorry things are going so poorly for you in class, and I will read a long litany from a prayerbook – for you – Cato said a long time ago: *Ego censo, Carthaginem esse delandam,* that is, I will pray to the gods for you. *Vale! Ego maneo* (It is my opinion that Carthage must be destroyed).' On another occasion he commiserated with Thuille for having failed his exams ('This can happen to the best of students...') and then proceeded to gloat: 'Recently we had a Greek exam, a Greek quiz, a Latin and a math exam, of which [I] passed the first with a one/two, the second with a one, the third a two...'

Richard made frequent reference to prayer (mainly in connection with Thuille's ailing performance at school) and it would seem that Franz's orthodox Catholicism, from whence stemmed a muscular anti-Semitism, was sufficient to inspire a childish Christian reverence in his son. It didn't last. By December 21, 1878, he was writing to Thuille: 'Regarding the saying of twelve rosaries [Thuille was facing yet more exams], I am unable to fulfil your request since, first of all, I don't know the rosary and, second, I have no particular desire to learn unintelligent blather.'

Richard's youthful Judaeophobia was another matter. In March 1878 he sent a long and tedious letter to Innsbruck in which he railed against Munich's Subscription Concerts. Of one he wrote: 'A lightening-quick Jew, name of Josephy [sic] from Vienna, played the splendid E-minor concerto by Chopin, in which I especially liked the Adagio ... Josephy is a good pianist but (says Papa) a Jewish slob.' He then describes a Scherzo by Goldmark – 'another Jew' – as 'Junk'.

In most things, 'Papa's' influence was stifling. When Thuille suggested that Saint-Saëns was a dolt and an ass, Richard replied: 'On the contrary he is a genius ... a G-minor piano concerto of his that he performed here himself this winter was very much praised *by my father.*' Richard later writes to Thuille: 'Papa advises you to give up playing Chopin and to concentrate ONLY on classical music' and when he mentions having stripped three of

his song settings[7] of 'any special modulations' he confirms that the rewrites
were '. . . ergo to Papa's satisfaction'.

Towards the end of October 1878 there were signs that Franz's hold over
his son was beginning to waver, the most conspicuous being Richard's conversion to Wagner. Six months earlier he had written to Thuille: 'Recently I
was in *Siegfried* and I can tell you, I was bored stiff, I was quite horribly
bored, so horribly that I cannot even tell you.' But in October, the same boy
who had recently announced 'You can be quite sure that in ten years' time
nobody will have heard of Richard Wagner' informed Thuille: 'I have become
a Wagnerian; I was in *Die Walküre*, I am in raptures; I don't even comprehend
people who claim a Mozart might be beautiful, who can go so far as to do
harm to their tongue and their gullet by expressing such a thing . . . damn
the simpleton M—, impudent that he is; and may Wagner, in his splendour,
be raised to his magnificently portrayed Wotan as a god in Halvalla [sic].' His
change of heart was formidable, and all but complete by the following year
when, to his father's dismay, he attended his first performance of *Tristan und
Isolde*.

Richard's initial reaction to the work in the theatre (where he took no
notice of the composer, who was sitting only a few yards away) was one of
bafflement. Indeed, it is difficult to imagine how a young boy, addicted to
the 'genius' of Auber and Boieldieu, would have reacted to a work as daring
as *Tristan* when performed by the under-prepared and uncomprehending
Munich forces; but after smuggling a copy of the score into his room he
began to understand the significance of Wagner's achievement. A few months
later, he carried the score to the piano and began to play through the opera,
scene by scene. As Richard started playing, Franz, who was practising in the
next room, realised that his son was airing the dissonant evils of Wagner's
most controversial score. Bursting in, he found not his son but 'a mule', and
as he told his colleagues the following morning, he was powerless when
confronted by such enthusiasm. As the weeks passed, Richard's passion for
Wagner deepened: the more of his music he heard in Munich, the more he
understood the gulf that separated Wagner's intentions from the Opera's
second-rate performances.

Richard's conversion on the road to Bayreuth marked the beginning of the
end of Franz's creative influence over his son, and from the age of sixteen
Richard determined to break with his father's musical authority. Though he
never regretted his classical upbringing, his letters and the experiences he
sought from 1880 confirmed a commitment to modernity that precluded
almost any contribution by Franz. During his sixteenth year Richard grew to
understand the potential, as well as the achievement, of Wagner's scores, and
even if his conversion to Wagner remained incomplete until the emergence
of the composer Alexander Ritter, Wagner helped Richard take his first
tentative steps towards creative autonomy.

3   A FAMILY AFFAIR

January 1880–October 1884

'Do not care for the piano pieces by R.S.[1] in the least – immature and precocious ... Fail to find any signs of youth in his invention. Not a genius in my most sincere opinion, but at best a talent, with 60% aimed to shock.' Not for the first time Hans von Bülow's insight was cripplingly sound. He had used similar words to dismiss the 'talent' of Felix Mendelssohn, and although he would later modify his criticisms, paying Strauss the compliment of the nickname 'Richard the Third',[2] there was nothing in his music before March 1881 to suggest what lay ahead. As far as Bülow was concerned there was no reason to admire music that carried almost no reflection of its composer, and Strauss's early scores are distinguished by everyone's finger-prints but his own.

Fearful that his teenage son might well not realise his potential, and as someone well acquainted with the realities of life as a jobbing composer, Franz pushed him towards as complete a general education as possible. He implored Richard to resist the spell of the Munich Conservatory and see out his time at the Ludwigsgymnasium: 'Then you will be free to take advantage of every opportunity. Whether your talent will last has yet to be seen. Even good musicians find it hard to earn a crust. You'd be better off as a shoe-maker or tailor.' True to his father's wishes Richard stayed the course, and he went on to enjoy his international career having never attended music college. In an age when graduation from a conservatoire was considered mandatory for anyone wishing to pursue a life in music, Franz's counsel and Richard's capitulation were exceptional.

The young Strauss's musical career prospered regardless. During the autumn of 1880 he began sketching his first major concerto, for violin (in D minor, Op. 8), and he heard his *Festive Chorus* performed with piano accompaniment, as well as a setting of a chorus from Sophocles' *Elektra*.[3] The latter had been inspired by his classics master, Laroche, who drew his atten-tion to the third stasimon, which Richard scored for the unusual combination of male chorus, clarinets, horns, trumpets, timpani and strings. Although the work was simple in design and routine in character, the performance at the end-of-year concert in 1880 brought its composer to a wider public than any previous work. During his last two years at the Gymnasium he produced a huge amount of music. Like Mendelssohn before him it was a time of exceptional creativity, and if he failed to produce his own 'Octet', as had Mendelssohn, he made up for the lack of quality with quantity.

During March 1881, no fewer than four different Munich concert halls witnessed performances of the sixteen-year-old's music: on the 14th, Benno Walter, Richard's cousin, with Michael Steiger, Anton Thoms and the celebrated cellist Hans Wihan,[4] premièred the A major String Quartet, Op. 2 (which was dedicated to them). Two days later the soprano Cornelia Meysenheim, part of the company at the Munich Court Opera, performed three of Strauss's songs – *Waldesgesang, O schneller mein Ross* and *Die Lilien glühn in Düften*[5] – and on the 26th the *Festive Overture* was given its first performance by Franz and the Wilde Gung'l.

Finally, on the 30th, Richard's most daring work to date, his D minor Symphony, Op. 69, was played for the first time at the Odeon in a Munich Akademie Hoforchester concert, conducted by Hermann Levi.[6] Scheduled as a new work by 'a youth who has not yet completed his seventeenth year', the symphony opened the concert[7] – which continued with Brahms's *Variations on the St Anthony Chorale*, Mozart's Concerto for Three Pianos and Beethoven's infamous 'Battle Symphony' (*Wellingtons Sieg, oder die Schlact bei Vittoria*). The three movements were enthusiastically received, and Levi brought their composer to the stage to acknowledge the audience's applause.

The work's critical reception was encouraging. The *Münchner Neueste Nachrichten* reported:

> The third of the Musical Academy's subscription concerts included one new work, a symphony in D minor by Richard Strauss. The recent performance of his String Quartet had already drawn our attention to the significant talent possessed by this still very young composer. The symphony, too, shows considerable competence in the treatment of the form as well as remarkable skill in orchestration. It must be said that the work cannot lay any claim to true originality, but it demonstrates throughout a fertile musical imagination, to which composition comes easily.

The symphony's accomplishment was very much a family affair. Had Franz not exercised such wide-reaching influence over the city's musical life, Richard's public emergence would have taken considerably longer and, in all probability, brought him much less. Franz enjoyed 'working' relationships with Hermann Levi,[8] Hans von Bülow and Hans Richter. To varying degrees he was on speaking terms with both Wagner and Brahms, and he was personally known to Munich's most influential critics. He was a major force within amateur musical life and he was considered, by concert- and operagoers at least, one of Munich's cultural vertebrae. In short, it was Franz's status, as much as Richard's talent, that enabled the sixteen-year-old to thrive as promptly as he did.

On May 16, 1882, Richard played two works from his piano pieces, Op. 3, at a school concert in the Great Hall of the Museum, and later that same month three of his manuscripts were sent to Karl Klindworth, a pupil of Liszt and a leading Wagnerian. Of the three, the most important was the Violin Concerto in D minor, Op. 8, which had yet to be premièred. Klindworth was impressed: 'So far as the form of the pieces are concerned, there is little to find fault with, but I could wish for content of greater significance before the young composer embarks on a public career. Even so, I liked the Violin Concerto best, and I should be delighted if it turned out to be effective and viable enough to banish Bruch's G minor from our concert halls.'

Strauss was largely unaffected by his precipitate success. His self-confidence remained acute, and his schooling continued uninterrupted – even if the standard of his overall academic performance began to deteriorate. Towards the end of his penultimate year at the Gymnasium he received the following evaluation: 'Keen, tries hard, but is in too much of a hurry, lacks the capacity to reflect.' His final report, dated August 5, 1882, was no less unremarkable, with no marks for his religious knowledge. The remaining subjects were rated as follows:

Latin   *good*
Greek   *good*
German   *nearly good*
French   *nearly good*
Mathematics and Physics   *middling*
History   *very good*
Gymnastics   *exempted*

Ten days earlier, as a school-leaving treat, Richard had accompanied his father to Bayreuth where he was playing in the first production of *Parsifal* for Wagner. At the dress rehearsal Richard saw 'the Master', but failed to appreciate the gravity of the event or the significance of the composer; only later did he cherish his good fortune at having been there. When Strauss began to conduct *Parsifal* himself – recalling, through his performances, the 'ideal' state in which he had heard it conducted by Levi – he realised how close he had come to the musician who, more than any other, dominated his musical life. It was one of his few adult regrets.

In August 1882, at Franz's request, Richard entered upon a brief and ultimately fruitless period of study at Munich University. Just as the conservatoire – an institution hampered by its regard for the consonant certainties of eighteenth-century theory – would have been a waste of time for a musician of Strauss's abilities, so the university was in no position to teach someone for whom the process of learning was interior and self-motivated. He had been studying aesthetics, philosophy and the history of art long before his contemporaries even began to consider attending university, and he learned more about Schopenhauer and Shakespeare from private study than he ever could have done from 'listening to the drone of a professorial voice for three-quarters of an hour at a time'.

With Franz's blessing, he left at the end of the winter term. Resigning himself to his son's now inevitable course as a musician, Franz urged Richard to undertake his first journey as an adult composer, to Berlin, Dresden and Vienna. He took with him his three most recently completed works: the Sonata for Cello, Op. 6, and the Concertos for Violin, Op. 8, and Horn, Op. 11.

From Vienna, Richard informed his parents that it was an 'ordinary city like Munich, only the houses are bigger [and] the girls aren't any prettier'. He had been prompted by his father to make the best of Franz's contacts and, recalling his own difficult, hard-fought youth, Franz excited in Richard a cynical enthusiasm for making 'friends', an awareness of the blight of politics and an aptitude for self-promotion that were at odds with the propriety and detachment of middle-class tradition. Beginning with Wilhelm Jahn, director of concerts at the Gesellschaft der Musikfreunde, whom he managed to talk into allowing him the use of his private box, Richard set about following up the numerous introductions from his father.

He also paid a courtesy call on Hans Richter, Director of the Vienna Court Opera and the Vienna Philharmonic. He failed to find Eduard Hanslick at home, but did track down Max Kalbeck, another acquaintance of his father's, whom he persuaded to write an article in the *Wiener Allgemeine Zeitung* about his Violin Concerto, due to be premièred on December 5.

Richard's reputation had preceded him – not least because of the successful premières of his Serenade, Op. 7,[9] and his *Concert Overture* in C minor[10] – but he was still required to bolster the audience at his concert on December 5 with complimentary tickets. In the first performance of the concerto he played the piano with his cousin Benno Walter (to whom it was dedicated) as soloist, and with typical openness he wrote to his parents: 'My violin concerto was very well received; applause after the first F major trill, applause after each movement, two bows at the end. Otherwise Walter and Meyer took only one bow after each item, both played wonderfully, I at least didn't make a mess of the accompaniment.'

In June 1883 Richard celebrated his nineteenth birthday. He was over six foot tall, with a long and beautiful face and a flowing head of thick, light brown hair. He was the son of Franz Strauss, the cousin of Benno Walter, and a veteran composer of two concertos and a symphony. He was known to many of Germany's most influential musicians and, despite having composed nothing out of the ordinary, his work was already being published and his music was being played. Franz again determined to see his son make the best of the family name and in September he packed Richard off to Dresden to stay with the in-laws of his friend and advocate, Hans Wihan, and Ferdinand Böckmann, the principal cellist at the Opera.

These were among the most valuable weeks of his life since leaving school. Böckmann went out of his way to introduce Richard to as much of the city's music as possible. As his wife Hélène later recalled: 'He went with my husband to the opera, sat in on rehearsals, and accompanied him to the Musical Association.' In a move worthy of Beethoven, Richard revealed a precocious flair for duplicity when he asked Ferdinand Böckmann to give 'the first performance' of his new Cello Sonata on December 5, 1883. According to Hélène, this 'première' was given at the Musical Association 'to great applause'. But it was not, in fact, the première: as Strauss well knew, it had been given its first performance by the work's dedicatee, Hans Wihan, ten days earlier in Nuremberg.

Strauss spent almost every night at concerts or the opera, while by day he called upon as many of the city's conductors and impresarios as would see him. He played for anyone willing to listen (notably Franz Wüllner[11]) and promoted his recently completed *Concert Overture*. During any free time he sat at the Böckmanns' Bechstein, practising or composing. As Hélène remembered: 'I had to close the grand piano on several occasions ... he used to give it such a pounding.'

Richard now began to take an interest in conducting, inspired by the work of Ernst von Schuch, the Artistic Director at Dresden Opera. On one occasion, according to Hélène, 'He practised conducting with one of my large wooden knitting needles, modelling himself on our celebrated von Schuch; my husband was in the middle of long and demanding rehearsals of Wagner at the time – he took the needle away from him with the words: "My dear Richard, just stop that! I've had Schuch fumbling about under my nose for three hours today, and I've had enough of it!" '

On December 1 Strauss was informed by the publisher Eugen Spitzweg that Hans von Bülow had expressed an interest in performing the Serenade for 13 Wind Instruments, Op. 7. This caught Richard by surprise, since Bülow had shown no interest in his music; but the conductor had been nudged towards Damascus by Franz's persistent advocacy. Regardless of Bülow's feelings for the prickly horn player, there was no denying the security of his judgement, and Bülow was confident of success when he programmed the Serenade for a concert in Berlin on Boxing Day, 1883. Spitzweg further advised Strauss of Bülow's plans to take the Meiningen Court Orchestra to Berlin during the first quarter of 1884 – all of which suited Richard, since he had already resolved to leave for Berlin on December 19, 1883.

The Berlin of 1884 revelled in its prosperity, with the frantic construction of ever grander homages to unification cluttering the city's horizon. The architect of Germany's passive revolution, Bismarck, was proving also to be the architect of brick and stone, advocating a burst of growth unprecedented in the country's history. He remained the Reich's father figure, while the Kaiser served as its military guardian. But, beneath this façade, cosmopolitan elements of unrest, born of unification, were growing. A socialist attempt on the Kaiser's life in 1878 had brought about severe parliamentary suppression of left-wing ideology which, when rejected, led to mounting dissatisfaction with the day-to-day running of the country as a democracy. Pre-empting the Nazis' political negativism, Bismarck's suppression of socialism and, effectively, of liberty caused a noticeable rise in emigration. Between 1878 and 1884, when Strauss arrived in Berlin, this grew fivefold – leaving Germany with fewer 'true-born' patriots and many more Jews.

Arriving on December 21, Strauss stayed with Fritz Fischerdick, the brother of his aunt Johanna Pschorr, before moving into his own rooms above a girl's boarding school on Leipziger Strasse. Five days later he heard his Op. 7 played by the Berlin Philharmonic Wind Orchestra conducted by Bülow, who subsequently commissioned him to write a similar work for the Meiningen Orchestra. The success helped launch Strauss in the capital. Never failing to exploit his father's name and influence, he made many friends and acquaintances, notably the violinist and composer Joseph Joachim, the conductor Robert Radecke, the musicologists Philipp Spitta and Karl Klindworth, the soprano Désirée Artôt de Padilla, the publisher Hugo Bock, the impresario Hermann Wolff and Baron Georg von Hülsen-Haeseler (the Intendant of the Berlin Court Opera).

Living above the giggling and screaming of a girls' school, Strauss began to reveal an enthusiasm for older women. His relationships with girls of his own age, such as Lotti Speyer whom he met on holiday in September 1883 at the Heilbrunn Spa and to whom he had dedicated the song Rote Rosen, were fleeting. For most of his life Richard wanted substance, not sex, and from the outset he appears to have had little interest in women as purely physical creatures. Certainly, the greatest love of his life before, and possibly during, his marriage was a married woman nearly five years older: Dora Wihan-Weis, the wife, for four years, of his friend Hans Wihan.

There were exceptions. Among his friends in Berlin was the novelist Friedrich Spielhagen, whose three daughters were the embodiment of cosmopolitan self-confidence. Richard was particularly drawn to: a 'wonderfully pretty, eighteen-year-old bluestocking with a delightful figure, perfectly beautiful throat and face, shining grey eyes'. She was also blessed with an acute and disciplined mind: 'She really is the most beautiful, piquant and clever girl I've seen for a long time ... I'm frightfully bored with the usual herd that you meet at the balls, that at a pinch you can talk to about the German theatre and – if they've money and you're desperate – you can marry.

But with her you can go on all evening without running out of subjects ... We talk about French plays, Spinoza, the existence of a Higher Being, then we poke fun at the other people there – in short, it was delightful, and I shall not waste the invitation to call on her.'

Another of Strauss's older flames, Grethe Begas (married to the much older Rheingold Begas, a popular sculptor in Berlin), was recalled by Hélène Böckmann, who wrote that Richard 'composed some lovely songs at the feet of the beautiful Frau Begas'. Richard himself wrote to his parents telling them of the 'many agreeable evenings chatting with the amiable lady'. He saw Begas regularly, and it is clear from his letters that she found Strauss irresistible. On January 11, 1884, he wrote to his father that he had 'spent a delightful evening with Frau Begas (unfortunately her husband wasn't there!)', and two days later he wrote to Thuille in Munich that he had been 'received in the most delightful manner by the beautiful Begas – I will give you fuller details when I see you.'

His relationship with Dora Wihan-Weis was more complex. It is uncertain at what point she and Richard began to fall in love, but fall in love they did – and during her marriage to Hans Wihan. They probably came to know each other during the early part of 1883,[12] when Dora's husband, then a member of the Munich Court Orchestra, began to discuss with Strauss the première of his Cello Sonata. As the daughter of a Dresden diplomat, Dora had been well educated and was musically literate, with some talent as a pianist. Five years younger than her husband, she was also strikingly beautiful.

Richard's sister was also fond of Dora. As Johanna recalled: 'She was like one of the family. Herr Wihan was insanely jealous over his pretty and already rather coquettish wife. I often witnessed scenes. For instance, she often asked me to spend the night with her, when her husband came in late from the opera, and sometimes had had a drop to drink, so that she wasn't alone all evening.' Although Richard and Dora exchanged dozens of letters, both agreed that these should be destroyed (Strauss burning his half of the correspondence long before Dora), allowing posterity little first-hand evidence for the relationship.

A photograph of Strauss, inscribed 'To his beloved and only one, R.', has survived, along with a single letter from Richard and three from Dora – one of which, dated October 15, 1889, contains the petition: 'I would like so dreadfully to go to Venice for a few days, tell me, Richard, would you go there with me?' He refused, and by 1890 their relationship had crumbled beneath the dual strain of uninterrupted absence and Richard's fiancée, Pauline de Ahna.

It is hard not to feel sorry for the gentle, kind, eternally dignified Dora. She had wasted her youth on a violent, alcoholic spendthrift, and she would have made an ideal wife for Richard; but the social stigma of a divorce would have been too damaging for the ambitious Strauss. Indeed, the gossip alone had been bad enough. In a letter to Richard after he moved to Meiningen in 1885, Franz warned him to keep his private life in good order. 'Don't forget', he reminded his son, 'how people here talked about you and Dora.'

After the divorce proceedings (during which no mention was made of the absent Strauss) Dora left Germany for America and, later, Greece, where she worked as a lady's companion and piano teacher. They met for the last time in 1911 when Strauss made the mistake of inviting her to dinner with Pauline. The latter was openly hostile, and Strauss was compelled to take her side. Dora accepted the circumstances with grace, and she remained content to follow Richard's career from afar, never losing sight of his precious photograph. She never remarried.

During his three-month stay in Berlin Strauss was able to push Dora to the back of his mind. She may well have been his Marschallin, but nothing could have distracted the young Octavian from the whirl of parties, meetings and performances that monopolised his attention. He saw many new plays, including Sardou's *Fédora*, which impressed him as a work by 'the greatest dramatist (not dramatic poet) since Shakespeare',[13] and dozens of new opera productions, including stagings of Auber's *Domino Noir* and Mozart's *Die Zauberflöte*. No gallery was left undiscovered and no musician escaped his judgement. He was impressed by the pianist d'Albert, awed by Bülow, whom he heard both as a pianist and conductor, and despite the inevitable prevalence of revivalism, then dominating every European capital, he was overwhelmed by Berlin's appetite for new music.

With his father's approval Richard continued to make acquaintances, most of whom found him compelling company. 'I note with pleasure', Franz wrote in January 1884, 'that you are moving in good social circles; it will be of extraordinary benefit to you in your general development; nothing else gives such refinement to the mind and the sensibilities as association with cultivated men and women of fine refinement and nice feeling. What is an artist without a refined mind and warm sensibility?' Richard proved to be of particular interest to the painters Carl Becker, Emil Teschendorff, Ludwig Knaus and Anton von Werner, a latently homosexual group who saw the young composer as a Eusibius or a Florestan, raising his unsullied talent as a beacon for the metal masses. On one occasion von Werner threw a costumed artists' ball, which he asked Richard to attend dressed as 'a virgin maid offering a laurel wreath to Germania'. With his father's conscience in mind, he resisted this imaginative suggestion and, instead, arrived as 'an angel of peace in a Greek tunic'.

It must have been a remarkably distracting time for someone raised by two such conservative parents, and yet at no point did Richard neglect his work. At the back of his mind he never lost sight of the reason why he had gone to Berlin in the first place: to establish himself as a composer. In a hastily written letter to the pedestrian Thuille he described his day: 'In spite of never getting up before 11 (I seldom get to bed before 1.30, very often it's 3 or 4, and it was 7 after the Artists' Ball) and spending every evening in society or at the theatre or a concert, and paying calls most days or writing letters, I have not been idle, and I hope that by the time I return to Munich you will have decided on the tempo and key of the Adagio.' This last comment was a reference to Thuille's slow progress with his own symphony, in F minor, which he would not, in fact, complete for another two years. At the time of writing Strauss had managed to finish his own Second Symphony, also in F minor, as well as a number of the piano pieces, Op. 9.

In February 1884, Bülow's promised performance by the Meiningen Court Orchestra of Richard's Serenade, Op. 7, was announced in the Berlin press for the 27th. Strauss well understood the importance of the concert, which grew dramatically when Benjamin Bilse, a hack conductor at the Konzerthaus, decided to steal a march on Bülow by giving the Serenade's first performance ten days earlier. Strauss was horrified, since Bülow's sensitive nature might well have caused him to back down from his initial promise, but the performance went ahead – even if it was conducted by the less prestigious Franz Mannstädt. As Strauss wrote to his parents, Bülow was 'very amiable, very well-disposed and very witty and told me to come to the rehearsal on Wednesday, so that I could hear him conduct my Serenade himself. He lavished unusual praise on it and afterwards invited all the players to give me a round of applause, and himself joined in.'

Strauss left Berlin at the end of March. He spent Holy Week with friends and in April he was back in Munich, playing with the Wilde Gung'l – a considerable step backwards for someone who had only recently heard one of his works performed in the German capital by the world's greatest orchestra. He tried to maintain a steady flow of new work, concentrating on his technically ambitious setting of Goethe's *Wandrers Sturmlied* for Chorus and Orchestra; but Munich was a staid and conservative city for the wide-eyed composer.

Returned to the bosom of his family, he was absorbed into the unchanging Strauss–Pschorr pattern of life; having recently sat at the feet of musical figures like Richter, Spitta and Klindworth it must have been difficult listening to his father's potted wisdom: 'When you are doing something new, make sure that it is melodious and not too heavy, and that it's pianistic. Increasingly, it's my experience that only melodious music makes a lasting impression on musicians and amateurs, and melody is the most viable element in music.' On occasion Franz revealed unusual perception. Writing to Richard shortly before his return to Munich, he announced: 'In art ... truth is the principal determining factor. There is no art which does not rest on deep, inner truth. External stimuli may excite the audience but they will not give an inner spiritual quality. In art, the world of the sensibilities is the primary factor, the critical element must, if it is to be true art, take the second place. This is the only thing that enables art to bestow the inner spiritual quality. All the head has to do is put things in the right order, but where both factors complement each other, a work of art can be created.'

Throughout the spring and summer months Franz continued to hand down his learning to his son, and Richard appears to have allowed something of a return to the father–son routine which had existed before his visit to Berlin. On October 22, however, he received breathtaking news from his publisher, Eugen Spitzweg. Hans von Bülow wanted to programme the Serenade, Op. 7, for a matinée performance by the Meiningen Court Orchestra at the Odeonsaal in Munich. More importantly, he wanted the composer to conduct the work himself.

This marked the end of Franz's influence over his son and also brought Richard's insulated family life to a close. None of Franz's contacts, and nothing within his experience, could rival the promise of Spitzweg's letter. With this invitation, Strauss's life was to take a determined course away from his family, and towards one of Europe's most influential musicians, Hans von Bülow – the man who, three years earlier, had denounced Strauss as 'at best a talent'.

4   MENTORS

October 1884–April 1886

Though celebrated as an autocrat, Hans von Bülow was also prone to bursts of extravagant generosity: his offer to schedule Strauss's Serenade in 1884 was not without precedent, but his suggestion that the composer conduct it himself was. Not only had Strauss never conducted in public, he had never seriously expected to. Like Wagner before him, he was happy to allow others the pleasure of bringing his music before the public. To his critics, Bülow was turning the hallowed Meiningen podium into a sacrificial altar. Having next to no experience of playing in an orchestra, and having never worked as a répétiteur, Strauss's limited understanding of conducting had been gleaned from seeing others do it. Being able to write for eighty players does not necessarily mean that a composer will know how to conduct them.

Of course, the prospect of such a responsibility terrified young Richard. His father had never allowed him in front of the Wilde Gung'l, and now he was being asked to conduct an orchestra that had worked for Wagner, Brahms and, more worryingly, Hans von Bülow.[1] Strauss's foremost concern was rehearsal time. Even for a work as linear as the *Concert Overture* it was clear that he would need considerable time to prepare, and since Bülow was famed for working his players to the point of exhaustion he felt confident of being able to make his mistakes prior to the performance.

On the morning of November 18, 1884 – the day of the concert – Strauss collected Bülow from his hotel, and the two made their way to the Odeon. The conductor was in a fearful mood and, according to Strauss, 'as we went up the steps of the Odeon, he positively raved against Munich, which had driven out Wagner and himself ... he called the Odeon a cross between a church and a stock exchange, in short, he was as charmingly unbearable as he could only be when he was furious about something.'

Strauss's recollections of his performance (which took place 'in a state of slight coma') are vague, but he remembered having made 'no blunders'. Bülow chose not to listen but, instead, paced up and down the green-room chain-smoking. When Strauss returned from the podium, his fit-to-burst father emerged through another door and the two headed towards the cloud of smoke that was Bülow. As Franz began to thank him for having helped his son, the conductor whirled on his adversary and hissed, 'You have nothing to thank me for. I have not forgotten what you have done to me in this damned city of Munich. What I did today I did because your son has talent and not for you.' Franz turned and marched from the room, leaving his son's debut 'thoroughly spoiled'; but Richard made no attempt to follow his father; instead he remained with Bülow who was suddenly, if not unsurprisingly, in 'the best of spirits'.

Only the cynical would suggest Bülow had helped Strauss purely for the pleasure of humiliating his father; but the conductor must have been aware that of all those who could have assisted Richard's career he was the last person Franz would have wished upon his son. After all, Bülow was wholly ignorant of Richard's skills as a performer, and it is worth noting the relative mediocrity of the Serenade that drew master and student together in the first place. Richard claimed that Franz 'bore no grudge against his son's benefactor', but there is no evidence for any such atonement. Indeed, of the two, Bülow was demonstrably the more forgiving. In 1886 Bülow informed Richard of his intention to visit Franz in Munich. Richard thought it best to warn his father in advance and wrote, asking him to be on his best behaviour; when Bülow arrived he found only Josephine. Franz had gone out, leaving his wife to engage the famously terse conductor in what must have been painfully small talk.

While Franz conceded the benefits of Bülow's unique authority, he was overjoyed when Theodore Thomas announced his plan to mount the world première of Richard's new Symphony in F minor. A German-born American conductor based in New York, Thomas had called on Franz shortly before Richard's return from Berlin. Having discussed the varying merits of contemporary music, Franz drew Thomas's attention to Richard's latest symphonic effort. The American was instantly captivated by the work's grand, contrapuntal gestures and he agreed to take the score back with him to America.

The première, given by the New York Philharmonic Society Orchestra[2] on December 13, 1884, was the first American performance of anything by Strauss. Unfortunately, neither the audience nor the critics were much impressed, and the hoped-for triumph failed to materialise. The German response to the symphony (conducted in Cologne by Wüllner on January 13, 1885) was less muted, and the performance and its reception – witnessed by Bülow – justified Strauss's faith in the work and its spurious novelty ('Papa will open his eyes wide when he hears how modern the symphony sounds').

On May 26, 1885, Richard was informed that Bülow's assistant at Meiningen, Franz Mannstädt,[3] had been summoned to Berlin by the Philharmonic. This left a much-sought-after vacancy, for which Felix von Weingartner, Jean Louis Nicodé and Gustav Mahler all made applications, but Bülow had by this stage taken a paternal interest in Strauss and, via his publisher Spitzweg, he inquired whether or not the twenty-year-old composer was interested in conducting the Meiningen Orchestra while he was away – 'gratis and interimistic, in the interests of his education – as a practitioner'.

It was an extraordinary offer, and to an outsider, such as Gustav Mahler – already a bitter rival – Strauss's good fortune was irritatingly consistent. After all, Nicodé had been a professor at the Dresden Royal Conservatoire since 1878 (he would be appointed conductor of the city's orchestra shortly after Bülow made his offer to Strauss); Weingartner had been a student of Liszt's, a conductor at the Königsberg Opera for nearly a year, and in 1884 had seen his first opera, *Sakuntala*, staged in Weimar. Either man would have made a more logical first choice than Strauss, since both had sufficient conducting experience to warrant the respect of the Meiningen players; but Weingartner was proving unpopular in Königsberg and Nicodé was of French stock, and a favourite of Bülow's rival Wüllner. Mahler was Jewish and did not even make the short-list.

Bülow needed no convincing. Strauss appealed to him not only as 'an uncommonly gifted young man',[4] but as someone in whom were embodied many of the human qualities dearest to Bülow's Prussian heart. These ranged from good stock (he promoted Richard to Duke George of Meiningen as 'the grandchild of the famous beer Pschorrs') to trenchant anti-Semitism. Bülow would have never tolerated a 'Jew-lover' and he would have expected any protégé to adopt his philosophies, whether social or musical. But for someone, such as Strauss, for whom anti-Semitism had been a part of daily life throughout his childhood, Bülow's hatred of the Jews must have seemed sympathetic, if not obligatory. Strauss had already heard from Bülow how the Jews had supposedly made life for him and Wagner unbearable in Munich, and he must have known about Bülow's association with Bernhard Förster,[5] the celebrated anti-Semite who in 1880 had enlisted the conductor's support (and signature) in attempting to convince the Reichstag that all German Jews be categorised as second-class citizens. Strauss can have been in no doubt as to where he was expected to place his allegiance.

He immediately accepted Bülow's offer, admitting that it had come as 'the most joyous surprise imaginable'. With his ambition between his teeth he asked if he might 'occasionally conduct preliminary rehearsals', and he added the flattering hope that, by attending all Bülow's rehearsals, he might 'study closely your interpretations of our[6] symphonic masterpieces'.

Richard's success provided a potent distraction from the one blot on his otherwise model landscape. A month before Bülow's offer, Josephine Strauss was admitted to a sanatorium for psychiatric treatment. Franz's tyrannical behaviour, his ranting and raving and general unpredictability had finally proved too much for his fragile wife, and she had begun to believe her family was conspiring against her. The Pschorrs had taken the only course available to them, and paid for her to be sent as far away from Franz as possible.

But the treatment, which initially lasted two months, was medicinal, not psychological, and Josephine was flooded with morphine, resulting in frenzied attacks of delusion and hysteria.

As Josephine's condition continued to resist treatment, Franz grew increasingly despairing. Richard was at home in Munich with his father, doing what he could to alleviate the poor man's guilt. As he wrote to his sister on April 26: 'My optimism and spirits seem to be slipping gradually, there's a limit to everything, I'm afraid, and when I pull myself together as best I can and comfort Papa, it's a waste of time trying to distract him – that's the sad thing – he's becoming more and more unsociable, I think he feels that he's doing dear Mama a moral wrong of some kind if he allows himself to be distracted and doesn't sit all day brooding on our misfortune.'

Gradually, Josephine's condition began to improve. But she never fully recovered and spent the rest of her life in and out of care, sometimes remaining in hospital for up to a year at a time.

At the end of May Richard prepared to leave for Frankfurt where Bülow was teaching at the Raff Conservatory. After a rather subdued twenty-first birthday, he was encouraged by Bülow to make the acquaintance of the Duke's sister, Princess Marie of Meiningen, who was then staying in Frankfurt. He spent the rest of his time dashing between theatres and galleries, making friends and contacts and generally enjoying himself. He saw productions of Wagner's *Die Walküre* and Massenet's *Hérodiade* and he was particularly struck by a performance of Heyse's latest tragedy, *Don Juans Ende*. On June 18 he received official notification from the court that he had been appointed to the orchestral staff, and on October 1, 1885, he arrived in the small duchy town of Meiningen[7] as second conductor to 'the world's greatest performing musician'[8] Hans von Bülow.

Gustav Leinhos[9] outlined Strauss's duties, as dictated by Bülow:

> He envisages your post as non-stipendiary to begin with . . . he would take most of the rehearsals himself in the month of October, in preparation for the tour, but he thinks that would be the best thing for you too, and give you the chance to get to know him and the orchestra . . . Herr von Bülow will also hand over to you the direction of the subscription concerts in the Court Theatre, and would be very willing for you to introduce some of your own compositions into the programmes if you wished. There will be a tour of Holland and Belgium in November, during which period the preparation of an oratorio will be [assigned] to you.

Richard was also charged with the Choral Society,[10] in which sang many of the town's 'finest' ladies, including Bülow's second wife, Marie;[11] but it was Bülow himself who made the greatest impact on the novitiate Kapellmeister. As he recalled a quarter of a century later:

Every day, from nine o'clock until noon, were held the memorable rehearsals such as Bülow alone could conduct. Ever since that time the memory of the works he then conducted, all of them by heart, has never been effaced for me. In particular, I found the way in which he brought out the poetic content of Beethoven's and Wagner's works absolutely convincing. There was no trace anywhere of arbitrariness. Everything was of compelling necessity, born of the form and content of the work itself; his captivating temperament, governed always by the strictest artistic discipline, and his loyalty to the spirit and the letter of the work of art (these two are more akin than is commonly believed) ensured that by dint of painstaking rehearsals these works were performed with a clarity which constitutes for me to this day the zenith of perfection in the performance of orchestral works. The gracefulness with which he handled the baton, the charming manner in which he used to conduct his rehearsals – instruction frequently taking the form of a witty epigram – are unforgettable.

Or perhaps not. Strauss's recollection of Bülow's rehearsals is clouded by distance and sentiment. There is significantly more evidence for the conductor having been a vicious despot, than for his having been a charming sage. Strauss admits that 'when he suddenly turned away from the rostrum and put a question to the pupil reading the score, the latter had to answer quickly if he were not to be taunted by a sarcastic remark by the master in front of the assembled orchestra'; but he overlooks the screaming and the abuse, the humiliation and the capriciousness for which Bülow is otherwise generally remembered.

Bülow was loath to pass compliments – Brahms said that even his praise brought salt to his eyes – and he was always the first to resort to insults. During his time in Munich, for example, he was informed that two rows of stalls would need to be removed in order that the theatre pit might be enlarged. Bülow turned on his messenger, remarking, 'Then there will be fewer *Schweinhunde* in the audience.' Bülow's motives may have been noble, and he may well have fostered unimpeachable artistic standards, but he was not a pleasant man to work with, and it is a measure of Strauss's savoir-faire that he was able to navigate the great man's mercurial temperament.

Richard wisely became a favourite of Bülow's second wife. Whether by design or simply because he liked her, he established an unusually close, familial tie with the childless Marie. She seems to have wielded some influence from within the Chorus, for just seven days after his arrival he wrote to his father: 'Frau von Bülow was absolutely enchanted by the capital way I acquitted myself with the sixty ladies at the first rehearsal of the Choral Society.' Her letters to her absent husband confirm that she, like Bülow, was finding the new addition difficult not to like.

On October 13 she wrote: 'Strauss keeps up his frenetic rehearsing. Three hours yesterday morning on his symphony alone. At the end applause from the orchestra – which he received sceptically and yearns for criticism. Very sensible. Once again the choral rehearsal went very well. I sang so energetically that Strauss paid me the charming compliment of asking me to step out and listen in some of the difficult passages, so that he could find out how the others manage without my assistance.' Flattery got him everywhere. By the middle of November Marie was bursting with affection for the young lion: 'He went to the Casino Ball here on Monday and danced till he dropped. It goes without saying that he has made some conquests, of course the slyboots won't breathe a word about them, but he has not yet been conquered to the point of engagement ... Yesterday Strauss brought me a song-cycle[12] he has written ... I was "critical", i.e. I did not simply praise it, but I also said which bits I didn't care for, which bits struck me as not having been really felt. The young man went away well pleased.'

Amidst all the activity Strauss continued to receive his father's advice. Referring to one letter – in which Franz urged him, 'Don't forget, my dear Richard, what I have often told you, to make the last notes in a figure clear and not to dash them off in too much of a hurry ... devote a little more care to the bass line ...' – Strauss wrote to Thuille: 'Papa amuses me capitally with his affectionate admonitions.'

His confidence was now absolute, and Bülow took to surprising his protégé with ever more formidable challenges. During the second week of October, for example, he informed Strauss that he would have to leave Meiningen for a day during the last fortnight of the month. Strauss was to take his place for a rehearsal of Brahms's A major Serenade. The day arrived and Strauss was doing his best to remain one step ahead of his players when in walked Princess Sachsen-Meiningen, wife of the orchestra's patron George II. Probably at Bülow's request, the Princess asked Strauss to conduct the Overture to Wagner's opera *The Flying Dutchman*. Strauss knew the music, but not so well that he would be able to keep his head out of the score, and so he hesitated. This irritated the Princess who inquired whether Strauss knew of Weber's Overture to *Der Freischütz*. Strauss swiftly reconsidered the initial challenge and, beating time 'with the courage of desperation', he managed to get through without obvious difficulty, thanks mainly to the orchestra, who knew the work intimately, having played it with the composer.

Less than a week later Bülow threw yet another gauntlet at Strauss's feet. He knew Strauss had been practising the solo part of Mozart's C minor Piano Concerto K. 491, and that he had also written a cadenza for the last movement. Bülow scheduled a performance of the concerto, with Strauss as soloist, which was startling enough, but he then informed Strauss that he was also to conduct, for the first time, his Symphony in F minor. To make matters worse, Brahms had asked for tickets.

By his own standards Strauss was not 'a fully-trained pianist'. He had never studied technique with a Liszt or a Leschetizky, and his left hand was weaker than the right.[13] Come the concert,[14] however, all went well: 'When we had negotiated the first movement quite creditably, the master encouraged me with the words, "If you weren't something better, you might become a pianist." Although I did not think that I fully deserved this compliment, my self-confidence had been increased sufficiently to enable me to play the last two movements a little less self-consciously. After this I conducted my F minor Symphony.'

It was here that Strauss scored his greatest success. Critics and audience warmed to the young man's enthusiasm, and the applause was led by Brahms. As Richard recalled: 'In his laconic manner he said to me "Quite nice", but added the rejoinder "Take a good look at Schubert's dances, young man, and try your luck at the invention of simple eight-bar melodies." ' It was sound advice. Strauss's symphony is overwritten, and there is throughout its four movements a reflection of someone trying hard to impress, but his musical training to date had been no less grounded in classical theory than Brahms's. Indeed, it was due to Strauss's feelings of theoretical fraternity that he entered a fleeting but intense period of devotion to Brahms and his music.

In this he was strongly influenced by Bülow; but it seems that the deciding factor in Strauss's conversion was Brahms's new symphony, his Fourth, in E minor. On October 24 he wrote to his father, describing it as 'beyond all question a gigantic work, with a grandeur in its conception and invention, genius in its treatment of forms, periodic structure, of outstanding vigour and strength, new and original and yet authentic Brahms from A to Z.' Although he would later dismiss all four of Brahms's symphonies, his appreciation of the scale and daring of the Fourth was unusually perceptive and balanced for a 21-year-old. The first performance was conducted, on October 25, by Brahms himself, although the rehearsals were directed by von Bülow.

As Strauss remembered: 'Bülow's rehearsals were outstanding and his enthusiasm and touching conscientiousness had often contrasted strangely with the indifference which Brahms himself manifested towards the dynamics and presentation of his work.' This legendary concert included a performance of the same composer's Violin Concerto (with Adolph Brodsky as soloist) and his *Academic Festival Overture*. In order to redistribute money to the wanting string section Strauss played the bass drum and Bülow the cymbals.[15] Neither could count the rests. Strauss cheated by placing a full score on his stand, but Bülow must have cut an extraordinary figure, dashing between his seat and that of one of the trumpet players to find out where they had got to.

Strauss's admiration for Brahms seems to have waned the more he got to know him. After sharing a hotel with the composer for a few days following the première of the Fourth Symphony, he concluded that he was 'quite pleasant and very well read without exhibiting particular signs of genius'. Ironically, much the same would be said of Strauss within less than a decade.

Another of Brahms's transitory disciples, Ludwig Thuille, was in the audience for Strauss's concert and it seems he was able to enjoy some small revenge against his friend by reporting an amusing, if less than charitable, account of Richard's podium manner to his father. Franz immediately wrote to his son, admonishing him: 'It is ugly to make those serpentine gestures when conducting, especially for a bean-pole like you. It's already not pleasant to look at in Bülow, and his is a small, graceful figure. Fieriness in conducting lies somewhere else altogether.'

Thuille also conveyed the advice Brahms had given Richard, which provided Franz with further grounds for earnest counsel: 'My dear son, I beseech you to take this truly good advice to heart. I have been very worried by the fact that in all your more recent things you have paid more attention to contrapuntal affectations than to natural, wholesome invention and execution. Craftsmanship should not be discernible ... You have enough talent for something better than affectation.' Strauss must have begun to sympathise with his mother's erstwhile feelings of persecution; leaping to his own defence, he wrote to his sister: 'Who told Papa that I have developed silly habits when I conduct, I'm not a clown, and who told him so precisely the advice Brahms gave me? I didn't write to tell him the details.'

Soon after, Bülow, Brahms and the Meiningen Orchestra left to tour the composer's new symphony around Germany and Holland. It was during this tour that Bülow and Brahms's friendship suffered a serious and long-sustained rift. The composer had, somewhat thoughtlessly, accepted an invitation to conduct his new work with a rival orchestra in Frankfurt – at which Bülow took such great offence that he handed his resignation to Duke George.[16] It is unlikely, however, that Brahms's dalliance in Frankfurt was the sole reason for the split. There seems to have been a misunderstanding involving Bülow's wife and her desire to begin acting again at the Meiningen theatre, and Bülow was also beginning to tire of the Duke's financial restrictions. Bülow's departure meant that, at the age of twenty-one, Richard Strauss was Principal Conductor of one of Germany's greatest orchestras.

Under normal conditions Strauss's promotion would have demanded another fifteen or twenty years' effort. But with Bülow's departure on October 31 Strauss found himself presented with an extraordinary opportunity to learn his craft with an orchestra of unrivalled technical skill. The Meiningen tradition was one of total mastery – they had been the first orchestra to play an arrangement of Beethoven's *Grosse Fuge*[17] – and Strauss had no intention of allowing the opportunity to pass him by. As he recalled, he conducted 'an orchestral rehearsal every morning at ten o'clock' when he 'made the orchestra play the whole of their concert repertoire ...' By December 20 he was able to write to his father: 'With rehearsals every day I am becoming adept at conducting, I have a very good sense of tempo and I've already conducted at sight a few times, Schubert B minor, the *Manfred* Overture, without having to look at the score first, and I've got the tempos and all the modifications

spot on.' He also conducted Mozart's D minor *Requiem*, Beethoven's Ninth
Symphony and Berlioz's *Harold en Italie*, as well as a fair amount of contemporary work, including Thuille's completed Symphony in F minor.

In November Strauss was officially offered Bülow's position, at a salary of
2,000 marks.[18] But the loss of Bülow's popular appeal prompted the Duke to
siphon funds away from the orchestra and plough them into his own cherished hobby – the theatre.[19] Cuts inevitably meant a reduction in the orchestra's numbers and, while Strauss was honoured by the Duke's trust, he felt
unable to apply himself to the direction of an orchestra of just thirty-nine
players – a body that could have done justice to almost none of its established
repertoire. As he wrote to Hermann Levi: 'It looks as though everything here
will soon be breaking up, after the business arrangement that the art-loving
duke made with Bülow comes to an end. It's all the same to me, I'm still
making the most of my opportunities, try out whatever I like, I've had a
chance to savour Bülow, achieved everything I wanted, and when there's
nothing more to be done here [I shall] depart consoled, with my wishes
fulfilled.'

He agreed to stay until a successor could be found, and it seems that he
thoroughly enjoyed the stay – not least since he was able to further his
acquaintance with Alexander Ritter. A composer, theorist and Wagnerite,
Ritter was also the single most significant influence on Richard Strauss's life
as a composer. The two first met shortly after Strauss's arrival at Meiningen,
although the young conductor is unlikely to have taken much notice of the
older man, simply because at that time Ritter was hacking out a living as
Second Konzertmeister.

Many years before his slide into Meiningen, Ritter had promised considerably more. He had shown conspicuous talent as a child in Dresden but,
like Strauss, he attended a Gymnasium rather than a specialist music school.
It was there that he became friends with Hans von Bülow. Together, they
entered the hallowed circle surrounding Liszt, who made a point of introducing them to a little-known composer called Richard Wagner. During the
1840s Ritter's mother Julie[20] (his father died when he was seven) befriended
Wagner, later becoming one of his most valued patrons, and after his flight
from Dresden in 1849 the two corresponded regularly. In that year Ritter
entered the Leipzig Conservatory as a violinist, where he was adopted by
Mendelssohn's friend and champion, Ferdinand David.

After three years he returned to Dresden, where he divided his time
between composition and playing in the city's orchestra. By the age of twenty-
two he could boast a pedigree of extraordinary distinction, but not even
marriage to Wagner's niece, the actress Franziska, in 1854, could kick-start
his career. Ritter was rarely happy. No one wanted to hear him conduct and
few wanted to play his music. In 1869 he and his 'long-standing friend' Bülow
fell out when it was rumoured that Bülow was broadcasting a less than

favourable opinion of Ritter's musicianship. Hearing of the fracas, Bülow's first wife, Cosima, wrote to Franziska: 'I consider it a duty to speak to you about the unfortunate misunderstanding which has arisen ... My husband was supposed to have said that he thought little of Alexander's talent. If Alexander believes this he does Hans a great wrong ...' She later wrote to explain, with not a hint of irony, that 'Hans's cutting and peremptory behaviour is no sign of disdain'. When, during the late 1870s, Ritter began to suffer serious financial difficulties Bülow bailed out his old friend[21] by inviting him to join the Meiningen Orchestra as Second Konzertmeister. It was there that he met Strauss, in whom he saw the man he wished he had been, and through whom he channelled his hopes for a new beginning.

Strauss had, by this stage, come to accept Wagner for who he was. It is a mistake to imply, as many do, that Ritter led Strauss to his understanding of Wagner's achievements for, as is demonstrated by his letters to Thuille, Strauss had come to just such an understanding, albeit one in need of refinement, long before his arrival in Meiningen. Where Ritter proved invaluable was in his grasp of music's potential as pure expression. Inevitably Wagner was central to Ritter's thesis and, as Strauss eloquently recalled:

> I hardly knew Wagner's writings[22] at all. Ritter, with patient explanations, introduced me to them and to Schopenhauer; he made me familiar with them and proved to me that the road led from the 'musical expressionist' Beethoven ('music as expression' in Friedrich von Hauseggers's phrase as against Hanslick's 'Of Beauty in Music') via Liszt who, with Wagner, had realised correctly that Beethoven had expanded the sonata form to its utmost limits – in Anton Bruckner, the 'stammering cyclops', it actually explodes these limits – and that in Beethoven's epigones and especially in Brahms, sonata form had become an empty shell.

Strauss had grown up with an anti-Semitic father. Bülow's views on the subject were no less widely known, and Ritter took pride in his condemnation of the Jews, probably more openly than Wagner, who worked with Jews and willingly took their money if it suited him. Ritter's deranged nationalism, in which there was no room for the insidious impurities of the Wandering Jew, must have had the same sort of impact on Strauss's perception of himself as a German, as Ritter's denigration of classicism had on his enthusiasm for Brahms. 'One has to study Brahms carefully,' Ritter informed his young protégé, 'in order to understand that there's nothing in it.'

Ritter probably introduced Strauss to the wide and intellectually predicated literature of hatred that constituted German philosophical anti-Semitism, beginning with Luther and graduating to Eisenmenger's essential 'set text' *Judaism Unveiled*, published in 1700 and still widely read some years into the twentieth century. In discussing Schopenhauer the conversation stumbled on to the great man's considered attitudes towards the 'sickening, low and degrading' optimism of the Jews. Indeed, pre-empting the Establishment writings of Heinrich von Trietschke and Adolph Wagner, both of whom produced rampant anti-Jewish tracts during the late 1880s, Schopenhauer's critiques sat at the heart of contemporary anti-Semitism.

The whole of German metaphysics, as dictated by Ritter, was directed towards the raising of the Germanic above the Jewish spirit, which was considered foul and corrupting. As the philosopher Ludwig Feuerbach wrote in 1841: 'The Jews have preserved their peculiar character to this day. Their principle, their God, is the most practical principle in the world – selfishness; selfishness in the form of a religion.' Eugen Dühring, the philosopher/economist and a violent opponent of Jewry and Christianity, went much further, and during Strauss's years in Munich and, later, Weimar, he became the leading torch-bearer for anti-liturgical German nationalism. His *Die Judenfrage als Frage der Rassenschänlichkeit* advocated a systematic eradication of the Jews because, so he claimed, 'On the basis of equality it is impossible to live with the Jews, because this tribe stands by nature on an unequal level, a much lower level, as regards talent and morality . . . The Jews are the most evil expression of the Semitic race in the form of a nationality that is particularly dangerous to other nations . . . Hence there would still be a Jewish question even if all Jews turned their backs on their own religion and went over to one of the dominant Churches.'

Ritter echoed Wagner's inferiority complex as far as the spread of Jewry was concerned, and he fostered in Strauss an active sense of guardianship, a feeling of protection for the German spirit, the German people and German culture. Forcing the Hegelian world-view, Ritter believed in the 'two ages of Man'. The first, represented by antiquity, involved the weeding out of 'the Negro stage of the soul' during which Man was dependent and weak. The second, represented by the development of a strain of Christianity that had nothing to do with Judaism, involved Man's evolution from dependency into philosophy, whereby he directed his own destiny through ideas and, eventually, collective freedom.

According to Dühring and his followers, the Jews had yet to pass out of the Negro state and, consequently, they were poison to the purity of the German mind and soul. For someone like Ritter, the beautiful and brilliant Strauss must have appeared the very embodiment of that purity and he was in need of protection and nurturing. The ultimate expression of this madness was Nietzsche's *Der Antichrist*, published in 1888, a text dear to Ritter, and one that Strauss probably read before leaving Munich in 1889.

Ritter's musical ideology was no less captivating. He argued that all music should carry some form of internal poetic momentum. As with the Wagnerian principle of leitmotif, everything should carry within it some greater, extra-musical significance. It was not a question of mere narrative. No one, least of all Ritter, was suggesting that a work of Absolute music should portray every character and represent every action in a story, which was impossible, presupposing a narrative refinement absolutely the preserve of vocal forms of music such as opera and the Lied. It was rather more a question of suggestion, so that, as Strauss put it many years later, the 'basic principle of Liszt's symphonic works in which the poetic idea was really the formative element, became from that day on the guiding principle for my own symphonic work'.

Strauss was under no illusion as to who had been the most influential of his mentors. During the 1890s he presented a photograph of the bearded, serious-looking Ritter to the American writer Arthur Abell with the words: 'Here you see how the man looked to whom I owe more than any other human being, living or dead.' We know that Strauss and Ritter enjoyed a lengthy correspondence, which probably stretched to hundreds of letters; but only a handful have survived. 'One day', it is claimed,[23] the complete correspondence arrived in a package at Garmisch where it was received by Strauss's wife Pauline. Presuming it to be an unsolicited libretto for her husband, she returned it to the post office, who are supposed to have lost it on the return trip.

Ritter's influence might have ended with Strauss's departure from Meiningen on April 10, 1886; but he was fortunate in being able to follow his protégé to his next position, in Munich, where he had been appointed Third Conductor at the Opera by the Intendant Karl von Perfall. Bülow had strongly advised against the move, considering it a step backwards for someone of Strauss's talent.[24]

> The problem of counterpoint in the Ninth would be easier to solve than to impart by letter decisive advice in matters of such prime importance as you lay before me. My impulse would be to advise you to stay on for the time being, in the interests of the duke as well as the Ex-*mine*-ingen orchestra. But it really depends on what part the duke is disposed to play in the full cultivation of music on the banks of the Werra ... If you want to go to Munich out of patriotism or homesickness – well, that is your business. But I in your place should refuse for the time being. You are one of those exceptional musicians who need not serve from a private on upwards; you have the stuff in you to be promoted at once to a commanding officer...

After reluctantly agreeing to Perfall's terms, Strauss signed a three-year contract with Munich Opera and, on April 3, 1886, he bade official farewell to Meiningen with a tearful speech and a private performance of Bülow's *Nirvana*. His new appointment was to begin in August. But first, he accepted his father's offer of 5,000 marks[25] for a holiday. Summer was approaching and Strauss decided to follow one of Brahms's suggestions and visit Italy.

5   THE HERO'S ADVERSARIES[1]

April 1886–March 1888

Strauss's life in Meiningen proved to be of great value to him as a conductor, but it brought him little as a composer. By the time Ritter's Expressionist philosophy had begun to take root, his term at Meiningen had come to an end. There is some doubt as to how, exactly, he benefited from his mentor's learning. It was rumoured at the time that Ritter was a half-baked academic, that he dealt in abstract theories and lacked the wit to direct someone of Strauss's talent. Certainly, were one to judge Ritter by his music, such a conclusion might be valid, but there is no denying the change in Strauss's direction during and immediately after the Italian holiday he took between April and August 1886. Even if the immediate result of this vacation, *Aus Italien*, lacks the personality and conviction of his later tone poems, the very fact that he attempted a tone poem at all underlines the immediacy of Ritter's influence.

Probably at Ritter's urging, Strauss took Schopenhauer's *World as Will and Idea* (1819) with him to Italy. Like Wagner, he was swayed by the philosopher's thesis that music was superior to all the other arts because of its direct relation to the will. Schopenhauer believed that music was the only medium through which man might be able to traverse the physical and phenomenal world. Oracular, literary and visual arts objectified the world whereas music, Schopenhauer proposed, 'passes over the Ideas' freeing the listener from preconception. It is 'as immediate an objectification and copy of the whole will as the world itself ...' Like the will, music 'gives the innermost kernel preceding all form, or the heart of things'.

Schopenhauer was writing at a time when Absolute music[2] was the prevailing aesthetic. The move towards Pictorialism had taken hundreds of years and while many attribute the 'creation' of the tone poem to Liszt, he was no less sensitive to his inheritance than anyone else. Musical picture-painting had been around for a long time prior to the nineteenth century, and such works as Telemann's *Don Quixote Suite* and Vivaldi's *Quattro stagioni* are merely well-known examples of earlier works in which music conveyed extra-musical meaning. With the nineteenth-century rise in cognitive expression it became necessary for music to convey more than itself, and many commentators overworked their attempts to find meaning in music.

Beethoven encouraged the greatest interpretive licence. In 1813 E. T. A. Hoffmann suggested that Beethoven's instrumental music opened up 'the realism of the monstrous and the immeasurable. Burning flashes of light shoot through the deep night of this realm, and we become aware of giant shadows that surge back and forth, driving us into narrower and narrower confines until they destroy us.'

Hoffmann's credo did much to liberate those who, in the hope that order and reason might prevail, still clung to the raft of Enlightenment rationality. But such voices were drowned by the wave of emotional release that sustained writers and composers during the first half of the nineteenth century. Just as poetry was freed from the strictures of couplets, alexandrines and hexameters, so music broke with the dogma and formulae by which it had been bound throughout the three preceding centuries.

The extra-musical images applied to some of Beethoven's works (*Moonlight, Tempest, Emperor, Appassionata, Eroica, Pathétique, Les adieux,* etc.) underline the increasing importance of unambiguous representative significance; and yet it was one of the great paradoxes of nineteenth-century aestheticism that music was capable of fathoming depths that precluded definition or analysis. It was no coincidence, for example, that only one of Beethoven's *late* piano sonatas suffered christening, and not without reason did the composer of the *Grosse Fuge* pre-empt audiences by explaining that his 'Pastoral' Symphony was 'more an expression of feeling than a painting'. According to Mendelssohn, 'the thoughts that are expressed to me by music that I love, are not too indefinite to put into words, but on the contrary, too definite'.[3]

In his essay 'Beethoven' (thought by Mahler to be the 'only thing of value', besides Schopenhauer's *World as Will and Idea,* written 'about the nature of music') Wagner plays with Schopenhauer's assertion that music is the only possible means by which man can express his 'inner nature'. Wagner emphasised the failure of language to provide anything more potent than an approximation of true feeling; despite having composed semi-programmatic overtures and regardless of the wealth of musical alliteration in his operas, he maintained that a programmatic description of a work of music – devised *ex post facto* – could only ever be a 'mere analogy'. In spite of his promotion of Liszt and his work, Wagner insisted[4] that it was preposterous for a composer to try and imitate the sounds and experiences of real life. Rather he 'sublates its chance occurrences and details, and sublimates whatever lies within it to its concrete emotional content, which indeed allows itself to be decreed solely in music'. Strauss read Wagner's writings while in Meiningen with Ritter, and he took many of his sentiments with him to Italy where, for the first time since joining Bülow, he was able to concentrate on his own work.

In the weeks prior to his departure he had shown no obvious signs of exhaustion, but his responsibilities in Meiningen had been intense. Even if he had been able to continue working for the Duke he would have been incapable of worthwhile composition; more than anything he needed inspiration if Ritter's nebulous theories were to prove of enduring value. Considering his financial security it is, therefore, surprising that Strauss chose to take his first major holiday in Italy rather than in Greece. The ancient world was already dear to the composer and, in addition to Goethe and the early Romantics to whom he turned for his Lieder, it was for Hellas that he felt the greatest sympathy. Despite his admiration for Renaissance art and architecture, he had been raised to think little of post-Renaissance music. Of course, Italian composers were represented throughout Germany, with more than a few German composers paying homage[5] to the country and its heritage; but Verdi and the *bel cantisti* were generally ridiculed – not least by Strauss himself.[6]

Travelling with the two sons of the Bavarian ambassador to Rome, Strauss looked for an Italy of lore, exercising an almost fairy-tale perception of the 'home of Dante and Pirandello'. He began his tour in Bologna, where he was moved to tears of joy by Raphael's *St Cecilia*, and to tears of anguish by a performance of Verdi's *Aida*, which he denounced as 'dreadful, Redskin music'. In Rome he 'wallowed in works of art' and walked through acres of ruins. He wrote with self-righteous indignation of his horror at finding the fashionable world beating a path to St Peter's:[7] 'All these people strolled up and down ... during the *Miserere*, chatting and laughing as if they were walking round the Chinesischer Turm.'[8]

His indignation was exacerbated by the locals. His suitcase was stolen in Naples; his laundry disappeared in Rome; and on June 23 he wrote to Bülow: 'Such a bumbling German as I, not knowing a word of Italian and very little French, alone and for the first time in Italy, quite overwhelmed by the magnificent landscape and art – such a fellow is an easy prey for the Italians, who could quite compete with any Jew.'

Just as he appealed to Bülow's anti-Semitism, so he bowed to his father's hatred of 'foreign' music, bemoaning his experiences of the Italian theatre: 'I don't think I shall ever become a convert to Italian music, it's such trash. Even Rossini's *Barber of Seville* could only be enjoyed if the performance was outstanding.' He remained in touch with his father throughout the trip, and they continued to exchange prickly letters in which Franz's shaky wisdom received ever shorter shrift from Richard. At the end of April he visited Naples where he was as transfixed by the art (chiefly the Pompeian murals) as by the landscape. He wrote to Bülow: 'I've never fully believed in the idea that natural beauty acts as a stimulus, but in the ruins of Rome I learned better, the ideas just simply come, in flocks.' On May 10 he returned to Rome, where he heard a 'tolerable performance' of Verdi's *Requiem* and, avoiding cholera-ridden Venice, he made his last protracted stopover at Lake Como, where he enjoyed 'some wonderful days'. Having returned to Munich, rejuvenated by his travels, by nature and by Italy, Strauss began developing an idea for a 'Symphonic Fantasy', to be called *Aus Italien.*

He completed the score on September 12, 1886,[9] eighteen days before making his conducting debut at Munich Opera.[10] As Bülow had warned, Munich represented a slide backwards for someone who had only recently been chief conductor of one of the world's leading orchestras. As Third Conductor Strauss was little more than a glorified répétiteur. He was expected to prepare the company and its major productions for Hermann Levi and Franz Fischer, and with the exception of Mozart's *Così fan tutte*[11] and Verdi's *Il trovatore*, his assigned repertoire was decidedly unremarkable: Cherubini's *Les Deux Journées*, Boieldieu's *Jean de Paris* and, during the 1886–7 season, Rheinberger's *Des Thürmers Töchterlein*, Auber's *Domino Noir* and *La Part du diable*, Delibes' *Le Roi l'a dit*, and Lortzing's *Die beiden Schützen*. It was a cheerless time for Strauss, and his enthusiasm for the post rapidly deteriorated to a point where his performances began to suffer and standards began to fall. As he later admitted:

> I was not a particularly good third conductor. Although I was adept at taking over at short notice – even in the first few months I took over one of Rheinberger's operas – my lack of the 'routine', in which many less talented colleagues were vastly superior to me, my idiosyncratic insistence 'on my own tempos', on occasion often hindered the smooth dispatch of operas in the approved manner. The result, more than once, was what we call a 'Schmiss', when singers and orchestra get out of time with each other, the more so because the operas I had to conduct in those days did not interest me sufficiently to study them properly, and really required much more careful preparation than I gave them – work which I found much too boring in the case of operas like *Nachtlager* and *Martha*.

Within just a few months he started to feel under-appreciated. Aside from an invitation to conduct his F minor Symphony for the Frankfurt Museum Concerts on January 7, 1887, the political jockeying between his senior conductors, the company singers, the social benefactors and the Intendant Perfall made life difficult and unfulfilling. To make matters worse, Strauss had to contend with the interventions of a horn player, one Franz Strauss, whose boldly expressed opinions fractured the relative peace and harmony of rehearsal time.

Franz's temper was particularly inflamed by his son's predilection for quick tempi. As is often the case, age corrupted Franz's perception of musical time and proportion. Anything that reminded him of Wagner's podium manner, whereby everything was played with corresponding urgency, indicated decay. Because Richard hurled himself bodily into his work, Franz grew despairing of his son's journey down music's *via dolorosa*. But having read Wagner's penetrating monologue 'On Conducting', Richard was convinced of his responsibilities to the expressive, as well as the metronomic, markings of a score, and he injected a novel degree of character and personality into his readings of what was then considered innocuous music. Although he was, at best, mercurial about his feelings for non-German repertoire it seems he was capable of generating equal measures of excitement and controversy simply through the application of *tempo rubato*[12] and the overemphasis of dynamic markings.

In short, Strauss was propelling Wagner's theories on conducting towards the ultimate late romantic expressivity typified by Mahler, Abendroth and Furtwängler, and it divided audiences as completely as had Spontini, Nicolai and Wagner a generation earlier. In a letter to Bülow, Strauss reported the astonished reaction of an audience when, during a performance of the Overture to Nicolai's *Lustigen Weiber von Windsor*, he introduced some 'perfectly harmless novelties'. Curiously, his arm was said to be 'too long' by one colleague[13] which would suggest, as it has done ever since, that his tempi were slow. But every other report of Strauss's work as a young man leads to the conclusion, later confirmed by his recordings of his own music, that he adopted uniformly rapid tempi.

Perfall was not enamoured of his new conductor's licence, and Strauss's youthful self-confidence did little to dispel the Intendant's suspicions. Having had his fill of Wagner[14] during the 1860s Perfall was understandably wary of charisma, and Strauss was not only charismatic, but truculent, argumentative, confrontational and fiercely independent. During the spring of 1888 matters came to a head when, with Levi on three months' sick leave, Strauss was entrusted with the preparation of Wagner's *Die Feen* – but not the honour of conducting its first night, which was given to Franz Fischer. Strauss wrote to Bülow: 'I'd placed colossal hopes on the work, as the first one which I'd rehearsed from scratch – it was my chance to show at last what I can really do; all that's gone by the board, thanks to the disgraceful malice of Fischer (who calmly stood by while I took all the rehearsals) and the spineless insolence of that scoundrel Perfall...'

It would have been surprising had Fischer allowed such a golden opportunity to pass; but he was not the villain of the episode. The cause of Strauss's humiliation was Perfall. It is possible that Strauss's talent, and his awareness of it, simply rubbed the right people up the wrong way; but in his letter to Bülow he suggested an alternative explanation: 'He [Perfall] can't abide my Bülowish [sic] conducting, so I had to listen to the usual abuse of you, and how your school had got to be rooted out once and for all, and so on and so forth... It's all more than I can stand, as you will appreciate. I've now at last realised that this is not the soil to nourish a musical life which is to give any kind of joy. I'm not capable, on my own, of pulling the cart out of the mud that everything here is stuck in. The whole place is a waste land, a swamp, a beery swamp.'

That his problems had anything to do with his association with Bülow was unlikely. Had Perfall wished to antagonise Bülow he could have done a lot worse than offer a much-valued post to Bülow's most favoured pupil. The truth was that Perfall's sense of failure as a composer/conductor[15] was painfully heightened by his popular, handsome, talented and successful novitiate. Strauss was working in his home city; most of his colleagues were family friends, many having known him from birth. Perfall's sense of isolation must have been suffocating.

While life inside the Opera dragged for Strauss, life on the outside thrived as he and Ritter grew ever closer. The two met whenever Strauss could get away – at Ritter's house in the evenings and at Leibenfrost's wine bar during the day – and together they pursued a semi-academic study of Ritter's favourite subjects: 'the topics of our conversation were reminiscences of Wagner and Liszt,[16] the gospel of Schopenhauer, Ritter's new works, songs and operas, among which the score of *Wem die Krone?* came in for its fair share of critical and constructive interest.'

They also discussed the merits of the ailing Jewish conductor Hermann Levi, whom both men considered musically redundant, and fit for retirement. Only a few years earlier Levi had been a valuable friend to Strauss. He had paid him the honour of conducting his D minor Symphony and C minor *Concert Overture* when neither work was known or published. Influenced by Ritter, Strauss grew to detest Levi, condemning the man and his work. At the end of 1887, for example, he heard Levi conduct 'the most demeaning, the most abominable' performance he had ever heard of Beethoven's last symphony. With Franz adding weight to the witch hunt (which became increasingly aggressive after he was pensioned off early, in 1889[17]), Richard was unlikely to consider Levi innocent of the charges against him. With Richard's eventual departure from Munich, his friendship with the man who had gone out of his way to help him as a youth ended in acrimony and name-calling.

Max Steinitzer, an old schoolfriend and one of Strauss's first biographers, understood the nature of Strauss's relationship with Ritter: 'The very facts of his marriage to a niece of Wagner and his acquaintance with Liszt in the Weimar days placed Ritter, with all the incandescence of his temperament, in the progressive camp, and the burden of his teaching to Strauss was all too often: "Burn what thou has worshipped!" ' Besides Brahms, the established romantics of the concert hall, Mendelssohn and Schumann, and their 'puerilities', fared particularly badly at Ritter's hands; at times he sounded more like a tub-thumping party man than a musician weighing composers' merits and demerits.

Even at the end of his life, when he had wisely revised many of his more juvenile opinions, Strauss upheld his faith in Ritter: 'Let me add here that the true importance of Alexander Ritter in the history of music, as a bold pioneer in the aftermath of Wagner, has yet to be recognised. Ritter's songs are new in their treatment of language and in the origination of the melody in the word, in a manner for which Wagner's creation of vocal form was the model ... What can be said to be derived from Wagner [in my work], without imitating him, I owe from the first to Ritter's teaching and his songs, and to his two one-act operas.'

But as someone who had not looked beyond Wagner – as is demonstrated by his music – Ritter was forced to juggle mystical generalisations which must have seemed very grand indeed to Strauss, whose musical experiences were still relatively narrow. Building so openly on his selective interpretation of Schopenhauer's writings meant that Strauss was still denied the concrete wisdom of someone – like Liszt – who had managed to see beyond nineteenth-century design. Wagner had liberated opera from the canon of self-slaughter represented by 'numbers' formulae, and he had, in *Tristan*, opened up unimagined harmonic possibilities. But in stuffing his libretti full of Schopenhauer, Wagner had widened the gulf between art and its audience, and it was this reality that so animated Ritter, for whom conceptual aesthetics carried a potential prohibited by Absolutism. If Ritter had been willing or honest enough to clarify his credo, bringing shape and detail to deductible theory, it is probable that Strauss would have had nothing to do with him. But Ritter dealt in a conjectural, semi-mystical humanism which would have better suited the composer Hans Pfitzner who was, in youth as in maturity, the incarnation of Ritter's 'visionary' Teutonism.

Strauss maintained that Ritter's understanding of vocal metre and his 'treatment of language and ... the origination of the melody in the word' were in some way revolutionary. But the scores support no such claim; tragically, the pretext for Strauss's devotion to Ritter would seem to have less to do with cultural didacticism than with loneliness.

For someone burdened by such a definite sense of his own importance, making and keeping friends was proving difficult. Ritter, and his family, offered him friendship ('What splendid, notable, dear people they are!'), encouragement and flattery; Ritter served as the father figure denied Strauss at home. Whenever Franz joined them at Leibenfrost's, the evening invariably suffered from tension between their conflicting aesthetic camps. Just as Richard had sided with Bülow against Franz, so he stood by Ritter, alienating his father who must, by this stage, have begun to resent Ritter's hold over his son.

At the end of 1886 and during the early months of 1887 Strauss began to receive conducting invitations from across Germany. Perfall took no pride in his Third Conductor's blossoming popularity and he made it difficult for him to get away. But Strauss had done his job and kept his word, and there was nothing Perfall could do to stop him from accepting both Bülow's offer to visit Hamburg and an invitation to conduct a performance, in Frankfurt, of his F minor Symphony on January 7.

He was to be allowed two rehearsals in Frankfurt which, at close to six hours, was a distinct improvement on recent experience. The concert was warmly received by, among others, Clara Schumann, and he arrived in Hamburg stimulated to meet Bülow whom he had not seen for some months. Bülow was busy working on a new production of *Carmen*, but he was also preparing to give a performance of Strauss's F minor Symphony on January 18. Immediately after this concert Strauss wrote to his parents: 'Symphony found favour yesterday and went very well. Bülow conducted very affectionately without a score, but was within a hair's breadth of letting it fall apart in the last movement ... I was called for after the Scherzo and last movement.'

Strauss conducted the work again on October 17, 1887, in Leipzig, where he met Gustav Mahler, whose adaptation of Weber's *Die drei Pintos* intrigued him. He was much taken with Mahler whom, so he wrote to Bülow on October 29, he considered 'a highly intelligent musician and conductor, who understands the art of tempo modification and subscribes to some splendid views altogether, especially on Wagner's tempos (by contrast with the accredited Wagner conductors of our day'.[18]

On March 2, he readied himself for one of the most demanding challenges of his life as a composer/conductor: the first performance of *Aus Italien*, his first orchestral work since meeting Ritter. Although the tone poem's impact was reduced by its separation into four movements, Strauss had written a work the inspiration of which had been his own emotional experience; but lacking the necessary confidence to allow the work to speak for itself, he prepared a programme for each of the movements. Strauss would never again provide such a detailed narrative for any of his works, but he remained committed to the predetermined programme until at least 1915.[19] As he wrote in 1890:[20] 'Programme music: real music! Absolute music: can be written with the aid of a certain routine and craftsmanship by any moderately musical person. The first: art! The second: craft!'

There were many who would have agreed with Strauss, but the popularity of programme music was already on the wane. To the critic Arthur Seidl, for example, Mahler wrote in 1893: 'You have quite accurately characterised my goals in contrast to those of Strauss; you are right that my music finally arrives at a programme as the last, ideal clarification, whereas with Strauss the programme stands as a given task.' Strauss and Mahler never saw eye to eye on the subject, which contributed to Mahler's negative feelings towards his rival, but their dissension created a curious bond that unconsciously led them towards the same philosopher, Nietzsche, and the same work of philosophy, *Also Sprach Zarathustra*.

This subject concerns a later chapter, but it is worth noting here the attitudes that separated Mahler, whose Third Symphony attempted to develop the non-corporeal and spiritual within Nietzsche's thesis, from Strauss, whose tone poem sought to explicate the evolution of Man through illustration and suggestion. Mahler considered Strauss's presumption absurd, while Strauss delighted in mocking the irony of Mahler's aesthetic conversion to Nietzsche's Catholicised doctrine. After hearing of Mahler's death in 1911 he noted with disdain how 'The Jew Mahler could still find elevation in Christianity...'

After the première of *Aus Italien* in Munich, Ritter's chest must have swelled with absolution. With the exception of the last movement, in which Strauss made vulgar use of Denza's Neapolitan song *Funiculì, funiculà*,[21] the prevalence of motifs, counterpoint, lush orchestration and pictorialism confirmed his suitability as guardian of Wagner's achievements. In later life Strauss was careful not to overestimate the importance of *Aus Italien* ('The first timid experiment ...'), but he was greatly encouraged at the time, not least by the Munich audience's bafflement: 'Some of them applauded furiously, some of them hissed vigorously, in the end the applause won. The opposition have pronounced me half crazy, talk about going astray and all that kind of rubbish. I felt immensely proud: the first work to have met with the kind of opposition of the multitude; that proves it must be of some significance.' To a friend he wrote: 'The first steps towards independence!'

Like many other progressives Strauss interpreted his public's hostility as approbation ('There has never been a great artist yet who thousands of people didn't think was mad'), although he was less cheered by Bülow's[22] failure to understand the work's relatively lucid demands. After reading the score Bülow wrote to Ritter: 'Is age making such a reactionary of me? The author is a genius, but I find he has gone to the utmost limit of what is musically possible (within the bounds of beauty), and has often, indeed, gone beyond the limit, without any really pressing need for it. A wonderful, enviable mistake, the prodigality of the ideas, the abundance of associations ... what I deplore more than anything are the colossal difficulties for the performers.'

For Bülow to consider *Aus Italien* a threat to the 'musically possible', when twenty years earlier he had prepared and conducted the first performances of Wagner's *Tristan und Isolde*, is barely credible. *Tristan* contains considerably more dangers, and makes many greater demands of its participants, than anything in *Aus Italien*. Strauss summed up his feelings – if not his entire credo – in a letter to the musicologist and critic Karl Wolff:

With the horrifying lack of judgement and understanding typical of a large proportion of today's pen-pushers, many of them, like a large proportion of the general public, have allowed some of the external features of my work, which may be dazzling but are of *purely secondary importance*, to deceive them as to its real content, indeed to overlook it altogether. It consists of *sensations evoked* by the sight of the wonderful natural beauties of Rome and Naples, *not descriptions* of them – in one review I read 'a musical Baedeker of Southern Italy'. It really is ridiculous to suggest that a present-day composer, whose tutors have been the classics, especially late Beethoven, as well as Wagner and Liszt, would write a work three-quarters of an hour in length in order to show off with the kind of piquant tone painting and brilliant instrumentation that almost every advanced composition student still at a conservatory can write nowadays. *Expression* is our art, and a piece of music which has nothing truly poetic to convey to me – content that is, of course, which can be properly represented *only in music*, a content that words may be able to *suggest but only suggest* – a piece like that in my view is anything you care to call it – but not music.'

Six days after the première, on March 8, 1887, Strauss travelled to Cologne to conduct a performance of his *Wandrers Sturmlied*, and in April he returned to Munich to hear Levi conduct Verdi's latest opera, *Otello*, and to assist him with preparing a staging of Berlioz's *Benvenuto Cellini*. Aware that Bülow had conducted a production of Berlioz's opera in Hanover nine years earlier, Strauss kept him informed of Levi's efforts.

Strauss used these progress reports as an opportunity to ask Bülow for deliverance from his hated routine, but Bülow was determined that Strauss should counter his restlessness and stay put. Strauss turned to composition for solace, writing to his friend Lotti Speyer on June 23, 1887, about a new work, after Shakespeare's *Macbeth*, 'which is, of course, very wild in character' as well as a violin sonata. *Macbeth* would occupy Strauss, on and off, for many years to come, but the remarkable Violin Sonata in Eb, Op. 18,[23] was completed with speed during the second half of 1887, and first performed on October 3, 1888.

Towards the end of August he decided to take a holiday, which he spent at the Pschorr family villa in the small village of Feldafing.[24] While there he was introduced to Major-General Adolf de Ahna, a respected local[25] patriarch, who delighted in introducing the elder of his two daughters, Pauline, to the famous young conductor. Her musicianship and soprano voice were well above the average, and as a graduate of the Munich Conservatory it was expected that she would make her career as a singer. The ambitious general knew Richard was unmarried, and while a musician would have normally been considered beneath the daughter of a general, Strauss had been born into the Pschorr family, which added breeding to his prodigal catalogue of qualities.

Pauline was plain to look at and some way from matching Strauss intellectually. Lacking Dora Wihan's beauty, sexual charisma and intelligence, she was liberated only by her social status and the extreme self-confidence it allowed her. Even as a young woman of twenty-five[26] she spoke her mind with alarming frequency and withering directness. There was nothing erotic or suggestive about Pauline; she was muscular in her dealings with everyone and everything, which appears to have touched an enigmatic, uncomfortable malaise within Strauss. He seemed to have needed, even enjoyed, her bullying and hectoring, and throughout their prolonged courtship Pauline revealed a candour and, if one believes contemporary reports, a spirit that swept the cynical conductor off his feet. Forthright, talented and fiercely independent, Pauline was the ideal Euridice for the perfect Orpheus.

They first came to know each other as tutor and pupil. Pauline had been studying privately with Richard's old friend, Max Steinitzer. As Steinitzer recalled two years before his death: 'I complain to Strauss, who is on a visit to his uncle Pschorr, that I am having musical difficulties with a very pretty, charming young lady, who lives across the road, almost opposite ... I assure him that the family are wild about his works and would certainly be glad to receive him. Strauss agrees, and everyone is thrilled; after the very first lesson with Pauline, Strauss tells me: "She is much more talented than you think, we have only got to bring her gifts out." '

In 1949 Strauss recorded his own account of their first meeting: 'Pauline had already spent some months studying at the Munich School of Music, and with the courage of a complete amateur had naïvely stormed her way through the aria from *Der Freischütz* at an examination-recital in the Odeon, to the thunderous applause of her military admirers! Her father ... handed her to me for tuition.' Strauss also did what he could for Ritter by recommending that Pauline take acting lessons with his wife Franziska, a move that is said to have done much to improve her limited dramatic talents.

For all that was happening in his private life, 1887 was proving one of the least productive years since Strauss's graduation; but possibly as a result of his feelings for Pauline he was inspired to write some of his most perfect songs during the last quarter of the year – famously his Op. 17 which included the exquisitely beautiful *Ständchen* and *Traum durch die Dämmerung*. The year 1887 also saw Strauss making references to an idea he and Ritter had been discussing for an opera. Ritter's obsession with myth, nationalism and the German identity led to a similar fascination in his young protégé.

Strauss told Arthur Seidl that the idea had come to him via a 'small and unremarkable reference in a *feuilleton* article in the *Neue Freie Presse*[27] to the existence of secret, artistic-cum-religious orders, which were founded in Austria to combat the worldliness of the Minnesang'. The fusion of fact (Minnesingers) and fantasy, with its deliciously heady mixture of Wagnerian/Norse philosophy and attenuated non-Liturgical Christianity must have struck the impressionable young composer as the perfect vehicle for his divine responsibility as defender of the (supposedly) modernist faith.

The shadow of Wagnerism loomed over Strauss, as it did over everyone else, and he was encouraged by Ritter to look upon the idea of a Wagnerian parable as the means by which he might carry the torch of German music into the future. He was being invited – by one of 'the Master's' friends – to protect Bayreuth's grail. The original title, 'Guilt and Atonement', was an obvious gesture towards Nietzsche, and the first drafts of the libretto were littered with all sorts of corrupted Nietzschean philosophy. Before long he was overtaken by good sense, and revised his title, adopting the Wagnerian penchant for naming operas after the leading male character. Richard's hero was to be Guntram, the title of his first opera. During the summer of 1887 Ritter drew Strauss's attention to an article in the *Wiener Neue Presse* in which were described a number of secret societies that had thrived in medieval Austria. These sects differed in their religious and aesthetic convictions, but were united in opposition to the prevailing, secular *Minnesängers*. One in particular attracted his attention since they called themselves 'Contenders for love', an irresistibly seductive ideal for anyone captivated by Wagner and Schopenhauer. Strauss quickly conceived a plot and a hero figure in the Wagnerian mould whose name was a fusion of Gunther (from *Götterdämmerung*) and Wolfram (from *Tannhäuser*).[28]

Work on *Guntram* occupied him throughout the remainder of the year, although he was overtaken by events in Munich when Perfall asked him to conduct the house production of *Carmen* from October 28. He wrote to Bülow, telling him how 'Bülowish' his performances had been, and in a notable gesture of kindness to a fellow composer, enclosed a copy of Mahler's arrangement of Weber's *Die drei Pintos*.[29]

In December Strauss returned to Italy where he made his foreign debut as a conductor. He had been invited by Count Antonio Freschi to conduct two concerts in Milan, on the 8th and the 11th. The programme, for which he was to be allowed six rehearsals,[30] was the same at both concerts: Weber's Overture to *Euryanthe*, his own F minor Symphony, Beethoven's *Leonora* Overture No. 1, Glinka's *Kamarinskaya* and the Prelude to Wagner's *Die Meistersinger*. Each appearance brought scenes of triumph, and Strauss delighted in the jubilant Milanese greeting, particularly since he was 'far from spoiled by recognition and benevolence' back in Munich.

The 'willing and very capable' orchestra played magnificently and after the first concert Strauss wrote to his parents: 'I am the lion of the hour. Everyone in raptures, concert went excellently and a great success, especially the symphony ... everyone delighted by my compositions and my conducting.' He considered the second concert an 'even greater success', and his sense of achievement was complete when the orchestra presented him with an inscribed silver baton.

During the first quarter of the new year, 1888, Strauss began to make references in his letters to two new works for orchestra. One of them, *Macbeth*, had already occupied him for some months, but the other, *Don Juan*, was new to his correspondents. With Ritter sitting at his shoulder, Strauss was pursuing musical theories that craved deserving subject-matter and, having attempted the representation of landscapes and generalised recollection through music, he grew – through his understanding of Schopenhauer and Nietzsche – towards the realisation that tone painting and the symphonic poem could only ever find their fulfilment through the portrayal of individual psychologies.

6 CERTAINTY OF VICTORY

March 1888–June 1890

To an impartial onlooker, the life and career of Richard Strauss up to 1888, in which year he celebrated his twenty-fourth birthday, might well have appeared Faustian. When he began working on *Don Juan* his orchestral works had been heard in Italy, America and over ten German cities, including Berlin, Dresden, Hamburg, Cologne and Frankfurt. He was fast growing in reputation as one of Germany's most promising young conductors, and he was esteemed by many of the country's foremost musicians, including Wagner's triumvirate Bülow, Richter and Levi. His music was being published by Spitzweg, his songs were popular with amateurs and professionals alike, and he was about to compose his first and most enduring orchestral masterpiece at an age when Beethoven, Brahms, Schumann, Berlioz, Wagner and Verdi had been struggling to find their voices. He may not have shone with the precocity of a Mozart, but following a relatively fleeting cycle of experiment, and with only a handful of orchestral works to his name, Strauss revealed through *Don Juan* a harmonic imagination, melodic sympathy and orchestral virtuosity that would have been prodigious in someone ten years his senior.

Don Juan occupied a central, inductive position in Strauss's life, but the theories which led him to that remarkable work were cultivated through the experiment of *Macbeth*. The idea for a one-movement symphonic poem after Shakespeare's play had probably first occurred to Strauss during the spring of 1888. Shakespeare was considered an honorary German within educated circles and, like most cultured Germans, Strauss had been brought up reading Schlegel and Tieck's celebrated translations.[1]

When he first considered the project he was acquainted with most of the better-known musical settings of Shakespeare's plays, such as Mendelssohn's Overture and incidental music to *A Midsummer Night's Dream*, Nicolai's *Die lustigen Weiber von Windsor*, Tchaikovsky's Overtures to *Romeo and Juliet* and *Hamlet*, and Berlioz's *Tristia*, *Lélio*, *Roméo et Juliette* and *Béatrice et Bénédict*. He greatly admired Verdi's *Otello* but it is unlikely that he knew the same composer's setting of *Macbeth*, which failed to secure an enthusiastic German audience until 1928 when Kutzchbach conducted a celebrated revival in Berlin. After Shakespeare, his most immediate model for a tone poem was Liszt's symphonic treatment of *Hamlet,* the closest anyone had yet come to translating the psychological concentration of a Shakespearean drama into a work of non-operatic music.

Strauss's first attempt, which has never been published, caused him some distress, not least because Bülow, to whom he sent the score, ridiculed Strauss's bizarre decision to end the work with a triumphal march for Macduff. A more unlikely end to a less triumphant tale could not be imagined, and yet Strauss evidently considered Macduff's Pyrrhic victory of greater significance than the prevailing misery of a drama in which death, betrayal and despair negate any sort of celebration. As Bülow wrote to Strauss: 'It is quite in order for an *Egmont* overture [Beethoven] to end with a march celebrating the triumph of Egmont, but a symphonic poem called *Macbeth* ...' Strauss later admitted that his work had needed altering 'in accordance with the correct stylistic principles of the genuine composer of programme music'; but in spite of the architectural similarities to *Don Juan,* it barely anticipates the later work.

After completing the second draft of *Macbeth,* and midway through *Don Juan,* he wrote a long elucidatory letter to Bülow, in which he attempted to spell out his intentions as far as *Macbeth* and his theories were concerned. Dated August 24, 1888, it is one of Strauss's most graphic aesthetic testimonies:

... It seems to me that the only way in which a self-reliant forward development of our instrumental music is possible, is in carrying on from the Beethoven of the Coriolanus, Egmont and Leonore III overtures, of Les Adieux, from late Beethoven in general, all of whose works in my opinion could hardly have come into being without a pre-existing poetic model. If I should prove to lack the artistic strength and gifts to achieve something worthwhile along this path, then it is probably better to leave it at the great Nine[2] and their Four celebrated successors[3] ... If it all comes to nothing – well: I still think it's better to follow one's true artistic conviction and to have said something wrong up a blind alley than something superfluous while keeping to the old well trodden high road ...

... From the F minor Symphony onwards I have found myself trapped in a steadily growing antithesis between the musical-cum-poetic content that I have wanted to communicate and the form of the ternary sonata movement which we have inherited from the classics. In Beethoven the musico-poetic content generally fitted exactly into that very 'sonata form' which evolved in his hands to utmost perfection and is the exhaustive expression of what he felt and wanted to say ... But the 'form' which was absolutely fitting for the highest and most sublime kind of content in Beethoven has been used for the last sixty years as a 'formula', regarded as inseparable from our instrumental music, and purely 'musical content' has simply to adapt itself, by force if necessary, to fit the formula or, worse, the formula has been filled in and filled out with contents unworthy of it.

Now, if one wants to create a work of art, the mood and structure of which are of a piece and which is to make a vivid impression on the listener, then the author must also have had a vivid image of what he wanted to say before his inner eye. This is only possible as a consequence of fertilisation by a poetic idea, whether appended to the work as a programme or not ... Making music according to the rules of pure Hanslickian[4] form is in any case no longer possible; from now onwards there will be no more beautiful but aimless phrase-making, during which the minds of both the composer and the listeners are a complete blank, and no more symphonies (Brahms excepted of course), which always reminds me of an immense garment, made to fit a Hercules, which a skinny tailor has tried on in the hope that he will cut a fine figure in it.

The precise expression of my artistic ideas and feelings and stylistically the most self-reliant of all my works to date, the one in which I was most conscious of my intentions, is *Macbeth*. Perhaps a newer work by me, one with a less brutal or gruesome content than *Macbeth*, will reconcile you to the path that I have now set out along. If not, then please pardon and forget this feeble and perhaps incoherent attempt 'not to remain unheard' by you at least.

Bülow was dismissive of Strauss's philosophising (writing across his August 24 letter 'Theory grey or green – in practice, what's important is to write beautiful melodious music') and he openly disliked the completed work, which was too 'grey and tuneless' for a conductor whose ears had been formed playing Mozart and Beethoven. Even though he is said later to have thawed towards *Macbeth*,[5] its inspiration and Strauss's presumed fixation with colour, counterpoint, programmatic detail and dissonance continued to present intractable obstacles.

Strauss conducted the first performance in Weimar on October 13, 1890. It was coolly received. As an experiment it was a triumph, enabling Strauss to take another step towards maturity, but as a work of isolated music it was a failure, and it has remained the least often performed of his tone poems. Many of those at the première rejected the work simply because experience had taught them – via the first performance of *Don Juan*[6] – to expect more of the composer; and Franz Strauss, with typical indiscretion, implored his son to reconsider his course.

When he finally revised *Macbeth* in 1891 he did so not because of his father's urgings but because private performances in Mannheim and Weimar allowed him to register defects that his inner ear had failed to notice. These were mostly textural anomalies, reflecting a weakness for instrumental counterpoint that, lacking a necessarily sophisticated technique, prevented 'the principal themes from standing out as clearly' as he wished. The final version enjoyed a spell of popularity during the early 1890s, by which time

Strauss was the *enfant terrible* of modern music, but *Macbeth* is still little more than a stepping-stone towards the cumulative brilliance of his maturity.

In May 1889 he paid another visit to Italy, travelling to Bologna where he attended the first Italian performance of *Tristan und Isolde*, conducted by Martucci and sung, in German, by Italians. It demonstrated the intrinsic lyricism of Wagner's most sensual work, and helped him understand how 'the whole Tristan is a most beautiful bel canto opera'. The experience informed not only his subsequent performances of Wagner, but also the substance of his current project, *Don Juan*.

Later that month he returned to Munich and his hated routine, owing to which, during the first week of July, he began to suffer from depression. *Macbeth* was confined to his desk and *Don Juan* was months from completion. He had not enjoyed an important première since March 1887[7] and he was perpetually troubled by the lack of respect accorded him in the opera house. As the month drew to an end he began to despair, whining to Bülow about the 'churlish priest' Perfall and the 'Taktjuden' ('Rhythm Jews') who were making his life so difficult.

Salvation again came from Bülow, who had promised to try and arrange for a new appointment, to begin when Strauss's contract in Munich expired on July 31, 1889. True to his word, he recommended Strauss to Hans Bronsart, a friend and colleague since the 1850s; like Bülow, Bronsart had become friends with Liszt (who dedicated his Second Piano Concerto to him) and later Wagner (who praised him for his tolerance and good nature in *Mein Leben*). In Munich, Bronsart succeeded Bülow as conductor of the Gesellschaft der Musikfreunde in 1865, and after a brief spell as Intendant at Hanover during the two years that Bülow conducted there, he moved to Weimar in 1887 where he set about restoring the standards for which Liszt's directorship had been celebrated.

Bronsart trusted Bülow. After Bülow's recommendation of Strauss he wrote to Munich's Third Conductor on August 25, 1888, asking him to visit Weimar for 'a chat'. Official negotiations did not begin until January 1889, and shortly before their conclusion on March 7, Strauss wrote to Bronsart setting out his terms:

After being engaged three years ago, without any knowledge of the theatre and without any of the routine essential to every aspect of it, as a third conductor in this swamp of antiquated fifty-year-old traditions ... I very soon recognised, to my great distress, that I had made a fundamental miscalculation in the extent of the influence I had hoped to exercise here ... These experiences have convinced me that, if I am to obtain that influence which will set a new standard for the orchestra, I must insist in Weimar on a full and varied share of the work (enough to bring me into intimate association with the whole company), on co-ordination with Lassen [Hofkapellmeister in Weimar] and also on the title and rank of a Hofkapellmeister.

Strauss was determined not to allow a repetition of his experience in Munich. He knew how important his official position within the house hierarchy would be to ensuring a productive and happy engagement:

> With members of the orchestra and the company in the theatre, it is not the artistic authority but the authority of the rank that counts first and foremost, and it is through the plenipotency of the rank alone that artistic influence can be acquired ... To revert to the unimportant subject of myself, as far as concerns the theatre, of which I knew virtually nothing before I took up my present position, the experiences I have had were some of them very painful (especially with producers), and my careful study of Wagner's writings and dramas has forced me to recognise how urgent the need is for reforms in this sphere too ... Here, the unconditional, strict authority of a first conductor is almost the only thing that carries any weight.

While all this made sense, it is unlikely that Bronsart welcomed having the obvious spelled out to him by a privileged young man of twenty-four. Strauss further soured his deposition by asking for too much money. He had been living with his parents in Munich, and they had assisted him financially throughout his tenure at the Opera, but a move to Weimar would demand living quarters and he wished to ensure, as well as he could, financial independence. Bronsart offered him an annual salary of 2,100 marks – less than he was being paid by Perfall; but Strauss was desperate to leave Munich, and so he accepted the meagre terms as well as Bronsart's decision not to grant him the title Hofkapellmeister. His contract was to be dated from August 1, although he would not be expected at the theatre until the following month. This interval was introduced not to accommodate a holiday; rather, Bülow had once again put himself out for his protégé by recommending to Julius Kniese, Cosima Wagner's musical adviser, that she engage Strauss as an assistant for the 1889 Bayreuth Festival.

During his final year as Third Conductor in Munich he enjoyed some good fortune outside the theatre. He conducted *Aus Italien* in Meiningen and heard it played in Frankfurt and Cologne. The Violin Sonata and Piano Quartet were played in Mannheim, as was the F minor Symphony; he completed the full score of *Don Juan* on September 30, 1888, and on February 1, 1889, the Wilde Gung'l gave the first performance of a C major *Festive March* that Strauss had written to commemorate the orchestra's twenty-fifth anniversary. Accompanied by his two closest friends, Thuille and Ritter, he travelled to Berlin in March 1889 to hear Bülow conduct Wagner's Overture to *Tannhäuser* and Beethoven's Ninth Symphony. On the 5th he reviewed the concert for his father:

'A glorious concert yesterday, Bülow conducted like a god, orchestra played like angels ... the *Tannhäuser* brought the house down, Bülow was called back ten times.' He also wrote candidly, on April 9, to Dora Wihan-Weiss, eulogising Bülow's performance as well as his own development: 'Rich. Str. the artist is in the pink ... With Ritter's help I am at least now well provided with a solid philosophy of life and art, I have firm ground under my feet ...' Indeed, Ritter's social and racial aphorisms had greatly enlivened Strauss, who boasted of his theories to Dora: 'now I can even dare to take up the cudgels on my own account against the Jews and the Philistines...'

In June 1889, at Bronsart's invitation, Strauss travelled with Thuille to Wiesbaden where he conducted the orchestra of the Allgemeiner Deutscher Musikverein in a programme that included Brahms's D minor Piano Concerto and his own *Aus Italien*. While there, he heard from his sister of their father's ignominious dismissal by Perfall. Considering Franz's open distaste for Levi, and Jews in general, it is probable that Levi had a hand in the matter – particularly since Franz learned of his retirement via a letter pinned to the opera house notice-board. Richard needed no convincing that the 'despicable' deed was Levi's. Franz's demeaning departure was typical of conduct befitting Richard's perception of Jews, and he wrote to his father: 'Now dear Papa, use your retirement to take a good rest and look after your health and strength, so that we shall have you with us in good health as our loving and beloved father for a long time to come.' When Johanna sent news of their father she reassured Richard that he was coping well: 'I was afraid that Papa's exaggerated jollity was only a front and might make him feel even worse inside, but he's really cheerful...'

Strauss finally left Munich on July 31, 1889, and headed straight for Bayreuth where he was to assist, among others, Hermann Levi. It was a delightful irony, one probably lost on Strauss who was, initially at least, too amazed by his good fortune to worry about 'Taktjuden' such as Levi. The other conductors for the 1889 season were Felix Mottl and Hans Richter; his fellow assistants were Carl Armbruster, Otto Gieseker, Oscar Merz, Hugo Röhr, Heinrich Schwarz, Arthur Smolian and Engelbert Humperdinck, who had lived with Wagner as a copyist for *Parsifal*, the first production of which he helped stage in 1882. The chorus-master was Julius Kniese. Above them all, and the undisputed master of Bayreuth, was Wagner's widow Cosima.

Bayreuth was a complex, stressful environment, particularly since one of the doctrinal prerequisites, at least as far as the Bayreuth aristocracy was concerned, was a healthy suspicion of the Jews. Cosima, like her husband, was a determined anti-Semite. She was known to employ staff on this basis alone, and her feelings for Levi – by then the most important of the festival's conductors – were as distressing as they were contradictory. Wagner had tried to force Levi to convert to Christianity before conducting *Parsifal*, and only after being told that he could not have Levi's orchestra without Levi did he accept the tragicomic irony of having a Jew conduct his pseudo-Christian parable. Wagner had been praised by King Ludwig for making no 'distinction between Christian and Jew ... at bottom all men are brothers, whatever their religious differences', to which Wagner had answered that this was all very well, but that Jews were to Ludwig 'only an idea' whereas 'for us they are an experience'.

The Wagners' anti-Semitism was unshakeable. At the beginning of December 1881, for example, a fire at the Vienna Ringtheater killed hundreds in the audience. Cosima noted in her diary: 'That 416 Israelites perished in the conflagration does not increase R.'s sympathy for the tragedy.' She would warn her children to stay away from Jews and, despite her admiration for Levi as a conductor, and regardless of their ostensible friendship, she could never bring herself to treat him with respect. Of course, she and Wagner were willing to make exceptions whenever it became necessary. The conductors Karl Tausig, Angelo Neumann, Anton Rubinstein and Hermann Levi were therefore tolerated in spite of their handicap.

Cosima was fanatically protective of her husband and, after his death in 1883, her Judaeophobia grew steadily more intense. Certainly, she made more references to 'the evil' of the Jews in her correspondence than almost any other historical figure prior to the late 1920s. Ernest Newman noted that her letters to Prince Hohenlohe-Langenburg, for example, 'might have been written yesterday by any leading Nazi'. He continued: 'The "Jew" leitmotif, combined with that of "Regeneration through Bayreuth", runs through these letters with the persistency of the "Gold" motif in *The Ring*; the only difference is that Cosima repeats her leitmotifs a thousand times without the slightest variation.'

She hated Mahler for his race[8] and opposed his appointment to the Vienna State Opera for this reason alone. When Mahler cut some of her son Siegfried's opera *Der Bärenhäuter* for a production of the work in Vienna, Cosima wrote to Hohenlohe: 'My son asked him [Mahler] in front of the entire personnel "Does the religious content bother you?" ...' She explained this situation, and almost everything else to do with German racial destiny, through a close study of the writings of Houston Stewart Chamberlain: 'The incident fits in curiously with a book I am reading, Chamberlain's XIX Century, in which the author explains that what distinguishes the Germans from the Semites is that the former have a strongly developed penchant for religion while the Semites lack it altogether.'

Levi suffered more than most as a result of the racial discrimination at Bayreuth, just as he had in Munich. In 1894, on the eve of his retirement, he wrote to Cosima, 'I believe that everything centres on one point: I am a Jew and in and around Wahnfried [the Wagners' house in Bayreuth] it has become a dogma that a Jew appears a certain way, thinks and acts in a certain way and above all that a Jew is incapable of selfless devotion to anything; as a result everything I do and say is judged from this point of view and therefore anything I do and say is considered indecent or at least alien.'

Strauss's introduction to the atmosphere of prejudice at Bayreuth presented no obstacles, and he positively delighted in the humiliation of Levi. In 1891, having worked at the festival during the previous three years, he wrote to Cosima: 'Yes, the Jews have come a long way with us ... Is it really too much when I say from the bottom of my heart "too bad"? So is poor *Parsifal* never to be let out of the Jewish torture chamber; why must the poor work suffer from the "services" of Levi?'

It might be assumed that the ambitious Strauss was hoping to win Levi's post for himself; but Bülow had recommended Strauss to Kniese, not to Cosima, who was increasingly determined not to engage anyone who had known and worked with her first husband. Within days of his arrival, Strauss and Kniese were good friends – and would remain so throughout his and Pauline's time at Bayreuth. They shared much, by way of time and philosophy, and they would grow closer after Richard's marriage to Pauline, when she and Kniese's wife developed their own private understanding. Strauss's affection for Kniese might suggest a poor judgement of character. Given their close friendship, however, it is improbable that Richard was ignorant of Kniese's all-consuming anti-Semitism, not least since Kniese was proud of his convictions. In his memoirs he boasted of his treatment of Levi: 'He pretended to be hurt, but he knew perfectly well and admitted that it had less to do with him personally than with his and his race's tragic destiny.'

Strauss revelled in life as a Bayreuth assistant. He was surrounded by devotees of the 'New German School', and Ritter's social and musical theories were daily confirmed by everyone and everything around him. Mottl and Richter were respectful and he was allowed visitors – chiefly Thuille, Ritter, Pauline and her father Adolf. After the festival Cosima invited Richard to study the scores of *Tannhäuser* and *Lohengrin* with her, confirming his popularity at Bayreuth where he was the 'only one besides Levi and Mottl' to play at the piano rehearsals. Having returned to Weimar, he wrote to Cosima: 'Today, as yet, I can only use words to clothe what I enjoyed, experienced and learned in Bayreuth; but it is my most ardent wish to have the chance eventually to prove my sincere and loyal devotion to the Bayreuth cause through action.'

It is not difficult to imagine what it must have meant to the 25-year-old Strauss to be working on 'the Master's' scores with his widow; and as Richard grew in fame and notoriety Cosima proved to be one of the few friends who were willing to pass honest judgements on him and his music. His compliance was especially remarkable as Cosima delivered her wisdom with a sledge-hammer, and Richard endured a bizarre weight of well-meaning abuse.

After hearing *Don Juan*, for example, she administered a long corrective,[9] imploring him to allow his heart supremacy over his intellect: 'Restlessness harms clarity and restlessness is a product, it seems to me, of a capricious intellect ... We have experienced the perfection of art: that very perfection

teaches us simplicity ... Even the choice of your subject shows the predominance of intellectuality. You could not have been truly moved by Lenau's
poem ...'; when, in 1905, he introduced her to *Salome* – ironically on Good
Friday – she was so stunned that it took her six months to write down her
feelings: 'The famous French poet Rostand wrote a play for the equally
famous actor Coquelin in which the chief protagonist is a cock. Are you
going to set it to music? You see, I'm joking to comfort myself: on rit pour
n'en pas pleurer!'[10] ... No doubt it was the demonic element which attracted
you to the subject. I can only keep quiet and continue to hold you in
affection ...'[11]

Strauss left Bayreuth for Weimar where, on paper at least, he found himself
in a situation not dissimilar to life in Munich. His official title was Third
Grand Ducal Kapellmeister, which again placed him at the bottom of
the conductors' hierarchy. He was to answer directly to Eduard Lassen,
and had Lassen been another Fischer then Strauss's term in Weimar would
have been as frustrating as in Munich. But Lassen was 'a splendid fellow',
the embodiment of everything that Strauss could have wished for in a
superior.

By contemporary standards Lassen was old for a Hofkapellmeister.[12] The
responsibilities of the job were demanding, the workload relentless, and it
may have been with some relief that Lassen greeted the young and enthusiastic
Strauss, for whom responsibility and work were the stuff of life. Certainly,
Lassen showed laudable maturity in his handling of his young assistant, for
not only did he treat him as an equal, consulting him over decisions that Levi
and Fischer would have considered none of his business, he also took a
generous interest in Strauss's music. Furthermore, within weeks of his arrival
Lassen invited him to adopt almost all the house's German repertoire. Any
other Hofkapellmeister would have parted with blood before allowing a
subordinate near the masterworks of Mozart and Wagner, but Lassen gave
Strauss free rein, with only four exceptions: *Fidelio*, *Der fliegende Holländer*,
Die Meistersinger and *Der Ring*.

History has been kind to Lassen, but there was more to his benefaction of
Strauss than mere respect and admiration. Not long after their first meeting
Lassen made the mistake of borrowing a fairly considerable sum from Strauss,
to whom he had also lost heavily at the card table. Strauss ensured that Lassen
was under no pressure to settle his account,[13] but Lassen felt the weight of
obligation, and despite fierce ideological differences[14] he became Strauss's
most vociferous advocate in Weimar.

Lassen was among the first to hear Strauss play through the score of *Don
Juan*. His reaction was characteristic, and at the beginning of November 1889
Strauss described in a letter to his father how his Hofkapellmeister had been
'quite beside himself with admiration'. So admiring were Lassen and Bronsart
that they urged Strauss to squeeze the world première into the second of

the season's Subscription Concerts a few days later, on November 11, to be conducted, of course, by its composer.

The rehearsals have entered musical legend. The Weimar orchestra had to be heavily augmented to meet Strauss's requirements, which included sixteen first violins, four horns, three trombones, three trumpets, three flutes, double wind, contra-bassoon, bass tuba, percussion, harp and glockenspiel. The score also demanded an outstanding concert-master, a pre-eminent first oboe and world-class virtuosity from every desk. As Strauss recalled: '... it's dreadfully difficult. I felt sorry for the poor horns and trumpets. They blew till they were blue in the face, it's such a strenuous business for them.' One of the players, soaked with sweat, lowered his instrument, having blown 'with utter defiance',[15] and demanded, 'Dear God! What sin have we committed, for You to send us this rod for our backs.'

The première itself was a triumph. Strauss wrote to his father: 'Don Juan was a magnificent success, the piece sounded magical and went excellently and unleashed a storm of applause fairly unprecedented for Weimar.' Bülow, in a letter to his wife, confirmed the work's 'quite unprecedented success'. As the first genuinely popular orchestral work by a German composer since Brahms's Fourth Symphony of 1884, *Don Juan*'s success catapulted Strauss towards international celebrity, bolstering his already considerable ego.

On October 13, 1889, Dora Weiss risked a criticism: 'I don't want to make you vainer than you've already grown with all the homage you receive, my old friend, and if that displeases you, console yourself with the very true words of Goethe: "Friends reveal to one another more clearly than anything else the one thing that they do not say to one another." Or write?!' Strauss's self-confidence kept pace with his popularity; the more he came to believe his criticism, the less he heeded the advice of those who had helped bring about his success in the first place.

Even Bülow was at risk. He had heard *Don Juan* played in Dresden by Adolph Hagen on January 10, 1890, a performance he considered 'a failure',[16] but he none the less determined to conduct the work himself in Berlin, scheduling the city première for the seventh Philharmonic concert of the season, on January 31. Berlin were no less appreciative of Strauss's work than Weimar and Dresden, but Strauss was outraged by Bülow's performance, and his dissatisfaction brought their long friendship to the point of collapse. Bülow 'had no inkling of the piece', and in a letter to his parents Strauss spelled out his dissatisfaction:

What use to me is success based on misunderstanding? Bülow has a total misconception of my work, in tempos, in everything, no inkling of the poetic content, and he treated it like any other piece of melodious music, rejoicing in subtle instrumentation and interesting combinations and harmonies. No question that he approached it with great diligence, the greatest application and

with a holy fear of failure (which he can't take any more, as he's become awfully
vain), put the rehearsals mainly into the hands of his abominable Jewish wolves,
oxen and cooks,[17] and introduced the public to a very interesting piece of music,
but it was not my *Don Juan*.'

Richard continued to denounce Bülow (despite having acceded to his
specific request for metronome markings), and a variety of explanations
were given for the cooling of their friendship: Strauss was popular at Bayreuth, Bülow was not; Strauss was a thriving composer, Bülow had tried and
failed; Strauss was embraced almost everywhere he went, Bülow was reviled
for his rudeness, over-confidence and short temper; and Strauss was an
increasingly fanatical Wagnerian at a time when Bülow was growing more
and more devoted to the 'beery Brahms'. Strauss also admitted to his pique
at Bülow's supposed intimacy with an 'ugly Jewish circle'[18] in Berlin, where
Ochs and Koch had rehearsed *Don Juan* for the promoter of the Philharmonic
concert, Hermann Wolff. Strauss blamed the Jews for having heightened
Bülow's vanity, and it was these same Jews who had, claimed Strauss, turned
his podium manner into a caricature of exaggerated ticks and mannerisms.

Strauss's anti-Semitism was growing worse, a development traceable to
the influence of one of his oldest friends, Friedrich Rösch. They had known
each other since their schooldays in Munich, when Rösch had entertained
musical ambitions alongside his more talented colleague. A scholarship to
law school led him to pursue a legal career, whereupon he became celebrated
as a champion of composers' publishing rights.

While Rösch cultivated his friend's racial paranoia he was also central to
Strauss's changing attitude to Bülow. *Don Juan* had convinced Strauss of
his artistic course, towards which Bülow could contribute little more. Had
Strauss's hostility been limited to the single concert in Berlin, then his outburst might easily be attributed to youth and precocity. But when, a few days
after the Berlin concert, in February 1890, Bülow travelled to Weimar for
a piano recital and symphonic concert the uncertain atmosphere turned
decidedly hateful. As a pianist, Strauss conceded, Bülow was beyond comparison, but when Bülow stood before the Weimar orchestra and invited the
players to 'give a cheer for Brahms', the Wagner-obsessed young Strauss drew
a line under their once intimate relationship.

From this point onwards Strauss kept Bülow at arm's length, even if he
never actually broke all ties with him. To his father, however, he continued
to denounce Bülow as a reactionary, repeating his opinion that Bülow had
never been a progressive, but that 'the powerful personalities of a Wagner
and a Liszt' had borne him in their wake. Bülow turned the other cheek, and
continued to conduct Strauss's music whenever the opportunity arose.

Strauss tried to forget the incident and returned his attention to Weimar
where, surrounded by friends and sympathisers, he was revelling in the

positive climate. On October 24, 1889, he wrote to Spitzweg: 'I feel very happy here. Herr von Bronsart is the most delightful intendant imaginable, Lassen the most charming of colleagues and, like Bronsart, a sensitive artist; the orchestra is good and has taken me to its heart, and the singers too have been as co-operative as you could imagine.'

Four months later, he was finding less free time in which to pursue his own interests. Bronsart was a hard taskmaster and Lassen was surrendering more of his responsibilities. Significantly, he now asked Strauss to take over his four Subscription Concerts, even allowing him carte blanche to schedule his own programmes. Had Bronsart not intervened, Weimar would have been prescribed a concentrated diet of Liszt and Wagner (whose music was already well represented by Lassen). As Strauss wrote to his uncle, Carl Hörburger, at the end of the year, he had been ordered to lighten his 'insanely modern programmes' with 'one or two works by Beethoven in three of the concerts and Schubert's C major in the last'. Ironically, after the second concert, in which he had conducted Beethoven's *Pastoral* Symphony, Bronsart criticised Strauss for his 'Bülowish' performance. Whereas this criticism, from Perfall, had been received by Strauss as the highest praise, from Bronsart it was a crushing dismissal.

Strauss's arrival in Weimar signified a change of direction unprecedented since Liszt's tenure forty years earlier.[19] He retired many of Lassen's regular players and set about retraining the orchestra, which was ill-suited to tackling Bronsart's catholic tastes. Strauss's repertoire for the 1889–90 season – his first – included works by composers he had never heard of, far less played, and his survival testifies to an extraordinary facility for sight-conducting. German composers accounted for the bulk of his work: three operas by Mozart (including *Don Giovanni*), three by Weber (including *Euryanthe*), three by Lortzing (including *Undine*), two by Wagner (*Tannhäuser* and *Lohengrin*), Beethoven's *Fidelio*, Gluck's *Iphigenia in Aulis*, Nicolai's *Die lustigen Weiber von Windsor*, Marschner's *Hans Heiling*, Flotow's *Stradella* and a new work of Wagnerolatory, *Der Meisterdieb*, by a local Weimar singing teacher Eugen Lindner. Strauss took little pleasure in preparing his French and Italian repertoire, which was exclusively populist, and although he detested Meyerbeer[20] and his music, he was expected to conduct two of his most long-winded operas, *Le Prophète* and *L'Africaine*. Thereafter, he had the pleasure of learning Auber's *La Muette de Portici*, Aimé Maillart's *Les Dragons de Villars* and Bellini's *Norma*. Taken as a whole, his schedule demanded that he prepare and conduct no fewer than twenty-two operas in a single season. An average repertoire conductor one hundred years later would have programmed no more than half a dozen.

His work on *Lohengrin* gives a clear indication of the effort he made to meet Bronsart's expectations. With Cosima's advice propelling him towards a duplication of the 'Bayreuth style', Strauss worked furiously to rid his new production of all the bad habits and 'insinuated ... traditions' that had become standardised over the previous thirty years. The Bayreuth tradition, as far as Wagner was concerned, had nothing to do with *Lohengrin*, which he never saw staged there, and the irony, for Strauss at least, was that while Bayreuth provided a huge string section for all its productions, he had to make do with an orchestra almost half the size, in which there were roughly the same number of strings as had played in the original performances conducted by Liszt in 1850.[21] He enjoyed numerous full-company piano rehearsals, private sessions with Heinrich Zeller (*Lohengrin*), Franz Schwarz (*Telramund*) and Louise Tibelti (*Ortrud*), a lengthy stage-movement rehearsal and two five-hour orchestral rehearsals.

Sadly, his exhaustive preparation paid few dividends. The orchestra played competently and the leads kept pace with Strauss's furious tempi, but the staging was archaic, and the chorus and supporting cast fell back on the bad habits that Strauss had tried so hard to eradicate. As he recalled, 'None of the entrances went right, they sang out into the audience, ignored the Master's stage directions! The stage director is a totally incompetent, elderly, bass-singing, theatrical hack!' Strauss seems to have been highly praised for his work and, despite Bronsart's assertion that the production was in need of a complete overhaul, he relished the applause for his Third Conductor.

On October 7, 1889, Strauss wrote to his sister: 'The *Lohengrin* was a brilliant success. Colossal praise from Frau W., who was quite enchanted and said that only in Karlsruhe (among all opera houses) had she been so profoundly impressed as the day before yesterday by my *Lohengrin*. All the tempos wonderful, the modulations of them sensitive and unobtrusive, there was great breadth in the performance, the orchestra finely shaded and discreet ... In short she was full of praise, quite moved and even kissed me, she herself began to applaud after the prelude, and in fact I have never conducted so well in my life as I did the day before yesterday.'

His affection for Cosima grew with every encounter: 'I was frightfully interested in her perfectly correct judgement of Bülow, of whom we talked a great deal ... She has completely finished with Levi and is waiting for the first good opportunity to get rid of him in some adroit way ... I am completely enchanted by her amiability, by all that she stands for and by her profound understanding.' This extended to a favourable opinion of Pauline de Ahna, and Richard endorsed her as a valuable addition to the Bayreuth *corps d'opéra*, preparing her for an audition,[22] after which she received an invitation to 'contribute' to the 1890–91 season as either the Shepherd Boy[23] in *Tannhäuser* or as one of the Flower Maidens in *Parsifal*.

As well as Pauline[24] (and the tenor Heinrich Zeller, whom he also brought with him from Munich), Strauss was expected to take other singing pupils, and so he accepted a small number of Weimar locals; but so demanding a workload, combining teaching, opera rehearsals, performances, private cast rehearsals and public Subscription Concerts, was beginning to tell on him. In 1892 he described to his parents his life during 'a few busy days'. On Tuesday evening he conducted a performance of *Tristan* in Weimar, after which he left by train for Leipzig. On Wednesday morning he rehearsed the Gewandhaus Orchestra in a programme of music by Liszt. He returned to Weimar the same day and, on Thursday evening, he conducted a performance of *Lohengrin* in Eisenach. He returned to Leipzig at one o'clock on Friday morning and from 10 to 1 and between 3 and 6 the same day he rehearsed for a two-hour concert, with Siloti as the piano soloist. In short, during the seventy-two hours separating the Weimar *Tristan* from the Leipzig concert he travelled over four hundred miles and conducted over eighteen hours of music. 'I am a little tired', Strauss wrote, 'but well, gay, and in good spirits. I relish such battles.'

The pressure of his schedule and the needs of his pupils left him little time to pursue a social life or to further his ambitions as a composer. This is surely one of the reasons why he and Pauline waited so many years before marrying. With the exception of a new tone poem, *Tod und Verklärung*,[25] and a handful of songs, he produced nothing of significance between *Don Juan* (November 1889) and *Guntram* (May 1894), a period of four-and-a-half years. He finished the score of *Tod und Verklärung* on November 18, 1889, having conceived of the programme during the previous winter, and the first performance was arranged for June 21, 1890, when it was performed alongside an earlier work, his *Burleske* for piano and orchestra.

Strauss also did his best to further the music of Alexander Ritter. *Der faule Hans* (Idle Hans) had been produced in Munich in 1885 when, as a precursor to Humperdinck's *Hänsel und Gretel*, it was praised for its cultivation of the principles of *Märchenoper* (fairy-tale opera). Although Ritter's text lacked wit, bogged down as it was by questionable theorising, the music was praised for its skill and originality, so much so that it warranted a variety of new productions before Strauss determined to stage it alongside Ritter's latest opera, *Wem die Krone?* (Who is the Crown?).

Strauss remained devoted to both operas for the rest of his life, going so far as to recommend them, in his testament to Karl Böhm, as works of pivotal significance to the future of the German operatic repertoire. Neither Böhm nor anyone else has revived them. Blinded by his faith, Strauss looked upon Ritter's operas as the 'only' viable development of Wagner's work, which stood 'like a gigantic colossus of pure ore on the swampy ground of the German theatre'. He conducted the first performance of *Wem die Krone?* in a double-bill with *Der faule Hans* on June 9, 1890, in front of an audience largely made up of the composer's friends and admirers. If the first night was considered a 'tumultuous success, constantly reaffirmed at every performance' by Ritter's son-in-law Siegmund von Hausegger, then his somewhat prejudiced opinion must be set against the commercial realities of the production which, for all Strauss's efforts, warranted only seven additional performances.

Both works were adopted by a number of German theatres in the wake of the Weimar productions, primarily thanks to Strauss's heartfelt recommendations.[26] Ritter's gratitude to Strauss, the son he never had, was beyond measure and the two grew closer as each looked to the other for salvation. They were even painted together by Leopold von Kalckreuth, a portrait which shows Strauss bending his head towards his wizened mentor. When Ritter returned to Weimar for one of the last of the eight performances in February 1892, Strauss wrote to his sister: 'It's happy days with me at present, as at last, in my wonderful Ritter, I again have a friend with me to whom I can unburden myself in complete confidence and with whom I know I am completely at one! I can't tell you all how much good it does me to talk everything over with him in the thick of the chaos that reigns in the theatre here. Aah! It's like a breath of fresh air.'

Strauss valued their shared social and racial philosophies as much as their musical congruence, and his kinship with Ritter continued to dominate his life. It was a relationship beyond discord and must have seemed one of the few certainties which their godless lives had to offer. Considering their intimacy, it must have been doubly painful when this precious rapport began to decay. Before the trials of *Guntram*, however, one last creative liaison lay before them: *Tod und Verklärung*.

THE HERO'S BATTLEFIELD

June 1890–October 1892

On June 21, 1890, Strauss conducted the second major première of one of his own works since his arrival in Weimar. As with *Don Juan,* the first performance of *Tod und Verklärung* was an occasion of triumph for Strauss, emphasising his reputation both as a composer and a conductor.[1] *Le tout Weimar* heard the work at the third concert of the 1891 season when Strauss conducted it in a programme that included Mozart's *Jupiter* Symphony. He later conducted the Berlin première with the city Philharmonic on February 23, 1891, after which Hans von Bülow confessed his total incomprehension of the work and its composer.

Like *Don Juan, Tod und Verklärung* followed a detailed programme. Strauss was loath to give too much away, but in 1895 he was asked by Friedrich von Hausegger to provide a comprehensive guide to the work's underlying narrative. Strauss replied:

> It was about six years ago when the idea occurred to me to represent the death of a person who had striven for the highest ideals, therefore very possibly an artist, in a tone poem. The sick man lies in a bed asleep, breathing heavily and irregularly; agreeable dreams charm a smile on to his features in spite of his suffering; his sleep becomes lighter; he wakens; once again he is racked by terrible pain, his limbs shake with fever – as the attack draws to a close and the pain resumes, the fruit of his path through life appears to him, the idea, the Ideal which he has tried to realise, to represent in his art, but which he has been unable to perfect because it was not for any human being to perfect it. The hour of death approaches, the soul leaves the body, in order to find perfected in the most glorious form in the eternal cosmos that which he could not fulfil here on earth.

Forty years later, when he was keen to distance himself from the anti-abstraction that possessed him as a young man, Strauss claimed that *Tod und Verklärung* was 'purely a product of the imagination – it is not based on any kind of personal experience ... It was an idea just like any other, probably ultimately the musical need – after *Macbeth* (which begins and ends in D minor) and *Don Juan* (which begins and ends in E minor) – to write a piece that begins in C minor and finishes in C major! *Qui le sait?*

As an explanation, this is narrow when applied to a work with a title as *fin de siècle* as 'Death and Transfiguration'.[2] Ritter had instilled within Strauss an awareness of his destiny as a German musician as well as an acute sense of responsibility as the only real heir to Wagner's legacy. The 'Death' of the title can be applied as easily to German music post-Wagner as it can to the passing of a mythical artist, and the Transfiguration is as likely to be a metaphor for the transformation of German music at the hands of Richard Strauss as it is a literal representation of the human faith in an afterlife. Strauss, like Wagner and Schopenhauer before him, was much taken by the idea of rebirth through death.

Tod und Verklärung invites another, more intimate reading. It is no coincidence that 'the artist', as portrayed by Strauss, is a young man. He reflects upon his 'past life', his 'childhood' and his 'youth', but there is no mention of a lifetime's experience and 'the artist's' terms of recollection would have been the same had the 25-year-old composer been the work's subject. Consequently, *Tod und Verklärung* can be read as a metaphor for the passing of the influence of his father and Hans von Bülow, and the transfiguration of his life and work as directed by Ritter.

Furthermore, the 'ideal' referred to by Strauss in his letter to Hausegger is as much the ideal of programme music as it is the representation of aesthetic perfection. Strauss understood that both faiths were subject to the limitations of original sin and, on this level, *Tod und Verklärung* is an involuntarily theological composition. It betrayed a frailty that defied the contemporary sympathy for Nietzsche's muscular gospel, favouring a Judaeo-Christian philosophy of humility and compassion. Strauss was celebrated for neither quality and by this stage his atheism was unshakeable; but his own reading of *Tod und Verklärung*'s programme shows him moving away from the bombast of *Don Juan*, and towards a more reasoned, vulnerable aesthetic.

Judged purely as a work of programme music *Tod und Verklärung* is an unerring evocation of the inevitability of death. It paints a vivid portrait of the final stages of an irreversible illness and, in 1949, Strauss remarked to his daughter-in-law Alice: 'It's a funny thing, but dying is exactly like I composed it sixty years ago in *Tod und Verklärung*.' The irregular breathing and faltering pulse of the introduction, the resignation of the opening C minor melody, the vivid stabs of pain, the grandly expressed life-struggle and the C major denouement may well appear hackneyed to a century inured to late Romanticism, but for the 1890s *Tod und Verklärung* was a startlingly bold composition, and in its structure and narrative it secured Strauss's reputation as the most inventive composer since Liszt.

This innovation, and the success of the first performance, gave Strauss unexpected leverage in his dealings with his publisher. On November 19 he wrote to Spitzweg:

> I am rather embarrassed as to what to ask you for *Tod und Verklärung*, since the work is the latest and most mature thing I have written, and since I do not expect to compose anything more for a while, as I am turning my back on absolute music altogether,[3] in order to seek my salvation in drama, therefore I should like a tidy little sum for it, which I need on my damn small salary, but, since it's you, only half what I would ask another publisher for ... perhaps we could come to some arrangement whereby you pay me in instalments spread over three or four years, that way it will last me longer. I can't and won't ask you straight out for a particular sum, since I don't know how our shares stand, and the confounded thing about my business is that one can never be sure that it won't take ten years for something to start showing a profit and I really wouldn't want to do you any injury.

Strauss asked for 2,000 marks. Spitzweg offered 1,600 – 400 less than Strauss's annual salary at Weimar, but twice as much as he had received for *Don Juan*. As with all such transactions, and in line with nineteenth-century publishing practice, Strauss surrendered all rights to the work, as well as any future arrangements or revisions, for a single payment. There were to be no royalties and he relinquished all rights over production, presentation and performance. Already, there were tensions developing between Strauss and his publisher, particularly since he was beginning to consider placing his works with wealthier, more generous rivals. When, in 1891, he took *Macbeth* to C. F. Peters with a price-tag of 1,500 marks Spitzweg asked him to reconsider. Strauss informed Spitzweg that he could have the work if he paid the asking price. Reluctantly, Spitzweg added it to his Aibl imprint, temporarily resisting the obvious commercial magnetism of the older, more powerful competitor, but Strauss's success was outgrowing Spitzweg's ability to pay for it.

There was also friction of a more serious nature developing in Weimar between Strauss and Bronsart. Well before the première of *Tod und Verklärung* Bronsart had begun to find Strauss's inflated self-importance a strain on house morale. Bronsart couldn't fault Strauss's abilities, and he was the first to admit to the beauty and skill of his music, but the administration of a theatrical establishment as grand as that in Weimar was simply too involved to allow for the sort of licence that Strauss was beginning to expect from his colleagues and employers.

It appeared he had determined to reverse the accepted theatrical polarity by which a conductor was subordinate to the producer and, whenever conducting, he made it clear that his was the only opinion worth heeding. This dictatorial approach, anticipating the ruinous autocracies of the 1920s and 30s, worked for Bülow and a small number of his peers, but for a Third

Conductor to adopt the manner and expect the latitude of a general music director was disastrous. On July 8, 1890, Bronsart took action: 'Some modi-fication of your ultra-radical views would be altogether desirable, and although I hope that, with more experience, the forces which drive you to over-hasty overthrow will settle into a harmonious equilibrium, yet I am obliged to say, in some alarm, that ever since you assumed your office I have, in fact, seen you advance further and further along that path.'

Weimar had been home to Goethe and Liszt, Bronsart reminded Strauss, and he wielded their names as panaceas, urging Strauss to take his time and soak up some of Weimar's tradition. He traced the source of Strauss's mission to Bayreuth and Cosima Wagner: 'Every good musician who had a close association with Wagner has a better and more reliable knowledge of [the performance of his works] than the Master's unmusical widow. But above all, everyone who knew Wagner at all well knows how liable the Master himself was to change his mind about a host of things – staging, tempos, etc. – and you yourself, my dear Strauss, sometimes select tempos (let me remind you of the end of the *Tannhäuser* Overture among many other instances) which notoriously contradict Wagner's known intentions, in other words, to use your own argument, which cannot be reconciled with correct performance style.'

An awareness of his burgeoning genius had left Strauss insensitive to the feelings of his subordinates. This brusqueness was not in itself remarkable but there was something brutal in Strauss's vehement dismissal of weakness. The compassion hinted at in *Tod und Verklärung* was scarcely evident in a disposition so devoid of restraint that Bronsart was forced to write:

> You must learn to control yourself at least enough, even when you are excited, to stop using at every moment turns of phrase which you would condemn severely in the mouth of another person. You must learn to respect indi-vidualities in your dealings with your artists at least enough, even though they are working under your general direction, to acknowledge their entitlement to a certain degree of independent artistic judgement, and you must not call it 'style-less' every time that somebody feels differently from you about a matter. Finally, you must learn to control yourself enough not to lose sight altogether of our respected positions, however excited you may be ... If your temperament – whether innately or by upbringing is immaterial – is so immoderate that you cannot control it, then you have no future in circumstances which rest on subordination.

Although his reply is lost, Strauss was evidently furious and expressed his amazement at having received so candid a reproach from someone who only a week earlier, on July 1, had praised him for his 'truly noble attitude ... friendly goodwill and fatherly indulgence'. Strauss's letters to his friends and family conveyed none of these tensions. Rather, he reinforced a positive image of life in Weimar and punctuated lengthy descriptions of his routine with glowing accounts of triumphs and plaudits. There is throughout a strong sense of over-protestation, particularly whenever making reference to the atmosphere in the opera house. By the end of August 1890 this must have become stifling. Bronsart was despairing of Strauss's devotion to the 'fanatical Bayreuth cult'; boosted by Cosima Wagner's admiration, his self-confidence was leading him towards an egocentricity wholly inappropriate to his position and responsibilities.

Despairingly, Bronsart urged Strauss to remember his place: 'The expressions of your extreme tendencies would cause me no alarm as to your future – I regard them as no more than the symptoms of a certain *Sturm und Drang* phase which natures of genius customarily go through in order to work off a certain excess of vigour, and from which you will emerge in time with a harmonious equilibrium restored, if you are fundamentally sound – but they do represent a danger to the sphere of influence you enjoy in your position.'

During these combustible times Strauss made the mistake of turning to Cosima for guidance, to whom he raised Bayreuth as the ideal against which all other theatres, including Weimar, were to be measured:

There is a need for the true pursuit of art at least for two months a year[4] for what we 'accomplish' in our court theatres amounts with few exceptions (e.g., the fortunate Mottl[5]) to nothing more than attempts so modest that one's whole courage simply goes overboard – apart from that the 'German people' – but forgive me, is there such a thing? I think that now there's only a German public and that's pitiable enough – so let's at least speak of a German people, even if it no longer exists, so, the German people needs 'once a year' a reminder, in letters of fire, that it could have a German art if it wanted.

Throughout the winter of 1890–91 Strauss tried to avoid collisions with Bronsart, and attempted to suppress his anxiety by concentrating on work, Pauline de Ahna, and *Guntram*. He broadened his repertoire to include more of Liszt's music (chiefly the A major Piano Concerto, the symphonic poem *Orpheus*, the fantasy for piano and orchestra *Todtentanz*, and the *Faust Symphony*[6]) and he indulged a fleeting infatuation for the music of Emmanuel Chabrier, a French composer celebrated for his hefty Wagnerian *hommages*, *Gwendoline* and *Le Roi malgré lui*. Of German composers, his favourites remained Beethoven, Liszt and Wagner, but he also conducted music by Schumann (including his Third Symphony, which he greatly disliked), Rheinberger, Nicodé, Bülow, Raff, Humperdinck, Draeseke and Ritter. In September 1890 Strauss emulated Berlioz and Wagner's youthful passion for Gluck when he prepared a new edition of *Iphigénie en Aulide* for modern performance. On April 18, 1891, he wrote to the publisher Adolph Fürstner:

> Taking Richard Wagner's version of Gluck's *Iphigenia in Aulis* as my model, I
> have completed a revision of the same composer's *Iphigénie en Aulide*, which I
> hope to see performed here next season. My revision consists of a completely
> new translation, actually a new text in parts (with some elements taken from
> Goethe's play), especially in the first act, in which the order of the scenes has
> been entirely changed, and the last act, for which I have composed a new ending,
> as well as changes in the scoring, to bring it into line with modern requirements
> ... My only purpose in writing now is to inquire whether you might be interested
> in publishing this version, which has given new life to a beautiful work?

Fürstner did, indeed, want to publish Strauss's arrangement, although it did
not appear until 1895, and remained unperformed until 1900 when, on
June 9, long after Strauss's departure from Weimar, Rudolf Krzyzanowski
conducted the first and, as things turned out, one of the last performances.

Strauss also programmed a small number of works by Lassen, one of
which – the incidental music to *Faust* – provoked tension between him and
his pupil Pauline de Ahna. Pauline evidently paid more attention to the
work's composer (who was standing in the wings) than its conductor, and at
one point she entered a bar early. Strauss was visibly furious, and three days
later he wrote: 'Most respected Fräulein, By all appearances you are now so
set on going your own way that my presence and the influence it inevitably
exercises could only seem a burden to you; I regret therefore that I must
gratefully decline your kind invitation both today and in the future, and I
remain with best wishes, yours most sincerely, Richard Strauss.'

After hearing of their separation Franz urged his son towards reconciliation: 'Do it to please me and put things straight again ... Fräulein de
Ahna seems to be rather given to over-exciting herself, and a man of good
breeding can always allow some latitude to a lady of that kind, without
lowering himself. Also I am sure she is the singer who will come closest to
realising your intentions.' Strauss resented anyone, far less a singer, taking
the upper hand, but he was captivated by Pauline's mood-swings. To him at
least, her fearsome pugnacity and capriciousness were irresistibly seductive.

In truth, Strauss was in no position to criticise Pauline for resisting him.
Her strides for independence were reminiscent of his own, and throughout
the 1890–91 season her growth in popularity was so rapid that she was now
quite able to thrive outside Strauss's influence. He doubtless had a hand in
promoting her talents to Bronsart and Cosima, and he had contributed much
to her headlong improvement as a *dramatischer Sopran*, but Pauline was, and
would always remain, her own woman.

She made her successful Weimar debut on May 22, 1890, as Pamina in
Zauberflöte, a role for which her voice must have been a size too large;[7] Strauss

had nothing but praise for her performance: 'de Ahna had a tremendous success and sang capitally, as well as acting and moving on the stage with a boldness and assurance that amazed everybody. The voice blended wonderfully with the orchestra, in short, her success exceeded all expectations. Such a shame that Frau Ritter wasn't here, she would have had enormous pleasure from the fruits of all the hard work she had in teaching her.'

So successful was Pauline that Bronsart offered her a five-year contract at a modest salary of 1,200 marks. Despite the meagre financial rewards, the artistic benefits were enormous, for the contract enabled her to develop and master her repertoire. This continued to set Mozart's gentle lyricism against Wagner's trenchant declamation, but she successfully bridged the conflicting demands, studying Pamina in *Zauberflöte* and Elvira in *Don Giovanni* alongside Elsa in *Lohengrin*, Elizabeth in *Tannhäuser* and Eva in *Die Meistersinger*. She was unsuited to the heavier demands of Brünnhilde and Sieglinde, and she could never have seriously attempted Isolde.[8]

In May the effects of his stressful private life, compounded by professional restlessness and an oppressive workload, proved too much for the wiry, chain-smoking Strauss and he contracted pneumonia. During six days in hospital he lived out his own *Tod und Verklärung*. As his condition deteriorated he unburdened himself of his fears and regrets, the most pointed being his lament that he had not been able to conduct *Tristan und Isolde*. Between bouts of unconsciousness he repeated lengthy passages from the opera to himself, as if the mantra of Wagner's genius would somehow restore him to health. His reaction to so close a brush with death demonstrated that his detachment from religion was now complete. At a time when even the most lapsed Catholic would have been reaching for a rosary, Strauss turned to Wagner for salvation.

He recuperated at his uncle's[9] house in Feldafing, where he engaged in a voluminous correspondence with friends and family. So fearful was he of not being invited to conduct at the 1891 festival he signed one of his letters to Cosima 'dying of longing for Bayreuth'. He made much of his plans to remain healthy in the future. These included giving up smoking and slowing his pace of life, but at a time when thousands died yearly from influenza, much less pneumonia, his assurance to Cosima that his convalescence was 'proceeding apace' signified little. In a worthy gesture of goodwill, Cosima and her daughter Eva travelled the 160-mile journey from Bayreuth to visit Richard in Feldafing. It must have been a rejuvenating sight for him to see his father walking around the gardens arm-in-arm with the widow of his most hated enemy.

With no word from Cosima, Strauss grew desperate. On June 12, 1891, he informed her that 'the most beautiful panorama of mountains and the most glorious view seem to mock me as I think of the view from the Festival Hill'. He signed himself 'most tractable and in need of instruction, Richard Strauss'.

The day before, on his twenty-seventh birthday, he was visited by 'Dear uncle Ritter', who brought with him a message from Cosima informing him that she, Pauline and Zeller would be celebrating the occasion in his absence at Bayreuth. By June 20 it was obvious to everyone except Strauss that he would not be conducting at that summer's festival. On July 1 this was officially confirmed when Cosima invited him to return as an assistant.

There was more to her reservation than concern for Strauss's health. Hermann Levi was mistrustful of advancing him to a position of influence within the Festspielhaus at such a young age; he was also wary of his self-confidence and resentful of his anti-Semitism. Although he would later woo Strauss back to Munich he was then concerned that Strauss might upset the subtle balance that existed between himself, the conductor Felix Mottl and Cosima.[10] While Strauss did not conduct that year, he was none the less treated as a member of the inner Bayreuth circle. On July 7 he wrote to his uncle: 'She [Cosima] says she would be so worried and would not be easy in her mind listening to a note conducted by me. She says the doctors have written to her that I need to be spared as much as possible and suchlike nonsense and that is why she is so fearfully worried. Although I'm not conducting I'm treated like M[ottl] and L[evi], eat luncheon and dinner with the Wagner family, and am cared for and watched over like a small child. I must console myself with the thought of next year.'

Strauss's time was monopolised by preparations for the first ever pro-duction of *Tannhäuser* at Bayreuth. Well remembering his dying remark that he 'still owed the world *Tannhäuser*', Cosima had vowed to bring her husband's most maligned and misunderstood drama to the stage of the Festspielhaus. With the solid financial backing provided by the success of the 1889 festival she threw herself into the project with a zeal unseen since the first production of *Parsifal* nearly a decade earlier. Cosima had forty-four designs prepared for Venus's costume alone, and she researched every minor point of historical detail down to the giving of historical names and titles to the 116 guests for the song contest.

In addition to the noblemen there were sixty-five huntsmen, a pilgrim's chorus of thirty-two, forty younger pilgrims, thirty knights and sixty-four dancers for the Bacchanal. There was also a pack of hounds, specially trained to bark on command. Added to an orchestra of around one hundred, this meant that Cosima and her assistant, Richard Strauss, were overseeing a theatrical company of nearly four hundred and fifty – not including the dogs.

The festival was a huge commercial success, with tickets being sold on the black market for up to four times their marked price, but the critical reception was brutally dismissive. According to Houston Stewart Chamberlain, of the three hundred papers to publish reviews of the new *Tannhäuser* only one saluted Cosima's efforts. That she had chosen to stage the Paris edition of the opera – i.e., that version for which her husband had been vilified in France –

rather than the Dresden edition was in itself provocative, but her (mis)interpretation of the work as a Christian mystery play caused a sensation. The performances were no more than satisfactory. Mottl conducted well and the orchestra played magnificently, but the alternating Tannhäusers – Max Alvary, Hermann Winkelmann and Strauss's pupil Heinrich Zeller – were a disappointment. The indisposed Pauline was outshone by Elisa Wiborg, a young and inexperienced Norwegian soprano, who replaced her at two hours' notice.

In September 1891 Strauss proudly informed Cosima that he had talked Bronsart and Lassen into allowing him to mount a new production of *Tristan und Isolde*, which he would prepare, rehearse and conduct. It was to be the first mounted in Weimar. On October 5 he wrote to his father: 'Yesterday I rehearsed *Tristan I* [the first act] with the whole orchestra for the first time, it's going very well already and even though the rehearsals are very painstaking and precise, with all the details being worked out in the most meticulous manner, the orchestra almost seem to enjoy it. How times change! My nuances are proving to be capital, there is no point now where the singer is swamped.' His ecstasy was so great that, as he wrote to Cosima two weeks later, he was 'delighted by the least good, or good-intentioned, thing that we bring off artistically'.

The rehearsals, including seventeen with full orchestra,[11] continued into January 1892. Franz urged his son to take it easy:

> *Tristan* will cause you much work and worry. I'll be glad when it is all over. Do not hold overlong rehearsals. It's no use tiring everybody, for then a lethargy sets in which works to the disadvantage of the project. A rehearsal of five hours is too long. *Tristan* contains no moments where one can coast and pull oneself together ... I know it from my own experience ... Consider that your orchestra is small and everyone has to contribute to the utmost of his power. And quite a few of the orchestral members are elderly and cannot stand such extraordinary exertions. Be sensible, dear Richard!

Strauss conducted the première on January 17, 1892. Four days later he wrote to his parents that the performance had been 'wonderful; the orchestra of the greatest refinement and elasticity, the staging done by Brandt as beautifully as it could be without any money, and all the singers excellent ... In spite of some things on which I disagreed with him, Brandt proved himself a superb producer, the performance was thoroughly unified and aroused the greatest enthusiasm. Brandt and I took a call after the first act, and after the third, and I look back on our great deed with the greatest satisfaction.'

To Cosima he wrote that 'the great event' had 'aroused a tempest of enthusiasm among the audience and the artists ... I was really pleased with the orchestra; they played with exceptional finesse, very free and elastic, so that my *alla breve* could respond as I wished to every modification of the singer's parts ... Now I've conducted *Tristan* for the first time, and it was the most wonderful day of my life.'

With *Tristan* behind him, Strauss came to believe an appointment at Bayreuth was a foregone conclusion, but in March 1892 Cosima announced her intention to invite Wiborg and Alvary instead of de Ahna and Zeller to that summer's festival. Strauss was horrified. As far as he was concerned Wiborg had no voice and Alvary was a 'miserable ham-actor'. He demanded of Cosima to know why, since both sopranos had sung at the previous year's festival, she had asked only one of them to return: 'if a new Elisabeth appears, who really is better than Wiborg and de Ahna, then drop both.'

As Strauss must surely have known, Wiborg was the better artist, but if Alvary lacked theatricality he more than compensated with vocal weight. Strauss fired off a series of ever more indignant letters to Cosima, who responded by offering Strauss the opportunity to rehearse *Die Meistersinger*[12] for Hans Richter, after which he would be allowed to conduct the season's last two performances. Strauss received the offer as an insult[13] and replied: 'I shall not achieve anything if I am "squeezed in" as a stopgap. I'm a newcomer in Bayreuth and need time and a chance to make myself at home in the work entrusted to me slowly and in collaboration with all the people involved; preparing a work for somebody else is beyond me, my nature's not pliable enough for that.'

To study an opera he had never conducted with the man who had copied the score for the composer was, indeed, a stroke of rare fortune, but it was one that Strauss considered beneath him. As he proudly announced, he was 'nobody's stand-in'. The success of *Tristan* had inflated his perception of himself to a point where he was barely in control, and when Cosima's patience finally snapped she expressed herself in terms that brought the 27-year-old temporarily back down to earth. This letter has been lost, or destroyed, but Strauss's reply makes it clear that Cosima had ridiculed his presumption.

He was now ready to serve Bayreuth as 'a lamp-cleaner or orchestral attendant' if that was what she wanted, but only days later he proceeded to ask for his own production of *Tristan* or *Tannhäuser*. Were she to accede, he would happily rehearse *Meistersinger* for Richter. On April 18 she duly conceded Mottl's *Tristan*, only to revoke the offer two days later.

Strauss made further demands, this time belittling Richter. Cosima was furious, but conciliatory: 'Should Richter spoil your intentions then I assure you that Others have befouled Mine ... as long as I continue to work you too shall continue to conduct here, even though your reputation has been torn to shreds.' In his letters to his family Strauss painted a different picture of events: 'I was infernally vehement and actually won my point. Frau Wagner yielded and will talk to Mottl (only now!) about his letting me have *Tristan* ... Frau Wagner's letters at first full of refusals and reproaches, then offering a few loopholes and then giving in. I shall have whatever I wish and a grand reconciliation.'

Franz blamed the whole affair on the Jews: 'It looks as though only slaves are wanted in Bayreuth. In my opinion she'd better take Jews, there are enough of them about ... let the Jews get on with it. As I see it, everything points to a greater interest in making money than in purely artistic matters, how else could they prefer a comedian like Alvary again? The whole business looks to me like a kind of Jewry in "Aryan" clothing.'

By the end of May, Strauss was flagging beneath the pressure. He had achieved nothing with Cosima and remained at loggerheads with Bronsart. He had composed nothing for months, and was contracted to rehearse and conduct a new opera, *Loreley*, by Hans Sommer, a friend who had moved to Weimar in 1888. The five orchestral rehearsals were exhausting, as the work was 'insanely difficult', and on June 5 he was again confined to his bed, this time suffering from pleurisy. Although doctors advised him to stay in bed, *Loreley* demanded his attention and he cut short his recuperation. On June 10 he returned to work, conducting the world première just two days later.

To his sister Johanna he wrote on June 14: 'It was a gigantic slog, but it went capitally and was well received. Sommer was called to take a bow after the love duet and several times at the end, after the fourth act I too was applauded so much that I had to take a bow ... Sommer, I'm afraid, will never grasp that nowadays one can't just haul Loreleis out of the romantic attic ...' Strauss, none the less, felt that the exercise had proved worth while since he had 'once again done a little honour to a German composer who isn't a Jew'.

A few days after the last performance in the run Strauss's health began to worsen, and shortly after returning to the family home in Munich he suffered a serious attack of bronchitis. His doctors ordered him to withdraw from work and take the waters in Reichenhall, where he was later joined by Pauline and her family. As a result, circumstances ensured that he could not even visit Bayreuth, far less conduct there; he wrote to Cosima: 'Two performances of *Meistersinger* were not enough for me, I wanted to play the lion too, and now? I am not conducting a note, I do not hear a note, I devote myself to the curing of his eminence my health and sit in Reichenhall, surrounded by Berlin Jews, taking saline baths and drinking whey.'

Reichenhall proved insufficiently curative and he was advised to move to warmer climes where uninterrupted sun was more likely to dry up the water on Strauss's lungs. As before, his uncle George came to the rescue. He offered his nephew the sum of 5,000 marks if he agreed to undertake a grand tour of Greece and Egypt. Richard was pale, dangerously thin, and many seriously feared for his life. He was also physically exhausted and battle-worn. His uncle's offer was too good to ignore, and at the end of October 1892 he took the money and left.

Strauss's exhaustion and frustration were not solely engendered by his immediate circumstances. For all his bourgeois resignation Strauss was as sensitive to the health of his country as he was to his own condition. En route to Greece he left behind a Germany struggling with economic hardship, social uncertainty, political ambiguity and cultural passivity. As he wrote to his father after a few weeks away: 'I can no longer stand Germany. It makes me ill.' In short, he thought Germany was going to the dogs and Greece's unrelieved sunshine and ingratiating populace heightened his disgust for life back home.

Strauss's feelings for his own people were unusually capricious. Condescending in private, he was gracious in public, extending a generous hand whenever his own works were well received; but his defining impulses were fatalistic. In 1893, for example, he received a vocal score of Leoncavallo's *Pagliacci* while staying in Palermo: 'What a paltry, botched thing it is! Yet another work worthy of the German public! And that's the crew for which Wagner worked and suffered for fifty years!' And yet Strauss considered the German spirit and German culture of immeasurable significance, so much so that when, in 1933, the conductor Fritz Busch wrote to Strauss: 'Just think, *Tristan* is beginning to be less of a draw at the box office,' he replied: 'Even if only one person pays for a seat at *Tristan* it must be performed for him, because he must be the last surviving German!'

His perception of the Fatherland – a mythical utopia husbanded by Goethes and Wagners – appealed to him more than the reality, which brought him greater concern than confidence. In 1885 the polemicist Heinrich Hart wrote an infamous attack against 'Prince Bismarck and his relationship to German literature'. The article was, in fact, a rampant assault on the Chancellor's failure to make the arts a priority of his new government. Hart amplified the increasing dissatisfaction with Bismarck's apparently conscious decision to do nothing to further German cultural activity. His attitude towards musicians, painters, poets and writers, Hart claimed, seemed to include them among his hated *Honoratioren*, the sponges of a society in which everyone was to serve a purpose.

Strauss was one of many who feared the objective imperialisation of German culture. Privately, at least, he mirrored the young man in Conrad Alberti's novel *Die Alten und Jungen* (The Old and the Young) who screamed, 'I'll tell you what we need. We need a Sedan in which we play the part of the French. We need a Jena that will tear us out of this stinking, fouled, slovenly bed upon which the bourgeois has thrown us – so that the rabble that has ruled the fatherland since 1870, jobbers and NCOs will learn that there is something higher than stock-market swindling and close-order drill.'

There was a lesson here for those Germans who, cherishing Wagner as the apogee of German creativity, failed to see how far their idol had turned himself, and his art, away from the responsible reflection of contemporary life. Having drawn potent inspiration from the struggle for unity in 1848, Wagner's early philosophy had benefited from a strong sense of social cognizance. The ideas behind *Der Ring* and, to a lesser extent, *Die Meistersinger* were socialistic, but only a small and highly educated section of the German public could understand what was being said: in expression and detail Wagner's music dramas were prohibitively internal, and this created a gulf between the composer and his audience.

Unlike Italy, where Verdi and his Risorgimento contemporaries targeted the working classes in an attempt to further their political ambitions, Germany fostered a culture in which, apoliticised, artists created a '*Jenseits von Gut und Böse* . . . that was accessible only to genius and demigods.'[1] This withdrawal from contemporary value-systems sparked the general adoption of remote times, mythical histories and nebulous philosophies that circumvented the interests of living Germans. Myth and magic, epitomised by the vagaries of *Märchenoper* and the centaurs and tritons of modern painting, were the height of fashion, and political or socially conscious art began to fall from currency.

As a reaction to these concerns, Strauss's extended tour of Greece brought him closer than ever to an awareness of his responsibilities as a German composer, as someone to whom his contemporaries might turn at a time when cultural beauty and national identity were less valued than material prosperity. It was the philosophical mantelpiece of *Guntram*, and Strauss expended considerable time and thought on his place within the progress of Germany and her people.

The cheapening of culture was one of Strauss's most pressing anxieties. Writing to his sister in 1893 he lamented: 'One is supposed to write "lightly and agreeably" so that, as dear Papa maintains, it will be performed at lots of theatres. But by whom and for whom? For that miserable bunch in the audience? Certainly not! One composes for oneself and for a few friends, for the rest – I couldn't care less!' Strauss's condescending, almost hostile attitude, and the hierarchical arrogance allowed by class and station, was entirely in keeping with a value-system that advocated German pre-eminence; at the heart of this Aryanised faith was a concern with, and wariness of, the persistent rise of the Jews.

Sensitivity to this 'loathsome progress'[2] had been pivotal to his father's tuition; and von Bülow, Ritter and Rösch had happily reinforced Strauss's inherited prejudice. But to place the responsibility for the young man's anti-Semitism with his friends and mentors undermines his absorption of wider attitudes and opinions. Strauss did not live in a bubble; he was as susceptible to the climate around him as anyone else, and it was on his travels that his father's intolerance and Ritter's teachings received their most enduring confirmation.

Succumbing to Nietzsche, Strauss abandoned his once unshakeable faith in Schopenhauer before leaving for Greece; and as his nationalism grew increasingly extreme he embraced an undiluted Bismarckianism that resented Christianity almost as much as it did Jewry. Racial purity and the furtherance of German ideals and culture were of escalating significance for Strauss; the Jews were thought to represent a threat to the stability and purity of the unified empire. With the financial crash of 1873 the majority began to see the Jews as the all-pervading evil within contemporary Germany. As the widening industrial boom dissipated the regional influence of the Church, the German-wide perception of the Jews as Christ's murderers gave way to the more pragmatic impression of the Jews as grasping and covetous Shylocks, interested only in monopolising the country's banking and stock markets.

During the 1850s and 60s this ancient stereotype was revived through the popular writings of Gustav Freytag,[3] Wilhelm Raabe[4] and Felix Dahn, whose *Ein Kampf um Rom*, published in 1867, proved highly influential with Strauss's generation. The world-Jewish conspiracy was traced to the heart of Germany's financial community, and radicals and extremists fuelled the moral majority by haranguing all 'good Germans' – which included the bourgeoisie – for allowing such a disgraceful situation to get the better of them.

Hatred for the Jews ran so high during the 1880s, in fact, that it was the one faith to which all Germans could apply themselves regardless of their class or profession. When Adolf Stoecker, an Evangelical pastor turned politician, ran for office in Berlin in 1878 he implored his audience, which was largely working class, to resist the blandishments of the Social Democrats because 'They hate their Fatherland ... to hate one's Fatherland is like hating one's mother.' This convinced few of those for whom the Fatherland had brought nothing but misery, and he secured less than 1,500 votes at the election.

But when, over the following five years, he began to appeal to his audience's anti-Semitism, his popularity grew exponentially, generating a large populist following and causing serious concern inside the Reichstag. In 1880 there were 45,000 Jews in Berlin;[5] a year earlier Konstantin Frantz had dismissed the city as the capital of a Jewish Reich: 'because one meets here in all areas of public life the arrogant Jew ... the flea-market and marts-of-trade and stock-market Jew, the press and literature Jew, the theatre and music Jew, the culture and humanity Jew ... Almost half of Berlin's city councillors are Jews ... and, hand in hand with their kept press and stock market, they actually control the whole city government.'

In September 1879 Stoecker gave a widely reported lecture entitled 'Our Demands on Modern Jewry' and just two months later Heinrich von Treitschke published a vicious attack in the *Pressische Jahrbücher* in which he denounced the Jews as 'our national misfortune'. In 1881 Treitschke founded one of the most widely subscribed and vehemently hateful anti-Semitic organisations in all Germany, the Verein deutscher Studenten. This influential body of opinion was directed against tolerance and liberality, particularly whenever a voice of reason was raised against the German-wide Judaeophobia; Treitschke and his like did much to reinforce a general consensus that because a small number of 'Israelites' had involved themselves in a variety of banking and stock-exchange swindles, and because an equally slight percentage of Jewish writers had criticised the Catholic and Evangelical churches,[6] all Jews were swindlers and heretical subversives.

As a young man Strauss must have come into contact with a huge variety of opinions and faiths. The educated, if not quite intellectual, society in which he moved encouraged the prevailing wariness of the Jews, and yet it is most unlikely that Strauss's contact with Jewish Germans, either in or outside the opera houses in Munich and Weimar, reinforced his prejudice. There was little at his level of society, beyond appearances, to distinguish a non-orthodox Jew from an Aryan, and one must assume that Strauss's anti-Semitism carried little racial animus against the Jews. Rather, his disdain was nationalistic, the product of a centuries-old fear that labelled any outsider as a subversive. Unlike Stoecker, however, Strauss saw through the Jews' attempts to disguise their origins, refusing to accept them even after they had embraced Catholicism, taken up an 'honest' trade, changed their names and become good German patriots. This much is clear from his relationship with Gustav Mahler.

There was a general German-wide move during the 1880s and 90s against the supposed materialism of the age. Unification and the consequent bedrock of middle-class values gave a moral and nationalistic edge to the accumulation of wealth. Inherited affluence was acceptable, and encouraged by those who considered Germany's future dependent upon the preservation of tradition and heritage. Jewish prosperity, however, offended all good German patriots, for whom the purity of German life was sacrosanct. 'The Jewish question' was embodied in the public war of words waged between Theodor Mommsen and Heinrich von Treitschke, who argued that Jews were unfit for public office or educational responsibility. Mommsen vehemently defended the rights of any German, Jew or not, to rise to public office if his talents and abilities merited the appointment.

But the prevailing social tide opposed such enlightenment. Strauss had not known a single Jewish professor during his time at university, and although Jews were employed as 'instructors', few were ever engaged as professors. In Berlin in 1909, for example, there was not one single Jewish professor at the university. While the curriculum pandered to industry and the sciences, there was a massive and wide-reaching intellectual sympathy for the humanities and, in spite of an inclination for creative endeavours, the Jews were identified with mercantile aspiration. Consequently, not even exceptional talents, such as Levi, could escape the simplistic Jewish stereotype.

Germany's seats of learning may have fostered some legendary minds, but they also fostered prejudice. Sitting at the feet of Germany's greatest thinkers, students absorbed a remarkable weight of parochial indoctrination. The future of the Fatherland was, therefore, entrusted, during the 1870s and 80s, to a body of young men in whom a hatred of the Jews had been cultivated alongside a respect for the ancient world, Beethoven and Goethe.

Treitschke and his imitators played up to these limited beliefs and, 'glorifying war as a German destiny, provided by a beneficent Deity as a means of purging the nation of the sins of materialism',[7] a relatively small body of intellectuals successfully whipped up Germany's somnolent anti-Semitism into a frenzy of formalistic hatred. Treitschke's influence on Strauss's generation is incontestable, and it can just as easily be traced to the writings and speeches of Alfred von Tirpitz, Carl Peters and, ultimately, Adolf Hitler. When Heinrich Class founded the Pan-German League in the 1890s Strauss unquestionably sympathised with the society's doctrine, even if he never enrolled as a member, and if his music and aesthetic principles were thought radical, then his politics were conservative.

He was drawn to the values of the Verein deutscher Studenten as a step towards reviving the moral and cultural principles of the Burschenschaft,[8] and he strongly sympathised with the Verein's aim, to see restored 'the ancient sound foundation of our national character'. As someone who had studied the philosophy of Max Stirner, Strauss was convinced that this national character was inextricably dependent upon the individual, and individual responsibility. Stirner's nihilistic attacks against the 'old orthodoxy' buttressed his faith in an all-embracing reality of 'the ego'. A thing of value could only be judged, so he claimed, through its relation to, and support of, the self. The individual had to come to terms with his importance without losing sight of his responsibility to the demands of the ego and, like Bauer, he elevated the self-conscious to a position reminiscent of pre-Hegelian romanticism.

In short, Stirner offered Strauss a validation of his egomaniacal behaviour.

Compounded by everything he had been raised to believe as an adolescent, he saw in himself and his situation a Wagner-like destiny for which he, like Wagner, would have to suffer for his beliefs and his work. As far as Strauss could see, and this was not very far, his cultural inheritance, if not all German life, was under threat, and as someone with an obvious and unique gift, he believed himself of defining significance.

In June 1892, shortly before resolving to undertake his Mediterranean sabbatical, Strauss was given reason to write openly about himself. As a frank and, one must assume, honest confession, it provides a valuable reflection of Strauss's self-image as a German composer prior to his 'thought-collecting' grand tour. The impetus for this burst of openness was the composer Eugen Lindner, whom Strauss had been stabbing in the back during the first half of 1892. Having conducted Lindner's opera *Der Meisterdieb* in Weimar during his first season at the Opera, it seems that he regarded the work as weak and as redundant as its composer. His slanderous remarks got back to Lindner, who responded with under-standable offence. Strauss replied:

There could be hardly any remaining doubts as to my true artistic convictions, even if I do happen to have studied, as a curiosity, Max Stirner's philosophy of egoism. I believed at least that I had always applied my ethical principles in practice to the best of my ability. You should not forget, my dear Lindner, that this honest application often meets with the most remarkable obstacles, even in my own breast, which put all my good intentions at risk and, with the help of my distinctly overwrought nerves, often encouraged the most extraordinary blossoming of paradox or, if you want it in plain language, *nonsense*. One of these obstacles is a devil of opposition, who means well but has three powerful enemies in the world, and he goes crazy at the sight of them; those three enemies are *hypocrisy*, the impudence of *dilettantes* and *philistinism*.

When I meet with hypocrisy, for instance, if someone always has the religion of love on his lips and is himself the crassest of egoists, with no consideration for the best and most self-sacrificing of friends, when the exaltation of his own person is at stake – When I hear that impudent, uninformed laymen judge our most sublime works of art as if their creators were no better than they –

And as for philistinism with its hired aesthetic sense and its traditions – if I collide with these three devils then it may very well come to pass that I utter things which, taken out of context, sound quite extraordinary . . . next time you hear of something crazy originating from me, make a few enquiries as to whether one of the above-mentioned three devils was lurking in the vicinity!

However, I really must put up a serious defence of myself against the charge of intolerance; I do not believe that there are many people who make a more honest and sincere attempt to do justice to everything that is beautiful . . . In other circumstances it can perhaps come to pass that, if somebody holds up

Mozart's *Don Giovanni* to me as a more formally perfect, profounder work of art than *Tristan*, I may declare Mozart's *Don Giovanni* to be utter trash, or, if somebody praises *L'amico Fritz* to me I may reply that *Der Trompeter* is a very respectable work of art in a decent German sort of way. That can happen, and has happened to me in the heat of battle! But it has nothing whatever to do with my serious, settled view of art... I'm only human, and if neither the performers nor the audiences show as much interest in the venerable old warhorses as they do in *Lohengrin*, devil take it, there is nothing I can do about it. What incomparable pains I took with Mozart's *Entführung*, and what a barely mediocre performance it was in the end!

Strauss comes close to an apology, but the essence of the letter is self-justification. He did not deny Lindner's accusations. He merely claimed that his words had been taken out of context, which is not unlike a politician announcing that he wishes to spend more time with his family. Strauss's self-confidence, which so frequently bled into arrogance, made it difficult for him to rationalise his behaviour towards others since, so it appeared, he held little respect for anyone with differing opinions and values.

While a holiday abroad was essential for Strauss's health, taking it in Greece was, potentially, a mistake. For most German late Romantics, and for all committed Wagnerites, Greece was the godfather of German supremacist culture. The 'ancients' were raised on to a pedestal from which their collective achievements were viewed through the most rose-tinted spectacles, and academic study reinforced the defining influence of the classics on 'German civilisation'. Strauss's travel diary makes it clear that he, too, embraced this overestimation of ancient Greek society as the servant, rather than the master, of its art.

Classical Greece was the backbone of German curricula, and a large proportion of university students went on to study Greek dramaturgy as a precursor to their studies of German poetry and theatre. Wagner, like most German composers, had perceived opera as an invention of the Greeks, not the Italians, who had, anyway, been attempting to recreate Greek drama; the classics were no less central to Strauss's libretto for *Guntram*. It is no coincidence that this was the only work which occupied him during his travels.

He left Germany for Brindisi on November 4, 1892. Arriving a few days later, he boarded the *Mediterraneo*, which took him to Capri (where he was forced to remain in quarantine for five days after an outbreak of cholera) and, later, to Corfu. On Corfu he visited 'the beautiful poetic villa of Empress Elisabeth [of Austria]' whom he reproached for introducing 'an ugly discord into the whole' by allowing her 'unhappy notion, born of misguided, feminine, emotional silliness, to erect a monument to Heine'.[9]

Before his arrival in Athens, on November 16, Strauss visited Olympia where, drawing an indiscreet analogy between Greece and Bayreuth, he entered a hymn of devotion in his diary:

> Uplifted by the heavenly, divinely-inspired peace of this hallowed spot, I praise the good spirit who has led me hither ... What harmony of nature and art: the greatest contrast to our Christian-German development which finally, in the greatest inward assumption of the religious idea, brought forth the music of the nineteenth century. Bayreuth – Olympia! There, a great genius rising far above his race, who creates from his own innermost strength the loftiest monument yet erected in the cultural development of all races; a *lone genius*! ... Philosophical, world-transcending sublimity, profoundest inwardness – Bayreuth! A great race! A great genius!

And so on. Strauss was in his element. Regardless of the filth and the disorganisation, and despite being constantly disappointed by the 'Greeks of today', nineteenth-century Greece did not detract from Strauss's watery-eyed vision of the Ancients. He lapped up the mythology, allowing a 'most hallowed mood' to overcome him at Olympia. This mood infused many of his letters, especially those addressed to his mentors Ritter, Bülow and Cosima. Bayreuth's pre-eminence was a constant motif, just as race, and the understanding of race as the product of culture (rather than the other way round), constantly occupied his thoughts. Echoing Wagner's view of the Jews as parasites, incapable of ever becoming true Germans, either through language or culture, Strauss saw in ancient Greece the model for modern Germany. To Cosima he wrote: 'Race, art, nature, religion, unite in a harmony of optimism which, through the perfection of its representation exercises a truly fascinating effect on the spectator, and to which one must surrender, whether one will it or not!' Even so, he thought *his* Germany lacking: 'The definition of "race" as those who share a common need applies, in my view, only to the Greeks; now there is no longer a "race", now there are only lonely geniuses.'

Arriving in Egypt at the end of November, though impressed by the Pyramids and surrounded as he was by the luxury of Shepheard's Hotel in Cairo, Strauss sniffed at the 'monumental naïvety of the ancients' and bemoaned the primitiveness of the country and its people. In fact, he was unreservedly dismissive of contemporary Greeks and Egyptians, who failed to meet his Olympian standards of society, art and culture, and many of his letters contain dismissive references to their 'backwardness'.

As far as Egypt was concerned, it was the absence of 'artistic effect' that so bothered him. Motivated by his study of Schopenhauer (to say nothing of the writings of Aeschylus, Sophocles and Plato), he revelled in a Teutonic superiority that judged the world and everything in it by the measure of art, an attitude that not only allowed for egoism and arrogance but, more importantly, apoliticism. 'The world has so little to offer', he wrote to Ritter, 'but art is eternally new, eternally beautiful.'

The warmth of the climate was as kind to his body as it was conducive to his mind, and he began to consider prolonging his stay in the Middle East since 'in the solitude of the glorious desert' he was free of the pressures of conducting, the perfidy of Bronsart, and his disillusionment with modern Germany. Even Ritter was determined to see his disciple make the best of his time away, particularly as he too saw Bronsart as a serious threat to the preservation of Strauss's health. 'The most important thing', Ritter wrote to the singer Rosa von Milde, 'was to get him through his twenty-eighth year ... and that above all he should not be exposed to any kind of emotional disturbances ... unfortunately the extraordinary attitude of his superior has caused him some very unnecessary emotional disturbances on a number of occasions.'

In February 1893 Strauss left Cairo for Luxor, where he met the blind Landgrave of Hessen and the young English composer Clement Harris. While there he gave an interesting outline of his daily routine:

> My day's work is very simple; I get up at 8 o'clock, have a bath and breakfast; 3 eggs, tea, 'Eingemachtes',[10] then I go for a stroll for half an hour by the Nile in the palm grove of the hotel, and work from 10 till 1 ... At 1 o'clock I have lunch, then read my Schopenhauer or play Bezique with Mrs Conze for a piastre stake. From 3 till 4 I work on; at 4 o'clock tea, and after that I go for a walk until 6 when I do my duty in admiring the usual sunset. At 6 o'clock it gets cool and dark; then I write letters or work a bit more until 7. At 7 dinner, after which I chat and smoke (8–12 a day), at half past 9 I go to my room, read for half an hour and put out the light at ten. So it goes on day after day ...

After five weeks in Luxor he returned to Cairo where he found a letter from his father, from which he discovered that Franz had been talking to none other than Hermann Levi. Remarkably, Levi had contacted his old enemy to find out whether or not Richard would be interested in returning to work, as Hofkapellmeister, in Munich. He would have to free himself from his contract at Weimar, and this would do even more harm to his reputation, but he would be on equal footing with Levi and the superior of Franz Fischer. Levi's one request of Richard was that he treat him, Levi, with respect and kindness. That Levi even considered giving him such a post is extraordinary, and some commentators have interpreted the invitation as a sign that Strauss's behaviour was better than it appeared. But Levi was insistent and, uniquely perhaps, able to divorce Strauss's personality from his talent.

Levi had also considered Felix Weingartner, whose contract in Berlin bound him until 1896, and Felix Mottl, whose life in Karlsruhe was disintegrating as rapidly as his marriage. Though flattered by the offer Strauss was rather more excited by the possibility of succeeding Mottl at Karlsruhe, where the Opera had been transformed into one of the finest in all Europe. While pretending to consider Levi's offer, he wrote to Mottl asking if the 'rumours' that he was to leave Karlsruhe were true. Mottl replied: 'Nothing is to come of Munich. I am to stay on here peacefully, with my wife, and enjoy life. If I had left, I would have thought of no one but you...'

It is possible that Bronsart and Levi had been in consultation prior to Levi's offer to Strauss of a position in Munich. Bronsart was tired of having to restrain his Third Conductor, who was equally tired of being restrained. Whether or not there was any outright collusion is impossible to say, but by the time the issue was finally resolved, during the summer of 1894, the interested parties had made their positions clear.

Five weeks after his return to Cairo, during the second week of April 1893, Strauss left Egypt for Taormina in northern Sicily. He had originally considered travelling overland through Jerusalem, the only Jewish city in Palestine; for whatever reason, however, he chose to take the sea route, port to port – a ferry crossing of nearly one thousand miles.

From Palermo, on May 6, 1893, he wrote to Ritter: 'I have been completely restored to health, of body and soul, on this wonderful journey. I almost rejoice in myself.' Richard was back to his normal self and he rushed around Sicily with renewed confidence, writing to his father on May 9: 'I do not know the meaning of nerves any more.' He was able to flex his aesthetic muscles for the first time in weeks when he was invited by the Countess Gravina[11] and her husband to stay at their 'extremely charming and idyllic' monastery at Ramacca. Strauss and the Countess played four-hand piano duets, including Thuille's arrangement of *Macbeth*, which Bülow had sent to her with the inscription 'Very significant'.

On June 7, having spent two weeks at Ramacca and six months away from Germany, Strauss left for home. He took his time, stopping in Florence to meet Hermann Levi with whom he discussed 'pleasantly, frankly and amiably' the possibility of his return to Munich. He crossed the border into Switzerland on June 20, detouring briefly to climb the 9,000-foot Gornergrat at Zermatt. The seven-and-a-half-hour trip up and down left him 'rather tired' but it demonstrated that he was fit enough to 'face the German winter with confidence'.

On July 15, 1893, he arrived at his family home in Munich. He divided the remainder of the summer between *Guntram* and his family, who were delighted to have him back, and on September 5 he completed the score of his first opera. A week later, having enjoyed a year's uninterrupted holiday and with the complete restoration of his health, Strauss buoyed himself for a new start at Weimar, relishing the prospect of fresh air and forgotten grievances. Less than two weeks after his return, however, he wrote to his father:

'The whole ménage here is too trifling to get myself excited about, it's a relief to be past that stage. Cool and indifferent is my motto, and it really seems quite easy to live up to it ... Everything here is as it was a hundred years ago...'

September 1893–February 1894

On September 24, 1893, Franz Strauss wrote to his son: 'Fancy giving way to depression like that! Think what a wonderful year you have experienced and enjoy it again in your memory.' Astonished at his son's failure to confront the realities of life in Weimar, Franz admonished Richard for allowing the city to get the better of him after his long and fruitful break. 'Don't forget', he wrote, 'how few people could compare themselves with you for fortunate experiences.'

Strauss was not to be swayed.[1] His tolerance had, if anything, dwindled during his year away. Never one to suffer fools, he now grew despairing as friends and colleagues failed to meet his expectations. His relationship with Ritter was on the wane and even the glow of Bayreuth was dimmed by revelations that Cosima Wagner's son, Siegfried, was a homosexual. Aside from any moral issues, Siegfried was also something of an idiot, and his surviving correspondence with Strauss indicates a trying acquaintance.

In one particularly obeisant letter Siegfried proposed, to 'Dear Expression', *The Merchant of Venice* as a possible theme for a symphonic poem. He went so far as to advise Strauss on matters of detail. 'Four strands:' he speculated, 'melancholy Antonio, dissolute Venice, captivating Portia and (!) Shylock (e.g. six bassoons, muted trumpets and horns and humming basses); that would be something for you!' The outlining of his ideas on how Strauss might characterise a 'theatrical' Jew failed to interest the composer, who gave the suggestion no further thought.

Siegfried had been studying with Engelbert Humperdinck at Bayreuth where he was a regular festival assistant, having been encouraged to take up music by Felix Mottl the year before. Strauss and Humperdinck were friends as well as colleagues, and Strauss was drawn, as many were, to Humperdinck's subtle wit. It was an act of friendship, as much as a gesture of goodwill to contemporary German music, that Strauss threw himself and the weight of the Weimar Opera behind Humperdinck's first opera *Hänsel und Gretel*.

So confident was Strauss of its quality that he convinced Bronsart to mount the opera, even though he had yet to see or hear anything of the score. By the end of October an arrangement was reached, including a tentative agreement on casting, and on the last day of the month, having finally read through the score, Strauss wrote to its composer:

> Truly, it's a masterpiece of the highest quality, and I lay at your feet my fullest admiration and my sincerest congratulations on its happy conclusion; it's the first work that has impressed me for a very long time. Such heart-refreshing humour, such deliciously naive melodies, such art and refinement in the orchestration, such perfectionism in the overall shaping of the work, such vital invention, such resplendent polyphony – and all of it original, new and so authentically German. My dear friend, you are a great master, and have given the Germans a work they hardly deserve, but let us hope all the same that they will very soon learn how to appreciate it fully.

The world première had originally been planned by Levi for Munich, but a singer's postponement gave Weimar the edge, and Strauss was able to stage the first performance a week ahead of Levi. The only concern was a late cast-change. Pauline de Ahna, who was to have created Hänsel, twisted her ankle three days before the dress rehearsal, and as the role demanded a fair degree of athleticism she had to be confined to her bed while Arabella Schubert, a coloratura soprano, stepped in and saved the day. Schubert found the role's pitch a problem, but the overall performance was satisfactory and the composer was delighted.[2]

As an interpreter, Strauss was allowed considerable freedom by Humperdinck. After the first run he wrote to the composer: 'The orchestration is always a little thick, the thematic writing is a little too rich, which always overpowers the singers a little, especially in the third act, and I shall sit down now and alter the parts a little, in order to muffle the wind even more; may I perhaps cut a little from the score if it seems to serve the clarity?' It is not difficult to imagine the ferocity of Strauss's reaction had he received such a 'little' letter in connection with one of his own compositions, but his self-possession was total. By the end of the run he was writing to Humperdinck: 'On Sunday we at last had an excellent performance of *Hänsel und Gretel*.'

Midway through his preparations for Humperdinck's opera Strauss had to cope with the added strain of conducting lengthy rehearsals for *Lohengrin*, as well as composing some small pieces for his uncle, by way of thanks for his sabbatical. Consequently, he had to turn down an invitation from Mahler to hear him conduct a concert of his own music[3] in Hamburg, something that Strauss would have enjoyed, especially as he was under pressure to find a conductor and an opera house willing to commit to a production of *Guntram*. Mahler and Hamburg would have been more than satisfactory, although at this stage Strauss was still banking on Levi and Munich.

Indeed, Munich was once again proving central to Strauss's ambitions. Three months on, Levi's provisional offer of the Munich Hofkapellmeistership was no nearer fruition. As Bronsart and the provincialism of Weimar continued to reinforce Strauss's monomania, he began to despair. On October 11, 1893, he wrote to Humperdinck: 'I am utterly dissatisfied with my present job and yet I'm almost afraid that if I leave it I shall find it even worse elsewhere.' He explained to Humperdinck how Levi's offer had been dependent upon the interest, or otherwise, of the conductors Mottl and Weingartner, and that he would take just about anything to free himself from Bronsart's interfering, the producer Brandt's egotism and a theatre orchestra which frequently boasted no more than four second violins for productions of works that demanded no fewer than ten.

With the ghosts of Meiningen gathering around Weimar, Strauss turned for succour to his small band of friends, chiefly Heinrich Zeller and Pauline de Ahna. Anyone who was not for him, was against him, and even those who seemed to be trying to help came under fire. In spite of his considerable efforts, even Levi's motives were called into question. The longer Levi prevaricated, the more Strauss came to suspect that Munich was using him as leverage in its negotiations with Weingartner and Mottl. In truth, Levi and Possart, the Intendant at Munich, were more interested in securing either rival, and despite Strauss's concern they continued to delay their decision in the hope that either Mottl would give up Karlsruhe or Weingartner would break his contract in Berlin.

As Mottl had personally assured Strauss he was staying put, Cosima Wagner advised him to play them at their own game: bid for the post at Munich and, simultaneously, make inquiries in Berlin as to the possibility of succeeding Weingartner in 1896. On June 19 Strauss and Levi agreed generous terms: Strauss was to receive a salary of 7,000 marks (4,000 more than he was recently paid in Weimar), a three-year contract from October 1, 1893, half the Academy Concerts, equal power with Levi over repertoire and a generous two months' annual leave. But by the end of July Strauss was still waiting for written confirmation. Weingartner continued to vacillate and Levi was growing embarrassed. Possart was running out of time and had no option but to inform Weingartner that if, by October 1, Berlin had not agreed to free him from his contract he would give the post to Strauss, beginning on January 1, 1894.

On July 29 Levi urged Strauss to be patient, but when October 1 passed with no confirmation of his appointment the composer's forbearance buckled and he began to consider litigation against the Munich Intendant. Cosima handed down more bad advice, urging Strauss to air his grievances in the press, while Franz pleaded with his son not to rush to judgement. The whole affair seemed to drag on interminably, and Strauss began to lose interest in Munich, although he kept his eyes open for alternative possibilities.

During the early months of 1894, with the painful Munich episode seemingly behind him, he found himself embroiled in another, equally taxing incident, this time involving Gustav Mahler. During the last two months of 1893 Hans von Bülow fell seriously ill. It was obvious to Hermann Wolff, the promoter of Bülow's Berlin and Hamburg Philharmonic concerts, that substitutes would need to be found if the concerts were to go ahead. Out of consideration for Bülow a different conductor was engaged almost every night. Richter, Levi, Mottl, Maszkowski, Strauss and Mahler all happily agreed to help out. Strauss conducted two concerts in Berlin, and he and Mahler each conducted one in Hamburg. Both received high praise, although it seems that Bülow was happiest with Levi.

Towards the end of January 1894, during their time together in Hamburg, Strauss and Mahler found an opportunity to get to know each other better. Previously they had had little to do with one another;[4] but having seen each other at work, and after sharing each other's free time, Strauss wrote to his father on January 22: 'I spend much time with Mahler, who is very charming and conducted a capital performance of the *Bartered Bride* ...' Mahler was anxious to impress Strauss, who was well placed to advance his fortunes both as composer and conductor. On October 20, 1893, he had informed Strauss that he was 'the only living conductor who is interested in my compositions'; both men well knew that, as composers, they were almost wholly reliant on their immediate contemporaries for support, since the older generation was unlikely to take an interest in anything unreasonably modern.

On December 24 Mahler had offered to stage the première of Strauss's *Guntram*, and he repeated this offer when they met in Hamburg. In January 1894, shortly before their meeting, Strauss sent Mahler the libretto for *Guntram*, and around the 24th or 25th he invited Mahler to hear him conduct the seventh of the season's Philharmonic concerts in Berlin, although by this stage Strauss seems not to have offered to conduct anything by Mahler.

In 1888 Strauss had played, with Levi, through a four-hand piano reduction of Mahler's First Symphony – which, as Strauss noted in his diary, contained a 'very original, humorous funeral march'. Six years on he must have realised that, with Mahler making constant reference to his plans for *Guntram*, he was honour bound to offer something in return. At the beginning of February he announced his intention to conduct the Symphony in Hamburg,[5] but this was little more than a gesture, since Strauss was only offering to cover for Mahler, who feared his own indisposition.

By this stage each was beginning to grow wary of the other. A certain amount of shared suspicion was to be expected at a time when top conducting positions were so fiercely contested, but while Mahler praised *Guntram* to its composer, he simultaneously wrote to a colleague that he had 'never met with anything so childishly immature and at the same time so pretentious'.

When they met in January 1894 Mahler made the mistake of telling Strauss that his contract at Hamburg was coming to an end. Mahler knew that

Strauss was tired of Weimar but he assumed, with good reason, that Strauss would move back to Munich, and if not Munich then Berlin or Karlsruhe. But Strauss was more jaded than Mahler knew, so much so that he decided to bid for Mahler's post at Hamburg. It is not known who contacted whom. The Intendant at Hamburg, Bernhard Pollini, admired Strauss, and he may well have considered him a more attractive proposition than the fussy, over-sensitive Mahler. In any event, Strauss and Pollini opened negotiations immediately after the Bülow Hamburg concerts in January 1894, and terms were agreed before the end of the month. Strauss was able to write to his father: 'Whether I have a lot of work and vexation here[6] or in Hamburg makes no difference; but it does make a difference whether I have a salary of 12,000 marks in Hamburg or 3,000 in Weimar.'

Mahler was also in negotiation with Pollini who, like Possart, seems to have used Strauss as leverage. Mahler's demands must have been greater than Strauss's, for Pollini made it clear that if Mahler refused to modify his expectations Strauss would get his job. Strauss chose not to inform Mahler of his discussions with Pollini until February 1st or 2nd, by which time they had agreed terms. Strauss shrewdly chose to break the news the day after he had written offering to conduct Mahler's First Symphony. Mahler was none the less furious. On February 3 he replied: 'I am quite dumbfounded by your news. – Only a few days ago Pollini asked when I wished to sign my contract. He remains extremely polite towards me. – I am therefore quite unable to form a judgement on this matter. – Pollini is up to all sorts of tricks ...'

Mahler was also put out by Strauss's refusal to stay with him on a forth-coming trip to Hamburg. He had been invited by Mahler before the Behn family even thought of asking him. Mahler ended his letter of the 3rd: 'Behn told me yesterday that you had agreed to stay at his house; this of course cancels my invitation, since it is best for you to accept Behn's. You will feel very much at home there.'[7]

Later the same day Mahler wrote another anxious letter: 'Your news has plunged me into a state of considerable agitation ...' and by the 6th he was clearly exhausted by all the duplicity: 'Dearest Friend, I no longer know where I am! The day before yesterday Pollini came up to me during a per-formance and said in a jocularly blunt way: "I'm fed up with waiting. Come to my office tomorrow so that we can get our contract straight at last!" I gave him a nonplussed look and said nothing. To be honest, I had already prepared myself for my departure. (In such matters I am somewhat fatalistic and believe everything that happens to be for the best.)'

Eventually, Pollini offered Mahler the contract, which made Mahler think that Pollini wanted both of them for Hamburg. This theory provoked an extraordinary response from Mahler, who wrote to Strauss: 'I know of no one with whom I feel such affinities, and in face of whom all petty promptings in me would be stilled. I should with the greatest pleasure relinquish the *Nibelungen* to you, and all else can be settled amicably between us.' Mahler then informed Strauss that his contract at Hamburg was secure for five years, and ended his letter with news that he had sent Bronsart a copy of his First Symphony.

It is surprising that Mahler did not take greater offence at Strauss's behaviour. Even if he did secure his position in Hamburg, Mahler's terms were less beneficial than they might have been had Strauss not played such a dirty game. Although it was the last time either man tussled so openly, enough seeds of doubt were sewn for Mahler never to trust his colleague again, and less than six months later he was casting more private aspersions. He had been sent some poor reviews for a performance of his 'Titan' Symphony at the thirtieth festival of the Allgemeiner Deutscher Musikverein in Weimar. Having read them, Mahler wrote to a friend: 'Many thanks for sending the reviews. I found them most diverting. You do not know the drollest of them, which came to me from another quarter . . . Str. is *not* entirely above suspicion! His favourite critic is the author of the *worst* reviews!'

Mahler's and Strauss's aesthetic paths were now wholly divergent and it is by no means inconceivable that Strauss had influenced Arthur Seidl's vicious review since both men were known to share anti-Semitic as well as musical values. Seidl was a close personal friend and Strauss held more than a few reservations about the structure of the symphony, some of which he expressed to its composer. But what these episodes prove is that, far from being the naïve and enthusiastic ingénue portrayed by some, Strauss was first and foremost a player. The path of righteousness led to obscurity and provincialism, and he had had enough of both.

On February 12, 1894, Hans von Bülow died of a stroke. Strauss saw him for the last time in Hamburg on January 20 when, gravely ill, the old man was preparing to recuperate in Egypt.[1] For some months before this final meeting Bülow had grown increasingly unmanageable. Whether as a result of his illness or the morphine to which he had become greatly attached, his attitudes and the vehemence with which he expressed them demanded his retirement from society. This was not, of course, the reason for the distance that had long since divided him and Strauss as friends, and to the end Bülow was alone in pushing for a reconciliation.

Strauss's attitude to the proposed memorial concerts confirmed the extent to which he had withdrawn from their friendship. Some months earlier he had been engaged to conduct a concert in Hamburg on February 26. When the chairman of the Philharmonic concerts, Hermann Behn, asked Strauss to change his programme in honour of Bülow he submitted 'a purely symphonic funeral celebration' of *Hérodïde funèbre* or *Orpheus* (by Liszt), Bülow's *Nirwana* and the Preludes to *Tristan* and *Meistersinger*. He added that Mahler – who had inherited Bülow's post – could 'perhaps follow with the Funeral March from *Götterdämmerung*'. The omission of anything by Beethoven or Brahms, and the overtly New German bias[2] resulted in the programme being rejected. Strauss then refused to conduct the concert, causing further tension. It was eventually conducted by Julius Spengel and Mahler, who directed a 'sombre' performance of Beethoven's *Eroica*. Bach, Beethoven and Brahms were the featured composers and, according to Behn, 'the ceremony took place in a worthy manner . . . with strong public support'.

Bülow's body did not arrive in Germany until the middle of March. The funeral, together with an official memorial concert, was planned for the 29th. During the weeks running up to the first memorial of February 26, when the papers gleefully reported Strauss's 'refusal' to conduct, rumours began to circulate that he had also announced his intention not to conduct at the funeral. Cosima Wagner was furious:

The thought will not leave me that you are not to conduct the memorial concert in Hamburg. Would you not write to them again, to say that on such occasions one does not celebrate the changing opinions and views but the merits of a person. And those merits undoubtedly include the championing of an art, at a time when it had enemies, which now has friends and many important ones to boot ... Please write a very wonderful letter, my dear Expression. Perhaps it will work, if not, at least the right words will have been offered to his memory. People are lamentable! If they want to celebrate someone, they have to drag him down first!

As a postscript Cosima added: 'I would have nothing against your conducting something by Brahms as well. It's a concession you could well make and there must be some piece or other.'

Strauss unbent a little but refused to omit the proposed works by Liszt – even though Bülow would not have wanted them there; it was clear that he was using the event to promote his own interests and ideals, rather than those to which Bülow would have joined his voice. The conductor's family did their best to change Strauss's mind, and on March 5 Bülow's son-in-law Henry Thode reported Marie von Bülow's belief that: 'It would be against his [Bülow's] wishes to include Liszt in the programme. I have been forced to accept that there is hardly any hope of carrying the proposal through ... It is now my opinion – after repeated consultation with my wife – that it would be advisable not absolutely to insist on it, in order to achieve a thoroughly worthy musical celebration. Perhaps you could bring yourself to let the Liszt drop, in return for your insistence that Brahms in turn be abandoned.'

The funeral, on March 29, was a grim affair.[3] Mahler had warned Strauss: 'Be sure to come to Bülow's funeral service, it is *very important* for *your opera!*'[4] – but Strauss had dug his heels in, and stayed away. The snub greatly offended the family, who knew how much Bülow had contributed to Strauss's good fortune, and it left his already uncertain reputation in tatters. Fortunately, the management in Munich were oblivious to the uniformly critical press reports, and on March 20, some thirteen months after he had first been offered the post, Strauss was finally invited to join Levi at the Court Opera.

Confirmation of his Kapellmeistership arrived during the same month that Bülow, who had implored him never to work in the city again, was buried. Even for those who hardly knew Strauss, his decision to return to the city of his birth was the triumph of optimism over experience, but he was tired of poverty, and if he was ever to marry Pauline de Ahna he would need Munich's generous salary to keep them both afloat. Moreover, Munich was the only city to have expressed a genuine interest in staging *Guntram*. Mottl had promised to mount the work in Karlsruhe, and Mahler had made grand claims for his influence in Hamburg, but Strauss wanted to see his first opera brought to life in Munich, where there were scores to settle.

Over *Guntram* Possart again proved untrustworthy. To his father, Strauss lamented: 'So I've got to look out for myself over the opera as well, have I? It's getting richer all the time. Possart asked me if the second week in February [1894] would suit me for *Guntram*, I said yes, now is that, or isn't it, a definite commitment? The way these people in Munich think fit to treat me trumps everything.' He was persuaded to delay the première until May 1, although he demanded the sort of contractual assurances that would normally have been considered unnecessary so far in advance of rehearsals. Possart's unreliability made Strauss nervous and, as ever, he blamed Levi for the slightest hiccup. On the whole, Levi weathered his colleague's suspicion with patience and good grace, but at times of exceptional stress even he was seen to wilt. On March 19, 1894, for example, he wrote to Possart:

> When I was conducting negotiations with him [Strauss] last year, I wrote that our collaboration would only work if he had faith in the possibility of not merely a superficial relationship with me but a genuine friendship as between colleagues ... Now I realise, however, from his present attitude towards me, that he is as distrustful as ever, for he has written to Fuchs: 'The matter will only be settled if L. does not cause any confusion and does not pile up new difficulties.' That's the *comble* of injustice ... I've done everything in my power to smooth his path, have made every possible sacrifice, and yet I now have to discover that he scorns even to establish a rapport with me. This opens up such a sorry prospect of our future collaboration that I now almost regret having made so many concessions to him, although that does not prevent me from keeping my word ... The only thing I want is a binding declaration that he intends in future to work with me and not against me, and that he will drop this really totally unjustified distrust towards me.

Why did Levi persist? What compelled him to keep faith with such an openly hostile subordinate when all the evidence suggested they could never work together 'as friends'? Levi was uncommonly devoted to his work (his criteria for any colleague was first and foremost artistic) and he used their relationship to demonstrate how even the deepest, most rooted suspicions could be conquered through a shared faith in the inviolability of music. In other words, Levi tried to raise himself above it all and defy the contemporary expectation that Jews were as unforgiving as their persecutors.

Even during preliminary negotiations, however, Strauss was impossible. He demanded 9,000 marks instead of the original 7,000, although this would have given him the same salary as Levi who had been at Munich for over twenty years. He insisted on the Hofkapellmeister title, even though only one of them could have held it, and he made demands over repertoire and the Academy concerts that he knew to be unmeetable. Throughout, he placed ultimate responsibility with Levi even though this rested with Possart. On one occasion he openly threatened Levi: 'If the repeated delays in the matter give rise to any consequence on my part, I would have to hold you alone responsible for them.'

Even after his appointment at Munich had been officially approved at the beginning of April 1894 Strauss was bitter towards Levi, blaming him for the coincidental announcement that *Guntram* would not be staged in Munich after all. This forced Strauss to turn back to Bronsart, whose offer to stage the opera he had grandly rejected on the grounds that the Weimar orchestra was insufficiently large to accommodate his scoring. With Mahler and Mottl's assurances failing to materialise, Weimar was Strauss's only hope.

Since he had only recently asked to be released from his contract it was a testament to Bronsart's good nature that he agreed to the production, but the Intendant cannot have failed to enjoy Strauss's dissatisfaction with the theatre's limited forces. Indeed, what should have been an occasion of great joy for the composer was a sustained process of disappointment and humiliation. *Guntram* requires a Wagnerian orchestra with a minimum of sixty-two strings. Bronsart could provide a full string complement of no more than twenty-one. He was further compelled to limit the wind and brass, so that Strauss had to prepare the orchestra with roughly a third of the players prescribed by his score.

He was forced to turn to the local military band, who provided the 'third' of each wind and brass section, but so difficult was the writing that the players quickly came to resent the physical demands almost as much as the enormously lengthy rehearsals which, on one occasion, lasted nearly eight hours. Strauss's friend and pupil Heinrich Zeller created the title role, probably the most demanding ever written for a tenor, and Pauline de Ahna created the soprano lead of Freihild. As Strauss recalled many years later, *Guntram* bore witness to his 'hair-raising naïvety in those days ... my poor, valiant pupil Heinrich Zeller went through agonies with his insanely demanding role – at the time somebody calculated that the part had so-and-so many more bars than that of *Tristan* – each rehearsal made him hoarser and hoarser and at the first performance he had a struggle to last out to the end. My fiancée knew her part faultlessly and her performance was vocally and dramatically outstanding.'

Conducted by Strauss, the première was given at the Grand Ducal Court Theatre on May 10, 1894. Many of the composer's friends made the trip to Munich, including Weingartner, Sommer, Ritter and most of the De Ahna clan.[5] His parents, to whom he dedicated the opera, did not attend. Strauss later remembered the performance as a '*succès d'estime*', but the work's overstated Wagnerism – from the cod-religiosity of the libretto to the deliberate quotation and mimicry of style[6] – was outdated even by 1894. Neither the audience nor the critics could see the wood for the World Ash Trees. In particular, the echoes of *Lohengrin, Tannhäuser* and *Parsifal* gave the entire opera an historical aspect that left most wondering what the point had been.

When Strauss began sketching plans for his first opera he did so under the influence of Ritter, Wagner and Schopenhauer. His thirst for philosophical redemption and his passion for the aesthetic of the *Gesamtkunstwerk* ('total work of art') led him towards a dramaturgy in which the themes of *Tristan* and *Parsifal* exerted a suffocating influence. Strauss knew that he 'lacked poetic talent', but the Wagnerian model demanded a composer write his own libretto. For Strauss to satisfy his mentors in Bayreuth as well as his own yearning to further Wagner's experiment, it was necessary for him to turn to the same strain of myth and legend as had his idol.

In one of his long explicatory letters to Ritter, Strauss outlined the story's significance:

> *Guntram* is the product of an order that has taken upon itself the task of uniting art and religion in the sense that it seeks to convey Christian teachings in artistic forms (using the effect of art on the human spirit) and so to make them clearer to the emotional understanding than ecclesiastical dogma can make them – in short, it seeks to improve mankind through art, that is, works of art with ethical tendency (in our language, you understand me!) This is something which has always proved to be a Utopia, a very attractive Utopia – but alas a Utopia (our friend Schopenhauer also takes this view in volume 3 of *The World as Will and Idea*); will it ever be different, will the Almighty Will, with its unchanging intelligible character, ever really allow itself to be captured by the 'illusory image'?

Strauss first mentioned his plans in a letter to Bülow in August 1887 and just six months later he could boast that he 'had a complete first draft of an opera text ready'. Other projects interrupted his progress – as they would, on and off, until his sabbatical – and not until November 1889 did he return to the libretto. In October 1890 he sent the finished draft to his father, and two years later he began composing the short score. During his year away he noted in his diary every passing milestone. On November 19, 1892, the day before his first visit to the Acropolis, he wrote: 'After dinner the scene between Guntram and Freihild, third act, completed in outline.' Four days later: 'Third act *Guntram* text (second final version) finished' and on Christmas Eve, while staying in Cairo, he rejoiced in being able to write the magic words '*Guntram* ready'.

The gestation of the libretto in its first draft provided a clear reflection of his reading of Schopenhauer's celebration of individual freedom within a secure and organised environment.[7] Strauss took comfort from Ritter, the opera's moral guardian, and the two appeared to share identical value-systems; but after immersing himself in Nietzsche's writings, chiefly *Der Antichrist*, Strauss began to regret his earlier 'naïvety', so much so that he transformed the final act – and the entire dramatic axis – to suit his new-found philosophy. Where Guntram had originally been sent back to be tried by his brotherhood – the exemplification of a collective society – the second draft saw him become his own judge, embracing individual responsibility as the ultimate truth.

Nearly fifty years later Strauss recalled how it had been Ritter who had encouraged him 'to write the text of *Guntram* which became, however, the reason for the inner estrangement between us. In Egypt I got to know Nietzsche's work, whose polemics against the Christian religion in particular struck a chord with me, and reading him strengthened and corroborated the antipathy which I had unconsciously felt since my fifteenth year for this religion which frees its believers of responsibility for their own actions (through confession).'

Advocating the primacy of the ego (Max Stirner) and Everyman's right to behave as he wished (Nietzsche), Strauss's new draft circumvented God and the merits of organised religion, presenting a direct challenge to the place and purpose of the Church and the place of confession within daily life. Through the character of Guntram, Strauss gave voice to his rapidly evolving beliefs: 'My life is governed by my spirit's law; my god speaks to me through myself!' Ritter was a confirmed Catholic, and he read Strauss's revision as 'an immoral mockery of every ethical creed'. On January 13, 1893, Strauss confessed to his father that he had long been afraid 'that Uncle Ritter wouldn't approve of the new version of Act III, and I'm sorry, but I can't do anything about it. The present denouement is the only course that makes the most of the material to any extent and Guntram must be like this and not contritely return to the fold.'

Ritter wasted no time in stating his case:

> The impression I had and still have after reading your new third act [is] one of the most *profoundly painful* things that I have experienced in the whole of the last decade of my life ... By the form you have given your third act you have thoroughly ruined your work, because: 1. The work has now been robbed of any kind of *tragedy*. 2. It is now bereft of the essential minimum amount of artistic unity. 3. The character of the hero has been transmogrified into a hazily patched together, psychologically quite impossible characterlessness ... Weighing all this, I have no hesitation in addressing the following urgent, imploring entreaty to you from a full heart: my dear friend! come to your senses! do not ruin your work, which is so very fine in the first two acts, beyond repair! take this new third act – even if the music has already been written – and throw it into the fire! Having done that, for your inner purgation read a chapter from the Gospels or from Schopenhauer's *Ethics* or Wagner's *Religion and Art*. Then set to and make a new third act according to the earlier draft, but restore Guntram's heroic deed of self-mastery, let him humbly submit himself to the judgement of the brotherhood. And when you have done that, let a Magnificat

be sung. Oh, if only God would lift up your soul to this resolution!...'

Ritter was ill-advised to submit such openly religious grievances to a composer so hostile to all non-secular religion. By urging Strauss to read from the Gospels, and through his invocation of God, Ritter was inviting friction, and it is a measure of Strauss's friendship that he replied in such generous, sympathetic terms:

According to Schopenhauer the artistic contemplation and representation of ideas are independent in themselves of all ethics; and even though Wagner succeeded in the case of *Parsifal,* that does not mean to say that every other artistic undertaking which intends too strong an ethical tendency from the first does not already, insofar as it is art, contain the seeds of death in itself. Be that as it may – at all events, in an artist whose works have this strong ethical or religious tendency the religious emotion always outweighs the artistic emotion. So it is with my brotherhood: the men who had those ambitions were better Christians than artists. Perhaps you will object that the two cannot be separated; but I believe that they are separate, in principle!...

You say that he blasphemes the Faith. But where? His actions are pure Christianity, which in its essence has nothing to do with the 'Communion of Saints' and the Catholic Church. 'In the end he loves only himself', you write! NO! He *hates* or *recoils* from himself. He has recognised his true self; naturally he can only do that *completely alone.* But there is nothing un-Christian or immoral about that. In the last resort each one of us is the only person who knows *what* he is. But what he does with himself after he has recognised himself is his business! So whose business? Here too, please do not confuse me with my dramatic figure! I am not giving up art; and I'm not Guntram either...

Ritter's inhibition and the whole *Guntram* affair punctuated Strauss's growing certainty that his old friend was not as devoted as he had once been Regardless of his later assurances that their falling out had been purely 'internal', they never again entertained the sort of closeness they had enjoyed during Strauss's youth. Ritter attended the first performance, and he was much affected by the music, but the air of corruption that had so turned him away from the libretto was not expunged, and like most of the critics Ritter dismissed Strauss's presumption.

Max Hasse amplified this apprehension when he wrote in the *Münchner Neueste Nachrichten:*

One can only expiate the guilt of existence: renunciation. [Guntram] enjoins compassion on the duke, while himself in the grip of self-seeking. He sang for enslaved freedom and was yet the slave of his own desires, he wanted to save an oppressed people and slew the husband of the woman he loved...

Does the librettist [Strauss] intend him to do penance for the sin in his heart, by leading from henceforth a life of Christian asceticism, or does he subscribe to the Schopenhauerian theory of the denial of the will to live and send the hero to a life of 'renunciation in compassion'? The text gives no certain indication. The music transfigures this last scene of decision to such a pitch that at the moment of listening to it one simply believes and only later turns to these critical deliberations.

Guntram was given only four performances in Weimar. Strauss was distraught, although he claimed to Ritter that the realisation of his score had fulfilled his every expectation. His one regret was that he had been unable to hear the work given in a covered pit.[8] If he was disappointed by the general response to it in Weimar, it was as nothing compared to his feelings for the people of Munich when *Guntram* received its solitary performance there in 1895. As he later recalled: 'The principal singers had refused the roles, the orchestra went on strike under the leadership of my own cousin and violin teacher Konzertmeister Benno Walter, and a deputation asked the General Director Perfall to free the orchestra from this "scourge of the gods". The tenor, whose memory had failed him at times during the première, declared afterwards that he would sing at further performances only if he received an increased pension . . .' Strauss traced the opera's failure to a conspiracy among the critics, most of whom were Jewish, and only after he moved into his villa in Garmisch in 1908 did his anger recede. Tongue in cheek, he erected a memorial stone in the villa's gardens to his operatic first-born: 'Here rests the honourable and virtuous young man GUNTRAM – *Minnesänger* – who was cruelly slain by the symphony orchestra of his own father. May he rest in peace.'

Guntram may have earned Strauss a funeral stone, and he never really came to terms with its failure,[9] but the opera's first production coincided with another, more lasting milestone in the life of its composer. Two days before the première, during a famously heated rehearsal, he and Pauline de Ahna became engaged.

11 GENERAL DE AHNA

May–October 1894

If the course of Strauss's life up to his twenties was defined by a succession of trenchant male mentors, the remaining sixty years were shaped by a single woman: Pauline de Ahna. None of his librettists, champions, friends or family exercised a comparable influence over his life after their marriage in September 1894. In certain respects it was an enviable relationship, for while Pauline may have lacked the intellect, wit and sensitivity he had found in Dora Wihan, Strauss appears to have loved her, and she him, with an almost mythological devotion.

Quite why he loved her as he did is unclear. Many of Pauline's contemporaries saw her as the embodiment of Wilhelminian hubris. She was loud, aggressive and fiercely proud. She delighted in reminding her audience that she was the daughter of a general, even if she did not always behave like it, and she suffered nobody, having neither grace nor patience. Even her own family thought her a handful. During the weeks prior to her engagement to Strauss, Pauline's father urged her to behave in a manner befitting her age[1] and breeding: 'Take heed that I am tired of having my old age soured by you. At your age and when one has been making one's way in the world for some years, one ought to know what one wants and not promise today to be a good and loyal wife and suddenly declare tomorrow that one has changed one's mind ... if you want to make yourself unhappy and cast a shadow over whole families, then do so, but thereafter I wash my hands of you.'

Externally, Pauline's personality appears to have been extreme in every respect. Many, including the Austrian poet Hugo von Hofmannsthal and the French writer Romain Rolland, were as repelled by her treatment of her husband as by her own brashness. Strauss's preferences were the cause of widespread bafflement. Franz led the family in recognising the positive aspects of marrying a woman 'so well placed to interpret' Richard's songs, but the majority considered Pauline inappropriate as a wife. In her memoirs Alma Mahler recalled a dinner party at which she and Gustav were joined by the Strausses. Gustav and Richard disappeared to talk shop – leaving Alma and Pauline to their own devices:

From this moment she began to rage. 'Yes, you can laugh – but it's no joke being the wife of a misunderstood genius. I tell you, it's frightful! We never have a penny and I never see him to speak to. Soon as he's done working, out he goes to play skat[2] and I'm always alone.' She burst into tears and laid her head on the table. We felt most uncomfortable. To soothe her was not easy.

I got up quietly, and brought Mahler and Strauss back into the room. Her face cleared at once. Strauss asked her what was the matter. 'Nothing,' she replied. 'Good,' he said, turning to Mahler. 'Then we can continue our conversation.' They stayed in the room with us after that and began discussing Mommsen's *History of Rome*. Mahler loved it. Strauss thought it unsound. They argued the question at length. Pauline sat in a corner and beckoned me to her. 'I say, which is the best hairdresser in Vienna?' I could hardly reply. Next they discussed Beethoven. Strauss preferred early Beethoven to late, to which Mahler replied that a genius such as he could only get better as he grew older. Strauss maintained the contrary: inspiration often failed him in his later years. The spontaneity of youth was worth all the rest. Mozart, for example – 'And blouses – where do you go for them?' I got up and left her to herself. I was not going to miss another word of that evening's talk.

Ida Dehmel, wife of the poet Richard, noted in a diary entry addressed to her husband, that Gustav Mahler had spoken of the Strausses' marriage 'with contempt, even with disgust' and that 'he thought it verged on masochism'. Her own observations led to similar conclusions: 'I was only once in Frau Strauss de Ahna's company ... She and her husband paid a call when Kessler and Hofmannsthal were there too. The exhibition she gave in that short space of time and in the presence of perfect strangers exceeded in tactlessness and vulgarity the worst I have ever known any woman guilty of. "Oh – men! Keep them on a tight rein, that's the only way"; and she went through the motions of holding the reins in one hand and the whip in the other.'

Why did the famous, handsome and talented Richard Strauss pursue, for seven years, a woman whose most striking qualities were defiance and pugnacity, when so many equally famous, more attractive and talented women found him irresistible? The surprisingly simple answer may well be that Strauss needed her. Dora Wihan and the other women with whom he had enjoyed sexual affairs while a young man personified an ideal of womanhood that left him unfulfilled and unchallenged. He wanted a matron, not a mistress, and he recognised – early on – that if he was to pursue his life and work to the best of his abilities he needed someone capable of providing him, and his family, with domestic security – something for which Pauline had rare talent.

According to Pauline, Strauss was uninterested in sex. He seems to have found it easier to translate his carnal energies into his music, and the absence of extra-marital affairs or scandals of any sort attest to a curious mixture of high principle and sexual apathy. As Pauline once delighted in explaining to a group of Strauss's friends, her husband's failure to produce a sibling for their son had nothing to do with his anatomy; rather, she had been unable to return him to her bedroom.

That Pauline was not a handsome woman may well have had something to do with Strauss's reticence. Unlike the striking Dora Wihan, her face and body were heavily set and her visage, as betrayed by the majority of photographs, was unsympathetic. Her attraction, for Strauss, was the personality that most others found so unpalatable. If Mahler was drawn to his wife's capriciousness – in spite of her anti-Semitism – then Strauss positively fed off Pauline's. Such danger and unpredictability were irresistible to a man bound by the routine and discipline demanded by a life of conducting and composing. Pauline struck the pose of an inner demon.

Like Alma, she was famed for her directness and many were alarmed by the absence of loyalty that both women displayed whenever their husbands' works were under discussion. But Alma was blessed with a compensatory beauty and charm that allowed her greater licence. There is also no doubting the influence of the De Alma family, whom Pauline considered superior to the Strausses in both pedigree and status. In 1926 the Strausses were invited to a dinner party in Berlin during which Pauline attacked Georg Büchner's Expressionist masterpiece *Woyzeck* (only recently set as an opera by Alban Berg). Asked to explain why she so detested the work, Pauline announced that she could never 'preoccupy herself with the troubled soul of a squalid non-commissioned officer'.[3]

Decades later Pauline would enjoy telling anyone willing to listen that her family had advised her not to marry Strauss. One of those with an ear for her dubious memoirs was the violinist Otto Strasser, who recalled how, in 1941, she had told him that 'her parents were very much opposed to her marriage, as she, the daughter of a Marshal of the Court and a General, wanted to marry a man whose father blew the horn in an orchestra!'

This was a lie. If any of the De Ahnas were opposed to the marriage then it was Pauline herself. As a singer, and a successful one at that, she had a long and glorious career ahead of her, and like Alma Schindler she intended to fill her own shoes before tending to those of an illustrious husband. Alma was a composer of some talent, but almost immediately after she and Mahler began courting he sent a huge epistle in which he explained that if they were to continue their relationship she would have to sacrifice her ambitions for his. On December 19, 1901, only a month into their relationship, he announced: 'You have only one profession from now on: to make me happy.' Pauline was at least fortunate in having a more tolerant suitor in Strauss, but his forbearance was by no means unqualified. Shortly before the birth of their son in April 1897 Pauline was retired from the operatic stage at the age of just thirty-four.[4]

As with Alma, this was the cause of an irrevocable resentment; but at least Pauline confronted her fears while she still had the chance. Strauss visited General de Ahna on March 22, 1894, to ask for his daughter's hand in marriage. The old man was delighted to have a son-in-law of such promise and he happily consented, writing to Pauline two days later: 'So the good loyal friend has been here to ask for your hand and we answered that if you and he were of one mind about your wishes and desires then we could only say "yes" and give "our blessing", for we know of nothing in the whole business that does not give us cause for joy . . . When I reflect on the uncertain, worrying future that you will now escape, by marrying a husband of good artistic repute, an interesting man and one devoted to you, I can only rejoice yet again with my whole heart that your destiny has taken this turn.' On the same day, presumably after having absorbed her father's counsel, Pauline sent an extraordinary letter to her fiancé in which, addressing him with bizarre formality as 'Mein lieber Herr Strauss', she attempted to rationalise herself and her situation:

> It's all suddenly descending on me like a shower bath; I beg you for God's sake not to rejoice so excessively, you know better than anyone how many faults I have, and I tell you in all honesty that in spite of the happiness I feel, I am sometimes terribly afraid. Will I be capable of being what you want and what you deserve? May I not first fulfil my guest engagement in Hamburg, so that I shall at least have a triumph to show off proudly to my respected teacher? . . . You should not overestimate me, and your parents and Hanna know my moods too. Oh God, and now I am suddenly supposed to turn into a model housewife, so that you do not feel disappointed. Dear friend, I am afraid that it will fail, and the more everyone else rejoices the more oppressed I feel . . .
>
> Will your parents like me, and Hanna, if she only knew how I have tried to dissuade you from everything. My dear friend, we really don't need to marry so soon; if each of us could first get accustomed to finding all the happiness we can in our careers; you in M[unich] and I in Hamburg . . . Please allow me at least to sing a lot more parts here; that will help me to get over some of my difficulties . . .

The defining obstacle was Pauline's future as a soprano. According to her sister Mädi, Richard was happy for her to do whatever she wanted, although Pauline appears not to have believed this. Furthermore, Pauline demanded that Strauss make it a condition of his agreement with Munich that she be engaged as a repertoire soprano. Strauss had no intention of giving anyone at Munich cause for criticism, and outright nepotism would have done nothing for Pauline's career, so he refused. In response, she penned an ever more obtuse series of letters to her intended, her parents and her sister, arousing anxiety in her father and accusations of madness from Mädi, who wrote to her sister: 'Papa was really annoyed and not in a fit state or mood to write to you, and told me that he wishes you would spare him enquiries about his health!'

Mädi wrote again on March 25, cautioning Pauline that to reject Strauss would stand as one of the greatest mistakes of her life: 'Everyone's patience gradually wears out in the end, and it might happen with Strauss too if you keep [him] in suspense for eternity ... don't go on playing this purely superficial role, and don't go on putting yourself in the foreground all the time.' Her father warned her to think of 'the social and the professional harm' that her refusal might bring her. Later on he demanded that she hold her tongue, and urged a 'little more self-control – for when the boorish words are out you always regret them at once'.

Things came to a head at the end of April, during rehearsals for the first production of *Guntram*. According to Strauss:

At one of the last rehearsals, during which I had to rap with my baton to stop Zeller countless times, we at last came to Pauline's scene in Act III which she knew perfectly well. All the same she felt unsure of herself and apparently envied Zeller because of his frequent 'repeats'. Suddenly she stopped singing and asked me: 'Why don't you stop me?' I: 'Because you know your part.' With the words 'I want to be stopped', she threw the vocal score which was in her hands at that moment, aiming it at my head, but to general hilarity it landed on the desk of the second violin.

Strauss makes no mention of what happened next but, in 1948, the soprano Lotte Lehmann recalled a version told to her:

He laid down his baton, interrupted the rehearsal which had been so violently disturbed, and without knocking entered Pauline's artist's room. Those waiting outside heard through the closed doors wild shrieks of rage and fragmentary insults – then all was quiet ... Strauss opened the door and stood in the doorway beaming radiantly. The representative of the orchestra stammered his speech: 'The orchestra is so horrified by the incredibly shocking behaviour of Fräulein Pauline de Ahna, that they feel they owe it to their honoured conductor to refuse in the future to play in any opera in which she may have a part' ... Strauss regarded the musicians smilingly. Then he said: 'That hurts me very much, for I have just become engaged to Fräulein de Ahna.'[5]

There is no primary evidence for this having happened, although Strauss well knew the story and enjoyed hearing it told. The truth was that, although Strauss had asked for Pauline's hand at the end of March, she had wilfully refused to give it. The confrontation was, therefore, typical of Pauline. He had waited years, and with *Guntram* nearing production his patience at last gave out. An ultimatum was delivered and, finally beaten at her own game, she yielded to his insistence. Cards were sent out officially announcing their engagement on the same day as *Guntram*'s première: May 10, 1894.

There were several reasons for Pauline's prevarication. She wanted to develop her voice and further her career; she felt threatened by the responsibilities of marriage, particularly marriage to one of Germany's most charismatic musicians, and she feared the loss of her identity. If she was not the sharpest woman to whom Strauss might have offered his hand, then Pauline was certainly the strongest in will and temperament. It was her desire to compensate for the flaws in her personality – to which she readily admitted – which led her to give vent to such extremes of emotion. In Strauss's autobiographical opera *Intermezzo*, Storch (Strauss) excuses his wife's behaviour by exclaiming, 'I must have life and temperament about me!' During their half-century together Pauline did mellow, but her ferocious disposition, intractable attitudes and short fuse were never subsumed. Away from home Strauss would frequently receive abusive letters from his wife, to which he would reply with endless patience and resignation. On December 9, 1896, for example, he sent the following to Pauline: 'Have just received your wrathful missive – ah, that's my old, cutting little woman again, signed "Bi" this time too, that always portends something of a tempest! It doesn't matter, my dear Bauxerl, I've had so many dulcet letters by now that I can perfectly sustain the occasional one that modulates into the minor.' In October the following year he referred to yet another explosion for which Pauline had, this time, apologised: 'Thank you once again for your adorable contrition: but you really ought not to make so much of these things ... scenes like this are never going to be able to shake my trust in you. The only thing is that I'm often distressed for you, because your nerves are not strong enough to help you stand up to these bursts of feeling as you should...'

Most of these outbursts were caused by insecurity. The soprano Viorica Ursuleac recalled how, after a performance of *Elektra* in Berlin, she and the conductor Wilhelm Furtwängler were invited to dinner by the Strausses. Ursuleac was a handsome woman and perhaps this riled Pauline, who proceeded to heap praise on Furtwängler's head, extolling his physical presence over and above his musical gifts – the softness of his hair, the beauty of his hands, his noble height and so on. Strauss lost his temper, leapt from his seat, cursed his wife and stamped from the room. As soon as he had left, Pauline began to sob: 'I only wanted to make him jealous.'

Whenever Richard mentioned a soprano as famed for her beauty as her voice, such as Maria Jeritza, Pauline's mood would darken – not because she doubted her husband's constancy, but because she secretly wanted him to reinforce his masculinity. His aversion to physical intimacy was an obstacle, and it is no surprise that Pauline's sexual appetite diminished as their relationship deepened.

If Strauss endured his wife's aggression he did so because he knew that, fundamentally, she was devoted to him, and that she only ever wanted the very best for them both. Lotte Lehmann, who created the 'Pauline' character in *Intermezzo*, remembered with 'astonishment' the huge paradoxical swings of mood and sentiment that possessed Frau de Ahna. She noted how Pauline would berate and criticise Richard for anything and everything and how, whenever she tried to intervene on his behalf, Strauss would urge her to stay out of the way, exercising 'angelic patience and adaptability'. But almost immediately after one of these fits of anger, when Strauss would sit at the piano and begin to play through his songs, Pauline 'would embrace him sobbing in one of her violent outbursts of tenderness'. Even her affection was rudely expressed, and yet it was obvious to Lehmann, at moments such as these, that they loved each other like 'a couple of youngsters'.

Strauss claimed to be indolent by nature and Pauline motivated him, ensuring that he remained focused and on top of his work. There is no denying that she acted like a bully, but there were times when he retaliated, if only to remind her that there were limits. For the most part, however, he cherished his wife's military bearing, and they enjoyed an intimacy and a mutual sympathy that transcended understanding and defies interpretation.

They were married, exactly four months after the official announcement of their engagement, in Marquartstein[6] on the morning of September 10, 1894. The service followed a Catholic order – presumably to satisfy the De Ahnas' social probity – although Strauss refused to allow it to be held in a church.[7] The wedding photographs reveal a stone-faced couple, as starched and tightly bound as their parasols, with neither betraying the slightest affection for the other. Strauss looks down on her while Pauline stares fixedly at the camera. As a wedding present Strauss gave his wife four songs: *Ruhe, meine Seele, Morgen!, Heimliche Aufforderung* and *Cäcilie*. More than Pauline can have known, these were to become cornerstones of the Lieder repertoire and they entered the mainstream almost immediately after their publication as Op. 27.

The couple left soon afterwards for their honeymoon in Italy. Finding their original destination, Bellagio, impossibly cold they moved to Pegli and later Venice before returning to Munich on October 6 and their first apartment together, provided for them by Pauline's ever-generous family.

October 1894–November 1896

The year 1894 was an auspicious one for Strauss, even if the first production of *Guntram* had to be considered a failure. He was officially released from his Weimar contract on April 13 and shortly afterwards Munich confirmed his new appointment. On June 3, ten days before his thirtieth birthday, he conducted the première of Mahler's First Symphony. The same month, the Allgemeiner Deutscher Musikverein held its congress in Weimar which ensured more work for Strauss the conductor, notably in productions of *Guntram* and *Hänsel und Gretel*, and he also heard Siegfried Wagner, Engelbert Humperdinck and Mahler in performances of their own works. Strauss conducted a celebrated performance of *Tristan* in Munich, as part of what would become the annual summer festival. Thus was he introduced to the orchestra which he was soon to share with Levi.

He left Weimar under a cloud of rumour and allegation. So outspoken were some newspapers that Strauss wrote officially to deny that his relationship with Lassen had contributed towards his decision to leave Weimar. To the *Deutschland* he protested: 'In order to counter the manifold rumours that seem to be swarming throughout Weimar at present . . . I will be obliged if you will publish the declaration that not only does Herr Hofkapellmeister Eduard Lassen have no connection with my departure from Weimar, but that on the contrary I gladly seize this opportunity to confirm that during the five years I have spent engaged in artistic activity Dr Lassen has always shown me the greatest possible co-operation . . .' In his memoirs[1] Strauss conceded: 'On the whole, people were very nice to me[2] (Bronsart, Lassen, the Court); but I recklessly squandered some of the good will they bore me, by my youthful energy and love of exaggeration, so that people were not sorry to see Pauline and me leave . . .'

Between their departure from Weimar and their arrival in Munich came the 1894 Bayreuth Festival, which gave rise to yet more political affliction. In the winter of 1893–4 Cosima had invited Strauss to conduct although, at the time, she had yet to decide on details of repertoire and casting. As Strauss correctly surmised, Cosima's hesitancy had less to do with him than with his imminent arrival in Munich. There had been rivalry between Bayreuth and neighbouring Munich ever since Possart and Wagner had crossed swords during the latter's turbulent stay in the city in the 1860s; but while Cosima and the Bayreuth clan were happy to co-operate with Munich, if for no other reason than that they needed access to the Court Opera's orchestra, Possart was determined to bring Munich to the fore of Wagner performance by announcing the establishment of an annual festival not unlike that staged in Bayreuth. His ambition guaranteed a measure of difficulty for Strauss, who found himself caught in the middle.

When Cosima failed to react Possart raised the stakes by announcing, for Munich's festival, a new production of *Lohengrin*[3] – the same work that Cosima had scheduled for Bayreuth's opening night. She demonstrated admirable wisdom and restraint in her handling of the affair, for although she warned Strauss that his invitation from Possart to conduct *Tristan* in June (and, in September, *Meistersinger*) had been designed to cause 'confusion between Munich and Bayreuth' she stood by her word, and invited him to conduct the festival production of *Tannhäuser*.

Cosima decided to oversee the new production of *Lohengrin* herself, and summoned Mottl from Karlsruhe to conduct. Her casting was outstanding but controversial. In defiance of the Bayreuth conservative movement she chose to cast non-German singers from around the world, finding the very best regardless, with one exception, of their nationality.[4] As she proudly announced: 'We want a German theatre of all nationals except for the chosen people.'

The press was uniformly hostile; one newspaper even questioned Cosima's racial suitability: 'How the Master was angered when his wife preferred to speak to her father Liszt in French ... half Magyar, half French she is hardly appropriate to hold a key in matters of German art.' Another wrote: 'Foreigners now come with their arrogance and their money and shove aside the children of the nation.' Cosima's lack of regard for Bavarian xenophobia was incautious, and Strauss was one of many who considered her judgement suspect. Like everyone else, however, he had his own agenda. By the time she announced her casting Cosima had still not decided whether to ask Pauline to return. This excited further antagonism, particularly in the light of Pauline's earlier usurpation by Elisa Wiborg. But on June 3 Cosima yielded, and wrote to ask Strauss if his fiancée would be willing to sing one of the six Flower Maidens in *Parsifal* and Elisabeth in 'his' *Tannhäuser*.[5]

Despite the politics, the atmosphere was convivial. Not even the presence of Hermann Levi (who was, again, in charge of *Parsifal*[6]) could overshadow Strauss's happiness at being back in Bayreuth, where art was 'treated seriously'. Pauline triumphed, and aside from some unflattering reviews,[7] Strauss felt like a 'Lion at Olympia'. His dream had come true, and another of his longest-standing ambitions was realised.

On October 1, 1894, Strauss began his second term at Munich Court Opera.

His responsibilities were greater than they had been in Weimar and, in theory at least, he should have found the climate conducive. But as Strauss noted in his memoirs, his return to Munich was spoiled 'by the bad feeling between Possart (Court Theatre), who was well-disposed towards me [!], and Perfall (Hofmusikintendant), who became more hostile towards me with every new work...'[8]

His arrival in Munich none the less heralded a fresh start as a conductor and, more importantly, he was back in the town of his birth. Having failed to establish any lasting relationships in Weimar, he was relieved to find himself again among friends, but it was the very proximity of so much unconditional affection that made his second spell in Munich such a disappointment. His misery had less to do with his own conduct than with the conduct of those around him, or so he liked to believe. Just as Jews were responsible for bad criticism, so the obfuscation of colleagues and administrators was motivated by jealousy and resentment, rather than by his arrogance and obstinacy. Strauss attributed his unhappiness to the strain between Possart and Perfall simply because he was incapable of seeing himself as its root cause. 'As a conductor one needs the success of the moment', he wrote to his father, but 'as a composer one has to be somebody. Nothing else matters.'

This need to be 'somebody' weakened his judgement, and left him vulnerable. By allowing himself to be tempted back into the fray by Levi, for example, Strauss seems not to have realised how much this would weaken his position in Bayreuth. Levi resented Strauss's rapid ascent with the Wagners, and he well knew that an offence against the occupants of Wahnfried, was rarely forgiven and never forgotten. Consequently, his invitation to Strauss, and his 'gift' of the Wagner repertoire[9] (coincidental to Possart's plans for a new Bayreuth in Munich) was a decidedly poisoned chalice.

Levi's divided loyalties were tolerated because of his connection with *Parsifal*,[10] and because many of those buying the tickets wanted to hear 'the Master's' works performed by the original creators. For Strauss, such a workable symmetry was inconceivable. Neither Cosima nor the increasingly resentful Siegfried were going to give an inch. Siegfried, in particular, saw in Strauss's alliance with Possart all the evidence he needed to leap to the wrong conclusions. Strauss was not against Bayreuth, although he was only ever for it if he had his own way, and yet by attempting to juggle responsibilities to both theatres he was inviting calamity. Strain was evident almost immediately after Strauss's arrival at the Court Opera. Neither Cosima nor Siegfried approved of *Guntram* and they were equally affronted by the announcement that Strauss was to conduct three 'model productions' of Wagner's works during the Munich summer season.

It has been suggested that the Strauss–Bayreuth rift occurred because Cosima disapproved of Strauss's music, but prior to 1895 she had applauded even his most daring compositions and it was not until the emergence of *Salome* ten years later that she would turn against him as a composer. Rather, it was Siegfried's jealous[11] influence that made Strauss an unacceptable presence within the Bayreuth circle, the more so since he was soon to begin conducting in his father's theatre. In fairness to Strauss there was little he could have done, short of resigning from Munich, to secure his place by Cosima's side. They had begun collaborating on an operatic setting of Goethe's *Lila* during the summer of 1895 and this assured Strauss some measure of protection, but Cosima was sufficiently devoted to her son to do as he asked, and he asked that Strauss not return to Bayreuth as a conductor. Furthermore, Strauss had been careless in his criticism of Cosima and her family – the disclosure of which added to the rumours that Strauss was by nature treacherous and manipulative. To the Wagner family and their confidants, disloyalty was unforgivable.

Strauss's difficulties with Bayreuth peaked on January 12, 1896. As he noted in his diary, he enjoyed a 'Momentous conversation with Siegfried Wagner' which resulted in an 'unspoken but none the less irrevocable separation from Wahnfried-Bayreuth'. In a letter sent to Strauss a few days after his conversation with Siegfried, Arthur Seidl traced the reasons for the Strauss–Bayreuth rift to Cosima and her fondness for tradition and quasi-religious deference:

> I hear that you are now talking of a period in your life, called 'Wahnfried', as being closed for good, and it grieves me in the depths of my soul that I have been proved right. I will only remind you of our long and animated conversation about Frau Wagner and the Wagner Societies the first time you came to see us, and of your denial when I identified you with Guntram, Friedhold with Ritter and Bayreuth with the Brotherhood in the *Rundschau*. I was quite sure about it even then and I foresaw all this ... These strict *Wahnfriedists* around the Meisterin, on the conservative right wing, who always have to run to her for all their answers and offer up one *sacrificium intellectus* after another to their own convictions are ... pitiful milksops, sad marionettes ... without the guts to live their own lives ... an empty nothing when Cosima has spoken and brandishes her terrorism over their heads...

On March 8, 1896, Cosima confronted the rift by writing to Strauss that her son had 'told me about his argument with you and even though I was very sorry to learn that you had been disturbed in that way, yet I was pleased to think that you had had that opportunity to learn to know him in all his frankness, simplicity and friendship for you'.

Strauss and Cosima remained in touch, doing their best to put the episode behind them, but his scrapping of *Lila* and Cosima's refusal to invite him back to conduct at the festival meant the beginning of the end of their friendship. Strauss returned to Bayreuth as a member of the audience, in August 1896,[12] to hear Siegfried conduct his first *Ring*.[13] On the 16th he wrote to Pauline, telling her that Cosima was 'very amiable and took me and Vogl and [H. S.] Chamberlain to Fantasie.[14] In the evening to a soirée in Wahnfried, everyone, Siegfried included, very amiable, I ditto, we behave as if nothing happened.' His reviews to Pauline veered between reverence (of the production of *Das Rheingold* he wrote that it was something 'that can be done only in Bayreuth') and disgust (he dismissed Siegfried's conducting as 'miserable') and, perhaps influenced by his proximity to Chamberlain, he damned Lilli Lehmann's 'atrocious' Brünnhilde in a letter to Pauline as an 'old Jewish grandmother without acting talent and without [a] trace of feeling'.

There were two further reasons for Strauss to resent the 'worthless, dandified fop Siegfried'.[15] The first was that tickets were being sold for the *Ring* cycle before it was clear who would be conducting – forcing audiences to risk four nights with Siegfried when most wanted to hear Richter. The second was the more lasting. Shortly before making his debut as a conductor Siegfried sent a letter to a cultural journal, which was later printed in a semi-official festival handbook, in which he stated his belief that ultimate authority in the theatre at Bayreuth lay with the stage director, who was to give the conductor his orders. In other words, conductors were sheep to be shepherded, an opinion that Strauss considered a personal affront.

His split from the Wagners did not signal the end of Strauss's association with their festival. While he had come to denounce Bayreuth as a 'pigsty to end all pigsties' he was still devoted to the ideas that had established it, and he never wavered in his admiration for its founder. In fact, locking horns with the family served to intensify his faith in the festival's role as cultural *imprimatur* for all German art. In Strauss's eyes the festival had been sullied by the Cosima/Siegfried regime and he decided to stay away until such time as he might return in a position of strength and authority.[16]

Family tension also marred Strauss's first year in Munich. Pauline was proving an unpopular choice with his parents. Franz began referring to her as 'the actress' and in his typically outspoken fashion he freely criticised her tempestuous manner. It is unlikely that Franz actually disapproved of his son's wife, but Pauline appears to have lacked respect for her father-in-law, who took servility for granted. If her later comments about her husband's family are anything to go by, Pauline was probably quick to vilify Franz's poor social heritage and pedestrian trade while, in turn, he attacked her conceit and vulgarity. There were many rows, and Franz and Pauline delighted in undermining each other. During the autumn of 1896 Richard resolved to draw a line under the affair:

Many thanks for the beautiful lilac plant. It gave me much pleasure. But, really, it would give me more pleasure if my continuous endeavours to effect an understanding between my wife and my family were not so totally unsuccessful. I assure you that my wife intends sincerely to correct her faults, faults which are minor and harmless and of which she herself is aware. You, on the other hand, I must note with sorrow, are not willing to understand the peculiarities of her nature nor to condone them. When I realise that gossip, miserable lying, old-woman Jew's gossip, suffices for you to raise such awful accusations against Pauline as you did this morning and to nullify all of my endeavours, as well as Pauline's, to arrive at an understanding, then I must ask myself if it wouldn't be better to cease any relationship between Pauline and you. To be sure, Pauline's nature is impulsive, violent, and brusque. But at the bottom she has a good, childlike, and naive nature. Even with the best will in the world, she can't quickly and radically change the way she behaves. That behaviour doesn't please you: very well, from now on she wants to avoid disturbing your peace and tranquillity – even though at the bottom of her jealous heart she feels true love and admiration for you.

I haven't the slightest intention of continuing to explain, unfortunately unsuccessfully, the character of my wife while you don't take the least trouble to get to know her ... In short, I propose that you erase your rambunctious [sic] daughter-in-law from the family book and content yourself with your much more accommodating son-in-law. Both Pauline and I want dearly to see you, my beloved parents, peaceful and happy. I conclude with much pain that cannot be the case, so long as the woman whom, after much deliberation, I have chosen as my wife, and whom in spite of her faults I love and admire, irritates you and embitters your life ... she will submit to voluntary banishment from your family circle and remain by the side of her husband ...

Whether or not they resolved their differences is impossible to say. On the one hand, Franz and Josephine realised that, for the sake of their relationship with their son – and any children he might father – they must do their best to arrive at some sort of conciliation. On the other hand, Franz was an old man with an unstable wife. That Richard addressed his letter to her, and not his father, suggests he was using his mother's emotional instability to get to Franz, who bore the brunt of her anxieties. If his letter was sent in late September, Pauline was almost certainly pregnant; in which case Strauss's threat to banish Pauline from the Strauss family circle implied the exclusion of any children. A reconciliation was swiftly exacted, although Franz and Pauline never fully suppressed their mutual contempt.

Aside from these family politics, the first eighteen months of Strauss's second term in Munich were monopolised by conducting responsibilities, which included a season of ten concerts as guest conductor in Berlin with the Philharmonic, who were looking for a full-time successor to Bülow. It was an unhappy partnership, and his contract was not renewed. This failure to win favour with Germany's greatest orchestra further dented Strauss's confidence at a time when the failure of *Guntram* and his unhappy departure from Weimar had already left him feeling vulnerable. He later confessed to having been unprepared to stand before the Berlin Philharmonic at so comparatively young an age, and he registered no complaints when Arthur Nikisch was appointed principal conductor at the end of the 1894–5 season.

Strauss's Berlin programmes were predictably New German, but he did what he could for living composers when he scheduled works by Schillings, D'Albert, Glazunov, Dvořák, Ritter, Johann Strauss, Widor and himself. Earning the disgust of Berlin's critics, he also invited Mahler to conduct the first three movements of his Second Symphony on March 4, 1895. It was on this now famous occasion that the aggressively anti-Semitic Otto Lessmann voiced the widely endorsed opinion, in the *Allgemeine Musikzeitung*, that 'the altar consecrated by Bülow has now been defiled by pygmies'.

Mahler had been frantically scratching Strauss's back in Hamburg in the hope that he might reciprocate in Berlin or Munich. As part of the 1894–5 Subscription Concert season in Hamburg Mahler conducted the Prelude to Act I[17] of *Guntram*, while continuing to make grand claims for his plans to mount a complete production. References, by Mahler, to the Hamburg public's supposed affection for what little it had heard of *Guntram* were bolstered by Mahler's hinting at Pollini's aspirations for the opera.[18] In his own way Strauss did his best to repay Mahler's generosity. On February 22, 1897, for example, he wrote to his 'Dear Friend': 'I had been thinking now and then that you had quite forgotten the first "Mahlerian"!' – a statement that was at odds with Strauss's apparent reluctance to conduct Mahler's music.

In fairness to Strauss, Munich in the 1890s was not the place to be promoting avant-garde music, particularly not the work of a Jew. Cultural parameters were notably wider in Berlin, where the promoter was Jewish and by whose audiences the principle of new music was widely embraced. Strauss's first production in his new post was of Lortzing's *Der Waffenschmied*, on October 24, 1894, which must have come as something of a disappointment having so recently conducted *Tristan* and *Meistersinger*. He was then entrusted with Weber's *Oberon*, Mozart's *Die Zauberflöte* and Ignaz Brüll's *Das goldene Kreuz*. The second half of the season, beginning in January 1895, saw him conduct twenty-nine performances of a further nine operas, a body of work that stood in homage to middle-class Bavarian values, at the middle of the cultural highway: Maillart's *Les Dragons de Villars*, Flotow's *Martha*, Humperdinck's *Hänsel und Gretel*, Bizet's *Carmen*, Nicolai's *Die lustigen Weiber von Windsor*, Wagner's *Tannhäuser* and *Rienzi*, Verdi's *Il trovatore* and Kreutzer's *Das Nachtlager von Granada*.

With just two exceptions every opera conducted by Strauss during the 1894–5 season was by a dead composer. Wagner was now part of the Establishment and there was nothing contemporary about Brüll or Humperdinck's works, which meant that Munich's operatic diet was monopolised by archaisms and confectionery. Later, in 1897, he managed to bring two new works by German composers to the Munich stage: Heinrich Zöllner's *Der Überfall* and Ludwig Thuille's *Theuerdank*.

The latter, composed by his childhood friend to a libretto by Ritter, was staged as part of the celebrations for the birthday of the Regent, Prince Luitpold, and it was one of three new works[19] to win the Luitpold Prize for new operas. Their failure was absolute, but Strauss persevered, and during the remainder of his stay in Munich he did his best to champion as many composers as the conditions allowed, including Schillings's *Ingwelde* and Siegmund von Hausegger's *Zinnober*.

As more of the opera house's responsibilities devolved on to Strauss he was forced to learn much of his repertoire in rehearsal, a constructive and illuminating process, but one that left him exhausted. On top of these professional pressures he had to cope, in June 1895, with Pauline's[20] guest appearance as Elisabeth in *Tannhäuser*, and during the August Wagner Festival he conducted no fewer than twelve performances, three each of *Rienzi*, *Tannhäuser*, *Tristan und Isolde* and *Die Meistersinger*, which went some way towards compensating him for having to conduct operas by Brüll, Kreutzer and Verdi.

Although Verdi was derided by German aesthetes, he was popular with audiences, and not even Strauss could deny the Italian composer's effortless vitality; indeed, his professed aversion to Verdi's music seems unlikely in the light of a letter he sent to the composer, together with a copy of *Guntram*, on January 18, 1895:

> Although I know from my own experience how troublesome dedications can be, I nevertheless venture to ask you to be so kind as to accept a copy of *Guntram*, my first essay in the genre, as a token of my respect and admiration for the undoubted master of Italian opera.
>
> As I can find no words to describe the deep impression made upon me by the extraordinary beauty of *Falstaff*, and have no other means of expressing my gratitude for the enjoyment it has brought me, I beg you to accept this score, at the very least. I should count myself happy indeed, if I ever had the occasion to talk with you about the divine art, music, in order to receive new stimuli for my inspiration and my artistic creation. My friend and patron Hans von Bülow was unhappily denied the privilege.

So too was Strauss, but nine days later the 81-year-old Verdi replied:

> I received a few days ago the work you so kindly sent me, and which has had such success. I leave today for Milan, where I shall spend several weeks, and so I have not had the time to read your score; but from dipping into it here and there I have seen that *Guntram* is the work of a very expert hand. It is a shame

that I do not understand the language of its text, not with an eye to pronouncing judgement on it (which would ill become me, and which I would never venture to do), but so that I could admire it and share in your joy.

On May 6, 1895, Strauss completed his first major orchestral composition for five years, the tone poem *Till Eulenspiegels lustige Streiche*, Op. 28. He had first considered using the myth of Till as an opera during the summer of 1893. On November 4 of that year he wrote to his father lamenting the absence of good operatic subjects, and twelve days later sent the news that he was 'working hard on a new libretto ... *Till Eulenspiegel und der Burghers von Schilda*. Considering the mood of the country during the late 1880s and early 1890s, Strauss's attraction to such a banal subject was curious. The legend of Till concerned a mischievous prankster – the German equivalent of the Hungarian Hárry János and the English Owlglass – whose rebellious antics result in his death by hanging.

Strauss was uninterested in the original myth's implicit social commentary; he ignored the elements that would have appealed, for example, to Voltaire or Dickens and he sidestepped the Naturalistic possibilities that informed the likes of Gerhart Hauptmann and Arno Holz. In fact, there is nothing in Strauss's interpretation to divorce it from a simple painting-by-numbers portrayal of a *Schalk* (a smiling scoundrel), apart from the genius of its construction. In short, Strauss appears to have been indifferent to the world around him, and blind to the growing contemporary predilection for Naturalism. Launched from within the intellectual circles of Munich and Berlin, German artists took their lead from the French movement in prose fiction and drama whose chief exponent, Emile Zola, defined the common objective in a series of twenty novels[21] in which life was portrayed through the eyes of experience, subject to natural laws, rather than through an idealised impression of existence, as had traditionally been the case.

Artificiality was rejected as decadent and irrelevant; accuracy and documentation were celebrated as the primary objectives. As fiction was transformed, and as real life was opened up before a gallery of enthusiastic consumers, it was necessary for artists to appeal to an increasingly wide cross-section of the educated public. If man was the product of his environment, so too was his art. Many of the finest French Naturalist dramas were created for the Théâtre Libre,[22] which toured to Berlin in 1889. Their impact was comparable in significance to the steady influence of Henrik Ibsen and August Strindberg, whose greatest German disciple, Hauptmann, transformed the German stage of the 1890s through a series of shocking dramas, famously *Von Sonnenaufgang* (1889) and *Die Weber* (1892). Of equal impact was Theodore Fontane, who revolutionised the German novel with the monumental social critique *Frau Jenny Treibel* (1892), an ironic parody of class hypocrisy, and

Effi Briest, a vicious satire on the small-mindedness of the German middle class.

This passive revolution added considerably to the liberation of German artists from the idealised, pseudo-classical stylisation of Romantics such as Caspar David Friedrich. A new, Naturalist school of German painting, centred in Munich and Berlin, emerged during the late 1880s, and by 1892 it had organised itself into a self-styled Sezession. Inaugurated in 1892 in Munich by Franz von Stuck and Wilhelm Trübner, the Sezessionists believed that contemporary art had outgrown the traditions and conventions favoured by the Establishment. Reorganising themselves into a genuine avant-garde, their defining characteristics were a social conscience, an awareness of the realities of the world about them and a defiance of the State's pressure to restore nationalistic monumentality and artificiality to the canvas.

To what extent German writers and painters genuinely sympathised with the downtrodden is difficult to say. A lack of sincerity is certainly noticeable in some of the more famous dramatic works and there was frequently a sense that scepticism was being substituted for true anger, as if change were something that might be written about and wished for, but never initiated. An element of fashion doubtless prevailed, and the impact of Bismarck's repressionary social reform provided more than mere provocation; but there was also a sense that artists were looking to shock the security of the bourgeoisie for the sake of it. It was no coincidence that, with Bismarck's laws repealed, many of the more aggressive social critics reverted to the security of their middle-class roots, renouncing the sex, violence and filth common to 'ordinary' life.

This reversion to an active apoliticism was thought inevitable at the time, particularly since the younger generation of talent, led by Richard Dehmel, Stefan George, Rainer Rilke and Hugo von Hofmannsthal, was either middle class or aristocratic. These writers found the Naturalism of Hauptmann and his colleagues objectionable. Exchanging political Naturalism for apolitical nationalism suited the style of the new school, whose foremost thinkers subordinated reality to feeling, favouring a detached humanism in which reflection and contemplation were more important than social truth and dramatic veracity. The darkest recesses of society were less exotic than the darkest recesses of the human soul.[23]

In music, of course, cogent locution was much harder to realise. Narrative detail in Absolute music – with neither words nor programme – was entirely subjective. Emotion or meaning in music could be understood by anyone, but whether or not it was the emotion or meaning intended by the composer was another matter. Similarly, composers could not be expected to translate Naturalism, *per se*, without resorting to words or a programme. The seventh of Beethoven's symphonies, for example, has been variously interpreted as an impression of village life, the inside of a cathedral, 'the love dream of a

sumptuous odalisque',[24] a tale of Moorish knighthood, a masquerade, a
military celebration and, perhaps most implausibly of all, a musical homage
to Walter Scott's novel *Ivanhoe*. With good reason, opera, the symphonic
poem and the Lied were the only means by which a composer could be
expected to convey anything specific.

Bruckner and, to a greater extent, Mahler had succeeded in delineating
a variety of human and societal enigmas. Mahler's obsession with non-
programmatic narratives – particularly in his Second and Third Symphonies – was typical of the general shift towards the subjective philosophy
exemplified by Beethoven and venerated by Wagner. Those composers raised
in the wake of Naturalism, notably Zemlinsky, Schoenberg and Schmidt,
determined to bring artistic definition to their century as it neared its end.
The seriousness of their music, and that of their hero Mahler, reflected the
overwhelming solemnity of *fin-de-siècle* aesthetics, and if German composers
began to resist the Programme as early as the middle 1880s it was only because
Absolutism allowed for a far greater variety and depth of expression.

It would seem, therefore, that Strauss lacked the necessary self-confidence
to break with programme aesthetics. Like Berlioz before him, Strauss feared
letting his invention speak for itself. *Till Eulenspiegel* typified his intellectual
and political detachment and reinforced his disregard for the aesthetic revolution that was unfolding about him in 1895. In spite of his supposed
modernity Strauss was essentially a conservative, a quality that bound him
to the romanticism of Fichte, Wagner, Nietzsche and Spengler rather than to
the modernity of Hauptmann and the Naturalists. As such, *Till Eulenspiegel*
was almost a declaration of independence. Had he not applied his genius to
such a reductive subject, engaging an absolute rather than a programmatic
formula, Strauss might have escaped the bourgeois associations that dog him
to this day.

The strong leaning towards 'cultural despair' which coloured Strauss's
attitudes throughout his life facilitated a disengagement from social and
political affairs rather than a healthy and proper involvement. His withdrawal
into his own private world of sensibility is not, however, synonymous with
the stereotype of the 'unpolitical German', defended by Thomas Mann during
the First World War. With hindsight, such resignation amounted to an indictment of the German bourgeoisie. Its irrationalism, inwardness and cultural
pessimism now appear as burdens that contributed more than anything else
to the bourgeoisie's failure to develop and fight for its own worthy objectives.

There was no pressure on Strauss to foster a conscience. He was, after all,
committed to the egoism of Stirner and Nietzsche, and the myth of Till was
no more or less valid a subject than Macbeth or Don Juan. But his satisfied
reliance on a comic, semi-moral folk-tale for inspiration at a time when so
much of greater significance was going on about him strikingly anticipates
his later actions. The gravity of his withdrawal, at such a young age, cannot

be ignored, just as his ultimate statement of indifference, *Capriccio*,[25] has to be evaluated within the context of the year in which it was written: 1942.

The son of a peasant, Till was supposedly born in 1300. His antics gave rise to a series of German and Flemish satirical tales, first published in German in 1519, in Flemish two years later and translated into English by William Copland in 1555 or 1560.[26] A poor relative of Chaucer's Tales,[27] they are directed against the pillars of society – chiefly noblemen, the clergy and tradesmen. Strauss targeted just two quarries: Academia, when Till confounds the 'philistrious [sic] professors' after setting off a 'Babylonian linguistic confusion'; and the Church when, oozing 'unction and morality', Till disguises himself as a priest. Otherwise, Strauss told his friend Wilhelm Mauke, he concentrated his attention on Till's jolly tricks – his riding on horseback through the 'market-women', his charging about in 'seven-league boots', his 'courtesies [sic] with pretty girls', his condemnation of 'the Philistines', his 'trial' and his eventual death at the gallows.

It has been suggested that the satire in *Till* was aimed at Strauss's enemies in Munich, whose reception of *Guntram* caused the composer such anguish. But the score was completed six months before the Munich performance. In reality, Strauss imagined himself as something of a Lochinvar, standing tall against the laggards in love and dastards in war that had caused him such distress in Munich, Weimar, Bayreuth and just about every other city in which his reception had been less than resounding. His lack of respect for the general public, for 'the mob' which he believed to be unhealthily dominated by 'bankers and tradesmen of low tastes', was as lifelong as it was regrettable. Not even his most ardent admirers can support some of his sweeping judgements on the very people who would ensure the continuing popularity of his music.

That there was a critical subtext beyond those generalised targets conceded to Mauke cannot be denied, but its message is uncertain and subjective. Writing about Strauss and *Till Eulenspiegel* in 1896, Arthur Seidl noted: '*Epater le bourgeois!* War against all the apostles of moderation, against the old guild of the merely virtuous and comfortable, all good Philistines and the safe schools of restraint! – that could well be the motto of the entire shoot [sic] ...' Strauss himself, in notes he made for his proposed opera on the same subject, again revealed his weakness for Nietzsche, nihilism and autobiography: 'Till: despises mankind, defies nature, has not yet worked his way through to reason, an idler, a lazy-bones, who does not cheat the good Lord of His time by spending it in useless work, who makes a fool of the men and plays tricks on them, despises the women because he thinks the love of every one of them is easily obtained ... Till ugly – misanthropic – loves nature "without human beings" who were the first to bring stupidity into the world ... Till, despiser of the world, fruitless sceptic and laughing philosopher.'

Clearly, these notes are more detailed and candid than anything implied by the tone poem. Properly developed, Strauss's references to man's paradoxical inability to reconcile a faith in humanity with an aversion for its people could well have led to a fascinating work of reflective, contemporary art. But his tone poem was born of more modest instincts. Shortly before the première he wrote to the conductor Franz Wüllner: 'Let the gay Cologners guess what a rogue has done to them by way of musical tricks ...' The work's defining function was to amuse and provoke. For everything he might have said or written in private, Strauss's primary concern was always his audience. Many years later Joseph Gregor, his long-suffering librettist, asked him whether or not he was aware that *Till* had reached 'the metaphysical boundaries of humour', to which Strauss replied: 'Oh, no – I only wanted to give the people in the concert hall a good laugh for once.'

The full score was completed on May 6, 1895. He sent it to his publisher, Spitzweg, demanding 1,500 marks (for which he would throw in three songs), but Spitzweg was still reeling from the costs incurred by *Guntram* and offered no more than 1,000. Strauss 'gratefully' accepted. The first performance was given in Cologne six months later on November 5, by Wüllner, at the second of the season's Subscription Concerts. It was cheered to the rafters by the audience and acclaimed by the critics. Before the year's end it had been performed in Mannheim, Berlin, Dresden, Eberfeld and, on November 29, by Strauss himself in Munich. It was his most popular orchestral work to date and, with the exception of *Don Juan*, it has remained so.

On November 17, 1895 – the day after the disastrous Munich première of *Guntram* – Possart rewarded Strauss with a pay-rise of 5,000 marks; but it was going to take more than money to dispel Strauss's dissatisfaction. In his diary on February 8, 1896, he wrote: 'Possart's knavery grows more and more blatant. After promising to put on *Guntram* once a month, whatever the circumstances, he has not scheduled the work in spite of Mikorey[28] having declared himself ready to sing G. five weeks ago. He promised my wife a guest contract from 1 January 1896 (6,000 marks, 40 appearances). He doesn't make a move. Offensively ignores my wife and sets the press on her and me, to make us compliant.'

Relief came from Mozart, whose operas received under Possart strikingly fresh and revitalising treatment in Munich's rebuilt Residenztheater. The first of these landmark productions, of *Le nozze di Figaro*, took place under Levi on May 29, 1896, and was followed by a production of *Don Giovanni* which, as the first on a revolving stage, invited international comment. The impact of these performances, to which Strauss made sizeable contributions, led to the establishment of the annual Mozart Festival which endures, like that devoted to Wagner, as one of the city's most consistent musical attractions. Strauss's performances of *Don Giovanni* and *Così* were considered exceptional, especially his improvisations of the *secco* recitatives; but of the three

Mozart operas he conducted in Munich it was *Così* that excited the most comment.

Although it is now considered among the finest of Mozart's operas, this was not the case during the first hundred years following its première in 1789. Da Ponte's libretto dramatised the erosion, by sexuality, of proper behavioural codes – as *outré* a social commentary to the eighteenth century as it was to the nineteenth – but Strauss and Possart delighted in the 'superior ironies' of Mozart's setting and their new production helped raise the opera to its rightful place alongside *Le nozze di Figaro*, *Don Giovanni* and *Die Zauberflöte*.

During his second spell in Munich Strauss conducted seventy-five performances of operas by Mozart[29] and forty-six performances of operas by Wagner[30] (a total of one hundred and twenty-one). Viewed against the number of performances he gave of other composers' works – just twenty-four – Strauss's allegiances appear more than a little archaic, but neither Possart nor the Munich public were naturally predisposed towards modernity.

With the Munich Mozart Festival and invitations to conduct overseas monopolising his time (including a concert of his own music in Moscow on March 16), the 1895–6 season was proving exceptionally busy. The ever-present burden of in-house politics was giving Strauss's overseas invitations an air of opiate irresistibility, and the new year gave him cause to reconsider the value of his appointment. In February he began making inquiries at rival opera houses in Mannheim and Karlsruhe, where Felix Mottl still held the musical reins, but they came to nothing.

In April he was snapped from his malaise by the death of Alexander Ritter. Although their relationship had come to an end during the *Guntram* crisis, they had done their best to put their differences behind them after Strauss's return to Munich. They could hardly avoid one another since both moved in much the same circles and Ritter was one of Strauss's few long-term friends. Indeed, Strauss appears to have held the curmudgeonly old man in unique affection and, as he later recalled, his second term in Munich benefited from 'precious hours in the company of Friedrich Rösch and Alexander Ritter'. Strauss's debt to his one-time mentor was enormous. In philosophical and aesthetic terms it was lifelong, and although Ritter never accepted Strauss's hardline atheism and failed to understand his attraction to Nietzsche, he was loyal and incorruptible. Strauss was right to look back on their relationship with fondness and gratitude.

Had Ritter lived another seven months he would, again, have had cause to admonish Strauss for his weakness for Nietzsche. Strauss began the score of *Also Sprach Zarathustra* on February 4, 1896. The idea, and the first sketches, date back to his time in Weimar, exactly two years earlier; but Strauss did not commit himself to the tone poem until July 1895. His attraction to *Zarathustra* was predictable. Strauss saw in Nietzsche's writings an extension of his own study of Schopenhauer. According to Roger Scruton: 'Nietzsche's philosophy arose out of art and the thought of art; it involved an effort to perceive the world through aesthetic value, to find a way of life that would raise nobility, glory and tragic beauty to the place that had been occupied by moral goodness and faith.' Nietzsche's belief that higher humanity could only be achieved through the expression and furtherance of artistic endeavour was in essence Strauss's life credo. Even on a small scale, argued Nietzsche, art could provide a lens through which an idealised perception of life might be viewed, thus providing a glimpse of a perfect humanity.

Strauss also relished Nietzsche's 'perspectival' theorising. Like many a 'creative' philosopher, Nietzsche refused to contemplate a life defined by Absolutism ('there are no facts,' he wrote, 'only interpretations') and he engaged Strauss's weakness for allegory, detachment and individuality. These were, after all, the very qualities elevated by *Guntram*, an opera in which the humanistic ideal of a collective society is supplanted by the 'ultimate truth' of individual responsibility. The absence of intellectual doubt and the certainty with which Nietzsche expressed his 'perspectival' ideas appealed to Strauss's self-image, and *Zarathustra*'s hysterical anti-Christian ravings were irresistible.

Zarathustra's uneven style, curiously reminiscent of the Bible, posits a series of brief, allegorically expressed aphorisms and reflections (eighty in all) in place of the traditional reasoned narrative. Nietzsche set considerable store by the four completed parts, so much in fact that, in his autobiography, he wrote: 'With *Zarathustra* I have given humankind the greatest present that has ever been made to it so far.' The work is best known for Nietzsche's pronouncement 'God is dead', which dominates each of the four volumes. Believing that Man faced a vertiginous future, he predicted a century of wars ('the like of which have never yet been seen on earth'), the Holocaust ('among the spectacles to which the next century invites us is the decision on the fate of the European Jews') and a period of undiluted nihilism. Nietzsche died in 1900, on the eve of a century that was to prove every bit as horrifying as he had foretold.

Having prophesied the death of God, and the inevitable failure of science to yield anything akin to absolute knowledge, the philosopher convinced himself that not only was it his responsibility to overcome the essential irrationality of the world and the weakness of the 'God-hypothesis', but that he must also find a way of helping mankind come to terms with the nihilism resulting from the abandonment of religion. Strauss recognised a soulmate in Nietzsche. Here was a man brave enough to acknowledge the limitations of humankind, a man with the strength and wisdom to see humanity within the context of a Darwinian universe that placed Man within that of an earthbound Nature.

Nietzsche saw Man's 'Dawn' through the translation of 'Man back into Nature'. As part of a naturally determined cycle of survival and experience, he was drawn to stress the differences between 'higher types' and 'the herd'; and through *Zarathustra* he proclaimed the existence of the Superman as 'the meaning of the earth'. His was not the pantheism of the romantics, who resisted a break with the security of God as omnipotent creator. Rather, he understood the need for man to acknowledge his place within Nature so that he might embrace a 'higher humanity' through which existence might be genuinely redeemed. Underlying all this, Nietzsche argued, was a 'Dionysian value-standard' that placed man within the context of an eternal battle, that raged between his Dionysian and Apollonian sides.

To the disgust and despair of Alexander Ritter, *Zarathustra* became something of a bible for Strauss. He read and memorised entire sections of the work, applying Nietzsche's theories as assiduously to himself as to the world about him. By the summer of 1896, when he composed the bulk of the score, he was convinced not only of his own superiority, and the philistinism of the '*Untermensch*', but also of a new aesthetic path that was to replace the reductivism of *Guntram* and the flippancy of *Till* with a pioneering musical aesthetic that engaged his thoughts as completely as his feelings.

Strauss initially intended to give the work the ironic subtitle 'Symphonic optimism in *fin-de-siècle* form, dedicated to the twentieth century'. He dropped this for the less illustrative 'Freely after Nietzsche'. In a letter to Romain Rolland, sent in 1905, Strauss clarified the use of Nietzsche's philosophy as merely 'the starting point, providing a form for the expression and the purely musical development of emotion'.

The absence of a determinate narrative, as had characterised each of the four preceding tone poems, confirmed what appeared to be a move by Strauss away from the confines of the Programme and towards a hybrid form of Absolutism that invited a thousand members of an audience to reach a thousand different conclusions. But Strauss could not entirely subsume his fear that audiences would fail to understand, and he gave each of the eight sections unambiguous subheadings: 'Of the Backworldsmen'; 'Of the Great Longing'; 'Of Joys and Passions'; 'The Song of the Grave'; 'Of Science'; 'The Convalescent'; 'Dance Song'; and 'Song of the Night Wanderer'. It was an understandable move. Nietzsche may have been contemporary, but Strauss held out little hope for 'the mob's' capacity to understand anything more complicated than nursery stories and folk-tales. By adding signposts to each section he was circumventing the inevitable cross-examination to which he would have been subject had he provided nothing more illustrative than a title.

Zarathustra is the least programmatic of Strauss's mature orchestral works, and the closest he came to writing an Absolute orchestral score, but the pressure of having, by his own admission, to 'write philosophical music or to portray Nietzsche's great work musically' was counterproductive and contradictory. In notes written for the Berlin première, conducted by Arthur Nikisch, he claimed he had intended to 'convey in music an idea of the evolution of the human race from its origin, through the various phases of development, religious as well as scientific, up to Nietzsche's idea of the Superman'. Such concision, with the possible exception of the opening Sunrise, could not possibly be conveyed through something so arbitrary as music. The use of a fugue to represent the world of science within Zarathustra's thinking says nothing more profound than that most scientific thought is founded on logic and the application of form and formula.

The only truly programmatic aspect of Strauss's work is its tonality. His intention was to develop the Lisztian symphonic poem to its natural conclusion, whereby the work's subject was transformed into pure music. But one does not need to know that the first twenty bars of the work, resulting in one of the most impressive C major cadences in all music, signify the Dawn of Man in order to enjoy the wondrous naïvety of the defining three-note (C-G-C) C major triad. Strauss therefore distilled the opposing forces of Mankind and Nature as two separate harmonic worlds: C major for Nature and B major for Man. The extreme opposition of these keys – the scales of which include all twelve notes of the chromatic scale – and the comparably symbolic opposition of motives made up from the basic intervals of a fourth, a fifth and a triad, result in a score of astonishing wizardry, in which every consequential theme stems from the same source. It is the work's only convincing philosophical metaphor.

If Strauss's fondness for the absolutism of a programme was typical, it was by no means unique. Concurrently, Gustav Mahler was also working on an orchestral exploration of *Zarathustra*. Like Strauss, Mahler had been transfixed by Nietzsche's writings and in 1891, referring to *Zarathustra*, he told a friend that he had been 'reading something so remarkable and strange that it may very well have an *epoch-making* influence on my life'. Ultimately, the impact of the work on Mahler was much slighter than on Strauss and he later renounced both *Zarathustra* and its author.

Strictly speaking, Mahler's Third Symphony, which is three times longer than Strauss's tone poem, is the more programmatic of the two works. It makes more concessions to pictorial allusion, and Mahler's expressed desire to give shape to the whole of Nature – detailing the various 'stages of evolution' – confirms the extremely narrow compass of interpretation. By the time he came to publish the symphony – which is, unsurprisingly, the most disorganised of the nine – Mahler had conclusively rejected programme aesthetics and withdrew the allegorical movement headings.

Throughout the eight months during which their work on *Zarathustra* overlapped, neither Strauss nor Mahler wrote anything to the other about their respective studies of Nietzsche's book. This reticence betrayed a deepening mistrust. Mahler, in particular, had grown unreservedly suspicious of his 'Dear Friend'. According to Josef Foerster, a colleague in Hamburg, Mahler had become obsessed with the 'Strauss case' and, in one letter, he lamented: 'They now proclaim with mighty complacency that the days of unrecognised genius are over. For behold: hardly has he appeared than we trumpet his praises! Hurrah: from now on geniuses will be paid forthwith in cash.'

Mahler's reference to Strauss's easy talent for business was only to be expected of someone who appeared doomed never to thrive as a composer during his lifetime. The situation was compounded for Mahler when, to his amazement, Strauss not only secured the publishing rights for *Zarathustra* with Spitzweg for 3,000 marks, but also successfully arranged for the work's first performance, with the Frankfurt City Orchestra, just three months after completing the manuscript. Mahler's symphony was not played complete until 1902, and only then with Strauss's help.

On November 27, 1896, Strauss conducted the first performance of *Also Sprach Zarathustra*. The programme included three other symphonic poems, by Liszt, Gustav Brecher and Strauss (*Aus Italien*), as well as items from *Guntram* and three of Strauss's songs. After the first full rehearsal Strauss wrote with unbridled satisfaction to Pauline: '*Zarathustra* is glorious – by far the most important of all my pieces, the most perfect in form, the richest in content and the most individual in character. The beginning is glorious, all the many passages for the string quartet have come off capitally; the Passion theme is overwhelming, the Fugue spine-chilling, the Dance Song simply delightful ... Faultlessly scored ... orchestra is excellent – in short, I'm a fine fellow, and feel just a little pleased with myself ...' The première brought the house down. Three days later Nikisch gave the first Berlin performance and, before the year was out, it had entered the repertoire of another three orchestras. It was soon Strauss's most popular orchestral score.

He was finding life a great deal more rewarding away from Munich (*Zarathustra* was performed in Liège and New York before it was heard in the city of his birth) where politics were, again, producing a contrary, unworkable atmosphere. In September 1896 – two months before the première of *Zarathustra* – Levi announced his retirement for October 1, which left Possart no choice but to offer Strauss the position of Hofkapellmeister. According to Strauss's diary, however, Levi's retirement was the cause of yet another confrontation with Possart:

Taking advantage of my difficult position over my appointment for October 1, on which no definite decision has been taken yet, he expects me to annul the contract for my wife to make twenty guest appearances, which is supposed to be valid from 1 March to 30 September, by making the options which have already passed without being taken up by Possart available for him to use later as he chooses. When I wouldn't agree to that, he threatens, on the grounds of being my only friend here, which I utterly deny, not to take my part at Friday's meeting. Ugly scenes over *Guntram* etc. In short – dirty, rotten trickery.

Strauss and Munich were simply not prospering as Levi had hoped, and the restriction of his new contract to just two years reflected this uncertainty. It was in October, during a month's holiday in Italy, that he heard of Mottl's appointment to the Munich Academy Concerts. Strauss is said to have responded to the news with the words '*Auch gut*' ('Also good') but he never forgave Mottl what he considered to be an act of treachery and duplicity.

Strauss put the disappointment behind him and concentrated on enjoying his holiday with Pauline. Together, they paid two visits to the Swiss painter Arnold Böcklin in Fiesole outside Florence, on October 8 and 10, and on the 11th they marched up the Via dei Colli to the church of San Miniato where Strauss wrote in his diary: 'First idea for an orchestral piece: Don Quichotte, mad, free variations on a knightly theme.' Even before the parts of *Zarathustra* had been printed Strauss was preparing a new work for orchestra. The stress of life in Munich, and the news that he had been pipped to the Munich Academy Concerts by Mottl, seem to have forced his hand. Strauss knew that, without the eternal dissonance of a conducting post, he could not afford to keep his wife, and any family, in comfort. But the dawning realisation that he seemed naturally unsuited as a house Kapellmeister led him to make his work as a composer his life. If this was every composer's dream, then for Strauss it was soon to become a reality.

13   TILTING AT WINDMILLS

November 1896–November 1898

Since his death in 1949 it has become increasingly common for Strauss's series of tone poems to be viewed within the context of a new and shocking modernity, with references to the 'daring' of the young Strauss submitted as a prelude to the ultimate audacity of the operas *Salome* and *Elektra*. This need to locate a sweep of causality in Strauss's aesthetic progress reflects the widespread determination of well-disposed critics and commentators to enhance his significance as an innovator, and to amplify his contribution to the history of music. Indeed, the only way that *Der Rosenkavalier* can be viewed as a step away from the 'brink' of *Elektra* is if one views *Elektra*, and the works that preceded it, as steps towards an ultra-radical avant-garde. But Strauss was too much the bourgeois and too concerned with the success and prosperity of his music to move very far from the interests and appetites of his ticket-buying public.

Strauss was a product of his times. Just as Wagner had reflected the wider emergence of the bourgeois as social hero, so Strauss epitomised the bourgeois as antisocial artisan. Of course, there was nothing aberrant in Strauss's concern with securing for himself the best financial rewards for his work. At the root of the social changes that had created the German middle-class revolution was the emergence and consolidation of a capitalist economic system that thrived off the skill and determination of individuals working within, not for, a social collective.

Strauss's music spoke for, and represented, nobody but its composer. Each of his tone poems, and the detail of their expression, was scrupulously middle class and consciously addressed to the sympathies of middle-class audiences. Even *Also Sprach Zarathustra*, while contemporary in its inspiration, was founded upon the conservatism of a C major triad. His daring was neither philosophical nor, in reality, musical. Rather, recalling Max Weber's belief that Germany had produced a parvenu bourgeoisie, a parvenu aristocracy and a parvenu working class, Strauss might be seen as the parvenu composer. His extraordinary technical skill, which could have been used as a weapon of conscience, was instead applied as a means towards an entertainment. As is proven by the majority of Strauss's first-night criticism, the shock of his music was not the shock of the new, but of its audacity.

The values and fears that had motivated Beethoven and Wagner meant little to Strauss. His maturity coincided with the maturation of the German bourgeoisie, for whom art was now as much an amusement as it was an instrument of social reflection. Strauss and his tone poems were read about and enjoyed by a class of people that had not even existed during Beethoven's lifetime. The death of patronage and the simultaneous rise of market economics inspired a popular art to which Everyman could legitimately apply himself. This slowly-forming public expected to find entertainment as well as profundity in its concert halls and opera houses. Two-hour symphonic paradigms by Bruckner and Mahler were unlikely to grab the attentions of a general tax-paying audience. They wanted to be distracted, and anyone craving success was going to have to pander, at some point in his creative process, to the interests of the many.

Until 1896, *Zarathustra* was the longest of Strauss's tone poems by nearly ten minutes. The others lasted no more than twenty-five, which perfectly suited the budgetary limitations of his publishers, the logistical capacity of orchestras and the attention span of audiences. No one would suggest that Strauss wrote to order, but he must have learned from the experiences of Bruckner (who died less well known than the 32-year-old Strauss just one month before the première of *Zarathustra*) and of Mahler that distended symphonic outpourings, denied the crutch of a programme, were not going to make their composers wealthy. Indeed, if Mahler – one of the most famous conductors of the younger generation – could not arrange for performances of his own conspicuously superior music, then something was clearly amiss.

A certain amount of the resentment endured by Strauss can be traced to the simple fact that his music was immediately popular. When Wilhelm Mengelberg invited Strauss to conduct a concert of his own music with the Amsterdam Concertgebouw Orchestra in November 1898 Strauss was welcomed as if he were Wagner: 'It was the most beautiful performance of *Zarathustra* I have ever experienced,' he wrote to his father, 'it had been rehearsed in sectional rehearsals for three weeks. It was fabulous!' After Mengelberg conducted *Tod und Verklärung*, the audience gave Strauss a standing ovation. They 'rose as one', he wrote to his father, and applauded me where I sat in the middle of the hall. With the applause thundering in my ears I made a slow progress up to the conductor's desk and was called back more times than I can count . . .' In a prescient gesture of respect, Mengelberg and the directors of the Concertgebouw had Strauss's name added (in place of Gounod and next to Liszt and Wagner) to the celebrated roster of composers whose names adorned the concert hall.

Amid the revivalism of the late nineteenth century it was relatively easy for young and untested composers to reach an audience. The sort of popularity enjoyed by Brahms took him forty years to acquire, but Strauss's rise to international prominence occurred within just seven. Had he not been such a respected conductor the process might have taken him a great deal longer. The ability to champion his own music contributed greatly to the rapidity of his ascent and, in particular, his concert tours brought him and his music before a vast number of what Strauss referred to as 'the mob'. His affection for these tours is easily understood in the light of his workload in Munich. Having been denied the opportunity to conduct the Academy Concerts he was condemned to spend the majority of his time in the opera house, and as he had written only one opera, and a failed opera at that, he was unable to apply his authority to the promotion of his own work.[1]

On tour he was able to enjoy a repertoire, a freedom of expression and an acoustical experience denied him in Munich. He had spent most of his conducting life in opera pits where, with the sole exception of Bayreuth, the orchestral sound was dry and constricted. A concert hall such as the Concertgebouw in Amsterdam brought forth a spatial warmth not available to a conductor in an opera pit. Indeed, one of the miracles of Strauss's early tone poems is the virtuoso grasp of instrumental balance and colour – a sympathy which should have been greatly inhibited by so many hours spent working in opera houses.

The first of Strauss's 1896 conducting excursions came soon after his holiday in Italy with Pauline. After conducting a performance of *Meistersinger* on November 1, he set off for Berlin, where his single concert for the Berlin and Potsdam Wagner-Verein included music by Wagner, Liszt, Wolf and his own *Till Eulenspiegel*. On the 11th, 14th and 17th he conducted operas by Mozart, Liszt and Rossini in Munich and on the 20th he travelled to Leipzig where he directed a concert for the Liszt-Verein. On the 27th he took a train to Frankfurt where he gave the world première of *Also Sprach Zarathustra*. Returning to Munich, he could look back on a month in which he had travelled more than a thousand miles and conducted three concerts, four operas and the première of his longest and grandest orchestral work to date.

During the first week of December he went by train to Brussels where he was to conduct the orchestra of the Théâtre de la Monnaie. He had requested, and received, 1,000 marks for the single concert and, with the conductor Joseph Dupont's blessing, he scheduled three of his own tone poems (*Macbeth*, *Tod und Verklärung* and *Till*) and two new songs. The only music not by Strauss was from *Tannhäuser* – two arias sung by the evening's soloist Milka Terina. Dupont acclaimed Strauss a genius and stated, without qualification, that Strauss was the only true composer since Wagner.

This baptism followed him around the country. Here was a man whose music grabbed people and shook them into feeling, if not into thought. Inevitably, therefore, Strauss was the man of the hour; he was fêted by the famous and honoured by the young, for whom he epitomised the German aptitude for aesthetic renewal. Brussels and La Monnaie were home to many of the leading Wagnerites of the day – a group known as 'Le petit Bayreuth'.

The opera house was, in particular, regarded as among the few genuinely Wagnerian institutions outside Germany, and its support of living composers – particularly those concerned with the furtherance of Wagner and his *Gesamtkunstwerk*, such as Chabrier, Chausson and D'Indy – was a model to opera companies around the globe. Strauss was predictably fond of the place, and he warmed to La Monnaie's idealism, to Dupont's enthusiasm and the irresistible goodwill of the Belgians.

Strauss left Antwerp for Liège, where he conducted *Don Juan*, *Zarathustra* and Beethoven's *Eroica*; on his way back to Munich he stopped at Düsseldorf where, as part of the Niederrheinisches Musikfest, he again performed *Zarathustra*. The year ended for Strauss in Munich with a performance of *Tannhäuser* on Boxing Day; after only seven days' rest he was back at work conducting a performance of *Hänsel und Gretel* on January 3, 1897. Adolphe Adam's *Die Nürnberger Puppe* followed on the 9th, Nicolai's *Die lustigen Weiber von Windsor* on the 14th and Gluck's *Orphée et Euridice* on the 21st. Amidst all this domestic activity he was working on the manuscript of his latest tone poem *Don Quixote* as well as preparing scores for foreign engagements.

The more capable he proved himself, the more Possart expected of him. On February 10, for example, he began a gruelling week's work with a performance of Possart's new *Die Entführung aus dem Serail* at the Munich Residenztheater, followed by a performance of *Tannhäuser* on the 13th and another of *Die Entführung* on the 14th. The following morning he travelled to Heidelberg to conduct *Zarathustra*, and on the 16th he worked on preparing Ludwig Thuille's new opera *Theuerdank*[2] for its première in March. On the 17th he conducted his third *Die Entführung* of the week.

Aware that he would have to mollify Possart if he was going to improve his lot, Strauss resolved to bribe his way into his Intendant's affections. Possart had been an actor of some renown before taking over the running of the Munich Opera. He had played throughout Germany and travelled as far as New York; despite relishing life as an Intendant he preferred working on the stage to organising life behind it. Strauss appealed to Possart's vanity by writing a piano score to accompany public readings of Tennyson's *Enoch Arden*,[3] a weak poem for which Strauss provided even weaker music. On February 26, 1897, he entered the following disclaimer in his diary: 'Finished *Enoch Arden* (melodrama) for Possart. Remark expressly that I do not wish it ever to be counted among my works, as it is a worthless occasional piece (in the worst sense of the word).'

Strauss saw nothing wrong in spinning musical persiflage for Possart if it was going to improve life for him and Pauline. That he had to write such a work should have told him more than enough about the value of his position, but Possart's reaction was so enthusiastic and his pleasure so great that he and Strauss soon found themselves on friendly, almost intimate terms. After the first performance on March 24 – during which (Strauss wrote to his father) he 'unleashed with Possart whole rivers of feminine admiration' – they were 'one heart and one soul'.

For just 1,000 marks he sold the work to Robert Forberg, who published it as Strauss's Op. 38 with a dedication to Ernest von Possart. In a letter to Spitzweg (July 23, 1898) Strauss explained his reasons for taking this 'worthless occasional piece' to another publisher: 'As I knew you were ill, I wanted to spare you new offers which would make your head ache ... Forberg will pay exceptionally well ... for *Enoch Arden*, which has been ready for two years without your having asked for it ...!'

Together Strauss and Possart toured Germany with *Enoch Arden* headlining a repertoire of melodramas by Schumann/Shelley, Liszt/Strachwitz, Schillings/Schiller and Ritter/Dahn. They were well paid for their work (300 marks a performance) and this, as much as their popularity with audiences, ensured Strauss's continuing interest. But Possart, together with a variety of publishers, wanted to develop the relationship and he clamoured for a sequel. They eventually agreed on Uhland's *Das Schloss am Meere*, which they premièred in March 1899, but it was the last of Strauss's melodramas.

Considering what was demanded of him in Munich it is no surprise that Strauss yearned to live entirely from composition – particularly since the pressure on him to do so was growing in proportion to the girth of his pregnant wife. In March 1897 doctors informed him that she was going to give birth to twins. In fact, there was only one, very healthy boy. The news of his son's birth was telegrammed to Strauss while he was on tour with Possart: 'A giant boy just arrived safely. Pauline well.' In reality, the birth had been difficult and protracted, and Pauline had suffered. Immediately upon waking, however, her first words were 'Doctor, would you like a cognac?'

When it had seemed as if the child might die it was baptised Richard. This was overturned by his father, who wrote to the proud grandparents: 'I shall overrule the emergency baptism and call him *Franz* Alexander, as he was born on the anniversary of Ritter's death.' In fact young Franz was known, almost from the outset, as Bubi – a generic German nickname which everyone, friend and family, used during the boy's childhood. Cosima Wagner was delighted by news of the birth and telegrammed 'the Expression family – beg not Zarathustra as teacher, offer self as governess'. Strauss replied to 'the greatest and most inspired of teachers that the delighted parents, with their hearts full of gratitude, accept the most kind offer of governess-ship for "Franz Alexander", in all the pertinent knowledge of the nineteenth and preceding centuries'.

Exactly one month before the birth of his son, on March 12, 1897, Strauss premièred *Theuerdank* for his old friend Thuille. It was a sad chapter in their friendship since Strauss knew, long before the public, that it would fail. The première aroused moderate applause, and some patronising criticism, but after the third performance, on March 27, Strauss wrote to his father that he had 'conveyed Thuille's *Theuerdank* to the churchyard, where he will probably be interred for good tomorrow evening'. In fact, it received its final performance in April when, together with the weight of Thuille's theatrical ambition, it vanished.

Eight days after Franz's birth Strauss was back at work, again conducting *Die Entführung* in Munich. He must have felt the sting of jealousy in May when, in the face of appalling anti-Semitic protest, the baptised Gustav Mahler was appointed conductor at the Vienna State Opera, then Europe's most prestigious theatre. In October, after six months of extraordinary music-making, Mahler was promoted to Director in place of Jahn, making him the most influential conductor in the German-speaking world.

While Mahler's star continued to ascend Strauss stuck his ground in tedious Munich, churning out the same old repertoire until June 19, when he escorted Pauline and Bubi to Marquartstein for their first holiday as a family. He returned to conduct Possart's new production of *Così fan tutte* on June 25, 27 and 29 and then went back to Marquartstein, where he remained until the first week of August. Back in Munich, Strauss regressed to the routine of Mozart and Wagner, and during August and the first two weeks of September he endured a leviathan workload, conducting eighteen performances of five operas[4] – eleven of them in just fifteen days.

In late September his spirits were lifted when he received an invitation from Edouard Colonne, France's most celebrated conductor and impresario, to conduct in Paris on November 28. A few days later he was invited back to Amsterdam for concerts on October 7 and 11, to Hamburg on November 4, to Barcelona on November 11 and 14 and to Brussels on November 21 – all the while juggling his responsibilities in Munich, which included eight performances of operas by Mozart and Wagner in September alone. He and Pauline finally arrived in Paris on November 24, whereupon he made straight for the most influential figures in the city's cultural life, including Alfred Bruneau, Ernest Reyer, Charles Lamoureux, Claude Paul Taffanel, Vincent D'Indy and, of course, Colonne. He then received Charles Widor, Bruneau, François Servais and the publisher Jacques Durand at his hotel.

Strauss's first impressions of Paris were of 'a great deal of old junk and a great deal of tradition and just a little of the present', but he delighted in Colonne's 'outstanding' orchestra. Two days after the concert, he informed his father that it had been 'a colossal success, for Paris sensational. Pauline made a great impression and had to repeat *Morgen* in the middle of the sequence, in response to tempestuous demand ... we were called back three times, ditto *Tod und Verklärung* (performance wonderful).' While in Paris he saw Sarah Bernhardt at the Théâtre Renaissance and enjoyed an 'unbelievable' *Don Giovanni* at the Opéra Comique. He left Paris, buoyed by the city and its people, and headed straight for Calais, where he crossed the

Channel for a concert in London on December 7, at the Queen's Hall. As with Wagner's first experience of the British Isles, Strauss's was accompanied by a storm, which whipped up a fog and emphasised the less appealing aspects of England in the winter. He would return, on and off, for fifty years but his opinion remained unaltered: England was damp, dark and gloomy. Apart from *Tod und Verklärung* (the first London performance) and *Till Eulenspiegel*, his programme was predictable fare, fusing bleeding chunks of Wagner to a grand orchestral performance of Mozart's *Eine kleine Nacht-musik*. *The Times* noted that the concert had been 'conducted with great skill by Herr Strauss who, in spite of a not very inspiring beat,' secured an admirable performance of his immensely difficult works.'

He was back in Munich for Christmas (again conducting *Tannhäuser* on Boxing Day) and on December 29 he completed the score of *Don Quixote*. January 1898 took him back to Paris for another Colonne concert, at which he was seen for the first time by the writer and musicologist Romain Rolland:[6]

A young man, tall and thin, curly hair with a tonsure which begins at the crown of his head, a fair moustache, pale eyes and face. Less the head of a musician than that of any provincial squireen ... It was enough to see him at the end of the Beethoven Symphony [No. 7], his great body twisted askew as if struck by both hemiplegia and St Vitus's dance at the same time, his fists clenched and contorted, knock-kneed, tapping with his foot on the dais – to feel malady hidden beneath the power and the military stiffness ... Well, well! I've got an idea that Germany will not keep the equilibrium of omnipotence for long. In her brain there are dizzy promptings. Nietzsche, R. Strauss, the Kaiser Wilhelm ... there's Neroism in the air.

In January Pauline travelled to Bayreuth to sing the title role in Liszt's oratorio *St Elizabeth*, under Julius Kniese, on the 29th. Richard could not go as he was conducting a performance of Adam's *Die Nürnberger Puppe* on the 30th, but Pauline triumphed without him, earning considerable praise from Cosima. She returned with a splendid anecdote, which Richard delighted in retelling: 'Pauline ... was invited to Wahnfried several times. At one tea-time she came out with: "Oh, my Richard is just too bourgeois for words", whereat the worldly-wise Wala [sic] Cosima promptly replied: "Be glad of it, dear girl!" '

In February Richard and Pauline travelled to Spain via Paris, where they saw Emile Zola on his way to the Palais de Justice where he was being tried for 'J'accuse', his attack on governmental anti-Semitism motivated by his defence of the Jewish army officer Alfred Dreyfus.[7] Strauss noted[8] with bitter delight that there were 'a lot of policemen, but of the crowds they were there to control not a sign. The Parisians have given up interest in the trial after a week.' Arriving in Madrid he conducted three concerts on

February 27, March 6 and March 13, with a 'pretty good' orchestra in which, so he wrote to his father, the horns were 'quite bad'.

Two days after the second concert, on March 8, *Don Quixote* was given its first performance in Cologne, conducted by the ever loyal Franz Wüllner. Strauss was informed of the audience's enthusiastic reception, although one of the generally matter-of-fact critics considered the new work a 'complete negation of everything that I understand music to be'. Otherwise the reception was typified by the Leipzig *Musikalisches Wochenblatt* which reported that the work 'aroused the greatest interest in all musicians, without always gaining their sympathy at the same time'. In March 1900 Romain Rolland saw Strauss conduct *Don Quixote* in Paris and noted how, in spite of all the shouting – for and against its aesthetics – the 'placid and drowsy' composer 'seems indifferent to it all'.

Strauss didn't hear the work himself until March 18, when he conducted it at a Museum Concert in Frankfurt. To his mother he wrote: 'It's very original, utterly new in its colouring and a really jolly snook cocked at all the muttonheads who, however, didn't recognise as much and even laughed at it.' His pleasure in his achievement was justified. In wit it is more subtle than *Till Eulenspiegel*, in construction more imaginative than *Don Juan* or *Tod und Verklärung* and in substance it is, with the single exception of *Ein Heldenleben*, the most consistently beautiful of Strauss's works for orchestra. Furthermore, it is the most successful of his experiments with programme music, perfectly reconciling the need for narrative clarity with a musical detail that succeeds in defiance of the subtext. While decisively programmatic, it is necessary only to know the title to appreciate the work, its characters and its meaning.

Like its predecessors, *Quixote* was immediately popular. That much of it said nothing at all ensured its appeal to a section of the public that neither wanted nor could absorb anything more profound than the *Schlagobers* (whipped cream) parodied by Strauss in his ballet of 1923. After hearing *Also Sprach Zarathustra* Hugo Wolf remarked that 'with his crazy posing, he [Strauss] achieved only an addition to public merriment, so far as connoisseurs were concerned, that is, for the darling multitude naturally cheered him to the echo. For the latter it was a sensation of the sort the kindly Viennese will always buy . . .' Mahler was no less distracted by the popularity of Strauss's works – and the skill with which he profited from them. Writing in December 1896 to thank Max Marschalk for an article in which he had characterised the differences between him and Strauss, Mahler sneered: 'Permit me to differentiate myself completely from [Strauss] – and to differentiate what you write about me from what the shallow Corybants say about that – forgive the term – knight of industry!'[9]

Don Quixote is entertainment, and it was conceived as such. The appeal of Cervantes' novel, which Strauss first considered setting in 1896 while holidaying in Florence with Pauline, was simple. Programme music, especially as understood by Strauss, thrived off psychological characterisation, the key to which was a popular, sympathetic source. The singularity of *Macbeth, Don Juan* and *Till Eulenspiegel* necessarily restricted programmatic interpretation, and with *Zarathustra*'s posturing behind him Strauss realised that his ever-increasing mastery of the orchestra would be better employed annotating a dramatic duality – as embodied, for example, by Quixote and his manservant Sancho Panza.

With *Don Quixote* Strauss decided to take 'variation form *ad absurdam*' and shower 'tragicomic persiflage upon it'. The Introduction, theme, ten variations and Finale are for a huge orchestra, with the Don portrayed by a solo cellist and Sancho Panza by a solo viola – both to be taken from within the orchestra. The uninterrupted score, for which Strauss provided the definitive title *Don Quixote, introduzione, tema con variazioni, finale. Fantastic variations on a theme of knightly character, for large orchestra*, Op. 35 – lasts some forty minutes. Again, Strauss charged Wüllner with the honour of conducting the world première, but his confidence in his programmatic abilities had not improved since *Zarathustra*. Having identified the themes for Quixote and Sancho, which would have been more than sufficient, he felt it necessary to provide a full synopsis. He instructed Arthur Hahn to write it, and advised Wüllner to distribute it among the first-night audience.

Within twelve months the work was, like its predecessors, cropping up all over the world. In a retrospective analysis of Strauss's tone poems, published in 1906, the Munich critic Rudolf Louis stated: 'What prevented *Don Quixote* from becoming the masterpiece that is just as perfect, in its own way, as *Eulenspiegel*, was ... the striving for the greatest possible realism in the aural depiction of the poetic events caused the instrumentation of *Don Quixote* to remain mired, in more than one place, in unsuccessful experiments.' Recalling Mahler's reference to *Zarathustra* that '*what* you write has always seemed to me more important than what it is scored *for*', Louis reinforced the cliché that Strauss was competing with, rather than complementing, the visual and literate arts.

And yet *Don Quixote* is the most perfectly constructed, the most elegiac and the least flawed of all Strauss's narrative tone poems. It is the only one in which the composer's technique is consistently overshadowed by the strength of his material; and for once the content survives its depiction. The cohesive architecture, delicate thematic table, effortless characterisation and swooning melodies conspire to produce a work of music that thrives regardless of any programmatic detail. No one listening to Don Quixote's musings to Dulcinea in Variation V, or the heart-rending tenderness of the Finale, could fail to be moved by the simple beauty of Strauss's writing. Indeed, it is music of perfectly judged sentimentality, a critique not often applied to the works of Richard Strauss.

Don Quixote did little to improve Strauss's lot in Munich. Eight months earlier his loyalties to Possart had, again, been diminished by an offer from Bernhard Pollini in Hamburg to join the staff, now that Mahler had gone to Vienna. The terms were generous: 15,000 marks per annum with three months' summer leave. Strauss took the offer seriously enough to deliver an 'ultimatum' to Possart and Perfall in which he spelled out his terms. He wanted a permanent appointment as Hofkapellmeister from November 1, 1897, with an annual salary of 12,000 marks and six weeks' summer leave. Shrewdly, he did not make his wife's engagement as a company soprano part of his terms, but he made it known to Possart that he was more likely to stay if she were engaged. To her enormous credit Pauline, having been informed by Richard of all 'this eternal theatrical chicanery', demanded that he not let the question of her future influence his judgement. Keen to leave Munich, he gave Pollini's offer careful consideration, but even after Possart agreed to a pay-rise of no more than 10,800 marks a year, with just four weeks' extra holiday, Strauss's fear of a move to a new city with a young child was sufficient to keep him where he was.

The confidence and goodwill invested by Strauss in his new agreement with Possart was quickly dissipated. In March 1898, unbeknown to Strauss, Possart had initiated negotiations with Felix von Weingartner who had resolved to leave his post in Berlin to take over the Kaim Orchestra in Munich, promising that if he agreed to join the opera house as well he would be appointed to a position *above* Strauss, for which he would be paid accordingly. When Strauss heard of Weingartner's plans he realised his days in Munich were numbered. Through an intermediary he inquired whether the Artistic Director of the Royal Theatres in Berlin, Georg Henry Pierson, would be interested in taking him on as Weingartner's replacement. To his delight, Pierson hinted that he would, but asked Strauss to make the first move.

On April 7, 1898, he travelled to Berlin to give a performance of *Enoch Arden*. Two days later he had agreed terms with Pierson. His contract was to run for ten years, from November 1, 1898, with an initial salary of 18,000 marks, a guaranteed pension of 4,200 marks and a pension of 2,000 marks for his widow. Amazingly, he was then approached by Hermann Wolff, the Berlin concert agent, who asked him if he was interested in taking over the New York Metropolitan Opera House from Anton Seidl for the staggering annual salary of 42,000 marks. On April 8, Strauss wrote to Pauline: 'If they will meet the conditions here, Berlin is the more practical proposition for me at the moment, so that I can broadcast my name abroad a bit longer in Europe and not lose my place in the queue too early, which would be the risk in going to America.'

Contracts were exchanged within a week, and on April 16 news of Strauss's resignation was published in the Munich press. Intoxicated by his success, Strauss noted in his diary: 'The city of Munich calm and dignified as always on great "tragic occasions".' At the end of June he took a month's holiday in Marquartstein with Pauline and Bubi and in September he directed the conference at which the Genossenschaft deutscher Tonsetzer was founded. On October 17 he wrote to Pauline: 'Tomorrow, *Fidelio* for the last time! Then finis! Off and away – into your arms!'

Strauss's final performance as Hofkapellmeister in Munich was a moving affair. He was received with an unusual display of mass emotion by the normally reserved audience and, as a mark of respect, his head was crowned with six laurel wreaths. After numerous concerts and almost continuous work on *Ein Heldenleben*, he arrived in Berlin on November 1, 1898. The following day he was introduced to his new orchestra by the General Intendant, Count Bolko von Hochberg, and paid calls on Pierson and his new colleague, the conductor Karl Muck.

Strauss was to spend more than two decades in Berlin, from where he would initially look back on his years in Munich with a mixture of regret and disgust. With the passing of time, however, he came to regard his second spell at the opera house as a period of personal and artistic growth. Bizarrely, on his eighty-fifth birthday, he claimed that the happiest memories of his life were inextricably bound up with his native city. This was imprecise, to say the least, but Strauss never denied that the four years between October 1894 and October 1898 had been among the most productive of his life, both as a composer and a conductor. Berlin, however, provided him with a stability and an influence denied him in Munich, and it was this authority, rather than the accommodating management or the cosmopolitan audiences, that allowed him to devote so much of his time to composition. As such, the Royal Theatres appointment was the single most significant development in the life of Richard Strauss.

14   PROTECTING THE MERCHANDISE

September 1898

In his biography of Strauss, published in 1908, Ernest Newman noted that 'a number of his songs may be frankly written off as not music but merchandise'. The *Enoch Arden* episode was typical of Strauss's questionable aptitude for business, and well before the crowning successes of *Salome* and *Rosenkavalier* he had earned for himself a reputation for greed incompatible with the necessary idealism of the true artist. Then, as now, composers were expected to suffer for their art simply because the majority prior to the Romantics Mendelssohn, Bellini, Meyerbeer, Paganini and Verdi had enjoyed creative success as a consequence of, and not despite, their pain.

The truth is, of course, that composers were no more and no less mercenary than the next man. There was never a more avaricious composer than Beethoven, and it would be absurd to think that someone like Schubert would not have embraced personal wealth had it been made available to him. Strauss's presumed avarice was criticised because he got what he wanted; he was abused for being successful, not greedy, and while he was unquestionably driven by self-interest it is as well to remember his work on behalf of his peers through the foundation of the first German performing rights society.

During his second spell in Munich he had grown increasingly aware of the difficulties facing all composers, not just himself, and he had come to realise that the best means of protecting his own interests was to protect those of his colleagues at the same time. His conclusions were not as revolutionary as some commentators would like to believe. As in so much else within German bourgeois society, the French had led the way, in this case nearly fifty years earlier when, in 1851, a small group of aggrieved composers formed themselves into SACEM – the Société des Auteurs, Compositeurs et Éditeurs de Musique.

Strauss took his inspiration from Goethe. During the first quarter of the nineteenth century there were no federal copyright laws, which left German writers vulnerable and underpaid, since publishers' fees were dictated by the omnipresent fear of piracy. Because each state was governed by provincial law a book of poetry published in one state could be bought by a rival publisher from a neighbouring state and republished, gratis, just a few weeks

later. Like most of his colleagues Goethe considered this a hopeless environment in which to foster German art, and in 1825 he became the first writer
to submit a successful application to the Federal Diet for protection from
piracy. This application foreshadowed the publication, between 1827–30, of
Goethe's celebrated *Vollständige Ausgabeletzter Hand*. Goethe avowed that
every author had a right 'to some advantages and reward for his work, which
however is generally denied to the German writer'; but it was to be another
decade (and three years after Goethe's death) before the first law against
piracy was passed by the Confederation. Even then, the ruling was ineffectual
and not until 1886, when Strauss was twenty-two years old, did the Berne
Copyright Convention finally pass enforceable legislation. But the Berne
Convention was of little significance for composers.

On July 14, 1898, midway through his work on *Ein Heldenleben*, Strauss
submitted an open letter to all German composers, care of Spitzweg, in which
he drew attention to a pamphlet by Hans Sommer arguing that the Imperial
German Law (protecting composers' intellectual rights for just thirty years
after death) should be extended. This law, passed in 1870, was up for renewal
and Strauss wanted the Reichstag to hear what composers had to say before
any concrete decisions were made. At the heart of Strauss's interest, and
central to his ever-growing chain of tone poems, was his belief that concert
works – e.g., tone poems – should receive a royalty 'such as at present is
already enjoyed by the authors of dramatic works in their lifetime'. Shrewdly,
he realised that this would count for nothing if the copyright law of 1870 was
not altered to incorporate the works of already dead composers, just as it
would have to be extended beyond thirty years in order to prove of any value
to surviving relatives.

At an 1898 session of the Allgemeiner Deutscher Musikverein in Mainz
these proposals, presented by Strauss's friends Sommer, Friedrich Rösch and
Otto Nietzel, were rejected by seventeen votes to fourteen. Strauss recognised
that every composer with an interest in preserving his copyright would have
to join his name to the fight if they were to enjoy any success and, leading by
example, he instigated what was to prove a long and painful battle by refusing
to offer his own publisher, Spitzweg, the performing as well as the publishing
rights to his music.

On November 11, 1898, he wrote to his 'Dear friend': 'It is with regret that
I learn of your refusal to take *Heldenleben*, because, as I have said before, it
is absolutely impossible for me to give the performance rights of my works
to the publisher in future. This is the cardinal point in our whole movement,
and as instigator I cannot set a bad example. *Publishing rights to the publisher.*
Author's rights to the author.'

This was all very well, but Strauss was asking his publishers for increasingly
large advances. Spitzweg, or whoever Strauss offered his work to, was having
to pay up to five times the going rate for half the privilege. Strauss had asked

for, and received, 5,000 marks for *Guntram*, a three-and-a-half-hour opera, in 1894–5. Just three years later he received 10,000 marks for *Ein Heldenleben*, a forty-minute tone poem for large orchestra; and for his next tone poem, *Sinfonia Domestica*, published by Bote & Beck in 1903, he was paid the princely sum of 35,000 marks – nearly one-and-a-half times his annual salary at the Berlin Court Opera.

During the course of 1898 Strauss's attitude to his publishers grew ever more combative. The surviving correspondence between Strauss and Spitzweg contains some forthright testimony; neither was happy with the other's contingent terms, but to be fair to Strauss he could well remember a time when he had sold his works to Spitzweg for derisory one-off payments – as was common practice for much of the nineteenth century – and his recollection of this 'exploitation' strongly influenced his attitude as an adult composer with over a dozen works in continuing, worldwide circulation.

From 1897 he offered Spitzweg no more than print rights (but never performing or arranging rights), for which he demanded a healthy advance and a sizeable 25 per cent royalty on everything assigned to the Aibl imprint, up to and including *Guntram*. Of course, Spitzweg had accepted Strauss's work during his less than miraculous adolescence; as he was never slow to remind the composer, the publication of his Lieder in high-, medium- and low-voice editions, individually as well as in collections, and with singable translations – each of which needed to be separately engraved – was a costly affair. By the third quarter of 1898 Strauss's fees were forcing Spitzweg to think about selling Aibl to another publisher; and at the same time as Strauss began looking for a new imprint[1] he started to work on the foundation of a nationwide lobbying group to support him – and his contemporaries – in his war against the State-supported publishing monopoly.

Supported by Rösch and Sommer, Strauss sent out his open letter on July 23, 1898, to 160 German composers. He received 119 replies, sufficient to reassure him that he was on the right lines and enough to warrant an official conference. At the beginning of September Strauss sent out another circular, this time announcing a seminar to be held later that month at the Kaufmännisches Vereinshaus in Leipzig. The event was a great success, considering the official opposition raised against Strauss and his colleagues, and having painstakingly outlined their ambitions for the protection of composers' rights it was unanimously agreed that an official body should be founded to ensure the maintenance of a workable legislation.

This conference paved the way for the establishment, five years later, of the Genossenschaft Deutscher Tonsetzer (GDT) – the first ever German society established to protect and administer composers' performing rights, and the first to acknowledge and defend the melodic content of individual works, thus ensuring a return for composers on lucrative collections and anthologies as well as guarding against quotation and theft by rival composers. It continues to this day.

Strauss saw no shame in self-interest and, with the death of Brahms in 1897, he was among the few German composers with anything significant to protect. But his efforts were to prove double-edged, for with the Leipzig conference Strauss was now definitively categorised as a greedy, money-obsessed bourgeois. He was to spend the rest of his life defending an entirely reasonable aversion to poverty, and even when his work rose high above such secondary considerations, as with the first production of *Elektra* in London, critics and commentators consistently settled on Strauss's royalties, his conducting fees and his general wealth as subjects of greater interest to the reading public than the genius of his work or the skill with which he performed it.

Of course, Strauss was, and would always prove himself, tactless in matters relating to money. There are many more anecdotes concerning irrefutable avarice than there are confirming selfless generosity, and everyone from Mahler to the conductor Fritz Busch verified his apparently defining obsession with the financial prosperity of his work. But such instincts were exceptional only in their fruition. Born to relative prosperity, Strauss knew little of the sort of struggle endured by Gustav Mahler, for example,[2] and it is odd, to say the least, that someone born with silver-plate in his mouth should have devoted so much time and energy to the prosperity and security of his own interests.

Consequently, his 'efforts on behalf of other composers' – as his work towards the GDT is now so often represented – must be viewed with caution. He may have enjoyed a childhood in which frugality in the midst of wealth was a way of life, but his youth was distinguished by the realisation that money brought status and respect – benefits which he and his father valued more highly than money itself. Whatever his instincts and regardless of his motivation, the foundation of the GDT was a milestone in the history of German music, and of enormous significance for German composers. Like his beloved *Don Quixote*, Strauss's intentions did little to hinder the good they achieved.

15   FROM HERO TO SCHALK

November 1898–November 1901

With *Don Quixote* galloping around Europe, few were surprised when Strauss's next work, *Ein Heldenleben* (A Hero's Life), became an instant success. Strauss's passion for appropriately psychological material had developed so rapidly that, immediately after resolving to compose an orchestral homage to Quixote, he began toying with ideas for a new project. Alongside his work on Cervantes' novel, he began a tone poem provisionally titled *Held und Weld* (Hero and World), for which he, his wife, his critics and his achievements would provide the inspiration. Almost from the outset, the two works were seen by Strauss as companion pieces; to the director of the Frankfurt Museum Concerts, Gustav Kogel, he wrote: '*Don Quixote* and *Heldenleben* are conceived so much as immediate pendants that, in particular, Don Q. is only fully and entirely comprehensible at the side of *Heldenleben*. Since this is also the very first (decisive) performance of *Heldenleben*, I feel it is very important. Of course it would then be an extremely progressive programme ... But for the very first performance of *Heldenleben* I think I may be allowed a little licence.'[1]

The rumour that Strauss had written another tone poem for which his own life had provided the stimulation was greeted with a mixture of bewilderment and delight. Such a combination of nerve and talent was unprecedented.[2] Neither Beethoven nor Wagner, whose opinions of themselves inclined towards hyperbole, indulged in any outright musical autobiography. Indeed, it was the irony of the gesture that distinguished *Heldenleben* as probably the boldest work of self-deprecation in the history of music, for Strauss was, in every respect, the least heroic figure imaginable. While he thought himself intriguing as a man as well as an artist,[3] his portrayal of himself as a hero was no more sober than was his characterisation of 'The Hero's Adversaries' as baying and spiteful nemeses, and, consequently, any criticism of the work's perceived arrogance is misdirected.

This irony was compounded by the presence of autobiography in all but one of the preceding tone poems. Strauss had never looked far from home for inspiration and, not surprisingly, his final two tone poems – *Sinfonia Domestica* and *Ein Alpensinfonie* – were also stimulated by diurnal experience.

The only shocking aspect of *Heldenleben* was its effrontery, and so it was the author's shameless self-indulgence, rather than his musical language, which provoked the most heated criticism.

Writing in 1906, Rudolf Louis[4] – who applauded Strauss whenever 'his splendid, lovable human personality expresses itself purely in his music, where he presents himself actually as he is'[5] – attacked the composer for presuming 'to elevate his own person' and, like Rolland, he lamented the apparent brutality of Strauss's Teutonism. When not brawling with his 'Adversaries' Strauss's yearning for 'emotional depth' was diminished by 'a shallow, even trivial sentimentality' which made *Heldenleben* a 'repellent' experience.

Despite Louis's reservations Strauss revealed little about the tone poem's inspiration and gestation; his only recorded explanations are weighed down by sarcasm. Writing from Marquartstein on July 19, 1898, for example, he wrote to Spitzweg: 'Beethoven's *Eroica* is so little beloved by our conductors, and is on this account now only rarely performed, that to fulfil a pressing need I am composing a largish tone poem entitled *Heldenleben*, admittedly without a funeral march, but yet in E flat, with lots of horns, which are always a yardstick of heroism.'

Strauss's sarcasm was partly aroused by his vexation at the recidivistic tastes of German audiences. If he was to compete with Beethoven, he would have to write his own *Eroica*, and Strauss was probably playing with the notion, current in the 1890s, that Beethoven had composed his Third Symphony in praise of himself, not of Napoleon Bonaparte. There is much within the *Eroica*, as there is in *Heldenleben*, that can be related directly to their authors, and many years later Strauss admitted that a comparison between the two works 'would produce some interesting studies of experience'.[6] There is no reason to believe, as he later claimed, that *Heldenleben* was the 'general and free ideal of great and manly heroism' since he was, at the time of composition, hostile to anything so inclined towards abstraction. References to Carlylian or Wagnerian theories on the nature of heroism lead nowhere since Strauss's movement headings (compiled with the help of Rösch and Wilhelm Klatte), and the general bombast and exaggeration of the score, are more sardonic than serious: I. The Hero; II. The Hero's Adversaries; III. The Hero's Companion; IV. The Hero's Deeds of War; V. The Hero's Deeds of Peace; VI. The Hero's Retirement from the World and the Fulfilment of His Life.

In spite of the translucence of these headings *Heldenleben* was the nearest Strauss had come to writing abstract orchestral music since his *Festmarsch* nearly a decade earlier. Although he had always maintained that abstract and programme music were really one and the same – that all music was in essence programmatic – each of the preceding tone poems, without exception, relied upon a narrative in which individual characters thought and behaved in a recognisable fashion. *Heldenleben* invited no such narrative. Rather, the autobiographical character, established through the movement headings, is vague to the point of conjecture. The listener may well understand the third movement, and the solo violin, as a portrayal of Pauline, but how many will recognise the detail and incident within that portrayal? Strauss happily confessed to having characterised his wife in the piece and although, according to Rolland, some thought her 'a depraved woman, others a flirt' she was neither. 'It's my wife I wanted to portray,' Strauss told him. 'She is very complex, very much a woman ... never twice alike, every minute different from what she was the minute before...'

Although the work is openly satirical – of itself, heroism and its composer – the line dividing the real from the imagined is so thin that no one other than the composer himself can have known or decoded its true nature. Like its contemporary, Elgar's *Enigma Variations*, *Heldenleben* is as much a mystery as it is a reflection of the pomp and circumstance of Edwardian/Wilhelminian society, and because it leaves so much to individual perception it continues to transfix audiences over a century after its first performance. Years later Strauss bemoaned the 'search by the musical theorists for "personal experiences" and "confessions" ', and yet he was the first to admit that all music, not only programme music, was born of individual experience. A few weeks before his death, prompted by his anguish at the dehumanising face of the more extreme elements within modern music, he despairingly acknowledged the 'confessional' aspects within his music: 'Why don't people see what is new in my works, how in them, as is found otherwise only in Beethoven, the human being visibly plays a part in the work – it begins already in the third act of *Guntram* (renunciation of collectivism), *Heldenleben, Don Quixote, Domestica*...'

The buffoonery of *Eulenspiegel* and the didacticism of *Zarathustra* were here rejected in favour of a freedom and a wistfulness unimagined by Strauss's disciples. *Heldenleben* left many expecting ever greater symphonic adventures, which would take Strauss away from the absolute and towards the ethereal. For all its inflation and sentimentality *Heldenleben* is an almost perfect fusion of genius and talent. It was the summit of Strauss's experiments with the tone poem, embracing a universe of ideas on which he would not be able to build until he began work on *Salome* four years later. The squealing of the critics (The Hero's Adversaries) and the thunder of the battle scene (The Hero's Deeds of War) stirred some to objection (chiefly the critics), but few disputed the beauty and invention of the two final movements, in which, during the Hero's works of peace, Strauss quoted some thirty times from his own catalogue, including passages from *Guntram*, the songs *Befreit* and *Traum durch die Dämmerung*, and all but one of his tone poems (*Aus Italien*).[7]

The glory of these last two movements is the ease with which Strauss fuses so much disparate material into a symphonic passage that thrives independently of the material's origin. Unlike the Fugue of *Domestica*, which is pure muscle-flexing, these passages touch an emotional depth anticipated only by the closing pages of *Don Quixote*, and conductors have to work very hard not to allow the sentiment to get the better of them.

It is worth noting that the gigantic chordal ending which incorporates the infamous rising fifth to a fourth of *Also Sprach Zarathustra* was not Strauss's original conclusion. The first edition of the score contains an ending reminiscent of the conclusions of most of his earlier tone poems in which, after the love duet between the horn (Strauss) and the violin (Pauline), the concertmaster leads a gentle, yielding orchestra towards a whispered, almost embarrassed resolution.

Reputedly over breakfast with Strauss, Friedrich Rösch lamented yet another quiet conclusion to one of his works and demanded, on behalf of audiences everywhere, that he replace it with something more in keeping with the music's general complexion. Strauss is said to have asked for pen and paper and, amidst tea and toast, he scribbled out a new ending, which was published, and is now played at all performances. To be fair to Rösch, the original lacks architecture and is far too subdued for a work of such grand proportions, and yet the new ending – a little like Beethoven's replacement for his *Grosse Fuge*, Op. 133 – is a parody of what was requested;[8] something between the two would have been ideal.

Not without reason, *Ein Heldenleben* is still upheld as one of the peaks of the symphonic repertoire, as much a benchmark for a conductor's skills as it is a showpiece for an orchestra's virtuosity. Strauss well understood that most European orchestras would struggle to cope with the violent counterpoint of the battle, that the horn parts were the most punishing he had ever written, that the violin solo demanded a virtuoso for a concert-master and that the sheer number of players required to perform the work – over sixty strings, eight horns, five trumpets, two tubas, quadruple wind, offstage band and full percussion including a wind machine – would exclude all but the very wealthiest cities.

With this in mind, Strauss dedicated the work not to one of his friends, or to a member of his family, but to the conductor Wilhelm Mengelberg *and* the Concertgebouw Orchestra of Amsterdam.[9] Mengelberg was delighted, not least because the dedication admitted him to a small and significant band of dedicatees that included Bülow, Levi and Wüllner. Significantly, however, Mengelberg was not entrusted with the première. Having completed the short score on July 30, 1898 (a date of extra-musical significance since, as Strauss noted in his diary, 'the great Bismarck has been dismissed!'[10]), Strauss worked on the orchestration throughout the summer, finishing the full score on December 1, by which time he was Hofkapellmeister in Berlin. As he was on good terms with the director of the Frankfurt Museum Concerts, Gustav Kogel, and as he had enjoyed working with the orchestra during preparations for the first performance of *Zarathustra*, it seemed only right that Strauss should conduct the first performance of *Heldenleben* in Frankfurt, which he did on March 3, 1899.

The critical response was understandably varied. Many misread the meaning (taking the movement headings literally), most misunderstood the structure (failing to appreciate the classical foundations), and almost everyone deplored the 'noise' of the battle (the more outraged sections of the first-night audience contributed whistles and hisses to the cacophony). But an equal number roared their approval. Romain Rolland, who attended what he thought was the first performance,[11] saw 'people shudder ... suddenly rise to their feet, and make violent and unconscious gestures'. They were not alone, for he had himself 'experienced this strange intoxication, the dizziness of this heaving ocean' and he thought then that 'for the first time for thirty years, the Germans had found their poet of victory'.[12]

After the Berlin première Strauss wrote to his father: 'Of the reviews so far, the *Lokalanzeiger* (Klatte[13]) and the *Vossische Zeitung* (Urban) are very good; the rest spew gall and venom, principally because they have read the analysis (by Rösch) as meaning that the hideously portrayed "fault-finders and adversaries" are supposed to be themselves, and the Hero me, which is only partly true.'

Mahler heard *Heldenleben* for the first time in January 1901, conducted by Strauss in Vienna.[14] He enjoyed Strauss's company at an after-concert dinner, where he found him 'modest, likable, not particularly profound, but hard-working and decent'; he privately considered *Heldenleben* unworthy of its composer, oscillating, so he believed, 'between the abstruse and the banal'.[14] In particular, he must have choked on Strauss's depiction of the Hero's struggles with the world. As possibly the most fortunate, least criticised composer of his generation, Strauss's artificiality must have seemed the height of bourgeois angst. To someone like Mahler – born 'crippled' by his race, forced to fight tooth and nail for everything he had achieved, and compelled to endure the sort of hatred and persecution of which Strauss knew nothing – the posturing of *Heldenleben* must have been difficult to swallow.

Heldenleben did much to smooth Strauss's path to the cosmopolitan heart of Berlin. Wisely, he performed it with the city's Philharmonic, at the Widows' and Orphans' Fund concert (three weeks after the Frankfurt première) where the Berliners were as taken by his noble appearance as by his talent. Aged thirty-five, he represented a considerable change for audiences used to the aristocratic Weingartner and the forbidding Muck whose appearance was almost as offensive as his personality. Broad-shouldered, well over six foot tall and crowned by a thick mop of hair, Strauss's refinement perfectly offset the fiery manner that possessed him on the podium – even if, as Rolland noted, all was not as it seemed:

'A face without a wrinkle, unblemished and clear, like that of a child. A big shiny forehead, pale eyes, a fine nose, frizzy hair; the lower part of the face is slightly twisted; the mouth often makes an ugly pout, from irony or from displeasure . . . his hands attract one's attention, delicate, long, well-kept, and with something rather sickly and aristocratic about them, which doesn't correspond to the rest of the individual, who is plebeian on the whole, and rough and ready.' At the end of February 1900 Strauss invited himself to Rolland's house for lunch, during which the Frenchman was able to add to his portrayal of the composer as proletarian:

'He behaves very badly at table, sits by his plate with his knees crossed, lifts his plate near his chin in order to eat, stuffs himself with sweets like a baby, etc. . . . His conversation shows me how right I was to see in him the typical artist of the New German empire, the powerful reflection of that heroic pride, which is on the verge of becoming delirious, of that contemptuous Nietzscheism, of that egotistical and practical idealism, which makes a cult of power and disdains weakness.' Rolland, a Germanophile and determined pacifist, was equally horrified, if less surprised, by Strauss's politics. The composer confessed to Rolland that he cared nothing for the Transvaal war, how at the beginning he had taken sides, but that he rather favoured the English since 'they are very agreeable when one is travelling . . . when I was in Egypt I was very glad that the English were there, instead of the Egyptians; one is always sure of finding clean rooms, every comfort . . .'

Strauss pronounced the Boers 'a barbarian people, backward, who are still in the seventeenth century'. The English, on the other hand, were 'very civilised and very strong. It is an excellent thing that the strongest should prevail.' When Rolland demanded to know how Strauss felt about Boer and Egyptian suffering he replied, somewhat prophetically, 'Oh! I don't know anything about it; I don't think about it; Egypt doesn't exist when I am not there.'

Strauss now relocated to the German capital, an arrogant city littered with imperial aphorisms such as 'A German owns the world'. It was a city in which *fin-de-siècle* expansionism had brought about a capitalist revolution to foreshadow William James's mockery of Nietzschean psychology whereby 'a man's Self is the sum-total of what he can call his, not only his body and his psychic powers, but his clothes and his house, his wife and his children, his ancestors and friends, his reputation and works, his lands . . . and bank-account.' Berlin was a Domestic Symphony waiting to be written, and Strauss loved it.

'I'm happy and very highly satisfied,' he wrote to his father a few weeks after settling in. 'I like Berlin with its splendid transport facilities, my apartment in its wonderful position, every domestic convenience, the servant problem solved satisfactorily . . .' Strauss was a whirlwind of energy and motivation at the Court Opera. Having fathomed something of the need to reconcile self-interest to the general good, he enjoyed considerably greater popularity in Berlin than had been his fortune in Weimar and Munich. Doubtless due to the success of his music, he was less prone to impatience and intolerance, and he seemed to acquire there a sense of proportion and an internal equanimity that precluded the need to humiliate or bully.

He was particularly fortunate in having Dr Karl Muck as an assistant, since even the cruellest despot would have appeared mellow beside this most feared of Bayreuth's scions. Muck had been chief Kapellmeister at the Court Opera since 1892, and by the time Strauss arrived during the winter of 1898 the orchestra, chorus and staff had been crushed beneath the unrelieved austerity and discipline that were Muck and Weingartner's trademarks. Strauss's manner improved in direct proportion to his growing exposure to Muck, and within a matter of weeks he was menacing recalcitrant players with the threat: 'I'll send for the Doctor!'

Strauss rarely inclined towards friendship, and in spite of their shared devotion to Wagner (Muck was a major force at the Bayreuth Festival from 1892 until 1930) they enjoyed no more than a distant working relationship. For his part, Muck was suspicious of Strauss long before his arrival in Berlin. As a non-composing conductor his priorities were the preservation of Wagner's art, the furtherance of all things conservative and the maintenance of an orchestral precision that was considered obsessional even then. In principle, Strauss's high standards should have made him an ideal colleague, but Muck was mistrustful of modernism and he went out of his way to frustrate any attempts to further the work of living composers. Between 1850 and 1918 – a period that includes Strauss's twenty-year term – only three works were premièred at the Berlin Court Opera.

This is not to say that Muck's fear of the contemporary, or his reactionary disposition, were unique. The German capital may have enjoyed a cosmopolitan reputation, and in instinct it was the most open-minded of German cities, but the archaic influence of Wilhelm II and the passionate conservatism of its Artistic Director, George Henry Pierson, were sufficient to prevent Strauss, and his sympathetic Intendant, Count Bolko von Hochberg, from furthering the Court Opera's reputation as something other than a museum.

Strauss was now working for the Emperor and, less directly, the Emperor's wife. Wilhelm made few exotic requests, and so Strauss was, again, forced to endure the proclivities of those for whom he had neither time nor respect. His first six engagements were Bizet's *Carmen*, Humperdinck's *Hänsel und Gretel*, Lehár's *The Merry Widow*, Beethoven's *Fidelio*, Wagner's *Rienzi* and Auber's *La Muette de Portici*. Strauss enjoyed respect in the opera house (which, he wrote to his father, was 'a real blessing after Munich'), but this didn't lighten the burdens of patronage; and he endured an archaic environment, in which modernity was anathema, with unusual forbearance.

A few months after the colossal success of *Salome*, for example, Strauss was summoned by Wilhelm, who demanded, in all seriousness, to know why his chief Kapellmeister did not compose marches – the Emperor's favourite musical form. Not wishing to offend, Strauss circumvented the truth by telling Wilhelm that he was unschooled in the genre. The following day Strauss was again summoned by the Kaiser, this time to the palace courtyard, where stood two military bands. Strauss was directed to a chair, from where he was obliged to endure three deafening hours of imperial marches. Thanking Wilhelm for his consideration, Strauss staggered to his desk where he dutifully sketched out two decidedly graceful marches – published as Op. 57 and 'Most humbly dedicated to His most gracious Majesty Kaiser Wilhelm II, in deepest homage' – for which he was awarded the Crown Order Third Class.

If the composition of marches (or an Olympic Hymn,[15] for that matter) seemed likely to smooth his and his music's path to popularity, it was worth the effort; but this gesture to Wilhelm's taste bought Strauss no more than a temporary reprieve from court prudery. The first and most lasting conflict was born of Strauss's second opera, *Feuersnot* (Fire Famine[16]). In his memoirs he claimed that after the failure of *Guntram* he 'had lost the courage to write for the stage', which is only partly true since the years separating his first two operas saw Strauss work on at least half a dozen fledgeling operatic projects. It is easy to see from the pattern of his work between *Guntram*, Op. 25, and *Feuersnot*, Op. 50, a composer preparing for a return to the theatre. His opus numbers 27 to 49 – which reflect roughly a decade of work – contain four of his five most important symphonic poems and nearly seventy songs. Strauss relished the applied theory that his early fidelity to the tone poem and the Lied had, in some conscious way, served as an apprenticeship for the cumulative splendour of his operas, chiefly *Salome* and *Elektra*; but this seems unlikely in the light of his almost consistent toying with operatic subjects.

Of these, the most plausible was his proposed setting of the legend of Till Eulenspiegel, which he later adapted (to a libretto by Count Ferdinand von Spork) as the archly satirical *The Forsaken Women of Schilda*. He also toyed with a setting of Cervantes' caustic social parody *Persiles y Sigismunda*, another Wagnerian drama *Das erhabene Lied von Könige*, and a Singspiel after Goethe's *Lila*, to a libretto by Cosima Wagner. With *Schilda* Strauss worked on his last libretto for over twenty years. As he willingly admitted, he needed 'help with the words'.

He finally settled on *Feuersnot* after meeting Ernst von Wolzogen in Berlin. Wolzogen was an emotive, unpredictable satirist in the mould of Hauptmann, a dedicated critic of Wilhelminian stupidity and complacency and, like Strauss, one of Munich's most passionate antagonists. Among Wolzogen's greatest fears was the march of Germany's State-sponsored conservatism, reflected in every sphere of modern life and embodied by the Kaiser. In his 1892 play *Das Lumperngesindel*, for example, he railed against a university system in which all but a small number of fraternities had become 'beer-swilling, duel-fighting, song-bawling' mediocrities.

Wolzogen delighted in hurling stones at the middle classes. Bravely, he attempted to translate the French satirical cabaret to Munich, a city in which few enjoyed seeing themselves so aggressively parodied and which he, like Strauss, was compelled to leave. Taking his ideas to Berlin, he eventually stumbled upon the right mixture of criticism and burlesque with the hugely popular and influential *Überbrettl*,[17] but his first three years in Berlin reinforced his deepest fears, since only a handful of Berlin's twenty-five theatres was willing to risk the scandal of novelty or satire.

Strauss asked Wolzogen if he had any ideas for an opera libretto. Wolzogen drew Strauss's attention to a Flemish folk-tale with which he had been toying, suggesting it as the basis for a contemporary satire on Munich and the Munichers. Strauss would later claim that he had developed the idea as revenge against the city for its cruel rejection of Wagner and Bülow, rather than for its treatment of himself and Wolzogen, but in his memoirs he admitted that the legend had given him 'the idea of writing, with personal motives, a little intermezzo against the theatre. To wreak some vengeance on my dear native town where I, little Richard the third . . . had just like the great Richard the first thirty years before, had such unpleasant experiences.'

The Flemish folk-tale was published in a German book of *Sagas of the Netherlands* in 1843, and told how a naïve young man was humiliated by a local girl with whom he was in love. She invited him to her room at night, but only if he ascended in the basket outside her house. Halfway up the basket stopped, where it remained, with the boy inside, all night. The following morning, jeered by the crowds, he fled the town utterly humiliated. Wandering in a forest he met a sympathetic wizard who offered to help the boy exact revenge on the wicked girl. The wizard dimmed every fire in the town, announcing to the horrified townsfolk that his curse could be lifted only if they produced the girl responsible for the boy's humiliation, stripped her of her clothes and forced her to her hands and knees on a table in the middle of the market square. The people did as they were told. As they forced the girl to her knees a huge flame shot from her rear end. One by one, each of the townsfolk had to use this source to light their candles. It took many hours, and the girl endured much laughter before the spell was lifted.

In March 1900 Wolzogen attended a performance in Munich of *Also Sprach Zarathustra*. The heckling of the disapproving philistines inspired him to begin work on a libretto for Strauss, to whom he wrote: 'It [the performance of *Zarathustra*] has given me a powerful incentive to get on at once with our opera. I now have the following idea: *Feuersnot* in one act – setting old Munich in a legendary Renaissance period. The young romantic hero is himself a magician; the great old magician, his teacher, whom the worthy citizens of Munich once threw out, does not appear. At the end, in order to free the town from its dearth of fire, the town council and citizens beg the heartless girl to offer her maidenhead to the young magician, which she does. When love is combined with the magic of genius, then even the worst philistine must see the light...!'

Influenced by the proto-Expressionist Frank Wedekind (with whom Strauss briefly considered an operatic partnership), Wolzogen's synopsis was only slightly less shocking than the original fable. If young ladies blowing fire from between their buttocks seems sensational at the end of our century, young ladies sacrificing their virginity against their wills was a great deal more inflammatory for Wilhelminian Germany's middle majority. Wolzogen clearly enjoyed writing the libretto (which took him no more than 'a few days') and the 'fresh enthusiasm of a delightful love affair' permeates throughout.

Neither Strauss nor Wolzogen disguised the presence of yet another appearance by Strauss in one of his own works. Just as the opera's setting was modelled on Munich, so the handsome, mysterious Kunrad the Alchemist was shamelessly modelled on Strauss who, in turn, portrayed himself as the embodiment of the new art. Elements of the fiery Pauline were injected into the character of the maiden, Diemut, the townspeople were based upon the antiquated Munichers while Kunrad's 'Master Reichart, the Ancient of Laim' (who never actually appears) was clearly modelled on Richard I. Wolzogen ensured that the diction was 'satirical, rather archaic in style with local dialect', which conveys a measure of Strauss's resentment since his own speech was characterised by the distinctive Doric of his native Munich and, under normal circumstances, he was hurt by the slightest mockery of his accent.

Within the context of nineteenth-century theatre it was rare for *auteurs* to air their preoccupations so publicly, but Strauss did not have to look far for a precedent. In *Der Meistersinger* Wagner allowed pioneering licence to his personal, aesthetic and philosophical prejudices, and he created diametric icons in Beckmesser (a caricature of the bucolic pedant Eduard Hanslick) and Stolzing (whom he modelled on himself) that shocked many.

But the true significance of *Meistersinger* was its universality, its appeal to all Germans, and its timelessness for lovers of musical theatre, regardless of their age or nationality. *Feuersnot*, on the other hand, was irreconcilably dated within a few years of its première. Wolzogen's libretto suffers from a surplus of references to a now obsolete culture. Moreover, *Feuersnot*'s themes – typified by the concluding verse – were banal, self-conscious and devoid of the political conviction for which the *Überbrettl* was celebrated: 'All warmth springs from woman / All light proceeds from love / From hot, young womanly love / Alone comes the re-kindling fire.'

While Wolzogen claimed allegorical profundity, the truth was less precious. Strauss privately recognised this, urging the conductor of the première, Ernst von Schuch, to 'give due emphasis to the burlesque, impudent, brazen, parodistic element'. Elsewhere, he admitted that *Feuersnot* was 'pure Lortzing'!

In addition to the many allusions to *Meistersinger* (such as the 'Solstitial Fire' scene and Kunrad's magisterial Address), there is an entire conference of references to the *Ring* (including the appearance of the 'Valhalla' motif whenever Master Reichart is mentioned)' and a love duet which owes more than just its inspiration to *Tristan und Isolde*. Furthermore, a discernible contradiction in Strauss's musical identity manifests itself for the first time in *Feuersnot*. At various points in the score Strauss develops ideas of exquisite refinement only to mutate to an Offenbachian vulgarity, better suited to a Bavarian beer-hall, as if he were bored by the beauty of his invention. This impatience with his art, and the shame that seems to have accompanied his purest thoughts, isolates a detachment and dubiety that was as central to the man as to his music.

This is not to dismiss *Feuersnot*, which is consistently 'gay and audacious'.[18] The potent use of folk-song, the lively children's choruses and the aching love duet are, indeed, hard to resist, and *Feuersnot* undoubtedly represents a move away from the Parsifalian textures of *Guntram*. Even so, the shameless Wagnerism, knowing humour, aesthetic innuendo, hermetic symbolism and poorly disguised agenda demarcate Strauss's second opera, like Wagner's *Rienzi*, as something of a curiosity – of greater interest for its place within the history of its composer's development than for any intrinsic value.

Strauss completed the score in 1901 'on the birthday of and to the greater glory of the "Almighty".' Strauss dated his score May 22 – the birth date of Richard Wagner.[19] Four months earlier he had travelled to Vienna, as part of a tour with the Kaim Orchestra, where he conducted a concert of his own works on January 23. Mahler was in the audience to hear a selection of Lieder, sung by Pauline, *Till Eulenspiegel* and *Ein Heldenleben*, but it was for Strauss's new opera that Mahler revealed the greatest enthusiasm. After Strauss played excerpts at the piano Mahler announced his delight at the new-found sense of proportion and, there and then, offered to stage the première at the Vienna Hofoper.

Three days later Mahler sent a copy of his Third Symphony to Strauss who replied that he would not be able to study 'what seems, again, to be a very interesting work' because he had to cover for Muck, who had fallen ill. In March or April,[20] Mahler wrote: 'I am very sorry that you cannot have the première of your work in Vienna ...' It seems that, fearful of closing doors, Strauss had accepted Mahler's impulsive offer to stage *Feuersnot* before the question of its première had arisen. But when Mahler later refused to confirm a date Strauss grew restless and began to look elsewhere. Resigning himself to the conservatism of the Berlin Court, he offered the work to the sympathetic, admirably contemporary Ernst von Schuch and the Dresden Court Opera, who gratefully accepted what was now an honour for any Kapellmeister.

With characteristic audacity, Strauss then set Schuch and Mahler against one another, promising the première to whoever first secured a date.

Not surprisingly, Mahler was alarmed by Strauss's gambit – particularly since he thought highly of Schuch, who had given the Dresden première of his First Symphony in December 1898.[21] Mahler could commit the Hofoper to a production 'mid-November', but he could provide nothing more concrete, and so he politely withdrew from the fray: 'If I like a work, I accept it and perform it when I can. – But with your opera it is different ... I must decline to become involved in a "race" with another theatre ...'.

Mahler agreed to mount the opera immediately after the première, but begged Strauss 'not to be exorbitant in the usual way'. Strauss chose not to inform Schuch of Mahler's withdrawal, since they had yet to agree terms; but when the Intendant offered less than the 1,500 marks demanded by Fürstner (which was not, after all, particularly unreasonable), Strauss threatened to give the première to Vienna. Strauss admonished Schuch as if he were responsible, and many letters passed between them. Amusingly, Strauss vowed to change his name to Riccardo Straussino and have his works published by Sonzogno (the house of *Pagliacci* and *Cavalleria rusticana*) since contemporary Italian composers were, apparently, more popular in Germany than contemporary German composers. Eventually, after further difficulties concerning the work's morality and a small number of cuts to Wolzogen's libretto, Strauss secured his fee and the first performance in Dresden went ahead on November 21, 1901, with Karl Scheidemantel as Kunrad and Annie Krull as Diemut.

The première was a tremendous success. 'Schuch is a marvel,' Strauss wrote to his father, 'Schuch has let me see my work as it really is ...'. Bathing in his triumph, he erroneously believed that *Feuersnot* faced a glorious, international future. The prompt interest of the Frankfurt Opera did little to discourage his faith. Mahler fought a long and difficult battle with the Austrian censor for a production at the Court Opera. As he wrote to Strauss in August 1901: 'I am going to Vienna on the 26th, and will find out something about the fate of our *Feuersnot*. – So far I only know that our highly moral Intendant,[22] who manages to be on equally good terms with the Graces, the nine muses and with our holy patron saints, wishes to inhibit the performance ...'. The première was scheduled for January 1902.

Strauss persuaded Mahler to arrange the première for January 29, since he was already booked to give two concerts on the 30th and 31st, with Possart and Pauline respectively. He arrived in Vienna four days earlier, in order to keep an eye on Mahler's progress, and on the day before the première he wrote to his father: 'Yesterday, Monday, dress rehearsal of *Feuersnot* under Mahler's direction, which unfortunately, because of his terrible nervousness, did not go as well as I expected after Saturday's rehearsal, in which particularly the magnificent Vienna orchestra had delighted me in the highest degree ...

Mahler is very nice, the whole staff are making every possible effort. Theatre sold out.'

This was certainly the case prior to the first night. Siegfried Wagner, no friend of Strauss's, attended the final rehearsal and, according to Strauss, poured praise upon the new work, possibly because it came a lot closer in spirit to his own mediocre operas than it did to his father's music dramas. The quality of the performance, and in particular the portrayals of Kunrad and Diemut by Leopold Demuth and Margarethe Michalek, should have guaranteed full houses; as it was, Strauss failed to account for the ferocity of the Viennese critics who, launching 'salvo after salvo from right to left, conservatives and radicals . . . unanimously rejected the work'.[23] Max Kalbeck thought it 'indecent in the extreme' and denounced the knowing plagiarisms as 'the height of bad taste'. He was not alone in acknowledging the skill of Strauss's orchestration while at the same time dismissing the actual score as a wash of 'clever orchestral babble and uproar'.

Having recently endured the ritual destruction, by the same critics, of his Fourth Symphony, Mahler fully sympathised with Strauss's anguish: 'I am so disgusted by the attitude of the Viennese press, and most of all by the public's total acquiescence to them . . . At the première I still had some hopes. – This, alas, dear friend, is all I can tell you for now of the fate of your child (and my child of sorrow . . .).' It must have been especially difficult for Mahler to inform Strauss of the receipts for the first three of the four scheduled nights: I: 3,100 fl.; II: 1,600 fl.; III: 1,300 fl.

The fourth night, which fell on 'Shrove Monday' (traditionally one of the best days of the theatrical year), was cancelled at the last minute for want of an audience. Strauss's reply to Mahler has been lost, but Mahler's response suggests that Strauss must have accused him of having had some personal influence over the disaster. Mahler protested: 'To continue to perform an opera when the whole audience stays away does not depend on my *goodwill* . . .' Strauss took the Viennese failure harder than that which followed in Berlin – where, because of censorship difficulties, the production, scheduled for March, had been postponed at the last minute. The censor finally passed Wolzogen's libretto in August, and Strauss conducted the city première, with Emmy Destinn as Diemut, on October 28, 1902.

Neither the Kaiser nor the Kaiserin attended, but Strauss's enemies denounced the opera's supposed obscenity to Augusta, who saw to its removal after only seven performances. The resulting scandal surprised even Strauss, who had been delighted by the audience's enthusiastic reception; out of sympathy Count Bolko von Hochberg resigned as Intendant.[24] Strauss never forgave the world for its treatment of his second opera, and he would pester conductors to stage revivals until well into his dotage. Even in his memoirs of 1942 he defended the work's quality and blamed its rejection on the difficulty of the music.[25]

Feuersnot was largely ignored outside Germany until *Salome* and *Elektra* generated sufficient curiosity. Thereafter, it was heard in London (in English, conducted by Thomas Beecham) in 1910, in Brussels (in French, conducted by Sylvain Dupuis) in 1911, and in Milan (in Italian, conducted by Tullio Serafin) in 1912. The *Feuersnot* episode produced one defining anecdote, recorded by Mahler's new wife Alma. Even if her attention to detail is questionable[26] the thrust of her reminiscence can be trusted. There is ample corroboration.

Alma had been invited to join Strauss and his wife in their box for the Viennese première of *Feuersnot*. Pauline was on excellent form: 'Nobody, she said, could possibly like that shoddy work. We were simply lying if we pretended to, we knew as well as she did that there wasn't an original note in it, all stolen from Wagner and many others, yes, even from Schillings (Maxi, as she called him) whom she liked a great deal better than her husband. In short, she raved. We could only put on our silliest faces, taking good care not to speak, let alone agree with her, because she would be quite capable of turning round and exclaiming with equal vehemence against what she had just said herself.'

After the performance they adjourned to Hartmann's restaurant, where they were joined by the conductor Franz Schalk. There was a delay as Strauss enjoyed his curtain calls, but when he arrived he immediately turned to his wife and inquired:

' "Well, Pauksl, what do you say to that for a success?" But he had come to the wrong address. She sprang at him like a wildcat:

"You thief, how dare you show yourself in my presence? I'm not coming with you – you make me sick." '

Mahler's patience snapped and he pushed them into an office. Shouting and screaming rang from within. Eventually, after threatening to spend the night at the hotel on her own, Pauline agreed to walk to dinner, but only if her husband remained 'ten paces behind'. At the restaurant Strauss turned to Alma and remarked, 'My wife's a bit rough sometimes, but that's what I need, you know.' But there was a greater shock to come:

Strauss himself even in my eyes came out in his true colours that night. Throughout supper his mind ran on nothing but money. He tormented Mahler without ceasing with calculations of the exact royalty on successes great or middling, with a pencil in his hand the whole time which he now and then put behind his ear, half by way of a joke, and behaved in fact just like a commercial traveller. Franz Schalk, the conductor, whispered to me, 'And the sad part of it is that he is not putting it on. It's deadly serious.' He had become an unashamed materialist, weighing his own advantage at every turn, a gambler on the stock exchange and an exploiter of the Opera.

Alma was strongly influenced by her husband, and a certain amount of jealousy can be detected. Nor can everything be taken at face value. Fortunately, we know something of Strauss's thoughts. In 1946, having read a copy of Alma's memoirs, he dismissed her recollections of himself and Pauline as the 'inferiority complexes of a loose woman'; and in the margin beside her account of the Vienna première he wrote 'Alles Schwindel!' It would be foolish to ignore Strauss's comments but as far as the dinner at Hartmann's is concerned, confirmation is provided by Mahler himself who, in probably his most celebrated letter to Alma, defined his aesthetic and spiritual credo inverse as diametrically opposed to that personified by Strauss:[27]

The atmosphere Strauss creates is so disillusioning that one literally becomes a stranger to oneself. If these are the fruits of the tree, how can one love the tree? You were right on target with the remarks about him. And I am proud of you for having so spontaneously found the right words. Surely it's preferable to eat the bread of poverty and walk in the light rather than lose oneself in everything mean and base! The time will come when people will see the wheat separated from the chaff – and my time will come when his is past ... What could I possibly contribute to this coffee-house talk, at a moment so sublime as that of a performance which, after all, releases my creative energy too and ought to free one from everyday cares, instead of dragging one down into the mire in a conversation about royalties and capital (the everlasting dreams of Strauss's imagination, which are almost inseparable from his enthusiasm).

16 LULLABY BEFORE THE STORM

November 1901–June 1905

The vicissitudes of *Feuersnot* had little immediate effect on Strauss's daily routine. Indeed, with Muck's illness, he had never been busier. A typical day would begin with an hour's composition, an hour's administration (including the writing of at least ten letters in longhand) and a three-hour rehearsal at the Opera between 11 a.m. and 2 p.m. After lunch he would rehearse the Tonkünstler Orchestra between 3 and 6 p.m. followed by a full performance at the opera in the evening. There was also family life which, as Pauline was quick to remind him, required daily attention.

This schedule was constantly under threat from publishers, fellow composers, in-house auditions and, later, freelance editing work for the magazine *Monat*, the book series *Die Musik* and a new edition of Berlioz's monograph on orchestration. Moreover, in June 1901 Strauss travelled to Heidelberg for the thirty-seventh festival of the Allgemeiner Deutscher Musikverein (ADM) and 'a jolly fight'. Writing to his parents, he announced his intention 'to unseat Herr von Hase' and the old governing committee[1] from the General Assembly. For someone who had only recently claimed:[2] 'I am not a hero; I haven't got the necessary strength; I am not cut out for battle; I prefer to withdraw, to be quiet, to have peace ...' such outright pugnacity would seem uncharacteristic. Once again, however, Strauss's ambition prevailed and, successfully deposing all but one of the old guard, he was elected First President of the Musikverein.

Strauss was now governing the most influential musical body in Germany. He used his influence to good effect. Wary of post-Wagnerian aesthetics his predecessors had viewed modernity with suspicion, fostering an archaic identity that worked against young and aspirant composers. Strauss considered it his duty to propagate a living tradition, and even if he did not actually select the works to be played under the ADM's aegis, his influence was all-embracing. According to Strauss's first biographer, Max Steinitzer, he 'stressed in the most unmistakable way our common duty, *sine ra et studio*, to let anyone have his say who had any right to do so – however much our personal feelings might incline us otherwise. We should be on our guard against all cliquish preferences and invite not even a suspicion of one-sidedness.'

Among those to receive direct support from Strauss and the ADM was a young Austrian composer, Arnold Schoenberg, who had arrived in Berlin, from Vienna, in December 1901. With almost no conducting experience, a poor command of the piano and a self-possession that defied his years, he was hardly assured of work in a city flooded with talent; but Wolzogen took him on as a conductor / arranger at the *Überbrettl* in Berlin's Bunte Theater, an experience that led to his freelancing as an orchestrator of other composers' operettas. In his spare time he concentrated on his own music, chiefly the colossal *Gurrelieder*, and it was this score that brought him to Strauss's attention. As the Expressionist virtuoso *par excellence*, Strauss was intrigued by Schoenberg's ambition – so much so that he arranged for him to receive that year's ADM Liszt Foundation scholarship.

Simultaneously, Strauss recommended Schoenberg as a teacher to the Stern Conservatoire, who obediently engaged him as a professor of composition. Schoenberg was then greatly in awe of Strauss, who provided him with the idea for the only major work he completed during his twenty months in the capital.[3] He was to come to regret Strauss's kindnesses, and after falling beneath the spell of Mahler, he was also to forget them. Years later, after his conversion to dodecaphonics, Schoenberg was to revile Strauss, mocking him as the last vestige of a dying culture. Strauss, in turn, ridiculed Schoenberg's break with tonality, but he tried not to allow their aesthetic differences to influence his judgement as benefactor.

Only once did Strauss formally turn down a request from Schoenberg. In 1909 he received a copy of Schoenberg's Five Orchestral Pieces, Op. 16 (an early atonal work), with a note from the composer expressing his hope that Strauss would show 'the kindness that you have so often bestowed on me . . . The usual run of conductors has no idea what to do with them. It has to be the best or nothing . . . I hope they will make sufficient impression on you to persuade you to perform them. It would be the utmost help to me . . .'

Strauss replied: 'You know that I like to help, and I have the necessary courage. But your pieces are such daring experiments in both content and sound that for the time being I cannot take the risk of presenting them to my ultra-conservative public.' As Schoenberg well knew, Berlin was much less conservative than Vienna (where he was at 'daggers drawn with practically everybody') and he read Strauss's rejection as a personal snub – even though Strauss later donated 100 marks of his own money to a fund established to support him, twice recommended the ADM to administer payments and three times (in 1913, 1914 and 1918) lent his support to Mahler Foundation endowments.

After Strauss gave his consent to the first of these grants, in 1913, he qualified his support in a letter to Alma Mahler: 'The only person who can help poor Schoenberg now is a psychiatrist . . . I think he'd do better to shovel snow instead of scribbling on music-paper . . .' Alma related Strauss's comments to Schoenberg who, the following year, remembered them when he was asked to write something for Strauss's fiftieth birthday: 'I have no intention of damaging Herr Strauss[4] "morally" ... He is no longer of the slightest artistic interest to me, and whatever I may once have learned from him, I am thankful to say I misunderstood ... Since I have understood Mahler (and I cannot grasp how anyone can do otherwise) I have inwardly rejected Strauss.'

Strauss's difficulties with Schoenberg typified his feelings for the Second Viennese School, but this conservatism was by no means representative of the general feelings for contemporary music, at least during the first decade of the twentieth century. Even Strauss was inspired to work against type, and in 1905 he inaugurated his own new music series in 1901,[5] with an augmented Tonkünstler Orchestra. Largely ignoring the classical / early romantic repertoire favoured by Nikisch and Weingartner, Strauss promoted dozens of works by living composers,[6] some of whom, such as Hans Pfitzner, he detested.

The extra work caused his friends and family concern. Franz, in particular, implored his son to take things easier: 'We're very unhappy to see the way you assault your health ... in order to earn enough money to be able to live from your savings later, so as to do nothing but compose. Do you imagine that anyone can create anything of the spirit when the body is enfeebled?'[7]

After returning from Switzerland at the end of December 1901, Strauss was thrown into the usual round of opera-house business, but not so much as to interfere with his composing. In March 1902 he began working on a setting of *Taillefer*, a poem by Uhland about the Battle of Hastings, for 'chorus, soloists and orchestra'. The inflated verse (reminiscent of Tennyson) and the simple narrative[8] appealed to Strauss's sentimentality, and he scored his grandiose setting for over 170 players.[9] It is an indulgent work, and deserves its obscurity.

In April 1902, Strauss conducted *Feuersnot* in Bremen, and in May he was invited by Julius Buths to conduct at the Lower Rhine Festival in Düsseldorf. For once he did not perform his own music; instead he conducted a large choral work by a little-known English contemporary called Edward Elgar. This concert, on May 20, comprised only two works: Liszt's *Faust* Symphony and Elgar's *Dream of Gerontius*.[10] Elgar and his wife Alice attended the rehearsals, during which Strauss devoted most of his attention to Liszt's tone poem, irritating Elgar who rightly considered the imbalance unfair. Elgar was none the less satisfied with Strauss's performance, and he positively glowed with pride when, during a banquet held in his name, Strauss gave the following toast: 'I raise my glass to the welfare and success of the first English progressivist, Meister Edward Elgar, and of the young progressivist school of English composers.' Strauss and Buths then presented Elgar with a copy of Beethoven's death mask. Ironically, when reported by *The Times*, Strauss's noble sentiments caused their recipient more harm, and gossip, than good. As Elgar wrote to his publisher, Jaeger: 'I always said British musicians were several kinds of fool and ignoramus – but this is worse than usual from them.'

From Düsseldorf Strauss travelled to London for 'A Grand Musical and Lyric Festival'. On June 2, at the Queen's Hall, he conducted the first English performance of Schumann's *Manfred* (together with a performance of that 'worthless occasional piece' *Enoch Arden*), with Ernst von Possart. Two days later Possart 'dramatised' poems by Heinrich Heine while Strauss conducted the Queen's Hall Orchestra in *Don Juan, Tod und Verklärung* and *Till Eulenspiegel*. For their final concert Possart read poetry by Goethe and Schiller while Strauss conducted popular 'musical selections'.

On June 6, 1902, Strauss returned to Krefeld in Germany for the annual festival of the Allgemeiner Deutscher Musikverein.[11] Earlier in the year Strauss had discreetly suggested to the committee, and the conductor of the Krefeld Concert Society, Theodore Müller-Reuter, that they engage Mahler to conduct the première of his Third Symphony.[12] Under normal circumstances the Krefeld Städtische Kapelle numbered only thirty, but the celebrated Gürzenich Orchestra[13] was engaged to join forces, bringing the total number of players close to the stipulated complement of one hundred.

The atmosphere in the concert hall was reminiscent of a first night at Bayreuth, with celebrated musical luminaries crammed alongside inquiring locals. Strauss was joined in the audience by Schillings, Humperdinck, D'Albert and Thuille – each of whom was in Krefeld to play or hear something of their own. Also present was the small band of Mahler disciples, such as Mengelberg, who followed the composer's progress with religious fidelity.

In his 'badly tailored coat', Mahler appeared to one critic as a 'defrocked priest', but when he began to conduct he revealed the 'superhuman calm of a snake charmer facing his cobras'. The first movement was heard in silence, but as the final mighty chord faded Strauss flamboyantly marched from the back of the hall to the foot of the podium from where he shouted his approval. This fuelled the audience's confidence, and with each succeeding movement the mood grew increasingly favourable. As Mahler lowered his baton on the sixth and final movement ('Perhaps the greatest Adagio since Beethoven,' wrote William Ritter) the audience burst into a riot of applause.

According to the *Krefelder Zeitung* the ovation lasted over a quarter of an hour, during which Mahler was called back to the stage no less than twelve times. It was, as he later recalled, the greatest day of his life. For some bizarre reason Strauss, having shown such enthusiasm for the first movement, had not stayed to congratulate the composer after the sixth and when they met for dinner later that evening Strauss did no more than politely shake Mahler's hand. During dinner Strauss made no mention of the concert or of Mahler's success. Wounded by this omission, Mahler then sulked throughout the meal.

One possible explanation for Strauss's snub is that, until the Krefeld concert, he had been one of the few to recognise Mahler's worth. Like most others, he expected the audience to greet the new symphony as coolly as they had its predecessors. When, for example, Strauss had conducted the Fourth Symphony in Berlin it was glumly received by the audience and savaged by the critics, so there was little reason for Strauss to expect anything different in Krefeld – particularly since Mahler's was the penultimate concert of a festival devoted to contemporary music. Strauss's march to the podium was probably designed to reinforce his allegiance to modernity as well as to Mahler; but by the end of the performance, with the audience united in its admiration, Strauss's support must have seemed peripheral and ostentatious, his virtue no longer as singular as he would have liked.

If Mahler had always considered himself morally superior, then Strauss had always relished his greater success, but now Mahler was winning over previously hostile composers and critics, and the same orchestras that readily scheduled Strauss's music began to fight to perform Mahler's. Whatever the reason for Strauss's behaviour, it caused his friend much anguish. As Alma recalled: 'The whole outward success now seemed worthless to him.'

Strauss was the first to break the silence that followed this bizarre episode. Sent on July 21, from Marquartstein, where he and his family were on holiday, Strauss's letter suggests a guilty conscience: 'Dear Friend, As you need a horn player – my father, whom I am just visiting, recommends one: Max Müller, first horn at the Spas Orchestra at Bad Reichenhall. I have written to Herr Müller, saying he should apply direct to you. Perhaps you could have the young man come to Vienna and blow for you! How are you otherwise? Contented and industrious? How long does *Das klagende Lied* last? Is it very difficult for the chorus? I should like to do it this winter in Berlin! How is your dear wife?' He signed himself 'Your dear friend, Richard Strauss'. Mahler appears not to have replied, and he did not return to the correspondence until early February 1903 – some six months later.

In May Strauss began another tone poem, the first since 1898. With so much else to attend to, progress had been slow and not until September was he able to pull the new work into shape. He was careful not to reveal the subject of his latest work since this too was flagrantly autobiographical; but where the confessional within *Heldenleben* had been buried beneath a third-party narrative, his *Symphonia Domestica* positively revelled in its indiscretion.

On the cover of the symphony's sketchbook,[14] dated May 2, 1902, Strauss outlined his 'Idea for a domestic scherzo with a double-fugue on three subjects' which he identified as himself (F major), Pauline (B major) and Bubi (D major). His stated narrative embraced a domestic sequence recognisable to everyone; but beneath this surface lies an abundance of revelation of which few (possibly, even, Strauss himself) were aware at the time. The most unusual disclosures emerge during the third of the four 'movements', an Adagio portraying life for Richard and Pauline after Bubi has gone to bed.

Beginning with Strauss alone at his desk, enjoying the solitude of creativity, the movement ends with husband and wife making love. Strauss does not deny the '*scène d'amour*', and he gives explicit detail to their orgasm by fusing together the relative motifs, both in their original keys (F major and B major). Audible too is the author's pallid detachment. Separated by a tritone, F major and B major cannot be resolved, and so their lovemaking ends brutally, without the slightest suggestion that they have consummated anything deeper than selfish desire or duty. This implicit allusion to Strauss's distaste for physical contact is reinforced by the immediacy with which an entirely new and disparate episode takes over.

In addition to the real and imagined clarity within this symphonic confessional, the composer can be seen coming to the end of a cycle of personal and aesthetic discovery that finally led him to a recognition of the limits of the purely orchestral tone poem. Throughout *Domestica* he grapples with the irreconcilable properties of literal pictorialism and psychological characterisation. On the one hand, he goes to extreme lengths to portray himself as 'affable', 'morose' and 'fiery', and Pauline as 'emotional' and 'angry' while, at the same time, doing his best to recreate the complexion and vitality of domestic life, from chiming clocks to goodnight kisses.

Such details seem doubly pointless in the light of Strauss's bewildering virtuosity. Indeed, that one of the greatest technicians in the history of composition squandered his gifts on such banal subjects seems almost too painful. No amount of skill can compensate for the elemental vulgarity of *Domestica*'s theme, and the means are absurdly disproportionate to the ends.

Strauss claimed a higher purpose: 'What can be more serious than married life? Marriage is the most serious happening in life, and the holy joy over such a union is intensified through the arrival of a child. Yet life has naturally got its funny side, and this I have also introduced into the work in order to enliven it. But I want the symphony to be taken seriously ...' The score monopolised his attention well into 1903, creating an internal clash of interests with the Berlin Court Opera and his work as a guest conductor. Between January and March he toured Europe, chiefly France, Holland and Switzerland, and in April he was back in Berlin for concerts with the Tonkünstler Orchestra. In June he took the unfinished work to London, where he was to attend the first British festival devoted entirely to his music. Strauss and Mengelberg shared the conducting, and each of his major works was heard, all played 'magnificently' by the Concertgebouw Orchestra.

The strain on Strauss's health was beginning to tell, and immediately after the final concert he collapsed. It was agreed that he should take a recuperative holiday on the Isle of Wight. The weather was consistently glorious and Strauss described to his parents scenes of appropriately domestic bliss, with 'Bubi running about all day in the hot sand and going in and out of the sea'. Strauss told no one of his latest, unfinished symphonic poem and, defying his doctors, he managed to complete the short score before returning to Berlin at the end of July. While on the island Strauss was informed that he had been awarded an honorary doctorate, in philosophy, by the University of Heidelberg. Since he had never completed a degree course, and had come to resent this absence of academic endorsement, thereafter he wore his degree like a chest of medals[15] and signed himself 'Dr Richard Strauss'.[16] As a double-edged gesture of gratitude for his degree,[17] Strauss dedicated *Taillefer* to Heidelberg University's Faculty of Philosophy shortly before he conducted the first performance at the town festival, on October 21, 1903.

From Heidelberg he went again to Britain for more concerts in London, Birmingham and Edinburgh, and then to Warsaw for a performance of *Heldenleben*. He arrived back in Berlin (and a new apartment on Joach-imstaaler Strasse) for Christmas and performances of *Samson et Dalila, Die Meistersinger* and *Fidelio* at the Court Opera. He also managed to complete the orchestration of *Domestica*, on December 31, in time to prepare the parts for his 1904 tour of the United States.

Although this was to be his first trip to the New World, it was not for want of invitations. Not only had the concert agent Hermann Wolff offered him the music directorship of the New York Metropolitan Opera six years earlier, but Theodore Thomas, Strauss's first American champion, had yearly advocated a grand 'introductory' tour. Strauss wisely postponed a visit until he was ready, as composer and conductor, to stand before the largest, fastest-growing audience in the world. With *Domestica* under his belt he was able to submit a repertoire of eight tone poems, two operas and a festival-worth of songs, which was more than sufficient, even for a tour of thirty-five concerts.

Richard and Pauline left Berlin on February 1, 1904 – leaving Bubi in the care of family. The eleven-day crossing, on the *Moltke*, caused Strauss a mixture of boredom, irritation and curiosity. But he relished the luxury, and delighted in the variety of onboard attractions, such as massages, electric camel- and horse-rides and the Marconi telegraph, which 'works without wires, with electric waves out of the air'. After arriving in New York Strauss's letters home vividly reflected his excitement and curiosity, and true to form, the cost of hotel rooms, travel, flowers, food, concerts, indeed almost everything for which they had to pay, was recorded for his own and Franz's bourgeois fascination.

In many respects he was the ideal tourist. America was the hearthstone of capitalism, fostering a people for whom culture and the arts were a reflection of prosperity and a measure of civilisation. Nothing was taken for granted in a country that, prior to the 1850s, had enjoyed almost no serious music, and Strauss found himself surrounded by people who, not knowing what they liked, were still more than willing to pay for it. America was a proud and booming country; unlike contemporary Germany, however, she had good reason for her pride. When Theodore Thomas first arrived in New York in

1845, for example, he found pigs roaming the streets. Stepping off the *Moltke* on February 23 Strauss was confronted by a city vibrating with energy and glistening with aspiration.

Like the majority of first-time European visitors, Strauss's jaw dropped at the amplitude of American life. The cars, the trains, the buildings, the bridges, the people, the extremes of wealth, the ambition and the enthusiasm were on a scale unimagined, even by someone as well travelled as Strauss. As he wrote to his father: 'The entire country makes a quite magnificent impression, but a bit wild. Hotels, railway stations, the railways, commerce and industry are on a grandiose scale, all practical installations dazzling, the twenty-storey giant buildings sometimes make a beautiful and magnificent effect, even in my eyes, because of their felicitous proportions.' Strauss had finally found a home for his musical skyscrapers, an audience for whom bigger was frequently better, a country in which heroes were the stuff of everyday life. He was a giant in Brobdingnag.

He was met at the harbour by a crowd of journalists, photographers, admirers (some of whom presented Pauline with flowers), and the tour's promoter, Hermann Hans Wetzler. He made his debut in Carnegie Hall on February 27, 1904, conducting the Wetzler Symphony Orchestra in *Ein Heldenleben*. Wetzler himself conducted *Zarathustra*. At his second concert, five days later, Strauss presided over a performance of *Don Quixote* with a young, little-known Spanish cellist, Pablo Casals, playing the solo part.

Thereafter, his schedule allowed for little freedom. When not travelling, rehearsing or conducting, or attending interviews, photo sessions and conferences, he was forced to endure the well-meaning, if insistent, attentions of sponsors and society hostesses.[18] Besides his concerts for Wetzler, he accompanied numerous recitals by Pauline, and made guest appearances with the New York Philharmonic and the Chicago and Philadelphia Symphony orchestras.

He was also engaged to conduct in Boston, where the orchestra's competitive music director Wilhelm Gericke blocked the engagement. After news of Strauss's triumphant performance in Philadelphia reached its founder and patron, Henry Lee Higginson, Gericke was ordered to extend another invitation. The concert almost floundered again when Higginson was told of Strauss's fee, but after gentle negotiations it went ahead – to enormous satisfaction on both sides of the podium. Strauss thought the Boston orchestra 'Wonderful, both in sound and technique, of a perfection such as I have almost never experienced'.

The main event of the tour, for Strauss at least, was the first performance of his *Symphonia Domestica*, which dominated his penultimate concert at Carnegie Hall. There were no fewer than fifteen three-hour rehearsals. To his father, Strauss reported a 'colossally enthusiastic success; perhaps eight recalls; two laurel wreaths'. But New York's critics sat firmly on the fence, neither eulogising nor condemning. One headline proclaimed 'Home Sweet Home as written by Richard Strauss – Papa and Momma and baby Celebrated in Huge Conglomeration of Orchestral Music.'

It was another matter entirely when he accepted an offer of $1,000 to conduct two matinee performances of *Domestica* in Wanamaker's department store. The concerts were given in the store's first-floor auditorium, well away from the ugly realities of commercial life. Responding to accusations of avarice, Strauss remarked, 'True art ennobles any building and to earn money for one's wife and child is no disgrace to an artist.' His German critics were less easily convinced. Few defended his actions, even fewer the *Domestica*, and for the first time in his mature creative life Strauss endured a comprehensive critical assault on a new work.

Since the days of *Aus Italien* he had enjoyed startling his audiences; but *Domestica* merely repelled and disappointed. Many thought it marked a downturn in Strauss's fortunes, chiefly Ernest Newman who wrote in his biography of the composer: 'After *Ein Heldenleben* it looked as if some subtle poison had entered into Strauss's art, and one began to have fears for his future. The *Symphonia Domestica* did not dispel these fears ... At present his greatest admirers cannot help admitting mournfully that for some years now he has shown a regrettable lack of artistic balance.'

After Hans Richter conducted the English première on February 8, 1908, Newman amplified these sentiments in a letter to his friend, Herbert Thompson: 'Great works are harmoniously balanced throughout. I am afraid there is something wrong with the man who now can only get us to say that the beautiful parts of his symphony outweigh the ugly parts and the stupid parts, and the ineffective parts of the music, and the miscalculated parts. Isn't that really damning it with faint praise, isn't there something wrong when you can only commend him for doing something or other and apologise for his having done something else?'

After the première in New York Strauss celebrated his achievement in a letter to his father: '*Domestica* is splendid, brilliant, too, although it lasts about forty-one minutes, yet it holds the public in breathless suspense. The double fugue comes off magnificently, the virtuoso coda with its colossal build-up is most grateful to play, the Adagio sounds wonderful; in short, I am content.' Perhaps; but the bourgeois obsession with himself (wry and sardonic though it may have been) had run out of both steam and admirers. Moreover, his sympathy for the programmatic had outlived its age, clashing with the new century's growing inclination for psychological involution, emotional asceticism and aesthetic restraint. With *Domestica*, another chapter in Strauss's life came to an end. But at a time when many were seriously proclaiming him a has-been, he confounded his critics, hypnotised his supporters and astonished audiences with a new work that stands as the greatest comeback in the history of music.

June–December 1905

That Strauss was one of the fathers of modern music and the leading voice of Germany's avant-garde is one of the least credible myths concerning his early life. The avant-garde was never likely to embrace a composer so openly seduced by himself. Hanslick's accusations of 'hedonism' were atypical of the general attitude; the younger generation of commentators, for whom Wagner was the beginning and not the end of musical culture, were rather less bewildered. By 1902 Strauss's operatic ambitions were proving as much of a cul-de-sac as his tone poetry and he found himself at odds with an avant-garde for whom the confines of Pictorialism, the vanity of self-glorification and the generic weakness of the Programme were the deadest of ends. As such, *Domestica* confirmed Strauss's status as Germany's leading reactionary.

With the Berlin Hofoper monopolising his time there were few opportunities for meditation, but at some point during 1902 he was approached by the Viennese poet Anton Lindner with an idea for an opera after Oscar Wilde's *Salomé*. Lindner offered to prepare Hedwig Lachmann's German translation for Strauss and as a taster sent the composer 'a few cleverly versified opening scenes'. According to Strauss, he was incapable of work on the score until the music for the opening line '*Wie Schön ist die Prinzessin Salomé heute Nacht*' came to mind. Thereafter he claimed, 'It was not difficult to purge the piece of purple passages to such an extent that it became quite a good libretto.'

Some weeks later he attended a performance of *Salomé* at Max Reinhardt's 'Kleines Theater' with Gertrud Eysoldt in the title role. In his memoirs Strauss recalled how, after the performance, he met a friend, the cellist Heinrich Grünfeld, who announced, 'My dear Strauss, surely you could make an opera of this!' He replied, 'I am already busy composing it.' Reinhardt's production of *Salomé* was the second in Germany, and only the third since the play's completion in 1891. In Berlin it ran for some two hundred performances, in a repertoire of works that reflected the contemporary vogue for sexual deviance and moral decadence in art.[1] This growing obsession with the forbidden was no less prominent in the visual arts, with Franz von Stuck, Ferdinand Khnopff, Edvard Munch and Gustav

Klimt producing huge, lurid canvases with explicit titles. Strauss was at liberty to settle on any number of subjects for his third opera. It is significant that he chose Oscar Wilde's *Salomé*.

Those who view Strauss's attraction to *Salomé* as the height of daring fail to account for the popularity of Wilde and his play in turn-of-the-century Germany. If his choice of source is judged in the light of contemporary British attitudes, then the setting to music of a play about an abused, necrophilic teenager would appear consciously provocative. But *Salomé* was not the unmentionable obscenity in Germany that it was in Britain. Strauss's attraction to Wilde's heady symbolic perfume was determined as much by business as by aesthetic considerations. If the man who composed *Tristan* did so 'with a mind of ice', then the same may be said of the man who chose to set *Salomé*. Strauss rarely acted on impulse.

After the failure of *Feuersnot* in 1903, and during the composition of *Domestica*, he had begun to hanker after avant-garde approval. *Salomé* was the ideal means to this end. When Strauss first considered turning Wilde's play into an opera the fashion for decadence was of defining centrality in German art. It has been suggested that Strauss's commercial sixth sense enabled him to see in *Salomé* a populist – and consequently financial – potential unrecognised by his peers, but this is unlikely when considering the daring of the finished score. It is more probable that Strauss enjoyed the primitive rush of infamy. The mature Strauss had always enjoyed his notoriety. During his youth he had relished upsetting the conservative apple-cart, but he was not, and was never considered to be, an experimental composer. Until deciding to write his third opera Strauss's choices had strayed increasingly towards the middle ground of populism, a cultural atoll generally thought incompatible with sincere artistic adventure.

Wilde's play furnished an aesthetic legitimisation that was denied Strauss by his own conspicuously Wagnerian tastes; and he would have to break with high Romanticism if he was ever to connect with the avant-garde. His given reason for adopting *Salomé* was unequivocal: 'I had long been criticising the fact that operas based on oriental and Jewish subjects lacked true oriental colour and scorching sun.' His repudiation of biblical operas, such as Verdi's *Nabucco*, Saint-Saëns's *Samson et Dalila* and Massenet's *Hérodiade* was legitimate; but the 'orientalism' craved by Strauss, and his desire to do justice to a Jewish subject, carried within it a deeper, much darker, reflection of his cultural perceptions.

Oscar Wilde wrote *Salomé* in French, for Sarah Bernhardt,[2] at the end of 1891. It was premièred in Paris in 1896, but within the contemporary context of a thriving Symbolist movement the reception was indifferent. Not until its first performance in Germany[3] was the play fully appreciated. During the 1903–4 season Wilde's plays enjoyed 248 performances in Germany, 111 of them of *Salomé*; between 1900 and 1934 there were more than 250 publications of his writings in translation.[4] After his conviction on charges of homo-sexuality in 1895 Wilde's German popularity grew sharply. Every detail of the trial was reported by the liberal newspaper *Der Zeit*, and a series of outspoken articles – defending Wilde, his work and his behaviour – rallied support from within the German literary avant-garde at a time when he was despised in his own country.

Indeed, by reason of his persecution, Wilde polarised German society into those who saw his 'perversion' as endemic of an exclusively British decay, and those for whom homophobia was yet another characteristic of German middle-class hypocrisy. Strauss had no time for homosexuality, but he was aware of the social and aesthetic undercurrents that made Wilde and his Symbolist play an ideal conduit for avant-garde approval. For Strauss, orien-talism, as a specific manifestation of Eastern European Jewishness rather than some generalised allusion to Middle Eastern culture, embraced all avant-garde aesthetics since, in Germany at least, the avant-garde was principally directed by Jews. Strauss was no less aware that many within the avant-garde, such as Reinhardt, were homosexual as well as Jewish, and that for most educated turn-of-the-century Germans homosexuality and Jewishness were considered analogous within any specific reading of the Semitic 'disease'. Wilde, a homosexual, and *Salomé*, a 'Jewish subject', presented model cre-dentials for an anti-Semitic composer eager to advance his art.

The promotion of Wilde as a tortured innocent encouraged artists to indulge their individuality as never before. The poet Hofmannsthal, in par-ticular, empathised with Wilde's uniqueness, as much as his suffering, and his celebrated epitaph, that Wilde's life and art were inseparable, was embraced at a time when court austerity was suppressing more than it was conceding. The sympathetic image of the persecuted artist was furthered through the writings of Karl Kraus, mainly those published in the periodical *Die Fackel*.

Probably the most influential of these appeared in December 1903, around the time that Strauss first began to take a serious interest in the *Salomé* theme. 'The uncomplicated German can only gaze upward jealously at the British nation,' Kraus wrote, 'so far above the Continent in the culture of sexual perversion and the development of sexual hypocrisy, which, as well as murder, can bring forth the genius of Oscar Wilde, and which has flagellation-bordellos and laws that can threaten the nuances of sexual activity with a ten-year jail sentence.' In this powerful article Kraus tethers the anti-homosexual attitudes of the British to the anti-Semitic attitudes of the Germans, mirroring the duality reflected in *Salomé* itself. Kraus, like most, but by no means all Jewish-German critics considered Wilde's representation of the Jews disgraceful. Friedrich Schütz dismissed the play, and its author, for reducing his race to 'a quintet of tottering Jews represented with ugly gestures that fulfil the deepest sense of subjugation'.

This hateful portrayal of stereotypes divided the Jewish critical community into those for whom all anti-Semitism was repulsive, and those, like Kraus, who considered perversion, as an aesthetic ideal, of greater significance than the immediate concerns of a hounded minority. Bearing all this in mind Strauss must have known his opera would lead to controversy. When Mahler submitted it to the Viennese Court censor he underlined his own personal objections to Wilde's drama despite his all-consuming admiration for Strauss's music: 'Aside from the fact that the representation of actions from the New Testament raises difficulties for the Court Theatre, the presentation of perverted sensuality, as incorporated in the figure of Salomé, is morally repugnant'; but this was the very quality to which Strauss was probably drawn, and he urged the first Salomé, Marie Wittich, to indulge the role's 'perversion and outrage'.

It appears that no one understood Strauss's attraction, as an anti-Semite and an aspiring modernist, to the perversions of Wilde's drama. Not even Romain Rolland, normally the most perceptive and honest of the composer's friends, saw beyond the 'nauseous and sickly atmosphere': 'Wilde's Salomé and all those who surround her are unwholesome, unclean, hysterical or alcoholic beings, stinking of sophisticated and perfumed corruption. I fear that you have been caught by the mirage of German decadent literature ... You are worthy of better things than *Salomé*.'⁵

Rolland failed to appreciate (or chose to ignore) the connection between Strauss's interpretation of the play as a German composer, and his understanding of it as an anti-Semite. The unmistakably Freudian subtext – in which the abused becomes the abuser – mattered to Strauss only inasmuch as it enabled him to extend his characterisation. The conventional understanding of Salomé's degeneration focuses on her final scene, in which she kisses the decapitated head of Jochanaan; but this is merely one, albeit significant, aspect within a portrayal of alienation and incongruity at the heart of which was a study of perversion – of the place and nature of Jews and homosexuals in modern society.

Like many of his closest friends, such as Rösch, Strauss will have been exposed to the contemporary propaganda in which it was argued that Jews were prone to hysteria and naturally predisposed to mental illness, to degeneration, corruption and neurasthenia. Despite having 'wandered' across Europe, the physical and emotional characteristics considered typical of all Jews were thought to reflect their predilection for inbreeding. The physiognomical similarity between the Jews of the West and the Jews of the East pointed 'unmistakably' towards incest, and a wealth of 'evidence' was produced to demonstrate the higher incidence of 'moral crime' amongst Jews.

The differentiation between good Christian incest and Jewish 'incest' well illustrates the hypocrisy of German anti-Semitism. It was acceptable for Wagner to allow Siegmund and Sieglinde to commit incest on stage – in the full knowledge that they are brother and sister – but it was unacceptable for Herod to marry his brother's widow. As Romain Rolland asserted in a letter to Strauss: 'The incest in the *Walküre* is a thousand times more healthy than the conjugal and legitimate love in such and such a dirty Parisian comedy, which I don't want to name.'[6] Like Wilde, Rolland was touched by an unconscious, inherited anti-Semitism. In a diary entry for March 9, 1900, for example, he described Pierre Wolff's *Le Béguin* as 'a typical Jewish comedy: witty words, utter immorality'. On May 28, 1907, Rolland recorded in his diary a dinner, with Strauss, 'at the house of a certain X who is, I don't know how, a friend of Strauss. One of those Jews who are good sorts, not very trustworthy, toadying and a bit sticky, whom it is impossible to shake off once they have stuck themselves to you.'

Wilde reinforced through *Salomé* the Europe-wide notion of Jews as inbreeders since he too parodied the 'heretical' Jewish law that required an unmarried man to marry his brother's widow. Jochanaan berates Herod and Herodias for their 'incest' – and, in turn, Herod for lusting after and, one must assume, abusing his stepdaughter – in the same way that Elektra attacks her mother for marrying Aegysthus. These Shakespearean triangles allude, in *Salomé* at least, to the then popular anti-Semitic notion that sexual abnormality (from circumcision and legitimised incest to child abuse and homosexuality) was in some genetic way a province of the Jews; Strauss's editing of Wilde's play leans towards an interpretation of the opera as a study in Jewish depravity.

This is supported throughout the score. The quintet of Jews consist of four high tenors and a bass – a comic ensemble, with its roots in *opera buffa* – and they are characterised, as a group, by the discordant and whining tones of forced oboes and clarinets. Strauss may have confined them to one major scene, but their leitmotif is introduced early in Scene I. There is a cacophonic offstage explosion of dissonance, reminiscent of Strauss's portrayal of his critics in *Heldenleben*; beside the passage in the score Strauss wrote a single word: 'howling'. The theme returns in an even less subtle guise to caricature the arguments and protestations of the Five Jews, this time allied more closely with the wailing tones of the oboe, but the cacophony reaches its peak when the first and second soldiers intone the words 'howling' and 'Jews'.

Just as Strauss assigned different sound worlds to his protagonists (a solid diatonicism for Jochanaan; glittering chromaticism for Salomé) so he cast his Jews in a near-atonal traffic accident of sound, with the Jews making lots of noise, but never any sense. Their 'screaming' appears yet more hysterical when Strauss sets it against the solemnity of Jochanaan's Aryan prophesies.

Furthermore, Strauss allies Herod to the quintet by scoring him as another high tenor. Herod cultivates the dissonant style of the Pharisees, extending the emasculated tone of their high, hysterical writing. Indeed, Herod and the Five Jews support the contemporary 'scientific' theories through which it was argued that circumcision was the Western equivalent of castration. Wagner had reinforced this doctrine in *Der Meistersinger*, in which he scored the Jewish caricature Beckmesser as a baritone while forcing his voice into the realms of the *Heldentenor*; and in *Siegfried*, in which Wagner's most vicious Jewish parody, the tenor Mime, is required to abandon any notion of tonal sweetness for the squealing that Wagner, and his peers, considered characteristically Jewish.

Salome's high tenor parts cannot be sung mellifluously, which is not to say that they are unmelodic. Herod, in particular, forces any but the most exceptional singer towards strain and unintelligibility – even in his most significant scene[7] – and Strauss's high pitching points towards the contemporary belief that, through circumcision, male Jews were feminised. Otto Weininger's *Sex and Character* – published in 1903, the same year that Strauss began the music for *Salome* – was influential in advancing the populist argument that Jews were incapable of clarity of thought and expression: 'his [the Jew's] shyness about singing or even speaking in clear positive tones has nothing to do with real reserve. It is a kind of inverted pride; having no true sense of his own worth, he fears being made ridiculous by his singing or his speech.' This type of speech was described at the time as *Mauscheln*, and a number of the more offended Jewish critics regretted Strauss's dogmatic reliance on this pejorative to characterise the drama's Jews. In addition, a high-pitched voice was considered emblematic of homosexual degeneration, which brings Strauss's caricatures full circle: they, like all Jews, are emasculated perverts.

That Strauss intended to mock the Jews is indisputable. In 1935 he wrote to his librettist Stefan Zweig: 'I tried to compose the good Jochanaan more or less as a clown; a preacher in the desert, especially one who feeds off grasshoppers, seems infinitely comical to me. Only because I have already caricatured the Five Jews and also poked fun at Father Herodes did I feel that I had to follow the law of contrast and write a pedantic-Philistine motive ... to characterise Jochanaan.' Productions of the work during the first years of National Socialist rule heightened the grotesque and parodistic, and even in England, as late as 1936, the director Hans Strobach was forced to write to the manager of Covent Garden, Percy Hemming, urging that 'contrary to the usual presentation' the Five Jews should 'NOT be caricatures! Serious, learned, interesting heads.'

Remarkably, a small number of Nazi fanatics considered *Salome* a Jewish opera. In spite of the work's unambiguous malice, a production in 1939 in Graz was banned. Strauss wrote to his nephew, the conductor Rudolph Moralt: 'The idea that *Salome* is a Jewish ballad is very humorous. The Führer and Reichskanzler himself told my son in Bayreuth that *Salome* was one of his first operatic experiences, and that he raised the money to pay his fare to go to the first performance in Graz by begging from his relatives.'[8]

If it seems odd that Strauss should have ridiculed the very people to whom he was directing his aspirations it is worth remembering that the Jews of Western, 'civilised' Europe – particularly the avant-garde – attempted to protect themselves from the mass of anti-Semitic prejudice by distinguishing themselves from the 'comedic', 'filthy' Jews of the East – those 'oriental' Jews incapable of assimilation. Wagner had attacked the Jews for their inherent inability to be or become German, and this was a belief passionately upheld by all committed anti-Semites; but for any second-, third- or fourth-generation Jew, assimilation was possible as long as they were not considered in any way oriental.

For as long as they allied themselves to the avant-garde, civilised Jews could rise above the prejudice and hatred. For Western Jews Strauss's *Salome* was understood as an attack on everyone else – new money, conservatism, reactionism, materialism and so on. Furthermore, Strauss was appealing to a strain of Jewish self-hatred that transgressed natural assimilation. Indeed, the number of prominent Jewish anti-Semites in Strauss's circle is astonishing. One of Hans Pfitzner's closest allies, for example, was the Jewish intellectual Paul Nikolaus Cossmann, who converted to Catholicism in 1905. Having founded the mainstream periodical *Süddeutsche Monatshefte* in 1903, Cossmann became a powerful spokesman for Establishment anti-Semitism, giving 'wide circulation to the stock slanders about Jewish "corrosiveness", "materialism", "hatred of tradition" ' ... the *Süddeutsche Monatshefte* was 'a vivid, if depressing reminder of how far some German Jews could go in escaping from their past'.[9] The paradoxes are many and complicated, but the reasoning is unequivocal: *Salome* is a stridently anti-Semitic opera. In itself, this invites yet another paradox, for *Salome* is also one of the five or six greatest works of operatic art of the twentieth century and Strauss's most enduring contribution to the history of music.

By 1904 he could look back on the première of *Feuersnot* with considerable happiness. The work may have failed, but the production was a success. The Dresden Opera's high standards, and the open minds of Dresden's audiences, made it an ideal home for *Salome*. Strauss offered the work to Schuch (reassuring him that there were none of *Feuersnot*'s awkward choruses). Even Schuch, the pre-eminent champion of new German music, hesitated after reading the score, but after many hours' study he gave his consent and summoned Strauss from Berlin to assist with the casting.

As Strauss later recalled:

At the very first piano run-through the singers assembled in order to give their parts back to the conductor – all except the Herod, a Czech singer named Burrian who, when asked last of all, answered: 'I already know my role by heart.' Bravo! At this, the others felt rather ashamed and the work of the rehearsal actually started. During the rehearsals the dramatic soprano Frau Wittich went on strike. She had been entrusted with the role of the sixteen-year-old princess with the voice of an Isolde, on account of the strenuousness of the part and the thickness of the orchestration ... In righteous wrath she protested like any Saxon Burgomaster's wife, 'I won't do it, I'm a decent woman.'

Long before the première Strauss was to rue the day he engaged Marie Wittich. According to a letter from Strauss to Mahler he settled on her because of her 'style and power', but he failed to take into account her capricious personality. She prevaricated over learning her part to such an extent that Schuch had no choice but to ask Strauss for a postponement of the planned November première.[10] Strauss was furious and wrote to Schuch:

So now everything has come out blissfully just as I had feared. Editor, printer and myself, we have all fallen over ourselves to get you the piano score by September 1, and the high and mighty Frau Wittich has left the rotten thing lying around for five weeks and can't even do it in the end; but you mustn't be cross with me if, under the circumstances, I can no longer guarantee you the first performance. In Leipzig, Nikisch is already hard at work at it. Mahler tells me today that, in Vienna, the piece has at least been pushed past the censor[11] and the work is now forging ahead ... should he stage it before you, there is nothing I can do about it. As I have already wired you, I will reserve the first performance for you until 9 December at the latest, and if you can't manage it by then, whoever is ready first can do it.

In truth, Nikisch had hardly looked at the score. His assistant, Albert Coates, was doing most of the work and it would be Coates, not Nikisch, who conducted the Leipzig première.[12] The situation in Vienna was more complicated. After having fallen out in 1902, Strauss and Mahler returned to friendship during the first quarter of 1903, after Mahler wrote to Strauss asking if he was entitled to join the GDT. As a member, since 1897, of the Viennese Gesellschaft der Autoren, Komponisten und Musikverleger (GAKM) Mahler saw in Strauss's organisation a route to the sort of professional security denied him in Vienna. The GDT represented composers and only composers, whereas the GAKM included publishers among its directors and membership, a situation which militated against the interests of someone like Mahler.

While fully recognising the commercial benefits of defection from the GAKM, Mahler must have realised that so public a renunciation of one of Vienna's most powerful musical bodies for the Berlin-based GDT was going to invite trouble. His concerns were justified. Nailing his colours to Strauss's mast nearly caused the planned Cologne première of his Fifth Symphony to be called off, while in Leipzig the second performance of the new work was cancelled because the promoter, Ernst Eulenburg, was fiercely opposed to the GDT.

Mahler was also conscious that while the GAKM propped up many of Vienna's more vocal anti-Semites, the directors of Strauss's GDT were not exactly celebrated for their equitability. Alma Mahler remembered one occasion in Strasbourg, in 1905 – more than eighteen months after Mahler defected to the GDT – at which they joined Strauss and his GDT allies:

> The Association of German Composers made a point of avoiding Mahler. Schillings gave him only a timid greeting, Rösch looked the other way. Anti-Semitism was in the ascendant and Mahler was made to feel it. There was no mistaking it; we saw how they made up parties at neighbouring tables. We did not begrudge them; we were very glad of our enforced quarantine. We went for walks in the country and over the old entrenchments. They were all overgrown and green, and breathed the spirit of peace, not war.[13]

Not long after Mahler's defection his correspondence with Strauss began to dry up, with only one letter exchanged between February 3, 1903, and February 15, 1905. Strauss's frequent tours and his stay in the United States obviously prohibited close personal contact, but such a prolonged silence is unusual in the context of their renewed friendship. Strauss probably upset Mahler, who was quick to take offence at the best of times, and Mahler's ill-disguised competitive spirit was greatly in evidence throughout 1904, particularly at times of personal triumph. Writing to Alma from Amsterdam in October 1903, for example, he reported how, after a concert of his own music, there followed 'a quite imposing burst of applause. Everyone tells me there has been nothing like it in living memory. Strauss, who is much in vogue here, has been beaten handsomely.'

By the time Strauss began looking for a home for *Salome* they seem to have resolved their differences. The 1905 Alsatian Musical Festival provided them with a good opportunity for reconciliation. Strauss was there to conduct his *Domestica* and a concert of Mozart; Mahler was there to conduct his Fifth Symphony and a concert of Beethoven. Alma's detailed recollection of this event contains a typically vitriolic memoir of Strauss. Mahler's performances, so she claimed, were 'glorious'; Strauss's were 'wretched'. She alleges that Strauss attended only the last of his scheduled rehearsals (leaving the remainder to an assistant) and that he was, as a result, 'filled with alarm at the prospect of his performance'.

That he conducted at all is extraordinary. According to Alma: 'He foamed at the mouth' and 'became violently angry'. She described how, having rehearsed Brahms's *Rhapsody* prior to his *Domestica*, he publicly insulted the alto Adrienne Kraus-Osborne, calling her 'a cow' and suggesting she was better suited to the Venezia in Vienna[14] than to a serious music festival.

Hearing of Strauss's remarks, Osborne's husband Franz von Kraus confronted him during the concert interval and demanded an apology. Failure to provide one would necessitate a duel. Strauss apologised, although his mood was not much improved when, after the concert, he joined the Mahlers en route to a festival banquet. As they walked towards their hotel Gustav and Alma chastised Strauss for making such an exhibition of his temper. Strauss replied: 'I must write and tell my wife that. She doesn't believe I've got a temper at all. But you must tell her too – give her a good fright.'

At the end of May Strauss passed through Vienna, joining Mahler for the journey to Graz and the annual meeting of the Allgemeiner Deutscher Musikverein. To Alma, Mahler reported that during the journey he and Strauss 'talked very agreeably as in the old days. Unfortunately he [Strauss] was called away the next day by the sudden death of his [84-year-old] father and did not hear my songs.'

Franz's death caused Richard considerable anguish. As father and son they had been divided by their aesthetic differences ever since Richard's first trip to Berlin in 1884, and much as he admired his father, Richard had, as a young adult, grown calluses over those parts of his psyche receptive to criticism. This intractability exacerbated Franz's conservatism which, in turn, amplified their dissidence; but parent and child remained close despite their unreconciled differences. During one of their last meetings Richard played through the short score of *Salome* for his father. His recollection of Franz's response is selective: 'Oh God', the old man is said to have exclaimed, 'what nervous music! It sounds as if a swarm of ants were crawling through your trousers.' Richard did not, as one might have expected, dedicate *Salome* to his late father. Instead it was dedicated to his banking friend Edgar Speyer,[15] who would handle most of Strauss's investments prior to 1914.

Strauss also played *Salome* to the Mahlers, in a Strasbourg piano shop. Alma's memoir of the event is detailed; it is also surprisingly equable and, on occasion, approving:

Strauss was cheerful and communicative at that time. His *Salome* was finished. He asked Mahler whether he would like to hear him play the opera from the manuscript ... He had located a piano shop and the three of us made our way to the place, where there were dozens of pianos. The room had big gleaming windows on all sides, with people constantly walking past or stopping to look in – pressing their noses against the window as they tried to catch the sound. Strauss played and sang incomparably well.[16] Mahler was enthralled. We came to the dance. It was missing. 'I haven't done that yet!' said Strauss and after this big hiatus played on to the end. Mahler asked, 'Isn't it risky simply to leave out the dance and do it later when one is no longer in the mood of the work?' But Strauss laughed in his carefree way, 'I'll manage.' ... Mahler was entirely won over. One can risk anything if one has the genius to make the preposterous possible.

In fact, for the first time in his life Mahler was convinced of Strauss's genius. If he had despaired at his choice of source, then he marvelled at its setting. As he wrote to Alma after first seeing *Salome* in Berlin: 'It is emphatically a work of genius, very powerful, and decidedly one of the most important works of our day. A Vulcan lives and labours under a heap of slag, a subterranean fire – not merely a firework! It is exactly the same with Strauss's whole personality. That's what makes it so difficult to separate the wheat from the chaff.'

So certain was Mahler of the opera's quality that, overcoming his own repugnance, he took it directly to Vienna where he did everything in his power to try and persuade the censor to allow him, and the Royal Court Opera, the honour of the Austrian première. As far as Mahler was concerned there was no possibility of his stealing a march on Dresden, and so when Strauss wrote to Schuch threatening to allow Mahler the first performance he did so in full knowledge that the Viennese censor had not, and was unlikely to, pass sanction. As with *Feuersnot*, Mahler was again the unknowing axis of Strauss's collusion – thanks to which Schuch coerced Wittich and her colleagues into meeting the deadline of December 9.

Mahler never gave up the struggle. He knew he was fighting a lost battle (at one point, he offered to resign over the matter) and the affair was emblematic of his impossible situation as Director of the Court Opera. He continued to advocate *Salome* throughout 1906 and, having endured a decade of almost constant frustration, he resigned in the spring of 1907. If the *Salome* affair was but one of many challenges to his authority in Vienna, then it was certainly among the most painful; there is no doubt that his failure to bring Strauss's opera to the Viennese stage was decisive in forcing his resignation. Mahler never did conduct the opera, and the Viennese censor (directed by one Archbishop Piffl) successfully fought off popular demand until October 1918, when Franz Schalk conducted the city première in what was then the Vienna *State* Opera.

Having panicked Schuch into action, Strauss suffered a harrowing rehearsal process. Since their last meeting, Wittich had added generously to her already considerable girth, and while this seems not to have bothered Strauss,[17] she had still to learn her part. Only Carl Burian and Karl Perron (the baritone, singing Jochanaan[18]) were able to rehearse without making constant reference to the score and, to make matters worse, Schuch was proving incapable of achieving the right balance between stage and pit: whenever Strauss was able to hear the singers, the orchestra was too quiet; whenever he was unable to hear them, the orchestra was too loud. The producer Willi Wirk was reduced to tears of frustration by Wittich, from whom he could generate not even a glimmer of sexual tension (a ballerina was engaged for the 'Dance of the Seven Veils'), and yet Wittich managed ultimately to generate a frenzy from both sides of the pit that secured *Salome*'s celebrity long before the last of the thirty-eight curtain calls.

Strauss's opinion of the première is uncertain. His praise to, and of, Schuch was doubtless intended to keep the work in repertoire, and years later he claimed that *Salome* had succeeded 'in spite of Auntie Wittich'. In his memoirs he wrote that: 'The first performance was, as usual, a success, but the critics gathered together in the Bellevue Hotel after the performance, shook their heads and agreed that the piece would perhaps be performed by a few of the largest theatres but would soon disappear.'

The Kaiser is said to have remarked, 'I am sorry Strauss composed this *Salome*. I really like the fellow but this will do him a lot of damage', to which Strauss replied, 'The damage enabled me to build my villa in Garmisch.' For the publishing rights alone, Strauss obtained the vast sum of 60,000 marks from Fürstner (at which Franz had remarked, 'Do remain modest – at that price the publisher won't make anything from it') and within two years *Salome* had enjoyed over fifty new productions around the world, hundreds of performances and a reputation that forced the once hostile critical Establishment to revise their opinions.

As Strauss had predicted, the Kaiser was opposed to the representation of biblical figures on 'his' stage. His wife considered the whole thing immoral, and both of them were warned against sanctioning such dangerously 'modern' music. Hülsen cleverly pacified Wilhelm and Augusta by suggesting that at the end of the opera the Star of David be shown against the backdrop, to herald the birth of Christ![19] In 1907 the Court Opera celebrated its fiftieth performance.

By 1911 *Salome* had been played in most of the world's opera-producing countries. The general response, outside Germany, to the shocking nature of the drama (which would have been exacerbated by the association with the 'degenerate' Wilde) was predictable. In the United States, where Strauss was much in favour since his grand tour, Heinrich Conried, manager of the Metropolitan Opera, secured the first American performance in January 1907. The audience was ecstatic, but Mrs Herbert Satterlee, the daughter of millionaire banking magnate J. P. Morgan, was appalled by the representation of hedonism in what was really her family's opera house. Morgan told Conried to cancel the work; Conried did what he was told. Twenty-seven years passed before *Salome* was again seen at the Met.

Rival theatres were quick to exploit Conried's predicament. In 1909 Oscar Hammerstein produced it at his Manhattan Opera House, with Mary Garden in the title role. He then toured it around the country, raising almost as much money as dust. 'No account of what Miss Garden did in *Salome* can so much as faintly mirror what Salome did to Chicago,' wrote one critic, while another described Garden's dance as 'like a cat in a bed of catnip'. She was, claimed another, 'a conception of incarnate bestiality'. All this helped raise the price, and demand, for tickets, bringing Strauss a fortune rivalled, in the history of music, only by the success of Verdi and Puccini.

In London, Thomas Beecham struggled to force the work past the British censor. That Debussy, Dukas, Ravel, Puccini, Schoenberg and just about every noted composer, with the exception of Stravinsky, had come out in its defence seems to have made no difference. The Lord Chamberlain officially banned the opera in 1907, and refused a production of the work until the day before its fifth anniversary, when Beecham conducted a heavily revised libretto in which Jochanaan became the prophet Mattaniah, the action was moved from Judaea to Greece, and the Jews and Nazarenes became Learned Men and Cappadocians. There was no head, and no platter. Salome sang her final scene to a bowl of blood. Each of the ten performances was sold out.

Salome brought Strauss unprecedented celebrity as well as extraordinary wealth. He was rivalled in popularity only by Puccini, and hundreds of cartoons and thousands of articles were printed in celebration of his and his opera's notoriety. *Salome* also brought him into direct contact with many of the world's leading conductors, most notably Arturo Toscanini. The story of the first Italian *Salome* is long and complicated, and it reflects little glory on the composer, who promised Toscanini and La Scala, Milan, the première while, at the same time, signing an agreement with the rival Teatro Regio in Turin.[20] Thinking there had been a mistake Toscanini arranged to meet Strauss on October 9, 1906. Since there was, Strauss claimed, no way for him to rescind his agreement with Turin, Toscanini asked if he would agree to a simultaneous première in both cities. Strauss replied that if Milan was willing to pay him the same fee as Turin then he was sure this would present no difficulty.

Before Strauss could finish his sentence Toscanini stood to his feet, claimed that Strauss's 'respect for his word was evidently just a question of money' and stormed out of the room. Strauss then wrote a pitiful letter to Toscanini, spelling out in painful detail his financial interests in the hope that these might clarify, if not dignify, his behaviour. Initially, Toscanini seems to have put the matter behind him, but within a matter of weeks his anger resurfaced and he began to scheme against the composer, setting the date for the Milanese *Salome* on the same day as the Turin performance. Turin responded by moving its première to the 23rd and, later, the 22nd of December. All seemed satisfactory until Toscanini produced his ace.

Unbeknown to Strauss, who had been engaged to conduct the première in Turin, Toscanini had arranged for a public dress rehearsal on the 21st – the day before the Turin première – to which he invited the majority of Italy's critics, his own friends, La Scala's subscribers and many of the country's leading socialites. Strauss was furious, for while Turin rightly claimed the

Italian première, Toscanini was the first to play it, and the Milanese were the first to hear it. Toscanini continued to conduct a number of the tone poems until the end of his life, but he never again conducted an opera by Strauss.

With hindsight, the 'modernity' of Strauss's third opera was something of a smokescreen. When played on the piano, or whenever vocal passages are isolated from their orchestral and harmonic surroundings, *Salome* is a nine-teenth-century music drama, rich with melody and indulgent chromatic extremes undreamed of, even, by Liszt. Like Mozart, Strauss was blessed with a unique sympathy for the human voice, and it was impossible for him to write anything anti-vocal. Even at its most hysterical, the writing for Herod is dictated by a fundamental consonance that, while not quite fulfilling Brahms's eight-bar strictures, owes unmistakable debts to *Don Giovanni* and *Tristan*. Beyond Strauss's harmonic palette, there is nothing particularly modern or shocking about *Salome*.

Within the context of any study of Strauss's life, probably the most remark-able thing about his third opera is that he was able to amplify the hysterical sexuality of *Salome* while, at the same time, depicting the frigidity of his bedroom in *Sinfonia Domestica*. *Salome* is, indeed, nervous music, and many of its contemporaries found it shocking and unintelligible; but it was popular, more popular in fact than anyone could have predicted and, ninety years later, it is possible to see how, aside from questions of detail, there was little to distinguish the portentous, shimmering world of the 'modernist' *Salome* from the indulgent escapism of the supposedly 'recidivistic' *Der Rosen-kavalier*. Before *Rosenkavalier*, however, Strauss would shock his audiences one last time.

18　　THE ELEKTRA PARALLAX

December 1905–January 1909

Salome confirmed Strauss as Germany's leading 'modernist'. Paradoxically, it also established him as the most popular German composer since Wagner, a position that compelled the Munich Opera to give the city première of *Feuersnot* a few days before Christmas 1905.[1] Strauss took his celebrity in his stride. He had, after all, been at the forefront of German music for nearly two decades, and the euphoria of a first-night success was no longer the novelty it had once been; but for the first time in his life he was enjoying an income comparable to his standing, and as *Salome* flashed across the stages of most of the world's opera houses Strauss petitioned Hülsen for a new contract befitting a composer of international standing. Strauss was not yet sufficiently secure to retire from his post (*Salome* might have proved to be an isolated success) but he was willing to devote no more than half of his year to the Opera – without, of course, any cut in salary. Hülsen was piqued, not least because Strauss had been absent for much of 1905. Even *in absentia*, however, Strauss was an irreplaceable asset, and Hülsen did not allow his frustration to disguise his faith in Strauss's value as Court Hofkapellmeister:

> I treated this unusual request as favourably as possible, because I could very well sympathise with your wishes ... But we have an official establishment to run, and the way things are now being managed has proved both inartistic and impossible. The lack of artistic discipline among almost the entire personnel has been, and still is, attributable, first and foremost, to the fact that often no example has been set ... You promised me in writing, and as a personal undertaking, to devote your entire strength to the Royal Institution in the remaining six months of the year, unreservedly. Your letter now – in a way that touches me in the most painful manner – places your own interests in the forefront again, to such an extent that I must ask you whether you will keep your word and dedicate your entire strength to the much needed betterment of the Royal Institution.

Strauss was outmanoeuvred. Needing the money, he stayed in Berlin and embraced the advantages of a routine that, as he well knew, would be of incomparable benefit after the family's move to Garmisch. Strauss had known Garmisch-Partenkirchen since childhood. Surrounded by mountainous, snow-covered terrain, 720 metres above sea-level, it provided a ready means of escape from city life, as well as a point of easy access for Munich (50 miles), Salzburg (100 miles) and Vienna (180 miles). Strauss determined to build a villa in which he could happily spend the rest of his days, a place where his family would have sufficient room to lead their lives while, at the same time, allowing him to work on his music.

He began making local inquiries shortly after having negotiated his fee for *Salome* with Fürstner, which he used as a down-payment towards the building of the villa. Having decided where and on how much land he wished to build, and having instructed the architect Emanuel Seidl to draw up plans, Strauss left the project almost entirely in the hands of others.

It is a beautiful house. On three floors, it contains some nineteen rooms, including an enchanting study that hardly changed during the more than forty years Strauss lived there. The family added more rooms in the 1920s, but the house is by no means extravagantly large; there is sufficient space to accommodate staff as well as the many guests that would become a fixture of Strauss family life and it is, like his finest works, perfectly formed. The decorative style was, and remains, an eccentric mixture of Biedermeier elegance, Deco refinement and bourgeois vulgarity – the latter manifested by Strauss's questionable fondness for Bavarian glass-painting and Catholic iconography. His son's affection for hunting added little, apart from trophies, to the prevailing air of warmth and geniality, and the house is now a living museum, with Strauss's souvenirs, medals, honours and busts providing a constant reminder of the house's progenitor.

Excited as he was by the project, Strauss had little time to worry about the finer details of domestic architecture. *Salome* had thundered into 1906 and for the first month-and-a-half of the new year his time was monopolised by negotiations with Intendants, promoters, publishers and conductors. In February he was back at the Court Opera, beating his way through the standard run of pot-boilers, and in March he travelled to Paris for a series of concerts in the frostbitten capital, including the first French performance of *Domestica*. He did not relish the trip, particularly as the weather was so cold, but he was able to enjoy the company of Pauline and Bubi, and he greatly looked forward to catching up with Romain Rolland, who had recently done so much to help prepare the French-language *Salome*.

Rolland wrote a detailed memoir of their time together. On March 23, Strauss had endured a long and freezing car journey to see the palace at Versailles, thanks to which he had woken the following morning with a severe cold. Rolland joined Strauss at his hotel, in order to accompany him to the Châtelet [concert hall], where he was to rehearse *Domestica*; but having packed no winter clothes Strauss's condition worsened, and he spent most of the journey launching a stream of invective against the weather, Paris, the Parisians, the Opéra and Gounod whom, he maintained, even 'the most serious Frenchman still loves above everything'. He then turned on the 'monotonous' Debussy whom, Rolland reminded him, he was scheduled to meet on the 25th; and only when Strauss began to talk of *Salome*'s enormous financial success did his mood improve.

They arrived at the Châtelet in time to hear the fifteen-year-old Mischa Elman rehearsing ('with amazing vigour and precision') the second movement of Beethoven's Violin Concerto ('I would like to have written that,' grumbled Strauss), after which Strauss stepped on to the podium to begin *Domestica*:

> He conducts with his whole body – arms, head and behind together; at moments he seems to dance on his knees; he crouches down; he makes tense and pulsating movements, like electric vibrations, with his hands. He gives explanations in very bad French gibberish, and sings out of tune passages that he wants played again; he cares nothing for ridicule; he always looks bored, sulky, half-asleep – but nevertheless lets nothing escape him. – His music stirs me to my very depths. To me the finale is a flood of strength and of joy. One always wonders how *that* can have come out of *this*.

The concert on the 25th was a triumph, and Rolland, having once expressed his opinion that *Domestica* heralded a downturn in Strauss's creative fortunes, now announced: 'There's been nothing like it in symphonic music since Beethoven.' He concluded his diary entry with another sketch of his friend:

> Just now, looking at the big portrait of Strauss which I have at home and which Strauss gave me, I was thinking: it's very idealised; they've credited him with a character which he does not possess. Strauss, in real life, hasn't that vigour of expression; the impression he gives is pale, uncertain, eternally youngish, a little inconsistent. – But when seeing him close to, at the concert, conducting his orchestra, I was struck by the other Strauss; his face is ageing, hardening, shrinking; it is acquiring and retaining an intense seriousness, which not the slightest gleam of gaiety illuminates for an instant. In profile, with his thick crown of hair, set very high up, and framing a monk's tonsure, with his enormous bulging forehead, his nose which appears small and short, and his sulky mouth, he looks like a barbarian from Asia, one of those Huns who founded a family in Germany. – But there is one thing which his portraits do not convey at all: that is the pale blondness of hair and complexion.[2]

Elsewhere he wrote: 'There is a Bavarian indolence in him ... One catches glimpses ... his eyes vague and half asleep.'

Pschorr Beer Hall at Altheimer Eck 2, Munich, where Strauss was born on June 11, 1864.

Father and son in a portrait taken towards the end of Franz's life.

Husband and wife in a portrait taken after their wedding in 1894.

A publicity photograph of Strauss the conductor in 1888.

Strauss and cast on stage in Dresden for the first production of *Salome* in 1905.

Strauss and the production team of the first *Der Rosenkavalier*, gathered in Dresden in 1911. *Standing, left to right:* Oberinspektor Hasait, Hoftheatermaler Altenkirch, Max Reinhardt, Hugo von Hofmannsthal, Alfred Roller, Leonhard Fanto, Oberregisseur George Toller. *Sitting left to right:* Nikolaus Graf von Seebach, Strauss, Ernst von Schuch.

In the gardens outside the family villa in Garmisch, c. 1912.

Strauss, Pauline and grandson Richard, photographed in Strauss's study at Jacquingasse, Vienna, c. 1929.

Strauss and cast at rehearsals for the first production of *Intermezzo* in Dresden, in 1924.

At Bayreuth in 1933 with Heinz Tietjen and Winifred Wagner.

At Bayreuth in 1933 with Franz, and Adolf Hitler.

In Berlin on February 18, 1934 for a concert by the Berlin Philharmonic Orchestra. *Left to right;* Dr Julius Kopsch, Friedrich-Christian, Prince of Schaumburg-Lippe, Dr Joseph Goebbels, Strauss, Franz Strauss and Wilhelm Furtwängler.

Conducting at the first *Reichsmusiktage* in Düsseldorf on May 28, 1938.

In Dresden playing
Die Schweigsame Frau
to the conductor Karl
Böhm in 1935.

In Vienna for the first
performance of
Gerhard
Hauptmann's
Iphigenia in 1943.

Edward Steichen's demonic, hand-finished portrait of Strauss, taken in New York in 1904.

Much of Rolland's portrayal contradicts the wider perception of Strauss at the time. That he should have thought him lacking 'vigour of expression' is extraordinary. Had Rolland any insight into Strauss's itinerary he might have extended more sympathy, for there was no harder-working musician in Germany. Mahler was one of many to marvel at his energy, expressing open astonishment at Strauss's ability to produce such a wide-ranging body of music while, simultaneously, sustaining an opera house, an orchestra, guest tours and a family. For Rolland to call Strauss indolent was absurd, particularly in the light of Rolland's closeness to Maurice Ravel, whose aversion to hard work was as comprehensive as his talent. The droop of Strauss's eyelids owed less to weakness of character than to exhaustion.

Strauss was none the less capable of inexplicable lapses. His meeting with Debussy provides a good example. Having been criticised for greed and self-interest in Germany and the United States, and knowing something of Debussy's indigent circumstances, Strauss devoted a long lunch with the French composer to talking, almost without interruption, about the business of music. Not only was Debussy permanently tortured by debt, but he had been invited to meet Strauss in the hope that, together, they might enjoy a sparkling discussion of contemporary aesthetics. The host, Jacques Durand,[3] could not believe his ears, any more than Debussy[4] could understand how the composer of *Salome* could be such a mercenary bore. He barely spoke during the meal, and each left with unshakeable perceptions of the other: Strauss thought Debussy dull; Debussy thought Strauss odious.

Strauss and his family returned to Berlin at the end of March 1906. He had to oversee productions of *Salome* in Prague, Cologne and Graz, and Pauline was keen to visit the site of their villa in Garmisch; but Strauss had another reason to relish the journey home. Shortly before leaving for France he had begun an exchange of letters with Hugo von Hofmannsthal.

Strauss first met the Austrian poet and dramatist on March 23, 1899, at Richard Dehmel's house in Berlin. Their paths crossed again the following year in Paris, where Hofmannsthal offered Strauss a ballet, *Der Triumph der Zeit*. In November 1900 Hofmannsthal wrote to Strauss, reminding him of their discussion, but Strauss was working on his own ballet, *Kythere*, and politely declined. But around the time that Strauss saw Wilde's *Salomé* at Reinhardt's Kleines Theater in 1902, he also saw a performance of Hofmannsthal's transformation of Sophocles' *Elektra*, again with Gertrud Eysoldt in the title role.

In 1905, with *Salome* nearing completion, Strauss began to contemplate a new opera. At some point during the second half of the year he contacted Hofmannsthal and suggested a possible operatic setting of *Elektra*. The first of Hofmannsthal's surviving letters on the subject dates from March 7, 1906, and begins: 'How goes it with you and *Elektra*?' Strauss's reply, sent four days later, is uncharacteristically revealing:

I am as keen as ever on *Elektra* and have already cut it down a good deal for my own private use. The only question I have not finally decided in my mind (no doubt this will be settled in the summer, the only time when I can compose) is whether, immediately after *Salome*, I shall have the strength to handle a subject so similar to it in many respects with an entirely fresh mind, or whether I wouldn't do better to wait a few years before approaching *Elektra*, until I have myself moved much farther away from the *Salome* style.

That is why anyway I should be glad to know if you've got anything else in stock for me, and if I might perhaps have a go at some other subject from your pen, farther removed from *Salome*, before doing *Elektra* ... I would ask you urgently to give me first refusal with anything composable that you write. Your manner has so much in common with mine; we were born for one another and are certain to do fine things together if you remain faithful to me. Have you got an entertaining renaissance subject for me? A really wild Cesare Borgia or Savonarola would be the answer to my prayers.

While not unreasonable, Strauss's fear of repetition is significant. The common assertion is that *Salome* and *Elektra* represented a conscious move by Strauss towards the 'abyss' of atonality and the severity of Viennese modernism, and that *Der Rosenkavalier* represented an equally conscious retreat. Belief in this 'volte-face' presupposes an awareness within Strauss of a responsibility to his cultural environment, a sensitivity to history (and his place within it) and, most importantly, an aesthetic agenda. In order for Strauss to step away from the abyss, he had actually to step towards it.

Convenient as they are, such theories clash sharply with what we know of Strauss. If *Salome* and *Elektra* were consciously experimental *Der Rosenkavalier* might represent a slide sideways, if not actually backwards; but Strauss cared nothing for aesthetic movements or ideologies. This is not to suggest that he wasn't aware of cultural transitions, or that he did not think about them; but Strauss was untouched by idealism. As he frequently admitted, his foremost concern was the success and popularity of his work, and this was defined by the need to do a good job – to entertain, move and, if necessary, shake his audience. In December 1907, for example, he wrote to Hofmannsthal concerning a possible setting of Pedro Calderón's *Semiramis*: 'I would urge you to consider where those Hanging Gardens might be installed – in the décor, of course – since, after all, they are the only thing the general public knows about Semiramis, and so they will all want to see them on the stage. You've no idea how the public still falls for decorative art ... Do therefore spare neither cost nor effort, please, on a lavish spectacle ...'

Strauss was writing for 'the mob', not himself; and if *Salome* and *Elektra* represented a move forwards, and *Der Rosenkavalier* a move backwards, it would only be natural to expect his correspondence, especially with Hofmannsthal, to reflect a variety of diverse, and deeply felt, cultural concerns.

Predictably, however, it does not. Strauss's letters are incisive, witty, self-deprecating and often entertaining, but they tell us little about his aesthetics. In fact, they make a mockery of the notion that Strauss took a conscious or considered view of his artistic significance. He was simply too self-motivated, and far too talented, to care anything for progress or 'movements'. He was a law unto himself, indifferent to the world outside his immediate interests and devoid of a social conscience. His choice of *Elektra* was defined by his taste, by Hofmannsthal's popularity, and by his need for a stimulating subject. His treatment of *Elektra* was, in essence, conservative. Like *Salome*, it embodied the particular genius of its composer. It presented no credo or testimony; Strauss was simply fitting the music to the subject, a musical tailor of very colourful suits.

In isolation, Strauss's attraction to *Salome* and *Elektra* suggests a composer alert to the modernity of contemporary literature, and yet, having broached a collaboration with Hofmannsthal, Strauss began to withdraw from *Elektra*. Instead he latched on to *Semiramis* until the exasperated Hofmannsthal's patience began to wear thin: 'In the far distance the vision of a *Semiramis* theme emerges rather like a mirage, but it is not possible for me to drag it up by force.' To Strauss's suggestion of a subject from the Renaissance, Hofmannsthal replied: 'Subjects taken from the Renaissance seem destined to transport the brushes of the most deplorable painters and the pens of the most hapless of poets.'

But Strauss remained restless, and while struggling with *Elektra* he continued to badger Hofmannsthal for alternatives. On June 5, 1906, he wrote to the poet: 'I read Rückert's *Saul and David* today ... there's a lot in it that might be usable ...' Moreover, Strauss could not rid himself of the suspicion that *Salome* and *Elektra* were sisters. Hofmannsthal replied: 'Both are one-act plays; each has a woman's name for a title, both take place in classical antiquity, and both parts were originally created in Berlin by Gertrud Eysoldt; that is, I feel, all the similarity adds up to.' His argument was unconvincing (the similarities between the two dramas are multitudinous), but it strengthened Strauss's resolve, and on June 16 he announced that he was 'busy on the first scene of *Elektra*' – even if he added, as a postscript, 'How about a subject from the French Revolution for a change? Do you know Büchner's *Dantons Tod*? Sardou's (*horrible dictu*) *Ninth Thermidor* has been warmly recommended to me ...'[5]

Cesare Borgia, Savonarola, Semiramis, Saul and David, Dantons Tod, Ninth Thermidor ... Strauss's pebble-dash sympathies confirm what is already known: that the composer wrote according to the subject in hand. He was no modernist, as was Mahler, and he cared nothing for prevailing literary trends (typified by the repertoire at Max Reinhardt's theatre in Berlin). There was no 'volte-face' since taking a stand never occurred to him.

Having begun sketching the first scene of *Elektra*, Strauss was summoned by Mahler in late June to conduct in Salzburg during the celebrations commemorating the 150th anniversary of Mozart's birth. Strauss was a last-minute replacement for Karl Muck, who was again ill, and he joined Mahler between August 16 and 20 to conduct the Vienna Philharmonic in opera and concert. Mahler triumphed with *Le nozze di Figaro* and Strauss enjoyed success with a concert of Mozart's Overture to *Die Zauberflöte*, his Sinfonia Concertante and Bruckner's Ninth Symphony.

Mahler wrote numerous letters to his wife during the festival. On the 16th he told Alma how, having been to a festival gathering, an 'elated' Strauss entered the hotel:

> We then discoursed for an hour about fees and royalties etc., after which I went to bed. But not to sleep – the devil only knows why ... Strauss has already composed a few scenes of *Elektra* (Hofmannsthal). He will not part with it for less than 10% a night and 100,000 marks down. (This, I confess, is only a supposition of mine.) As he made no further enquiry I told him nothing of the antiquated life I led in the summer.[6] I don't think he would be greatly impressed to hear what old-fashioned rubbish I was busy on.

Strauss divided the remainder of 1906 between *Elektra*, preparations for performances of *Salome*, and conducting engagements. He worked steadily on the new opera, a process to which, as their correspondence demonstrates, Hofmannsthal contributed little. Indeed, to refer to the creation of *Elektra* as a collaboration is to stretch a point. They met several times during 1907, but never for very long, and the correspondence yielded nothing between October 1906 and December 1907, by which time Strauss had completed well over half the score. Not until January 1908 did Strauss demand anything of his partner, and then Hofmannsthal did little more than furnish padding.

On December 15, 1906, Strauss travelled to Vienna, where he had lunch with Mahler and conducted another concert with the Philharmonic Orchestra; a few weeks later, during the second week of January 1907, Mahler travelled to Berlin for a concert with the BPO. After his first rehearsal, of the Third Symphony, Mahler visited the Strausses' flat on Joachimstaaler Strasse. He was met at the door by Pauline:

> She greeted me with 'Sh! – sh! Richard's asleep,' and pulled me into her (very untidy) boudoir, where her old mother was sitting over coffee, and let loose a flood of nonsense about all the financial and sexual events of the last two years, rapidly interjecting questions about 'a thousand and one' things without waiting for the answers. She would not hear of my going, told me Richard had had an exhausting rehearsal yesterday morning in Leipzig, had then returned to Berlin to conduct *Götterdämmerung* at night, and today, being reduced to pulp, had lain down to sleep in the afternoon, while she kept strictest watch. I was quite

touched. Suddenly she leapt up: 'But now to wake the brute.' Before I could stop her, she dragged me by both hands into his room, and roused him with a stentorian shout: 'Get up. Gustav's here.' I was Gustav for an hour, and after that Director. Strauss got up with a patient smile, and the torrent of nonsense was resumed as a trio.

Under normal circumstances Mahler did not embellish his accounts in this way, but knowing how much Alma detested Pauline he may well have garnished his narrative for her benefit. Two days later he endured another burst of Pauline: 'To lunch with Strauss afterwards. And besides that, a dinner-party for the Blechs. There was no one there when I arrived, but a moment later in came Frau Strauss, and began a temperamental conversation, which fell steeply to this abysmal outburst: "My God, for a million – well no, that's not enough – five million! And then Richard can stop manufacturing music." '

The remainder of his letter is unusual. Mahler had joined the Strausses knowing full well that the dinner was in honour of Leo Blech, who had recently joined the conducting staff at the Court Opera; and yet he plainly resented the scope of Strauss's largesse. Like a jealous lover, he continued: 'The respectful and friendly consideration which I show him on such occasions awakes no echo, is not, probably, so much as noticed, is simply as though it had never been. – If I am to experience this sort of thing again, I feel I know neither myself nor the world about me. Are other men made of a different clay?'[7] In the margin of his copy of these letters, next to Mahler's rhetorical question, Strauss wrote 'Yes'.

Mahler's apprehension was briefly assuaged when, on January 14, he met Strauss at the Opera where he found him 'his agreeable self again'; despite the 'temperamental intermezzi contributed by the eternal feminine'[8] he enjoyed an 'exhaustive and most agreeable discussion' at dinner later that evening. The bubble burst when Strauss failed to attend Mahler's concert in Frankfurt on January 15: 'It was unkind of Strauss not to be present,' he wrote to Alma. 'I found the enclosed card when I got home.' Strauss's scribbled apology was heartfelt, and Mahler was probably right when he blamed Pauline whom he imagined confronting her husband: ' "You'll stop here and play your skat and then go to bed". '

Mahler failed to penetrate the lack of connection between Strauss the man and Strauss the composer; such an inexplicable polarity was incompatible with Mahler's romanticised view of creativity and, as he wrote of *Salome* to Alma, 'I cannot make out the drift of it, and can only surmise that it is the voice of the "earth-spirit" speaking from the heart of genius, a spirit which does not indeed make a dwelling-place for itself to suit human taste but in accordance with its own unfathomable needs. Perhaps in time I shall gain a clearer understanding of this "cocoon" it has spun for itself.' Elsewhere he simply admitted, 'I don't know what to make of Strauss. How is one to explain his unequalness and jumbling together of bad and good?'

With his resignation from the Vienna Court Opera in May 1907 Mahler's correspondence with Strauss was suspended until June 1909, and their relationship all but ended with his departure for New York at the end of the year. A small number of letters were exchanged (of which four have survived), and there was a final meeting on September 12, 1910, at the first performance of Mahler's Eighth Symphony ('of a Thousand'). Before then, in August 1909, the two families met ('almost as between potentates' noted Mahler) and, for comic value alone, Alma's recollection of Richard and Pauline is indispensable:

> They arrived in Toblach and expected us to dinner. But first Mahler went down at midday. Frau Pauline greeted him in the square in front of the hotel by shouting out at the top of her voice: 'Hello, Mahler. What was it like in New America? Filthy, eh? Hope you got a pile anyway' ... Frau Strauss was very wrought up that evening. Her son, who was still a boy, got first a slap on the head and next a glass of milk. We all stood awkwardly round and Strauss, to get the company seated, motioned to Mahler to sit next to his wife. At this Pauline exclaimed 'Yes, but only if he doesn't start fidgeting, because I can't put up with it.' ... She excelled herself that evening. We trailed home exhausted in mind and body.

At the same time as Mahler was preparing to resign from the Vienna Court Opera, Strauss was on his way to Paris for the French première of *Salome*. The production was mounted by Gabriel Pierné, who magnanimously extended the honour of conducting the first night to Strauss. He was shadowed throughout by his self-proclaimed chronicler, Romain Rolland, whose portraits of the composer are of more value for their anecdotes and references to his physical appearance than for their aesthetic or psychological insights. On May 15, he visited Strauss in his hotel room, where he found the composer 'very nice, very good-natured, as perfectly simple and natural as ever; not a second of posing, not a single artificial word, not a premeditated gesture'. Of Strauss's appearance he wrote: 'I am always surprised how tall he is; he is thin, well-built; a tired face, still young, although the forehead (and part of the head) is very bald. He complains of his heart, and of excessive tiredness ...' Strauss also bemoaned the corruption apparently endemic within Parisian musical life. His cast for the Châtelet *Salome*, for example, had been chosen for him on the basis of who was sleeping with whom.

In a remarkably portentous outburst, he went so far as to attack the French for their republicanism which, according to Rolland, 'he cannot bear'; and it is clear from Rolland, and others, that the unlimited freedom enjoyed by the French press was a source of considerable anguish for the much-gossiped-about composer. *La Libre Parole*, in particular, laid siege at his door – asserting, to Strauss's 'contempt', that he was a Jew – and much was written against him and his wife, who was particularly despised for her arrogance and 'military' disposition. Rolland referred to one incident in which 'this foolish woman' supposedly 'went about saying in Paris society that there was only one way of getting the French to do something, and that was with fixed bayonets'. Consequently, Strauss was compelled to exhibit a quite false measure of discretion as 'everything one says in Paris is in the newspapers the next day, but distorted'.

At the end of the month, with Richard and Pauline en route to Germany, Rolland was able to collect his thoughts. Having shared their company on and off for a month, his assessment lacked grace, although his opinion was coloured further by Strauss's failure to understand Debussy's *Pelléas et Mélisande*:

> Strauss is a Shakespearean barbarian; his art is torrential, producing at one and the same time gold, sand, stone and rubbish; he has almost no taste at all, but a violence of feelings which borders on madness … And he himself is greater than his works, sincere, loyal and absolutely open. He is a good judge of himself … Unfortunately he has a terrible wife who has done him great harm here … Strauss himself has shown a deplorable clumsiness of speech, slinging abuse at the Republic and bitterly criticising Paris. In a word people have come to hate them. And yet what fine and beautiful qualities they possess …'

Suffering from chest pains and fatigue, Strauss spent most of June and July 1907 at Bad Nauheim, twenty miles north of Frankfurt, before returning to Berlin, his routine, and *Elektra*. If his disposition was gloomy, it was much improved by an invitation from the board of the Vienna Philharmonic to become one of the orchestra's guest conductors – an honour partially facilitated by a warm recommendation from the outgoing Mahler. How he was expecting to combine such a weight of conducting work with the needs of *Elektra* was, and remains, a mystery; yet Strauss appears to have been incapable of saying no. He agreed to patronise 'Strauss Weeks' all over Europe, he promised his personal support to a dozen new productions of *Salome*, and in May 1908 he was offered and accepted the post of conductor of the Court Orchestra – the Berlin Philharmonic – after Weingartner resigned to take up Mahler's position in Vienna. In October the same year he was promoted from Royal Kapellmeister to General Music Director of the Berlin Court Opera which meant that, at the age of forty-three, Strauss was Germany's most powerful musician.

Something had to give. Pauline feared it would be his heart and so, probably at her 'suggestion', Strauss made yet another appeal to Hülsen for compassion. Aware that he might resign his post should his petition be rejected, Hülsen agreed to a year's sabbatical, so long as Strauss concentrated on *Elektra*. Duly, at the end of 1907, Hofmannsthal visited Joachimstaaler Strasse where he and Strauss discussed, at great length, *Semiramis*.

A few days later Strauss wrote Hofmannsthal a long and convoluted letter in which he outlined his ambitions, and his hopes that Hofmannsthal – the most refined of poets – would provide him with a drama 'full of action and contrasts, with few mass scenes, but with two or three very good rich parts'; only towards the letter's end did he turn to *Elektra*. Betraying something of his sensitivity for popular theatre, Strauss outlined his reasons for wanting to keep Aegysthus, Klytemnestra's husband, in the opera: 'He is definitely part of the plot and must be killed with the rest, preferably before the eyes of the audience.' In February 1908 Strauss amplified these requirements when, referring to *Semiramis*, he reminded Hofmannsthal: 'And don't forget plenty of ballet, martial music and victory marching: these, apart from the erotic elements, are my strong suit.'

They met again in March, when Strauss visited Vienna for three days between the 6th and the 8th, but nothing more passed between them until June 4, when Hofmannsthal made references to a new idea for a comedy based upon the exploits of Casanova.[9] It is clear that, at some point since (or, indeed, during) their meeting in March, Strauss and Hofmannsthal abandoned all plans for *Semiramis*; and that, long before any direct allusion to *Rosenkavalier*, and while Strauss was working on the great 'Recognition' scene of *Elektra*, Hofmannsthal and Strauss had decided that their next work should be comic.

During May Strauss endured a punishing conducting tour of Europe, and for most of June and July he concentrated on the final scenes of *Elektra*, from Orestes' entry to the climactic duet between the sisters. Hofmannsthal provided the few changes demanded of him – most unforgettably, the exquisite 'Recognition' scene, on receipt of which Strauss wrote: 'Your verses when Elektra recognises Orestes are marvellous and already set to music. You are the born librettist – the greatest compliment to my mind, since I consider it much more difficult to write a good operatic text than a fine play.' Hofmannsthal provided three pages of new verse for the concluding duet, while at the same time working on 'their' comedy.

In August Strauss moved into his villa at Garmisch and on September 22, 1908, he drew a line beneath the full score of *Elektra*. Weingartner made a doomed bid to première the new work, but Schuch, and Dresden, were Strauss's first and only choice for *Elektra*'s proud parents. Again, the composer's impatience made life for the conductor miserable. Strauss wanted the première as soon as possible; Schuch wanted more time than he had been allowed to prepare *Salome*. However, the composer knew that Dresden had scheduled a 'Strauss Week' for the end of January 1909; and so, with a little negotiation, it was agreed that the première of *Elektra* would make a memorable opening night.

Strauss devoted most of the last three months of 1908 to preparations. In October he travelled to Dresden to audition the company's leading singers. Much of his work had been done for him, since many of the prospective cast had worked on *Feuersnot* and *Salome*. Karl Perron was cast as Orestes, Ernestine Schumann-Heink as Klytemnestra and Margarethe Siems (later to sing the first Marschallin in *Rosenkavalier*) as Chrysothemis. Carl Burian was still Dresden's leading tenor, but both Strauss and Schuch considered his voice and appearance too heroic to portray the snivelling Aegysthus. The *Spieltenor* Johannes Sembach was granted this questionable honour.

According to Strauss, the title role demanded 'the highest and most dramatic soprano who can be found'; he was fortunate in being able to turn to Annie Krull, Dresden's leading soprano. Schuch did little to disguise his preference for Krull, a singer blessed with intelligence as well as voice; and both he and Strauss were thrilled at how quickly and professionally she grasped the psychology of the role as well as the complexion of the music. There were many rehearsals and, as Strauss later recalled, the production was 'extremely carefully prepared by the conscientious Schuch'.

There were also meetings between Strauss and the director George Toller, the designer Emil Rieck and the costumer Leonhard Fanto, but it was to the rehearsals that Strauss paid the greatest attention. This was, after all, the most contrapuntally complex work of music ever written, scored for sixteen named singers, a chorus and 111 orchestral musicians playing over 140 instruments including piccolos, a Heckelphone, two basset horns, clarinets in E flat, B flat and A, tubas, bass trombones and tubas, eight timpani, a vast percussion section incorporating glockenspiel, triangle, tambourine, side drum, twig bush, cymbals, bass drum and tam-tam, a celeste, two harps and a string section of sixty-three – divided into ten sections.

Schuch worked strenuously, honing individual sections until something approximating the right sort of balance was achieved; but it was never more than approximate for, as Strauss conceded, he had forgotten that 'such complicated polyphony will only become quite plastic and lucid after years, when the orchestra has it almost by heart'. Schuch did not help matters, since his compassion for the struggling singers compelled him to moderate the scale and clamour – dissipating the theatrical immediacy of a score that Strauss had already heard to perfection in his head. The composer's disappointment was habitual and frequently obvious. Strauss recalled: 'My continued insistence on secondary thematic parts annoyed Schuch so much that he played with such fury during the dress rehearsal that I was forced to make the humbled confession ' "The orchestra was really a little too strong today." "You see," said Schuch triumphantly, and the first performance had perfect balance.'

The première was reported internationally. The critics conceded the work's technical mastery, and most applauded the stamina and perseverance of the cast; but, as Paul Bekker noted, it lacked 'the element of the piquant, the titillating, the sensuality torn between voluptuousness and fear found in *Salome*'. There was also a general sense that, musically, he had gone too far, that *Elektra* was simply too much noise and bluster. Strauss attempted to defend his ambitions, remarking to one journalist: 'When a mother is slain on the stage, do they expect me to write a violin concerto?'

The myriad cartoons, puns and jokes to which the opera was subjected at the time established *Elektra*, for the earliest audiences as well as for our own, as the apogee of modernity. Strauss himself enjoyed telling how, during a rehearsal, a cleaner had entered one of the boxes and begun to rummage while Schuch was talking to his players. Irritated by the interruption, Schuch turned and yelled at the poor woman, 'What are you looking for?', to which Strauss replied, 'A triad.' Elsewhere, the popular press published images of elephantine orchestras, 'electrocuted' musicians and, in one cartoon, an Intendant informing the composer that there was no one in the auditorium to hear the performance as everyone was in the pit. One paper claimed that for his next opera Strauss was planning to score for four locomotives, ten jaguars and a herd of rhino.

It is easy to see how the popular impression of *Elektra* was fostered. Even today, critics and biographers persist with an analytical vernacular in which the ugly and the shocking are emphasised as if these were the opera's cardinal qualities. This misreading of *Elektra* has done irreparable damage to Strauss's reputation, allowing the work's surface to define its substance. As Bekker wrote shortly after the première: 'Seldom, I think, has the outward success of a work of art, its public reception at the moment of its performance, had less in common with its artistic value than was the case with Strauss's *Elektra*.'

With hindsight, *Elektra* is a work of almost conventional lyricism, and probably Strauss's most fluid score, as singable and melodious as anything by Mozart, as traditionally inclined as *Guntram*. Strauss recognised that any genuine appreciation of *Elektra* would take time, study, routinely ideal performance conditions and a conductor able to execute the work as if it were 'by Mendelssohn: Fairy Music'. Strauss knew that if contemporary music were looking for a champion he was not the man. In 1907 he embarked on a three-month spell as editor of *Der Morgen*, a weekly music magazine, and in his first issue he wrote an essay entitled 'Is there an avant-garde in music?', the content of which can be easily guessed at.

Coincident to this essay, and some six months before *Elektra* was played to the public, developments were unfolding in Vienna which replaced Strauss as the 'Leader of the Moderns'. In 1908 Schoenberg started to refine the path that led him to atonality, and with his Three Piano Pieces, Op. 11 and the song cycle *Buch der hängenden Gärten*, he became the darling of the progressive musical establishment. The controversy encircling these works reached many more ears than did the works themselves, but their impact was considerable for the younger generation of composers, for whom Strauss was still pre-eminent. With his monodrama *Erwartung*, completed the same year as *Elektra*, Schoenberg was established, amongst his immediate contemporaries at least, as the new Messiah of German music.

Erwartung, Schoenberg's first work for the stage, provides a perfect foil against which to consider *Elektra*'s conjectural modernity. It was inspired by personal experience – the suicide of the painter Richard Gerstl – and written as a private confessional. Schoenberg's librettist Marie Pappenheim was a medical student as well as a poet, and her 'stream of consciousness' text provides little narrative since the drama's 'unnamed woman' is alone and near to madness. Schoenberg matched Pappenheim's nebulous language with music of an almost improvisatory expressionism; the rapidity of the mood-swings, the rhythmic freedom, the *Sprechgesang* declamation and the absence of pulse and tonality generate a haunting sense of timelessness, as if the drama were unfolding inside the woman's head.

Conversely, Hofmannsthal's *Elektra* is a work of symbolist naturalism. His use of language is pictorial and suggestive, but the dramatic narrative is both exhaustively theatrical and unmistakably coherent. The wealth of symbolic imagery is overshadowed by a weakness for his characters and their circumstances. A concern with motive, character and – most importantly – event precluded a genuinely contemporary interpretation of Sophocles' tragedy. Strauss responded to motive and character considerably better than to the uncertain human frailties being revealed by Freud.

It is frequently stated that Hofmannsthal read Freud and Breuer's *Studies on Hysteria* (1895) before writing *Elektra*, as if this provides sufficient ordnance to support a 'modernist' interpretation of his play. He was also conversant with Freud's psychoanalytical interpretation of *Hamlet*, and with Hermann Bahr's psychoanalytical reading of Greek tragedy. There are clear parallels between Hofmannsthal's drama – in which is depicted Elektra's father-fixation, her abused sexuality and the 'trance-like state' of her dance – and Freud's (and Jung's) explorations of the human subconscious; but they tell us little about the opera.

Hofmannsthal was creating cogent and intelligible narrative dramas at a time when, in response to Freud's theories of repression and the unconscious, most of his contemporaries were amplifying, not containing, human neuroses. As such, *Elektra* owes more to the tragic nobility of Sophocles in its pacing and construction than to the fractured neurasthenic horrors revealed by Freud. Elektra and Orestes are grand, driven creatures, motivated by cognitive emotional stimuli that allow for a bravery and heroism incompatible with Expressionism.

Strauss wanted a return to fluency, to the sort of principles that cried out for his skills as a tone poet. There is more naturalist pictorialism in his score (such as the representation of barking dogs and the jangling of Klytemnestra's jewellery) than psychoanalysis (as typified by Schoenberg's representation of 'the Woman's' stumbling through a forest), and he evidently found the more shocking parts of Hofmannsthal's play unsettable. While at ease with Hofmannsthal's luminous Symbolism (the blood that runs through the drama also saturates the score), he was less comfortable with its potent sexual imagery – most of which he cut. Elektra's explicit delight in her own body, her celebration of sexual as well as emotional and physical impotence (her failure to bring forth children being set against her failure to dig up the axe and kill her mother), the inherent sexual tension between mother and daughters and the psychosexual cruelty of Aegysthus are all excised. Strauss was left with a narrative shell, to which he asked Hofmannsthal to add appropriately nineteenth-century formulae, such as the Recognition scene and the final duet – both of which soften the drama's edges.

The stage directions for the final dance – set to a near-hysterical waltz – require Elektra to throw 'back her head like a Maenad, thrusting her knees high in forward movement, flinging her arms wide apart: it is a dance of indescribable intensity.' This allusion to the Bacchantes, worshippers of the god Dionysus who manipulated the vulnerable through the primeval urges of Nature, attests to Strauss's romantic pantheism; Elektra is no 'Rat-Man', rather she is the embodiment of a Nietzschean belief in strength and per-severance, of loyalty and commitment, of rebirth through tragedy.

Like *Salome*, *Elektra* is a tragedy of the passions, not the psyche. Each of the characters is defined by an emotion: Elektra is hatred, Chrysothemis is longing, Klytemnestra is fear, and Orestes is love. Hofmannsthal even confessed, in 1911, that he had written *Elektra* as 'a vehicle for emotions', and if the drama lacks event (there is only one scene of consequential action – the murders – and these occur offstage) the text makes constant reference to past and future events – inviting Strauss to score the drama, and the *dramatis personae*, as a tone poem. In this respect, Strauss's music is decidedly nineteenth-century.

While it is true that he employed a remarkable, frequently bitonal har-monic range – sailing close to atonality during Klytemnestra's harrowing monologue – his score represents the fulfilment of late Romanticism, not the deposition of modernism. It is hard for many, when first seeing the opera, to hear the birdsong for all the traffic, as the wealth of dissonance and the variety of orchestral sound can easily disguise the score's hypnotic simplicity. Indeed, even those used to the work can mistake the *Schwung* of Strauss's all too easy virtuosity for empty gesture. But there is not one ill-considered bar in the score. Only when played to perfection or, better still, at the piano, is it possible to appreciate fully its paradoxical curiosities. Like a modern-day film composer, Strauss was tailoring music to a libretto, and Hofmannsthal's libretto demanded hysteria and violence. What makes *Elektra* so remarkable is that Strauss was able to amplify these qualities without once surrendering his genius for expressive melody; it is the very regressiveness of the score's construction that makes its achievement as a work of 'modernist' opera all the more astonishing. That *Elektra* is not the modernist credo understood by received opinion does Strauss's reputation no harm. Indeed, his ability to create such a powerful, psychologically affecting opera while remaining true to his romantic convictions is confirmation, if any were required, of his stature as one of the greatest composers in the history of Western music.

His box of tricks is endlessly fascinating, and the skill with which he created such a complicated, multi-voiced backdrop against which to set his unique style of through-composed lyricism is bewildering; but it is necessary to understand that the 'innovations' of *Elektra* stemmed, for the most part, from the innovations of Richard Wagner. This in no way lessens Strauss's accomplishment, it merely illustrates the direction in which he was looking at the time. Each of the score's tonalities comes in contrasted tonic major/minor pairs, mirroring Hofmannsthal's dramatic parallels. For example, while the opening D minor establishes the horror of the first scene it is also the defining tonality when Chrysothemis cries out 'Orestes is dead'; later it is used to announce Orestes's arrival and, finally, it ushers in the denouement. Such cyclic tonalities are typical of Wagner, as of all late Romantic music, but it is the constant play of contrasts, both harmonic and tonal, that emphasises *Elektra*'s romantic bedrock. There is much use of deliberate contradiction – whereby line and chord are consciously thrust against one another – and the seven sections are constructed along the lines of the earlier tone poems, with each passing episode adding more and more layers to the dramatic canvas until, sixty-three leitmotifs later,[10] Strauss brings everything together in his own climactic immolation scene.

The broad, singing lines, the concordant metre and the prevailing tonal consonance tie the work yet further to the cyclical, melodramatic world of Wagner, and – in the right hands – the horror and violence of Hofmannsthal's drama is couched in music of extravagant beauty. The opera's finest scenes – Elektra's soaring monologue, Chrysothemis's hymn to motherhood, the Recognition scene and the final duet – are irresistibly powerful expressions of emotional states; and, in particular, the denouement underlines Strauss's consuming obsession with beauty. The sweep and majesty of this duet, viewed purely as the product of technique, is a miracle; but it is a miracle animated by traditions already established by Mozart and Wagner – whereby the finale consolidates most, if not all, of the preceding episodes, emphasising the opera's concentrated, cyclic progress. Nowhere is the orthodoxy of *Elektra* more evident than at its end, when Strauss brings the 6/4 waltz grinding to a halt with a triumphant plunge into C major – the most consonant and positive tonality in music. The anxiety and atonality of *Erwartung* are joyfully rejected, and with Elektra lying dead before the gates of Agamemnon's palace, Strauss confirmed both the conventions of his past and the conservatism of his future.

January 1909–January 1911

Hofmannsthal had been the first to applaud Strauss's *Elektra*. He was also the first to admit that it was not, and could not be referred to as, a collaboration. Aside from his limited contribution to the creative process he winced at the overpowering character of Strauss's music. A comedy would necessitate a less inflated approach from the composer if audiences were to understand events on stage. It is not difficult to imagine Hofmannsthal's delight when, with reference to an earlier conversation, he was able to write to Strauss:

> Before I tackle this new task ... we must get entirely clear between us the style in which you mean to write this opera. If I rightly understand the hints you threw out and which struck me as immensely promising, you intend to create something altogether novel in style, something which (since every development in the arts proceeds in cycles) will resemble more closely the older type of opera[1] ... You intend, unless I wholly misunderstood your hints, to alternate set numbers with passages which approximate to the old secco recitative.

He added triumphantly, 'I very much hope that the result will earn me the proud title of librettist which I shall value most highly.'

Hofmannsthal toyed with various ideas, each of them a reflection of his consuming obsession with the past. Many of his poems, particularly those written during his precocious adolescence (when he signed his work 'Loris'), comment on the present through a romantic fascination with obsolete cultures and civilisations ('Weariness of long forgotten races I cannot brush off my eyelids'). This longing for a sense of historical connection, allied to an almost paranoid fear of contemporary association, runs through his work up to and including *Rosenkavalier*, notably *Das kleine Welttheater*, *Das Bergwerk zu Falun*, *Oedipus und die Sphinx* and *Cristinas Heimreise* – the title he eventually gave to *Casanova*. When he finally decided on the idea for *Rosenkavalier* it came to him as a completed canvas – with the language, period and characters in place – rather than as an isolated character-driven scenario; and like each of Hofmannsthal's librettos it was as animated by its setting as by its plot.

The idea was drafted during the first week of February, 1909. On the 11th Hofmannsthal wrote to Strauss:

> I have spent three quiet afternoons here drafting the full and entirely original scenario for an opera, full of burlesque situations and characters, with lively action, pellucid almost like a pantomime. There are opportunities in it for lyrical passages, for fun and humour, even for a small ballet. I find the scenario enchanting and Count Kessler[2] with whom I discussed it is delighted with it. It contains two big parts, one for baritone and another for a graceful girl dressed up as an old man, à la Farrar or Mary Garden. Period: the old Vienna under the Empress Maria Theresa.

Hofmannsthal began work soon after, and on March 16 he wrote to Strauss informing him of progress on Act I, and of his concern for Strauss's needs as a composer. It is clear from this letter that Hofmannsthal had finally resigned himself to the singular complexion of the operatic libretto. No longer was he attempting to write a stage play to which music might later be married; he had come to see himself as the ostensible saviour of contemporary operatic theatre, the one man capable of restoring intellectual rigour to an art form that had long been the bastard child of European literature. But Hofmannsthal was under no illusions. He understood the significance of his contribution, later writing to Strauss: 'Your music only adds something very beautiful, something which is naturally far more than actors or the designer of the scenery could ever offer me.'

From Garmisch, on April 21, 1909, Strauss acknowledged receipt of the first 'delightful' scenes: 'It'll set itself to music like oil and melted butter: I'm hatching it out already. You're Da Ponte and Scribe rolled into one.' Hofmannsthal reacted politely to this ambivalent compliment, noting that 'Scribe as well as Da Ponte worked perhaps within a somewhat simpler convention...'

While Hofmannsthal concentrated on their eighteenth-century 'distraction', Strauss flew around Europe after *Elektra*, which was proving almost as popular as its established sister *Salome*. In February Leo Blech conducted the first Berlin production at the Royal Court Opera, and Felix Mottl conducted the first Bavarian performances at Munich's Court Opera; Weingartner, who was now openly hostile towards Strauss and his music, none the less gave the first Austrian performance at the Vienna Court Opera in March, and in April Strauss travelled to Milan to hear Tullio Serafin give the Italian première at La Scala. He reported to Hofmannsthal that this last performance had been 'surprisingly good: Krucziniska as Elektra first rate in every respect, the other parts vocally excellent – I've never heard the opera sung so beautifully. Orchestra very good, success colossal, the biggest taking of the season. I think we've now definitely turned the corner with *Elektra*. Congratulations to you and myself.'

The poet replied 'As *Elektra* has slain her thousands, I look forward to our slaying with this comedy tens of thousands'; probably as a gesture to Strauss he added, 'rather like Saul and David in the Bible, and they like us had to face the Philistines'. In a carefully worded postscript he warned Strauss that not everything in his libretto would prove as conducive to music as the first scenes: 'There are bound to be sticky passages too, but none I hope where I have not explored with much thought the possibilities of musical interpretation ... and the "good" passages will, I believe, outnumber the others.' That Hofmannsthal was now thinking as a librettist as well as a poet is further confirmed by his now legendary advice to the composer: 'Do try and think of an old-fashioned Viennese waltz, sweet and yet saucy, which must pervade the whole of the last act.'

Hofmannsthal addressed everything to Strauss at his villa in Garmisch. The sabbatical from Berlin did not expire until October 1909; apart from new productions of *Elektra*, and a small number of guest conducting engagements, Strauss was free to divide his time between Pauline, their twelve-year-old son and *Ochs von Lerchenau*, as *Rosenkavalier* was known during its composition. The collaborators met infrequently, mainly because Hofmannsthal cared little for Strauss's company, and positively detested his wife.

On March 16, for example, Hofmannsthal wrote to Strauss, suggesting times when they might meet at his rococo castle in Rodaun, near Vienna: 'It would be very nice of you if you could come out here for an evening, we could talk everything over at leisure and that would be a real gain. But if your wife were to come too, we could not do that, for she would of course be bored: and we have nothing whatever to offer her out here except melting snow. And since I am sure you prefer to play skat in the evening, I should also willingly come to town one of these days between six and eight.' Strauss's reply, in December, referred to a recent visit by Hofmannsthal to the apartment on Joachimstaaler Strasse, during which Pauline evidently lost her temper: 'I hope you will come again to Berlin – and I promise you that my "original" of a wife won't throw her keys into the room.'

Garmisch was a mere 260 miles from Rodaun. Both men had access to cars, Strauss to a chauffeur, and they made regular use of the excellent railway system for business, but neither went out of his way to visit the other. Pauline appears to have reacted badly to the over-sensitive poet, and Strauss well knew how even the most robust souls found her intolerable; but Hofmannsthal went out of his way to avoid Strauss even if he knew Pauline would not be joining him. When, in 1919, the composer moved to the Vienna Court Opera, and a short drive from Rodaun, Hofmannsthal still found excuses for not welcoming his colleague. Eventually, caring little for Strauss's feelings, he was reduced to submitting candid, humourless rejections: 'It is most kind of you to offer to come out here, but please don't think of it under any circumstances; the tram journey of one and three-quarter hours each way is torture, and I do not enjoy visitors.'

In character and personality Strauss and Hofmannsthal could not have been more different. Hofmannsthal was an aristocrat and an aesthete. Self-consciously emotional and famously quick to take offence, he was also prone to severe depression, endured extended bouts of self-hatred, and suffered crises of confidence during which he was incapable of confronting the world outside his study. On September 9, 1909, he admitted to Strauss that he was suffering 'a tiresome interruption in the middle of my work, a slight but most deplorable nervous depression. As a result I have done practically nothing for the past three weeks...'

Having inherited wealth as a young man, Hofmannsthal had no need for an income, a freedom that allowed him to produce work unsullied by commercial instincts; he was an unadulterated snob, as aware of his genea-logical superiority as was Pauline, and he would inwardly cringe if reminded of his paternal grandfather, whose Jewish ancestry was a cause of shame and irritation. He despised small talk, craved encouragement and fed off flattery. He feared the cold, refused to allow central heating to ruin his castle's period charm, and was incapable of working if the temperature in his study was a degree above or below ideal. He was repelled by the vaguest suspicion of vulgarity. His comic play *Der Schwierige* depicts an Austrian aristocrat whose aversion to coarseness leaves him incapable of self-expression; Hofmannsthal was so liable to embarrassment, and so fearful of middle-class society, that he felt it necessary to stay away from Garmisch if he and Strauss were ever to enjoy a successful collaboration.

Strauss, on the other hand, was irredeemably bucolic. He relished light conversation and generalised debate. He was insensitive, on occasion pain-fully so, and prickled at the first sign of pretension. He was confident, seemingly untouched by self-doubt, and possessed an earthy sense of humour – and all in spite of Pauline's public and determined admonitions. Regardless of his extensive travels Strauss's instincts were unmistakably prov-incial and as Bavarian as his birthplace, while the Austrian Hofmannsthal – though less travelled – spoke five languages, read as many non-German as German authors and embraced the world, not merely those parts of it in which German was the mother tongue.

For all this, the working relationship was well balanced, with each bols-tering the other's weaknesses. Strauss's instinctive flair for the theatre ensured that Hofmannsthal was periodically reminded of his audience ('I do not find anything more distasteful than plays which do not draw, and are written for the proverbial five perceptive spectators'), while Hofmannsthal raised

Strauss's game, helping him to resist the vulgar and meretricious, and urging him to develop some small measure of sophistication.

Mutual incomprehension precluded friendship. Hofmannsthal failed to penetrate the paradoxical tensions between Strauss's diffidence and the rapture of his music. He never understood, or accepted, that the composer of *Elektra*'s barely contained ecstasy was simply not a romantic – or, at least, not sufficiently romantic to embrace the mystical, quasi-religious theorising dear to Hofmannsthal. The creative process for Strauss was a means to an end. For Hofmannsthal, like Mahler, that process *was* the end.

Ochs von Lerchenau occupied them throughout the spring of 1909. On May 4 Strauss received the completed first act from Hofmannsthal. He wrote to say that he was 'simply delighted. It is charming beyond measure: so delicate, maybe a little too delicate for the general mob, but that doesn't matter.' A few days later Hofmannsthal replied: 'Your apprehension lest the libretto be too "delicate" does not make me nervous. Even the least sophisticated audience cannot help finding the action simple and intelligible: a pompous, fat, and elderly suitor favoured by the father has his nose put out of joint by a dashing young lover – could anything be plainer.' He urged Strauss to remember that their work must be 'free from anything trivial and conventional. True and lasting success depends upon the effect on the more sensitive *no less than* on the coarser sections of the public, for the former are needed to give a work of art its prestige which is just as essential as its popular appeal.' Hofmannsthal was already sensing something of Strauss's 'poor taste', even if he lacked the confidence to confront it.

At the end of May Richard and Pauline were visited in Garmisch by Edward Elgar and his wife, who admired the 'beautifully fitted & kept' house; Elgar was less taken with Pauline, who controlled access to the manuscripts, securing the key on a chain beneath her skirts. On June 1 Strauss left Garmisch for music festivals in Aachen and Stuttgart. He returned a week later, whereupon Hofmannsthal made one of his rare visits, to hear Strauss play through his music for the first act. Writing on the 12th, Hofmannsthal confirmed his satisfaction: 'Everything you played me from the first act of the opera is most beautiful and has given me great and lasting pleasure'; typically, however, his compliments prefaced a storm of indignation: 'Allow me to speak quite frankly: a detail in the aria of Ochs distressed me profoundly when I heard it. The line "Muss halt eine Frau in der Nähe dabei sein" can never conceivably be acted or sung in any but a sentimental manner. Ochs must whisper it to the Marschallin as a stupid and yet sly piece of coarse familiarity, with his hand half covering his mouth; he must whisper, not bawl it, for God's sake! It cut me to the quick to hear him shout the word "hay" at *fortissimo*.' To Kessler he wrote, 'Strauss is such an incredibly unrefined person, he has such a frightful bent towards triviality and kitsch ... vulgarity rises as easily in him as ground-water.'

In his reply, dated June 26, Strauss made no reference to Hofmannsthal's outburst, but his eyebrows must have risen, since he was unused to anyone, far less a collaborator, invoking such strong terms over an issue of transient significance. Strauss was beginning to realise that Hofmannsthal's disposition was singularly delicate, and even the slightest misjudgement on his part was an occasion for outrage. For this reason alone, Strauss's demands of his librettist were often audaciously pragmatic: 'Could you possibly write me some 12 to 16 lines in the following rhythm ...' he wrote, 'can't think of anything better at the moment: it's the rhythm that matters. Some such popular vaudeville poem: about 3 verses, 12 lines. On the above pattern!'

Strauss's pragmatism was all-pervading. Throughout the dozens of letters that passed between them during the summer months of 1909 he urged Hofmannsthal to remember for whom he was writing his play. On July 9 he sent a long and complex letter in which he demonstrated the acuteness of his theatrical perception: 'I hope you won't be angry with me. But I feel that, as it now stands, I can't do anything with the second act. It's too much on one level. I must have a great dramatic construction if I want to keep myself interested for so long in a particular setting.' The letter was so astute and so comprehensively unarguable that Hofmannsthal had little choice but to 'make the alterations ... as soon as possible'. For his part, Hofmannsthal nurtured Strauss's sense of proportion, at one stage imploring him to protect Octavian and Sophie ('who have nothing of the Valkyries or *Tristan* about them') from the 'Wagnerian kind of erotic screaming' for which Strauss, post-*Elektra*, was celebrated; but there was little reason for any such apprehension. Apart from the second act, which caused considerable anguish, the process of composition flowed, as Strauss noted to Hofmannsthal, 'like the Loisach' running through his garden.

At the end of September Strauss wrote to Hofmannsthal: 'Act II is now composed and, I believe, has turned out a first-class hit ... I am satisfied with myself.' He hoped to begin orchestrating the short score in Berlin where, from October 1, he was again Music Director of the Court Opera. In Berlin, Strauss was fortunate to enjoy the support and good offices of Leo Blech, who was happy to take on an ever greater weight of responsibility. Without his help Strauss would not have so quickly completed *Rosenkavalier*'s orchestrations, and neither would he have so much enjoyed conducting *Elektra*, which Blech had honed to a point just short of perfection. So well prepared was the production that Strauss conducted twenty-seven performances between October 1909 and March 1910.

The characteristically passive Hülsen raised no objections to Blech shouldering Strauss's duties. Allowing his music director unprecedented freedom, Hülsen granted Strauss leave whenever it was requested. Strauss duly gave notice that he would be taking a week off in February to attend the first production of *Elektra* in Holland and a week off in March to attend the

English première. To Hülsen's relief Strauss resisted an invitation, from Oscar Hammerstein, to attend the American première of *Elektra*, also in February.

In an attempt to ape the rival New York Metropolitan Opera, Hammerstein had, at enormous expense, bought the rights to *Elektra*. It was a questionable investment. He appears not to have appreciated the number of players required by the score, and the ten weeks of rehearsals cost him a staggering fifteen thousand dollars at a time when a balcony seat at his Manhattan Opera cost just one dollar. The unfortunate man was forced to proceed (convinced, in part, by the house conductor Cleofonte Campanini), although he grumbled incessantly that the work was upsetting 'both my singers and my orchestra'.

The first night, on February 1, was played (in French!) before a full house. As the curtain fell the audience of three thousand rose, producing an unbroken cheer that, according to one observer, became 'almost hysterical in quality'. Gustav and Alma Mahler were present although, if Alma is to be believed, neither of them enjoyed the experience: 'Mahler disliked it so much that he wanted to go out in the middle. We sat it out, but agreed afterwards that we had seldom in our lives been so bored.' Neither she nor her husband seem to have been impressed by the evening's Elektra, Mariette Marazin,[3] who invested so much effort into the part that she visibly fainted at the point in the score where she was supposed to drop dead. Upon waking for her curtain calls she stated that she fully expected to faint after every performance. It was, she noted, entirely worth it. In Boston, a few weeks later, the city première was heard in 'a silence so tense that the orchestra seemed at moments the expression of the answering emotions of the audience as well as of the emotions of the drama'. At the end there was 'an instant of recovering silence', followed by an 'applause so intense that it seemed a new and strange and exciting thing'.

The English première was mounted by Thomas Beecham, at Covent Garden, on February 19, 1910, with the American soprano Edyth Walker (and later Annie Krull and Zdenka Fassbender[4]) as Elektra, Anna von Bahr-Mildenburg (of Vienna) as Klytemnestra, Frances Rose as Chrysothemis and Friedrich Weidemann as Orestes. The extended run of nine performances was a colossal success. During the two weeks prior to the opera's première both popular and broadsheet newspapers daily devoted at least half a page to Strauss and his new work. On February 7 the *Daily News*'s 'Music Notes' mischievously reported: 'Dr Strauss I understand is to receive £200[5] for each night he conducts the work – and this apart from the royalties he draws for every performance.' Much was also made of the cost to Beecham of obtaining the rights to perform *Elektra* in London. Not only was Strauss to receive a royalty on every performance, but before the publishers released any music a one-off payment, in lieu of copyright, of £5,500[6] had to be paid. This vast sum[7] was expected of every opera house at which the work was being produced. In the five years following *Elektra*'s birth there were nearly forty such productions, the copyright for which amounted, in general terms, to somewhere around £220,000 between 1910 and 1914.[8]

No mention was made of *Salome* (which was still the victim of British censorship), of Strauss's obvious talent, or the opera in question. Elsewhere, society's conscience-ridden puffed out their cheeks with indignation, registering 'complaints about costs of the *Elektra* season, with £7,500[9] being given over to the new work which is costing £1,500 a night'. Strauss was being paid huge sums of money, but he was considered worth the investment. So much so that tickets for the first night were available on the black market for up to ten times their face value.

The critical response ranged from the adulation of the *Daily Telegraph* ('very beautiful') and the *Morning Post* ('splendid in force and conviction'), to the disdain of the *Evening Standard* ('we cannot resist the feeling that the vital spark of genius is wanting') and the *Daily News* ('seldom is the note of real tragedy sounded, and on the whole the music lacks conviction'). The most heartfelt criticism came from Ernest Newman, writing for the *Nation*, who furnished a bitter, misguided review: 'much of the music is as abominably ugly as it is noisy ... one would hardly venture to prophesy more than a few short years for *Elektra* ...' In response, George Bernard Shaw wrote to the *Nation*: 'May I, as an old critic of music, and as a member of the public who has not yet heard *Elektra*, make an appeal to Mr Ernest Newman to give us something about that work a little less ridiculous and idiotic than his article in your last issue ... this infatuated attempt of writers of modest local standing to talk *de haut en bas* of men of European reputation ... is an intolerable thing.'

In March Strauss arrived in London to conduct two performances of *Elektra*, on the 12th and 15th. An excellent report of his conducting, diminished only by its curiously disappointed account of Strauss's appearance, was published by the *Daily Mail*:

> The tall, pale man with the dome-shaped head, the huge, smooth brow, the steel-blue eyes, sat slightly bent forward with a glow on his delicate features which are those of a lyric poet, rather than of a musical giant. His thin, long hand held the tapering baton like a pen. His head was immobile; only his eagle eyes flashed from time to time towards Elektra or Chrysothemis on the stage, towards the strings at his feet around him, the brass on his right, the percussion on his left. His elbows seemed riveted to his body. The sobriety of his gestures was striking. The baton did not cleave the air with fantastic arabesques; he seemed a mathematician writing a formula on an imaginary blackboard neatly and with supreme knowledge.

Strauss's interpretation was predictably exciting. Accents were exaggerated, tempi were doubled and, despite the economy of his gestures, both orchestra and soloists had to work considerably harder for Strauss than for Beecham. Queen Alexandra, Strauss's foremost admirer in England, was in attendance. Less than an hour after curtain-down Strauss was whisked to the Savoy Hotel where 150 guests – including Lord Howard de Walden, Lady Cunard, the impresario Beerbohm Tree, the actor Henry Irving, Percy Pitt and Edward Elgar – had paid to dine with him.

Strauss returned to Garmisch towards the end of April, from where he wrote to Hofmannsthal that he was in 'agonies waiting' for the third act of *Rosenkavalier*. The poet replied: 'I am really quite upset to learn you are "waiting in agonies". In the first place I did not expect you to be at home and at leisure, for I seem to read constantly of your flitting here, there and everywhere.' He was none the less able to send Strauss a sizeable portion of the final act on May 1, and the completed draft was in Garmisch four days later.

Composition was interrupted by the death of Strauss's mother, Josephine, on May 16. The news came as no surprise: she had been weak and divorced from reality for some time; and since Franz's death Richard had found progressively less time for his mother – leaving the weight of responsibility with Johanna. Only four days later he was back at work, although Hofmannsthal may, at first, have wished he had taken a longer leave of absence. In his letter of May 20 Strauss explained how the final scenes were 'not at all' to his liking, and he outlined the changes he considered necessary if the final act were to have 'one thing bursting on top of another'. Hofmannsthal was sympathetic to Strauss's judgement, and agreed to most, if not all, of his proposals.

Work on the score was again interrupted in June by the demands of another 'Strauss Week', this time in Munich where, no longer a prophet in his own land, he was venerated as the city's greatest living son. On the 24th he conducted a performance of *Salome* with Edyth Walker as the princess. In a letter to his sister, Otto Klemperer drily noted that Walker's performance had been 'better than the work itself'. July saw considerable progress; Hofmannsthal was delighted, so much so that on the 4th he wrote to Strauss: 'Since we are now on the point of bringing our joint labours, so to speak, to a conclusion, I would like to tell you how much I have enjoyed working with you from the first discussion down to the last letter, not forgetting your occasional very valuable objections and to thank you most sincerely.'

On September 10 Hofmannsthal agreed that the honour of the first night should again go to Dresden. Schuch and his Intendant, Count Seebach, assumed that the process would be less traumatic than the three previous premières. They were mistaken. Far from resting on the laurels that bound him to Dresden, Strauss – doubtless encouraged by Pauline – decided to capitalise on his influence. Mottl (Munich) and Weingartner (Vienna) were keen to break the Dresden/Strauss alliance; how keen depended upon how much. Strauss considered all offers while at the same time presenting Dresden with an heroically enterprising set of terms: they could have *Rosenkavalier*, but only if they agreed to ten years' performances of *Feuersnot*[10] and *Elektra*. Seebach was dumbfounded; were he to agree, an impossible precedent would have been set for Germany's operatic culture.

Strauss was not the first composer to find himself with the influence necessary to hold an opera house to ransom, but he was the first to exercise it. Seebach took Strauss's threat seriously. It was inconceivable that a composer, even one so powerful as Strauss, be allowed to dictate repertoire to an Intendant. The only possible solution was to inform his colleagues, and the press, of Strauss's conditions. Strauss attempted to defend his position, claiming that it was only right that he do whatever he could to ensure the preservation of his music. As a composer, he was forever at the mercy of others (conductors, impresarios, producers, etc.) and it seemed only reasonable that he should try and retain some measure of influence over the fate of his less popular works. On September 12 he confirmed to Hofmannsthal that 'at the last minute Seebach did not sign the contract, and now the whole Bühnen-verein[11] is up in arms against me because of my unheard of conditions. I am still fighting, but whether I shall win is, to say the least, questionable at the moment.' At the foot of this letter he added, 'I shan't win but the world première is going to be in Dresden all the same.'

A few hours after writing this letter Strauss travelled to Munich for the first performance of Mahler's Eighth Symphony. The concert's presentation, by the 'Barnum and Bailey' impresario Emil Gutmann, was on a grand scale. No fewer than 1,030 musicians had been engaged to take part[12] (thus Gutmann's ascription 'Symphony of a Thousand'), and there were three days of rehearsals. Not even the most recent of Strauss's premières had attracted an equivalent number and variety of luminaries. Sitting alongside Strauss were Arnold Schoenberg, Anton Webern, Siegfried Wagner, Alfredo Casella, Bruno Walter, Leopold Stokowski, Willem Mengelberg, Oscar Fried, Anna von Bahr-Mildenburg, Alfred Roller, Max Reinhardt, Arnold Berliner, Kolomon Moser and Thomas Mann. Many other celebrated artists, thinkers, musicians, poets and writers attended – many queuing for tickets – and the air of ceremony and reverence was so potent that, according to Maurice Baumfeld, when Mahler walked on stage to conduct, 'the entire audience, as if responding to a secret signal, rose to its feet, initially in silence. The way a king is greeted ...' For whatever reason, Strauss made no mention of the event in his correspondence, and he appears not to have gone backstage after the concluding half-hour ovation had died down. If the two composers did meet, neither made mention of it to anyone. Strauss was never to see Mahler again.

A few weeks later the proprietor of the *Münchner Neuste Nachrichten* newspaper invited Strauss to a reception and musical soirée where he was encouraged to play excerpts from *Rosenkavalier*. When he asked for a page-turner, the Viennese critic Julius Korngold, one of the composer's most hostile adversaries, was pushed to the front. The irony was not lost on Strauss, but Korngold enjoyed vicious revenge six months later, in April 1911, when he penned his now famous assassination of *Rosenkavalier* for the *Neue Freie Presse*.

In Garmisch, on September 26, Strauss completed the music for *Rosenkavalier*. He left almost immediately for Berlin, where he remained throughout October. Once the date of the première had been agreed (January 26, 1911) Dresden began to take bookings and Strauss and Hofmannsthal were able to concentrate on the difficult matters of staging and casting. The first setting rehearsals were expected to begin in mid-November, and while they both feared the lack of a *buffo* bass able to carry the role of Baron Ochs, Strauss's primary concern was George Toller, the producer at Dresden. Strauss later claimed it was during the first stage rehearsals, in January 1911, that he realised Toller was 'incapable'. Strauss urged Hofmannsthal to make his way to Dresden 'as the producer there is only an ordinary run-of-the-mill operatic producer and presumably hardly capable of staging a comedy like ours'.

Exactly when Strauss contacted Max Reinhardt is not known, but that he did so before making his way to Dresden is certain. Strauss had long admired Reinhardt, and Hofmannsthal thought him the finest producer in Germany. His productions of new work at the Kleines Theater were celebrated for their imagination and subtlety, but he made his name with a series of spectacular productions of popular repertoire, the majority distinguished through the singular use of music. In 1910 he mounted *Oedipus Rex* in a Viennese circus ring, and the following year he brought *The Miracle* to London's Olympia. He was famed for his stagings of Offenbach's operettas (notably his 1906 production of *Orphée aux enfers* at Berlin's Neue Theater) and it was inevitable that he should translate his talents to the operatic stage. At a time when Bayreuth and Berlin were revelling in their puffy antiquarian theatrics, Reinhardt was cultivating an urbane and laconic dramaturgy that would revolutionise the production of opera around the world.

When Strauss asked Seebach to allow Reinhardt to work on the production of *Rosenkavalier* the Intendant refused, reminding Strauss that Toller was Dresden's producer and that to invite another, more famous rival to 'assist' with the production would be tantamount to having Mahler share the rehearsals with Schuch. But Seebach could not deny Reinhardt's celebrity, and on December 30 Strauss confirmed, to Hofmannsthal, that Reinhardt would arrive in Dresden on January 10, 1911. Toller was not informed of this development, but read about it in the local paper. His considerable anger was brushed aside by Strauss, who tactlessly remarked that, instead of

complaining, Toller should be grateful for the support of someone so conspicuously gifted.

The tension between Toller and Reinhardt was contained since the Austrian
producer was also Jewish, and not allowed on stage during rehearsals.
Dresden and Seebach were notoriously anti-Semitic; the inclusion of a Jew
would have been abhorrent to many of those at the opera house, and it is
likely that Reinhardt (born Goldman) was induced to accommodate the
hostile environment for the sake of the project. While Toller and Strauss
attended to matters on stage Reinhardt stood in the wings, whispering his
advice to the singers as they passed; when Seebach, a pragmatic anti-Semite,
saw the fruits of Reinhardt's muted influence it was decided that he be allowed
complete freedom. The production was transformed – resulting, as Strauss
recalled, in 'a new style in opera'. Reinhardt's name still appeared nowhere
on the programme.

If events on stage proved uneven, the stage itself was flawless. Alfred Roller
was a celebrated artist and draftsman and co-founder of the first Viennese
Secession in 1900. Three years later he began a five-year[13] collaboration with
Mahler in Vienna that revolutionised the performance of opera in Europe.
In particular, his production of *Tristan und Isolde* in 1903 – with its startling
use of colour, lighting and symbolism – ushered in a long-overdue age of
post-Wagnerian theatrical design. With Mahler's resignation from the Court
Opera it was only a matter of time before Roller followed suit; but rather
than move to the United States he concentrated on cultivating his relationship
with Reinhardt at the Deutsches Theater in Berlin; it was here that Hofmannsthal and Strauss came into contact with Roller's unique vision.

In May 1909, a year-and-a-half before Strauss completed the score of
Rosenkavalier, Hofmannsthal reported that Roller was 'literally burning to
produce a production book containing designs (sets and costumes)'. By July
he had completed 'ground plans of the sets', and Strauss finally saw the
'magnificent' costume designs in April 1910. Later that month Hofmannsthal
urged Strauss to send Roller a piano score so that he could 'produce a
production book that will make it virtually impossible for even the stupidest
provincial opera producer to get the least grouping or nuance wrong'.

Inspired by the detailed stylisation of the Meiningen Theatre,[14] and the
Japanese artist Katsushika Hokusai, an exhibition of whose work in Vienna
in 1901 impressed him greatly, the sweeping lines and exaggerated expressions
of Roller's drawings for *Rosenkavalier* anticipate the sweep and grandeur of
Strauss's music. He left nothing to chance and, having become acquainted
with the music, produced designs that have never been bettered. Thanks to
Roller, *Rosenkavalier* is one of only three of Strauss's operas (the other two
being *Salome* and *Capriccio*) to have consistently resisted the ambition and
vanity of modern operatic producers.

For the première, numerous singers were considered for the four leads.

Hofmannsthal wanted Marie Gutheil-Schoder for the part of Octavian since 'so far as acting goes, she is the only person worth considering, and she also looks the part'; but Strauss chose instead the young Wagnerian Eva von der Osten. They agreed on the casting of Minnie Nast (a regular from *Feuersnot* and *Elektra*) as Sophie, and of Margarethe Siems (who had done a marvellous job as Chrysothemis) as the Marschallin.

The process was less straightforward when it came to Ochs. Everybody wanted Richard Mayr[15] for the première. His was one of the finest acting voices of the century, but he was based in Vienna, at the Court Opera, where the conductor Franz Schalk (under instruction from the new director Hans Gregor) refused to allow Mayr leave. This left a choice of two:[16] Paul Bender (Munich) or Karl Perron (Dresden). On January 8, 1911, Hofmannsthal officially rejected Bender, wittily remarking that 'if all bass buffos are long and lean and the only Quinquins[17] thick and fat I may as well close down!' Perron, an old hand at Strauss premières, was comparably long and lean and, worse, a baritone; but time was running out. Perron was therefore honoured with his third consecutive Strauss première.[18]

Schuch conducted thirty-three full orchestral rehearsals (a total of some 100 hours), Reinhardt put the cast through dozens of acting classes and Roller invested unprecedented time, and money, to ensure that the costumes and sets were faultlessly realistic. On the morning of the première Strauss and Schuch were locked in discussion, working out last-minute details, when Pauline marched in and announced, 'You've talked enough.' She wanted a new hat for that evening's performance, and her husband would have to accompany her to Prager Strasse to buy it. Ever dutiful, he did as he was commanded, and that evening Pauline entered her box wearing an opulent gold turban.

The first night was, and remained, Strauss's greatest. At a time when contemporary operas were attracting progressively less interest, *Rosenkavalier* created a world-wide sensation – equalled only by the première of Puccini's last opera *Turandot* in 1926. There were ten curtain calls after the second act, twenty after the third, and each of Europe's significant news agencies confirmed that, with *Rosenkavalier*, Strauss's Midas touch was unspoiled.

The critical response was almost uniformly hostile. Hofmannsthal's 'humourless libretto' came in for considerable punishment, as did Strauss's 'superficial' music. But audiences marched to a different tune, and they marched in their thousands. So popular was *Rosenkavalier* that within its first year Dresden had seen over fifty performances – to say nothing of the contiguous productions mounted in Nuremberg, Munich,[19] Basel, Hamburg, Milan, Prague (in Czech), Vienna, Budapest and Amsterdam[20] – and all within ten months of the première. When Hülsen, fearful of the opera's implicit indecency, vacillated over mounting a production in Berlin, the Imperial Railways provided a special service to Dresden, offering a return train fare and a seat in the stalls for sixteen-and-a-half marks. Hülsen was informed by the Court censor that unless changes were made to the libretto Berlin would not be seeing Strauss's latest opera. The composer considered success in Berlin, and the attendant royalties, sufficiently tempting, and to Hofmannsthal's astonishment, Strauss sanctioned Hülsen's modifications of Hofmannsthal's poetry. At the first performance, on November 14,[21] the bed on which, during the Prelude, Octavian and the Marschallin make love was seen unoccupied and various objectionable innuendoes – chiefly the word 'bed' – were replaced with equally idiotic, but less scandalous, alternatives.

In Milan events took an unexpected turn. According to Strauss, 'Serafin had rehearsed the opera faultlessly with an excellent cast'. He and Pauline 'sat in the proscenium box with the Duke Visconti and his wife, with whom Pauline discussed French fashions'. No one expected anything more than another triumphant first night; but Strauss had not accounted for the expectation of Italy's young modernists: 'After the second act there was no applause, but hissing, whistling, and shouting, accompanied by the scattering of hundreds of pamphlets from the top balcony.' A group of 'Futurists' were indignant that the composer of *Salome* and *Elektra* could have produced something as apparently slight and insubstantial as *Rosenkavalier*. They were not alone in seeing the new work as a step backwards – that great 'volte-face' to which critics and historians have referred ever since. But *Rosenkavalier* was no U-turn.

If Strauss and Hofmannsthal had never met, it is generally argued, he would not have been 'dragged away from the vanguard of influential musical thought towards a product less provocative . . . and less popular'.[22] To suggest that Strauss's modernity – rather than the beauty and dramatic conviction of his music – was responsible for his ubiquity is absurd, particularly in the light of subsequent developments within European art music; Strauss's operas were popular because people liked them, not because they blew raspberries at the Establishment.

Hofmannsthal's leverage was considerable, but the notion that he precipitated Strauss's retreat from modernism presupposes there *was* a retreat. The truth is that Strauss neither progressed nor regressed. *Rosenkavalier* represented a decisive continuity of thought and style, not a withdrawal from some imagined vanguard. Indeed, the very absence of considered aesthetic shifts on the part of Strauss during his life accommodates more of what we know of his personality than those theories through which he is seen to toss and turn between aesthetic poles as if torn by uncertainty and self-doubt.

When, during the first half of 1908, Strauss and Hofmannsthal applied themselves to the possibility of writing a comedy Strauss was already halfway through the score of *Elektra*. He had resisted another psychological drama so soon after *Salome*, and had discussed various comic subjects with Hofmannsthal before finally committing himself to his play; but had he rejected *Elektra* for a comic subject, history would have judged Strauss and his illusory 'volte-face' quite differently. When he followed *Guntram* with a comic satire none of his many critics considered this, in itself, worthy of comment; and had he followed *Salome* with something lighter, along the lines of *Till Eulenspiegel* or *Casanova*, before tackling the House of Atreus, his aesthetic withdrawal would have been seen for the myth it is.

Strauss's detractors argue that, with *Rosenkavalier* behind him, he could have returned, via an appropriately lurid subject, to the coruscating sound-world of *Elektra*. Perhaps, but *Elektra* was not, as it seems to be for many, an aesthetic soapbox; its creators approached each successive idea anew, unconscious of a work's place or significance within their own or shared chronologies. The '*Elektra* Parallax', and its relation to *Rosenkavalier*, says more about the development and critical understanding of twentieth-century music than it does about *Elektra*, *Rosenkavalier* or their composer. Furthermore, by the time Strauss completed *Rosenkavalier* he was wholly committed to Hofmannsthal, who had no intention of allowing Strauss to regress to the 'erotic screaming' of *Salome* and *Elektra*.

Moreover, there is little precedent in music history for the sort of shift that *Rosenkavalier* is supposed to represent. No significant composer during the two centuries prior to Strauss's birth broke with his own tradition; rather, the majority ripened with experience – building on youthful experiments, not retreating from them. The very consistency of Strauss's progress appears to be something of a blind spot for his detractors, the more so since *Rosenkavalier*, and most of the Hofmannsthal operas, are the embodiment not of conservatism, but of post-modernism.

Strauss was instinctively sympathetic to Hofmannsthal's preoccupation with cultural history, and the sources for *Rosenkavalier* underline their shared delight in the sort of pluralistic, anti-modern attitudes that animated twentieth-century post-modernism. Vienna for Strauss and Hofmannsthal was the imperial Vienna of waltzes and sentimentality; neither felt the slightest connection with the contemporary city, or its foremost residents Schoenberg, Berg, Freud, Neurath, Schnitzler, Klimt, Kokoschka, Schiele and so on. The use of ornament, quotation and self-quotation (with which both the libretto and the score are saturated), the conscious allusion to obsolete tradition, the parodistic application of distorted cultural references, the general reordering of the past, and the manipulation of time as a narrative constituent attest to *Rosenkavalier*'s prescience as a work of post-modernism.

This is amplified throughout Hofmannsthal's libretto, for which he borrowed liberally from French eighteenth-century literature. The Marschallin – Marie Thérèse, Princess Werdenberg – is based on Beaumarchais's 1784 play, *Le Mariage de Figaro*. Hofmannsthal relocated the drama from Spain to the Vienna of 1745, then ruled by Maria Theresa. The scandal of Hofmannsthal's reinvention was the affair between the 32-year-old Marschallin and the seventeen-year-old Octavian, a creation resonant of Beaumarchais's Cherubino;

but Octavian is also indebted to Molière's 1671 *Les Fourberies de Scapin* and, in his sexual fantasies, Couvray's *Faublas* of 1781.

Baron Ochs, though coloured by the traditions of the Commedia dell' Arte and Harlequinade, is a fusion of Molière's 1669 Monsieur de Pourceaugnac, Shakespeare's Falstaff and Sir Toby Belch, Sheridan's Bob Acres and Goldsmith's Tony Lumpkin. Sophie's father, Faninal, is lifted wholesale from Molière's *Scapin* and, more significantly, *Le Bourgeois Gentilhomme*. The stage setting for the first act is an almost exact replica of Hogarth's 1745 *The Countess's Morning Levee*,[23] and Strauss's use of the Viennese waltz is as anachronistic (since the waltz was a nineteenth-century development) as it is inspired.

More remarkable is Hofmannsthal's invented language. Every character has a different, highly distinctive linguistic style – from the stylised eighteenth-century idiom of the court and the Marschallin's *Hochdeutsch*, to Ochs's self-conscious, sham nobility. The care and attention invested by Hofmannsthal, reflected by his decision to publish the libretto separately as a play, was the cause of much of his frustration with Strauss. As he wrote on July 14, 1910: 'A number of small alterations from the Viennese diction of the characters must be restored again, if at all possible, in the text as sung, but in any case *certainly* in the libretto. They look casual and accidental, but to me they are really distressing (for Octavian, for instance, to say "Therese" instead of "Theres" sounds altogether *impossible*). You may well consider such changes of a syllable here or there, or even only a single letter quite trifling; I am as mortified by them as you would be if someone were to fiddle about with the notes in your score.'

Strauss's weakness for the achievements of his ancestors, as well as his namesakes, was less categorical; and in certain respects the music for *Rosenkavalier* represents an emphatic continuation of *Elektra*. It advances his general approach to opera as a theatrical adjunct to the tone poem; it exploits extended tonal blocks and sudden shifts in harmonic colour to further the delineation of character and emotion; and even though most remember the opera for its melodies, chiefly the 'Presentation' duet of the second act and the exquisite Trio of the third, the orchestra is dominant throughout. Even Hofmannsthal knew this, writing to Strauss: 'The whole life of the thing is centred on the orchestra and the voice is only woven into it, emerging sometimes and submerged again, but is never – unless my impressions deceive me – wholly sovereign, never takes the lead.'

As an eighteenth-century pastiche, the counterpoint is necessarily less dense than in *Elektra*, but *Rosenkavalier*'s construction is, if anything, more complex. So too is the writing for the voices. In this respect, *Rosenkavalier* represents a considerable advance on the earlier work in that it crystallises Strauss's fascination for the patterns and varieties of human speech,[24] creating a vocal style that is, apart from the work's 'big numbers', less lyrical and more expressive than *Elektra*, in which the melodic writing is comprehensively linear. For the first time in his operatic life Strauss exercised a self-discipline and revealed a care for detail that – precluding the late Romantic, Wagnerian ecstasies of *Salome* and *Elektra* – enabled him to reconcile his affinity for pure Mozartian melody to a less archaic concern for expression that anticipates, but never quite adopts, the novelty of Schoenbergian *Sprechstimme* (speech-song).[25]

With hindsight, Strauss's achievement was the successful fusion of modernism – as an inexact belief in aesthetic progress – with the popular traditions against which modernism was supposedly a reaction. This resolution was manifested, not least in *Rosenkavalier*, through Strauss's extension of tonality, and its expressive compass, without ever needing to abandon it. The reinvention of tradition is significantly more challenging than its complete rejection and, as such, the aesthetic separation typified by Schoenberg was remarkable only for its totality. While many continue to see in the Second Viennese School the bedrock of late twentieth-century modernism, it can now be argued that Schoenberg's experiments were dated long before his death and that, starting with *Rosenkavalier*, Strauss prefigured the more lasting post-modern instincts that have come to dominate music since the 1970s.

Rosenkavalier was the first opera begun and completed by Strauss in Garmisch. The pattern of his life was now established, thanks mainly to Pauline, who governed his routine, prescribed his diet, supervised his wardrobe and administered that curiously sadistic unction to which Strauss was singularly disposed – and for which Pauline was incomparably well equipped. That she loved him cannot be doubted; that she liked him is less certain. His passivity and his willingness to compromise were a source of lasting irritation, and Pauline – like Hofmannsthal – would push and pester for want of a satisfying reaction. On one occasion they were taking a cab ride through Garmisch, during which Pauline systematically reproached her husband. Eventually, the astonished driver turned and asked Strauss, 'Are you going to stand for that?' When Strauss merely shrugged his shoulders the heroic driver recommended that he 'Throw the cow out!'

At home Pauline was omnipotent. She carried a weighty bunch of keys around her waist on a chain, securing everything from Strauss's library to the biscuits in the kitchen, and no one did anything, whether cleaning, shopping, cooking or decorating, without her supervision. Rationing was habitual, and Strauss had no choice but to stand by and watch family and friends conform to his wife's increasingly eccentric house rules. Everyone – including Strauss – had to wipe their feet before entering the house (in later years she placed a second mat in front of the first, just in case) and all dinner guests were required to wash their hands and comb their hair prior to sitting at the table.

Dusting was an almost religious fixation for Pauline. When staying with friends she would run her hands over furniture, open drawers, peer under beds and, on occasion, ask to inspect servants' finger-nails. Dirt of any kind in anyone's home was greeted with a look of disgust; and it says much about her feelings for Strauss that, after his death in 1949, the dust in Garmisch was finally allowed to settle.

Her administration suited Strauss's fondness for routine. He rose at nine, ate breakfast and began work at ten. He would remain in his study until midday when, regardless of the weather and for the good of his health, he would take an hour's walk around his estate. There followed lunch with the family and any guests who were staying, after which he would rest on the sofa in his study for half an hour. This was followed by another, shorter walk around the gardens with his sketchbook, and at least three more hours at his desk. After the evening meal he and Pauline would either retire to the drawing room or the study, where Strauss would play something from the work in hand. If he was playing skat – and he did so frequently – then he would stay up late, often past midnight. Of course, Pauline could disrupt the routine whenever she liked. Midway through a morning's work on *Elektra*, for example, he was ordered by Pauline to walk into town and fetch the milk as the maid was busy.

Strauss's routine was typical of a composer for whom composition was a process of pure expression, not self-expression. He claimed more than once that the composing of music was a business as much as an art, and because it came to him so easily he felt little sympathy for the effort and anxiety endured by the likes of Beethoven and Mahler. Strauss was not averse to articulating his own process. Possibly unconsciously, these explanations frequently provided an insight into his relationship with Pauline:

> The melodic idea which suddenly assails me, crops up without any external, sensual stimulus, or any internal emotion being present; it appears directly, unmediated, in my imagination, unawares, without the influence of the conscious mind. Is the imagination perhaps an intensification of the conscious mind, the highest flowering of the soul? ... In my experience, the artistic imagination becomes especially active at times of great excitement, anger or annoyance and not, as is often supposed, after receiving some sensual impression, from the beauty of nature, or in moods of great solemnity ... I am almost inclined to believe that there are chemical elements in the blood, which pass through certain nerves, or join up with certain parts of the brain, so as to produce the highest possible intensification in the activity of the spirit. There is ground for this belief in the fact that melodic ideas very often come in the morning at the moment of waking, when the brain, which has drained through the night, refills with fresh blood ... I work in the summer, very coolly, without hurrying, without emotion, and slowly. Invention takes time, if it is to lead to something new and exciting. The greatest art in the inventive process is the art of waiting ... I compose everywhere, taking a walk, driving, during meals, at home or in noisy hotels, in my garden, in railway carriages. My sketchbook never leaves me.

There have been few composers, or at least few honest enough, to admit to such unorthodox stimuli as excitement, anger and annoyance; the latter two are ordinarily the very death of creativity. Most of history's significant composers have coped with, and overcome, anguish and affliction. Few have

actively fed off them. Strauss's admission corroborates the general perception
of Pauline as a termagant, just as it amplifies his need for discipline; but it is
still difficult to reconcile his repudiation of sensuality as a stimulus to the
overt eroticism of his music.

Strauss was able to work under conditions that would have driven Mahler
or Schoenberg to madness. He had no need of seclusion or – so he claimed –
of Nature, and as the conductor Karl Böhm recalled he could quite easily do
two things at once, such as holding a conversation about one piece of music
while at the same time orchestrating another. This ability to sustain two or
three ventures simultaneously was reflected in Pauline's and, consequently,
Strauss's almost Protestant faith in the merits of hard work. Unsurprisingly,
therefore, Strauss began to discuss with Hofmannsthal potential subjects for
their next collaboration seven weeks before completing *Rosenkavalier*.

On October 8, 1910, he reminded Hofmannsthal of *Semiramis*, a subject
the poet had evidently counted on Strauss forgetting: '*Semiramis* is miles
away; no intellectual or material inducements could extract from me a play
on this subject, not even a most determined effort of will ...' Instead, Hofmannsthal proposed a 'fantastic play' based upon a fairy-tale by Wilhelm
Hauff, *Das Steinerne Herz* (The Stone Heart), which he hastily withdrew after
Strauss inadvertently revealed his complete misreading of Hofmannsthal's
intentions: 'What a confounded fool I was to tell you the title and the
subject...'

On March 20 Hofmannsthal grabbed the bull by the horns:

> If we were to work together once more on something (and by this I mean
> something important, not the thirty-minute opera for small chamber orchestra
> which is as good as complete in my head; it is called *Ariadne auf Naxos* and is
> made up of a combination of heroic mythological figures in 18th century
> costume with hooped skirts and ostrich feathers and, interwoven in it, characters
> from the commedia dell'arte; harlequins and scaramouches representing the
> buffo element which is throughout interwoven with the heroic.

In the same letter Hofmannsthal drew Strauss's attention to another idea
he had had for 'something big':

> It would have to possess colourful and clear-cut action, and the detail of the
> libretto would be less important. I have something quite definite in mind which
> fascinates me very much ... It is a magic fairy-tale with two men confronting
> two women, and for one of the women your wife might well, in all discretion,
> be taken as a model – that of course is wholly *entre nous*, and not of any great
> importance. Anyway, she is a *bizarre* woman with a very beautiful soul, *au fond*;
> strange, moody, domineering and yet at the same time likeable; she would in
> fact be the principal character and the whole thing a many coloured spectacle

with palace and hut, priests, boats, torches, tunnels through the rock, choruses, children.

This was to be their fourth opera, *Die Frau ohne Schatten* (The Woman without a Shadow).[1]

Before that, however, Hofmannsthal wanted to develop *Ariadne*, an idea he was approaching almost as a sorbet between courses: 'I am also inclined to think that this interim work is necessary, at least *for me*, to make myself still more familiar with music, especially with your music, and to achieve something which brings us even closer together than in *Rosenkavalier*.' He was determined that everything should 'follow a definite line of development in the matter of style', and reminded Strauss that the continuity of their work together signified 'a new genre which to all appearance reaches back to a much earlier one, just as all development goes in circles'.

Hofmannsthal later confessed that his original idea for *Ariadne* had been to 'give her a framework of my own devising: a little comedy which takes place at a castle in Bohemia, a young heiress with three suitors who, to please her, bring an opera company and a troupe of harlequins to the castle. I suppressed this idea deliberately so as not to endanger your work by combining it with the première of a Hofmannsthal comedy' – the implication being that his play would have obscured Strauss's opera! Hofmannsthal had originally conjured the idea of a play followed by an opera as a response to the claims of his circle that his reputation was suffering from the Strauss collaboration. A spoken rather than a sung play, for which Strauss could none the less provide incidental music, was the ideal route to autonomy; but he backed away from the idea at the last minute, preferring the reinvention of a long-forgotten French comedy to the invention of his own work. Though secure in intimate company, Hofmannsthal was plagued by the Furies in private. *Rosenkavalier*'s success, and the critical dismissal of his libretto, had left him deflated. He lacked the courage to set his work against Strauss's.

When Hofmannsthal met Strauss in Vienna in April, to supervise the Court Opera's première of *Rosenkavalier*,[1] he outlined his ambitions for *Ariadne*: no longer interested in writing his own comedy, he planned to combine a translation of Molière's *Le Bourgeois Gentilhomme*[3] (for which Strauss would provide incidental music) with a thirty-minute chamber opera, provisionally titled *Ariadne auf Naxos*. He proposed to reduce the original five acts to two, omitting the Turkish scene and all secondary narration, thus allowing for Strauss's opera which would follow *Gentilhomme* as an 'after-dinner' entertainment. Hofmannsthal encouraged Strauss to read the German translation by Bierling, and to help him on his way he sent a variety of suggestions for vocal numbers together with the following imaginary playbill:

DER BÜRGER ALS EDELMANN
A comedy with Dances by Molière, arranged by Hugo von Hofmannsthal
from the old translation by Bierling (1751)
At the end of Act II
Divertissement:
ARIADNE AUF NAXOS
(Music by Richard Strauss)

At the beginning of May the genial atmosphere was threatened when Hofmannsthal learned that Strauss had been in contact with the dramatist Gabriele D'Annunzio (whom he met at the Milan *Rosenkavalier*) concerning a possible collaboration. Brushing aside Hofmannsthal's anxiety, Strauss took the opportunity to emphasise D'Annunzio's expendability: 'I had a few ideas passed on to him, in particular my wish for an entirely modern subject, very intimate and psychologically extremely nervous: let's wait and see what he brings off. I've no great hopes of him, but one's got to pull all strings.' In truth, he was bored; in the same bad-tempered letter he noted, 'I am waiting for you and am meanwhile torturing myself with a symphony – a job that, when all's said and done, amuses me even less than chasing maybugs.'

The work to which he referred was his long-considered *Ein Alpensinfonie*. Tortured by his attempts to quit smoking ('let the devil be cheerful in such circumstances') and fearful of boredom, Strauss was looking for something to keep his hand in while Hofmannsthal kept his head down. The idea for a pantheistic travelogue first occurred to him in 1878, since when he had toyed with the idea for nearly forty years. He had even made a veiled reference to it in *Heldenleben* in 1899 and the following year had written to his parents about a symphonic poem 'which would begin with a sunrise in Switzerland'. There is good reason to suppose that Strauss's unchanging devotion to Liszt (who wrote his own *Bergsymphonie* in 1848–9[4]) and his enduring contact with Hans von Bronsart (who wrote a Symphony with Chorus called *In der Alpen*) provided secondary stimuli.

The work's purely descriptive character, though typical of Strauss's achievements as a symphonist, is unique within his *oeuvre*. Whether operatic, pictorial or absolute, Strauss's music, with the early exception of *Aus Italien*, was animated by individual psychologies, but the *Alpensinfonie* was indiscriminately pictorial. For Strauss's champions, it represents the legitimate privilege of an orchestral virtuoso wishing to stretch his legs; for his detractors, it is a work of incontinent flamboyance, the exemplification of a composer, and a culture, whose time had come and gone.

The truth is somewhere in between. Considering his mood at the time, Strauss's approach to the new symphony was unavoidably dutiful; the gestation was necessarily difficult and protracted, and while the finished product was better than is generally claimed, it was dismissed at the time as academic, frigid and narcissistic, having struck a late romantic chord for which there was no longer an audience. And yet, for sheer inventiveness and dramatic conviction it is unsurpassed. The harmonic construction and melodic invention are irrepressible, the climaxes transcend anything written before or since, and the narration is irresistibly graphic. Had Strauss not so publicly devoted prodigious amounts of time, effort and talent to the portrayal of an afternoon walk in the rain it might have thrived. Heard within the context of European music at the time, however, and bearing in mind that it was completed and first performed thirteen months into the First World War, its unpopularity is easily explained.

Strauss was momentarily given cause to consider applying a subtext to the thunder and lightning. On May 18, 1911, news arrived from Vienna that Gustav Mahler had died. In his diary that afternoon Strauss wrote:

> The death of this aspiring, idealistic and energetic artist is a heavy loss. [I] read Wagner's memoirs with emotion. [I] read German history of the age of Reformation, Leopold Ranke: this confirmed very clearly for me that all the elements that fostered culture at that time have been a spent force for centuries, just as all great political and religious movements can only have a truly fruitful influence for a limited period. The Jew Mahler could still find elevation in Christianity. The hero Richard Wagner came back to it as an old man through the influence of Schopenhauer. It is absolutely clear to me that the German nation can only attain new vigour by freeing itself from Christianity ... I shall call my *Alpensinfonie* the Antichrist, since it embodies: moral purification through one's own strength, liberation through work, worship of eternal, glorious Nature.

Strauss's homage would have brought a smile to Mahler's lips. It provided definitive confirmation that Strauss had understood neither him nor his music. Nearly a year earlier, in June 1910, he had been invited by the musicologist Paul Stefan[5] to provide a tribute in honour of Mahler's fiftieth birthday. Strauss wrote that 'Mahler's work is in my view among the most significant and interesting in present-day art history. Just as I was fortunate to be one of the first to commend his symphonic works to the public, I see it as one of my most pleasant duties to continue by word and deed to help his symphonies attain the general recognition they deserve. The plasticity of his orchestration, in particular, is absolutely exemplary.'

That Strauss said more about his services to Mahler than about Mahler himself should be set against the facts: during Mahler's lifetime Strauss conducted only three performances of his symphonies (two of Number One and one of Number Four), whereas Mahler conducted all but two of Strauss's nine completed tone poems as well as his first two operas on twenty-six

separate occasions in five different countries.[6] There is no denying that
Mahler's death came as 'a great shock';[7] but his diary entry underlines their
fundamental disparity. Strauss was an unrepentant Nietzschean, advocating
the semi-hysterical prejudice of the Antichrist in which, to the question
'What is more harmful than any vice?', Nietzsche replied, 'Active pity for
the ill-constituted and weak – Christianity.' Even in his middle age Strauss
believed in the virtue of strength, and his hostility towards religion – whether
Jewish or Christian – hindered any genuine empathy between the two composers.

In August or September 1911 Otto Klemperer visited Garmisch. The conversation turned to Mahler, during which Strauss commented on Mahler's
obsession with redemption: 'That, he [Strauss] said, was a concept that meant
nothing to him, he had no idea what Mahler meant by the expression. To
quote his actual words: "I don't know what I'm supposed to be redeemed
from. When I sit down at my desk in the morning and an idea comes into
my head, I surely don't need redemption. What did Mahler mean?" '

As the years passed Strauss's opinion of his 'old friend' grew less admiring.
In 1923 he took Mahler's First and Fourth Symphonies on a South American
tour with the Vienna Philharmonic; less than twelve months later he
announced to the conductor Fritz Busch: 'As for Mahler he's not really a
composer at all – he's simply a very great conductor.'[8]

On July 2, 1911, another of Strauss's long-term colleagues, Felix Mottl,
died – as had been his stated preference, while conducting the second act of
Tristan und Isolde. They had known each other since the latter's childhood,
but since October 1896, when Mottl had been appointed conductor of the
Munich Academy Concerts, Strauss had kept his distance. Not without reason
did he send Hofmannsthal to supervise Mottl's preparations for the first
Munich *Rosenkavalier*. Strauss willingly took over a number of Mottl's commitments at the Munich Court Opera, including performances of *Figaro* and
Così fan tutte. These were attended by Otto Klemperer, who confirmed
the revolutionary character of 'Strauss's Mozart': 'He only made very small
movements, but their effect was enormous. His control of the orchestra was
absolute ... He accompanied the recitatives himself on a harpsichord[9] and
made delightful little embellishments ... He seemed to have a new approach
to Mozart.'

Back in Garmisch, Strauss's nicotine-free lifestyle was doing nothing for
his mood, although Hofmannsthal's progress on *Ariadne* gave rise to a furious
burst of correspondence which peaked on July 12 when Hofmannsthal dispatched a completed draft of his libretto. The composer's reaction was typically candid: 'The whole of *Ariadne* is now safely in my hands and I like it
well enough: I think there'll be some good use for everything. Only I should
have preferred the dialogue between Ariadne and Bacchus to be rather more
significant, with a livelier emotional crescendo.'

Having two weeks earlier addressed Strauss as 'My dear Friend', Hofmannsthal now wrote to tell 'My dear Doctor' that he was 'somewhat piqued' by Strauss's 'scant and cool reception of the finished manuscript of *Ariadne*, compared with the warm welcome' he had given 'every single act of *Rosenkavalier*...' He demanded that Strauss restore 'that sense of fine and intimate contact ... which I enjoyed during our earlier collaboration, and which has by now become indispensable to me'. The warmth of Strauss's reply does him credit: 'I am sincerely sorry that in my dry way I failed to pay you the tribute you had hoped for and which your work certainly deserves ...' For the first time in well over a year Hofmannsthal began to feel part of a collaborative effort: 'This frank exchange of views is most welcome to me; I am grateful to you for your letter. Nothing you might have said could have appealed to me more than that we must try to bring out the very best in each other.' Had they not reached such an amicable state, the ensuing months might well have proved unendurable.

The problem was symbolic; or, at least, it grew from Hofmannsthal's growing preoccupation with a symbolic mysticism of which Strauss was contemptuous. He believed, with good reason, that narrative and psychological clarity were indispensable for 'those asses of spectators' that made up their audience; it was simply too much to expect 'the mob' to decipher Hofmannsthal's poetics, and Strauss feared isolating the very people for whom he was writing his music. As he well knew, and as Hofmannsthal was soon to discover, the audience for opera was quite unlike the audience for theatre. Responding to Strauss's concerns, Hofmannsthal wrote a long and moving explanation of *Ariadne*'s meaning: 'What it is about is one of the straightforward and stupendous problems of life: fidelity; whether to hold fast to that which is lost, to cling to it even unto death – or to live, to live on, to get over it, to transform oneself, to sacrifice the integrity of the soul, and yet in this transmutation to preserve one's essence, to remain a human being and not to sink to the level of the beast, which is without recollection...'

Strauss was delighted: 'The piece did not fully convince me until after I had read your letter, which is so beautiful and explains the meaning of the action so wonderfully that a superficial musician like myself could not, of course, have tumbled to it.' However, that Hofmannsthal felt compelled to explain himself and his intentions was, in itself, an indictment of his libretto, and Strauss amplified his misgivings: 'Isn't some of the interpretation still lacking in the action itself? If even I couldn't see it, just think of the audiences and – the critics ... An author reads into his play things which the sober spectator doesn't see, and the fact that even I, the most willing of readers, have failed to grasp such important points must surely give you pause...'

Hofmannsthal was unconvinced. He blamed Strauss's lack of receptivity on his loneliness (Pauline and Bubi were away from Garmisch at the time) and on his attempts to quit smoking, and he repeated his faith in *Ariadne*'s coherence: 'The attractive style of this supporting opera, the bizarre mixture of the heroic with buffo elements, the gracefully rhymed verses, the set numbers, the playful, puppet-show look of the whole piece, all this gives the audience for the time being something to grab and suck like a child ... As for the symbolic aspect, the juxtaposition of the woman who loves only once [Ariadne] and the woman who gives herself to many [Zerbinetta], this is placed so very much in the centre of the action, and is treated as so simple and so clear-cut an antithesis, which may be heightened still further by an equally clear-cut musical contrast.'

Hofmannsthal conceded Strauss's concern for the cognitive abilities of their audience, and he drily reminded Strauss that it was 'on them, and not the critics' that their success depended. He nevertheless proposed a compromise: the two disparate worlds of Ariadne and Zerbinetta should be brought together, at the invitation of the host Jourdain. This would allow for ample comic potential, reconciling the solemn and the frivolous, and necessitating an explanation, to Zerbinetta (and the audience), of the opera's content: 'This offers us the opportunity of stating quite plainly, under cover of a joke, the symbolic meaning of the antithesis between the two women.'

On July 26 Hofmannsthal wrote to Strauss confirming his intention to visit Garmisch ('Please don't ask me to stay at your house ...'). In August, though tired and unwell, and despite having committed himself to a series of concert and opera engagements in Munich, Strauss managed to spend many hours with Hofmannsthal – a closeness that precluded any further correspondence until the end of October, when the poet was piqued into breaking the silence: 'After all those letters we exchanged in July, we both laid off for a while: what a pleasant surprise it was, therefore, at Neubeuern, suddenly to come across the most unexpected news in the *Münchner Neueste Nachrichten* that you have actually finished!' Strauss's failure to communicate the news that he had completed *Ariadne* in short score had less to do with rudeness than with an absence of time, an aggressive case of intestinal flu and the demands of the Berlin première of *Rosenkavalier*.

During rehearsals Strauss was able to discuss his new work, and its staging, with Max Reinhardt. Hofmannsthal had been so affected by the producer's contribution to the Dresden *Rosenkavalier* that he had always intended his next work as a vehicle for Reinhardt's talents; Strauss cared little for Hofmannsthal's sentimentality. The practicalities of staging a work like *Edelmann/Ariadne* were too involved to allow something so ephemeral as gratitude to interfere. Strauss had always known that Reinhardt's Deutsches Theater would prove too small, even for *Ariadne*'s diminutive orchestra of thirty-seven, but he seems also to have feared Reinhardt's reliability. As early as November 1911 Strauss inferred these concerns in a letter to Hofmannsthal, who flatly refused to consider a substitute.

On December 18 Hofmannsthal launched an hysterical attack against Strauss: if he were to allow the work to go anywhere but the Deutsches Theater, or if Reinhardt's involvement were in any way threatened, their collaboration would be at an end. The hostility of this letter (which suggests a certain amount of doubt in his own work) was unquestionably cumulative; its grievances were absolute and personal. Strauss, unlike Hofmannsthal, was disinclined towards professional loyalty, and he must have despaired at Hofmannsthal's melodramatic defence of Reinhardt's probity.

There had never been any real question of Strauss's forswearing Reinhardt, but his theatre was ill-adapted to the particular needs of their play/opera, and this was a matter that would have to be resolved, not by Strauss, but by the physical resources of the Deutsches Theater. The first half of Strauss's response to Hofmannsthal's assault has gone 'missing'; but it would be fair to assume that, for once, he gave as good as he got. Certainly, the second half confirms his unarguable refusal to consider the Deutsches Theater for the first night. The matter was resolved when Strauss proposed '*Dresden incl. Reinhardt*', a suggestion to which Hofmannsthal grudgingly agreed.

At the end of 1911 Strauss sent discreet inquiries to a number of Intendants, including Albert von Speidel at the Munich Court Opera, but the 'crisis' surrounding Reinhardt and his theatre would not go away; two days into the new year he was compelled to reassure Hofmannsthal yet again: 'Believe me it cost me a hard inner struggle before my conscience would let me tear the piece, which after all had been conceived from the start solely for Reinhardt and the Deutsches Theater, away from this destination.' At the end of January, having been informed that the smaller of Dresden's two opera houses was unsuited to *Ariadne*'s intimacy, and having decided not to place it with the cavernous Court Opera, Strauss offered the world première to his friend Max von Schillings, the Intendant of the newly built Königliches Hoftheater in Stuttgart. This pleased Hofmannsthal, although Reinhardt took some persuading,[10] and not until the beginning of February 1912 was Strauss able to apply himself to the delicate process of casting.

In his memoirs Strauss recalled: 'I was thinking of Madame Jeritza whom I had seen in Munich in *La belle Hélène*, of the splendid tenor Jadlowker and the coloratura Frieda Hempel.' His correspondence with Hofmannsthal adds considerably to this picture. Initially, for the role of Zerbinetta, he proposed Selma Kurz, Hempel and, somewhat surprisingly, the spherical, 'stout and ugly'[11] Luisa Tetrazzini. Hofmannsthal objected, claiming that such stars would constitute too great a drain on Reinhardt's finances, a stance which makes his own preferences – Geraldine Farrar and Mary Garden – all the more startling.[12] For Ariadne herself Strauss was convinced that the genius of Emmy Destinn would help overcome any critical reservations, and on January 27, 1912, he wrote to his 'Dear and honoured Fräulein!':

Unforgettable, unsurpassable Salome!

I have written a new little opera, *Ariadne auf Naxos*, with a small chamber orchestra accompaniment. Duration one hour. Will you create Ariadne for us? ... Two performances, second half of October, before you go to America: the choice of the exact dates is entirely yours. Eight days of rehearsals will suffice, the whole affair a matter of about ten days. You will learn the part in three. It is for you to command what fee you will! May I count upon you? ...

Destinn may have smelled a rat. Certainly, Strauss's letter reeks of desperation. That he was moved to offer one of the world's highest-paid singers a blank cheque, and that she turned it (and the honour of a Strauss première) down, speaks volumes about the gossip, and insecurities, surrounding *Edelmann/Ariadne* during the ten months leading up to the first performance – insecurities accentuated by Strauss's decision to conduct the première himself. For Ariadne he eventually settled on Maria (then Mizzi) Jeritza, a young, beautiful and newly minted dramatic soprano; for Zerbinetta he turned, for the third time, to Margarethe Siems after Hempel failed to free herself from American commitments; for the tenor role of Bacchus he was able to borrow Jadlowker from Hülsen in Berlin.

At the beginning of June, Strauss's chauffeur drove him to Stuttgart (a 'wonderful journey' during which, of all things, he composed a march) where he was immediately won over by the theatre, the orchestra and Ernst Stern,[13] whose stage and costume designs were a delight. For the first time since beginning *Edelmann/Ariadne* Strauss's confidence resurfaced. To Hofmannsthal he wrote: 'My score is a real masterpiece of a score: you won't find another one like it in a hurry'; to Pauline: 'It sounds splendid, beyond my expectations, more beautiful than anything I have written so far. A completely new style and new sound-world ... Am blissfully happy.'

It was to be a temporary state. Reinhardt – to whom *Edelmann/Ariadne* was dedicated – was a Jew, a Berliner and, consequently, an outsider in Stuttgart; his production team were compelled to work alongside a reluctant and bitter house staff who considered it an outrage that Strauss and Hofmannsthal should have imposed their own people on a theatre already prodigal with talent. The apprehension was compounded on stage, since the rehearsal cast for *Ariadne* was to be replaced ten days before the first night by Jeritza, Siems and Jadlowker. On June 19, and in apparent ignorance of any tension, Strauss returned to Garmisch.

His summer months were, again, monopolised by Hofmannsthal, who introduced him to a new idea on which he had been working with Harry Kessler: 'I have produced a short ballet for the Russians,[14] *Joseph in Egypt*, the episode with Potiphar's wife; the boyish part of Joseph of course for Nijinsky, the most extraordinary personality on the stage today.' But Hofmannsthal's *Joseph* proved ungrateful, and it was with palpable relief that Strauss was able to put the project to one side to attend the final rehearsals for *Edelmann/Ariadne* in October.

In his memoirs Strauss recalled how 'everything went well until the dress rehearsal'. This is not exactly true. In addition to the upset caused by the arrival of Jadlowker, Jeritza and Siems on the 15th, some nine days before the dress rehearsal, and the induction of five desk soloists from Berlin, Stuttgart's in-house producer, Emil Gerhäuser, was publicly humiliated by Strauss. Gerhäuser had done a fine job preparing the rehearsal casts, but there was still much to resolve and when he approached Strauss for guidance the composer simply waved him aside, as he had done George Toller in Dresden, remarking 'Reinhardt will settle all that.'

Gerhäuser complained to Schillings, who urged tolerance, but with the arrival of Reinhardt and the Deutsches Theater cast, the situation threatened to turn mutinous. Previously oblivious, Strauss's ire was roused when Schillings scheduled a performance of Lortzing's pot-boiler *Undine* in the larger theatre to coincide with *Ariadne*'s dress rehearsal. In itself, Lortzing's opera posed no threat, but Schillings withdrew a number of the Königliches's stage managers to assist with *Undine*.

Chaos ensued. Strauss recalled how 'the scene-designer Stern acted as stage manager, although he had no idea of stage management. Singers made their entrances either too late or at the wrong time, the sets were all wrong, and in short it was a mess.'[15] Strauss attacked Schillings, accusing him of sabotage and deception; Schillings demanded a public apology, without which he threatened to withdraw the new work. Strauss – who later exonerated the Intendant of all responsibility – was forced to apologise, and the opening went ahead without misadventure; but the damage had been done. Word leaked out that Strauss's latest opera was a failure.

The first night, on October 25, was successful as far as the performance itself was concerned, but the fine singing and witty staging were insufficient to negate the weight of preconception beneath which *Edelmann/Ariadne* had long been suffocating. Strauss blamed the immediate circumstances for its failure: 'The audience was looking forward to the Strauss opera so much that it did not show sufficient interest in the splendid Molière ... and after the Molière the amiable King Karl of Württemberg, with the best of intentions, held a reception lasting three quarters of an hour, which meant that *Ariadne*, which lasts an hour and a half, began two and a half hours after the beginning of the play, so that the audience was somewhat tired and ill-tempered.' That there was more curiosity in *Ariadne* than *Edelmann* cannot be doubted; neither can the audience's lassitude, but the reasons for its failure – which lasted well beyond the first night – owe more to the work's originality than to its unreasonable duration or local tension.

There was no modern precedent for *Edelmann/Ariadne*. Its construction, and the demands it made on theatres and impresarios, commanded world-class speaking and singing casts, a more than competent producer, a chamber orchestra of virtuosi and, most importantly, a small theatre with enough seats to subsidise Strauss's colossal fees. The theory – to which Strauss subscribed – that the audience for *Edelmann* was uninterested in opera, and vice versa, is nonsense. The very plurality of theatrical art at the time was central to Hofmannsthal's suggestion of the idea in the first place.

Once again, audiences and critics were unable to reconcile *Ariadne* to the composer of *Elektra*. In truth, of course, Strauss had produced a chamber opera of equal daring and modernity. He had created a work in which the musical and aesthetic styles were so diverse, and of such delicacy, that critics were unable to safely determine the opera's complexion; consequently, they chose not to like it. Its failure to adhere to aesthetic precedents, its paradoxical approach to tradition and history, and its uncanny variety of cultural reference yielded incomprehension and hostility. That audiences did not understand the work at the time is by no means surprising, but that later generations have failed to appreciate its defining influence is astonishing.

In one obvious respect, *Ariadne* emphasised Strauss's cultural pessimism. Anticipating Thomas Mann's *Doktor Faustus* by some thirty-five years, Strauss's fatalism conjures a world in which the only viable artistic gestures are those that look backwards. Though Strauss was raised in a culture in which composition was considered the purest form of self-expression, and although his earliest works, chiefly the symphonies and chamber music, reflect this innocence, the majority of his later music is shamelessly subjective.

Strauss's post-modernism had, by its very nature, to embrace the fantastic. Hofmannsthal understood this, and encouraged him to forgo any lingering affinity he might have felt for the world surrounding him. Strauss's recreation of earlier achievements – even in the supposedly avant-garde *Salome* and *Elektra* – helped stimulate less nostalgic composers, such as Schoenberg, towards a reinvention of the periods, styles and composers that were dearest to them. The ironic gestures of the post-modernist attempt to legitimise a withdrawal from modern life. Great art affirms the real, not the imagined, just as it animates the collective. A sense of shared experience and a belief in the viability of civilisation – as is heard throughout Mahler's work – is central to the success and durability of any cultural change. Strauss inwardly knew this, and the path of his creative life, through sixty years of composition, mirrors his increasing aversion to the air outside Garmisch.

Edelmann/Ariadne may have been typical of Strauss, but it was by no means typical of German music at the time. For all its nostalgia, and in spite of its evident suspicion of actuality, *Ariadne* was a musical landmark; but only with time and a rewrite did audiences and critics come to realise this. The wit and skill of an obviously twentieth-century work in which are quoted dozens of other composers – including bursts of 'La donne è mobile' from Verdi's *Rigoletto* – and which features a ten-minute coloratura *hommage* to the *bel cantisti* of the early nineteenth century, was lost on contemporary audiences – as was the work's vigorous expansion of *Rosenkavalier*'s pluralism.

But whereas *Rosenkavalier* adhered in complexion and period to the rococo world of Mozart and Molière, *Edelmann/Ariadne* symbolised a reinvention of three centuries of musical evolution within a framework that, as Hofmannsthal later conceded, was too subtle for the established conventions of contemporary theatre. Strauss was beating a path towards an aesthetic that would be refined by another school of composers, led chiefly by Stravinsky. This aesthetic was neo-classicism, and *Edelmann/Ariadne* was its prototype.

Most sources correctly claim that neo-classicism thrived between the world wars, but it is also held that Stravinsky was its father; yet Stravinsky's first neo-classical composition, *Pulcinella*, was written five years after *Edelmann/Ariadne*, in 1917. Stravinsky was publicly resentful of Strauss's success, and his views on *Ariadne* were far from complimentary. In 1958, for example, he told Robert Craft: '*Ariadne* makes me want to scream'; but Strauss's incidental music for *Edelmann* – with its minuets, gavottes, entrées, courantes and intermezzi[16] – surely influenced Stravinsky when he came to revise the music of Pergolesi for *Pulcinella*. It is fortunate that when Hofmannsthal revised *Edelmann/Ariadne* Strauss did not abandon his incidental music (as did Hofmannsthal the play), but chose to publish it in 1917 as a Suite.

By the end of the year Strauss and Hofmannsthal had resigned themselves to their first failure. While the work enjoyed a number of new productions – including one in England to a translation by Somerset Maugham – and although it fared relatively well in Germany, Hofmannsthal was deeply hurt. After the Dresden production he wrote to Strauss: 'The performance was very poorly attended, and there is something saddening in the comedy being acted in a vast half-empty hall.'

His first letter to Strauss after the Stuttgart production, on December 2, was written 'at the express request of Bruno Walter' (a disciple of Mahler's whom Strauss detested) and raved at the composer for having given Walter, then Music Director at Munich, permission to stage *Edelmann/Ariadne* in the city's cavernous Residenztheater. He concluded: 'There is something wrong between the two of us (you and me) which in the end *will have to be* brought out in the open; but to touch on it and discuss it is so extremely distasteful to me that for some three weeks I have put off the decision to mention it to you.' He declined to go into detail since 'the political situation seems to render everything else almost trivial'.

The year 1913 was the first in twelve during which Strauss did not work on an opera. Hofmannsthal was working on *Die Frau ohne Schatten*, and *Joseph* loomed, spectre-like, on the horizon, but Strauss was essentially free of the pressures that accompanied the gestation of his operas. This unexpected, and unwanted, latitude did little to change the patterns of his life. The routine into which he had fallen fitted like a glove, although he seemed incapable of freeing himself of his interminable conducting responsibilities. It has been suggested, and not without reason, that Strauss's avarice prevented him from giving up such a lucrative source of income. A more charitable interpretation is that Strauss genuinely doubted the lasting value of his work and that, like Wagner and Mahler, he wanted to institute his own performance tradition while he had the chance. It is also to be remembered that conducting demanded lengthy periods away from Garmisch, and Pauline.

Eventually, Strauss was forced to return to the score of *Joseph*. He had long wanted to compose a ballet. Since 1900 he had been adding, on and off, to a setting of his own synopsis (*Kythere*, after the paintings by Watteau and Fragonard), but the work had grown so out of proportion that it would have spanned three consecutive evenings – a sort of *Ring* for dance. Strauss felt little enthusiasm for Hofmannsthal's biblical fantasy, finding the character of Joseph dry and unreflective, but since it had been commissioned by Diaghilev (who, in turn, wanted Strauss to provide the music), and in the wake of the ballet revival inaugurated by Diaghilev's company, commissions for Stravinsky (*Firebird*, 1910; *Petrushka*, 1911) and Ravel (*Daphnis et Chloé*, 1912), Strauss saw an opportunity to become the first German composer since Gluck to write a significant ballet score.

On August 23, Diaghilev (accompanied by Nijinsky) helped Strauss subdue his reluctance by travelling to Garmisch with a contract for 6,000 gold francs. His acceptance allowed Diaghilev to confirm bookings in Paris and London for 1914. Money may have bought Strauss's compliance, but no amount could buy his inspiration. On September 11 he wrote to Hofmannsthal: 'Joseph isn't progressing as quickly as I expected. Chaste Joseph himself isn't at all up my street, and if a thing bores me I find it difficult to set to music. This God-seeker Joseph – he's going to be a hell of an effort! Well, maybe there's a pious tune for good boy Joseph lying about in some atavistic recess of my appendix.' The ever-earnest poet endeavoured to clarify his intentions, and in the course of this long and nebulous process he blamed the *Alpensinfonie* – a score of which he was ignorant, but for which he had nothing but contempt – for obstructing Strauss's clarity of thought.

As Strauss's first significant commission, the short score for *Joseph* was audibly a labour of necessity, and neither Pauline nor Hofmannsthal liked it. In Berlin, on December 12, Strauss played through various themes and ideas to the poet, who sent a long, overwritten indictment the following morning from Darmstadt. Strauss's music, so he believed, was 'dressed up, dolled up, pastoral, impossible for this [*Joseph*'s] atmosphere'. Joseph must bear no 'trace of another, dainty world, the world of the minuet, or else this whole work is ruined'. Strauss's lack of sympathy for the subject, and his overzealous approach to the rhythmic complexion of dance, led him to create a score that was almost a caricature of its subject. Hofmannsthal spoke for Nijinsky when he implored Strauss: 'Write the most unrestrained, the least dance-like music in the world. Put down pure Strauss . . .'

At the end of the month Hofmannsthal dispatched a barely disguised threat to his long-suffering colleague: 'For us to be rent asunder, or not to come together, that would be a major disaster . . . it would prove correct all those friends and strangers who incessantly, by letter and by word of mouth, directly and indirectly, tell me, write to me or get others to write that I ought to abandon this collaboration . . .' If *Joseph* was proving a cause of strain between Strauss and Hofmannsthal, then their earlier 'children' were a source of enduring balm. On January 29 Beecham conducted the British première of *Rosenkavalier* at the Royal Opera House, Covent Garden. The run of eight performances – which Strauss did not attend – were fabulously successful. The *Illustrated London News* trumpeted: 'Not only brilliant, it is beautiful; not only beautiful but finely considered – the ripe expression of genius'; the *Daily Telegraph* announced: 'It is the most prodigal and elaborate sacrifice ever offered to the Muse of Frivolity.' The public bought every single available ticket.

Coincident to *Rosenkavalier*'s conquest of London Hofmannsthal infor-med Strauss of the 'decisive progress' he had made on *Die Frau ohne Schatten*: 'The profound meaning of this plot, the effortless symbolism of all the situations, its immensely rich humanity never fail to fill me with delight and astonishment.' Buoyed by the prospect of Hofmannsthal's new libretto Strauss undertook the stressful journey to St Petersburg in February for the first Russian production of *Elektra*;[17] he returned to Berlin for the city première of *Edelmann/Ariadne* at the Schauspielhaus on the 27th. The competence of this production heightened Strauss's rage at Bruno Walter's 'assassination' of the work in Munich.[18]

In March Strauss persuaded Hofmannsthal to join him on a driving tour around Italy, en route to concerts in Rome on April 6 and 13. The poet was ordinarily opposed to conversation in a car, particularly when accompanied by Strauss. The composer knew this, and reassured Hofmannsthal, 'you'll have complete freedom: when we feel like it we'll chat – but silence and contemplative enjoyment also very welcome.' For fear of intimacy Strauss added the tragic addendum: 'Each of us to pay for himself, to choose the hotel as he likes – in short, complete independence.' The journey appears to have been a success inasmuch as they were able to discuss the new opera.

Finally, at the beginning of July, and with the help of Harry Kessler, *Joseph* began to take shape; by August the short score was complete and, at some point during September, the working title was changed to *Josephslegende*. At the end of December, as a 'New Year's gift', Hofmannsthal sent Strauss the first scene of *Die Frau ohne Schatten*. The prospect of another operatic collaboration was sufficient motivation for Strauss to push on with *Joseph*, and he completed the full score just over a month later, in his apartment in Berlin, on February 2, 1914. Three days earlier Diaghilev signed contracts with the Théâtre National de l'Opéra in Paris for the first production on May 14. Nijinsky, for whom the work had been written, was replaced[19] by choreographer Michel Fokine, and Leonid Massine and Marie Kussnetzoff were engaged to dance Joseph and Potiphar's Wife.

The new year began with Strauss attacking Hofmannsthal. The poet had confided in one of his closest friends, Baron Eberhard Bodenhausen-Degener, and Max Reinhardt, over *Die Frau ohne Schatten* – reading them the manuscript before it was sent to Strauss. Such a breach of trust may have been uncommon as far as Hofmannsthal was concerned, but Strauss was merely having done to him what he did to others. The composer frequently played his scores to everyone bar the housemaid before Hofmannsthal. Less than two weeks after Strauss's outburst Hofmannsthal wrote: 'When I came to Berlin, I looked forward to hearing something of the music for *Joseph*, and in the course of conversation I was always on the look-out for a turn of phrase which would indicate your willingness to let me enjoy some part of its still hidden beauty. But nothing happened; and I am always too diffident to ask outright.'

At the beginning of May, with Hofmannsthal still ignorant of the music for *Joseph*, Strauss and Pauline left for Paris where they took rooms at the Hotel Majestic beside the Arc de Triomphe. On the 10th, while directing rehearsals, Strauss was told of the death of Ernst von Schuch in Dresden.[20] He conducted the first performance of *Josephslegende* (which he dedicated to his friend Edouard Hermann – another banker) on the 14th, the same day as Schuch's funeral. Also on the programme were ballet productions of Schumann's *Papillons* and Rimsky-Korsakov's *Scheherazade*. According to Romain Rolland, the production was 'the most magnificent I have ever seen ... a production so perfect that the tissue of this long act (which lasts more than an hour) is not broken by any interruption, any failing of the action, even a fleeting one. Absolute harmony of the music with the slightest gestures or steps.' He endorsed the popular consensus that Fokine's choreography, José-Maria Sert's set designs and Léon Bakst's costumes were universally superior to the music, the composer of which appeared 'much aged, bloated, heavy and red'.

Rolland found himself sitting behind Gabriele D'Annunzio ('who boos Strauss's work when the curtain falls') and his then girlfriend Ida Rubinstein ('who must have quarrelled with Strauss'[21]). It is curious that D'Annunzio, of all people, should have booed a work so epic and opulent as *Joseph*. His delight in spectacle and voluptuousness (as reflected in his ballet scenario for Debussy's *Le Martyre de St Sébastien*) was more than satisfied by *Joseph*, and Hofmannsthal's preoccupation with the search for God was in complete accordance with D'Annunzio's own work, not least that for Debussy.

However, Strauss's rebuff of their tentative collaboration was more than sufficient to offend the peppery D'Annunzio, and the darkening political climate, the general lack of respect for Strauss and the awesome wake of Stravinsky's *Sacre du Printemps* did little to help.

Josephslegende deserved its failure. The heavy, overripe score typified the composer's tendency to note-spin, and with the exception of the final ten or so pages *Joseph* drags with exertion. After returning briefly to Garmisch, Strauss left for London and a festival of opera and ballet sponsored by Thomas Beecham's father, Joseph. In England Strauss's star was still in the ascendant, and his company was much sought after;[22] but because rehearsals demanded so great an effort, and because Tamara Karsavina was engaged to replace the 'hobbling' Kussnetzoff, the première was pushed towards the end of the season, by which time expectation was running even higher than normal. Few were surprised when *Josephslegende* fell to another critical death. Ernest Newman savaged the score as 'the funeral of a lost leader' – which provoked from Shaw a humiliating defence of 'a masterpiece' he had not, as yet, actually heard. To make matters worse, the eternally shifty Diaghilev failed to pay Strauss his conducting fee of 6,000 gold francs. The composer noted in his memoirs of 1942: 'nor has he done so to this day', which was a little unkind since the impresario had died in 1929.

The day after *Josephslegende*'s London première Strauss travelled by car to Oxford where he received from the University another honorary degree, although this time it was for his services to music. For Strauss, the sun was shining. Aside from the critical mauling of *Joseph* (a work hardly dear to his heart), all was well with his ever-shrinking world. Outside, however, the situation was less rosy. On June 28 Archduke Ferdinand and his wife were assassinated in Sarajevo. One month later, on July 25, the Ballets Russes brought their London season to an end with a performance of *Josephslegende*.[23] Three days later, as Strauss and his family enjoyed their holidays at San Martino de Castrozza in the Dolomites, Austria-Hungary declared war on Serbia.

July 1914–December 1918

The consequences of Germany's declaration of war against Russia and France in 1914 had little immediate effect on Strauss. He read the papers and listened to the gossip, and like every other 'true' German he willed his country towards their inevitable victory. However, his enthusiasm for Germany's triumph took on a different dimension on August 1 when the British government sequestered all German savings in London. Having invested most of his earnings through Edgar Speyer,[1] Strauss's loss was staggering. Some estimate the sum at £50,000; it was probably three times that amount.[2] Twenty-eight years later Strauss drily recalled how, after a week's 'severe' depression, he 'carried on with *Die Frau ohne Schatten* which I had just begun and started again from the beginning to earn money by the sweat of my brow'.[3]

Strauss's enthusiasm for the war was typically subjective. When Hofmannsthal joined the Austro-Hungarian army in 1914, for example, he wrote to the poet's wife Gerty: 'Does he really have to be involved in the fighting? Poets ought to be permitted to stay at home. There is plenty of cannon fodder available.'[4] Three years later he described in a letter to Pauline the course of his travels around Germany: 'Eight hours from Berlin to Bielelfeld in an unheated train – that came close to getting even me down. No restaurant car, nothing hot to eat or drink. There is only one train from Cologne to Aachen on a Sunday: packed of course, and one and a half hours late. What made it worse is that the war is so eerily close along that stretch of line. Trains full of wounded, trains loaded with whole fleets of aircraft or with ambulances that have been shot to pieces – appalling!'

He was unmoved by the abuses to which his own and his enemies' soldiers were victim; rather, he complained to Hofmannsthal, it was the treatment of artists that caused him despair: 'The Kaiser reduces the salaries of the Court Theatre, the Duchess of Meiningen turfs her orchestra out into the street, Reinhardt stages Shakespeare, the Frankfurter Theatre performs *Carmen, Mignon*, the *Tales of Hoffmann* – who will ever understand this German nation, this mixture of mediocrity and genius, of heroism and obsequiousness? ... We're bound to win, of course – but afterwards, heaven knows, everything will be bungled again!' To Max Reger he wrote: 'To think that the Duke of Meiningen has thrown out his old and famous orchestra on to the street: whoever heard of such a thing – that is German vandalism! How are the innocent citizens to summon up enthusiasm for all the fearful sacrifices the war demands of us, if the Kaiser's own sister sets an example like that.'

Strauss was hardly one for making sacrifices. When, in June 1918, the War Office requisitioned the lightning conductor from his villa in Garmisch he wrote to the offices of the regional government: 'My lightning conductor has been removed and replaced by an inferior one on the orders of the regional authority. As must be self-evident, if the state forcibly requisitions the citizen's property in this way, the state should also bear the costs that the citizen incurs.'[5]

Though he may have acted selfishly, Strauss rarely exhibited signs of stupidity, and he refused to add his name (alongside those of Richard Dehmel, Max Reinhardt, Engelbert Humperdinck, Felix Weingartner and Siegfried Wagner) to the infamous Manifesto of German Artists and Intellectuals of October 10, 1915. Rolland claims he resisted this opportunity to reinforce his solidarity because 'declarations about things concerning war and politics were not fitting for an artist'. It is more likely he thought the Manifesto ridiculous, feeble and penitent; he can have wanted no part of a document in which, with all seriousness, the signatories claimed: 'As in our love for art we cannot be surpassed by any other nation, in the same degree we must decidedly refuse to buy a German defeat at the cost of saving a work of art.' To Rolland he announced that 'he would joyfully send back his 'title of' doctor *honoris causa* of Oxford University if, in exchange, a British Dreadnought would be handed over or sunk'.

On August 20, 1914, having completed the first act of *Die Frau ohne Schatten*, Strauss wrote in the manuscript that this small personal battle had occurred on the same day as 'the victory of Saarburg. Hail to our excellent and courageous troops, hail to our German Fatherland.' Two days later he wrote to Gerty Hofmannsthal: 'Hugo has the damned duty not to die for the Fatherland before I get the third act . . . But joking aside – these are great and glorious times, and both of our peoples [Austrian and German] have shown themselves as magnificent; one is now ashamed of the nasty critical words which one has uttered about the brave, strong German nation. One feels exalted, knowing that this land and this people stand at the beginning of a great development, that they must and will assume the leadership of Europe.'

Elsewhere, and frequently in the company of liberals, Strauss would confirm his views with alarming animation. According to an entry in Hermann Bahr's diary in November 1915, for example, Strauss asserted: 'that he comes from peasant origin, that he had risen by his own efforts, and whatever he achieved he is willing to defend against others who have not succeeded. In general, and politically, he asserts the right of the strong. He is opposed to universal suffrage, wants a true aristocracy, a selection of the strong – believing that everyone can be strong if he disciplines himself.' While German to the core, Strauss's faith in his army's military superiority, and his general enthusiasm for Germany's pugnacity, were transient, and as much a product of propaganda as of principle.[6]

As with much else concerning his sensitivity to world affairs, it is not easy to reconcile the thoroughness of Strauss's education and the breadth of his experience with the ease with which he was able to bury his head in the ground – particularly as there were many artists for whom the war was something more than an irritation. His belief in Germany's cause and her stated aims diminished, but at no point did he surrender his belief in the sovereignty of artists and their work, a belief that held the mass of suffering and tragedy then materialising around Europe to be less deserving of concern and anguish than the preservation of a painting or a theatre. To Hofmannsthal, on January 16, 1915, he reinforced the balance of his priorities: 'Shall we ever see the Louvre, never again the National Gallery? And Italy?'

Only rarely did Strauss make reference in his correspondence to the realities of the human catastrophe engendered by the war. In February 1915 he was moved by indignation, rather than compassion, to complain to Hofmannsthal: 'It is sickening to read in the papers about the regeneration of German art, considering that only twenty years ago the most German of all artists, Richard Wagner, was accused of "Latin rut"; or to read how Young Germany is to emerge cleansed and purified from this "glorious" war, when in fact one must be thankful if the poor blighters are at least cleansed of their lice and bed-bugs and cured of their infections and once more weaned from murder! ... one feels a veritable revulsion against all this hypocrisy and ignorance.'

Irritated though he may have been by the official posturing he was, like most of his intellectual peers, confident of victory. Having railed against the propagandists (for whom, ironically, Hofmannsthal was working at the time), Strauss continued: 'As far as the war itself is concerned we have, I think, every reason to view the future serenely. In our Navy there is an unbelievable confidence; the Russians will soon cave in; and in England itself the popular mood is said to be very flat already.' It was always *we*. Strauss was, after all, cosmopolitan only in taste.

He made no direct contribution to the war or to the German propaganda machine, but if he was himself unmoved to patriotic expression he was happy to assist those of his colleagues who were. When, in 1915, Max Reger asked him to schedule an early work of tub-thumping jingoism Strauss replied, 'Of course it will give me great pleasure to arrange for the first performance of your *Patriotic Overture* to take place under your direction. What Beethoven symphony would you like to share the programme?'

While Reger and his like-minded peers saluted the Fatherland, Strauss occupied himself with his fairy-tale opera, *Die Frau ohne Schatten*, and his hymn to the view from his study, *Ein Alpensinfonie*. To the surprise of his friends and family, and the dismay of Hofmannsthal, Strauss orchestrated the massive, fifty-minute symphony in just three months, between November 14, 1914, and February 15, 1915. For his critics it was evidence, if any were needed, that Strauss was a spent force, even though the work is superbly written, marvellous entertainment and more than worth the 50,000 marks paid for it by F. E. C. Leuckart. He scored the symphony for an obscene number of players – 137 in total (of which sixteen are offstage[7]) – making demands that, to this day, stretch even the wealthiest orchestra. Not only did he call for twenty horns, an organ, cow-bells and wind and thunder machines, he also expected the wind section to sustain the score's long-held pedal notes, notably during the opening B flat minor section, by use of 'Samuel's Aerophon', a long-extinct pedal-pump that allowed a player to receive oxygen whenever his[8] lungs threatened to collapse. Such extravagance contributed to what many considered the symphony's grotesque lack of connection with the singular poverty and hardship of the times. Later, more affluent generations have spurned the work because it is fashionable to do so.

In truth, the *Alpensinfonie* contains some of Strauss's most beautiful music. Even if it harks back to the Pictorialism of his youth, Strauss never claimed anything for the score other than that it was 'really quite a good piece'. Heard for what it is – an indulgent exploration of the expressive capacity of a modern orchestra – there is much to enjoy, and it does not deserve rejection simply because it is aesthetically incorrect and spiritually vapid. Neither Mahler's death, nor the increasingly traumatic events of the war, were sufficient to make Strauss drop his *Alpine* title or the twenty-two distinctly programmatic subheadings; had he done so, it might well have entered the mainstream alongside *Don Juan* and *Till Eulenspiegel*.

Aware of the cost of a performance of his new work, Strauss decided, as with *Heldenleben*, to dedicate it to an orchestra. It was only right that he should 'give' it to the Dresden Hofkapelle,[9] Schuch's orchestra of forty-two years. He arranged for the first performance to take place at the Berlin Philharmonie on October 28, 1915. After the dress rehearsal he remarked to the Dresden orchestra: 'Finally, I have learned how to orchestrate.' The premère itself was given a roasting by the critics, a response that would have been unremarkable in peacetime, but which, given the prevalence of wartime jingoism, demonstrates how far Strauss's standing had plummeted.

Having completed the *Alpensinfonie* Strauss returned to Hofmannsthal's fairy-tale which, more than any other of their collaborations, warranted effort. He completed the music for the first two acts during January 1915; only a few days into February it became apparent that the third would take a great deal longer. The fractured postal service and Hofmannsthal's military responsibilities had interrupted what, under normal circumstances, was a linear process. In February he wrote to Strauss: 'I do not think anybody could have foreseen that during our most important joint work we would be cut off from each other for an indefinite period. Please God this stupendous affair, which possibly causes me more violent pain than most people, may soon come to a decisive issue.'

Hofmannsthal's progress was further hampered by his father's illness, and Strauss's wearing criticisms of the libretto did little to help. On one occasion he informed the poet that, having shown the texts of the first two acts to Hülsen in Berlin and Seebach in Dresden: 'Both displayed total incomprehension of the thing, and Seebach understood it only after I had once more orally explained the subject to him and played the first act to him on the piano. Everything tells me that the subject and its theme are difficult to understand and that everything must be done to make it as clear as possible.'

Not for the last time Strauss was confounded by Hofmannsthal's obstinate denial of commercial reality. Why, when having recently triumphed with his lucid morality play *Jederman* (Everyman), was he so averse to providing Strauss with an intelligible libretto? The answer lay in Hofmannsthal's belief that audiences were never likely, with Strauss providing the music, to understand more than half his words. The libretto for *Die FroSch*[10] compensated for this suspicion by relying for clarity on the weight of a parabolic scenario, a world divided between gods and man, and a wealth of literary and visual symbolism.

At the beginning of April Hofmannsthal sent the first draft of Act III. Strauss was delighted, despite returning four pages of 'criticisms and suggestions'. After a short conducting tour to Prague and Budapest he travelled to Vienna on April 23 for performances of *Elektra* at the Hofoper and meetings with Hofmannsthal. Two days later he played through the short score of Acts I and II at Franz Schalk's house, an experience that bolstered Hofmannsthal's confidence in their 'child of sorrow'.

Progress was again hampered by Hofmannsthal's transfer to Poland. Strauss moved back and forth between Garmisch and Berlin, conducting opera at the Hofoper and concerts with the Hofkapelle, where his programmes made a feature of the valorous *Heldenleben*. Having no idea if and where his work was being played overseas, and anticipating none of the attendant income, Strauss was compelled to continue conducting. These financial pressures heightened his antipathy for Bruno Walter and the Munich Intendant Clemens von Franckenstein.

Strauss believed that both were conspiring against him, and that their poor treatment of *Ariadne*, and their indifference to the earlier operas, reflected a policy of persecution. He was only partly right. Walter positively despised Strauss, perhaps even more so his music, whereas Franckenstein admired the music but not the man. Strauss had allowed himself to be pacified, firstly by Franckenstein, secondly by Hofmannsthal, with whom Franckenstein was good friends; but by September Strauss's patience, and financial security, had worn thin enough for him to demand 'written guarantees about the upkeep of my works in my native city – or else I shall not enter the Munich Hoftheater so long as its present directors are in office'. Hofmannsthal again urged caution, and Strauss finally retreated.

Concern for the prosperity of his music, and the paucity of his income, had in 1914 convinced Strauss to accept an offer from the Hupfeld company to record a series of piano rolls to be played on domestic player-pianos. He had made his first piano rolls in 1905, the year of *Salome*,[11] for the Welte company. At that time, it seems, Strauss's motivation was less acquisitiveness than inquisitiveness. Furthermore, Mahler, Grieg, Rachmaninov and many another star composer/performer had already 'recorded' rolls, and Strauss had no intention of being left behind. Nine years later Rachmaninov and Busoni were his only rivals as composer/performers, although their appeal was unquestionably more executionary than creative.[12] Since Strauss was no more than a competent pianist Hupfeld evidently believed that public interest in his music was sufficient to make them pay the considerable prices for which piano rolls were then sold. This confidence in Strauss's contemporary appeal is reflected in the repertoire, which consisted of excerpts from *Ariadne auf Naxos*, *Josephslegende* and *Heldenleben*.

On December 1, 1915, he travelled with Pauline to Vienna for the Austrian premiere of the *Alpensinfonie*. Hofmannsthal attended, and he and Strauss were able to spend many hours together discussing *Die FroSch*. Ten days later Hofmannsthal's father died, an event of immense significance for the poet, and over a month passed before he was able to return to Strauss's libretto. At the end of January, accompanied by Strauss and Reinhardt, Hofmannsthal saw a performance of *Ariadne* in Berlin. It reaffirmed his faith in the work, and he informed Strauss that he was 'full of hope that this hapless child will be rehabilitated'.

It was generally Hofmannsthal's practice to view each succeeding work as if it were his finest and later, having witnessed a failure such as *Ariadne* or *Joseph*, to act as if he had estimated its fate from the outset. This defence mechanism irritated Strauss, particularly in connection with *Ariadne*, which he considered his finest work to date; he was particularly delighted, therefore, when Hofmannsthal began to drop hints about rewrites and revisions, not least since he had prematurely dismissed the idea when Hofmannsthal had urged a rewrite shortly after the Stuttgart failure.

Hofmannsthal proposed that the Molière be replaced by a Prologue. This dramatic introduction, based upon a scene in *Gentilhomme* and relocated to the house of 'the richest man in Vienna', would allow a glimpse of events 'backstage' prior to the performance of *Ariadne*, and featured a Composer of whom Strauss was instinctively suspicious. Though he liked in-jokes, and encouraged Hofmannsthal to play with their celebrity, he was opposed to such an obvious caricature, and abandoned the revision until 1916 when Leo Blech suggested making the Composer a *travesti* (trouser) role. On April 6, Strauss forwarded Blech's idea of casting the Composer as a soprano, although with characteristic tactlessness he closed with the news that 'On Wednesday I am playing the second act of *Frau ohne Schatten* to Hülsen, since perusal of the "longwinded text" hasn't given him much of a clue.'

Whether Hofmannsthal's reply was prompted by his reaction to Strauss's suggestion, Strauss's dismissal of *Die FroSch* or his general despair at the course of the war, is uncertain; but the animosity of the response was unprecedented: 'I fear your opportunism in theatrical matters has in this case thoroughly led you up the garden path ... To prettify this particular character ... smacks a little of operetta, this strikes me as, forgive my plain speaking, odious ... Oh Lord, if only I were able to bring home to you completely the essence, the spiritual meaning of these characters.' Strauss's idea for the Prologue's end was 'truly appalling'; elsewhere his suggestions were 'rubbish ... nonsense, absurd and truly horrid'; Hofmannsthal felt 'faint in mind and body to see' them 'quite so far apart'.

Strauss absorbed the attack like any other, although he was moved to ask Hofmannsthal: 'Why do you always get so bitterly angry if for once we don't understand each other straight away?' He stood his ground over the *travesti* casting and continued to write as if there had been no breach. On May 25, for example, he sent his 'Hearty congratulations on Austria's fine success in the South Tyrol: we are delighted!' Strauss was also considering new ideas for operas which, despite the daily reports of casualties and suffering, were as remote as ever from world events. In May he proposed 'either an entirely modern, absolutely realistic domestic and character comedy of the kind I have outlined to you before, when you referred me to Bahr[13] – or some amusing piece of love and intrigue ... or some such rather amusing subject ... You'll probably say: Trash! But then we musicians are known for our poor taste in aesthetic matters ...'[14]

Only a few weeks later Strauss resumed: 'my tragic vein is more or less exhausted, and since tragedy in the theatre, after this war, strikes me at present as something rather idiotic and childish, I should like to apply this irrepressible talent of mine [to a comedy] – after all, I'm the only composer nowadays with some real humour and a sense of fun and a marked gift for parody. Indeed, I feel downright called upon to become the Offenbach of the 20th century, and you will and must be my poet ...' On July 28 Strauss confessed that his predilection was 'for realistic comedy with really interesting people ... something in the manner of Offenbach's parodies ...' He complained to Hofmannsthal: 'Characters like the Emperor and Empress, and also the Nurse [*Die Frau ohne Schatten*], can't be filled with red corpuscles in the same way as the Marschallin, an Octavian, or an Ochs'; having made gloomy reference to Pauline's criticism that his music for *Die FroSch* was 'cold', Strauss pleaded with his poet: 'let's make up our minds that *Frau ohne Schatten* shall be the last romantic opera.'

Unable to find a musical character for Hofmannsthal's symbolical obscurantism, Strauss retreated into a bloated post-Wagnerian sound-world for which he could muster neither invention nor enthusiasm. In September he conceded: 'I no longer know what's successful and what's bad. And that's a good thing, for at my age one gets all too easily into the rut of mere routine and that is the true death of art. Your *cri-de-coeur* against Wagnerian "note-spinning" has deeply touched my heart and has thrust open a door to an entirely new landscape where, guided by *Ariadne* and in particular the new Vorspiel [Prelude/Prologue], I hope to move forward wholly into the realm of un-Wagnerian emotional and human comic opera.'

Strauss's hopes were more than realised. His revision is a masterpiece of lyrical, elegant persuasion – his first successful collaboration with Hofmannsthal since *Rosenkavalier* six years earlier – and his greatest achievement prior to *Capriccio*. There was no question of placing the new work with Stuttgart. Strauss recognised that if the first performance was to make an impression it would need to be staged in a cosmopolitan musical centre. They settled, somewhat grudgingly,[15] on Vienna and the Hofoper. Maria Jeritza[16] was invited to recreate the role of Ariadne; Siems was replaced by Strauss's first choice for Zerbinetta, Selma Kurz, and Jadlowker was dropped in favour of the Hungarian tenor Béla von Környey, a newcomer to the Hofoper who pipped the much loved Alfred Piccaver to Bacchus. Strauss relinquished the baton to the Hofoper's music director, Franz Schalk.

For the new and equally sought-after role of the Composer, Strauss turned to Vienna's beloved Marie Gutheil-Schoder. The Intendant of the Hofoper, Hans Gregor, was concerned that the Viennese stalwart was neither reliable nor, at forty-two, young enough to play the role, and he secretly arranged for a new company member who had recently arrived from Hamburg, Lotte Lehmann, to learn the part. He told no one, not even Franz Schalk, and waited to see how events unfolded. At the first orchestral rehearsal, with Strauss and Hofmannsthal pacing about the stalls of the Hofoper, Gutheil-Schoder failed to arrive. Gregor seized the opportunity to present his 'understudy, musically prepared' to Strauss who, fearful of losing the day's rehearsal 'to the dogs', was compelled to agree.

The following morning, with Gutheil-Schoder nowhere to be seen, Strauss decided that Lehmann should sing the role of the Composer. Gregor had never expected Strauss to react so favourably to the young soprano, and he found himself obliged to tell Gutheil-Schoder the bad news. At first, the august soprano accepted her fate with stoic nobility; but after the first performance on October 4, when both the opera and Lehmann were cheered to the rafters, she revised her earlier resignation and accused Gregor of subterfuge and deception. She never spoke to the Intendant again, despite remaining at the Hofoper for another eleven years. Gutheil-Schoder bore Lehmann no ill-will,[17] but Lehmann's success did upset Jeritza, since her assumption of the Composer earned the loudest cheers of the evening.[18] The Berlin première of *Ariadne II*, staged two weeks later on November 1 and conducted by Leo Blech, was 'not a real success'[19] but the hostile critical response did little to hamper the opera's prospects, and productions followed soon after in Dresden, Breslau, Leipzig and Düsseldorf. Strauss remained in Berlin until the beginning of December when he returned to Garmisch and the final act of *Die FroSch*.

At the beginning of 1917 he embarked upon a gruelling, but 'magnificent triumphal' tour of Germany and Holland: 'first *Rosenkavalier* at the Hague and in Amsterdam with the Dresden crowd and Knüpfer; full houses at unheard-of prices; a Strauss Week in Mannheim with *Salome*, *Rosenkavalier* and *Ariadne*, staged very prettily and wittily by Dr Hagemann, the Vorspiel botched completely at the most heavy-footed pace by F., otherwise a very gifted conductor, and eventually put right by me for Switzerland in three rehearsals ... Finally *Ariadne* and *Elektra* in Switzerland, with a downright triumphal success.' The 'gifted' F. was Wilhelm Furtwängler, a young con- ductor whom Strauss was to have reason to know much better during the 1930s.[20]

In February 1917 he left Germany again, this time for Scandinavia. While away, the Kaiser announced his decision to wage unrestricted submarine warfare, and the United States finally joined the conflict. There followed food rationing throughout Germany, which led to starvation and crime in most of the largest cities. Berlin was visibly affected, and when Strauss returned to the capital on March 5 for a month's conducting he found a city under siege. He experienced little deprivation himself. In Garmisch he was always able to find food from the farms that surrounded his house; and with Pauline to ensure that the larder was stocked and the cellar was full, the villa was able to withstand the worsening deprivation around it.

In June Strauss completed the full score of *Die Frau ohne Schatten*. There was no question of staging such a monumental opera mid-war, so it was left to one side until the arrival of more propitious times. Strauss then turned his attention to Hofmannsthal's revision of *Der Bürger als Edelmann*, for which he had been asked to write more incidental music. During the course of July Strauss dared to make critical suggestions to Hofmannsthal regarding his adaptation of the play; on August 3 Hofmannsthal exploded: 'Your critical remarks and "proposals" reveal such absolute incomprehension, indeed such diametrical anti-comprehension of what I have tried to do, and have accomplished with the Molière adaptation by devoting to it for two months every effort of my imagination, my artistic sensitivity, my tact and self- effacement ...' Hofmannsthal later apologised and Strauss was able to make good progress; but his additions are uninspired, and many of them read, and sound, as if his only motivation was Fürstner's generous terms of publication.

A few days later Strauss travelled to Salzburg for the first Mozart Festival since 1910. Friedrich Gehmacher and Heinrich Damisch had, a few weeks earlier, founded the Salzburger Festspielhaus-Gemeinde[21] in Vienna with a view to establishing an annual festival of drama and music with an emphasis on Mozart's stage works. Both Strauss and Hofmannsthal were elected to the committee; other members included leading figures from Strauss's circle such as Max Reinhardt, Friedrich Rösch, Franz Schalk and Alfred Roller.

While in Salzburg Strauss found time to meet Hermann Bahr, who had some months earlier begged to be freed from his obligation to *Intermezzo*. Having been asked to set the opera in Garmisch, and having based the leading players on Strauss and his wife, the playwright had found the intimacy of the project a presumption, particularly as far as Pauline was concerned. Shortly after the première of *Ariadne II* Strauss adopted the libretto himself, completing it at the beginning of August.[22] In Salzburg Strauss showed Bahr his first draft, although Pauline's sullen presence inhibited a free exchange. Bahr recalled how Pauline was 'threateningly angered because of this marriage-libretto', which was putting it mildly.

The year 1917 ended for Strauss with his first orchestral recordings, for Deutsche Grammophon, with the Berlin Hofkapelle.[23] There are various reasons for DG's having engaged Strauss. The German financial climate at the end of the year was grim: individual buying power, especially among the gramophone-owning middle classes, was in vertiginous decline, and prospects for overseas sales were limited. In part, the sessions appear to have fulfilled something of an experimental purpose. The first ever recording of a complete symphony (Beethoven's Fifth, conducted by Nikisch) had been made only two years earlier, and it was important for the company to be seen to promote the latest techniques. Strauss was Germany's best-known musician at the time, making him an obvious choice as conductor, and both his concerts and those in which his music featured remained popular throughout the war. Concert and opera performances between 1914–18 brought almost as many people together as the Church; and it was culture (specifically German culture) to which the majority were apt to bow their heads. Whether or not the recordings made Deutsche Grammophon any money pales beside the historical value of the recordings themselves.

During the early months of 1918 Strauss was threatened with another extended period of inactivity, most worryingly during the summer months when he was at his least distracted. *Die FroSch* was finished and *Edelmann* was nearing completion;[24] he had only begun to toy with ideas for *Intermezzo*, and Hofmannsthal had broached nothing new. By May Strauss had no choice but to commit himself to *Intermezzo*. On June 6 he wrote to Hofmannsthal that he was 'making excellent progress. The whole thing is very well planned, and its structure and music will no doubt make up for what the piece lacks in poetic power.' His confidence was misplaced; he would not complete the work until 1923.

The second half of 1918 saw great changes, both for Strauss and the world around him. A few days before the Armistice of November 11 he was in Coburg for a production of *Rosenkavalier*, from where he wrote to Pauline:

> Things are starting to be really desolate. The war is over, definitely over! But what is to come may be worse. After a 12-hour journey I had a rehearsal ... this morning, with new sets. The King of Bulgaria and the Duke were present throughout the entire rehearsal. Afterwards lunch with the Duke: soup, pullets, mashed potatoes and apple sauce! Rien plus! Even dukes are having to tighten their belts. It's a scandal that we have to live through times like these. They say we shall all have to diligently learn new ways now. I shall not make the effort to do so until the whole situation has become a little clearer, otherwise there will be too much twisting and turning with every wind that blows. I am still holding my head high, in the belief that Germany is too 'diligent' to fall into such a complete decline – in spite of all the nonsense the worthy government has instituted. Bismarck's dream has suffered a rude awakening, at all events, and 200 years of Prussiandom are at an end. Let's hope that it will be replaced by better times. I don't believe that it will ... Please don't upset yourself unnecessarily ... we will think over everything calmly, although I wouldn't know what to do, even now, other than carry on as usual for as long as possible, according to plan, for as long as theatres and concerts keep going and pay fees.

Strauss's openly confessed self-interest underlines how little he and his values had been affected by sixty months of war; and yet, in the same breath, he professed a belief in the dignity, and destiny, of the German people, for whom he normally felt no more than a distant, congenital compassion. Whether he was privately disillusioned by Germany's plunge towards defeat in 1918 is impossible to say for sure, but his feelings for Berlin reached their nadir during the summer when, as the German army's advance was halted at the second battle of the Marne, he travelled to Vienna for a 'Strauss Week' at the Hofoper. During his brief stay in the Austrian capital the Opera's director Leopold Andrian-Werburg appealed to Strauss's disenchantment by inquiring whether he might be interested in succeeding him as joint director, with Franz Schalk. As a gesture of goodwill, and after thirteen years of wrangles with the censor, he offered to stage *Salome*.[25]

As with most of the significant changes in Strauss's life, this one owed more than a little to good fortune. He had been at odds with Hülsen, a man of resolute implacability, since 1915. That Hülsen was incapable of reconciling Strauss's arbitrary commitment to the casual terms of his revised contract to his unquestionable value as Germany's best-known musician was a source of frustration for Strauss and of misery for Hülsen. Both men knew that Strauss's heart rarely accompanied him to the Berlin Hofoper, and Hülsen came to believe that he was employing a composer for whom the Court Opera was little more than a platform from which to supervise performances of his own music.

During the spring of 1918 history repeated itself. Strauss's relationship with Hülsen disintegrated to a point whereby neither would speak to the other, and it became obvious that one, or both, had to go. When Hülsen announced his retirement a few weeks later overtures were made to Strauss to replace him, even though Hülsen's successor, George Droeschler, believed he could hold on to Strauss by tightening, not relaxing, the reins. By this stage, however, Strauss was some way down the road towards a contract with Vienna. At one stage he dared to suggest maintaining the directorship of both opera houses simultaneously. For Berlin's audiences this might have been an acceptable compromise – half a Strauss was better than none at all – but for the Viennese even the whole Strauss was less than they wanted.

The term 'poisoned chalice' might have been coined to describe the directorship of Vienna's Opera. Strauss knew this; he had watched a whole series of incumbents struggle, suffer and fall. Mahler's pain may have come to him as a Jew,[26] but Weingartner's miserable tenure underlined the impartiality of the rancour and intrigue that accompanied the post. Anyone tempted by the status and influence had also to remember the politics, claques and cabals. Andrian-Werburg asked for Hofmannsthal's help with negotiations, and the poet contributed much to the final agreement; he was none the less fiercely opposed to Strauss's appointment, and in August he wrote with characteristic frankness:

I cannot help saying that this plan has an opponent … I am that opponent … I believe that about fifteen years ago you would have been the ideal person to bring about the urgently needed renaissance of the Vienna Opera, but I cannot think that you still are today. I believe – and what has given me this impression is the manner in which yourself, with hundreds of little brush strokes, have painted the picture of your activity in Berlin – that today you would put your own personal convenience, and above all the egoism of the creative musician, before the uphill struggle for the ultimate higher welfare of that institution. I believe that, though you are still eminently *capable* of throwing yourself whole-heartedly into the task of building up the repertoire, into a Mozart or Wagner cycle, into protracted serious rehearsals (the ever-renewed youthfulness of your mind is the finest aspect of your personality and the most obvious assurance that you are a man of superior qualities), you would no longer be willing to do so. I believe … the advantage to your own works would be uppermost in your mind and not the advantage to the institution.

Strauss was now used to receiving such letters from his librettist, but even he must have been taken aback by Hofmannsthal's observation that he was 'very fond of the good and fine aspects of your personality where I meet them in the artist or, by sudden flashes, in the man as well. Without goodwill towards you I could not possibly speak so frankly ...' Without goodwill Strauss would not have let him, and it says much about his expediency that he was willing to tolerate such haranguing simply for the sake of a good libretto. Having confirmed that he wished Strauss well ('better than most people have done in your life'), Hofmannsthal brought his letter to an end with the fantastically presumptuous, but horribly accurate assertion: 'You have not looked for many friends and have not had many.'[27]

Strauss's reply was no less typical: 'The few years that are left to me I must devote principally to my productive work. Nevertheless, since I compose only in the summer, I have resolved to devote five winter months for the next ten years or so to my work as a conductor – and since Berlin claims a little more than two months, I could well imagine myself spending the other, longer, half – and if necessary even part of the spring – in Vienna in a kind of advisory capacity (*along with* a full-time director) in the building up of a truly artistic repertoire, with a say as to the manner of its execution.' He intended to conduct 'either such operas of the current repertoire as appear to me valuable or first performances of domestic and foreign works that are deserving of support ...' But since he was 'generally regarded as a very good Mozartian and Wagnerian conductor, the work of these masters (in addition to Gluck and Weber) would be the first to be chosen for revival'.

The hallmark of Strauss's term at Berlin had been conservatism. With good reason did Hofmannsthal and his circle fear the appointment of a music director for whom Mozart, Wagner and Strauss were priorities of repertoire. Those days during which Strauss had been an emphatic champion of the new were essentially mythical. Examples of Strauss actively championing – i.e., performing – new works were notable for their scarcity, and only two new operas were produced during his tenure.

Strauss claimed, to Hofmannsthal, that it had been his 'devoutest wish for the past thirty years to assume the *de facto* supreme direction of a big Court Opera House', which was simply not true. Prior to the outbreak of war he had done everything possible to free himself from the claustrophobia of the theatre. The loss of his savings compelled him to seek a long-term contract that paid sufficiently well to compensate for the misery and strain of any active directorship during what were, for most conductors, the twilight years of a working life.

That he was willing to accept a term in Vienna attests not only to his continuing fear of poverty, but also to his obdurate faith in himself. It is a peculiarity of the Viennese people that amidst the deprivation and turmoil that befell them during and immediately after the First World War they were able to devote themselves to the leading cultural concerns of the day. That the fabric of society was beginning to come apart at the seams, or that fellow Austrians and Germans were dying of starvation, mattered as much as, or indeed less than, the appointment of a Bavarian to the most parochial of Vienna's artistic institutions. At the end of 1918, with rumour and conjecture daily absorbing columns of Viennese newsprint, Strauss's appointment as joint director, with Franz Schalk, was made public. The uproar was unprecedented; Strauss might almost have been a Jew. Criticisms were many: his salary of 80,000 kronen was insane;[28] his international commitments would keep him away from the city; he would promote his own work above that of the more deserving and less established.

The assault was led by Julius Korngold, Vienna's most powerful critic, for whom Strauss was a first-rate conductor, a second-rate composer, and a third-rate human being. Korngold had already done more than anyone to harm Strauss's reputation in Vienna but his apparently unambiguous rivalry was complicated since the critic had in 1897 fathered a genius, christened Erich Wolfgang, who had emerged during the war years as probably the most precocious musical talent since Mendelssohn. The productions of the eighteen-year-old Erich's operas *Der Ring der Polykrates* and *Violanta* in 1916 had created a sensation, and their critical and popular success had, for the first time in nearly two decades, threatened Strauss's pre-eminence as Austro-Germany's leading composer. The Korngolds were, therefore, among the relatively few Viennese Jews to surmount the city's determined anti-Semitism, and Julius was more than aware that Strauss's Aryan disposition represented a threat to his son's advancement at the Opera.

Initially, Julius attempted to unsettle Strauss's appointment by highlighting his supposed intention to hold the directorships in Vienna and Berlin at the same time – a not unreasonable presumption since Strauss had agreed to be the caretaker director in Berlin for a year from December 1918 – but when Strauss reassured the public that he would only be conducting concert cycles in Berlin while director in Vienna, Korngold turned his sights on Strauss's weaknesses as a man and as an administrator.

Why, he asked, did Franz Schalk need help? Did not any partnership invite conflict? Strauss and Schalk claimed not, since each brought different qualities to the post. Moreover, following Weingartner's incompetent administration it was thought two heads might be better than one. Just as the storm appeared to be passing it was revealed that Strauss's latest opera, *Die Frau ohne Schatten*, was ready for its première. As if no warning shots had been fired, Strauss announced that it would be staged at the Vienna State Opera.[29]

December 1918–January 1925

In his diary for October 4, 1918, Thomas Mann wrote: 'Formal peace offer and armistice terms from the "New Germany" are impending. Belief in "power" is being solemnly abjured – though Germany's enemies are steeped in that belief. The self-abnegation, remorse, and penitence are boundless. We now say that the enemy is in the right, admit that Germany needed to be reformed by such an enemy, and out of fear we reformed ourselves. – Lethargic, tormented, half sick.' 'Germany', believed Mann, 'has truly preserved her honour.' The shock of defeat was enormous, the humiliation crippling, but peace allowed no time for mourning; indeed, life after the November Armistice was considerably harder for most Germans than it had been during the war. Socialism was welcomed by the disenfranchised as the people's right after so much monarchical abuse, and a Socialist government was established on November 10, 1918 – the day after the official proclamation of the Republic.[1]

When Friedrich Ebert's Social Democratic Party proved incapable of holding the country together the SPD separated into factions, one of which (taking its model from Lenin's Soviet revolutionaries) reformed as the Spartacists, later taking the official title of the German Communist Party. The threat of bloody revolution necessitated a pre-emptively bloody regime: Right and Left fought out their differences on the streets, and the consequences of gunfire were everywhere. The elections of the National Assembly in January 1919 reflected a victory – the first in Germany's history – for parliamentary democracy, but the revolution continued apace.

No one living in or near a German city could fail to be aware of the turmoil; even electricity was rationed. In January 1919 Hofmannsthal informed Strauss that he was working in 'almost unheated rooms, with no gas and practically no electricity'. The mail was reduced to a skeleton service and the public transport system was barely functional. At the end of February 1919 commitments in Berlin forced Strauss to leave the relative security of Garmisch. On March 1 he wrote to Pauline:

When I got to the station in Munich yesterday, people were running about, soldiers were loading their guns and I was told, 'There's going to be trouble, the

Spartacists are on the march.' It was impossible to leave the station again, so, like everybody else, I ran up the platform to the front of the train and, in the company of a very nice Consul from Bremen, waited for 'things' to happen. But of course, as usual, nothing happened, and so we left on time, three of us in the compartment, and the heating actually working! Dear old Berlin is much more orderly than crazy Munich. There are officers to be seen, soldiers, all in uniform ... This idiocy cannot last much longer.

He was wrong. Six days later he wrote again to Pauline: 'I've just come back from the theatre, where it should have been *Fidelio* but wasn't, as the lights went out. There was a lot of shooting today, the government troops won at Alexanderplatz, and did a thorough clear-out of the Spartacists.' Strauss's priorities were characteristically myopic; with reference to the GDT he wrote to Pauline: 'With these matters to think about, which are very important for the future of the arts, it is best to forget the whole idiotic revolution and enjoy the inner satisfaction of working selflessly for a good cause.'

Strauss was still sufficiently informed to ask the critic Alfred Kerr for a quasi-political burlesque tailored to his ambition to become 'the musical Aristophanes of today's Grand Operetta'. He wanted a text 'in Singspiel form, like the *opéra comiques* of Auber' against which could be parodied the 'state of the theatre today ... workers' soviets and works' committees, prima donnas' plots, tenors' ambitions, General Intendants of the old regime proffering their resignations, could provide the milieu of one plot – and the political operetta: National Assembly, Old Comrades' associations, party politics, while the people starve, a souteneur as Minister of Education and Culture, a burglar as Minister of War, a murderer as Minister of Justice, could form the background of the other comic scene.'

This leaning towards lighter subjects kept Strauss at odds with the times, and left him dangerously removed from the wider cultural sea change then absorbing the younger generation of German-speaking artists and musicians. During the first six months of 1919 there emerged within intellectual circles a sense that the new era necessitated a near-total break with Wilhelminian culture. The course of aesthetic and moral trends led away from the probity of German precedence, whereby everyone and everything was judged by its connection with, and responsibility to, the past. In contrast, Strauss dug his heels in, seeing in Vienna an opportunity to preserve the eighteenth- and nineteenth-century values supposedly under threat from modernity.

The dramatically rapid changes that affected Austro-German fashion, architecture, design, theatre, typography, poetry, painting, art and music during and immediately after the war, together with the concurrent rise of cinema, radio and jazz, created an unparalleled divergence from the national-istic legacy which had characterised German music throughout the nine-teenth century. The emergence of cosmopolitan tastes, allied to the advancement of successively greater numbers of Jews, threatened the Teutonic foundations on which Beethoven, Brahms and Wagner had raised their mighty edifices. Furthermore, German aesthetic isolationism was challenged by the growing popularity of non-Germans such as Bartók, Stravinsky, Ravel and Prokofiev – to say nothing of their promotion through gramophone records.

Despite the social consciences of Schoenberg, Berg, Webern, Krenek, Hindemith, Eisler and Weill the general public was always going to prefer its music with abundant melodies, rising fourths and relative keys. Not without reason were Schreker, Korngold and Strauss the most popular living 'German' composers of the 1920s. The political Left demanded that music reflect the society in which it was written, and for whom it was played, while arguing that any regeneration of German social and political life necessitated a coincidental renaissance of spiritual and artistic values. The growing radicalism of a product for which the market was obdurately conservative generated considerable tension throughout Austria and Germany, especially in Vienna: after all, the thrill of *Neue Sachlichkeit* (new objectivity), dodecaphonics and atonality was never likely to seduce audiences asked to choose between Schoenberg's *Erwartung* and Verdi's *Rigoletto.*[2]

The Weimar years were probably the most fertile of the German twentieth century as far as music was concerned, but the polarity between the cutting-edge minority and the mainstream majority meant that a composer such as Strauss could remain at the forefront of contemporary music while at the same time suffering almost routine critical derision. Reflecting the wider political concerns absorbing the German middle classes after the Republic's foundation, Strauss revealed a commitment to the preservation of a veiled status quo through which the bourgeoisie might ensure their own interests while at the same time accommodating the new order. Many of the younger generation – i.e., those from whom the war had demanded blood as well as belief – were also strongly opposed to such sour *realpolitik*, and urged a rejection of the processes of modernisation which, they believed, threatened Germany's spiritual identity. Ever the pragmatist, Strauss favoured elements of both, but chose the path of least resistance.

When, in 1919, he finally announced his intention to exact a 'thorough-going reform' of Vienna's State Opera, the Viennese public reacted with fear and disbelief. They did not welcome change, particularly when wrought by outsiders, and Strauss's ambitions were thought objectionable. Appealing to Vienna's now equivocal sympathy for its German cultural roots, Strauss blazed to Schalk: 'It is not necessary to give *Traviata, Un Ballo in Maschera, Mignon, Faust*[3] every week. That's why I'm coming to Vienna to make a new modest try at a repertoire which is lofty and German.'

Such privileged access to Europe's greatest opera house during a period of uncommon creative affluence should have stimulated a vivifying repertoire policy – as had existed during Mahler's directorship – but Strauss instituted an official programme that all but suppressed modernity. He sneered at the 'old-fashioned' ambition (that had, coincidentally, allowed him and his music to achieve success) 'to produce as large as possible a number of new operas every season', and promoted a course of celebrity-based revivalism through which the old was honed and mastered at the expense of the new.[14] Strauss was becoming his father; he was apparently blind to the irony of a situation in which he was seen to be fostering the very star system[5] against which he had so valiantly struggled as a young man.

Of course, new works were performed; but they were scarce, and composers frequently found their works removed from the repertoire the moment audiences appeared to lose interest. In his defence Strauss claimed: 'Our best soloists can be persuaded only with very great pains to learn and sing the usually extremely exhausting and difficult vocal parts of a new opera ... who today would want to? ... But, and this is typical of Vienna, a new work without stars is foredoomed to failure: the public has no faith in an opera which soloists will not touch.' Further to his announcement that the house was in need of reform Strauss pledged to overhaul every internal artistic and administrative office. He proposed pensioning off those orchestral players and singers whom he considered past their best; he threatened to change the terms and conditions by which players were able to enjoy generous salaries and lengthy holidays while abusing a deputy system that did little for production integrity. Most unexpectedly, he grumbled about the high fees[6] paid to the very stars with whom he had recently developed such unexpected empathy.

To the surprise of no one, except possibly Strauss himself, almost the entire orchestra, technical staff and opera/ballet corps signed a petition demanding the withdrawal of his contract. Probably sponsored by Weingartner, the petition was signed by all but two of the company's leading soloists (Jeritza and Kurz), which meant that Gutheil-Schoder, Richard Mayr, Karl Aargard Oestvig and Richard Tauber demanded the dismissal of a man to whom each was, for different reasons, personally indebted. What makes this all the more remarkable is that a number of the petition's signatories were pencilled to sing at the world première of *Die Frau ohne Schatten* in October. Strauss had offered to withdraw the work from the Staatsoper, but this was no more than a political gesture since no one was going to risk losing such a prestigious event – particularly Schalk, who was to conduct.

If Strauss had always wanted to stage the première in Vienna, Hofmannsthal had always opposed such a proposal. As early as February 1916 he wrote to Pauline urging the reconsideration of her husband's 'abrupt and sudden' decision: 'At first sight there is quite a lot to be said for Vienna, but also much, and weighty considerations, against it. This, above all, that Vienna cannot produce a verdict which will be accepted all over Germany; failure would be taken in Germany as settling the matter, but success not. Moreover: nowhere will Roller find worse soil, nowhere will the libretto meet with so little good will, with so much preconceived incomprehension as in Vienna.' The following year, in September, Hofmannsthal asserted: 'I am more and more convinced that Munich might be the one place which offers us at least a hope of finding an audience so composed as to appreciate a work like *Die Frau ohne Schatten*, concerned as it is with spiritual values far beyond the horizon of the average Viennese-Jewish crowd.'

Oblivious to Hofmannsthal's concerns, Strauss began casting the new opera shortly before the season's end, in June 1918. Having conducted a number of productions at the Staatsoper during the preceding six months he had been able to observe at first hand the wealth of talent available to him. There was no need for auditions since he had heard each of the cast in performances of operas by Mozart, Weber and Wagner. As with each of his operas post-*Feuersnot* Strauss conceived *Die FroSch*'s leading roles for women: a half-human, half-fairy Empress,[7] a Wife[8] modelled, by Hofmannsthal, on Pauline, and the Empress's malevolent, human-hating Nurse;[9] but he also created two extremely fine male roles in Barak 'the Dyer' (one of the opera's two named characters) which he scored for a baritone, and the Emperor, a horribly taxing part for *Heldentenor*.

The Nurse, Barak the Dyer, and the Emperor virtually cast themselves. Lucy Weidt was the company's most tenacious mezzo, and Richard Mayr was by this stage 'the' Baron Ochs, beloved of both Strauss and Hofmannsthal. For the Emperor, Strauss had little hesitation in engaging the handsome, vocally magnificent Norwegian Karl Aargard Oestvig who, though he had been with the company only a short time, had forged a considerable reputation as Don José and Bacchus. For the opera's two leading roles, the Empress and the Dyer's Wife, Strauss had long known his cast, although for a while he was undecided as to who should sing which role. He had composed the Dyer's Wife, at least to the end of Act I, expressly for the blood-and-guts Jeritza, but during the course of writing Act II he changed his mind and decided she was better suited to the higher tessitura – and greater physical beauty – of the Empress. The other soprano, Lotte Lehmann, was piqued when (as it seemed to her) she was asked to adopt a Jeritza cast-off. It took considerable diplomacy to assuage her; eventually, on July 22, 1919, Strauss himself wrote to Lehmann: 'Think, for God's sake, what a fuss there would be if you, the first youthful-dramatic singer, do not sing this most lovely youthful-dramatic role.'

As a show of faith Strauss invited Lehmann to Garmisch for private rehearsals. A few days later she received a copy of the piano score from Schalk, which she was fortunate in being able to study with the young conductor Jascha Horenstein and the pianist Leo Sirota. When she arrived in Garmisch, Strauss was astonished to discover that she knew the music, and her stay appears to have been as pleasurable for Strauss as it was instructive for Lehmann. She remained in Garmisch throughout the summer and was able to observe the composer, and his family, at leisure. At first Lehmann thought Strauss 'utterly aloof and impersonal'; but extended contact revealed 'an altogether different' complexion: 'The morning hours were given over to work, and work in a sense in which I had never known before. No hour was too long, no amount of sunshine could lure him from the piano ...' When not at work she was able to witness first-hand the 'hen-pecked and rather subdued husband'. Pauline, she recorded, 'derived an almost perverse pleasure from proving to her husband that no amount of fame could alter her personal opinion of him as essentially nothing but a peasant, a country yokel. Strauss himself warded her off with an indulgent smile, not even bothering to listen while she explained ... why their marriage constituted, in fact, a shocking *mésalliance* as far as she was concerned ... Nor was his music ... anywhere near comparable to Massenet. She in fact behaved like a shrew, snapping and snarling at him whenever and wherever she could.' It was apparent, however, that Strauss secretly relished the situation. As he confessed to Lehmann: 'The whole world's admiration interests me a great deal less than a single one of Pauline's fits of rage.'

A masseuse would arrive each morning for Pauline (precipitating the first of Strauss's daily walks), followed by a burst of rigorous exercises – a burden that Lehmann was compelled to share. On one occasion she and Pauline were 'lying half-naked on the floor of the terrace' when Strauss walked in. So acute was his embarrassment that he fled the room, slamming the door behind him, and marched from the house ignoring Pauline's bellowed commands for him to return. Lehmann was thankful that 'for once he had the courage of his cowardice', and did not do as he was told. The evenings were given over to Strauss accompanying Lehmann in performances of his own songs. During these impromptu sessions she frequently caught 'a glance or a smile' passing between Pauline and her husband, and slowly 'began to sense something of the profound affection between those two human beings, a tie so elemental in strength that none of Pauline's shrewish truculence could ever trouble it seriously'. She began to suspect they were 'putting on a kind of act for their own benefit as well as for that of outsiders', but Lehmann could never comprehend the oscillations between Pauline's 'violent outbursts of tenderness' for her husband and the 'tyranny' with which she otherwise tormented him.

The setting rehearsals for *Die FroSch* were held at the Staatsoper on August 28, 1919. Out of respect for Strauss the rivalry between Jeritza and Lehmann was kept in check, and thanks to the 'repertoire' policy that existed at the time the leading cast – probably the finest ever assembled for the first night of an opera by Strauss – persevered bravely with the punishing schedule. Alfred Roller returned for his second Strauss première, but it was an unhappy reunion. The designer was at odds with the new work, which he denounced as a 'machine-opera'. Although aware that he was required to accommodate Hofmannsthal's very specific stage directions, Roller simply ignored them and presented the work almost as if he disapproved of the magical setting.[10] No one could have faulted the skill with which he overcame the numerous technical obstacles,[11] but he appears not to have liked the work, its symbolism or, for that matter, Hofmannsthal.

The Viennese media's appetite for gossip was as insatiable as ever, but curiosity turned to resentment when it was announced that tickets would be sold at quadrupled prices and Strauss was again condemned for his implicit greed. For once, however, Strauss was blameless; Austrian inflation had left the kronen so unstable that a stalls ticket at the Opera cost the same in 1919 as had a season ticket five years earlier; prices suffered a further increase after it was announced that the première would be held in aid of the Opera's Pension Fund.

The performance itself, on October 10, marked a return to the sort of gala celebrity to which Strauss had become accustomed during the first decade of the century, and Vienna's shops and cafés were flooded with Strauss memorabilia. Although Julius Korngold spat poison at the new work ('Die Frau ohne Schatten has her shady side: the libretto . . .'), many of his colleagues set their grievances against an optimistic belief that Die FroSch represented a creative renewal for Strauss. The wealth of bitonality, dissonance and Sprechstimme appeased those for whom modernity necessitated an audible split with consonance, while romantic diehards warmed to Strauss's habitual reversion to the effortless melodies for which he was customarily celebrated. But the public (and secretly many of the critics) were baffled by the opera's dense symbolism. Strauss's refusal to conduct even one of the eight performances that filled the house during October reflected his own aversion to Roller's designs, and Hofmannsthal's manifest disappointment made it even harder for Strauss to enjoy their achievement.

After the euphoria of the première many began to question the opera's meaning; as Strauss predicted, few had any more than a vague idea what the work was about, and the underlying message – that marriages not blessed by children are barren and doomed to unhappiness – went largely unrecognised. Three years earlier, in May 1916, Hofmannsthal had reassured Strauss that Die FroSch's complexities were a blessing in disguise: 'You have every reason to be grateful to me for bringing you . . . that element which is sure to bewilder people and to provoke a certain amount of antagonism, for you have already too many followers, you are already all too obviously the hero of the day, all too universally accepted. By all means get angry with me and keep harping for a while on this 'incomprehensibility', it is a mortgage to be redeemed by the next generation . . .'

But this mortgage was not, and never has been redeemed. Strauss attributed the work's unpopularity to the quality of performance and calibre of production; but while his operas may suffer more than most from poor execution it would be folly to blame *Die FroSch*'s unchanging failure on those sporadic occasions (as occurred at the Dresden première) when nothing went right behind, beneath, or on the stage. Commentators have even presumed to trace its unpopularity to Strauss's own incomprehension. That the score denoted a reversion to the heavy Wagnerian universe from which he had fled with *Rosenkavalier* and *Ariadne* cannot be denied;[12] and his discomfort at working outside the parameters of neo-classical parody is evident throughout the score (as throughout the attendant correspondence with Hofmannsthal). But that Strauss did not understand the libretto is insupportable. The roots of this theory are to be found in the lack of connection between the music and words. Having advocated a score analogous to his libretto's Mozartian inspiration, Hofmannsthal looked on as Strauss wrote the most fulsomely Wagnerian music of his operatic career.

The bewildering catalogue of leitmotif and orchestral effect, the vastness of the orchestration[13] and the demands on the five leads marginalised the work for a post-war audience indifferent to anything reminiscent of pre-war bombast. The many passages of exceptional beauty are just that, and Hofmannsthal was not far from the mark when he later grieved: 'We have missed lightness of touch.'

Die FroSch's halting reception in Vienna failed to provide Strauss with a triumphant entrance into Valhalla – although a celebratory 'Strauss Week' did whip up a small degree of excitement. He none the less threw himself into the Staatsoper directorship. At first, his easy skill in decision-making made him an ideal companion for the indecisive Schalk; unfortunately, since neither thought to establish house rules, neither knew what the other was supposed to be doing. Consequently, there was tension from the outset. Strauss did not improve matters by refusing to forgo his freelance conducting work (including tours to Hungary and Romania), and since Schalk loathed any sort of confrontation – preferring to work out his resentment through the press – the situation became a great deal worse before it had a chance to improve.

Strauss's difficulties were compounded by the Opera's abnormally influential claques. This awful (now extinct) tradition served to provide singers with powerful vocal support from the third and fourth galleries – in return for a fee. Few novitiate singers could afford to operate without them (although Lehmann and, famously, Tauber prevailed through talent alone) and Strauss was forced to reconcile his interests as a music director to his responsibilities as a conductor. Even by German standards the Viennese gallery's influence was perverse. On April 11, 1919, when Strauss's position in Vienna was far from secure, the conductor, Leopold Reichwein – a noted opponent of the composer – was preparing to begin the Prelude to *Parsifal* when the theatre exploded with cries of 'We want Strauss'. This organised outburst clinched the directorship, but if the gallery could be manipulated to Strauss's advantage it could also work against him.

During the first four months of his tenure, between December and April 1920, Strauss trod carefully, winning many supporters with a dazzling production of *Lohengrin* that did much to sweep away the stylistic cobwebs that had returned since Mahler's departure in 1907. He emphasised the score's lyricism, modified the company's declamatory singing style and toned down the infamously noisy orchestra. He also conducted a *Ring* cycle, *Fidelio*, *Die Zauberflöte*, *Tristan und Isolde*, *Freischütz* and two of his own works – *Rosenkavalier* and *Ariadne* – earning equal measures of praise and derision in a situation that, as he was beginning to realise, was quite unwinnable.

He surprised everyone (including Julius Korngold) with an outrageous new production of *Carmen* – an inadmissibly 'Latin' work for German diehards, but one of the Staatsoper's most popular repertoire operas. Strauss recognised, as few had before, that the title role necessitated an excess of erotic absorption. Wearing a low-cut dress and a blonde wig Maria Jeritza certainly looked the part, but Strauss wanted more than the mere appearance of Carmen. He compelled her to learn the opera's dances as he had seen them practised in Spain, demanded that she play the castanets in time with the music and ordered her to conjure extremes of ecstasy, rage and lust. The Viennese had never seen a woman leap about a stage (far less on and off café tables) with such intemperate physicality, and the production caused a sensation. Jeritza secured her reputation as Germany's leading dramatic soprano, and Strauss was hailed as one of the world's greatest conductors.

In June 1920 his first season as joint director came to an end. Having received nothing more interesting from Hofmannsthal than a weak scenario for a ballet, Strauss was happy to accompany Schalk and the Vienna Philharmonic on a summer tour to South America. Joined by his son, Strauss left for Rio de Janeiro during the second week of August, stopping for an 'appalling'[14] fifty-one hours at the Cape Verde Islands for coal and supplies. After fifteen days at sea they arrived to find the local concert promoters embroiled in a battle that had led to the saturation of Rio's audiences with European art music. The VPO's promoter therefore presented the world's greatest orchestra and Germany's most celebrated conductor to half-empty theatres.[15] But as the tour gathered pace, and as news travelled faster than the orchestra, it ended better than it had begun. A few weeks before their return Strauss wrote to Hofmannsthal: 'There's one good thing in this kind of trip: one recovers one's full pride as a European and even feels nostalgic for hunger, fuel shortages and Bolshevism amidst all this material opulence!' He may well have come to regret these sentiments.

He returned to Vienna from Rio during the second week of December to find a city in economic turmoil, and himself the victim of criticism and conjecture. The prediction that he would abuse his position as joint director had, it was being claimed, come to fruition. In absentia Strauss proved an easy target. Guido Adler, Karl Kraus, Paul Bekker[16] and Julius Korngold – each of whom was Jewish[17] – sowed seeds of doubt as to Strauss's suitability as director; and when news leaked out in June 1921 that he was intending to travel to the United States for another tour – this time without 'his' Viennese orchestra – the indignation was all too predictable.

In particular, Schalk (who was not enjoying life in Strauss's considerable shadow) took this, and every other, opportunity to chastise him. Schalk demanded answers. In a letter, dated June 22, Strauss attempted to provide them: 'After England confiscated the chief part of my capital, having no pension to look forward to from any quarter, I have only the royalties from my works to fall back on if anything happened to me that stopped me going on conducting. Even operatic successes are unreliable if the royalties fail, which I hope will not happen for a while yet, I shall be a beggar and shall leave my family in "overty and shame".' Perhaps as a conscious gesture of reconciliation to the Viennese he began, during the summer of 1921, a ballet after his own scenario called *Schlagobers* and completed another neo-classical score, the delightful *Couperin Suite*.[18]

Having placated Schalk,[19] and in defiance of public and press opinion, he arranged to leave Vienna at the beginning of October. Again, Franz was his father's travelling companion, but on this occasion they were joined by Elisabeth Schumann – a soprano for whom Strauss had developed an uncharacteristically intense affection. They had first met almost exactly two years earlier, when Schumann had been engaged to sing the role of Sophie in the Viennese production of *Rosenkavalier*. Her great beauty, exceptional talent, ready wit, broad shoulders and willingness to perform Strauss's music made her an ideal companion for the composer, and she was as honoured by his admiration as Strauss was admiring of her voice.

Her diary of the trip contains much priceless disclosure. It was agreed that, en route to Cherbourg, they would stay in Paris:

He asks me about Vienna and the Opera, and listens very interestedly, grumbles about the rehearsals in Italian[20] – and Schalk ... When he hears that I intend to stay at the Majestic in Paris, he persuades me to go to the Grand Hotel with him instead. 'We're going to do some sightseeing in Paris, and so we must stick together.' So I go with him. At one we meet again in Prunier's – a wonderful place. Strauss sates himself on oysters, I feast on lobster ... he is wild about Paris – finds everything so tasteful and knows of no more beautiful city. I congratulate him on Prunier's and the marvellous lunch and he answers: Yes I'm a good courier, a moderate composer and a rotten theatre director.

They left Cherbourg for New York on October 19 aboard the White Star

Line's *Adriatic*. Also on board were H. G. Wells and the Russian bass Chaliapin, with whom Strauss played poker. To the delight of the passengers, Strauss, Schumann and Chaliapin gave an impromptu concert (mainly of Strauss's music) on the penultimate evening of the cruise. Schumann was encouraged by Strauss to indulge herself and 'hold on to the high notes a little longer'. Having done so she asked him if she had sustained them for long enough, to which he laughingly replied, 'Yes, but with a certain inward sense of shame.'

According to both Strauss and Schumann, their arrival in New York set the tone for the tour. The quayside was bursting with fans, reporters, photographers and cameramen – all eager to catch a glimpse of 'the world's greatest composer'. If there were any for whom Strauss symbolised the Imperial, warmongering Germany on whom the United States had so recently wished death and destruction, their grievances were engulfed beneath an overwhelming display of generosity, affection and respect. On October 31, when he was invited to an official reception in New York, Strauss and his companions were informed that someone would be sent to meet them at their hotel. 'At twelve midday,' Schumann recalled, 'approximately fifteen cars draw up outside the Hotel St Regis – all have the city coat-of-arms at the back. Strauss goes into the first with three gentlemen, Franz and suite go in the second, I in the third ... The cars are accompanied by policemen to left and right, riding on motor-bicycles and sounding their sirens all the time. That means that we go over every crossroads without stopping, all the other cars stand still ... Strauss drives throughout N.Y. "like a king".'

His first concert was given to a packed Carnegie Hall, with the Philadelphia Orchestra playing *Don Juan, Till Eulenspiegel* and *Sinfonia Domestica*. To Pauline, Strauss wrote: 'The applause as I entered went on for several minutes. I had to turn round and take a bow four times before I could even start.' He recorded every little detail of the modern American way (and cost) of life: '[I] allow myself to be fêted for the good of our dear country ... Apart from New York, which is really fabulous, staying in the land of universal mechanisation is deadly boring. All the hotels are overheated, while the weather remains mild. On Friday (when we leave for Chicago) we give up this expensive St Regis Hotel (38 dollars a night) ... and move into the Wellington Hotel, two bedrooms with bath and sitting room for 9 dollars a day. Bubi has worked out that it will save us the equivalent of the petrol for 500 trips to Munich.'

During the tour he was required to give almost as many interviews as concerts, in which he praised the beauty of 'all' American women and applauded the 'interesting' new music, jazz – when neither was, in reality, of the slightest interest. He told interviewers that his favourite (and most revealing) symphonic poems were still *Zarathustra, Quixote* and *Domestica*,[21] and he appeased the gossip columnists by making wry comments about his absent 'muse', Pauline. The concerts with Schumann were dominated by performances of Strauss's songs. The composer's creative instincts were so intense that, more often than not, he would deviate from his own piano score in performance. These changes were rarely more than cosmetic, but at a concert in Detroit on December 7 the loss of their luggage – and their scores – forced them to reschedule the programme, adding Schubert to the promised selection by Strauss.

Schumann was able to rely upon memory alone, but Strauss was unable to recall the detail of his accompaniments. When it came to *All mein Gedanken* he forgot his part and composed a completely new song. Schumann recalled how 'the words fitted perfectly, nobody in the audience suspected a thing and when we reached the end safe and sound, I looked to the right out of the corner of my eye to see . . . his mouth stretching from ear to ear in one huge grin.' In the artists' room after the concert she asked Strauss 'to write down the new version'. His reply was typical: ' "Oh, I've already forgotten it." '

The tour was exhausting, with the party spending the equivalent of fourteen (out of sixty-seven) days in trains. There is no reason to suspect an affair between Strauss and Schumann, although the stress of the tour might legitimately have driven them into each other's arms. Her affection for Strauss improved with familiarity, and not even his short temper or his tendency to fault everyone and everything about him could dampen her respect for 'this great man'. On November 10, 1921, she confided to her diary:

> Strauss bad tempered, takes it all out on Franz – grumbles about everything. I say that I don't understand his making the sacrifice this tour represents . . . 'Yes,' he says, 'I only do it so as to be able to live in Italy again one day.' I do not altogether understand why he couldn't do that without dollars. We sit at breakfast – his elbows are working – a bad sign – finally I break the spell and pour ridicule on the whole scene – especially his scolding of Franz – to such good effect that we all start laughing like lunatics. Otherwise it is simply unendurable when he sulks the whole time. But the morning is his bad time . . . He is so touching, the day before he brought me a tablet in my sleeping compartment, and when I couldn't swallow it he ran to fetch a glass of water and handed it to me with a gallant flourish. Our digestion and other discomforts often form the topic of our conversations.

Strauss's second tour of America ended[22] in the recording studio.[23] Earlier in the tour he had made his first radio broadcast (along with Schumann) as well as a small number of 'accompaniment'[24] piano rolls for the Ampico Company.[25] On December 30 and 31 he recorded performances with the Chicago Symphony Orchestra of the Dance from *Salome*, and the Minuet and Intermezzo from *Der Bürger als Edelmann*. He and Franz (but not Schumann, who did not return until February) left New York on the *America* on January 4, 1922.

Less than two weeks later, on January 17, Strauss conducted the London Symphony Orchestra in the Royal Albert Hall in a concert of his own music that included *Don Juan, Till Eulenspiegel* and *Tod und Verklärung*. Strauss was shocked by his reception in England, which was as disinterested as the United States had been captivated. The half-empty hall[26] attracted only a handful of critics, most of whom agreed that the programming was unadventurous. They, and probably the public, wanted to hear performances by the composer of his later tone poems, but since Strauss had agreed to record a number of sessions with the LSO at Columbia's London studios (which were to include *Don Juan*) he was understandably determined to preserve his rehearsal time. On the 19th he was back in the studio for recordings of the waltzes from Act II of *Der Rosenkavalier* and yet another recording of the Dance from *Salome*. The performances are magnificent,[27] as much a testament to the orchestra's virtuosity as to Strauss's stamina.

Back in Germany Strauss discovered that the mice had been at play. For the February 1922 issue of the British journal, the *Musical Times*, Paul Bekker provided an example of the sort of criticism to which Strauss was routinely victim in Vienna:

This house – which since the 1918 revolution has been under the management of Dr Richard Strauss in conjunction with Franz Schalk – is gradually assuming the character of a place of merely superficial amusement for the wealthy classes, and for those *nouveaux riches* whose taste is all too often heeded by the management. The once perfect ensemble of the theatre has become practically disorganised owing to a strong preference on the part of the directors for 'guest' singers whose mission is sensationalism, while some of the finest artists of the theatre are enjoying involuntary leave.

The consequent enormous outlay constantly increases the deficit of the Staatsoper, which now amounts to well over a hundred million crowns annually ... repertoire is now arranged according to the whims of visiting stars. Other [than Strauss] contemporary composers receive scant attention from the directorate with the possible exception of Puccini's all too pleasing operas and the works of Erich Wolfgang Korngold ... [neither can] possibly be said to represent present-day operatic tendencies.

Bekker was no lone gunman. During a visit to Vienna in May 1924 Romain Rolland recorded in his diary that the city had 'no inkling of new trends, of the accelerated rhythm, of the contribution of such people as Stravinsky, Honegger etc., of this frenzy which we can no longer do without in music, especially operatic music. – I feel here that I am with distinguished people half-asleep and habit-bound.' Rolland's concerns and Bekker's criticisms were valid, and Strauss knew it; but a knowledge of his failings as director was unaccompanied by the will to resolve them. He saw it as his responsibility to establish and maintain a set of artistic standards which were of greater significance than the city's ability to pay for them. Strauss believed that as a state-funded institution, and as a world-renowned symbol of Austro-German significance, the opera was there to lose money. Without conscience, therefore, he defied the commercial realities reinforced by Schalk, and carried on spending public money as if the country were in a purple state of prosperity.

So serious was the crisis that certain critics even began to talk of the 'good old days under Mahler'.[28] Korngold's shamelessly personal[29] campaign of denigration was especially damaging. Had Korngold not exercised such influence over the course of Viennese musical life the situation might have been different, but his was the most commanding voice in musical Austro-Germany, powerful enough to make or break a career within the course of a single article.[30] No one – especially not the directors of the Vienna State Opera – could afford to start a fight with the critic of the *Neue Freie Presse*. Unfortunately, Julius went out of his way to provoke Strauss, scorning his 'shameful' profligacy, his 'irresponsible' attitude to company homogeneity, his 'debilitating' predilection for visiting celebrities, his 'poor' management of schedules, and his 'weak' refusal to stamp out the deputy system. He cited one example in which a tenor singing the role of Paul in his son Erich's *Die tote Stadt* was forced to make cuts in the score because he was engaged to sing *Tannhäuser* the following evening.

On one occasion Strauss and Schalk summoned Erich Korngold to the Opera for a 'meeting'. Not unnaturally, he assumed that they wanted to discuss the company's successful production of *Die tote Stadt*; instead he found himself accused of using his father to promote his music. Strauss made the absurd claim that singers only performed in *Die tote Stadt* to avoid upsetting Julius (even though the three principal roles are among the most grateful in the German operatic repertory), and, most objectionably for Korngold, they reproached him for his father's public proposal that a Jew, Bruno Walter, and not Strauss, be appointed to the directorship of the Opera. The diatribe ended with the extraordinary announcement that, as a result of his father's constant criticism of Strauss and his administration, Erich would no longer be allowed to conduct his works at the Staatsoper.[31]

Erich expected prejudice in a city renowned for its hatred of Jews, but Strauss and Schalk's actions were hostile even by Austrian standards. Nevertheless Julius's attacks against the Opera's administration abated neither in number nor in severity; Erich was, therefore, obliged to endure the anguish of watching another, (deliberately) less talented conductor carve his way through his music. During a rehearsal of *Die tote Stadt*, at which the unfortunate conductor struggled to remain in control, the singers grew impatient, until one of them demanded to know: 'Why isn't Korngold conducting?' At this Erich leapt to his feet and not only repeated the question, but provided his own answer: 'Because my father writes bad reviews of the opera's directors!'

Strauss was informed of the outburst and summoned the composer to his office. Asked to explain himself, Korngold simply told the truth. Using a line from *Ariadne auf Naxos* to support his case – 'Lieber ins Feuer!' (Throw it into the fire) – he told Strauss that he could not sit by and watch his work suffer the agonies of incompetence. Strauss's sympathy for Erich's boldness brought about a temporary reconciliation, but when Korngold entered the pit for the first performance of *Die tote Stadt* since his clash with Strauss, the galleries exploded with whistling, stamping and shouts of 'Up Strauss, down Korngold!' Erich's supporters retaliated as best they could, and while the thunder continued he stood motionless with his arms raised. After ten minutes' commotion a woman in a stalls box turned the shouting to laughter by screaming 'Kusch!' at the top of her lungs.

Korngold was not the only living composer entertained at the Opera by Strauss. Puccini's works were enormously well liked in Vienna, and Strauss had little choice but to stage the Austro-German première of *Il trittico* in 1920; he also staged operas by Jan Brandts-Buys (*Schneider von Schönau*), Julius Bittner (*Die Kohlhammerin* and *Musikant*), Hermann Goetz (*Der Widerspänstigen Zähmung*), Richard Heuberger (*Opernball*), Wilhelm Kienzl (*Der Kuhreigen*), Hans Pfitzner (*Palestrina*) and Julius Zaiczek-Blankenau (*Ferdinand und Luise*). But these thoroughly German composers harked back to the nineteenth century and an aesthetic with which Strauss himself was manifestly sympathetic; so while living composers may have had their works performed at the Opera, contemporary music was all but circumvented.

Strauss made no attempt to pacify his critics. Productions of his own works continued apace, and on March 18, 1922, he raised the stakes by mounting the Viennese première of *Josephslegende*.[32] This lavish, enormously expensive staging precipitated the renewal of his friendship with Hofmannsthal, which had lain dormant since August the previous year. Absence had done little to improve the fondness of Hofmannsthal's heart, and on April 15 he wrote to the composer: 'Of course our relationship is now less easy, for the very reason that it was once something so very special and rich in content . . .' He repeated his warning that he and Pauline were to stay away from Rodaun; since 1918 his life had 'become, both in its economic aspects and in its mechanics, infinitely more difficult'. 'We live nowadays', he wrote, 'like very humble little people whose aspirations cannot go beyond leading a reasonably *decent* and *honest* existence . . . nobody has a car any longer.'[33]

He was keen to begin another opera, and Strauss's passion for all things ancient and Greek led to the development of another symbolic, semi-mystical idea, this time concerning Helen of Troy. With characteristic zeal, on March 21 the poet predicted a 'third work [after *Rosenkavalier* and *Ariadne*] certain of enduring for many years to come', but in the meantime he persuaded Strauss to collaborate on a 're-invention' of Beethoven's ballet *Die Geschöpfe des Prometheus* as a 'Festive Spectacle with Dances and Choruses'.[34] To these projects was added the 'great responsibility' of their plans for an annual festival in Salzburg. Max Reinhardt's proposal to the Austrian government in 1917 was 'lost',[35] and divisions between rival 'advisory' bodies led to a bastard festival in 1921, which was publicly denounced by the rival triumvirate of Strauss, Reinhardt and Schalk.[36]

Although the Strauss–Reinhardt proposal remained the best option for Salzburg, the city was in social and financial disarray, and local politics (administered by a conspicuously anti-Semitic council) made Reinhardt's role in the project the one obviously 'weak' link. Both Hofmannsthal and Strauss believed Reinhardt the only choice for the festival presidency, but as Hofmannsthal wrote to Strauss in early September: 'Never will these Philistines accept Reinhardt as president: they hate him, hate him three and four times over as a Jew, as lord of the castle,[37] as artist, and as a solitary human being whom they cannot understand.'

Strauss was persuaded by Hofmannsthal and Reinhardt to accept the post instead, and at the first full festival, later that year, he conducted two of the four stagings of Mozart with the Vienna Opera. The remainder of 1922 was monopolised by work on *Intermezzo*, Hofmannsthal's arrangement of Beethoven, ideas for *Helena* and, during the autumn, the completion of *Schlagobers*. But his heart was at the Opera, where he was overseeing a remarkable new production of Wagner's *Flying Dutchman*. The violinist Otto Strasser, who was later appointed manager of the Vienna Philharmonic Orchestra, recalled his first season under Strauss:

'It is amazing how ahead of the times he was in solving problems which are tackled by technology nowadays. The chorus of ghosts sat underneath a part of the stage that jutted forwards, and without the distortion caused by electroacoustic aids they sounded really ghostly. We had green lights on our desks ... and thus, without any disturbing reflection, the whole scene was truly spooky.' He also recalled, with affection, Strauss's improvisations of the recitatives in Mozart's operas at the harpsichord; and, with disappointment, Strauss's tolerance of Jeritza, whose severe cuts to *Salome* left 'only a torso' of the work.

The first five months of 1923 were, again, devoted to a new production of an opera by Wagner (*Tannhäuser*), but few Viennese were able to enjoy a night at the opera when the basics of food and fuel were barely affordable. When, in an attempt to force Germany to meet the reparation payments demanded by the Treaty of Versailles, the French occupied the Ruhr in January 1923, the resulting devaluation was so severe that what had once been annual salaries were insufficient to meet the demands of a single month's expenditure.

By February 15 wholesale food prices in Germany and Austria had suffered their 5,967th price increase since 1914.[38] Millions went without fuel, a joint of beef cost as much as had a field of cattle in 1914, and new clothes could not be bought at any price. The mortality rate began to climb and, due to the poor dietary conditions, a lack of hygiene and some disgraceful housing, disease began to spread. Oedema, dropsy, food poisoning and scurvy appeared in every major town and city, and the suicide rate rose dramatically, as did the number of deaths from 'old age' and 'weakness' – these being the terms used by coroners to account for the thousands dying from starvation.

With good reason did Strauss cherish his summer tour with the Staatsoper to South America,[39] during which he conducted productions of *Salome, Elektra, Rosenkavalier, Ariadne II, Bürger als Edelmann*[40] and a series of orchestral concerts in which he played music by himself, Brahms, Bruckner, Schillings, Korngold, Reger, Pfitzner and Franz Schmidt.[41] In Rio, Strauss was handed a letter from his son in which he announced his intention to marry Alice Grab, the daughter of a half-Jewish industrialist, Emanuel von Grab, whom Strauss had known since 1907.

On August 21, 1923,[42] Strauss completed the full score of *Intermezzo* in Buenos Aires. A month earlier he had written to warn Hofmannsthal that, upon his return to Garmisch in September, he would be 'without any work, and should like to find *Helena* (a delightful ballet in every act, please) waiting for me there!' From Dakar, on September 8, Strauss spelled out his desire for a 'second *Rosenkavalier*, without its mistakes and longueurs! ... Something delicate, amusing and warm-hearted!' Before receiving Strauss's note, Hofmannsthal wrote on September 14: 'Let me hope ... that you are now safely back at home ... Over and over again my mind has turned to this subject in propitious moments and now I have the whole piece worked out in my head ... You recall the chief characters of Act I: Aethra, the Egyptian sorceress and mistress of Poseidon, Helen, and Menelaus. The setting of the second act is an oasis in the desert adjoining Egypt to which the sorceress has carried off the rejuvenated couple for a short honeymoon, a beautiful spot to which neither the news of the Trojan war, which fills the whole of Europe, nor even the name of Helen has ever penetrated ...' He imagined Jeritza as Helen and Oestvig or Tauber as Menelaus, and urged an easy-flowing style 'as nearly conversational as the Vorspiel to *Ariadne*, sometimes coming close to the conversation scene in *Rosenkavalier*; never so heavy as in the opera in *Ariadne*'.

With *Helena* on her way Hofmannsthal and Strauss turned to the least likely of their collaborations – a film version of *Rosenkavalier*. It had originally been suggested by the director Robert Wiene (remembered for the Expressionist *Cabinet of Dr Caligari*), who would add to the silent film a live, purely orchestral reduction of the operatic score. Hofmannsthal's interest in the venture was financial. He believed a film would encourage Intendants to mount new productions of the opera, and urged Strauss to treat the project seriously; but Strauss was busy, and so he turned to Otto Singer and Karl Alwin (the second husband of Elisabeth Schumann, and a conductor at the Vienna Opera) for assistance. Together, they reduced the full operatic score to a selection of numbers and interludes[43] – leaving Strauss sufficient time to concentrate on mounting the premières of *Schlagobers, Intermezzo* and the *Hochzeitspräludium* (an epithalamium for two harmoniums, dashed off for Franz's wedding in January 1924).

A preoccupation with his various 'children' did not blind him to the worsening situation in Vienna. Aware that daggers were being drawn, and under siege from the ever-hostile Korngold, Strauss decided on consistency as the best form of defence and disappeared to Rome at the end of January 1924 to conduct a production, in Italian, of *Salome*. The move backfired and Korngold demanded Strauss's resignation as director. Before leaving for Italy he was able to enjoy Franz's wedding – and the première of his *Hochzeitspräludium* (which quotes themes from *Domestica, Guntram* and *Rosenkavalier*) – on the 15th. Franz and Alice were married in the Schotten-kirche, and honeymooned in Egypt, where they caught typhus. Franz nearly died, and remained extremely ill long after his return to Garmisch.

On February 1 Hofmannsthal's fiftieth birthday was celebrated throughout Austro-Germany. Strauss was in Rotterdam at the time (having stopped en route to enjoy 'exemplary' performances of *Ariadne* in Amsterdam) from where he wrote with unexpected openness:

> I have deliberately not participated in any literary demonstration in honour of your fiftieth birthday because I cannot escape the feeling that anything I could tell you in words would be banal in comparison with what, as the composer of your wonderful poetry, I have said to you in music. It was your words which drew from me the finest music that I had to give: this knowledge must fill you with deep gratification. Let therefore Chrysothemis, the Marschallin, Ariadne, Zerbinetta, the Empress, and not least, H[elena] – 'admired much and much reproved' – join me in calling on you and thanking you for all you have dedicated to me out of your life's work, and kindled in me, and roused to life.

Four months later, on June 11, Strauss's sixtieth birthday was celebrated throughout the world – nowhere more than in Vienna, where the composer basked in myriad honours, concerts, galas and a general air of reverence. Tributes came from the most unexpected corners, perhaps the most surprising from the Austrian government, to whose deficit Strauss had contributed so much. They made a gift to him of a plot of land in the Belvedere Gardens on which he was invited to build a house, his for the duration of a 24-year lease. In return he gave the city the original score of *Rosenkavalier*. Elsewhere there were 'Strauss Weeks' in Berlin, Breslau, Dresden (where a city square was renamed Straussplatz) and Munich, where he was made an honorary citizen, in return for which he gave the city the score of *Feuersnot*.

Hofmannsthal's tribute, rather than acknowledging Strauss's remarkable talent, or his unparalleled service to his own career, was a painstaking ration-alisation of his contribution as a librettist – thanking Strauss less for his music than for his recognition of, and sympathy for, his own achievements as a writer. Celebrations notwithstanding, Strauss's relationship with Schalk had deteriorated during February. Schalk accused Strauss of profligacy and dilettantism; Strauss dismissed Schalk as a Kapellmeister (in the worst sense of the word) and remained as oblivious of his criticisms as he was of the 'petty chicanery of the Ministry of Finance'. He none the less offered Schalk an olive branch in a letter of pliant reconciliation. When this was rejected Strauss refused even to talk to his co-director; he then informed Andrian-Werburg that if he was to stay in Vienna, Schalk would have to go.

On May 9, 1924, Strauss's tribulations were supplemented by another failure. The première of *Schlagobers*,[44] his 'Comic Viennese Ballet in Two Acts', had occupied Strauss and the choreographer Heinrich Kröller for most of the year; neither considered it a masterpiece, but much Viennese time and money had been expended on its first production. Many believed its reception would decide Strauss's future as co-director at the Opera. The scenario was his own, although it bears an uncanny similarity to Colette's ballet of 1917 *L'Enfant et les sortilèges*:[45] a young boy celebrates his confirmation by visiting the Viennese confectioners Demel's where he is encouraged to eat to his heart's desire. His greed makes him ill and while recovering on his bed at home he is tormented by a riot of dancing sweets and cakes from the 'realm' of Princess Praline and the cupboard of liqueurs.

That Strauss should have wanted to let his hair down after the symbolic concentration of *Die Frau ohne Schatten* was only to be expected, but that he should have let it fall to the ground was an error of judgement unworthy of the composer of *Elektra*. It was none the less consistent with the pattern of his development – always leading away from the tragic and towards the facile – and his expressed desire to become 'the Offenbach of the twentieth century'. Considering the poverty of the times, and knowing something of Strauss's fondness for diversity, *Schlagobers'* comic source has much to commend it, but for a composer whose reputation was founded, and main-tained, by serious dramas and even more serious comedies, the banality of a score in which the wittiest episodes are those quoting themes from operas by Wagner appeared to confirm the end of Strauss's career as a 'serious' com-poser. Of course, *Schlagobers* was superbly written. As he once predicted for himself, he was now able to portray through music the moving of a fork from the left to the right of a plate, but the very fluency and breadth of this talent served only to heighten the vapidity of the essential concept.

Worse, the piece was demonstrably anti-Semitic, and while Strauss was persuaded to drop the allusions before the première their origination did not escape the notice of the city's critics. Karl Kraus interpreted *Schlagobers* as a social commentary, in which 'the ordinary baked goods, pretzels, chips, cookies and suchlike proletariat – the latter, truly, incited by the intellectual matzohs[46] – until those circles who sit in the opera boxes ... have been pacified – until the resolute Munich beer – that's the way! – puts a conciliatory end to the class struggle ... the matzohs as rabble-rousers of the Revolution had been omitted at the première, so as not to offend anyone, even though everything ends well; instead the rabble rousing was done by "magicians" of no particular confessional stripe.' His contempt was not restricted to questions of discrimination: 'Now even his [Strauss's] famous versatility seems to have failed him, and even the Corybant critics cannot conceal the fact that there has not been a nastier desolation of the spirit even of the ballet or a more thoroughgoing degradation of theatre to the level of a preschool than this *Schlagobers*.'

Kraus did not waste the opportunity to turn his pen against Strauss the co-Director: 'a beggar state spends millions, while the city gives the master a piece of property on which to construct a castle in Vienna's most elegant park. All this and a week-long celebration in the ideal expectation that the creator of a musical world that has the Will to Tourism written all over its face should remain with us for a few months of the year in full nonconnection to the institute with which he has been entrusted.' The dedication of *Schlagobers* to Ludwig Karpath[47] – one of Vienna's most scheming critics, a good friend to Strauss, and a detestable man – did little to stem the stream of abuse.

On May 12, Strauss was visited in Vienna by Romain Rolland.[48] He found the composer

> surrounded by a circle of ladies and boring society people. Strauss, serious, heavy, affectionate ... Very preoccupied by nationalist follies, by our threatened European civilisation. Civilisation. Civilisation, for him, is concentrated in Europe, a little tiny Europe, three or four nations ... He doesn't understand ... He never has a smile on his face. No sudden bursts of gaiety, of fire, of unconscious 'raga-muffinery', as there used to be in the past ... The question of money preoccupies him. In Vienna he is reproached for, and people speak ungraciously of, the place this preoccupation now occupies in his life ... He appears to be absolutely indifferent to national questions and to national quarrels – Madame Strauss, who flutters about hither and thither, and who kisses him on the head whilst stuffing him with pastries, affects the same detachment from the German fatherland (which astonishes me).

With his birthday and *Schlagobers* behind him, Strauss turned to the serious matter of what to do with *Intermezzo*. Since Vienna was now out of the question he decided on a return to Dresden,[49] and the blessings of experience and provinciality. 'There was a kind of aristocratic unity and calm', recalled Dresden's conductor Fritz Busch, 'which was a great help to the works which were to be presented. All the light was focused on one point, resulting in an extraordinary brilliance.'

Into this spotlight Strauss was pushing more than just an opera. *Intermezzo*'s indiscretions were unprecedented. Where Strauss had once been the cause of scandal and outrage, *Intermezzo*'s confessional plot and open autobiography threatened embarrassment and ridicule. His enduring belief in the validity of his own life as inspiration surprised few who viewed him as a shallow, self-interested bourgeois; but in the eyes of those for whom Strauss had been Germany's greatest composer, the opera was a disaster. Even those summoned to work on the first production were shocked by the soul-baring, and yet *Intermezzo* was, and remains, a daring and adventurous achievement.

Completed five years after the end of the war, Strauss's eighth opera was his last, halting gesture of innovation. In the wake of Weimar's cultural revival, and amidst the surging changes that affected opera during the 1920s, Strauss finally recognised a need for musical theatre to keep pace with the changing social canvas against which he and his work were to be judged. *Intermezzo* forgoes myth and spectacle for a modern, everyday setting; gone are the weighty symbolic, motif-ridden washes of Wagneriana. In their place Strauss dramatised a realistic domesticity that would serve as the prototype for the *Zeitopern* (opera of the time) beloved of Hindemith and *Neue Sachlicheit*. In one of two Prefaces, written to be published alongside the score,[50] Strauss confirmed that 'by turning its back on the popular love-and-murder interest of the usual operatic libretto, and by taking its subject matter perhaps too exclusively from real life, this new work blazes a path for musical and dramatic composition which others after me may perhaps negotiate with more talent and better fortune'.

For the only time in his operatic career – and not for Hofmannsthal – Strauss composed his music with the clarity of the words uppermost in his mind. He instructed his own and later generations to forget the old-fashioned gestures required for the performance of Verdi and Wagner. To give the impression of improvised dialogue he urged aspiritic pronunciation (*ff* for consonants, *mf* for vowels), stipulating a rigorous attention to rhythmic detail: 'Don't let one word or one eighth note escape you.' With its cultivation of speech-led melody, cinematic use of time and setting (thirteen short, open-ended, rapidly changing scenes[51] separated by traditionally-inclined programmatic orchestral Interludes) and bold approach to 'real life', *Intermezzo* implied a new departure for lyric theatre. Even Schoenberg was forced to admit in 1926:[52] 'I find it inconceivable that he can play comedy and make himself appear better than he is. For all that, he knows far too little as a poet. And since this presentation leaves me with the definite impression that one is dealing with a very genial, warm person – a consequence not of his art, but of his personality – it convincingly reveals a side of his personality that has actually captivated me.'

But for all its implicit modernity *Intermezzo* is a work of determined conservatism. It typifies the detachment that Strauss brought to every aspect of his life, furthering, through a bizarre fusion of self-criticism and over-confidence, his suspicion of all things sincere. Unlike Brecht or Pirandello, Strauss was incapable of writing a truly daring or truthful social commentary since to do so would have required him to understand and, worse, empathise with his fellow man. Strauss the anti-modernist – for whom neither comic nor serious theatre were feasible without distance and objectivity – resisted the sentimental and loathed the familiar; anyone writing for the dramatic and lyric theatre had, he believed, to apply the same ambiguity and moral uncertainty to the mundane (*Intermezzo*) as to the extraordinary (*Salome*). In Strauss's universe there was no room for the partisan.

To create the role of Storch's Wife, Christine, Lotte Lehmann was summoned by Strauss from Vienna. Having 'eagerly set out to study the role' she was aghast to discover that both words and music 'seemed to present almost insurmountable obstacles'. To make matters worse Fritz Busch objected to bringing in Lehmann, since she was not part of the Dresden company. Strauss was then forced to threaten withdrawing the première if the 'ideal' Lehmann was not allowed to sing Christine; it was eventually decided she would sing only on the first night, and that to make the journey worth her and Busch's while she would also take part in four other company productions. Believing the situation resolved Lehmann was shocked to hear from Strauss that she was 'going to be in for trouble' since 'the local crowd would have much preferred one of their own'. Arriving at the Schauspielhaus, Lehmann discovered that Strauss would not be attending the first rehearsals – 'a fact not calculated to allay my apprehension'.

Lehmann not only 'made many mistakes' but 'swam'[53] through the score, 'a practice that drove him [Busch] to despair'. The conductor held his breath until Strauss's arrival at the end of October, whereupon he demanded Lehmann's immediate dismissal. Strauss asked to hear something for himself; as Lehmann began to sing she was able to watch the composer 'leaning on the piano, watching me, while I cast warning glances in his direction and tried to ignore Busch, who turned to him at every mistake, apparently expecting an outburst of Olympian wrath'. Instead, Strauss turned to the indignant conductor and remarked, 'Yes, I know that Lehmann likes to "swim". But even when she is "swimming" I prefer her to other singers. 'I could have hugged him,' Lehmann recalled, 'but I well knew how much he disliked displays of affection.'

Like Lehmann, Busch was mystified by the composer's ambiguities:[54]

Strauss was not in the least unsophisticated. At first glance he appeared a grand seigneur: he might have been taken for the president of a bank. No one would have imagined he was an artist ... The puzzle of Strauss, who in spite of his

marvellous talents is not really penetrated and possessed by them like other
great artists but, in fact, simply wears them like a suit of clothes which can be
taken off at will ... his decided inclination towards material things made him
an outspoken defender of capitalism, and with his complete disinclination to
any sacrifice, the sworn enemy of social changes. His materialistic pleasures ...
often seemed nearer his heart than his music.

Conductor and composer were to come to know each other much better over
the coming decade, and with time and through experience Busch was to
refine and revise his opinion of a composer whose 'amazing talents' he
admired 'too much to be seriously put off by his less attractive characteristics'.

In 1924, however, he was still easily shocked – not least by Strauss's enthusiasm for Adolf Mahnke's stage and costume designs for *Intermezzo*. With a
faithful attention to detail, Mahnke had reproduced, on stage, rooms from
Strauss's villa in Garmisch that were all but indistinguishable from the real
thing. Furthermore, the Storchs' maid, Anna,[55] was required to mimic her
impossibly stupid namesake;[56] Joseph Correck, who sang the role of the Conductor Robert Storch, wore a mask that heightened his already considerable
resemblance to Strauss, and while nothing could have been done to make
the hefty Lehmann resemble the diminutive Pauline, the soprano carried off
an impersonation of bizarre authenticity, imitating her mannerisms and
reproducing her voice without once stooping to caricature or mockery.

Conducted by the composer, the première on November 9, 1924, was a
huge local success, although the wider opinion was dismissive. Strauss's
responsibilities as conductor prevented him from exerting any influence over
Pauline, who yielded to a wholly legitimate fury at seeing herself portrayed
on stage as a shrew. Lehmann recalled how, with the première over, 'we
crowded into the hotel, surrounded by a mass of people who had all been to
the opera and were now ogling Pauline and her famous husband ... "This
opera," I said, "is really a marvellous present to you from your husband, isn't
it?" Tensely everybody waited for her answer. She looked round, cast a quick
glance at her husband, then said in a loud, clear voice: "I don't give a damn."
Embarrassed silence. Strauss smiled.'

Strauss had good reason to smile. During *Intermezzo*'s rehearsals he had
received a visit from Ludwig Karpath and Franz Kossak, a Viennese civil
servant, whose mission it was to 'resolve' the difficulties between Strauss,
Schalk, Korngold and the Vienna State Opera. For two days they argued the
merits and demerits of Strauss's position until Kossak produced a copy of
Schalk's new contract, in which he had been granted the authority to make
any and all decisions in Strauss's absence. Kossak wanted a resident director
for whom Vienna was the sole responsibility, and when he informed Strauss
that he had been charged to accept his resignation Strauss cheerfully gave it.

Just as Mahler had been crushed by Viennese anti-Semitism, so, in a bizarre reversal of influence, Strauss fell to the admonitions of a Jew. But he was glad to be rid of the post, the pressure and Vienna. Hofmannsthal urged him to remain on good terms with the city, writing on November 8: 'Since June 1923 I have foreseen this development and outcome as almost inevitable ... My only wish is that, among the various consequences which will flow from an eventual solution of this affair and in the status after the solution, it will be possible to avoid ... wholly hostile relations between the institution and yourself.' At the end of the month he again implored Strauss not 'to contribute to anything which might make the rift ... unbridgeable'.

Even after leaving the post he was subject to gossip, conjecture and hostility in the Viennese press. There was a particular frenzy of indignation when the *Neue Freie Presse* published details of Strauss's (rumoured) salary during 1924 – including a barely credible golden handshake – but Strauss simply let it wash over him. He retreated to Garmisch at the end of the year, from where he could reflect on the stormiest, least settled five years of his life; but if he was glad to be relieved of Vienna's poisoned chalice he was neither ready nor willing to forgive the manner in which it had been taken away from him.

January 1925–January 1933

A few days after the première of *Intermezzo* Strauss was visited in Vienna by the Opera's new Intendant, Franz Schneiderhan, to discuss the terms under which he might remain at Jacquingasse. In return for the 24-year lease for which he had already bequeathed the autograph scores of *Rosenkavalier* and *Schlagobers*[1] he would be required to hand over the autograph of *Helena*[2] as well as a commitment to give a hundred free performances at the Opera over a five-year period. Having paid huge sums for the designing (by architect Michael Rosenauer) and building of the house itself,[3] Strauss was not unreasonably piqued by the city's fresh demands for the equivalent of $60,000 worth of manuscripts[4] and 200,000 schillings' worth of conducting.[5] As he told his son, Strauss was happy not to receive any more 'gifts' from the city council.

He turned to work for distraction. In January 1925 the *Rosenkavalier* film was beginning to take shape; Hofmannsthal was convinced that the project would make them a fortune, and on New Year's Day he enthused: 'Wiene is (next to Lubitsch) the only German film director who has acquired an international reputation and whose work is accepted in America ... these people intend to invest what is for Europe a great deal of money, and they are sure they will get it back again with a substantial profit.'

Strauss was also preoccupied with *Helena*, and a commission from the pianist Paul Wittgenstein[6] (brother of philosopher Ludwig). Wittgenstein enjoyed a considerable private income that enabled him to commission works from many of the century's leading composers, including Prokofiev and Ravel. He was a difficult, confrontational man and his depressive character runs throughout Strauss's 'concerto' – the *Parergon zur Sinfonia Domestica*. Inspired by the drawn-out illness of his son Franz, it was to be Strauss's last work of outright autobiography; and while it is a strikingly powerful, earnestly felt work of catharsis, the unrelievedly dark and unsettled character has kept it in the shadow of its better-known parent-work.

In February Strauss was again touring, this time to Spain, via Paris. While in Barcelona he enjoyed a visit to a bullfight (which he embraced as the last ancient spectacle to survive antiquity), and conducted a huge massed band in arrangements of *Tod und Verklärung*, *Till Eulenspiegel* and *Don Juan*. He returned to Garmisch in March, from where he travelled at the end of May to 'take the waters' in Nauheim. During the summer he divided his time between *Helena* and the reduction of *Rosenkavalier*'s score for Robert Wiene's film.

Famed for his darkly Expressionist style, Wiene's predilection for *Stimmung* (the creation of mood through lighting), distorted spatial relationships and exaggerated perpendiculars were better suited to the neurasthenic worlds of *Salome* and *Elektra* than the Rococo idealism of *Rosenkavalier*. Wiene's *The Cabinet of Dr Caligari* was a non-narrative and poetic work of psychology; stripped of its libretto *Rosenkavalier* was its very antithesis and the director was required to jettison his theatrical sympathies in favour of a literal representation of Hofmannsthal's Vienna. Filming was arduous; Wiene, in particular, was out of his depth directing a cast made up largely of singers.[7]

Strauss completed his reduction in October, shortly before travelling to Italy and Greece (where he was made an honorary freeman of the island of Naxos). While Strauss was in Athens, Friedrich Rösch died; he returned to give a heartfelt commemorative address at the funeral: 'By dint of his great gifts . . . Rösch was destined to fulfil a lofty calling in the service of his German fatherland, and if Richard Wagner's saying "To be German means to do a thing for its own sake", may be allowed to stand, he was a genuine and great German.' The ever-diplomatic Hofmannsthal consoled Strauss: 'I have thought of you warmly, for I believe you have lost in him your only close friend of many years standing.'

In late November he left for Turin, where *Ariadne auf Naxos* received her city première on December 1; on his return Strauss wrote to Hofmannsthal that their work had scored 'an absolutely overwhelming success . . . Right after the first act — which is always a little chancy in Italy — there was tumultuous shouting for me, during the opera itself there was applause after the first masked quintet and after Zerbinetta's aria, and there was universal enthusiasm.'

Good news, according to Hofmannsthal, was always tempered by bad, and it followed just a few days later when Strauss announced his decision not to conduct the première of Wiene's film of *Rosenkavalier* in Dresden. Hofmannsthal convinced himself that this 'negative decision' threatened 'the loss of very considerable financial expectations – which was sufficiently threatening for Strauss to capitulate. Unfortunately not even his presence at the film's première on January 10, 1926, during a 'Strauss Week', could compensate for the absence of Hofmannsthal's poetry, and the film was a failure.

Hofmannsthal's mood swung again two months later, in March 1926, when Strauss played him the first act of *Helena*. He was overjoyed, writing by return: 'I am more delighted with this *Helena* music than, I believe, about any of your other compositions ever, and I feel I am right in this, even though I altogether lack the words to express myself properly. Yet, however inadequate my ear, I must have some sense for what matters in music, and this sense was most profoundly stirred by what I heard yesterday.'

The following month Strauss left for London and the Tivoli Cinema in the Strand where, on the 12th, he conducted the Tivoli Orchestra in the British première of the Wiene *Rosenkavalier*. According to *The Times*, Strauss was accorded the honour 'more of a film-star than a composer and conductor', but the critical reception was again negative. Many of the more hostile reviewers recalled an interview with Strauss, published by *The Times* in 1922, in which he was asked his opinion of 'cinematograph films with good music', and whether or not he had ever considered 'the possibility of writing original music to accompany films'. Strauss had replied 'emphatically that he had never entertained such an idea, and declared that good music was quite able to stand on its own, without the adventitious help of the film producer'.

The critic of *Musical Opinion* declared:

People who still need to be told what a strange mixture of boy, extraordinary genius and huckster Richard Strauss is can be sated at the Tivoli, where they will see a meandering *Rosenkavalier* film flickering along to music which, without the singing voices and operatic compactness of construction, is like a nigger troupe without the bones and banjo, and jazz without the kettle and mutes ... Think of his callow self-consciousness in *Feuersnot*, his infantile puerilities in his *Domestic Symphony*, 'Whipped Cream', and that recent opera of his alleged conjugal affairs [*Intermezzo*] ... and now this Tivoli affair ... A great work of genius ... disembowelled, then stuffed in order that it may leer like some mythical hybrid in the gilded shop window of a fashionable taxidermist.

Strauss remained in London until October 15 to record[8] his *Rosenkavalier* Suite for HMV at the Queen's Hall, again with the Tivoli Orchestra,[9] but he must have been glad to leave for Garmisch. Within weeks of his return, he left again for Greece, where he hoped to find 'a few beautiful tunes for Act II' of *Helena*. His travelling companions were Michael Rosenauer, the architect of his Viennese mansion, and Rosenauer's fiancée, the soprano Dora Kaiser. The Greek government – responding to the composer's countrywide popularity – had offered to help sponsor a Strauss Festival Theatre in Athens; attached to it would be a conservatory, through which would pass pupils trained specifically for the performance of operas by Strauss. The Greek authorities were sufficiently organised for Strauss to take the offer seriously, and when he arrived in Athens with Rosenauer they travelled the city looking for suitable sites. They eventually settled on a plot on the Museion hill, just south of the Acropolis, but political tensions and nationalist bitterness killed the project dead before Rosenauer could begin drawing up plans.

Meanwhile, Hofmannsthal was in Salzburg supervising a production of *Ariadne auf Naxos* with Lothar Wallerstein and the conductor Clemens Krauss. Although it had been decided that living composers would not be represented at the festival,[10] the temptation to mount an 'ideal' staging of his favourite libretto was simply too great. When Strauss arrived in August – via a 'triumphal Strauss Week in Leipzig' – he was delighted to find his friend Krauss presiding over a 'model' production and an 'ideal' cast. His mood was briefly soured when he learned that the festival's two most eagerly anticipated stagings (*Die Entführung aus dem Serail* and *Don Giovanni*) were to be conducted by Bruno Walter[11] and Franz Schalk, but *Ariadne*'s success, and Lotte Lehmann's performances as the Composer, were such that not even he could remain bitter for long.

In September the Strausses began their first winter as residents of Jacquingasse. The generally negative publicity surrounding Strauss's presence in the city – including the oft-repeated assertion that he was spending more time in Vienna now that he was no longer a director at the Opera – motivated Schneiderhan to send out an olive branch; he invited Strauss to conduct something of his own at the Opera, and after a 'staggering' performance of *Elektra*, even the press agreed to bury the hatchet.

Schneiderhan's efforts to build bridges continued into the new year, when the Staatsoper mounted the Viennese première of *Intermezzo* on January 15, 1927.[12] Strauss again stipulated Lehmann as Christine, but as a snub to Schalk he insisted on conducting the first of the six performances himself. The Viennese audience was surprisingly generous, but if many cheered the grand old man, few cheered his work. The critics praised Lehmann, and one or two acknowledged Strauss's contribution in the pit, but the opera itself was dismissed as decadent persiflage, and of total contemporary irrelevance.

Strauss's friends leapt to his defence, and even Hofmannsthal, who hated the opera,[13] stretched to words of consolation: 'It was with rather peculiar feelings that I was present at the première of a Strauss opera in the position of "librettist, without special duties *pro tem*" (but not "retired"!). The warmth of the success and everything this warm reception was meant to convey (to you generally) gave me real pleasure. About the work itself I cannot yet say anything upon this first hearing, because the whole thing, style, approach and all, interested and preoccupied me too keenly – I lack as yet the right perspective . . .' His refusal to pass comment over the libretto irritated Strauss, who replied, somewhat rashly, with his own critique: 'Harmless and insignificant as the incidents which prompted this piece may be, they nevertheless result, when all is said and done, in the most difficult psychological conflicts that can disturb the human heart . . . I presume that the smoothly-flowing, the naturally-flowing dialogue has not escaped the poet Hofmannsthal either.'

Four weeks later, in Paris, Strauss was given cause to reconsider Hofmannsthal's value when the Opéra mounted its first production of *Le*

Chevalier de la Rose (*Rosenkavalier*) on February 8. Almost unanimously the Parisian critics complained that the weight of Strauss's music hampered the clarity of Hofmannsthal's words, and that, despite the score's great beauty, the appeal of the opera was to be found in its almost anti-theatrical, extra-musical intimacy. Romain Rolland reached a similar conclusion in May:[14] 'Never did any musician have the good fortune, which fell to Richard Strauss, to work on a libretto like Hofmannsthal's. Even without the music, it's a feast to be relished. What subtlety of touch, what grace, and what malice! It is almost too rich and too delicately shaded to be fully expressed in the operatic theatre: the listener loses more than half of it.'

In March Strauss was invited to contribute[15] to the Germany-wide celebrations mounted in honour of the centenary of Beethoven's death in 1827.[16] Twelve months earlier, he had been asked to record the Seventh Symphony (together with Mozart's 39th[17]) by Deutsche Grammophon, as part of their plans to capitalise on the anniversary celebrations. These were Strauss's first electrical recordings – which makes a cut in the last movement of the Beethoven all the more terrible; they were followed at the end of 1926 with a recording of Mozart's last symphony, No. 41. During the first half of 1927 Strauss was back in the studio to record No. 40 – thus making him the first conductor to record the last three symphonies as a unit – but he disliked his performance, and demanded the opportunity to re-record. Both performances were eventually released, but their icy detachment adds nothing to his reputation as a Mozartian. Midway through 1928 he was asked to make what would be his last studio recording of music by a composer other than himself – Beethoven's Fifth Symphony.

Like most of the century's finest conductors Strauss took no pleasure in making records. The immutability of recorded interpretation was an aesthetic contradiction in terms, and he considered the masterpieces of Europe's classical tradition deserving of greater respect. He none the less continued to record his own music, justifying this apparent inconsistency as he had his performances at Wanamaker's store in New York.

In April 1927 Hofmannsthal began to nag Strauss about preparations for the first performance of *Helena*, the score of which was nearing completion. Strauss's preference was for Dresden; Hofmannsthal's was Vienna – even if, as he wrote to Strauss: 'Vienna involves for me as librettist a very definite vexation: Korngold. ... He has worked out for himself a regular system: to discredit each new work first of all by an attack directed against the libretto, while ostensibly paying homage to the composer ...' Strauss attempted to distract Hofmannsthal by urging him to consider ideas for a new opera.

On September 20, 1927, while orchestrating *Helena*'s final pages, Strauss complained to Hofmannsthal: 'But now I have no work: completely cleaned out! So please: write some poetry. It may even be a "second *Rosenkavalier*" if you can't think of anything better. If the worst comes to the worst, a little stop-gap job – a one-act piece – to keep my hand in – oil to prevent the imagination from rusting up.' At the end of the month Hofmannsthal composed his usual reply to such petitioning ('Without an original idea I can do nothing, and such an idea is a god-send ...'), but just two days later, on October 1, he wrote to Strauss with reference to a comedy that had occupied him two years earlier: 'It was called *The Cabby as Count* (*Der Fiaker als Graf*) ... in the *Rosenkavalier* style, but lighter still, still more French, if one can say that – still further removed from Wagner.'

All was well. There was new work on the horizon, *Helena* was days from completion, her première appeared fixed for Dresden in June 1928, and Maria Jeritza had expressed an interest in creating the title role. Strauss arranged to meet Schneiderhan, who agreed to sublet the soprano, but he was still concerned that Reucker, the Intendant in Dresden, would not allow another guest artist to steal his company's limelight. Fearful of losing Jeritza beneath red tape Strauss resorted to intimidation. On October 15 he informed Hofmannsthal that 'Mme Jeritza is in principle prepared to create Helen and [Schneiderhan] adds the hope that the first performance will therefore have to be in Vienna, if only because Dresden, under the rules of the Deutscher Bühnenverein, is not allowed nor able to pay her fee. That a first performance in Vienna is as good as out of the question I have already explained to Schneiderhan at some length. Nevertheless I have threatened Reucker with it, and Fürstner as a result is now negotiating with the Bühnenverein and with Reucker.'

When these negotiations collapsed Strauss forwarded to Hofmannsthal Reucker's proposal that Elisabeth Rethberg should take Jeritza's place.[18] On October 27 – the same day that Strauss completed the full score of *Helena* in Garmisch – Hofmannsthal exploded:

> I am utterly struck dumb by your letter. How am I to reconcile all this? You want me to write something new for you, and yet at the same time you inflict on me what I consider more loathsome than anything else that could happen. It looks as if, although we have known each other for so long and mean well by each other, you had not the least idea what it is in our collaboration that gives me pleasure and what has the opposite effect. I do not think there is anyone who knows me so little. I remember perfectly the energy with which, sixteen years ago in Dresden, you opposed, jointly with me, an impossible actor for Ochs ... *Helena* with a graceless Helen is simply ruined.

The following morning the poet sent a letter of apologetic self-justification; on the 29th Strauss replied:

> Just received your letter of the 27th! But why do you always turn so poisonous the moment artistic questions have to be discussed in a business-like manner

and you don't share my opinion? To accuse me immediately of not under-standing you is neither polite nor just. If I may say so, I think I understood you a good deal sooner than many other people: otherwise I wouldn't have put your books to music against the advice of the 'most competent' people – among whom theatre managers and critics are as a rule included, *though not by me* . . .

In truth, it was Hofmannsthal who did not understand Strauss. To the irredeemably romantic poet, who believed that art should transcend ques-tions of practicality, even the slightest compromise was tantamount to treach-ery and malfeasance, whereas pragmatism was second nature to the efficient, business-minded composer. The Jeritza question proved that Strauss was as ready as ever to stoop to 'tactics'; his feelings of contempt for the general public had, if anything, worsened. On November 2, 1927, he wrote to Hof-mannsthal: 'the present is generally a bad age for art and . . . the public who can afford a seat in the opera today is stupid and uneducated'; more alarmingly, he continued to hold to the politics of strength, in particular the patron saint of militarism, Friedrich Nietzsche, whose *Birth of Tragedy* he had recently reread 'with tremendous relish'.

Hofmannsthal felt sufficiently guilty to begin his three next letters to the composer with apologies; on November 13 his conscience suffered a further blow when he realised he had failed to congratulate Strauss on the birth of his grandson, Richard, ten days earlier. With guilt at his heels Hofmannsthal began working on their new comedy (*The Cabby as Count*, later titled *Arabella*), and on November 20 he determined to lay his conscience to rest:

The characters of this new comedy for music are cutting their capers under my very nose, almost too obtrusively . . . The comedy might turn out better than *Rosenkavalier*. The figures have taken very distinct shape in my mind and offer excellent contrasts. The two girls (sopranos) could develop into magnificent (singing) parts. They stand to each other roughly in the same relation – as characters – as Carmen and Micaela . . . As lovers a high tenor and a baritone. This latter is the most remarkable character in the piece, from a semi-alien world (Croatia), half buffo and yet a grand fellow capable of deep feelings, wild and gentle, almost daemonic, a part for – well, for whom? For Chaliapin? . . . Perhaps I shall be able to offer you once more, as I did seventeen years ago, something which lends itself to easy-flowing, happy creative labour.

Strauss badly needed another success. The 'Strauss Weeks' continued to follow on from one another, and he travelled the country conducting new productions of his operas, but he could no longer disregard the gulf that separated him and his music from Weimar culture – a separation that was having a conspicuous impact on his earnings. In 1928 he would be sixty-four years old. That he was producing operas at an age when most of his immediate contemporaries were either dying or sliding into semi-retirement was, in itself, a marvel; but his music was undeniably falling from popularity. In the five years prior to the collapse of democracy Strauss had conducted nearly half of the new productions of his works in Germany. Had he not invested such time and effort in maintaining the reputation of his music, there is no question that it would have begun to fall from the repertoire far sooner than it did.

The weight of influence exercised by the younger generation of con- ductors – such as Furtwängler, Klemperer, Busch, Kleiber, Reiner, Abendroth, Knappertsbusch and Tietjen[19] – further diminished Strauss's influence in that repertoire policy in later Weimar Germany was as often dictated by individual curiosity as by public taste. Nowhere was this more apparent than at the Kroll Theater where, in 1927, Otto Klemperer was appointed music director. Klemperer and the Krolloper typified the 'anti-Aryanism in the arts' reviled by Max Schillings.[20] Without the huge turnaround in Jewish influence which characterised the cultural achievement of the inter-war years Klemperer could never have been offered a contract to 'establish the Kroll with its own ensemble on as independent a basis as possible'. Not only did he promote the very latest musical sensations – including Stravinsky's *Marva, Oedipus Rex*[21] and *Petrushka*, Hindemith's *Cardillac* and *Neues vom Tage*, Schoenberg's *Erwartung* and *Die glückliche Hand*, Janáček's *From the House of the Dead* and Weill's *Der Jasager* and *Royal Palace* – but he also radically overhauled the nineteenth-century style and character of stage production favoured by the likes of Strauss, Pfitzner, Siegfried Wagner and Schillings.

When, in 1929, Klemperer mounted a new production of Wagner's *Der fliegende Holländer* he broke completely with the composer's instructions, provoking a reaction so hostile that two hundred policemen had to be summoned to prevent a group of Nazi thugs from razing the theatre to the ground. The *Allgemeine Musikzeitung* described Klemperer's Dutchman as 'a Bolshevist agitator', his Senta as a 'fanatical Communist harridan' and his Erik as 'a pimp'. It is easy to understand the apprehension felt by Strauss at the rise of what he, and the far Right, considered anti-German instincts. Hitler's earliest public speeches had appealed directly to this bundle of nationalist, anti-Semitic anxieties. In 1922 he made his widely publicised statement that 'the Right has completely forgotten that democracy is fun- damentally not German: it is Jewish. It has completely forgotten that this Jewish democracy with its majority decisions has always been without excep- tion only a means towards the destruction of any existing Aryan leadership ... there can be no compromise ... and there are only two possibilities: either victory of the Aryan or annihilation of the Aryan and the victory of the Jew.'

At a dinner party in June 1928, thrown by Hofmannsthal to celebrate the birth of *Helena*, Strauss (according to Count Harry Kessler's diary) 'gave forth his droll political views, the need for a dictatorship, etc.'. According to

Kessler, 'Nobody took it seriously', and Hofmannsthal was later compelled to apologise for his colleague's 'nonsense', but Strauss's confidence in doctrines of strength, and his blind faith in German superiority, were by then typical of the middle-class majority. He had always applied these beliefs to his working life out of instinct, breeding and self-interest. But now, as Busch recognised, 'He who in his inmost heart was in direct opposition to National-Socialist ideology had long before anticipated in practice one of its dogmas: "Right is what is of use to me." '

This was plainly demonstrated by the *Helena* affair, when – having squeezed Fürstner for $50,000,[22] the largest fee ever paid for the publishing rights of an opera – Strauss asked Reucker for a comparably fantastic royalty. When Reucker pleaded poverty, Strauss threatened to give the honour of the first night to the better-funded Schneiderhan. Reucker believed that Dresden, as godfather to most of Strauss's operas, deserved preferential treatment, but when Schneiderhan confirmed Jeritza's engagement as Helen, Reucker was forced to pay Strauss his fee. In return, he gained the première (and one-half of the dedication of *Arabella*[23]), only to be informed that Strauss had gone ahead and sold the rights to Schneiderhan anyway, who announced the Viennese first performance for June 11, 1928[24] – just five days after the première in Dresden. Strauss consequently received yet another massive fee, this time for conducting. Reucker was appalled – the more so when Strauss went public with his claim that while Dresden was mounting the first performance, Vienna would be staging the première.

This outrageous assertion hinged on the engagement of Jeritza as Helen.[25] But even she proved more trouble than she was worth. Schneiderhan had agreed to pay her fee of 6,000 marks,[26] only to be told that she was unwilling to sing in anything but the first performance. Strauss was trapped, and he wrote to the outraged soprano: 'I cannot reconcile myself to the news that you will not sing the part of Helen ... I perfectly understand your position, and I share your view that you are the one foreordained to create the role. But alas, you see things from afar ...' Having won her round, Strauss read of an interview in March 1928 in which she claimed not to have even looked at the new role and he promptly informed Franz of his suspicion that Jeritza 'wants to get out of it. She has probably found some snag, some hair in the soup.' But there was more to losing Jeritza and Vienna than money: 'What is at stake is having the première on my birthday. I have worked out the most precise timetable for the rehearsals, starting on 16 April, and there is no margin!'

Strauss emerged unscathed from these disagreeable events. Only Reucker and Busch thought his behaviour extraordinary. Busch's anxieties continued into the rehearsals, when he was again reminded of the inexplicable polarity between the composer and the man. Some weeks earlier Strauss had played his new opera to Busch in Garmisch. Asked for his 'sincere opinion', Busch replied, 'amongst other things, that I thought Da-ud's song in D flat major was cheap, and that he ought to weigh such "inspirations" more carefully. He in no way disputed this criticism but actually repeated it with enjoyment to his wife, who had just come into the room, but then added with disdainful cynicism: "That's what's wanted for the servant girls. Believe me, dear Busch, the general public would not go to *Tannhäuser* if it didn't contain 'Oh, Star of Eve' or to the *Walküre* without Winter Storms. Well, well, that's what they want."'

Midway through the difficult and frequently ugly rehearsals Strauss arrived to find Busch in a state of near panic. Not only was the staging proving over-elaborate, but Pauline's presence was making life impossible for everyone, particularly for the producer Otto Erhardt. Her interruptions and bellowed advice, coming from the wife of the composer, were impossible to ignore (at one point Erhardt reputedly screamed Herod's final words from *Salome*: '*Man tötet dieses Weib!*' 'Man kill that woman!'), and an air of formal sufferance pervaded what should, under normal circumstances, have been an enjoyable, instructive process. Furthermore, neither the cast – led by Rethberg as Helen, Kurt Taucher as Menelaus and Maria Rajdl as Aithra – nor Busch himself could come to terms with Strauss's vast orchestral apparatus. Taucher was especially harassed by the unfriendly writing for the tenor register; however, when Strauss politely asked Busch to lend him the podium he transformed the music, and the cast's understanding of it, to such an extent that Busch was humiliated before his orchestra. Strauss meant no harm – he was simply the better conductor – but the ease with which he advanced the rehearsal process starkly illustrated the contradictions of a character that fused the heights of artistry with the depths of self-interest.

The première, given as the opening night of a week-long festival of Strauss's music, was a triumph and Strauss basked in the adulation of a Dresden public for whom he could do no wrong. Unfortunately, the critics had, again, written their reviews in advance of the opera's performance,[27] and *Helena* remains the most unwarranted of Strauss's mature failures.

The majority balked at Hofmannsthal's libretto. Following a bourgeois comedy of manners, *Helena* was as chalk to *Intermezzo*'s cheese. The impenetrable array of mythological reference, the self-conscious profundity and characters as thin as Aithra and as absurd as the Omniscient Mussel/Sea Shell alienated audiences seeking an Elektra, an Octavian or a Composer. Hofmannsthal's dramatic framework – the psychological developments leading up to Helen's reconciliation with Menelaus after the Trojan War – inspired Strauss rather more than the actual libretto.

As with *Die FroSch*, Strauss worked to his own agenda, creating a self-contained musical narrative through another motif-riddled score. Much of the music, particularly during the first of the two acts, recalls *Elektra* and *Rosenkavalier* in its formal symphonic cohesion, and the abundance of

soaring lyricism, again chiefly during Act I when Strauss indulges his fondness for sopranos *a due*, presents some marvellous opportunities. The muscular orchestral fabric, scored for a huge number of players, is no less
reminiscent of an earlier style; but without the necessary inspiration Strauss
was forced to fall back on what he knew best. Like its composer, the opera is
a curate's egg: to episodes of extraordinary power and conviction (such as
the Finale of Act I) he lumped the weakest of note-spinning – at its worst
during Altair's big scene. In 1933, at Krauss's behest, Strauss revised *Helena*
for a production in Vienna. His changes did much to improve the flow,
but neither the Dresden nor the Vienna editions has managed to secure a
following.

The American première at the Metropolitan Opera, conducted by Arthur
Bodanzky, generated a frenzy of publicity. Ticket prices were raised for the
first night, and the theatre was crammed with the Great and the Good, but
neither the Olympian efforts of Maria Jeritza nor the outstanding conducting
of Arthur Bodansky were sufficient to dissuade the American critic W. J.
Henderson that *Helena* was 'the voice of an elderly man babbling his reminiscences'. His opinion prevailed, and the opera sank.

As always, Strauss turned for absolution to hard work. He immersed
himself in *Der Fiaker als Graf*, and during an unusually creative July in 1928
he and Hofmannsthal exchanged numerous long and complex letters in
an attempt to reach some point of mutual understanding. On the 3rd an
uncharacteristically sentimental Strauss wrote: 'I find we understand each
other better every year. A pity such good, continuous progress towards
perfection must come to an end some day and that others must start again
from the beginning.' And yet he was disappointed by what he read of Hofmannsthal's work, sending pages of suggestions in August, and he went so
far as to warn his poet that he was 'reconciled to not embarking on the job
until the whole thing is absolutely ready'.

At the end of September he attended the rehearsals in Munich for the
October staging of *Helena*. Knappertsbusch did 'his stuff excellently', and the
stage designs were 'very nice', although the cast was no more than 'good
lower-first class'. It was a different story in Berlin, where Heinz Tietjen
oversaw the launching of a 'magnificent' production on October 5. On November 19, and for no obvious reason, Strauss wrote to inform Hofmannsthal
of a Hamburg critic's commiseration 'for having my "marvellous music"
weighed down by your "incomprehensible text"'. As an addendum he drew
the poet's attention to Wagner's *Oper und Drama*, which he considered 'as
topical as it was eighty years ago' and a source of 'consolation and encouragement'.

Relations improved at the year's end when Hofmannsthal visited the
Strausses at Jacquingasse, and a return to cordiality was assured when Strauss
eventually confirmed his satisfaction with *Arabella*'s progress. Their spirits

were further lifted by the number, and quality, of new Strauss/Hofmannsthal productions during the last four months of 1928 – the highlights of which were Blech's new staging of *Salome* at the Berlin Staatsoper on September 5, followed on October 7 by the first Berlin *Helena* and Knappertsbusch's Munich première of *Helena* the following day.

The optimism and anticipation of the first few days of 1929 were tainted by sickness and death. Both Strauss and Hofmannsthal were taken ill in March and April, and Hofmannsthal registered Strauss's 'cooler attitude' towards both him and *Arabella* in May, which Strauss did little to assuage when, on the 9th, he wrote from Istria:[28] 'operatic texts can only be judged by the person who's got to set them to music. So don't go about asking any more people but write your poetry! ... In the past I never asked anybody but simply put to music whatever appealed to me. The public has always been a matter of indifference to me. And a good thing too!'[29]

Strauss spent May in Italy, returning to Germany, and a concert in Aachen, on June 1. He then travelled to Berlin for the 1929 festival. This now-legendary gathering[30] of musical life represented an assemblage of genius and invention that has haunted every subsequent generation. Between May 19 and 29 Arturo Toscanini conducted a season of six operas[31] with the La Scala company; between June 1 and 11 Strauss conducted productions of six of his operas, including *Helena*; Wilhelm Furtwängler conducted *Figaro* and *Tristan*; Leo Blech conducted the *Ring* and Busoni's *Doctor Faust*; George Szell conducted *Andrea Chénier*; Erich Kleiber conducted *La Clemenza di Tito*, *Wozzeck* and *Don Pasquale*; Bruno Walter conducted a solitary concert of *Das Lied von der Erde*, and Otto Klemperer conducted not only the world première of Hindemith's *Neues vom Tage*, but *Don Giovanni*, *Der fliegende Holländer* and a series of concerts with the Berlin Philharmonic. Ernest Ansermet conducted the Diaghilev ballet in a series of Stravinsky's scores, while Stravinsky himself played the solo part in a performance of his Piano Concerto, conducted by Klemperer.[32]

On July 4 Strauss returned to Garmisch, from where he informed Hofmannsthal that he was 'waiting impatiently' for the revision of *Arabella*'s first act; having received the new draft Strauss responded by telegram on the 14th: 'First act excellent. Many thanks and congratulations.' Hofmannsthal never read it. On July 13 his eldest son, Franz, committed suicide, and while dressing for the funeral two days later the poet suffered a massive brain haemorrhage. He died in Gerty's arms,[33] and in the presence of his younger son Raimund, aged fifty-four.

Strauss was deeply affected by the tragedy, and on the 16th he wrote to Gerty: 'This genius, this great poet, this sensitive collaborator, this kind friend, this unique talent! No musician ever found such a helper and supporter. – No one will ever replace him for me or the world of music ...' To general amazement,[34] Strauss informed Gerty that he would be 'indisposed'

on the day of the funeral, and he sent Franz and Alice to represent him in
Vienna on the 18th. Franz sat in front of Harry Kessler, who recalled in his
diary how the poet's 'coffin, altar and altar rail disappeared under a sea of
roses. Every rose garden in Vienna must have been pillaged to produce such
splendour. The church was cramfull . . .'[35] In his own, deeply felt eulogy Franz
Werfel, the husband of Alma Mahler, amplified the disaster for the wider
literary community: 'We have lost one of the very last *poets* – in the sacred,
classical sense – we had in this world. He was a seraph, a messenger of alien
powers in our midst. His timelessly youthful appearance confirmed that. In
the twenty years that I knew him, not a single feature changed in his beautiful
face.'

Strauss battled to come to terms with his loss. The day after Hofmannsthal's
death he called on his neighbours Elisabeth Schumann and Karl Alwin with
a copy of *Arabella*'s unfinished libretto, and read it through to them and their
house guest Clemens von Franckenstein, the Intendant at Munich Opera.
Unable to contain himself, the 65-year-old composer broke down as he
read through the poet's verses. It was a cathartic process, and his audience
understood how the ordeal was as significant as it was necessary. To all intents
and purposes, Strauss's operatic career was (for Strauss, at least) over. *Arabella*
would be his last opera, for how could he possibly follow such a pivotal
collaboration with another? Who could ever take Hofmannsthal's place?

Franckenstein, though no friend of Strauss's, was encouraged to help
keep the composer from reflection, and he offered a block of conducting
engagements as part of the Munich Summer Festival. These performances of
Strauss's favourite operas – *Figaro, Così fan tutte* and *Tristan und Isolde* –
helped him come to terms with his immediate future, and after a brief,
respectful sabbatical he returned to *Arabella*. As a mark of respect, Strauss
decided to set Hofmannsthal's second and third acts unedited.

In August, Schalk was forced into early retirement from the Staatsoper by
the same claque that had squeezed out Strauss. Rather than contribute to the
many written appreciations of Schalk's life and work, Strauss threw his
weight behind the appointment of his choice of successor – Clemens Krauss.
Unusually, Krauss was more popular with his employers than with his players,
many of whom found his manner over-polished and insincere; but these
were qualities that would serve him – and Strauss – well over the coming
decade. Krauss's responsibilities incorporated not only the Staatsoper, but
also the Salzburg Festival – of which he was made music director and administrator immediately after the 1929 event.

If Strauss had not by now quite recovered the massive losses of 1914, he
had saved enough to adopt a pace of life more fitting to his age and stature.
Krauss, and later Karl Böhm and Rudolph Moralt, considered Strauss Germany's greatest living composer; in the light of contemporary political and
philosophical fashion, that meant a great deal to anyone looking to prosper

within a fiercely conservative and nationalistic system. Had Krauss not played such an archly political game, and had his sympathies not so graphically accommodated prevailing attitudes and theories, then his attraction to Strauss might well have been purely aesthetic, but the National Socialists had long since made their cultural preferences crystal clear – and these embraced neither the progressive nor the exotic. Strauss was among Germany's most influential musicians, one of a handful guaranteed to find favour with a right-wing government.

Conversely, Strauss was careful to ensure good relations with as many conductors as possible. In spite of his anti-Semitism he was willing to make exceptions whenever it suited him and the furtherance of his music. He was happy, for example, to remain on constructive speaking terms with the Jewish Otto Klemperer for as long as Klemperer continued to perform his music – the more so after Klemperer's appointment to the influential Krolloper. But in 1924, soon after his departure from Vienna, Strauss dismissed Klemperer to his friend Ludwig Karpath as 'a notoriously bad conductor of my operas and famously lazy', adding that 'in Cologne they are glad to be rid of him'. None of this was true, but Klemperer behaved little better, passing all sorts of criticisms over Strauss's music while paying court to the grand old man – just in case.

Another conductor of whom Strauss was apparently fond was Erich Kleiber,[36] whose appointment to the Berlin Staatsoper had brought them into close proximity. When, after the Wall Street crash on October 28, 1929, Germany was forced for the second time in a decade to the brink of financial ruin, there was a drastic pan-German reduction of concert and operatic activity. The massive increase in unemployment, allied to the emergence of sound films (which put no less than 12,000 cinema musicians out of work), placed great strain on an economic system getting used to a return to prosperity. Composers felt the pinch more than anyone.

As a celebrated champion of new music Kleiber determined to use his influence in Berlin to launch the work of living composers; but unlike Knappertsbusch and Tietjen, Kleiber's altruism favoured only talent.[37] When he scheduled the world première of the French composer Darius Milhaud's spectacular opera *Christophe Colomb* – at a rumoured cost of 150,000 Reichsmarks (RM) – the German press whipped itself into a frenzy of nationalistic indignation. Strauss considered the move a personal affront and on March 24 he railed against

the abominable way in which your Staatsoper has treated me this winter. Dr Hörth[38] did, I admit, send me a black-edged letter of excuse and apology, and I quite understand that you have tenor-trouble and that your best singers may be temporarily in America. But what I don't understand is why Frau Kemp no longer sings *Elektra*, and why there should be no performances of *Intermezzo* and *Helena,* just because Herr Schützendorf and Frau Gusza have 'gone off'. A theatre like the Berlin Staatsoper should have four or five deputies who could learn the notes of those small roles in three days. Can't that be done? Or is it that you've forgotten me, just a little, in the stress and strain of all your advances? ... And I'd been promised a production of *Feuersnot* and *Josephslegende* for this March! But perhaps we shall see the *Nachtlager von Granada* instead?[39] It has a lovely violin solo in it!

A few weeks earlier he had written to praise Kleiber for his work on a Berlin production of *Rosenkavalier,* while at the same time anticipating the deepening of 'a relationship whose foundations, alike in the human and the artistic sphere, have been so firmly laid'. Kleiber failed to appreciate that the future of this relationship was contingent on his promotion of Strauss's operas. Strauss considered it his right to have his work played in Berlin, but Kleiber saw his responsibilities in a wider context – for which the composer was without sympathy.

While such episodes[40] may have been typical of Weimar theatrical life the 'elections' in September 1930, in which the Nazis gained 107 seats from the centre parties, were preface to a climate in which politics infected every quarter of German life. In 1925 Hitler had denounced, in *Mein Kampf,* the 'bolshevisation [sic] of art'; but Hitler was not, at this stage at least, keen to involve himself in the uncertain business of cultural legislation. Not until 1928, when his protégé Alfred Rosenberg steered his newspaper, the *Völkischer Beobachter,* towards the propagation of Nazi ideology, did the Party begin to take a serious interest in the doctrinal significance of art and music. The following year Rosenberg founded the Kampfbund für deutsche Kultur (KfdK Fighting League for German Culture), the sole aim of which was the discrediting of Weimar modernism; and in a series of attendant speeches he determined to analyse 'Today's Cultural Crises', thus informing the German people 'about the interconnection between art, race, knowledge and moral values' and of the need to give 'wholehearted support to genuine expressions of German culture'.

None of this was lost on Strauss. In October 1930, while in Paris, he was subjected to political and aesthetic hostility. The press was routinely spiteful, and there were rumours that his concerts would be disrupted by anti-German demonstrations, although as he wrote to Franz on October 25, 'everyone is being fearfully nice to me'. He nevertheless detected a grim atmosphere in Paris, which he related to 'those stupid Hitler elections' – since when everyone had started to talk 'of nothing else but the war that Germany is supposed to want to start at any moment'. Strauss demonstrated laudable judgement when he denounced Rosenberg as a 'pipsqueak ... who simply hasn't a clue and whose empty phrases about defeatism and pacifism Curtius[41] dismissed in a few brusque words!'

In Brussels, Strauss was embraced by government liberals as an 'effective apostle of peace';[42] in Paris, the German ambassador to France invited him to visit Aristide Briand, then Minister of Foreign Affairs, ostensibly to discuss the Paneuropa proposal, his scheme for the federal union of Europe, but probably to cheer the ailing statesman for whom Strauss's music was one of life's great pleasures. Back in Germany, the political mood was darkening in line with the financial crisis. Chancellor Brüning inaugurated a tough deflationary policy in 1930 in an effort to balance the country's increasingly unworkable budget. Income tax went up by five per cent, and taxes on domestic essentials such as sugar, beer, tobacco and coffee were pushed beyond the average wage of the middle classes. With government investment dramatically curtailed, the rise in income tax forced up the levels of unemployment,[43] and unemployment insurance, thus leaving all but the very wealthiest impoverished. All this served to heighten the demands within Germany for a change of leadership.

Alfred Heuss, the editor of Germany's most respected musical journal, the *Zeitschrift für Musik*, highlighted a *Zeitgeist* in February 1924 when he suggested that the country was 'dealing with a test of strength between Germanness and – now let it be said openly – a specifically Jewish musical spirit'. Heuss spoke for the conservative majority on most subjects, although as a Bach scholar his opinion on the Jews' 'perfidious influence' was less compelling than his denunciations of modernist musical trends, such as atonality and jazz. Both would be banned by the Nazis.

These sentiments were promulgated through the official Nazi press, frequently by respected musicologists and music historians. In one particular journal[44] Hans Ziegler declared that the only solution for the contemporary German composer was to reject 'cerebral constructivism' and 'racially-alien mental acrobatics in music'. His vision was of a utopian society in which all Aryan musicians might work in a secure political environment free from contamination – as had supposedly existed when Bach, Beethoven, Brahms and Wagner produced their Aryan masterpieces. It was a vision shared by Strauss.

Earlier, in January 1930, while Strauss was in Vienna giving concerts with the Philharmonic, Germany was given a taste of things to come when the Nazi Wilhelm Frick was appointed Minister of the Interior and Education in Thuringia. Although this breakthrough was short-lived, it provided a glimpse of the kind of programme of censorship awaiting Nazified Germany. The widely reported measures were relatively mild by later standards, but they drew a line in the sand that no one, regardless of their political complexion, could ignore.

The year 1931 was marred for Strauss by the perpetuation of Germany's economic and spiritual suffering, and during the first six months he succumbed to a bout of irresistible nostalgia which manifested itself, for the

most part, in his work on *Arabella*, but which also contributed to his decision
to make an arrangement of Mozart's early *opera seria*, *Idomeneo* (1781), for
the Vienna Staatsoper. The idea was Clemens Krauss's (who well knew the
composer's devotion to Mozart), but the impetus came from the
Czech/Jewish producer Lothar Wallerstein, who had joined the Vienna Opera
shortly before Krauss.

Strauss dragged his feet, fearing a resurrection of the ghosts of *Iphigénie
en Tauride*,[45] but when the publisher Hugo Bock, of the Berlin-based Bote
and Bock, offered a considerable fee in return for the publishing rights
Strauss capitulated, and threw himself into the project with an adolescent
enthusiasm. That he was amused by the irony of working on another composer's *Elektra*[46] cannot be doubted, but Strauss's motivation was his all-
embracing reverence for 'the divine Mozart' and the prospect of salvaging an
unjustly neglected masterpiece for the modern stage.

It is odd, therefore, that he did not show more respect for Mozart's intentions. Aside from cutting nearly half the score, which he completely re-
orchestrated, Strauss composed a new set of recitatives, an Interlude for Act
II and a new Finale. He even quoted from his own operas, most boldly the
chordal motif that describes the fall of Troy in *Helena*. Strauss believed his
additions and amendments would bring *Idomeneo* alive for a generation new
to Mozart, but even in 1931 (when Strauss conducted the first performance
in Vienna on April 16) his efforts were dismissed as anachronistic. Although
the revision remained in the Viennese repertoire until 1945,[47] it rapidly fell to
the growing post-war interest in historical veracity.

Apart from a brief trip to Switzerland and some guest appearances at the
Munich Festival, 1931 was marked only by the near completion of *Arabella*.[48]
With the end in sight, Strauss began to pine for inspiration. In the four years
between 1928 and 1932 he produced just one opera, eight songs, a patriotic
hymn and the arrangement of *Idomeneo*. In other words, his only substantial
achievement after Hofmannsthal's death was his setting of the poet's last
libretto. On October 27, with the almost finished score of *Arabella* open on
his desk, Strauss received a visit from Anton Kippenberg, a director of the
Insel Verlag publishing house, who was en route to a meeting with the
celebrated Jewish/Austrian writer Stefan Zweig. Strauss suggested that Kippenberg ask Zweig if he had any ideas for an opera. Having 'flirted and
negotiated with the best German poets', Strauss held out little hope of a
response, but only three days later Pauline opened a parcel from Zweig
containing a letter of introduction and, as a gesture of goodwill, a facsimile
of a letter by Mozart, from Zweig's unique collection of autographs.

Strauss and Zweig arranged to meet on November 20, 1931. In his autobiography, *The World of Yesterday*, Zweig recalled his delight at seeing 'how
quickly, how clear-sightedly Strauss responded to my suggestions. I had not
suspected in him so alert an understanding of art, so astounding a knowledge

of dramaturgy.' Zweig was taken with the idea of translating Ben Jonson's play of 1610, *Epicene, or The Silent Woman,* to the lyric stage. Since the drama involved feminine intrigue and boasted a strong female lead it seemed perfectly suited to the composer's predilection for portraits. Zweig was struck by the speed with which Strauss was able to envision the completed work, although he had never met a great artist 'who knew how to maintain such abstract and unerring objectivity towards himself'.

Strauss 'frankly admitted ... in the first hour' of their meeting that his 'musical inspiration no longer possesses its pristine power', and that he 'could hardly succeed in composing symphonic works like *Till Eulenspiegel* ... because pure music requires an extreme measure of creative freshness'. Words were still an inspiration – even if, since 'nobody could rise higher than Wagner', opera as an art form 'was dead'. Zweig was 'dumbfounded' by the composer's frankness, but Strauss liked his proposal and urged him to make a start as soon as he had completed his biography of Marie Antoinette.

Zweig was a self-effacing and gentle man; having admired Strauss and his achievements from afar he was overawed by the prospect of having not only to satisfy an intensely demanding composer, but also to fill the shoes of the dead Hofmannsthal, of whose memory Strauss was increasingly protective. Zweig's attitude to the poet was more complicated. He had, like many of his generation, grown up looking upon Hofmannsthal as 'Goethe's worthy successor'; but during the 1920s, he was to discover, Hofmannsthal had deliberately persuaded Max Reinhardt not to produce Zweig's plays, chiefly *Jeremiah, Volpone* and *Lamb of the Poor.*[49] According to his first wife, Fridericke, Zweig was 'shocked by the discovery of a one-sided rivalry which his own truly naïve trustfulness would have regarded as impossible'; if he knew of Hofmannsthal's treachery Strauss never let on, and neither he nor Zweig made mention of the regrettable incident in their correspondence. Strauss returned to Garmisch in a mood of heightened expectation. For the first time in four years he could look forward to the continuation of his operatic work, and he turned, reinvigorated, to the orchestration of *Arabella.*

Outside Garmisch the mood was no less expectant. In the presidential elections of March 12, 1932, Hitler procured 30 per cent of the votes cast – an 86 per cent improvement over the previous election. One month later the National Socialists increased their presence in the Prussian Landtag from 9 to 126 seats. Democratic government, and Otto Braun's position as Prussian Chancellor, were fatally undermined, and five weeks later Franz von Papen 'succeeded' Heinrich Brüning as Chancellor, making Hitler's rise to power now inevitable. The summer months saw a return to mob violence. Strauss escaped to Switzerland, and later Salzburg, where a different, but no less serious, battle was being waged between Clemens Krauss, and the Jews Bruno Walter and Max Reinhardt – both of whom Krauss wanted ousted.

The 1932 festival was predictably lavish, with productions of Gluck's

Orpheus und Euridice, Mozart's *Die Zauberflöte*, and Weber's *Oberon*, all conducted by Walter; a Carl Ebert production, conducted by Fritz Busch, of *Die Entführung aus dem Serail*, and a magnificently old-fashioned staging of *Fidelio*, conducted by Strauss, with the stellar casting of Franz Völker as Florestan, Lotte Lehmann as Leonora and Richard Mayr as Don Fernando.[50] Krauss kept the cream for himself, with productions of *Der Rosenkavalier*, *Così fan tutte*, *Le nozze di Figaro* and *Die Frau ohne Schatten*. His lover and future wife, Viorica Ursuleac, starred in them all.

While Salzburg revelled in her past Germany came to terms with her future. On July 20 – when Strauss was briefly in Schloss Elmau[51] to oversee a touring production of *Intermezzo*[52] – Von Papen dismissed the legally elected Prussian government as prelude to the establishment of unelected authoritarian rule. Three days later Otto Klemperer met Strauss in Elmau and requested an audience to discuss some points of detail in *Rosenkavalier* and *Ein Heldenleben*, both of which he was scheduled to conduct during the coming season at the Linden Opera in Berlin.[53]

Strauss invited the conductor and his wife to Garmisch, and over coffee and cake Klemperer outlined his concerns. 'He couldn't actually tell me much,' Klemperer recalled; he merely commented: 'You know, I'm always glad when I'm over those passages.' They were joined by Pauline, whereupon the conversation turned to Germany's changing political climate, and the future of the many Jews then occupying positions of influence in German artistic life. The indefatigable Pauline turned to Klemperer and, in her broad Bavarian dialect, boomed: ' "If the Nazis give you any trouble, Herr Klemperer, just you come to me. I'll tell those gentlemen who's who." ' At this, Strauss raised his eyebrows in astonishment and remarked, ' "That will be just the right moment to stand up for a Jew." ' Klemperer later recalled: 'The shamelessness was so naked one couldn't be angry. I said nothing and later we left.'

On September 14 Strauss received Zweig's draft of *Die Schweigsame Frau*. He replied: 'absolutely exquisite!' Four weeks later, on October 12, Strauss completed the orchestration of *Arabella*. The remainder of Strauss's 1932 was taken up with conducting. From October 19 until November 1 he was in Budapest; after three days' rest in Garmisch he left for Hanover, and from there he travelled to Munich. All the while Zweig worked on the remaining two acts of *Die Schweigsame Frau*, which he was able to complete on January 17, 1933. Exactly two weeks later, on January 30, Adolf Hitler was sworn in as Chancellor of Germany by President Hindenburg.

24 THE MIGHTY LEVERKÜHN

January 1933–July 1935

When Hitler came to power in January 1933 German unemployment stood at over 30 per cent. Within the musical community it was almost 60 per cent. At the end of 1932 the Berlin Philharmonic had been forced to abandon its fifty-year independence and accept reformation as a limited company, with a board on which were represented the orchestra, the Prussian State, the Republic and the Broadcasting System. This 'national catastrophe'[1] symbolised more than economic crisis. For the far Right it was the inevitable outcome of 'Weimar decay',[2] a process begun at Versailles and fostered by the dramatic acceleration of Jewish influence. That confessional Jews made up less than 5 per cent of Weimar Germany's professional musical community (which numbered 93,857 in 1933) mattered less than that Jews occupied many of the country's more influential administrative, educational and performing appointments.

Weimar's plurality heightened the spiritual and intellectual isolation felt by all 'true' Germans, and it was thanks in part to this atmosphere of paranoia that Hitler was able to secure such a powerful grip on a country desperate for scapegoats and solutions. The subversive social commentaries produced by Brecht, Werfel, Weill and Hindemith, and the demonstrable sympathy felt by most Jewish German musicians for non-German music, provided a focus for the widely promulgated belief that the only way forward for Germany, and her art, was a return to conservative and isolationist principles. The Jews were denounced as 'soulless'[3] since, as German anti-Semites believed, they possessed neither the historical nor the cultural roots necessary for the development of genuine German art.

It cannot be doubted that Strauss felt increasingly alienated during the 1920s. He welcomed the promised return to financial stability and national economic independence, and his genuine concern for the future of German music under Weimar rule buttressed much of his behaviour during Hitler's dictatorship. How many non-Jewish Germans paused to consider the wider cultural, political and humanitarian consequences of Nazi empowerment while at the same time enjoying the promised rebirth of Germany and her culture? Certainly, Strauss's son Franz was unconcerned by any such thoughts, and his membership of the Nazi Party was as much a manifestation of his own sentiments as it was a confirmation of his father's beliefs. The devoted Franz would never have acted against the family's wishes, and at least in 1933 his membership of the Party was entirely in keeping with his and his father's social philosophy. To Schillings, Pfitzner, Strauss and the majority of those opposed to pluralism, Hitler's pledge to 'make the trains run on time' mattered less than his promise to 'make German music German again'. Any lasting process of reformation was likely to be lengthy and complicated, but events during the twelve months following Hitler's appointment as Chancellor unfolded at a dizzying pace, and Strauss was neither adequately political nor sufficiently unselfish to resist developments that were the answer to every 'German' musician's dreams.

For Strauss, the first three months of 1933 were monopolised by preparations for *Arabella*. Neither he nor Zweig made mention of contemporary events. In January Fürstner signed a contract with Reucker in Dresden for a July première; an eventuality seemingly assured by Strauss when he dedicated the opera to 'My friends Alfred Reucker and Fritz Busch'.[4] But on February 12 a daringly unorthodox production of *Tannhäuser* at the Berlin State Opera, conducted by Otto Klemperer, provoked outrage from the hard Right; the Nazi press fumed at the conductor's 'offence' against Wagner's memory[5] and demanded his immediate dismissal.[6] The popular acceptance of these events triggered a series of disruptions, by Nazi mobs, of concerts and operas featuring musicians deemed threatening to the new regime, including a number of 'Aryan' artists, such as Fritz Busch.

In 1949 Busch recalled how, during the course of 1932, 'the Party realised that my co-operation in building up their Third Reich could not be relied on. On the principle they had adopted – "He who is not for me is against me" – they gave up the attitude they had hitherto maintained of expectant benevolence and went over to the attack.' It emerged in March 1933 that Reucker had inadvertently given employment to a Nazi spy, one Dr Börner, who conveyed to party headquarters Busch's publicly voiced criticisms of Hitler and the Nazis, as well as a library of mythical infraction. The Dresden office of the Nazi Party invited Busch to atone for his sins by taking membership; when he refused they cut his annual budget by a third and threatened to 'liquidate' his salary. The head of the Saxon government, Walter Schieck, summoned Busch to a meeting at which he outlined the conductor's options: ' "I am afraid that you, dear sir, will be sewn into a sack and thrown into the Elbe unless you decide at the last moment to change your behaviour completely and make concessions." '

On March 6, as Busch entered the orchestra pit to rehearse the following evening's performance of *Rigoletto*, a group of SA thugs charged forward and began to assault the conductor, forcing him out of his own theatre. When Busch announced his determination to conduct the performance half the tickets were bought by SA agitators, who shouted Busch down before a note of music could be played.

The following morning Reucker phoned Busch from a telephone box outside the opera house to say that he, Reucker, had been replaced by a fanatical Nazi actor, Alexis Posse, who refused to allow Reucker to enter the building in which he had worked for most of his professional life. Busch confronted the new Intendant, who calmly informed him that since he, Busch, enjoyed 'too many dealings with Jews', 'a too high salary' and provided 'advantageous conditions ... to Jews and foreign singers' he would not be allowed to continue as music director at the Opera. When Goering took his cause to Hitler, the Führer sent a telegram to Posse demanding Busch's immediate reinstatement, but it was too late. Not even his own company was willing to stand their ground, so that when, on March 12, a petition was raised for signatures in the opera house with the stated purpose: 'The undersigned request the Führer to take every means of preventing the former Musikdirektor Fritz Busch from returning to the Dresden Opera in any capacity whatever, as in personal and artistic matters he is incompetent', only seven, out of nearly fifty singers, refused to sign.[7]

When events were brought to Strauss's attention, Heinz Tietjen arranged a meeting in Berlin with Busch to discuss what might be done to save *Arabella* for the disgraced conductor. Busch recalled: 'Strauss declared it was to be taken for granted that the première of this work ... would only be allowed if produced by Reucker and conducted by me. My remark that he was not to take me into consideration he put aside with derision. If I positively refused to conduct in Dresden then it should be somewhere else. There was no question of any other solution as far as he was concerned.'

Strauss did, briefly, try to keep his word, but a contract had been signed, placing him in the impossible situation of having to choose between the opera and its conductor. It was not much of a choice. A few days later Strauss asked Clemens Krauss to conduct the première of *Arabella* in place of Busch. Josef Gielen was summoned as producer, and in defiance of the Saxon prohibition of visiting stars, Krauss's lover Viorica Ursuleac was engaged to create the title role. According to Lotte Lehmann, Strauss had asked *her* to create Arabella, an honour she turned down because of 'over-fatigue' after a 'heavy season'. In truth, Lehmann stood little chance of appeasing Dresden. She had won few hearts during the first production of *Intermezzo*, whereas Ursuleac had been singing to popular acclaim in Dresden since 1930. That Berlin wanted Krauss to conduct the city première of *Arabella* in October ensured Ursuleac's continuing security.

Security was otherwise in short supply. On March 8 the 'Aryan' producer Carl Ebert, a colleague of Strauss's in Salzburg, was hounded from his post as Intendant of the Berlin Städtische Oper after refusing to tone down his denunciations of Hitler's regime. He was replaced by Max von Schillings, whose return to influence was greeted by the Nazi press as a symbol of rebirth. Throughout March and April (when he conducted at a concert in Berlin to honour Hitler's forty-fourth birthday) Schillings grew in power via his presidency of the Academy and his honorary presidency of the music educators' organisation,[8] until he was in a position to exact revenge on his Jewish tormentors by contributing his authority to the 'Jewish purges' (*Entjudung*).

A sense of revenge permeated every corner of musical life during the early months of 1933. While considering the loss of Klemperer *et al.* a matter for 'regret', the Propaganda Minister Joseph Goebbels reassured readers of the *Berliner Lokalanzeiger* that this was a 'small matter when weighed against the countless true German artists who in the past fourteen years have not been allowed the opportunity of having their work appreciated by the people'. As Goebbels worked towards the 'purification' of German art, hundreds of Jewish and anti-Nazi Germans were attacked and run from the country. Dozens of Jewish conductors for whom Weimar Germany had been a cultural haven were threatened with violence, and worse. On March 16, having seen his friend Busch ousted from Dresden, the principal conductor of the Leipzig Gewandhaus, Bruno Walter, arrived at the hall for rehearsals only to find the doors locked. The concert had been banned by the Reichskommissar of Saxony because the safety of the orchestra's musicians could not be guaranteed with Walter, a Jew, on the podium. Four days later Walter arrived in Berlin for a concert with the Philharmonic Orchestra. Fearing a repetition of events in Leipzig, Walter requested police protection. When this was refused, he turned to Louise Wolff,[9] the widow of Hermann Wolff, for help. She advised Walter to submit an application for a public safety order, but this too was refused. The same day Walther Funk, Secretary of State (and future president of the Reichsbank), informed the orchestra's management that they would have to engage an Aryan conductor if they wished the concert to proceed.

Aware that collusion would represent a validation of Nazi racial policy, Furtwängler[10] refused to save the day and demanded that the management look elsewhere for their replacement. In a bizarre twist, and with only hours in which to find someone willing to save Nazi face, they approached Louise Wolff for help. She, in turn, approached Strauss (who was in Berlin conducting a production of *Elektra* at the Staatsoper), and asked him to salvage the concert 'for the orchestra'. Inviting conclusions that have haunted his reputation ever since, Strauss agreed. He changed the programme to include his own *Sinfonia Domestica*, but donated his fee[11] to the orchestra's charitable fund. Strauss had saved the new government from an embarrassment – which, with so many foreign journalists in Berlin at the time, would have been international news.

In his memoirs Walter recalled: 'The composer of *Ein Heldenleben* actually declared himself ready to conduct in place of a colleague who had been forcibly removed. This made him especially popular with the upper ranks of Nazism.' The following day Walter's friend Thomas Mann dismissed the composer in his diary as an 'arse-licker', and went on to rant against 'the strange phenomenon of an imaginary "historical moment" . . . Who has been conquered? The inner enemy – who after all made it possible for the national uprising to take place. Idiotic. But if only that were all it is and it were not compounded with so much base, murderous malevolence!'

Berlin's audiences were as appalled as Walter and Mann, so much so that many of the orchestra's subscribers returned their tickets for the concert on April 3 (which was to have been the last conducted by Walter that season) and the event had to be cancelled. But in taking Walter's place, Strauss had handed the Nazi propaganda machine its greatest cultural victory to date. Writing for the *Zeitschrift für Musik*, Fritz Stege reported that the audience had welcomed Strauss to the podium with 'overwhelming jubilation', while the *Völkischer Beobachter* announced that Strauss had saved the day as a 'salute to the New Germany'. Three days after this fateful concert Hitler stood before the Reichstag and announced that the government of the Reich would 'undertake a thorough moral purging of the body corporate of the nation . . . Art will always remain the expression and reflection of the longings and realities of an era. The neutral international attitude of aloofness is rapidly disappearing. It is the task of art to be the determining spirit of the age . . . respect for the great men of the past must once more be hammered into the minds of our youth, it must be their sacred heritage.'

Seven months later, in October, Strauss submitted an article to the *Münchner Neueste Nachrichten* in which he made some 'Contemporary Remarks on Musical Education'. He began by quoting, as a measure of his own cultural priorities, Confucius's 'principles of Chinese ethics' which he 'outlined in three fundamental tenets: (a) Cult of one's ancestors, i.e., pious conservation and study of the achievements of our forefathers; (b) Cultivation of good manners, i.e., our relationship with our fellow men; (c) Cultivation of music, i.e., achievement of an inner harmony.' That Strauss fervently believed in (a) is unquestionable; that he was able to reconcile (b) to the inauguration, on April 7, of civil service laws designed to remove all non-Aryans from employment in German opera houses, state orchestras and music academies is not so certain; and yet Strauss's value-systems accommodated the apparent contradiction between the cultivation of good manners and the expulsion of all Jews from cultural life.

Like so many others, Strauss was intoxicated by the promise of renewal, believing that enthusiasm, rather than wickedness, lay at the root of the Nazis' more extreme behaviour. For example, when Zweig wrote to Strauss on April 3 complaining that Goebbels had mistaken him for the dedicated anti-Nazi Arnold Zweig,[12] the composer replied that he had been in touch with his 'friend Hugo Rasch', of the *Beobachter*, who had promised that he would do everything he could 'with the highest chief, Rosenberg, to ensure that justice will be done to you'. Unfortunately, Strauss's naïvety bled, rather too easily, into denial. Having used the words 'justice' and 'Rosenberg' in the same sentence, he continued (in the light of the Jewish exclusion laws): 'I am doing fine. Again I am busily at work, just as ... a week after the outbreak of the Great War. I am in the midst of Act II [of *Die Schweigsame Frau*].'

Admittedly, few of those affected by the new legislation (such as Fritz Stiedry, Jascha Horenstein, Josef Krips, Emmanuel Feuermann, Fritz Zweig, Joseph Rosenstok, Wilhelm Steinberg, Eugen Szenkar, Gustav Brecher, etc.) had much to do with Strauss or his music. Neither were the teachers Bernhard Sekles, Hans Gál and Walter Braunfels more than acquaintances; but like Arnold Schoenberg and Franz Schreker – who were both dismissed from their Berlin teaching posts in May[13] – they had made an unquestionably valuable contribution to German cultural life.

Not everyone was so willing to compromise. Wilhelm Furtwängler took the remarkable step of writing an open letter of protest to Goebbels, which was published in the *Vossische Zeitung* on April 11, 1933. Furtwängler was not a brave man; indeed he was notoriously weak away from the podium, which makes his stand all the more heroic:

> Quotas cannot be placed on music as they can for bread and potatoes. If nothing worth hearing is given in concerts, the public will just stay away. For this reason, the quality of music is not merely a matter of ideology. It is a matter of survival. If the fight against Jewry is focused upon those artists who are rootless and destructive ... the fight is justified. But if this attack is waged against real artists too, it is not in the best interests of our culture. Real artists are very rare ... and no country can afford to renounce their service without enormous harm to its culture. Plainly, it must be said that men like Walter, Klemperer and Reinhardt and others must be enabled in the future to practise their art in Germany.

In his reply, which was also published, Goebbels built his arguments upon the nationalist legend: 'German musicians have been condemned to silence over the past fourteen years by their Jewish rivals.'[14] Many believed this, but anti-Semitism was not always the defining measure of prejudice. Jewish self-hatred was, unsurprisingly, on the increase, and even someone as apparently liberal as Thomas Mann could write, in response to an article in the *Beobachter* calling for the sterilisation of the Jews, 'Might not something deeply significant and revolutionary be taking place in Germany?'

Eight days later, in response to a lecture given in February 1933 by Mann entitled 'The Sorrows and Grandeur of Richard Wagner', the Munich *Neueste Nachrichten* printed a 'Protest of the Richard Wagner City'. The forty-five signatories were appalled that, having given the lecture outside Germany,

Mann was posing as a 'representative of German culture'; and they denounced not only the 'calumny' of his 'un-German' arguments but his anti-German adoption of a cosmopolitan and democratic position. The signatories were headed by Hitler's publisher Max Amann, followed alphabetically by many of the leading musical and intellectual names in Munich life, including those of Strauss, Pfitzner, Siegmund von Hausegger and the document's sponsor, Hans Knappertsbusch.

In May another crisis befell one of Germany's aesthetic cathedrals. Having agreed to conduct *Parsifal* at the 1933 Bayreuth Festival, Toscanini wrote to Winifred Wagner, the composer's daughter-in-law, informing her that he was unlikely to patronise the festival for as long as Germany embraced Hitler and his racial policies. Winifred persuaded Hitler to write a letter of appeasement, to which Toscanini replied that it would be 'a bitter disappointment' if 'circumstances' remained as they were. On the 28th, in the light of continued harassment of Jews and enforced emigration, Toscanini brought his association with Bayreuth to an end: 'The sorrowful events which have wounded my feelings as a man and as an artist have not undergone any change, contrary to my every hope. It is therefore my duty ... to inform you that for my tranquillity, for yours and for everyone's, it is better not to think any longer about my coming to Bayreuth.'

The festival was due to begin in a matter of weeks, and since Furtwängler had also spurned Winifred (if for different reasons), she was left without a conductor of international standing. She turned briefly to Fritz Busch, now living in Switzerland, but when he reluctantly turned her down, she was forced to approach Strauss. It was common knowledge that he had been nurturing a grudge against Bayreuth for nearly forty years; but with both Cosima and Siegfried Wagner dead since 1930, he was invited to step into the breach to save the festival and its new patron, Adolf Hitler, international embarrassment. German culture had to be seen to be strong enough to cope with the 'treachery' of non-German musicians such as Toscanini.

The invitation could not have come at a worse time. *Arabella* was mid-rehearsal in Dresden, a process that Strauss had planned to oversee, but his faith in Bayreuth compelled him to stand up for what he believed to be Germany's greatest artistic monument, and save the day. Of course, not a summer had passed since his last official visit during which he had not pined to conduct in Wagner's 'sacred' Festspielhaus; neither the forthcoming première of *Arabella*, nor the implicit political significance of his intervention, were sufficient to prompt the slightest hesitation.

Before going to Bayreuth, Strauss turned his attention briefly to *Arabella*. Krauss wanted him on hand for the final rehearsals. Leonhard Fanto and Johannes Rothenberger had created a stylised nineteenth-century Viennese backdrop, against which Josef Gielen's production forged an orthodoxy from which few producers have deviated since. Krauss did everything to appease the composer. Every rubato and each passing metre was calculated to keep the opera's sentimentality in check; Ursuleac and Alfred Jerger[15] brought an instinctive Viennese *Schwung* to Strauss's ardent, flowing music. The first night, on July 1, was no more than a moderate success, but the Berlin première on October 12, conducted by Furtwängler,[16] and attended by Hitler, Goebbels and Strauss, launched a sequence of triumphs that would make *Arabella* the most frequently performed new opera in Germany between 1933 and 1945.[17]

The Viennese première on October 21[18] was probably Strauss's greatest triumph since the first performance of *Rosenkavalier* twenty-two years earlier.[19] Before the end of 1934 there were productions in Olomouc (in Czech), Stockholm (in Swedish), Basle, Monte Carlo (in French), Buenos Aires (conducted by the exiled Fritz Busch), Amsterdam (conducted by Strauss), Budapest (in Hungarian) and London, where Krauss conducted most of the original cast during a visiting season by the Dresden company to Covent Garden. Only in London were the reviews anything less than adulatory.

To Zweig, on January 21, 1934, Strauss wrote of his surprise at the new opera's fate: 'Confidentially – I was not expecting too much of *Arabella*. I worked hard on it and now this enormous success, hardly less, so far, than that of *Rosenkavalier*. It is strange. The public is inscrutable. Despite all one knows about the art, one knows least what one is really capable of doing. Such bull's eyes as the *Arabella* duet and the *Rosenkavalier* trio don't happen every day. Must one become seventy years old to recognise that one's greatest strength lies in creating kitsch . . .'

Strauss's ironic dismissal of *Arabella*'s populism disguises the skill with which he and Hofmannsthal had managed, for the second time, to revive a Vienna of lore (1860); indeed, after *Rosenkavalier*, no other opera of the twentieth century enjoys such irrepressible Viennese *élan*. Not surprisingly, its mixture of operetta gaiety and farce, the fluency of its pacing (the opera's action takes place over a single day), the happiness of its ending and the all-pervading air of nostalgia provided an ideal distraction for a German public fearful of, and uncertain about, its future. Whether Hofmannsthal had given up trying to raise Strauss's sights and simply conceded to his requirements as an old-fashioned bourgeois is impossible to say for sure, but *Arabella*'s lightness of touch, its freedom from poetic abstraction, the scarcity of symbol and the richness of characterisation attest to a grudging, cumulative, accept-ance of his partner's strengths. Strauss rose to the challenge and created some of his most beautiful music for the soprano title role, her baritone and tenor suitors, Mandryka and Matteo, and her sister Zdenka.

The plurality of formative ideas, the inevitable touches of parody, the reappearance of the post-modern instincts first cultivated through *Rosen-kavalier* and the sweeping orchestral canvas add depth to the glittering surface, but it is for its calculatedly emotive vocal score that *Arabella* is remarkable. Strauss took his inspiration from a book of Croatian folk songs, and the melodies poured forth as though he had been saving himself for want of a suitable libretto. According to Viorica Ursuleac, in performance he would rush the duets 'Aber der Richtige' and 'Un du wirst mein Gebieter sein', and positively charge through the final scene, all the while muttering under his breath 'Agh! Such sentimentality!'

At the end of July 1933 Strauss and Pauline were driven to Bayreuth in their six-litre convertible Mercedes.[20] Winifred installed them in the recently-built guest house, where they were later joined by Franz and Alice. Both Friedelind and Wolfgang Wagner, Winifred's children, recorded their very different recollections of Strauss's stay; they coincided on just one point – that Strauss was without rival as a card player. Indeed, so excellent was he at skat that his colleagues from the orchestra would cry off and play on their own. When he complained to Winifred that there was no one willing to join him at the card table she secretly agreed to make good each player's losses the following morning.

The festival opened, for the first time since the 'laying of the stone' cer-emony in 1872, with a performance of Beethoven's Ninth Symphony – con-ducted by Strauss in front of Hitler and Goebbels.[21] On August 7 Karl Elmendorff conducted Heinz Tietjen's banner-waving production of *Die Meistersinger*, followed by Daniella Wagner's antiquated staging of *Parsifal*. While her interpretation of the drama accommodated house orthodoxy, Strauss's reading of the score broke with the solemnised conception estab-lished by Muck and endorsed by Toscanini.[22] Chopping a hefty forty minutes off Toscanini's time,[23] Strauss ran headlong into his critics, one of whom – Ernest Newman – dubbed him 'merely second-rate'. Even the Nazi press was at pains to find words of approval; he would none the less be back in 1934.

Shortly after leaving Bayreuth, Winifred wrote to thank Strauss for his help. She enclosed a page of sketches for *Lohengrin* from the Bayreuth archive of Wagner's autographs. Overjoyed, Strauss replied on September 23:[24] 'There was no need for further thanks: my modest help for Bayreuth was only a respectful repayment of the great debt of gratitude stored up in my heart for all that the great master gave to the world and to me in particular.'

The day before, Hitler and Goebbels had announced the creation of a Reichskulturkammer (RKK; Reich Chamber of Culture). This body became responsible for the supervision of all German art when the RKK Law was passed on November 1, 1933. Goebbels appointed himself president, but delegated administrative responsibility to seven autonomous chambers, each of which was empowered to supervise one aspect of German cultural life: Fine Art, Theatre, Literature, the Press, Radio, Film and Music (Reichsmusikkammer RMK). The RMK was itself subdivided into a ruling committee (consisting of a president, vice-president, business manager and inner council whose responsibility it was to decide policy), an internal administration (which dealt with publicity, cultural propaganda, finances and law) and seven departments relevant to various aspects of professional life (composers, performers, concert agents, amateur societies, publishers, retailers and instrument manufacturers). The RMK was unprecedented. Neither the Russians nor the Italians, and certainly not the British, had ever attempted such a thorough administration of musical life.

In September Goebbels asked Strauss by telegram if he would like to accept the presidency of the RMK. He was not, as most continue to believe, appointed without consultation. In fact, Goebbels needed the composer; Strauss's star may have fallen from the elevated position it had enjoyed during the first twenty years of the century, but he was still generally referred to as Germany's 'greatest' composer, and his real or imagined advocacy of Nazi policy would be beyond value. Goebbels knew that Strauss's sympathies were not, and never would be, political (he never joined the Nazi Party, or any other political organisation), and this placed him outside the squabbling and personality clashes likely to impede the RMK's presidency. Furthermore, it was evident that Strauss genuinely believed in the sacred primacy of German music – a belief to which the RMK and its stated objectives might almost have been tailored. Indeed, Strauss's values were so irrevocably nineteenth century that the eradication of modernism and Jewry were probably secondary, for Strauss, to the conservatory philosophy professed by Goebbels.

For Strauss, the Jews were not simply scapegoats; rather they posed a very real threat to the Bach/Beethoven/Wagner trinity on which both his work, and the work of all 'true' German composers, was founded. Consequently, Goebbels's appeal to Strauss satisfied not only his respect for the sacred relevance of German art, but his concern for the preservation of traditions that had suffered fourteen years of tacit infection.

At the RMK's inauguration ceremony, in Berlin, on November 15, 1933, Strauss thanked Hitler and Goebbels for initiating a return to the state of intimacy that had supposedly existed between music and the people during the sixteenth century. His *Festliches Präludium* was performed by the Berlin Philharmonic. When Strauss, accompanied by his son, addressed the first convention of the Chamber on February 13, 1934, he lauded the RMK as 'the dream and goal of all German musicians for decades' and heralded it as 'the most important step in the direction of the reconstruction of our total German musical life'. As a matter of course he thanked 'Reich Chancellor Adolf Hitler and Reich Minister Dr Goebbels in the name of the entire musical profession of Germany'.[25]

The speech continued along predictable lines, with references to 'the illustrious history of German music', the need to restore 'unity between music and the German people which has been marred in the recent past' and 'a community of destiny'. As a reminder of the RMK's political context, Strauss announced that the Chamber would serve as 'an organic, essential part' of 'our people and our National Socialist state'. He concluded: 'Since Adolf Hitler's seizure of power has not only resulted in a transformation of the political situation in Germany, but also of its culture, and since the National Socialist government has called to life the RMK, it is evident that the new Germany is not willing to allow artistic life to remain in isolation, but that new ways and means will be explored for the revival of our musical culture.' To Zweig he explained, 'I believe I should not refuse this task because the goodwill of the new German government in promoting music and theatre can really produce a lot of good; and I have, in fact, been able to accomplish some fruitful things and prevent some misfortune.'

At the first assembly of the RMK in Berlin's Philharmonic Hall, Gustav Havemann conducted the Landescorchester Gau Berlin in performances of Beethoven's *Consecration of the House* and Wagner's *Huldigungsmarsch.* This was followed by a speech from Strauss's press director, Dr Friedrich Mahling, in which the RMK's resolutions were hammered home; the ceremony ended with three '*Sieg-Heils*', all with arms raised, and a performance of the Horst Wessel Song.[26] Hitler may have been privately condemned as a clown, but he was a clown with a mission for which Germany's non-Jewish, conservative musical community could not help but feel enthusiastic. While Strauss, and everyone else affiliated with the RMK, was compelled to sanction overtly racist policies, the promise of a German musical revival seemed more than worth the small moral sacrifice required by any contract with Hitler and his government.

Strauss's vice-president was Wilhelm Furtwängler, then the most admired conductor in Germany, and another priceless coup for Goebbels. Although neither Furtwängler nor Strauss considered themselves political, everyone and everything in Nazi Germany was politicised, since any collaboration served an inevitably approbatory means to what was an unavoidably political end. Goebbels trusted neither man to toe the Party line, and appointed a council of Nazis[27] to 'assist' them in their work and oversee the day-to-day running of the RMK, leaving Strauss and Furtwängler time to concentrate on their unofficial duties.[28]

As president of the RMK Strauss was required to legislate membership, in line with a programme laid down by Goebbels. Questionnaires were sent to all registered German musicians in which they were asked to establish their racial purity and musical qualifications. The completed forms were scrutinised for weakness, in consultation with the Gestapo. A hint of 'non-Aryan' blood led to exclusion, which meant unemployment, since one of the Chamber's chief responsibilities was the purging of 'undesirables' from German musical life. Formal exclusion – and indefinite unemployment – came via a letter signed by Strauss, as stipulated by the First Implementing Ordinance of the RKK.

Strauss may have authorised the RMK's edicts, including its racial decrees, but he was still little more than a public face – a means towards legitimisation and approval. Living in Garmisch and Vienna (and spending much of his working time in Berlin) he was isolated from the dismal human instincts then pervading the RMK's administration, and he left the running of the Chamber's affairs in the questionable hands of Heinz Ihlert[29] and the RMK council. His vice-president, Furtwängler, took his responsibilities more seriously, and invested time and effort in the furtherance of the RMK's aesthetic programme – even if this frequently meant standing in opposition to every official suggestion. According to Bertha Geissmar, Furtwängler's secretary, the conductor's obfuscation was so deliberate that 'the bureaucracy, and last but not least, Strauss himself, began to conceal things from him' – which may well have been true but presupposed that Strauss had any more influence over the ordinary workings of the RMK than did Furtwängler.

The RMK, with Strauss and Furtwängler ostensibly at the helm, began regulating Germany's musical life on December 28, 1933 – while Strauss was sitting at home in Garmisch, enjoying the aftermath of Christmas with his young grandchildren. It is impossible to know the exact nature of his contribution to the first rush of laws, but they bore his name, and he raised no objection to their publication in the RMK journal *Amtliche Mitteilungen der Reichsmusikkammer*. The majority of RMK decrees confirmed Strauss's stated ambitions, but a number were purposefully limiting, including a series of laws requiring official permission to leave the country, the vetting of concert programmes, the prohibition of foreign pseudonyms and a whole batch of anti-Semitic measures. Strauss's contribution to the RMK's persecution of Jewish musicians must, however, be considered slight. That he was part of a wider Jew-hating culture, and that he was an anti-Semite who allowed himself to be manipulated by an anti-Semitic government, is indisputable; but though willingly accommodating and approving of the government's general attitude towards race, there is no evidence that he instigated or encouraged anything more than an awareness of the 'Jewish problem'. It is difficult, if not impossible, to know the full extent of what was being done in Strauss's, and the RMK's, name. If he read the minutes of those RMK meetings held in his absence, and it would be fair to assume he did, Strauss could make no claim to having been kept in the dark.

Certainly, he was informed of all significant policy changes, not only as president of the RMK but as a working conductor/composer, and he was doubtless aware of the fate of those musical associates and colleagues who were removed from their own businesses, deported from the country, or sent to concentration camps. As president he was also kept abreast of the conduct of the Chamber's agents, and he was required to sign numerous documents attesting to the usurpation, by racially pure Germans, of posts and positions[30] previously occupied by Jews – including businesses with which he had himself enjoyed prosperous working relationships.

The supplanting of his own publisher, Adolf Fürstner,[31] by the Nazi-approved Johannes Oertel, is a case in point. The demise of Louise Wolff is another. Strauss had worked with and through the Wolff agency for most of his life,[32] notably during his years in Berlin, and like most of Germany's leading musicians he had come to rely on Louise's influence and bearing as one of the country's leading agents and concert promoters. After the April 7 decree banning Jews from all state institutions Louise dispatched her two Jewish partners (Erich Sachs to Palestine, Erich Simon to Paris) and changed the company name from Wolff und Sachs back to Hermann Wolff Konzertdirektion. This was not enough to distract Rudolph Vedder.

A fanatical Nazi and friend of Hermann Goering, Vedder had worked as a secretary to the pianist Edwin Fischer and the violinist Georg Kulenkampff before moving to Steinway's, from where he was dismissed in 1927 for embezzlement. When the Nazis came to power Vedder set his sights on Wolff's agency. Helped by contacts in the SS (whose ranks he joined in 1941) to compile a largely fictional dossier on Wolff and her Jewish contacts, he used this to discredit the management of the agency. In February 1934 Vedder was appointed director of the concert division of the RMK.[33] While answering directly to Strauss (who, none the less, can have known little of his colleague's persecution of Wolff[34]), Vedder attempted to blackmail the old woman into relinquishing control of her agency; when this failed he began to make threats against the lives of her half-Jewish daughters. A combination of age, depression, fear and a short illness brought an end to Wolff's life on June 25, 1935, and to the agency she had run successfully for fifty-five years. A few days later the Nazis marched into her offices, sent one of her daughters to a concentration camp and handed over all relevant documents, monies and artists to Vedder at the RMK.[35] Strauss remained on the agency's books.

His commitment to the RMK and its policies[36] continued into 1934 when, at a council meeting in February, he reasserted his loyalty to Hitler, the Nazis, New Germany and the Chamber, which he believed would 'free the road to healthy creativity', and in so doing make the 'sick and harmful . . . disappear'. Such sentiments were superfluous to his overall plan as RMK president. Indeed, the Nazis were offering him the opportunity to expand upon the enterprise of the GDT. His long-held ambition to improve the lot of all German musicians, spiritually as well as economically, appeared to be at hand.

On February 23 Strauss wrote to Havemann:

> I have long been conscious of the abysmal quality of the programmes given by spa orchestras . . . I would like, through the Reich Music Chamber, to exercise an influence to the end that there should be some supervision of these programmes, and I would like to draw up a long list of entertainment music of

decent quality, for which our German publishing houses should be asked to furnish the performance materials.

1. I should like, in due course, to see two-thirds of such programmes made up of German and Austrian music, but excluding the worst rubbish from Viennese operetta; I would also like to see a total ban on potpourris compiled from all manner of works, while decent fantasias from just one operatic work should be permitted.

2. It is high time that a stop was put to the murder of pieces like the 'Funeral March' from *Götterdämmerung* in the stuttering performance which is all a band of sixteen can hope to give it. There are charming French and Italian pieces, the numerous divertimentos and serenades of Mozart, and of course the entire *oeuvre* of Johann and Josef Strauss, Lanner and – naturally – Schubert, from which a decent audience could draw real pleasure.

He failed to achieve a ban on 'potpourris', and the 'Funeral March' continued to be played in reduction, but his concern for the 'Germanness' of native opera and concert repertoires was widely endorsed by Goebbels and the RKK. Of course, the policy recommendations contained in his letter to Havemann were subsidiary to Strauss's wider ambitions for his country's musical life. He wished to see German composers favoured as a gesture towards the revitalisation of German culture, so that through a 'respect for the great men of the past', present and future generations might provide a firm foundation on which to build new and lasting achievements.

Strauss was understandably thrilled, therefore, to accept an invitation by Goebbels in February 1934 to head the Professional Association of German Composers. This subchamber of the RMK was, like the RKK, one of the models for many of the European Arts Councils that emerged after the war, and it promised to accelerate Germany's creative revival. Strauss was assisted by Hugo Rasch (deputy), Gerd Kärnbach (business manager) and Julius Kopsch (organisational and legal affairs), together with a Leadership Council of Nazis and Nazi sympathisers such as Max Donisch, Willy Geissler, Siegmund von Hausegger, Georg Schumann and Hans Pfitzner.[37] They, in turn, had the support of a General Assembly, most of whom were, again, sympathetic to Nazi political sentiments.

At the first Association meeting Strauss applauded the State's recognition of the need to encourage 'contemporary [musical] literature' and commended their [the Nazis] eagerness to acknowledge the legal status of the profession. 'Creative artists', he announced, 'are in need of the backing of law and corporate organisation.' Strauss's enthusiasm for the Association and its objective of 'creative rejuvenation' was to his credit; but his speech also confirmed the extent to which both he and the RMK were led by nationalist isolationism. Strauss urged German composers to acknowledge their responsibilities to the nation, and insisted on a heartfelt and constant solidarity with the principles and workings of the National Socialist State.[38]

It was necessary for the RMK and the Composers' Association to buttress their words and gestures of native encouragement with a thoroughgoing suppression of 'alien' influence. In a letter to Otto Laubinger,[39] dated December 12, 1934, Strauss suggested, without irony, that 'it goes without saying that Germany, with its universality and greatness of heart, affords generous hospitality to meritorious works of art from abroad . . .', as if coercive charity, rather than market economics, was forcing German impresarios and conductors to schedule works by non-German composers. He believed that an enforced diet of German music – balanced by 'a third, or perhaps once in a while, as an exception, half the scheduled programme' of 'foreign repertory' – would nurture the restoration of cultural immunity.

As a result, the Composers' Association proved to be less a call to creative freedom and administrative independence than a means of economic and ideological control. Under the terms of the Association's statutes, a living composer's music could be played in public only if the composer handed control of the box-office receipts to the RMK; earnings were sent to the composer only after administrative costs and profits had been deducted. This left most of Germany's composers less well off than during the Weimar years, when self-promotion had been the primary, and most productive, channel for the performance of new music. Strauss's conviction that it was 'not the proper cultural function of theatres in receipt of state and municipal subsidies'[40] to promote operas by foreign composers was informed not only by issues of race and identity, but also by his regard for the Nazis' offer of a 'generous' system of State subsidy.

Strauss advocated a 'Culture Tax', which he believed necessary for the rebuilding of musical life. It was a laudable, if undemocratic concept, since the money would be given only to 'German' causes that were considered deserving of support by a small and racially prejudiced committee of conservative, self-interested composers. Strauss suggested that funds be raised via the radio or through direct taxation. Either way, as he wrote to Bruno von Niessen, a colleague at the RMK,[41] distribution of monies had to be 'accompanied by strict admonitions about the theatre's role in raising cultural standards and the banishing of operetta from the big houses. These must retrench, the foreign repertory must be limited, and the performance of worthwhile, old, forgotten works recommended.' On February 23, 1934, Strauss finally managed to persuade the RMK to agree to help finance the production and playing of music by young German composers, even if, in his capacity as a conductor, he refused to do anything himself to further their work.[42]

Indeed, while Germany recreated herself in the image of National Socialist ideology, Strauss persevered with an almost unchanged way of life – conducting concert after concert of his own music, and almost nothing by the new breed of composer with whom he was apparently so empathetic. His habitual run of tours, cures and composing took him around Europe as if neither he, nor the country he represented, had undergone anything more traumatic than a mere change of government. *Die Schweigsame Frau* was a source of pleasure, and he relished Zweig's lightness of touch. Having completed Act I on January 21, 1934, he began scoring Act II in March and, in April, he drove to Kissingen for the waters. At the end of the month he travelled to Dresden for the Festival Week, which opened with a performance of *Arabella* on May 1.

Although Clemens Krauss was again conducting, Dresden had a new music director, Karl Böhm. Austrian born and exceptionally talented, Böhm had been a staunch supporter of the Nazis since 1933,[43] when he had been appointed to the theatre committee of the KfdK. Böhm had moved from Hamburg[44] to Dresden in January 1934, and began using the Nazi salute in public long before such gestures were officially required. Throughout his career under the Nazis he gave publicly voiced support to Hitler,[45] and although, like Strauss, he never took Nazi membership, he lent his services to the Party, the RMK and the government. Böhm would become one of Strauss's intimates during the late 1930s; in the meantime Strauss asked him to conduct the first performance of *Die Schweigsame Frau* in Dresden.

In May Krauss took the Dresden production of *Arabella* to London for three performances at Covent Garden on the 17th,[46] 21st and 25th – all with Ursuleac and Jerger. A fourth was announced for the 29th, in honour of the composer's seventieth birthday. Strauss was unable to attend, since he was supervising a production of *Intermezzo* in Berlin and had arranged a series of meetings with Goebbels, ostensibly to discuss the future of his relationship with the Jewish Stefan Zweig. The writer lived in Salzburg and was, consequently, untouchable; but Nazi law demanded that Strauss bring an end to their relationship. Having waited so long to find an eligible successor to Hofmannsthal, Strauss was not going to surrender such a vital creative advantage without a struggle. On the 24th he wrote to Zweig: 'I recently ... asked Dr Goebbels whether there are any "political objections" against you, to which the minister answered no ... All efforts to relax the stipulation against Jews here are frustrated by the answer: impossible as long as the outside world continues its lying propaganda against Hitler.'

Goebbels had no wish to upset Strauss, whom he dubbed 'neurotic'; the composer's co-operation and support provided invaluable international endorsement. At any rate, and at this stage in their relationship, Goebbels and Strauss appeared to be on good terms, the more so since Goebbels had in 1933 received the dedication of a new song by Strauss, *Das Bächlein*.[47] Moreover, Goebbels was keen to exploit his seventieth birthday as an excuse for the national celebration of a native genius.

Five days earlier, on June 6, Strauss was in Wiesbaden for the 1934 Allgemeiner Deutscher Musikverein. The Nazis had hijacked this internationally venerated festival the year before, when the programmed composers Walter Braunfels and Anton Webern were replaced by Hermann Unger and Max Trapp – both of whom employed the conservative, tonal aesthetics advocated by the KfdK. The 1934 festival, now fully Nazified, played up these sentiments, paying special homage to the music of Strauss, Pfitzner and Schillings, each of whom was lauded as the embodiment of the 'Aryan musical spirit'. Most of the festival's new music elevated the past, the heroic and the nationalistic through gigantic expressions of German pride, such as Gottfried Müller's *Heldenrequiem*.

The festival, therefore, provided a less than ideal setting for Strauss to unveil his Permanent Council (later 'Society') for International Co-operation amongst Composers (SICC) – Strauss's most noble attempt to break down the cultural barriers that had risen between Germany and the rest of the world since Germany's withdrawal from the ISCM in 1933. The first gathering of the SICC was held in September 1935, in Vichy. Strauss believed in the viability of this unworkable, but idealistic, venture; as he wrote to Hausegger on December 31: 'This first French, non-atonal, international festival of music is immensely important. It is the first step towards smoothing the way abroad for those of our composers who have not yet been performed in other countries.' But the SICC was little more than a vehicle for Nazi propaganda. Admirable though the aims of the Society were, it was a home for anti-democratic, Nazi-friendly and, with the sole exception of Strauss, second-rate composers. The Council's membership represented a glorious body of failed ambition: Friedrich Bayer (Austria), Emil Hullebroeck (Belgium), Peter Gram and Nils Raasted (Denmark), Yro Kilpinen (Finland), Carol Bérard (France), Maurice Besley (England), Adriano Lualdi (Italy), Ludomir Rozycki (Poland), Adolf Streuli (Switzerland), Jaroslaw Kricka, Kurt Attenberg (Sweden) and Jon Leifs (Iceland).

On June 11, when Strauss turned seventy, Goebbels hailed him as the father of the new wave of creativity that would restore Germany to the forefront of world culture.[48] Almost every major orchestra and opera house paid homage through performances of Strauss's works; Vienna (Krauss), Berlin (Blech), Munich (Knappertsbusch) and Dresden (Böhm) mounted celebratory Strauss Weeks; Dresden made him a Freeman of the City; German radio broadcast a cycle of his works, including another revision by Strauss of *Guntram*; and thousands of postcards, photographs, paintings, books and anniversary manuscripts were produced in honour of his achievements.

At the RMK celebration even Strauss must have blushed at the testimonies of his admirers – among whom were numbered Goebbels and Hitler. Each gave Strauss beautifully framed and inscribed photographs of themselves; Hitler's was addressed 'To the great composer, Richard Strauss, with deepest veneration, Adolf Hitler'. Goebbels later gave Strauss a bust of Gluck, which remains on display in the Garmisch villa. The RMK itself presented him with two original letters, one from Mozart to his wife Constanze, the other from Wagner to Mendelssohn. The following day President von Hindenburg awarded Strauss the Eagle Shield of the German Reich – the highest and most cherished of all German civil honours.

It cannot be doubted that, had the Weimar Republic continued beyond 1933, Strauss's birthday would have been honoured throughout Germany; but it is equally certain that the honours would have been lesser in both number and grandiloquence. Like Mann's Leverkühn, Strauss's pact with Evil centred upon renewal – both personal and national. Leverkühn's conditions may have been purely creative, and his music and personality bear few comparisons with Strauss's, but such was the composer's vanity, and so acute his sensitivity to the popularity of his work, that the respect and adulation of the Nazis brought with it a burst of confidence and optimism that blinded him to the wider issues of morality, identity and political reality.

As such he was delighted to return to Bayreuth in August 1934 for further performances of *Parsifal*, and more meetings with Goebbels and Hitler. During lunch at Wahnfried, Goebbels and Strauss discussed the future of *Die Schweigsame Frau*. In a memorandum, of July 1935, Strauss recalled:

> I received him, saying that it was perhaps significant that in the house of the 'great martyr' I too, the smaller man, had to suffer my martyrdom. I told him that I did not wish to embarrass Adolf Hitler and himself by performing my opera, and that I was willing to withdraw *Die Schweigsame Frau* altogether and to forgo all showings at home and abroad. Goebbels said later that this talk had 'deeply impressed' him – perhaps because I told him openly that the whole affair was a 'big disgrace'. In parting we agreed to submit the score to the Führer for a final decision . . .

Their discussion was sufficiently frank for Goebbels to inform Strauss that secret agents were tailing Zweig in London. On August 2 Strauss informed Zweig: 'In strictest confidence: You were shadowed in London and your magnificent conduct has been found "correct and politically beyond reproach". Please don't let anyone distract you from your attitude and everything will turn out all right with *Die Schweigsame Frau*.' Zweig must have pondered the motivation for Strauss's concern – Zweig's safety as a Jew, or the safety of his opera?

Strauss would not have been able to accept Winifred Wagner's invitation to return to Bayreuth in the summer of 1934[49] had it not been for the increasingly tense relationship between Germany and Austria. He would rather have been at the Salzburg Festival to hear Krauss conduct *Rosenkavalier*, *Elektra* and *Die Ägyptische Helena*, but on May 9 the Propaganda Ministry in Berlin received a request from the exiled branch of the Austrian

Nazi Party asking that Strauss and Furtwängler not attend the festival 'because of the political situation ... the festival has considerable propaganda value for the Austrians' foreign relations ...' On May 20 Goebbels wrote on his own copy of this report: 'Should not take part! Dr G.'. Five days later both Strauss and Furtwängler received an official letter from the Ministry of Propaganda demanding that they stay away from Salzburg, since their attendance would 'be contrary to the Führer's policy towards Austria, and so he requests in the interests of the political situation you do not participate'. Both men conceded without a struggle, but Strauss managed to work his way around Goebbels's edict. Having announced that he was ill, and thus indisposed, he managed to attend the festival as a member of the audience; to general bewilderment he was spotted during a performance of *Elektra* conducted by Krauss, who invited him on to the stage to acknowledge the audience's approbation.

Though musically expert, the 1934 Salzburg Festival was an anxious, unpleasant gathering. Of the festival's nine productions Krauss had kept six for himself; but his influence was not yet total and he failed to exclude Bruno Walter, who conducted the remaining three. The air of tension was palpable, and not only between the conductors: with the blowing-up of a railway bridge near the city, and the murder of Chancellor Dollfuss on July 25[50] there was rioting, shootings and a bomb explosion on July 30 in the Hotel Bristol during a performance, by Walter, of *Tristan und Isolde*. Not even Krauss's (reluctant) engagement of Toscanini for three concerts was sufficient to prevent many visitors from returning their tickets and leaving; and when the Italian and the Jew received adulatory reviews, Krauss's already sour mood turned poisonous.

The *New York Times* commented: 'Clemens Krauss and his partisans are greatly cut up over the unbroken succession of Walter and Toscanini triumphs and are excogitating counter-measures for future emergencies. Rightly or wrongly Krauss is convinced that the victories of his rivals have elbowed him into a shadowy background – an intolerable location for the Pooh-Bah of the Vienna Staatsoper.' When demand for Walter's *Don Giovanni* grew so great that Krauss's scheduled performance of *Die Frau ohne Schatten* had to be cancelled, more than one critic echoed the *New York Times*'s warning: 'The consequences of Krauss's present irritation may be far-reaching and, so far as the artistic direction of the Salzburg Festival is concerned, dangerous.'

Strauss was able to escape the politics for a brief, but gainful, meeting with Zweig, who proposed a new opera, after Calderón's *La redención de Breda*; but on August 18 an 'Aufruf der Kulturschaffenden' (proclamation by all artists) was published in response to the death of Hindenburg, with Strauss among the thirty-seven signatories. This unequivocally political document asserted *inter alia* a belief 'in this Führer, who has fulfilled our strong yearning for concord. We trust his work, which demands sacrifices which go beyond carping and hairsplitting, and we place our hope in this man who believes in God's Providence over men and things. Because the artist and the poet can only create if he also has the same trust in his people, and because he has the same deep conviction that the people's holiest right consists in the right to self-determination, we belong to the Führer's followers.'

On August 21 Zweig sent Strauss fresh suggestions for an opera, *Friedenstag*, based on episodes surrounding the Thirty Years' War. Having outlined the events and characters, Zweig gave the first hints that he was beginning to doubt the personal and moral consequences of a collaboration with Strauss. Sensitively he wrote: 'I do not mind *at all* if you pass this plan [for *Friedenstag*] on to someone else – Rudolph Binding could do it, for example – to save you all that cursed political bother ... I shall be just as pleased if somebody else carries out my suggestions – all that's important is that your creativeness finds the strongest stimulus to unfold.' Two days later he sent a postcard with news of another idea for an opera – a 'delightful' reworking of an Abbate Casti libretto with the title *Prima la musica, poi le parole* (First the Music, then the Words) which would eventually become the basis for Strauss's last opera, *Capriccio*.

Strauss's reply of August 24 contained the first signs of fear and uncertainty. Having made it clear that he 'would consider only' Zweig 'as the writer', Strauss suggested that 'for strategic reasons it might be wise, in case we should again collaborate on one or more works, not to say a word to anyone. If anyone asks me, I say: *I am not working on anything now, I have no libretto.* In a few years, when all projects are finished, the world probably will look different.'

His apprehension was justified. Shortly before Strauss's arrival in Salzburg, on July 20, Paul Adolph, the Intendant in Dresden was attacked in the local press for proposing to stage the première of Strauss and Zweig's *Die Schweigsame Frau* during the coming season. This outburst triggered nation-wide imprecation, and Strauss fled to Garmisch, where he attempted to concentrate on the opera's unfinished orchestration. Zweig too was finding concentration increasingly difficult. Art was starting to seem ridiculous in the light of German domestic policy, and so, on September 13, he encouraged Strauss to consider another new writer, Robert Faesi, whose festive play *Opferspiel* Zweig recommended as 'extraordinary'. Rejecting both the play and its author, Strauss reiterated: 'if you don't mind, I'll stick with Stefan Zweig.'

On October 20, 1934,[51] Strauss completed *Die Schweigsame Frau*. The following month, on November 25, he witnessed the transience of Nazi favour when an article by Furtwängler, entitled 'The Hindemith Case', was published by the *Deutsche Allgemeine Zeitung*. A defence of Hindemith, who had been the subject of unremitting and vicious scorn in the Nazi press, it caused a sensation; the first issue sold out within hours. Goebbels was enraged, particularly by Furtwängler's assertion that Hindemith's sensationalist one-act operas *Mörder, Hoffnung der Frauen, Nusch-Nuschi* and *Sancta Susanna* were no more 'perverse than ... the mature Richard Strauss's *Salome*'. 'Who', Furtwängler asked, 'is prepared to turn his back on Strauss because of the libretto of *Salome*?' The article implied that, since both Hindemith and Strauss were 'Aryan', neither, or both, should be considered guilty of un-German behaviour.

That evening when the conductor stepped on to the podium of the Berlin Philharmonie the theatre exploded into applause. The ovation continued for ten minutes, a reaction interpreted by Goebbels as a demonstration of support. Goering, who was present, telephoned Hitler and warned him that Furtwängler was 'endangering the authority of the government'; Hitler ordered the conductor's dismissal; Furtwängler resigned – from the Staatsoper, the Philharmonic, the State Council and the RMK. Erich Kleiber was alone among Germany's musicians in giving public support to Furtwängler. Kleiber then found himself under fire, and resigned from his post as staff conductor at the Berlin Staatsoper, eventually leaving for South America.

With Furtwängler gone, Goering took the opportunity to promote Clemens Krauss to the Staatsoper. On December 6, while Strauss was in Holland conducting *Arabella*, the Nazi's chief racial ideologue, Alfred Rosenberg, entered the fray in an article for the *Beobachter* in which he argued that 'Furtwängler ... had no sensitivity to the great national struggle of our time, and had to take the consequences.' Later the same day Goebbels gave a two-hour address at the Berlin Sportspalast, to coincide with the RMK's anniversary celebrations, during which he ranted against Hindemith and his 'purely German origin' as proof of how 'radically our own people have been infected with Jewish intellectual principles'. 'No one,' he raved, 'no matter how distinguished he may be in his own profession, has the right to limit the political field or to exclude these ideals from art.' As a grand finale to this speech, and as evidence of wider ideological support, Goebbels hailed the arrival of a telegram from Strauss. The short message contained the composer's thanks for the 'removal of undesirable elements' from Germany's musical life, and his 'Congratulations and ... full support for your marvellous culture speech'. He concluded: 'You have my admiration. Yours faithfully, Heil Hitler, Richard Strauss.'

This infamous telegram was not sent by Strauss himself, although he raised no objection to its contents until it became necessary for him to do so overseas. If Strauss was the author, he must have dictated it to his son, for he was its source. Claims that Franz was told what to write by a Nazi official are tenuous – even though Franz was a fully paid-up member of the Nazi Party; in any event, the wording of the telegram is typically understated, and by no means out of character, not least since Strauss had already publicly praised the Nazis' attempts to make the 'sick and harmful ... disappear'.

Whether Strauss understood 'undesirable elements' and the 'sick and harmful' as something other than the Jews, or whether they were simply naïve references to atonality and foreign influence, is uncertain, but the message was manipulated to imply that he supported not only the persecution of the Jews but the harassment of Furtwängler and Hindemith. His failure to deny its alleged origins, and his refusal to denounce the treatment of both musicians, was interpreted as approval by German and non-German commentators alike. If Strauss was not the author of the telegram, and if he was beginning to doubt the value of the Nazis' contribution to German musical life, he betrayed little sign of dissatisfaction. Rather, he continued to work for, and through, the RMK in the interests of his own and other German composers' efforts. At the end of 1934, for example, Strauss fulfilled an unusual commission for the RKK. 'I kill the boredom of the Advent season', he wrote to Zweig on December 21, 'by composing an Olympic Hymn for the proletarians – I, of all people, who hate and despise sports. Well, Idleness is the Root of all Evil.'

Having attempted to improve the lot of his Aryan contemporaries through normal concert/promotional channels, Strauss turned his attention to the radio. It was then German broadcasting policy not to play music by any composer, German or otherwise, on the RMK 'blacklist'. To be added to this roster of 'un-German' talent a composer had either to be Jewish or part-Jewish, an atonalist or 'stylistically sympathetic' to any of the aesthetic trends associated with the Weimar Republic. Not surprisingly, these criteria excluded the majority of Germany's most interesting young composers (many of whom were trying to leave, or had already left, the country), so that Strauss and Pfitzner were, again, upheld as paragons of German cultural virtue. While Strauss's concern for Germany's musical future was heartfelt, self-interest undeniably played a hand in the deal he struck with Eugen Hadamovsky, a fervent Nazi entrusted by Goebbels with responsibility for all German radio programming.[52]

Strauss proposed that the country's broadcasting network should sponsor a series of programmes featuring unknown orchestral works by (racially and aesthetically qualified) living German composers.[53] In defiance of Strauss's purely musical aims, Hadamovsky saw an opportunity to make anti-Semitic capital from the arrangement and announced that, henceforth, the radio would seek out worthy German music that had gone unnoticed because of the 'Jewish predominance' in recent German musical life. Strauss knew better than anyone that even the finest work of music needed to be played often, and to many, if it was ever to capture the general interest. Since Hadamovsky's ambitions were primarily doctrinal, new works were rarely ever played twice. In isolation, Strauss's motives were admirable, but when compelled to rely on people like Hadamovsky and Ihlert, not even the president of the RMK enjoyed workable influence.

For the time being, however, Strauss still believed in the future of National Socialism, and his relationship with his superiors, colleagues and subordinates in and around the RMK remained positive and cordial. On February 25, 1935, he set some verses by Goethe, 'Zugemessne Rhythmen', and dedicated them to his colleague (and successor as president) at the RMK, Peter Raabe,[54] in gratitude for Raabe's defence of Strauss against an attack by Walter Abendroth in his biography of Hans Pfitzner. While Strauss joked with Raabe about Abendroth's allegations of 'feminine voluptuousness',[55] Stefan Zweig's dismay at Strauss's cosy relationship with the new Establishment was growing conspicuous.

On February 23 – two days before the completion of 'Zugemessne Rhythmen' – Zweig wrote to Strauss of his prophetic concerns that the composer was 'not quite aware ... of the historical greatness' of his position ... Everything you do is destined to be of historic significance. One day, your letters, your decisions, will belong to all mankind, like those of Wagner and Brahms ...' Zweig rejected Strauss's proposal that they work in secret as 'beneath' them: 'Your grandiose work, incomparable in the world of the arts, imposes the responsibility on you not to allow yourself to be limited in your free will and your artistic choice ...' When Goebbels made it clear to Strauss at the beginning of April that he would not be allowed to set another libretto by Zweig, Strauss again begged Zweig to work with him in secret; Zweig again refused. On the 13th Strauss repeated his petition, this time with the reassurance that 'No one will hear about it ... I am protected on all fronts as far as Dr Goebbels is concerned.' Zweig persisted, and on April 26 he first introduced the cultural historian Joseph Gregor as his successor.

In March 1935 Strauss's loyalty to the Nazis was again put to the test. The Berlin Philharmonic was in difficulties, with many of the orchestra's subscribers returning their tickets in protest at Furtwängler's 'resignation'. The management engaged a succession of celebrated replacements, including Eugen Jochum, Carl Schuricht, Hermann Abendroth and Max Fiedler, and Strauss agreed to cover one of Furtwängler's Hamburg engagements, on March 8. Pfitzner was covering the ninth Berlin concert, on March 10 (repeated the following day), but when he cancelled his appearance the orchestra turned back to Strauss and asked him to conduct all three concerts for a fee of 3,000 RM. Strauss demanded 2,000 RM more. The management refused to negotiate, and the engagements went to Fiedler. A week later, on the 18th, the Secretary of State, Walther Funk, sniped that 'Fiedler was very good. It is well known that Strauss asks fantastic prices. It's his caste.'

Having willingly come to the aid of the Berlin Philharmonic two years earlier, Strauss may have deliberately priced himself out of the market to avoid further complicity. Certainly, only a few weeks later he must also have begun to realise that his presidency of the RMK, and his general prominence, were of little tangible benefit to Germany's cultural future. His propaganda value was illustrated on April 9 when he was invited to Berlin to join the celebrations accompanying the wedding of Hermann Goering to the actress Emmy Sonnemann. After probably the grandest, most extravagant non-political ceremony of the Third Reich,[56] Strauss was enticed to a gala performance at the Staatsoper of *Die Ägyptische Helena*. The reception in the foyer, and the banquet in the Kaiserhof, were the civilised face of Nazi power. Its other face was demonstrated earlier in the day when a young Communist was publicly executed as another sacrifice to the Horst Wessel myth. In his diary on the 10th, Thomas Mann wrote: 'A show of the power and pomp of this rabble would be incomplete without the taste of blood.'

At the end of May Strauss took part in the Munich Summer Festival (where he conducted *Feuersnot, Die Frau ohne Schatten* and *Arabella*), and on June 12 he travelled to Dresden for rehearsals of *Die Schweigsame Frau*. Hitler had been sent a copy of Zweig's libretto, to which he had raised no objections; indeed, so unconcerned was the Führer about the opera's Jewish librettist that he announced his intention to attend the first night. In Dresden, however, the Saxon Gauleiter Martin Mutschmann and the NSKG (National Socialist Culture Community) subverted the Führer's implicit approval, objecting that their country's leading composer was setting a bad example by working with a Jew. There were also mutterings about Strauss's quarter-Jewish daughter-in-law, and when Rosenberg contributed a serpentine letter to the protest the atmosphere turned decidedly nasty.

Having previously defied Hitler's express wishes regarding the handling of Fritz Busch, his subordinates in Dresden again disregarded the Führer's appeal for moderation, and went after Strauss, Zweig and the new opera with clamorous zeal. Strauss remained oblivious to the gathering storm clouds and concentrated on the rehearsal process. According to Böhm, this 'did not show his best side'. Even though Strauss was 'ceaselessly' critical and forever correcting conductor and cast, 'nothing satisfied him'. He was 'impossible ... He would fidget over every chord, every dynamic.' To Pauline he sent regular progress reports: 'My beloved! The opera is magnificent: both the work and its execution. Böhm and the producer have already done some splendid work ... It is the best comic opera since Beaumarchais ... You have nothing to worry about: nobody can raise any objections to this opera ... No dead spots anywhere, furious tempo, not a moment's boredom, yet full of feeling and the three finales are simply phenomenal! ... If possible, come to the dress rehearsal. The première could be sold out three times over. I am perfectly confident.'

On June 9 Zweig sent Strauss another letter advocating Joseph Gregor as his successor. Four days later Strauss replied: 'Your collaboration with good Gregor makes my skin crawl. Why do you insist à tout prix on saddling me with an erudite philologist? My librettist is Zweig; he needs no collaborators.' On the 16th he received a further letter from Zweig, which has not survived.

It is clear from Strauss's response, however, that Zweig's sense of shared grief, and of collective suffering, was growing as more and more reports emerged of the Nazi's enforced Diaspora. Understandably, Zweig began to consider his collaboration with Strauss a betrayal, and in his letter of the 15th he evidently gave voice to these concerns.

Unaware that he was being monitored by the Gestapo, Strauss's reply of June 17 betrayed a measure of his naïvety, and an insight into his priorities:

> Your letter of the 15th is driving me to distraction. This Jewish egoism! It's enough to make one an anti-Semite! This racial pride, this feeling of solidarity! Do you think that I have ever been guided, in any of my actions, by the thought that I am German? ... Do you believe that Mozart consciously composed as an Aryan? I recognise only two types of human being: the talented and the untalented. For me, the populace exists only from the moment it becomes an audience. Whether they are Chinese, Bavarians, New Zealanders or Berliners, it's all the same to me, so long as they've paid the full price of admission ...
>
> Who has told you that I have become so deeply involved in politics? Is it because I conducted a concert in place of that mean and lousy scoundrel[57] Bruno Walter? I did that for the sake of the orchestra. Because I substituted for that other non-Aryan Toscanini? That I did for the sake of Bayreuth. It has nothing to do with politics. How the gutter press presents it is none of my affair, nor should you worry about it. Because I pose as President of the Reichsmusikkammer? I do it to bring about good and to prevent greater disasters! Simply because I know my artistic duty, I would have taken on this tiresome honorary office under any government ... So be good, forget Herr Moses and the other apostles for a couple of weeks, and keep on working at your two one-acters.

Strauss foolishly posted the letter in the hotel's box. It was opened by the Gestapo who forwarded a copy, via Mutschmann, to Hitler in Berlin. The Nazi controlling mechanisms sprang into action, and on the 20th a memorandum was issued by the Office of the Cultivation of Art in Berlin to all district officers of the National Socialist Cultural Unit, in which *Die Schweigsame Frau*'s various Jewish connections – including its librettist, publisher and copyist – were highlighted as a prelude to the announcement that the 'National Socialist Cultural Unit has good cause to distance itself from this work'. In his diary for July 5 Goebbels wrote: 'The letter is impertinent and incredibly stupid to boot. Now Strauss must go too ... Strauss "is going through the motions ..." he writes this to a Jew. Damn!'[58]

Strauss remained oblivious of the fate of his letter until shortly after the dress rehearsal on the 22nd, when he was joined for a game of skat by the tenor Tino Pattiera, Leonhard Fanto and Friedrich von Schuch, Dresden's Administrative Director, and son of Ernst. About an hour into the game

Strauss asked to see a copy of the poster for *Die Schweigsame Frau*. Seeing Zweig's name omitted from the titles[59] he announced that unless the poster was reprinted with the librettist's name 'in type as large as Hofmannsthal's had been on the poster for *Rosenkavalier*', he would leave Dresden before the first night. The Intendant Paul Adolph had no choice but to concede to Strauss's request. Adolph's 'treachery'[60] was leaked to Mutschmann, who informed Berlin. Hitler was cornered. Neither he nor Goebbels wanted to cause trouble for Strauss, and with good reason they withheld judgement on the issue until it became clear that the regional offices of the Nazi Party were working independently of central office.

Reluctantly, Hitler announced that he would not be among the audience. Had the news reached him in time, Goebbels would have done the same, but he was halfway to Dresden when Hitler's note reached his office. A radio message was sent to his pilot who, at Goebbels's command, turned back to Berlin. The absence of Hitler's patronage did nothing to dampen the evening, which was broadcast across Germany.[61] Strauss and Böhm[62] were cheered to the rafters, and even Strauss's previously hostile critics conceded the work's mastery. It appeared to everyone that Strauss, for the second time in succession and despite the racial descent of his librettist, had struck populist gold. There were only four performances, however, after which the opera was shelved.

By this stage, Mutschmann had sent a copy of Strauss's letter to Hitler, who reacted by instructing Goebbels to see that Strauss's presidency of the RMK was brought to an end; Goebbels passed the assignment to Secretary of State Walther Funk, who delegated it to Ministerial Councillor Otto van Keudell. On July 6 the composer was visited in Berchtesgaden by Van Keudell who, according to Strauss, demanded 'that I resign as president of the Reich Music Chamber for reasons of "ill health". I did so at once.' In fact, the official announcement was not made until July 13, when Peter Raabe was appointed as his successor. In the meantime, everything was done to ensure a gracious transition, not least so that a successor could be found for Raabe in Aachen, where he had been General Music Director. His successor's name was Herbert von Karajan.

A few hours after Strauss's resignation had been broadcast to the world, he wrote to Adolf Hitler:

> My Führer. The mail has just brought me the notification that my request to resign from the presidency of the Reich Music Chamber has been granted. This request was initiated by Reich Minister Dr Goebbels, who originally transmitted it to me by special messenger. I hold my removal from the Reich Music Chamber sufficiently noteworthy to feel obligated to recount to you, my Führer, in brief, the whole development of the affair.
> The cause seems to be a private letter addressed by me to my last collaborator,

Stefan Zweig, opened by the state police and handed over to the Propaganda Ministry. I willingly admit that without a precise explanation and taken out of context of a long and artistic correspondence, without knowledge of its previous history nor of the mood in which the letter was penned, the contents of the letter could be easily misinterpreted and misunderstood. To understand my mood, it is first of all necessary to think oneself into my situation and to consider that I as a composer, like almost all my colleagues, suffer the continuous difficulty of not being able, in spite of frequent efforts, to find a German librettist of worth. In the above-mentioned letter, there are three passages which have given offence. I have been given to understand that these were that I have little comprehension of anti-Semitism, as well as the concept of a People's Community, and of the significance of my position as president of the Reich Music Chamber. I was not given the opportunity for a direct and personal explanation of the sense, content and meaning of this letter which, briefly put, was written in a moment of ill humour against Stefan Zweig and dashed off without further thought.

As a German composer, and in view of the sum total of my works, which speak for themselves, I do not think that I have to assert that this letter in all its improvised sentences, does not represent my view of the world or my true conviction. My Führer! My whole life belongs to German music and to an indefatigable effort to elevate German culture. I have never been active politically nor even expressed myself in politics. Therefore, I believe that I will find understanding from you, the great architect of German social life, particularly when, with deep emotion, and with deep respect, I assure you that even after my dismissal as president of the Reich Music Chamber I will devote the few years still granted to me only to the purest and most ideal goals. Confident of your high sense of justice, I beg you, my Führer, most humbly to receive me for a personal discussion, to give me the opportunity to justify myself in person, as I take farewell of my activity in the Reich Music Chamber. I remain, most honoured Herr Reichskanzler, with the expression of my high esteem,

Yours, forever devotedly,
Richard Strauss.

July 1935–September 1939

On July 10, 1935 – three days before his official resignation as president of the RMK – Strauss wrote a short memoir of the events leading to his dismissal:

> Herr Keudell pointed several times to a red-marked copy of a personal letter to my friend and, up to now, collaborator St.[efan] Zweig ... I did not know that I, the president of the Reich Music Chamber, was under direct police surveillance, and that I, after a life of creating eminent works 'recognised in the entire world' was not considered above criticism as 'a good German'. Yet, the unheard of has happened: Herr Minister Goebbels dismissed me without even asking for an explanation of the sequestered letter, which, to unauthorised readers not aware of the background, and part of an involved correspondence concerned with purely artistic questions, is bound to be misunderstood.
>
> The beginning of the letter about Zweig's Jewish stubbornness and his (understandable) feeling of solidarity with his persecuted tribal brethren contained the obvious answer that Teuton composers have never considered whether their compositions were sufficiently German and Aryan. We simply compose, ever since Bach, whatever our talent permits us, and we are Aryans and Germans without further being aware of it. This can hardly be construed as treason, but is loyal service to the fatherland, even though my libretto, like Mozart's, was written by a non-Aryan. About the passage most heavily marked in red, I may be in disagreement with Dr Goebbels who, as a statesman, naturally has to judge people differently; the passage says that for me – it's a personal view, expressed in a personal letter – the 'people' start when they become an 'audience', that is, people begin with the upper two million, the educated audience that paid their tickets in full – not those who for 15–30 pfennigs listen to *Meistersinger* or *Tristan*, causing great financial loss to the theatre and requiring ever larger subsidies from the government...

Does this apparent confirmation of his petition to Hitler mean that Strauss lied to Zweig? Were his assertions of reluctant complicity no more than a subterfuge designed to ensure Zweig's continued co-operation? What was the true nature of Strauss's relationship with National Socialism? Was he

Thomas Mann's 'Unpolitical German' or his Leverkühn? Did he engage in a full and conscious collaboration with a government he knew to be riddled with wickedness and stupidity in return for adoration and renewal, or was he an old man forced into an 'inner emigration' by events and personalities that defied comprehension and resistance?

After the war Strauss, and his apologists, produced various reasons for his having remained in Germany. The most oft-repeated were his age (despite maintaining a hectic conducting and composing schedule into the 1940s); that he feared for the safety of his 'Jewish' daughter-in-law (although his entire family could have left for America at any time before the war); and that he was able to achieve more by working inside Germany than outside it (even though turning his back on Hitler would have contributed much to the preservation of German cultural dignity). In response, his critics have tended to repeat Strauss's own declaration (made to Klemperer in 1933) that there were over fifty opera houses in Germany, and only two in America.

But to believe that Strauss gave himself up to the Nazis simply to ensure the propagation of his music is absurd. That such benefits occurred to him cannot be doubted,[1] but that they defined his philosophy as a man, as an artist and as a German is irreconcilable with someone of his intellectual and emotional refinement. Notwithstanding his infamous self-interest, such an argument would bear scrutiny only if Strauss had done everything in his power to avoid collaboration; it is evident, however, that even after July 1935 Strauss remained the Nazis' foremost cultural asset. His 'fall from grace'[2] immediately after his dismissal from the RMK lasted a matter of days,[3] and at no point did it constitute a period as *persona non grata*.[4] Neither Goebbels nor Hitler was willing to risk the loss of such an internationally celebrated German, and a vast cycle of his works was broadcast over the nation's radio just three months after his 'resignation'. In addition, Strauss was Germany's most valuable cultural ambassador, and he continued to travel about Europe with Berlin's blessing until 1944.

At the heart of Strauss's defence of his concessions to Nazi rule after the war, aside from any specific apologia, is his, and his music's, presumed apoliticism. Strauss himself maintained that he had persevered in the interests of German culture and that, since culture and politics were irreconcilable, he and his work were apolitical. But as early as April 1933, in an open letter to Furtwängler published in the *Deutsche Allgemeine Zeitung*, Goebbels left the reader in no doubt that apoliticism was incompatible with National Socialist government.

The message was clear: all art would, in future, serve a political purpose, regardless of its formative inspiration. Since Nazi politics were essentially ideological, Nazi Germany would be political only inasmuch as she used politics to realise her objectives. Because most of these were rooted in an idealistic antiquity of innocence, purity and righteousness, it was inevitable that Strauss's ambitions for German music would bring him crashing into line with the new order. There was no shame in conservatism as an aesthetic ideal; however, because Strauss's doctrine of insularity and purification was being applied to questions of race and creed it was impossible for him to avoid being tarred with the same brush.

Furthermore, Goebbels's reiteration of music's political complexion left no one – least of all Strauss – in any doubt that all claims to apoliticism were doomed to dismissal as empty rhetoric. Once the State had declared all art to be a means to a political end the only possible response, whether social or cultural, had to be politicised; in Nazi Germany, therefore, everything had a political aspect, and it was down to individuals to choose between reality or denial.

Initially, Strauss was his own worst enemy. In 1934, for example, some months into his presidency of the RMK, he wrote:

Art is a cultural product ... The bearing of witness of the culture of time and peoples ... For this reason the current reforms in the area of culture appear to us, as representatives of the musical world, of immense importance. We will be able to count on a new blossoming of our musical life only if we succeed in winning over the entire people to our music, saturating them with our music, and implanting within the heart of every individual fellow citizen a love for his German music. Thus the need for music will always increase, and it will be our highest task to satisfy it with the best music.

Such an unrealistic utopia would have been ridiculed before 1933, and it was Strauss's founding enthusiasm for much (but not all) of that promised by Hitler that led the composer to such inexplicable errors of judgement as, for example, *Das Bächlein*. Strauss wrote 'The Little Brook' on December 3, 1933, shortly after returning from the Berlin inauguration of the RMK. Its dedication to Goebbels 'in memory of the fifteenth of November', is well known, but the song itself is far more disturbing. Strauss almost certainly wrote the three verses, as well as the music, which read like a stylisation of Goethe. Considering the song's historical context, and Strauss's recent proximity to Hitler, there can be no mistaking the meaning, and significance, of the imagery:

Little brook, light and clear as silver,
you hurry along forever.
I hurry on the bank and ponder:
from where do you come, where are you going

I come out of a dark cave,
my path takes me over flower and moss.

The smiling image of the blue sky
Hovers gently on my mirror.

I therefore have the happiness of a child.
It drives me along, I know not where.
He who has called me forth from stone,
he, I think, will be my leader!

The last verse, in particular, provides an unmistakable amplification of Strauss's cultural philosophy[5] just as the repetition in the last line of the song ('wird mein Führer, mein Führer, mein Führer sein!) confirms his contemporary admiration for Hitler and his assurances of renewal. Similarly, the line 'I come out of a dark cave' tethers Strauss to the Platonic metaphor – admired by Heidegger and typical of the New Hellenism that characterised Hitler's Germany – of Man's emergence from 'the cave' of inwardness into socialisation, brotherhood, responsibility and unity.

Strauss's lifelong sympathy for the Ancients, his devotion to Hellas and his love of Greek philosophy coincided with the Hellenic trends in architecture, philosophy, art and politics that typified the Third Reich. Although they met rarely Strauss may well have read some of Heidegger's work, and he must have known something of the philosopher's stated wish to return to Greek beginnings so that Germany might 'gain distance for the leap into the present and beyond it'. Furthermore, Strauss's weakness for the quasi-Hellenic nationalism of Hegel and Hölderlin – both of whom had been politically seduced by Napoleon – attests to a sympathy with what one contemporary of Hitler's revolution[6] interpreted as 'an attempt to capture Hölderlin's dream'.

In 1921, two years into his administration of the Vienna State Opera, Strauss set three of Hölderlin's texts as Hymns, published as his Op. 71. The sentiments of these verses,[7] and Strauss's treatment of them, predate the intense ideological nationalism advocated by Hitler and the Nazis, and demonstrate how seriously Strauss treated his devotion to Germany. The second of the songs, 'Return to the Homeland', contains the unambiguous stanza: 'How long it has been, oh how long! / Childhood peace is gone, and gone are youth and joy and pleasure; / but you, my fatherland! holy – enduring! / see! you have remained.' The final song, 'Love', ends with the lines: 'May the language of lovers / be the language of the land, / their soul the sound of the people!'

In themselves, the settings prove nothing, but they reinforce Strauss's philosophical collectivism (contributing to the paradox of a man who was without sympathy for the suffering of people outside his immediate acquaintance); furthermore, his evident enthusiasm for the future of Germany in the light of contemporary democratic republicanism conforms

with what we know of Strauss's reasons for collaborating with Hitler's administration.

It should be noted that Strauss has left no written confirmation of his
supposed dislike of Hitler himself. That he loathed the Führer's aides and
minions is unarguable: he was the first to attack the bureaucracy and red
tape that slowed him and the processes of reformation down; but Strauss's
allegiance was to Hitler and his call to participation. Like Heidegger, who
remarked to his friend Karl Jaspers in March 1933, 'One *must* involve oneself',
Strauss believed in determined action. His hatred of apathy, in himself and
others, was total.

That there were many in Strauss's situation whose response was similar is
neither a defence nor a validation of his conduct.[8] However, the actions of
Busch, Kleiber, Furtwängler and – outside the field of music – Gerhart
Hauptmann prove there were solutions and alternatives. Armed with an
awareness of the scale, nature and ambition of National Socialism Strauss
should, at the very least, have attempted a withdrawal from public life. Yet
he took risks only when it suited him and his music; as such, the very novelty
of his defence of Zweig (which never stretched beyond the confines of *Die
Schweigsame Frau*) makes it harder to characterise his behaviour as decent,
brave or noble since it was unequivocally motivated by self-interest. Such
blatant calculation was less common than the general circumvention of
responsibility of which the majority of Strauss's contemporaries were guilty.

When Schoenberg's life began to fall to pieces in 1934, for example, he
turned to Furtwängler for help. The conductor could easily have ignored his
petition but instead he went to great lengths – even going so far as to contact
Hitler – to ensure the composer's safety. Many years later, Schoenberg's
widow remarked in an interview, 'How very different from Richard Strauss
...' Hauptmann also showed exceptional fortitude when he resisted Hitler's
adulation and turned down Goebbels's offer of a position as State Councillor.
To his wife Alma (née Mahler), Franz Werfel marvelled: 'In spite of all that
(in contrast to Strauss, Furtwängler etc.), he said no.' Like many other artists
loath to abandon Germany, but for whom collaboration was unthinkable,
Hauptmann sank his head into the sand, tacking along, Werfel noted, 'as
befits his non-combative nature, trying to avoid all risks ...'

Elsewhere, the majority simply looked the other way. Many failed to see
how they could have done anything else. Karl Böhm, for example, acknowledged no good reason for turning his back on Germany – even though
Bruno Walter, his mentor and the man who had given him his first and most
significant career opportunities, had been threatened with death and exiled.
In 1968 he told Hans Weigel: 'It was equally held against me that I did not
emigrate. People from abroad also asked questions on this subject, to which
it remained to me only to reply: at that time I had no invitations from the
Met or from Covent Garden.'

In truth, relocation was no simple matter. Even if, logistically, a public figure was at liberty to leave the country he had in Germany a life, family, friends, financial security and the certitude of national and ideological identity. Of course, he also had far better career opportunities for work overseas. For those better-known figures, lionised by the Nazis, all arguments for leaving were dramatically outweighed by arguments for staying. As Albert Speer told Gitta Sereny: 'I really don't think people understand what it was like. People like Furtwängler, Wilhelm Kempff, Richard Strauss and others were considered to be, well, national treasures. If they expressed disapproval or doubts, they would be argued with; if they remained unconvinced, they would be warned and put under open supervision. What would never have been allowed under any circumstance would be for them to leave. Nothing so damaging to Germany's reputation abroad could have been permitted.'

If this was so, then Strauss's freedom to travel outside Germany prior to his fall from official grace in 1944 suggests the Nazis never seriously feared his emigration. Had he and Pauline wished to leave, they could have done so via Switzerland and settled in England (like Hindemith), South America (like Kleiber) or the United States (like the majority). They would have struggled, particularly since neither spoke English well, but they would also have arrived as international heroes, and they had more than enough German-speaking friends and admirers to cushion the financial blow of relocation. One of Zweig's indictments of the Nazi system contains a reference to the obstinacy of his Jewish friends which could have been applied as easily to Strauss: 'They stayed because of loyalty or of indolence, cowardice or pride. They preferred being humiliated at home to humiliating themselves as beggars abroad.'

Strauss stayed because he saw no alternative. While his entire family could have relocated at any time prior to 1939 – with Garmisch ideally placed for a break into Switzerland, and Strauss sufficiently affluent to bribe his way past any number of officials – they were safer and more appreciated at home. Moreover, the first six years of the Reich coincided with a return to Elysian prosperity. It isn't necessary to detail German life in 1932, save to point out that seven million were unemployed, most of whom would have voted for the Devil himself had he promised an end to suffering. Strauss had never known anything akin to hardship, and he was insensitive to his fellow Germans' anguish, but where the unemployed were seduced by promises of bread and marks, Strauss subscribed to the assurances of cultural renewal that did so much to disarm the middle and intellectual classes on whom Hitler founded his authority.

The Führer's promises to exact revenge for the suffering of Versailles and to bring an end to Weimar democracy were assured through action. Like so many others, Strauss was impressed by public displays of brutality and suppression; as a devotee of Nietzsche and Stirner, such determination confirmed for Strauss the seriousness with which Hitler was leading the way in his call for 'boundless love and loyalty to one's nation'. The crushing of democracy advocated by Strauss was no less attractive for its eradication of politics. He may have recalled Wagner's 'A political man is distasteful to me', and he was certainly disgusted by the 'Jewish' political vagaries of Weimar Republicanism. Hitler's dictatorship may appear abhorrent to eyes opened after 1945, but it was widely believed to be the only possible means to achieving *Volksgenosse* in 1933.

Heidegger articulated this common perception: 'The German, at odds with himself, with deep divisions in his mind, likewise in his will and therefore impotent in action, becomes powerless to direct his own life ... As a nation of singers, poets and thinkers they dreamed of a world in which the others lived, and only when misery and wretchedness dealt them inhuman blows did there perhaps grow up out of art the longing for a new rising, for a new Reich, and therefore for a new life.'

Strauss's laconic personality saved him from making comparably determined endorsements – the absence of which serve for the composer's apologists as proof of disinterest – but his reticence in no way disproves his sympathy for Hitler and the Nazi administration. Indeed, to argue that his collaboration was motivated by something other than ideology and political sympathy leads inexorably to his having stayed in the interests of his music, and the wealth it brought his estate. Such reasoning would support his continued allegiance to the official Nazi publisher Oertel, just as his apparently unaffected creative process during the war attests to the clarity of his conscience at a time when even the most loyal and supportive Nazis were feeling the strain.

But while Strauss enjoyed his affluence, it is unthinkable that his collaboration was motivated by avarice rather than ideology. He is remembered for a pragmatic and calculating personality, but he was also prone to startling naïvety. This much was evident after the war when the horrors of the Third Reich mattered less to him than Wagner's writing for the bassoon in *Tristan*. During the course of his denazification he complained to Willi Schuh, in a mocking inversion of recent history, that he believed he was being persecuted simply for being German. Similarly, his sympathy for Nietzsche's belief that art was there 'to prevent the bough from snapping' – tenable only within the context of a nihilistic determinism that saw all human experience as painful – led him towards a cultural despair so suffocating that on February 12, 1944 (after Munich was levelled by Allied bombs), he could write to his grandson: '165 years ago people regarded the Lisbon earthquake as a turning point in history, ignoring the greater significance of the first performance of Gluck's *Iphigénie en Aulide*, which marked the conclusion of a process of musical development that had lasted for 3,000 years ...'

Anyone so convinced of the significance of an opera – even if, as he believed, it had enabled Mozart to reveal 'the secrets of the human spirit to a greater extent than thinkers have been able to, over the course of thousands of years' – was unlikely to think much of real life as it was understood by the majority of ordinary Germans.

The memoirs of many of those who met Strauss for the first time after the war attest to the reluctance with which he discussed the Reich and his association with its leading figures. The British music critic Felix Aprahamian visited Strauss at the Park Hotel in Vitznau on September 2, 1946. The significance of the meeting was not lost on Aprahamian, who noted in his diary his arrival at 11 a.m. and his departure exactly forty-seven minutes later. Their conversation pointedly circumvented life between 1933 and 1945, but as Aprahamian was leaving Strauss remarked, 'If you see the Vice-President [Furtwängler[9]], send the best wishes of the President.'

Such cynicism may seem shocking so soon after the war, but it was entirely in character. Bertha Geissmar recalled how, in 1936, she questioned Strauss about their mutual friend and colleague, the stage designer Leonhard Fanto. Geissmar was certain that Fanto must be Jewish, but could not understand how he managed to coexist with the Nazis. Strauss replied: ' "Well, Fanto, you see – Fanto has been clever, he has simply declared that he was a foundling and does not know anything about his parents." ' Geissmar's reaction to this was understandable: 'Considering the agonies which other people had endured on account of just one Jewish great-grandmother – at that time – it must be admitted that this statement, direct from the President of the Reichsmusikkammer, seems a piece of incredible cynicism. What desperate letters addressed to Furtwängler had I seen ... from people whose private and professional life had depended on the handling of the question of their parentage.'

Cynicism and selfishness merely buttressed Strauss's defining faith in Germany's rebirth, but to have collaborated as a matter of faith ultimately reflects better on his choices and actions than that he did so purely out of self-interest. Either way, the notion that after his 'resignation' from the RMK he spent the remainder of Hitler's Reich as *persona non grata* – propagated by the majority of Strauss's apologists – is almost total fabrication. Such attempts to defend Strauss have always reinforced the suspicion that there was something to hide. As the following chapters prove, this suspicion was entirely warranted.

Strauss's departure from the RMK was as much a source of relief as of distress.[1] Liberated from the strain of bureaucracy, he was again free to pursue his own interests.[2] But his relationship with Zweig was now definitely at an end. In his 'History of *Die Schweigsame Frau*', written on July 3, 1935, Strauss wrote: 'I almost envy my friend Stefan Zweig, persecuted for his race, who now definitely refuses to work with me in public or in secret because, he says, he does not want any "special privileges" in the Third Reich. To be honest, I don't understand this Jewish solidarity and regret that the "artist" Zweig cannot rise above "political fashions" ' – as if the Nazis' purging of Jews from German society could be considered a "political fashion". In conclusion, Strauss confirmed the consistency of his priorities: 'With *Die Schweigsame Frau* my life's work definitely seems to have come to an end. Otherwise I might have been able to create other works not entirely without merit. It is regrettable.'

In truth, the composer was suffering from probably the worst depression of his life. For the second time in six years he had lost an irreplaceable librettist, and as late as October 1935, he was warning Zweig from the Tyrol that he had 'better not write ... across the German border because all mail is being opened'. In a last desperate attempt to hold on to the writer Strauss proposed that Zweig sign his name as 'Henry Mor';[3] and that he should sign himself as 'Robert Storch'.[4] Zweig did, in December, write as 'Morosus', but it was his last direct contact with the composer, who heard nothing more of him until news of Zweig's death was broadcast on German radio in 1942.

The writer's 'desertion' left him with a single avenue of exploration – Joseph Gregor. From the outset Strauss made no bones about his professional aversion to this 'erudite philologist', and it seems extraordinary that, having worked with Hofmannsthal and Zweig, he was willing to settle for someone so patently unsuited to a theatrical collaboration. Gregor's lack of first-hand theatrical experience was compounded by his astonishing knowledge of world theatre, an asset that made it all the more difficult for him to come to terms with Strauss's pragmatic instincts. During the second half of July 1935 they spent many hours together discussing Gregor's draft of *Friedenstag*, and although Gregor was happy to suggest his own ideas for operatic subjects Strauss was sentimentally predisposed to stick with the first of Zweig's unrealised proposals.

Gregor's selfless enthusiasm and humble manner didn't help; Strauss was vain and sensitive to flattery, but he shrank from sycophancy. Gregor was clearly overwhelmed by his good fortune, and his regard for Strauss was almost devotional, but his eagerness to serve impaired an already suspect judgement, leaving Strauss frustrated and inclined towards attacks of bewildering rage and cruelty.

Strauss was happier talking to his librettist in person. Since neither man liked the telephone Strauss was forever urging Gregor to visit the villa in Garmisch – something that Gregor, like his predecessors, preferred to avoid. By September 3, 1935, Gregor had completed the second draft of *Friedenstag*, as well as the first draft of his own idea, *Daphne*, on which he was working with Zweig. Foolishly, Gregor introduced his own work to Strauss with the claim that Zweig preferred it to *Friedenstag* 'by far'.

Having had a chance to study Gregor's work at leisure Strauss wrote on the 25th: 'I have taken a more intensive look at *Daphne* and must, in contrast to the opinion of our friend [Zweig], regretfully confess that the more I read it the less I like it. It is nothing more than a sequence of events, not a trace of any dramatic climax ...' According to Strauss, *Daphne* was a collection of 'schoolmasterly *Weltanschaungs*-banalities ... the whole thing in its current form, as it simultaneously unfolds in a not particularly felicitous imitation of Homeric jargon, would not draw a hundred people to the theatre ... *Theatre* and not literature!'

On October 2 Strauss returned to Garmisch and the score of *Friedenstag*. While setting Gregor's verses Strauss continued to demand changes, all the time repeating his objection that the 'dialogues are much too literary, not theatrical enough ... everything is written and not visualised on stage!' In a letter to Strauss on October 10 Gregor put the composer's criticisms down to a 'momentarily depressed mood' for he 'could not imagine that everything I had accomplished in those many months, often in your presence and with your so valuable advice and directions, should suddenly be worthless'. He rashly defended *Daphne* as the product of 'true and genuine inspiration', and protested that Strauss's opinion was the cause of 'considerable pain'. 'The matter is behind us', wrote Gregor, 'and I shall never come back to you again with this plan.'

Five days later Strauss magnanimously apologised for hurting Gregor's feelings – 'but the surgeon's saw also hurts, when it is used without anaesthetic ... please do not be annoyed if I find *your* Daphne in its present form unusable, above all untheatrical, and not interesting for any public in the world ... above all, be mistrustful of this dangerous "TRUE AND

GENUINE INSPIRATION" in which you claim to have written the little piece. Such products neither stand up to sober artistic judgement nor awaken the same sentiments in the observer.' Strauss's hammer-blow diplomacy concealed a tempering of his feelings for Gregor, and he generously forwarded a well-disposed letter from Clemens Krauss. 'If you value corroboration from third parties', he wrote, 'the enclosed recognition should give you pleasure.'

By January 1, 1936, Strauss was nearing the end of *Friedenstag*, and Gregor the end of *Daphne*. Strauss's mood was greatly improved, and he sent his librettist a charming new year's greeting, with his affirmation that '*Daphne* promises ... to be outstanding. Congratulations.' He none the less continued to send Gregor all sorts of advice, the detail and insight of which was remarkable: 'more evenness in the lines, avoidance of feminine endings, avoidance of the little, usually superfluous expletives, avoidance of subordinate clauses that begin with "while" and "although" – you see what I mean.' He gave Gregor an insight into his creative process by revealing that he declaimed everything out loud to himself 'to see what is the best way to compose it'.

On the 13th Strauss completed the first draft of *Friedenstag*, whereupon he turned his attentions to *Daphne*. A week later he applauded 'the plan and structure' of the second part, but urged a revision of the 'many empty phrases and cheap commonplaces like clarity – truth – repentance – regret – confession – manliness – *culpable* passion – eternal – a just (?) and kindly tree?' On the 26th Strauss reinforced his concerns in another brutally frank letter: 'I don't know whether I express myself clearly enough – whether you understand me! If so, then I ask you to review every thought and every word exactingly – there is too much that is hasty and banal in it, the way one dashes something off in the first flush of enthusiasm!' Having worked on the script for over six months this was hardly true of Gregor, but he took the composer's criticisms on board, and agreed to make all relevant changes.

Meanwhile, Strauss left Garmisch for Munich[5] and a series of conducting engagements (*Rosenkavalier, Frau ohne Schatten* and *Lohengrin*)[6] before travelling to Italy, via France, for a Genovese production of *Arabella*. Despite an annual salary of around 1,000,000 RM[7] Strauss continued to undertake a schedule that would have burdened a man half his age. Aside from some mild rheumatism and arthritis, the 71-year-old composer enjoyed the rudest of health. The trip to Italy confirmed his capacity for tireless industry. Arriving in Genoa at the beginning of February he worked on *Arabella* until the end of the month, whereupon he drove to Monte Carlo, and from Monte Carlo to Milan for an 'excellent' performance of *Die Schweigsame Frau*. On March 12 he drove to Antwerp for performances at the Flemish Opera; en route he took a five-day 'detour' through France by way of Marseilles and Avignon. On the 27th he left Antwerp for Paris and another stay at the Hotel Meurice before returning to Garmisch on April 7 after a round trip of something like 1,700 miles.

All the time Strauss and Gregor corresponded over *Daphne*. The *entente* remained *cordiale* but Gregor was forced to endure much humiliation. On March 9, for example, Strauss informed him that, having discussed *Daphne* with the producer Lothar Wallerstein, he had asked his old friend to sort Gregor out. The now servile librettist replied: 'I must tell you that I am *enthusiastic* about your letters, since they reveal to me the most intensive and productive preoccupation with the material and are endlessly stimulating to me. I am completely in agreement with everything of importance to which you refer.' Strauss responded on the 12th with his urgent request that Gregor 'get in touch with Wallerstein immediately and revise the material *again with him*. I have discussed the work thoroughly with him and explained to him exactly what I want – namely something almost entirely new!'

Strauss began work on *Daphne* in June. Simultaneously, he completed the orchestration of *Friedenstag* on June 16. Two weeks later he made his way to Berlin for the inauguration ceremony of the eleventh Olympic Games.[8] At Goebbels's request, Strauss conducted his *Olympic Hymn* in the Olympic stadium on a vast platform, with the Berlin Philharmonic Orchestra and chorus (augmented by the National Socialist Symphony Orchestra), in front of Hitler, Goebbels and an audience of over forty thousand.[9] From Vienna, Gregor congratulated the composer, remarking that 'it must have been an exalting feeling for you'.

While in Berlin, Strauss assisted with a project dear to his heart – the International Composers' Contest, which Raabe had announced on April 16. While the games ran their course, dozens of young composers' music was judged for its 'Olympic spirit'; few were surprised when three of the four awards went to Germans (Egk, Thomas and Paul Hoeffer),[10] although the concept of aesthetic judgement must have seemed at odds with Goebbels's directive of the 23rd, banning all criticism of German culture. In June Strauss was again at liberty to cross the Austro-German border, and had his music been scheduled for performance at the Salzburg Festival he might have done so; instead he remained in Garmisch, working on *Daphne* and making the occasional trip to Munich for performances of *Così fan tutte* and *Don Giovanni*.

On September 20 illness prompted his second trip in twelve months to Dr C. von Dapper-Saalfals' sanatorium in Kissingen; when this failed to exact an improvement he underwent further treatment at the less exclusive resort of Baden-Baden. His strength restored, Strauss was able to embark upon another gruelling tour. He arrived in London at the beginning of November to support Karl Böhm and the Dresden company, who were giving a guest season at Covent Garden. Together with *Don Giovanni*, *Figaro* and *Tristan* they gave two performances[11] of *Rosenkavalier*. For the first of these, Strauss joined Joachim von Ribbentrop in his box. As everyone stood for the British National Anthem the ambassador raised his arm in the Nazi salute.

On the 6th Strauss conducted a single performance of *Ariadne auf Naxos*, with Martha Fuchs as Ariadne and Torsten Ralf as Bacchus. Ernest Newman applauded the composer's contribution, but disliked the work and its production. *The Times* commented on 'the ease with which in conducting it he [Strauss] obtained what he wanted from the singers and players without any physical effort on his part'. There was little sign of the anti-German fervour that had soured his season in Antwerp, and when he conducted a Royal Philharmonic Society concert in the Queen's Hall on the 5th[12] he was delighted to receive not only the approbation of the full house but, during the interval, the RPS's Gold Medal.[13]

Among Strauss's many admirers were those who saw him, and his recent history, in a different light, such as Bertha Geissmar, who had emigrated to England and found employment as Sir Thomas Beecham's secretary at Covent Garden. While attending rehearsals for the Dresden *Rosenkavalier* Strauss asked to meet Geissmar, ostensibly to discuss plans to stage *Salome* at the end of the year. She found the composer 'very good-looking in spite of having aged a little' and recalled how

> many thoughts shot through my mind as I sat opposite him. He had known my parents' house and myself for many years. Yet in spite of the fact that he was President of the Reichsmusikkammer, he had not made the slightest move to help either Furtwängler or me during all our difficulties in Germany ... He himself made use in foreign countries of his Jewish publisher, Herr Fürstner, who had emigrated to London ... and enthusiastic Jews had furthered and supported his work; but he only remembered those things in so far as they contributed to his own interests ... Why had he not, in his position ... supported all of us who were by tradition and merit entrenched within the traditional musical culture of the genuine Germany? Why had he not protected artists like Furtwängler and Hindemith, and also people like myself, against the Government? Why had he not protected the principles vital for Germany's musical life? I burned to express my opinion that had he not played into the hands of the Nazis, many tragedies in the field of music might have been avoided.

Needless to say, she did not. Rather, she was so 'bewitched' by Strauss's 'fabulous charm' that they discussed 'many topics, among which were casts for his operas ... the dangerous problems were carefully avoided'.

Strauss crossed the German border on November 7, only to leave for Italy eight days later. To Gregor he outlined his plans: 'Could be in Bozen (Hotel Greif) for lunch on the fifteenth, that evening in Verona, around the sixteenth in Florence, seventeenth Perugia, and eighteenth in the evening Rome (Hotel Russie). On the twenty-second and twenty-fifth concerts there, on the twenty-sixth beginning of the return trip by way of Orvieto, Siena, bringing me back to Garmisch again on the twenty-eighth or twenty-ninth.'[14] After five days' rest he left for concerts in Munich, Berlin and Salzburg. Shortly before Christmas 1936, having returned to find Hindemith's music banned, Handel's oratorios 'Aryanised', Mendelssohn's statue outside the Leipzig Gewandhaus torn down and the *Völkischer Beobachter* calling for the Aryanisation of Mozart's operas, Strauss invited Gregor to Garmisch to discuss the progress of *Daphne*.

In February 1937 Gregor mailed Strauss a draft of his third libretto. When they had first discussed ideas for stage works Strauss urged Gregor to read Hofmannsthal's scenario for an 'Offenbachiad', *Danae, or The Marriage of Convenience*, which the poet had sent Strauss in 1920. Unfortunately, Gregor failed to understand, even vaguely, Strauss's requirements as 'the Offenbach of the 20th century', and the text was rejected. But Strauss had nowhere else to turn, and persevered in defiance of Krauss's subtly-worded prediction that Gregor was not the man for the job. Throughout 1937 Strauss worked simultaneously on *Daphne* and *Danae*[15] which, inevitably, meant that he was spending more time in Garmisch, mostly at his desk. For no other reason than that he was tired and feared confrontations with the authorities, he was accepting fewer conducting engagements, and during the first half of the year he made only two excursions, to Berlin and Vienna, where he was able to enjoy the luxury of his house at Jacquingasse.

In July Strauss conducted a concert of his music and a performance of Wagner's *Fliegende Holländer* in Munich,[16] and at the end of the month he left for Salzburg and another glittering festival. He had not been asked to conduct (possibly out of deference to the wishes of Toscanini and Walter[17]) but *Rosenkavalier* was being staged, again with Lotte Lehmann as the Marschallin, conducted by Hans Knappertsbusch; Lehmann had also programmed a number of Strauss's songs[18] in two 'Liederabends' with Bruno Walter. On August 27 Furtwängler made his debut at the festival, conducting Beethoven's Ninth Symphony, an event that heralded the celebrated encounter with Toscanini in which the Italian grilled the German over the political significance of his continued support of Bayreuth. This unpleasantness aside, it was a matchless gathering of talent and imagination, and Strauss's chest must have swelled with pride to see his ambitions come to such fruition.

His chest was, otherwise, ailing, and illness forced him to withdraw from the Paris World Fair, where he had been scheduled to conduct *Rosenkavalier* and *Ariadne auf Naxos* in September. His withdrawal was a severe blow to Goebbels, who had advocated Strauss's participation in order to demonstrate Germany's cultural superiority. In his diary on August 27 the Reichsminister wrote: 'Richard Strauss is ill. Unfortunately he cannot conduct in Paris. A great loss for us.'

At Pauline's urging he agreed to retire to warmer climes, and in October they set off for Italy. Possibly without her knowledge, Strauss managed to smuggle out the manuscript of *Daphne*, on which he worked throughout

November and December. Shortly before Christmas, on December 17, Karl Böhm received from Taormina, Sicily, a postcard of the Apollo Citaredo in the National Museum in Naples.[19] On the back Strauss had written: 'Dear Friend, Hofmüller has told me enthusiastically about your wonderful performance of *Iphigénie*.[20] Heartfelt thanks and best wishes! The Sicilian summer suits me very well and I am working on *Daphne*, which will be dedicated to you: I hope this will bring you a little Christmas joy.'

From the start Böhm had shadowed the conception of *Daphne*. If, unlike Krauss, he contributed little beyond encouragement to its creation he had none the less publicly supported Strauss throughout the *Schweigsame Frau* affair, and in the months following Strauss's 'disgrace' he had continued to perform his music – a gesture of faith that went a long way with the composer. Böhm and his wife were welcomed on a number of occasions to Garmisch, when Strauss would invite the conductor to join him in his study. In 1968 Böhm recalled:

> He would write out the full score from the short score with everything, even new counterpoints, in ink in the final draft; very shaming – he never crossed anything out. If he made a mistake he would take out a pen-knife, carefully erase it, smooth the spot with his nail and write the note over the spot. But there were very few corrections to be done, for he rarely made a mistake; particularly with transposing instruments, where it is easy to go wrong. He would write just as the likes of us would write a letter.[21]
>
> Once, he was sitting at his desk, with me behind me. He was working on the score of *Daphne* and discussing a Mozart interpretation with me. Upon which I said, 'But Herr Doktor, you can't talk to me about other things while you are working.' 'Don't worry, carry on, my dear Böhm,' he replied, 'I am able to think of the two things at once.'[22]

Böhm owned four of the composer's precious sketchbooks, in which he mapped out ideas before taking them to short score. One of these contained material for *Ariadne auf Naxos*: 'It goes from the first half of the Prologue where the Music Teacher says, "Ich weiss nicht wo mir der Kopf steht", in exactly the right harmony, the vocal part with the right text and notes. Not one of them was later changed and the whole thing was more or less like a piano score.'

These abilities enabled Strauss to work just about anywhere, and under almost any circumstances. Consequently, work in Taormina progressed well, and he was able to complete *Daphne* on Christmas Eve, 1937. Instead of taking the score back to Germany, however, he remained in Italy until April 1938, by which time events at home had taken a noticeable turn for the worse. On March 11, while Strauss was in Rome, it was announced that Germany had annexed Austria.

As the swastika was raised over the Chancellor's office in Vienna, thousands began to plan their escape. On April 12 Hitler made his triumphant entrance into his native land, and that very evening the once politically discriminating Hans Knappertsbusch conducted a performance of one of the Führer's favourite operas, *Tristan und Isolde*. The following night Germany's troops arrived and the Opera was closed down. It reopened two weeks later, with Knappertsbusch in the pit and Goering in the audience, to a performance of Beethoven's hymn to freedom, *Fidelio*. Sitting next to Goering was Baldur von Schirach, a friend of the Strausses since childhood, and the future Gauleiter of Vienna.

Schirach was a career Nazi and rampant anti-Semite who would sign away 185,000 Jews to Polish concentration camps between 1940 and 1945. He had been a devotee of Hitler since his student days, when he helped establish the National Socialist German Student League. In 1931 he was nominated head of the Hitler Youth,[23] was later appointed Reich Youth Leader, and in 1937 he established with Robert Ley the Adolf Hitler Schools system. Unlike many of his Nazi contemporaries Schirach was a man of culture, and a noted music-lover, inheriting knowledge and enthusiasm from his father who had been an Intendant at Weimar. His sister, Rosalind, an averagely gifted coloratura soprano employed by the Berlin State Opera, was said to present the 'idealised replica of the Nordic-Aryan singer type'. Schirach admired Strauss, and Strauss was quick to realise that, as Gauleiter of Vienna, Schirach would make a valuable ally, particularly if he and his family wished to spend any time at Jacquingasse.

In the light of his presumed apoliticism, Strauss's return to Germany in April 1938 is baffling. Had he remained in Italy just a few weeks longer he could have avoided what was probably the Nazis' most flamboyant, heavily publicised cultural event of the pre war years. Instead, he returned to lend his services to the promotion of Nazi mythology through the first (and, as things turned out, penultimate) Reichsmusiktage. The Reich Music Festival (running between May 22 and 29) was the realisation of Goebbels's dream to mount a demonstration of the richness of pure German musical life. The massive emigration of the early 1930s had proved ruinous to Germany's reputation as the heart of European culture (an association that had transferred to the 'New Europe' of the United States) and Goebbels was determined to establish, as through the previous year's Olympics, that German life had flourished because of, and not despite, the departure and suppression of the country's Jewish talent.

The festival's overall director was Goebbels; to oversee matters of detail he enlisted Heinz Drewes, a conductor and presidium associate of Strauss at the RMK. It was decided that the festival should lead the dominant musical events of the summer season, chiefly Bayreuth, and it was staged in Düsseldorf, home of the national conventions of the NSKG.[24] Though running

for only seven days, the event was hailed as a 'musical Olympics' and 'a
military parade of German music'. The musical highlights were three concerts
of contemporary German works conducted by Hugo Balzer (including a
performance of Pfitzner's *Von deutsche Seele*), three operas (one of which was
Strauss's *Arabella*) and a performance of Beethoven's Ninth Symphony by
the Berlin Philharmonic, conducted by Hermann Abendroth.

Elsewhere, the festival provided a platform for numerous conventions,
with papers delivered on subjects as predictable as 'the nature of German
music', 'music and race' and 'the state and music'. With hindsight, the most
controversial event – even though it was independently mounted by Hans
Ziegler and Paul Sixt, and enjoyed only a minimum of assistance from the
Ministry of Propaganda – was the exhibition 'Entartete Musik' ('Degenerate
Music').[25]

This bewilderingly childish assembly of material attempted, through a
curiously typical mixture of scholarship, name-calling and derision, to highlight the evils of modernist, Jewish and un-German music. Both morally
and aesthetically, the contents[26] represented the nadir of National Socialist
cultural commentary. The chief targets were the influence of jazz (Höllander,
Stravinsky, Rotter, Korngold, Spoliansky, Jessel, Tauber, etc.), the Weimar
press (Bekker, Adorno, Bloch, Einstein, etc.), atonality (Schoenberg, Hindemith, Weissmann, Berg, Hauer, etc.) and the Jews, all of which was supported through the presentation of scores by Schoenberg, Stravinsky,
Hindemith, Weill, Schreker, Krenek, Eisler, Berg, Rathaus, Hauer, Toch,
Seckles and Reutter.[27]

Considering Strauss's aesthetic sensibilities, it is worth noting Ziegler's
official definition of musical degeneracy: 'The Entartete Musik exhibition
presents a picture of a veritable witches' sabbath portraying the most frivolous
intellectual and artistic aspects of Cultural Bolshevism ... and the triumph
of arrogant Jewish impudence ... Degenerate music is thus basically de-
Germanised music for which the nation will not mobilise its involvement ...
it is the last measure of snobbist adoration or pure intellectual consideration.'
While it would be wrong to suggest that Strauss had any interest in, or
sympathy for, the exhibition there is no question that he shared Ziegler's
concern to protect German culture from the impurities of the *Unter-
menschentum* (Nietzsche's 'Lower Human Type').

Whatever political misgivings he might have had, Strauss chose to accept
Goebbels's commission to write, and conduct, a 'Festival Vorspiel' as an
introduction to the Minister's formal address on May 28.[28] This was intended
to be the Reich Music Festival's highlight, and it attracted extensive publicity;
not unfairly, Strauss's compliance with Goebbels's wishes and his presence
during the speech were construed as an approval of its contents. Goebbels
took the opportunity to 'restate and recognise the principles which have
always been the source and driving strength of our classical achievements

here in Germany'. The third of these 'Ten Principles of German Music' stated:

> Like every other art form, music arises from deep and secret forces which are
> rooted in the people of the nation. Therefore only the nation's children can create
> and perform it in a manner which befits the desire and musical inclinations of
> that nation. Judaism and German music are opposites which by their very
> nature stand in sharp contradiction to one another. The fight against Judaism
> in German music, which Richard Wagner once took upon himself, quite alone,
> is for that reason still today the great and never-to-be-surrendered fight of our
> time, in which we can never surrender, and which is no longer being fought by
> one brilliant and knowing outsider, but by a whole people.

That evening Strauss conducted a concert with the National Socialist Symphony Orchestra in the Düsseldorf town hall with a forty-foot swastika, bearing the imprint of the NSDAP (National Socialist German Workers' Party), dominating his immediate horizon.[29]

These unequivocally politicised submissions smoothed Strauss's path, in July,[30] for the first performance of *Friedenstag* in Munich. He had originally intended to stage the premières of *Friedenstag* and *Daphne* in Dresden, as a double bill on the same night; Böhm later claimed he had promised as much, but pressure from Clemens Krauss,[31] and fallout from the badly handled *Schweigsame Frau* affair, brought about a temporary suspension of Dresden's right to first refusal. The honour of *Friedenstag*'s première thus went to its dedicatees, Clemens Krauss and Viorica Ursuleac.

Krauss slotted the new work into the summer festival, for which he had already programmed new productions of *Rosenkavalier* and *Ariadne auf Naxos*, and he cast Ursuleac as Marie – the opera's only named and female role.[32] Rehearsals began in June, and progressed favourably, thanks partly to the outstanding quality and professionalism of the cast which featured Hans Hotter as the Commandant, George Hann as the Cavalry Sergeant, Julius Patzak as the Rifleman, Peter Anders as the Piedmontese and Karl Ostertag as the Mayor.

As a filler it was decided to begin the first night with a ballet. Strauss and Gregor briefly toyed with the creation of an original work; but they eventually opted for Beethoven's *Die Geschöpfe des Prometheus* (The Creatures of Prometheus).[33] For all *Friedenstag*'s unmistakable shortcomings the first performance was a great success, particularly with Nazi officialdom since Strauss had proved to the world that he could persevere, indeed prosper, with a German author of pure birth. It was also enjoyed for its robust libretto, which appropriated every imaginable Wagnerian cliché, from the Citadel setting (Valhalla) to the reinvention of Brünnhilde and Wotan as Maria and the Commandant. The under-inspired score and absurd prevalence of self-quotation confirm Strauss's less than total commitment to Gregor's cardboard cut-outs, and the final C major apotheosis (recalling Beethoven's *Fidelio*) was probably the biggest compromise of his career.

Goebbels was delighted. In the light of Hitler's claims to international pacifism the opera could not have come at a better time, and he announced their intention to attend the first Austrian performance in Vienna the following year. The opera's critical reception mirrored the official response, so that the work's topicality and broadly idealistic Nazi stereotypes (namely the Commandant and his Wife) were thought sufficiently resonant for one commentator to hail the work as 'the first opera to be born out of the spirit of Nazism'. The Munich critic Alexander Bersche announced: 'This time we see only ourselves on the stage . . . each figure is a part of us. This inescapable reflection of ourselves is the most convincing proof of the artistic and human truth of the work, which shows courage and self-sacrifice, fear and denial, for what they are.'

Of course, the message could easily have been read quite differently. Gregor may not have been a Nazi but his political sympathies were anything but passive. As an Austrian he saw the positive aspects of the Anschluss, and as late as 1942 he was dedicating one of his books (*Das Theater des Volkes in der Ostmark*[34]) to the Gauleiter Baldur von Schirach. Strauss doubtless understood the implications of a drama in which assimilation and effective aggression were advocated as a prelude to collective peace and productivity, but his setting played down these transient sympathies and concentrated on the broader, less intemperate characteristics of Gregor's libretto. Given the official response, few were surprised when *Friedenstag* was embraced by Intendants throughout Germany, Austria and Italy: within its first two years it had received over a hundred performances.[35]

With this troublesome work out of the way Strauss could turn to the happier business of staging *Daphne*. Despite the constant struggle with Gregor he had enjoyed writing his fourth 'Greek' opera, and the music throbs with a youthful energy and compactness of style and intent absent from his two preceding operas. Strauss's own special preference for the music was shared by Pauline who, to the end, held it to be her husband's finest stage work. So fond of *Daphne* was Pauline that she accompanied him to Dresden for the première. Böhm recalled how, after the dress rehearsal, she 'took my head between her hands, gave me a little kiss and said: "You're not getting a second one now, you're too sweaty."' The rehearsals were difficult, however, since it had been decided that, as a curtain-raiser to the new work and in line with the creators' original intentions, *Friedenstag* should be played first. The strain of so demanding a double bill was enormous and Böhm later recalled, 'I would never do that again.'[36]

Had *Daphne* been played on its own, its impact might have been greater; heard at the end of a long evening, with a tired conductor, orchestra and chorus, the audience response was muted. Even with Goebbels's blessing, opera houses were slow in taking the new work into repertoire – a fact that might, in part, be ascribed to the simple logistical nightmare of needing to find two world-class tenors for the demanding roles of Apollo and Leukippos. *Daphne* is decidedly a singer's opera, and one of Strauss's most lyrical. The title role is especially grateful, although – as in her wordless final scene – much of what she says matters less than how she sings it. Gregor's text is a minefield of clichés; that Strauss was able to generate such electricity between Daphne and her suitors is a testament to the freshness of his abilities as a septuagenarian. The wonderfully inventive scoring adds magic to the already other-worldly atmosphere, and the excitement of the confrontation between Apollo and Leukippos stands comparison with the final scene of *Elektra*. It is a great shame that *Daphne* has failed to join the ranks of Strauss repertoire operas[37] since, as the composer himself suspected, it is a masterpiece.

Back in Garmisch he continued to work on *Danae* (the first act of which he had begun in June) in defiance of the obvious weakness of Gregor's doggerel verse. It is a wonder that either man persisted with such a transparently unproductive relationship. Gregor withered beneath Strauss's rudeness, while Strauss shrank from Gregor's servility, and it was by now obvious that the composer would have to look elsewhere for *Capriccio*'s libretto.

He spent the remainder of 1938 in Garmisch, from where he observed his country's increasingly frantic degeneration into repression and violence. On November 7 Herschel Grynszpan, a Polish Jew, murdered Ernest vom Rath, a secretary in the German embassy in Paris, in response to the mistreatment of his family and their fellow Jews by the Nazi government. Two days later[38] Hitler gave Goebbels permission to induce widespread 'demonstrations', whereupon the Propaganda Minister invited the SA to 'have a fling'. This licence to brutality set in motion what became known as 'Kristallnacht', a pogrom in which over a hundred Jews were killed by the SA, nearly 1,000 Jewish businesses were razed to the ground, 200 synagogues were smashed and burned and 26,000 Jews were rounded up and imprisoned in concentration camps. The Propaganda Minister then had the audacity to blame the Jews for the violence, and used the opportunity to seize one billion RM in insurance money paid out in recompense. Finally, on November 15, Goebbels passed laws prohibiting any Jew from further participation in German cultural life, while Jewish attendance at German theatres, opera houses, cinemas, concerts and public exhibitions was strictly forbidden.

On January 21, 1939, Hitler told the Czech Foreign Minister that he intended to destroy the Jews, on whom he blamed the 'disintegration' of German life after November 9, 1918; a week later, on the anniversary of his appointment as Chancellor, he stood before the Reichstag and announced: 'If the international Jewish financiers in and outside Europe should succeed in plunging the nations once more into a world war, then the result will not be the Bolshevising of the earth, and thus the victory of Jewry, but the annihilation of the Jewish race in Europe!' By the end of 1938 Paris, London and New York were inundated with refugees – inadvertently advancing the musical life of all three cities.

Musical life in Germany continued as if nothing had happened. Oblivious and seemingly en route to an inner emigration, Strauss buried himself in *Danae*. He briefly emerged at the end of 1938 when Munich Council (by way of the Ministry of Propaganda) asked him to write a short work for a film in honour of the city. He completed this 'Occasional Waltz' on January 3, 1939, which was duly added as background music. The film received a single showing (and the Waltz a single performance) on May 24;[39] since Hitler and Goebbels were planning a series of huge 'Führerbauten' they postponed the film's public release until these could be edited into the finished reels. The outbreak of war put an end to such grandiose plans, and the film (together with Strauss's waltz) was forgotten until Strauss revised it as a *Gedächtniswalzer* in 1945.

On June 11 Strauss celebrated his seventy-fifth birthday. It was, again, a date of enormous significance to the Nazis, given the attention being paid throughout Europe and America to the wealth of Jewish talent that continued to flee Germany in the wake of Kristallnacht. As *The Times* reported in February 1940, even German radio was broadcasting its fears for the future of its musical life.[40] Consequently, Goebbels capitalised on Strauss's continuing centrality and offered him godlike recognition, glory and deference in return for his ongoing collaboration. Festival weeks were organised in all the major Strauss centres, including Munich, Dresden (where Böhm mounted performances of no fewer than nine of the composer's operas, together with productions of *Josephslegende* and *Schlagobers*[41]), Berlin (where Herbert von Karajan conducted *Salome*[42]) and Vienna; German radio broadcast another cycle of his works and every major cultural journal knelt in homage.

In Garmisch he was presented with the Golden Ring of Honour, and the city of Vienna gave him a three-foot bronze copy of the Beethoven monument in Heilingenstadt. Aside from the many Lieder and chamber recitals devoted to his music, the Vienna Philharmonic Orchestra scheduled numerous tributes and, at the Opera, Clemens Krauss conducted the Austrian première of *Friedenstag* on June 10, attended by Hitler and Goebbels. German radio broadcast the performance, and Hitler and Strauss were applauded as they entered the auditorium to the imperial accompaniment of Strauss's own 1924 *Wiener Philharmoniker Fanfare* for brass and timpani.

The following morning Strauss and Hitler had breakfast together. News of the meeting was leaked, and different sources reported different meal times and places. Thomas Mann, for example, recorded in his diary on June 18: 'Haunted by what Landshoff[43] told us, namely that the 75-year-old Richard Strauss had lunch with Hitler the day after the gala opening of his latest opera in Vienna, which Hitler also attended.' That evening, Strauss conducted the

Philharmonic in a concert[44] of his Suite from *Le bourgeois Gentilhomme* and the *Sinfonia Domestica*. The violinist Otto Strasser later recalled how 'we had arranged for this music [*Le bourgeois Gentilhomme*] to be played by our youngest members, to demonstrate what would be lost if they were conscripted. During the interval I said how much this suite, in particular, had impressed me. He remarked that he had "written it with the left hand, so to speak".'

Swoboda, then conductor of the Vienna Philharmonic, had prepared an arrangement of the final duet from *Rosenkavalier* for flute, which he had rehearsed with Strauss's eleven-year-old grandson, Richard. After the presentation to Strauss of a painting, the boy stood and played his piece. Strauss remarked: 'Lovely, but no sense of rhythm – just like most flautists.' *Domestica* followed, after which, Strasser recalled, Strauss

> was stormily applauded, but when I met him at the exit from the platform, he suddenly threw the baton away, stumbled into the artists' room, sat down, visibly distressed, and murmured: 'Now it's all over', and began to cry bitterly. I was moved and at the same time had no idea what to do. He was a man who took such joy in life: was he thinking of the end at this moment of moments? After a short time his son arrived and put his arms around his father, who was growing calmer, and all was well again. The next morning Jerger[45] and I collected him from the Hotel Imperial, and as we strolled across the Ring together, he was fresh and cheerful and said that he would have to go to Dresden, the same day, to conduct *Arabella*. He had overcome his depression, and turned his face to the world.

Strasser's moving recollection invites various interpretations. That Strauss was beginning to sense the end of his creative life was obvious, the more so since his lingering collaboration with Gregor served to provide a painful reminder of what he had lost in Zweig and Hofmannsthal. He was also growing old, and there can be no doubt that the weakening of his health (which required two cures during the course of 1939) was fostering intimations of mortality. Of course, when considering the imminence of war, and in the light of his awareness that National Socialism was some way from producing the Elysian dream promised six years earlier, Strauss may well have been alluding to his loss of faith in Hitler and his assurances of unity, renewal and prosperity. While the country may have been thriving economically and, in certain respects, socially, there was little sign of Germany's much promised cultural renaissance; meeting Hitler again may well have brought home to Strauss the true place occupied by culture in the Führer's priorities.[46]

Indeed, there were sporadic indications that Strauss was beginning to understand something of the brutal practicalities of National Socialism but,

unless he and his circle were affected, he did nothing about them. Some
months earlier, in 1938, for example, a friend of the family, the industrialist
Manfred Mautner-Markhof, had been arrested and imprisoned, for reasons
that remain unclear. At his birthday reception, shortly after collapsing in his
dressing room, Strauss made an official 'anniversary request' that Mautner-
Markhof be released. 'The arrest can only be an error in any case,' he
remarked. The industrialist's crimes cannot have been too serious, since
the authorities acceded to Strauss's request. A free man, Mautner-Markhof
returned to his factories and later gave Strauss's grandson Richard a job in
Schwechat, near Vienna.

On July 16, as part of the continuing birthday celebrations, Krauss conducted a revised version of *Arabella* in Munich. Krauss had always considered
the end of Act II redundant, and after much badgering – and many small
revisions by the composer – he persuaded Strauss to cut the final waltz and
chorus. This allowed him to play the second and third acts as one, using
Munich's revolving stage to full advantage. From Munich Strauss travelled to
Salzburg and another production of *Rosenkavalier*. At the end of August a
serious attack of rheumatism necessitated another cure, this time in Baden
bei Zürich. Strauss was there when Britain declared war on September 3.

Strauss greeted the outbreak of war like so many others; he believed that, second time around, Germany would repeat none of her mistakes, that Britain's defeat was 'inevitable'.[1] But he was careful not to make any bold predictions, and his surviving correspondence contains none of the war-mongering common to his letters of 1914–15. If he did not expect defeat then he was wise enough not to think it impossible, and he reserved any judgement on the conflict until its outcome was decided six years later. As normal, he buried his head in the sands of work: the score of *Danae* was nearing completion and Gregor's draft synopsis for *Prima la Musica e poi le parole*[2] had been sitting on his desk since May.

Four years earlier Zweig had joined Gregor for a holiday in Zurich with a view to working out the details of Casti's thesis. According to Gregor:

> Strauss had expressed the desire for the sort of discourse set in dialogue after the manner of Plato over the old argument: is it the music or the text which in opera is the more important? Zweig came along with a bag full of history, with the little comedy of the Abbé de Casti ... neither of us knew what to do with it. A few radiant summer days changed our mood to one of wild dionysiac poetics. We became obsessed with an idea: a group of comedians come upon a feudal castle; they fall headlong into a delicate situation; a poet and a musician both sue for the hand of the lady of the castle; she herself does not know which to choose ... we were at once of the same mind that such a band of players must have a magniloquent director, a blunt caricature of that so much revered Max Reinhardt, full of his art, full of the theatre. As we laughed and sang on a wooden bench in a Gasthaus we found the original concept of the director La Roche ...

Gregor's nostalgia for those heady days with Zweig – so dissimilar to his collaboration with Strauss – hardly reflects the time and effort he invested in the first draft of *Capriccio*. On receipt the composer replied that it was 'a disappointment ... nothing like what I had in mind', that the project was only really 'worthy of a Beaumarchais, Scribe or Hofmannsthal!' The resolute and thick-skinned Gregor bore his humiliation, and set about revising the draft, describing it to Strauss as 'a little comedy in the manner of Eichendorff'. While Gregor flailed, Krauss gently prodded. In September he wrote his own scenario, which arrived in Garmisch concurrently with another from Gregor. On October 7 Strauss sent Gregor his own draft, in the hope that this might stimulate progress, but just five days later he resigned himself to the inevitable. Summoning Rudolph Hartmann and Krauss to Garmisch, he outlined his ambitions for *Capriccio*, ambitions that no longer involved Gregor.

Since they were still working on *Danae*, and because Gregor now openly despised Krauss,[3] Strauss had to tread lightly. On October 28 he wrote to thank Gregor for his hard work; but instead of telling him that he was to be replaced by Krauss he announced his intention to write the libretto himself. When Gregor learned of Krauss's involvement he was overcome with grief and shame; not surprisingly, he attended the premières of neither *Die liebe der Danae* nor *Capriccio*.

In truth, Krauss was the ideal collaborator. Gregor was learned and well-meaning, but hopelessly anti-theatrical. Krauss was no poet, but he was born to the stage, and his instincts, strength of character and robust self-respect precluded the humiliating master-and-servant routine enacted by Strauss and Gregor. Consequently, the genesis of *Capriccio* was a source of singular delight for the composer, and his surviving correspondence with Krauss is as jovial and good-natured as his correspondence with Gregor is strained and undignified.

In November 1939, Strauss was suffering from water on his lungs; work on *Danae* and *Capriccio* was suspended until the spring of 1940, when he took the draft to Italy[4] for another working convalescence. Meanwhile, he had to attend to a commission from the Ministry of Propaganda. Shortly before the commencement of hostilities the Japanese government had asked a number of French, British and German composers to write something in celebration of the 2,600th anniversary of the Japanese Empire. Strauss's *Japanische Festmusik*,[5] which he completed on April 23, 1940, in Merano, was the favoured submission – thus scoring a rare propaganda victory for Goebbels. Although the commission came via the Reichsminister's office, there is no evidence that Strauss's co-operation was unwilling; rather, it seems that his enthusiasm was enlisted by the Japanese government's fee of 10,000 RM.

That the 75-year-old Strauss was still interested in money should come as no surprise, particularly considering contemporary circumstances. Less comprehensible is the reconciliation of his aesthetic principles (to which he was then giving life through *Capriccio*) to the writing of such a crass and inflated work.[6] On his return Strauss played through the score to the Japanese ambassador,[7] who appears to have approved; the first performance was given in Tokyo by Helmut Fellmer and the United Symphony Orchestra on December 7, 1940.[8]

Back in Garmisch, Strauss concentrated on *Capriccio*'s libretto and the score of *Danae*. He managed to complete the latter on June 28,[9] whereupon Krauss asked for verbal reassurance that the première would be entrusted to him, regardless of where it was eventually staged; this Strauss gave, but on the condition that the first performance was delayed until at least two years after the war. When Krauss began to badger the composer to allow a première to be held in Salzburg Strauss wrote to the conductor:

> Do you really think that *Danae*, which is so hard and so demanding, could be at all adequately presented scenically or acoustically in that riding-school barn of a Festspielhaus? The old well-known operas can stand up to even a temporary set-up like that, but a new work whose whole future hangs on the way it is given at the first performance? You will yourself be the best judge of this when you have had a look at the enclosed score ... over the date I would really ask that the previous agreement stands: at least two years after the conclusion of peace-talks – that is to say, when the other stages are halfway to the point when they can guarantee a satisfactory production.

Strauss's caution, and his willingness to forgo the pleasure of seeing the première, stemmed from his attribution of the failure of *Die Frau ohne Schatten* to its having been 'put on in German theatres too soon after the last war'. Strauss none the less instructed Oertel to prepare the publication of *Danae* in full score, and Krauss may well have sensed the composer's private ambition to see the work staged during his lifetime; either way, just twelve months later Strauss was persuaded to sanction a wartime première.

With *Danae* to one side, Strauss was able to concentrate on *Capriccio*. For the last important piece of the jigsaw – the verse passage which was to serve as the opera's axis – Krauss turned for help to one of his assistants in Munich, Hans Swarovsky, who was a competent linguist as well as a fine conductor.[10] Having fallen foul of the Nazis, Swarovsky was dismissed from Berlin at the end of 1939; Krauss managed to secure his services as a translator in Munich, in which capacity he spent many hours digging through archives for a French couplet suitable to provide the basis of a discussion of the relative merits of words and music. He eventually settled on a sonnet[11] by the sixteenth-century poet Pierre de Ronsard, whose passionate advocacy of a reversion to classical form and tradition made him the ideal source.

Such was Strauss's enthusiasm that he began the score of *Capriccio* before the libretto was ready. Indeed, he had managed to complete the Introduction[12] and first scene by July 1940, whereas Krauss did not finish the libretto until January 18 the following year.[13] The music flowed out of Strauss as if bursting through a dam; the eloquence and fluency of his work was extraordinary for a man approaching his seventy-seventh birthday.

While Strauss waltzed with his imagination the German army invaded Holland, Belgium, Luxembourg and France, and in May Goebbels announced the founding of the Reichsstelle für Musikbearbeitungen for the purpose of bringing opera and operetta libretti into line with National Socialist ideology. Even for someone as single-minded as Strauss it is remarkable that he was able to tap such a rich creative well while his country violated almost every human right worth protecting. Of course, he was far from unique in this respect; most of his German contemporaries continued to work throughout the war, but very little of it was any good. *Capriccio*, on the other hand, is a masterpiece,[14] Strauss's *Falstaff*,[15] the most sparkling of his late works[16] and the finest opera produced by a German composer during the Third Reich.

That Strauss chose to write a 'conversation piece' set in eighteenth-century France denotes an inner emigration;[17] no one would blame him for turning away from the grimmer realities of the war, but that he could write music of such beauty and inspiration while so many crimes were being perpetrated in the name of a Germany to which he had contributed so much, and in which he continued to believe, suggests a near-total moral and ethical detachment. Such a conclusion owes little to hindsight; equivalent reasoning was common throughout the conflict; and many, from Thomas Mann to Albert Einstein, spoke of their despair at the continuity of German creativity during the war. Among the most insistent commentators was Stefan Zweig. On July 28, 1940 – while Strauss was working on *Capriccio*'s first scene – the exiled writer was interviewed for the *New York Times Book Review*:

> The artist has been wounded in his concentration . . . How can old themes hold our attention now? . . . The basic law of all creative work remains invariably concentration, and never has this been so difficult for the artists in Europe. How should complete concentration be possible in the midst of a moral earthquake? . . . even the happy few who are able to continue working at their desks cannot escape the turmoil of our time. Reclusion is no more possible while our world stands in flames; the 'Ivory Tower' of aesthetics is no more bomb-proof, as Irwin Edman has said. From hour to hour one waits for news, one cannot avoid reading the papers, listening to the wireless . . . From all sides every one of us who has found a haven is daily assailed by letters and telegrams for help and intervention; every one of us lives more the lives of a hundred others than his own.
>
> And the internal difficulty – what do psychology and artistic perfection mean at such an hour, where for centuries the fate of our real and spiritual world is at stake? . . . I would be suspicious of any European author who would now be capable of concentrating on his own private work. What was allowed to Archimedes, the mathematician, to continue his experiments undisturbed by the siege of his town, seems to me quasi inhuman for the poet, the artist, who

does not deal with abstractions but whose mission it is to feel with the greatest intensity the fate and sufferings of his fellow beings.

Despite the occasional interruption (such as the première of the revised *Guntram* on October 19[18] and another Berlin 'Strauss Week' in November), Strauss sailed through *Capriccio*. By the end of 1940 he and Krauss had agreed on the opera's title and at the beginning of the new year, in a move hardly designed to improve their relationship, Strauss sent Gregor a copy of Krauss's completed libretto. The following month, on February 24, Strauss finished the vocal score. At the beginning of April he interrupted work to make a film for the Propaganda Ministry of his conducting the *Alpensinfonie*, with interpolated views of Bavarian mountainscapes. A week later, on the evening of April 9–10, Allied bombers attacked Berlin, killing thousands of Germans and flattening hundreds of buildings, including the Opera unter den Linden.

On May 24 Strauss travelled to Munich for the Bavarian première of *Daphne*, conducted by Krauss, and on August 3, just over a year after having begun the short score, Strauss completed the final orchestrations of *Capriccio*.[19] He was now out of work; Krauss and the indefatigable Gregor would suggest dozens of ideas over the coming months, but Strauss already knew that *Capriccio* would be his last opera. As he wrote to Krauss: 'Isn't this D flat major [in which key *Capriccio* ends] the best winding up of my theatrical life-work? One can only leave one testament behind!'

Unemployment allowed Strauss to relax. Life in Garmisch was comfortable, so much so, in fact, that there were few signs of a country at war. There was ample meat and vegetables, and Pauline would ensure that everyone, including the chauffeur Theodor Martin, the maid Anni Nitzl and Pauline's aide de camp Anna Glossner, ate well.[20] If Pauline was busy – and she was known never to rest unless illness dictated otherwise – Strauss would lend a hand. Taking his instructions from her, he would leave memos around the house. One such note reads: 'Anni. There are chestnuts. Frau Bierling is to bring some, or whatever else there is. Anni is requested to bake a vanilla loaf and a double batch of Plätzchen [biscuits] for the children. If Martin has the time, ask him to come to Frau Doktor.'[21]

But as Allied bombing missions increased in number and severity it was obvious that Garmisch's distance from Munich was no longer a guarantee of safety. Furthermore, the family was encountering difficulties with the local Nazi Party – mainly, it would appear, as a result of Pauline's boldly expressed contempt for officialdom. The grandchildren, Richard and Christian, had been insulted and attacked by their peers at school, apparently on account of their quarter-Jewish mother. Strauss was able to garner a modicum of support and protection from Walther Funk,[22] whom he had known since 1933 and to whom he dedicated a short work for unaccompanied voice in 1940, *Notschrei aus den Gefilden Lapplands*, but with Franz and Alice spending most of their time in Vienna it seemed only sensible to relocate the rest of the family. In December 1941 Strauss, Pauline and the children packed up and left for Jacquingasse.

Shortly after their arrival Strauss contributed his services to a Mozart festival at the Opera in which his arrangement of *Idomeneo* was receiving an airing.[23] Six weeks later, motivated by his dread of apathy and inspired by the imminent fiftieth birthday celebrations of the poet Josef Weinheber,[24] Strauss composed two songs in his honour. In itself, there was nothing remarkable in Strauss setting verses by a living writer; he had done so throughout his song-writing life. But Weinheber was a devoted, officially honoured Nazi. Strauss set two of his poems (*Sankt Michael* on February 3, and *Blick vom oberon Belvedere* eight days later) dating from 1937, two years after Weinheber was awarded the Mozart Prize and catapulted to Nazi-sponsored celebrity. Both songs are unashamedly patriotic, and while neither is especially rabid – at least not when compared to Weinheber's more extreme work – *Sankt Michael*'s metaphor of a wind from the West cleansing a plague from the East would be difficult to misinterpret. They were first performed at an official celebration in the Palais Lobkowitz in Vienna on Weinheber's birthday.[25]

The Weinheber songs are extremely controversial; it is now clear that Strauss's family tried to suppress them after 1945, and yet neither was officially commissioned, as were some of Strauss's later curtsies to the administration. Their composition appears to have been a spontaneous and willing manifestation of Strauss's respect and admiration for Weinheber. Strauss may also have been trying to ingratiate himself with the Establishment, particularly Gauleiter von Schirach. In fact, it is now clear that there was more to Strauss's move to Vienna than fear of enemy bombs. Eighteen years earlier, in 1924, he had had his lease on Jacquingasse extended to sixty years; but it now dawned on him that while *he* would not live to see its reversion to the city of Vienna in 1984, his descendants would. He therefore approached the city with a new offer. In return for the freehold of Jacquingasse, he would donate to the city the autograph score of *Die Ägyptische Helena*, together with one hundred free performances in the Philharmonie or the Staatsoper. Remarkably, considering the obvious worth of the building and its land, his offer was accepted.

When, in 1940, Schirach was appointed Gauleiter he made much of his ambition to turn Vienna into the 'cultural heart of the Reich'. Such a claim was as catnip to Strauss, who had known Schirach's father and after whom Baldur and Henrietta had named their son, but Strauss also saw in the Gauleiter an opportunity to smooth his and his family's path to a life of sanctuary and prominence. In return for Strauss's endorsement, reputation, credibility and talent, Schirach would ensure a trouble-free stay in the city. Of course, Schirach had scant influence outside Vienna, and Strauss's vulnerability was demonstrated on February 10 when he and a number of his composing colleagues were summoned to a meeting with Goebbels in Berlin. Among the party was Werner Egk:

> Strauss saw the minister first, alone. Through the door we could hear Goebbels screaming. Then we were all ushered in. Goebbels ordered something that Strauss had written in a letter to be read out aloud: 'In accordance with our agreed statute, we ourselves will decide questions concerning the distribution scheme. It is not for Dr Goebbels to interfere.' Goebbels slapped the letter and screamed: 'Herr Strauss, did you write that?' 'Yes.' 'Be quiet! You have no conception of who you are, or of who I am!' Strauss had also made some derogatory remarks about Lehár, to which Goebbels exploded: 'Stop your clap-trap about the importance of serious music, once and for all. It will not serve to raise your own standing. Tomorrow's art is different from yesterday's! You, Herr Strauss, belong to yesterday!' None of us said a word, then he threw us all out. Strauss was grey, ravaged and exhausted. He hid his face in his hands ... Tears were running down his cheeks.

Twelve days later, as Strauss returned to the protection of Schirach's Vienna, Stefan Zweig and his wife Lotte committed suicide in Brazil.[26] They had left England in search of a fresh start, far from the ravages of Nazism and war, and even though Zweig had managed to complete his 'autobiography', *The World of Yesterday*, as well as a homage to his new home ('Brazil – land of the Future'), his despair was overwhelming. Lotte, twenty-seven years younger than her husband, could not imagine life without him, and they took poison together.

He left a brief and poignant declaration:

> ... I depart from this life, of my own free will and with a clear mind ... Every day I have learned to love this country better, and nowhere would I more gladly have rebuilt my life all over again, now that the world of my spiritual home is destroying itself. But one would need special powers to begin completely afresh when one has passed one's sixtieth year. And mine have been exhausted by long years of homeless wandering. It seems to me therefore better to put an end, in good time and without humiliation, to a life in which intellectual work has always been an unmixed joy and personal freedom, earth's most precious pos-session. I greet all my friends! May they live to see the dawn after the long night is over! I, all too impatient, am going on alone.[27]

German radio broadcast the news as a victory for Nazism. There is no record of Strauss's reaction. On April 16 he conducted the Vienna Phil-harmonic in a performance of his *Alpensinfonie* to celebrate the orchestra's centenary. Three months earlier he had set out to compose a work in honour of the date, with the Danube as its theme; he filled four sketchbooks with ideas but nothing came of them. Instead he wrote to 'My dear Philharmonic': 'For your fine festivities I can today only send my congratulations in heartfelt words ... I should like to put my words of praise today into one short sentence: "Only he who has *conducted* the Vienna Philharmonic players knows what they are! But that will remain my secret!" '[28]

On May 7 Schirach hosted a private concert in his house for the world première of the Introduction from *Capriccio*, with a string sextet from the Vienna Philharmonic. Later that month Strauss oversaw the first performance of *Daphne*, as part of a week-long festival of contemporary music patronised by Schirach; on June 13 he attended the Berlin première of the revised *Guntram*[29] and on the 19th the première of his orchestrated version of Goebbels's song *Das Bächlein*[30] – both as part of his seventy-eighth birthday celebrations. From Berlin he travelled to Salzburg for the festival, where he conducted a single concert of music by Mozart and supervised a new production[31] by Hartmann of *Arabella*. From Salzburg he drove to Baden bei Zürich for another cure and in September he made his way to Munich, where Krauss was supervising rehearsals for the first performance of *Capriccio*.

Strauss wanted to see his last opera open in Salzburg, where Krauss had been appointed music director. On October 12, 1941, two months after completing the score, he warned Krauss that *Capriccio* was 'not a piece to put before an audience of 1,800 night after night. Perhaps a dainty morsel for cultural gourmets, not very substantial musically – at all events, not so succulent that the music will compensate for it,[32] if the general public does not take a liking to the libretto. Your pleasure in the collaboration makes you overestimate the work out of the kindness of your heart ... I have no faith in its theatrical effectiveness in the usual sense.'

Krauss had other plans. Initially, he was determined to stage *Capriccio* in June, in Munich, as part of the largest festival of Strauss's music ever mounted in Germany. There were other reasons for favouring Munich, not least Krauss's cordial relationship with Goebbels,[33] who inevitably favoured a German musical centre; but when Krauss failed to get his 'Strauss-fest' off the ground the première was postponed until October, by which time Munich was sustaining almost nightly air raids.

The rehearsals were a joy for Strauss.[34] He marvelled at his achievement, almost as if it were by another composer, and after the final dress rehearsal on October 27 he announced: 'I can do nothing better than this.' The tenor Franz Klarwein[35] recalled that although Strauss was 'very moved [and] had tears in his eyes' he still invited everyone back to his hotel for a game of skat: 'The rehearsal finished at 3, and Hotter[36] and I had to present ourselves at the Vier Jahreszeiten at 4 – we then played until 11.30 at night. We both wanted to go to bed – after all, we had the première the next day! But he liked staying up late and in any case he was losing and didn't want to finish. So we let him win, as otherwise we would never have got to our beds.'

Krauss suggested playing the opera without an interval, so that the theatre could be emptied before the bombings began, usually between 10 and 11 p.m. Hartmann recalled:

> Who among the younger generation can really imagine a great city like Munich in total darkness, or theatregoers picking their way through the blacked-out streets with the aid of small torches giving off a dim blue light through a narrow slit? All this for the experience of the *Capriccio* première. They risked being caught in a heavy air raid, yet their yearning to hear Strauss's music, their desire to be part of a festive occasion and to experience a world of beauty beyond the dangers of war, led them to overcome all these material problems ... Outside the blackened city waited, and one's way homeward was fraught with potential danger ...

The first performance,[37] on October 28, 1942, was a critical and popular triumph. Many acclaimed it as the composer's finest work since *Ariadne auf Naxos*, which caused one commentator to lament that Strauss had waited thirty years to catch his second wind. *Capriccio* is a glorious achievement, a testament to the tireless genius of its composer and the perfect work with which to celebrate his life in the theatre. Not a bar is wasted, every phrase is made to count and the concision of the libretto inspired Strauss to a comparably economical setting. Throughout there is an underlying melancholy that owed less to circumstances outside Garmisch than to Strauss's realisation that he would write no more opera; the final outpouring for the soprano Countess is particularly bittersweet. Leavening this introspection is a deliciously understated wit, fusing dangerously subtle cultural *bons mots* to a panoply of musical jokes, quotations and puns – including a riotous parody of a classical Italian opera duet – and the fizzing central fugue cannot fail to leave audiences breathless. The defining question – words or music? – is left unanswered, although the Countess leaves the stage humming, surely pointing towards Strauss's own conclusion.

Almost exactly twelve months later Strauss wrote to his friend and biographer Willi Schuh: 'My life's work is at an end with *Capriccio*, and the music that I go on scribbling for the benefit of my heirs,[38] exercises for my wrists ... has no significance whatever from the standpoint of musical history, any more than the scores of all the other symphonists and variationists. I only do it to dispel the boredom of idle hours, since one can't spend the entire day reading Wieland and playing skat.' Strauss began the first of these 'exercises' a matter of days after the première of *Capriccio*. In a letter to Viorica Ursuleac, dated November 12, 1942, the composer informed her that he had 'just completed a little horn concerto, the third movement of which – a 6/8 rondo – has come out particularly well'.

For this far from 'little' work Strauss returned to a formula he had ignored for over half a century. His writing of a second concerto for horn, with a similar solo opening to the first, in his seventy-eighth year attests to his increasing aversion for contemporary life, but Strauss's was a pragmatic nostalgia. *Capriccio* had proved a masterpiece, even to *his* critical ear, and if he was to write no more operas he nevertheless recognised the need to capitalise on his renewed creative freshness, not least for the security of his estate and the benefit of his descendants to whom, were the war to be lost, he would leave little or no money. Schirach and the Viennese city authorities officially acknowledged Strauss's renaissance at the end of 1942 when they awarded him the coveted Beethoven Prize. Before then, he was one of three German composers – the other two being Paul Graener and Hans Pfitzner – to receive a one-off subsidy of 6,000 RM from Goebbels in recognition of their prominence and political commitment. Before the year's end he was also re-elected president of the German Composers' Society.

On January 2, 1943, Karl Böhm's successor[39] in Dresden, Karl Elmendorff, conducted the city première of *Capriccio*; ten days later Strauss began working on a commission for the Wiener Trompeterchor (Trumpeters of Vienna). Contradicting the myth of Strauss's isolation, he dedicated this *Festmusik der Stadt Wien* to the commemoration of the fifth anniversary of Hitler's annexation of Austria. Strauss himself conducted the first performance from the Rathaus Tower in Vienna at an official ceremony on April 9. So popular was the work with the city and the band's players that Strauss provided a shortened version to add to their repertoire as a Fanfare. In June Strauss was approached by Viktor Maiwald, the Director of the Vienna State Opera Chorus Concerts, for an *a capella* choral work. Perhaps to ease his conscience, he asked Gregor to polish up a choral finale he had dropped from *Daphne*. Unfortunately, history repeated itself as Gregor sent in his material only to have it returned by the composer; not until the end of August was he satisfied with Gregor's work. He began setting the verses soon after, and completed the scoring on November 13.[40]

Five months earlier, in February, Strauss had again yielded to nostalgia, writing a Sonatina No. 1 for 16 Wind Instruments as a companion piece to his 1884 Serenade for 13 Wind Instruments. He prefaced this as 'from the Studio of an Invalid' which, considering his and Pauline's recent medical history, was no exaggeration. During the summer of 1942 Pauline's eyes began to fail; Strauss then suffered a nasty bout of influenza – interrupting composition of the Sonatina – after which Pauline spent most of the spring of 1943 in bed. Further strain was brought to bear when Vienna was added to the list of Allied bombing targets, placing Jacquingasse and its occupants at serious risk. In July Strauss decided to relocate to Garmisch.

That summer's Salzburg Festival was an understandably muted affair. Strauss conducted only a single concert of Mozart's music, but he relished the enlightened atmosphere, as well as the company, friendship and devotion of Krauss and of Böhm who conducted the world première of the Second Horn Concerto on August 11. Six weeks later Allied bombing badly damaged the Munich National Theatre. To Willi Schuh, Strauss wrote: 'The burning of the Munich Hoftheater, the place consecrated to the first *Tristan* and *Meistersinger* performances, in which 73 years ago I heard Freischütz for the first time, where my good father sat for 49 years in the orchestra as 1st horn – where at the end of my life I experienced the keenest sense of fulfilment of the dreams of authorship in 10 Strauss productions – this was the greatest catastrophe which has ever been brought into my life, for which there can be no consolation and in my old age no hope...'

Over ten thousand Germans were killed and wounded in that same raid, and many more were left homeless; but Strauss did not (probably could not) come to terms with the human scale of the disasters befalling Germany. His indifference to the suffering of his fellow men was crudely demonstrated again later that year when the leader of the local Nazi Party, Herr Windeisen, requested the use of a number of his nineteen rooms for the billeting of wounded German soldiers. Strauss flatly refused. The Gauleiter declared, 'Even you must make sacrifices for our people's heroic struggle', to which Strauss replied, 'No soldier needs to fall on my account. I did not want this war, it is nothing to do with me.' The infuriated official screamed, 'Other heads than yours have already rolled, Herr Doctor Strauss' and stormed out. He went directly to Martin Boorman, who reported Strauss's defiance to Hitler. For the moment Strauss was protected by Dr Hans Frank, the Governor-General of Poland;[41] in gratitude, Strauss composed an unaccompanied song for Frank, 'Wer tritt herein',[42] which the Governor framed and hung in his office.

In October Strauss took another cure in Baden bei Zürich. Returning to Garmisch at the beginning of November he found Munich all but flattened;[43] in dismay, he scrawled a few bars as the basis of a work of mourning, to which he tentatively ascribed the legend 'Trauer um München'. Strauss was not present, on December 4, when a propaganda film *Philharmoniker* was given its first showing at the Tauentzien-Palast in Berlin. Goebbels had embraced the film as a means of glorifying the government's patronage of Furtwängler and the Berlin Philharmonic Orchestra, but when the conductor read the script (which made no mention of the many Jews to have contributed to the orchestra's fame) he was appalled to discover that Hitler and his government were credited with a founding influence, and he refused to have anything to do with the project. With Furtwängler out of the picture Goebbels approached Strauss, who readily agreed to be filmed conducting one of his own works.

He returned to Vienna for the winter of 1943–4, but in January a 'confidential report' from Boorman to the NSDAP Party Chancellery[44] seriously criticised him for refusing to allow wounded soldiers to be billeted in his house: 'Strauss has managed to sidestep all demands to give shelter to those who have been injured by bombs, and to evacuees. When it was pointed out to him that everybody had to make sacrifices, and soldiers on the front were putting their lives at risk all the time he answered that this did not concern him, and that he had not asked any soldier to fight for him ... The whole situation is being widely discussed by the citizens of Garmisch, and is being quite properly criticised.' The report made its way to Hitler, and living quarters above the garages at Garmisch were commandeered. Furthermore, on January 24, in a communiqué to all Reichsleiter and Gauleiter, Boorman ordered: 'The personal association of our leading men with Dr Strauss shall cease. However, the Führer, to whom Reichsminister Goebbels referred the question, decided today that no obstacles should be put in the way of his works.'

This remarkable document proves two things: that Strauss had maintained regular contact with high-ranking Nazi officials up to January 1944, and that Strauss's status as *persona non grata* after July 1935 and prior to January 1944 is pure fantasy. Ironically, there *is* evidence (much of it admittedly anecdotal) attesting to Pauline Strauss's less conciliatory attitude; indeed, it is said that after having seen Viorica Ursuleac wearing a fur coat given her by Goering she refused to allow the singer into the villa in Garmisch. Needless to say, she did not apply the same censorship to her son, whose membership of the Nazi Party provided valuable leverage for his father during the last two years of the war.

Strauss's subsequent difficulties with the Nazis were never very serious. Although he was prevented from leaving the country he remained on Goebbels's list of 'irreplaceable artists'. In making the mistake of appearing 'un-German', and for his expectation of 'special rights', he had provoked Hitler and Boorman. Hitler's resentment coloured Strauss's eightieth birthday celebrations: he decreed that while theatres and orchestras were at liberty to perform Strauss's music on and around June 11, there would be no official celebration. Strauss took this badly, and turned for support to Baldur von Schirach and Clemens Krauss. When both these 'friends' refused their help, Strauss approached Furtwängler who immediately sent Hitler a telegram and Goebbels a letter, warning that 'We Germans will make ourselves ridiculous in the eyes of the rest of the world if we neglect to honour the birthday of our greatest living composer.' Hitler saw the wisdom of Furtwängler's caution and sent Strauss a birthday telegram, signifying that the June celebrations could continue unhindered.

There were concerts, opera performances and broadcasts throughout the Reich, including Poland where Hans Frank mounted a lavish celebration at the Krakau State Theatre.[45] The two surviving musical centres most commonly associated with Strauss – Vienna[46] and Dresden – mounted week-long commemorations. The Strausses chose to join Karl Böhm in Vienna, where Baldur von Schirach had received a teleprinter message with a series of instructions from Goebbels as to how the celebrations should be handled. On the day itself Richard and Pauline invited the Böhms to join them for a private lunch party at Jacquingasse, before driving to the Musikvereinssaal where Strauss was scheduled to conduct the Vienna Philharmonic in a special daytime concert of *Till Eulenspiegel* and *Domestica*.

As Strauss prepared to walk on to the stage Böhm stopped him and said, 'We have a little surprise for you.' He then conducted the Prelude to *Meistersinger* and the *Rosenkavalier* Waltz. As the audience applauded, Strauss walked out to a rapturous greeting. Böhm gave a short address and presented Strauss with a baton of gold and ivory, tipped with a diamond, that had been designed on Schirach's orders by a local jeweller. The composer then conducted *Till Eulenspiegel*; afterwards, in the artists' room, he tapped Böhm on the shoulder, held out the baton and wheezed: ' "It's damned heavy. I shouldn't like to conduct *Götterdämmerung* with it. Give me another baton for the *Domestica*." '

Böhm recalled in his memoirs: 'At that point in the symphony which describes domestic relationships, where the theme of man and wife is heard, he looked at Pauline, and when the oboe d'amore enters for the first time and the birth of Franz is expressed in music he turned to "Bubi" ... After that Vienna gave its Richard Strauss a tempestuous ovation.' In the evening Böhm conducted a performance of *Ariadne auf Naxos*. Strauss also took time out to coach a young soprano called Ljuba Welitsch in the title role of Salome which, to the composer's delight, she sang at the State Opera on the 12th; he also attended a performance of *Elektra*, again conducted by Böhm. Strauss was sitting in his box next to the conductor's wife. During the Recognition scene he took hold of her hand and squeezed, saying at the end, 'I had quite forgotten that I wrote it myself.' There followed more concerts and operas, dinners, photo-calls, filming sessions and recordings.[47] Otto Strasser recalled: 'As always on such occasions, Strauss told us whether he intended to beat 2 or 4 in a bar, and then, without a break, we made the recordings.'

From Vienna, on August 7, Strauss made his way to Salzburg where Krauss had persuaded Goebbels to allow the première of *Die Liebe der Danae*. Two years earlier, on November 5, 1942, Krauss wrote to Strauss thanking him 'for having, during your recent personal visit, assigned the world première of *Die Liebe der Danae* to me for Salzburg. I shall then bring the work to its first performance in celebration of your 80th birthday.' True to his word, Krauss overcame extraordinary obstacles[48] to bring together the singers, designers, sets and, of course, the new and difficult opera while all the time attending to the many other demands on his life as a conductor and administrator.

On June 29 Krauss wrote to inform the composer that 'There were great difficulties with transport from Munich to Salzburg. We had to try and move the finished sections of the set in furniture vans which ran on wood-gas. The artists' work for the three sets of Act III was done in Prague and arrived here on schedule last week. The entire wardrobe department, who had to down needle in Munich because there were so many days without electricity or light, moved into temporary workshops in Salzburg last week, bringing with them all the costumes that had been started and the fabrics for the rest. I would very much like to telephone you, if only a connection was to be had for love or money.'

On August 1 Goebbels announced the closure of all Reich arts festivals; the Allies had opened a second front in Europe and every man and resource was required for the waging of 'total war'. As a measure of Krauss's influence over Goebbels, the Reichsminister was persuaded to allow the Salzburg Festival to proceed. Furtwängler would conduct the opening concert – of Bruckner's Eighth Symphony – on August 14, and two days later Krauss would conduct a dress rehearsal of *Die Liebe der Danae* in front of an invited audience. There would be no public première.[49]

It is unfortunate that Strauss's last operatic première should have been of such a troubled work. In 1920 Hofmannsthal had advocated Danae as a subject suited to his talents, adding that it called for 'light, nimble-witted music, such as you can write, and only at this stage in your life'. Unfortunately, while Strauss's talents were still undeniably nimble – as is proved by the delicacy and élan of *Capriccio*– Gregor provided verses heavy with intellectual good intentions. Strauss still needed inspiration, and Hofmannsthal may well have provided it; but Gregor's *Danae* brought forth intermittently average music, and ponderous characterisation that begin to outstay their welcome by the end of the second of the three acts. Ironically, the third act – while dramatically superfluous – contains the opera's finest music, a fact recognised by Strauss; but without substantial revision *Danae* will remain a curiosity.

The significance of the first production, not merely for Strauss but also for those taking part,[50] created an unforgettably emotional atmosphere. Strauss arrived in Salzburg to find Krauss rehearsing the opera's final act. Rudolph Hartmann was again the producer: 'Towards the end of the second scene Strauss stood up and went down to the front row of the stalls. His unmistakable head stood out in lonely silhouette against the light rising from the pit. The Viennese were playing the wonderful interlude before the last scene ("Jupiter's renunciation", Strauss once called it) with an unsurpassably beautiful sound. Quite immobile, totally oblivious to all else, he stood listening to the performance of his glorious work.'

And then something strange happened, which everyone present felt with the same intensity. As the last scene progressed the atmosphere became dense with a painful and melancholy seriousness. Out of the perfection of the scene, interpreted musically by Krauss with consummate mastery, out of the vocally and dramatically ideal performances of Ursuleac and Hotter, there grew and grew the undefiled purity of the highest artistic fulfilment. Profoundly moved and stirred to our depths, we sensed the almost physical presence of our divinity, art. We experienced one of the precious and very rare hours in which all trouble and effort sink into the darkness of the past, irradiated by the unique happiness of purest spiritual enjoyment.

Several moments of profound silence followed after the last notes died away. Then, clearly under the emotional impression of what we had all just experienced, Krauss spoke a few sentences outlining the significance of these last days in Salzburg. Strauss looked over the rail of the pit, raised his hands in a gesture of gratitude and spoke to the orchestra in a voice choked with tears: 'Perhaps we shall meet again in a better world.' He was unable to say more. Silent and deeply moved, everyone present remained still as he left the auditorium, carefully guided by myself.

In his dressing-room immediately after the performance Strauss was found leafing through the full score. 'When I make my way up there,' he said, pointing to heaven, 'I hope they'll forgive me if I bring this along too.'

Strauss was going deaf, his eyes were poor and he was audibly asthmatic; few – including Strauss himself – thought he would survive the war. With his twinkling eyes and baggy face he looked like everyone's favourite grandfather; and many of the younger members of the cast, crew and orchestra were as overwhelmed by the history of the man, as by the tragedy of his circumstances; a number spoke openly of their disgust that the composer of *Rosenkavalier* should have to endure so much at such an advanced age. Some were reduced to tears; they knew, as did Strauss, that the Germany of old was gone. With his heart all but broken, Strauss retreated to Garmisch to sit out his country's inexorable ruin.

Even for someone of Strauss's wealth and influence, life in Garmisch was now difficult. Bartering and the black market were the only real means of acquisition, but he lived in a mansion, was surrounded by luxury, and enjoyed the attention of servants. It could have been worse. He began to succumb to bouts of terrible depression and self-pity ('For me it's especially bad, having to talk about our misfortunes all the while' and so on), but in his letters to Franz and Richard in Vienna he made no reference to events outside his immediate concern. News of destitute and homeless friends and colleagues came almost every day, while all but a few of Garmisch's rooms remained empty. At times, his self-absorption bordered on the ridiculous.

On September 9, 1944 – the day before his and Pauline's golden wedding anniversary – Strauss wrote to Franz:

We shall celebrate it with tears and sorrow after weeks of worry and troubles! Early on Tuesday our poor dear Anna left us (probably for ever!). Mama gave her a last farewell kiss at 5 in the morning, has cried every day since then and I generally join in the blubber too. Frau Martin went with her as far as Nuremberg where she promptly vanished into the nearest bunker with her niece ... Naumaier gave her another jab on Sunday which gave her so much relief that on Monday she was able to hand over the entire housekeeping to Mama, keys and all, which was very moving. We have had no news since then ... The poor loyal soul, fifty-one years old, we are inconsolable. For poor Mama it is a catastrophe.[51]

To his grandson Richard he wrote: 'I am very happy to think that you are practising the piano diligently and have resumed lessons in harmony. You will realise the benefit later when you can read a score as easily as Christian can read his Westerns. For before long it will be impossible to hear – let alone see – the *Ring, Salome, Daphne,* etc. I myself have a purer pleasure from *Meistersinger* and *Tristan* today, when I read the scores with all the right tempos, than from having to listen to a mediocre performance with the wrong tempos from one of my respected colleagues.'

Strauss may have been down, but he was far from finished. On September 15 he was again in Vienna to conduct another concert with the Philharmonic (with Julius Patzak singing four of his songs)[52] and to stay at Jacquingasse. But the threat of bombing could no longer be ignored and he returned to Garmisch, followed a month later by Franz and Alice. Realising that the Reichsmark was again facing collapse Strauss began to make copies – from memory – of his tone poems that would later fetch large sums from collectors; on October 3 he wrote to Richard that he had begun 'to make a new copy of the score of *Eulenspiegel.* It is more sensible than continuing to turn out senile new works. *Don Juan* and *Tod und Verklärung* shall follow and ought to make a valuable Christmas present for you all. The work is giving me a lot of fun and at least it stops me thinking about other things, now that I don't even have an occasional game of skat to divert me, and poor Mama needs a lot of comforting.'

On January 30, 1945, Hitler made his last broadcast to the German people, during which he urged them to hold out to the end. Two weeks later that end came, for Strauss at least, when Dresden suffered the most savage and indiscriminate bombing raid of the war. The apocalyptic attack of February 13–14 on a city of no strategic significance, home to tens of thousands of refugees, and which left over 750,000 dead and wounded, caused Strauss unimaginable anguish: 'I am in a mood of despair!' he wrote. 'The Goethehaus, the world's greatest sanctuary, destroyed! My lovely Dresden – Weimar – Munich, all gone!'

He reached for his sketchbook containing the 'Occasional Waltz' he had written in 1939 for the 'München' film and, adding a middle section in a minor key, revised it as a banal depiction of the destruction of Dresden and Munich and the frantic efforts to suppress the flames. This *Gedächtniswalzer*

(Memorial Waltz), in which Strauss developed a motif of dotted quavers reminiscent of the Funeral March in Beethoven's *Eroica* Symphony, would resurface only a few weeks later as the thematic axis of his *Metamorphosen*.

After the terrible violence of the attack against Dresden, Goebbels promised a secret weapon that would turn the war, but it seems there was little need for such assurances since a vast number of Germans continued to believe in their Führer and his military genius, despite all evidence to the contrary.[53] Strauss appears to have expected the worst; any lingering hope was expunged shortly after midday on March 12[54] when a mixture of phosphorous incendiaries and high explosives passed through the roof of the Vienna State Opera and landed directly on the stage, consuming the building from within. Karl Böhm was among those who stood and watched the fire: 'Absurdly, I tried to drag valuable pieces of furniture out of the still burning building. We placed them opposite the Opera: the next day, of course, they were stolen.'

Strauss was grief-stricken. The following morning he began to orchestrate what many consider to be his greatest work – *Metamorphosen*. The idea for this extraordinary lament for twenty-three strings came to Strauss from a poem by Goethe:[55] *Niemand wird sich selber kennen*.

> No one can know himself,
> Detach himself from his Self-I;
> Yet, let him put to the test every day,
> That which is objectively finally clear,
> What he is and what he was,
> What he can and what he may.

In August 1944 Strauss had begun a choral setting of the verse. Simultaneously Willi Schuh met Karl Böhm and the conductor Paul Sacher in Waldhaus Sils-Maria, where it was decided that Sacher would commission a work from Strauss for his orchestra, the Collegium Musicum Zürich. Strauss accepted the commission and abandoned work on *Niemand wird sich selber kennen*. But the poem had a decisive influence over Strauss and his early work on the 'Adagio' (as *Metamorphosen* was initially known);[56] it is no coincidence that he copied it into the same sketchbook as the first twenty drafts of the *Adagio*. Significantly, this early work coincided with Strauss's first serious disillusionment with the Nazis, when Goebbels obstructed the world première of *Die Liebe der Danae* and, later, ordered the closure of all German theatres and opera houses. On September 30 Strauss sent a progress report to Karl Böhm before putting the score to one side in order to concentrate on other projects, such as the revision of the 'München' Waltz.

Strauss returned to *Metamorphosen* in January 1945, and completed the short score on March 8. He began the orchestration five days later, and finished the full score on April 12. Because of a thematic-rhythmic similarity between *Metamorphosen* and the earlier 'München' *Gedächtniswalzer* it has always been assumed that *Metamorphosen* (which contains oblique references to the Funeral March from Beethoven's Third Symphony as well as a direct quotation, to which Strauss ascribed the legend 'In memoriam') was written as a homage to his beloved Munich. It is unlikely, however, that the city's destruction had any direct influence over the work, especially when considering the chronology of its gestation, the obvious impact of *Niemand wird sich selber kennen*, and the common use of themes, ideas and inspiration. Strauss may well have been prompted to orchestrate the short score by the destruction of Vienna's Staatsoper, but there are less detached, more likely, explanations for *Metamorphosen*'s emotional and psychological intensity. The first and most controversial is that it was conceived as a memorial to the living, but doomed, Adolf Hitler.

Strauss's collaboration with the Nazis was motivated primarily by ideology, and Nazi ideology was personified by its Führer. Strauss began sketching ideas for *Metamorphosen* at the same time as Hitler began closing down all German cultural life in August 1944. Strauss had been wooed by Hitler's promises of cultural renewal, and not until he was able to experience for himself the effects of Hitler's failure as a social, military and cultural messiah, was he able to appreciate the scale of the tragedy that had befallen his beloved country. It has always been claimed that the inscription 'In memoriam', beneath the double-bass *Eroica* quotation, is a reference to Beethoven, whose music appears central to the work's thematic and illustrative complexion. It is worth remembering, however, that Beethoven had initially dedicated the *Eroica* Symphony to Napoleon Bonaparte, in whom he had seen such promise, only to cross it out when Napoleon crowned himself Emperor. Beethoven subsequently dedicated the work '*Per festeggiare il souvenir di un grande Uomo*' (To the memory of a great man) while Napoleon still lived. The parallels are unmistakable.

Even if Strauss saw in Beethoven a symbol for everything then being shattered by the Allies, Strauss's inscription 'In memoriam' is unlikely to be a reference to Beethoven himself. Similarly, there is no evidence that Strauss conceived *Metamorphosen* as a homage to the millions who had died since the Nazis' ascent to power in 1933. Strauss never apologised for his collaboration. Not even during his denazification did he admit to being misguided, weak, vain, or even human. But the significance of Goethe's *Niemand wird sich selber kennen* and the lines 'No one can know himself / Detach himself from his Self-I' allude to the possibility that Strauss was seeking penance or, at the very least, trying to rationalise his complicity.

His choice of the title *Metamorphosen* is itself a Goethean conceit – making obvious reference to the poems *Die Metamorphose der Pflanzen* and *Die Metamorphose der Tiere*. Goethe took an essentially optimistic view of the idea of transformation; similarly, the classical understanding of meta-

morphosis was that it provided a means towards a divine end – the understanding and experience of God, and the philosophical counteraction of
original sin. Throughout his life Strauss demonstrated a heartfelt cultural
pessimism and social fatalism that precluded religion and religious redemption; judging by the interrelation of *Metamorphosen*'s C major and C minor,
this negativism would appear incontrovertible.

And yet the solemnity and sadness of the music are so penetrating
(probably more so than in any other work by Strauss) that one is forced to
interpret his inversion of Goethe's metamorphosis (whereby self-knowledge
leads not to Heaven but Hell) as an admission of guilt and responsibility.
Strauss may well have recalled *The World as Will and Idea*, in which Schopenhauer wrote: 'The chief source of the most serious evils affecting man
is man himself; *homo homini lupus*. He who keeps this last fact clearly in view
beholds the world as a hell, surpassing that of Dante by the fact that one man
must be the devil of another. For this purpose, of course, one is more fitted
than another, indeed an archfiend is more fitted than all the rest, and appears
in the form of a conqueror.'[57]

An alternative, less inflammatory theory is that Strauss was simply grieving
for the aesthetic and cultural ruin of his world. It is significant that at no
point in the score does he develop the opening theme; there is no variation, no
progress and no metamorphosis. This nihilistic cultural despair[58] is enshrined
within a grimly negative stasis, so that the tiny modulations and modifications that do occur imply a scrutiny of, and meditation on, the past
rather than an expectation of, and ambition for, the future. In this respect
Metamorphosen serves as the ideal accompaniment to Mann's *Dr Faustus*
since Strauss, like Mann, saw in the end of ideology (as opposed to idealism)
the end of culture.

With the emotional turmoil of *Metamorphosen* behind him Strauss was
resigned to the inevitable course of events and took to mapping out his
cultural aspirations for Germany after his death. The most famous of these
testaments was sent, on April 27, 1945, six weeks after the destruction of the
Viennese State Opera, to Karl Böhm who shared Strauss's horror at the
destruction, not of life, but of bricks and mortar. It contained what he called
his 'artistic legacy' and makes for extraordinary reading. No gesture to the
future of German musical theatre could have included so little and omitted
so much. Strauss listed all his own stage works in preference to work from
Puccini, Debussy, Ravel, Bartók, Janáček, Stravinsky, and Schoenberg. Biographical portraits of Strauss as a grand old man, resigned to his fate, secure
in the immortality of his music are, at best, romantic. He ended his days
beset by doubt, unsure of his contribution to the German tradition, and
fearful for its future after his death. Three days later American tanks and
infantry arrived in Garmisch and parked themselves in a field beside Strauss's
villa. As they drove to the front door Strauss dressed in readiness to greet

them. The American army was requisitioning property for use by their men and Strauss's was by far the grandest building outside the town centre. As Alice supervised the packing of bags Strauss calmly opened the door and announced to the waiting soldiers, 'I am Richard Strauss, the composer of *Rosenkavalier* and *Salome*.' The commanding officer, a Major Kramer, was a music-lover and he ordered his men to stand down. Strauss then invited Kramer and seven of his officers to lunch. Anni Nitzl prepared a venison stew, and bottles of wine were brought up from the cellar. At midday the soldiers left, having mounted a sign at the front gate warning 'Off Limits'. Strauss was delighted: 'A complete victory of the spirit over matter.'

That afternoon, at about 3.30 p.m., Adolf Hitler took poison and received, either by his own hand or by that of Eva Braun, a gunshot to the right temple. In the evening German radio broadcast the news that 'our Führer, Adolf Hitler, fighting to the last breath against Bolshevism, fell for Germany this afternoon in his operational command post in the Reich Chancellery'. This was immediately followed by recordings, conducted by Furtwängler, of the Adagio from Bruckner's Seventh Symphony and the Funeral Music from *Götterdämmerung*. Sitting in his study, Strauss wrote in his diary:

Germany: 1945: Thus is the body dead, but the spirit is life.

Luther

On 12 March the glorious Vienna Opera became one more victim of the bombs. But from 1 May onwards the most terrible period of human history came to an end, the twelve-year reign of bestiality, ignorance and anti-culture under the greatest criminals, during which Germany's 2,000 years of cultural evolution met its doom and irreplaceable monuments of architecture and works of art were destroyed by a criminal rabble of soldiers. Accursed be technology!

28   IM ABENDROT

May 1945–September 1949

One of the many visitors who passed through Garmisch during the weeks following Germany's surrender on May 7 was a Mr Brown. Strauss immediately took to the young man, and they spent an hour in discussion, walking round the Garmisch estate. A few weeks later an interview with Strauss appeared in the American forces magazine *Stars and Stripes*. It transpired that 'Mr Brown' was Thomas Mann's son Klaus, author of *Mephisto*[1] and an outspoken anti-Nazi. Mann wrote of his 'extraordinary hour' with Strauss during which the composer spoke of the Reich as if it had existed outside his experience and influence. He expressed no regret and offered no sympathy. Pulling no punches, Mann condemned the composer for his 'moral obtuseness and callousness', and portrayed him to readers as 'completely lacking in the most fundamental impulses of shame and decency'.

Strauss was treated well by the American soldiers, and on May 10 he could write to Schuh: 'Eight days have now gone by since our poor, ravaged, ruined Germany was liberated from twelve years of slavery ... Today, I am taking advantage of the first available opportunity to let you know ... that Garmisch was spared any bombing attacks, and since, thank God, no resistance was offered when the Americans marched in, it has remained unscathed; it has simply been occupied ... the Americans are being extremely kind and friendly.'

Many soldiers came to Strauss for autographs (most asking for a bar or two from *Rosenkavalier*, some for a quotation from his '*Blue Danube Waltz*'), but there were those who wanted to talk music. One of these was John de Lancie, a 24-year-old conscripted oboist from Chicago[2] who, together with the Hamburg-born American musicologist Alfred Mann, visited Strauss at his villa in May. They talked for many hours, in French, about a wide range of subjects. De Lancie later recalled that he was

> overcome by shyness and a feeling of great awe in the presence of this man, and
> I remember thinking, at the time, that I would have nothing to contribute to
> the conversation that could possibly be of interest to the composer. Once,
> though, I summoned up all my courage and began to talk about the beautiful

oboe melodies one comes across in so many of his works ... I wanted to know if he had a special affinity for that particular instrument, and since I was familiar with his Horn Concerto, I asked him whether he had ever thought of writing a concerto for oboe. His answer was a plain 'No!' That was about all I could get out of him.

Strauss changed his mind. While still working on the score of his Second Sonatina for 16 Wind Instruments in Eb (which he completed on June 22, 1945) he began sketching a concerto in memory of De Lancie. On July 6 Strauss wrote to Schuh: 'In the studio of my old age, a concerto for oboe and small orchestra is being "concocted". The idea for this was suggested to me by an oboe player from Chicago.' Strauss's return to work could not disguise his misery: for his eleven-year collaboration with the Nazis he had been labelled by the American War Commission 'Class I – Guilty'. Of the five tribunal classifications, Class I was the most serious, and came with the threat of two to ten years' forced labour, the confiscation of all property, the permanent loss of civil rights and the removal of all pensions and savings. Article I of the Allied Control Council's Directive No. 38, published in October 1946, held Class I to signify 'Major Offenders' which it defined through ten points. Two related directly to Strauss:

> 4. Anyone who was active in a leading position in the NSDAP, one of its formations or affiliated organisations, or in any other National Socialistic or militaristic organisation.
> 6. Anyone who gave major political, economic, propagandist or other support to the National Socialist tyranny, or who, by reason of his relations with the National Socialist tyranny, received very substantial profits for himself or others.

According to the rules drawn up at the Potsdam Conference, some of which were modified by the Ordinance for Political Cleansing on May 28, 1946, membership of the Nazi Party would not be considered *prima facie* evidence of guilt any more than non-membership would be considered proof of innocence. Strauss was informed of the charges against him by the head of the American command in Bavaria, who also instructed him that he would be allowed to submit a defence.

While bearing the anxiety of retribution Strauss began to fear for his and Pauline's future in Germany. Allied countries were unlikely to programme his music, Germany's orchestras and opera houses were in disarray and his royalties were to remain frozen in America, as a consequence of the 'Washington Agreement'. With German production of domestic essentials at a minimum Strauss realised that he and Pauline would have to leave the country. He asked the regional commanding officer, Major Hayl, for permission to cross the border into Switzerland; when this was declined he turned for guarantees and references to friends in Switzerland and America. Their support, and Hayl's sympathy, proved sufficient,[3] and on October 9 Richard and Pauline packed their bags (including the short score of the Oboe Concerto, which Strauss had completed in Garmisch on September 14, 1945) and began the short, but eventful, drive into neutral territory.[4]

In his diary Strauss wrote: 'After having already said goodbye over the last few days to my dear little garden and the little wood, at 8.30 the last farewell to the dear children and the grandsons. 3.30 safe arrival at Bregenz in very good weather. Turned back by the last French post before the Swiss frontier because we lacked a last pass document. Nowhere to go. Put up by Prince Friedrich of Saxony (the rightful King) in his children's rooms…'

When, the following morning, Strauss and the Prince went to see the French commandant, Comte d'Audibert, Strauss donated a manuscript copy of the *Alpensinfonie* to the French National Library. He signed it there and then, and watched as 'the French enthusiastically carried the manuscripts from the cellar to the car'. In a gesture of glorious irony, Strauss donated the scores of his two Weinheber songs to D'Audibert and his aide, Major Moreau.[5] By 5.40 that evening they looked set to cross the border, when the Swiss authorities demanded that both Richard and Pauline visit the medieval Disinfection Unit. 'That too went off very smoothly', he confessed to his diary, 'with the aid of a dozen autographs.'

They were finally cleared at 9 a.m. on October 11. Willi Schuh met them at the station in Zurich at 11 a.m., and fifty minutes later they arrived at the Hotel Verenhof in Baden, where Strauss deposited a number of scores in lieu of payment. Strauss's diary betrays his relief at finding himself delivered from the horrible realities of post-war Germany. It also proves that, despite a knowledge of the Nazis' 'Final Solution', Strauss continued to mourn the Nazis' crimes against culture above their blackening of humanity, and it demonstrates the extent to which his perception of the world continued to revolve around materialism and self-interest:

> This is an earthly paradise. Exemplary, comfortable hotel with the best French cuisine (our 'menus' deserve to be perpetuated in writing), we have two beautiful, spotlessly clean south-east facing rooms, attentively equipped to meet our every need, a big bath, as well as a large chest of drawers. We are revelling in fruit again: grapes, pears, bananas, prunes. In short, for us two sad Germans, who have lived only for art, and have fled from chaos, misery, slavery and the shortage of coal, this is heaven; driven by the destruction of our poor ravaged homeland to leave our dear children and grandchildren and the beautiful things we have owned for decades, to come far away from the ruins of our burnt-out theatres and other seats of the Muses – we can pass the rest of our days in peace and quiet, in the company of good people and friends.

The following morning the first post-war performance of an opera by Strauss was mounted in Dresden's Tonhalle, when Keilberth conducted *Ariadne*. This sign of rebirth inspired Strauss to proceed with the Oboe Concerto, which he finished orchestrating on October 25, in the Hotel Verenhof. At the end of December Strauss was visited by Ernst Roth, of the music publishers Boosey & Hawkes.[6] Roth had acquired the rights to Strauss's music in 1942 from the Nazi-hijacked Fürstner, and he promised to try and help Strauss, whose failure to settle his account with the Verenhof was beginning to make the hotel management more than a little nervous. Friends came and brought presents, doctors ministered to Richard and Pauline's various ailments – curing months of discomfort with simple injections of a new drug called penicillin – and Strauss met and negotiated with Switzerland's leading musical figures.

But public opinion was turning against Strauss, noticeably so after Zurich Opera announced a new production of *Arabella*. When Maria Cebotari was engaged to sing the title role, a leading Swiss rival publicly announced that, having collaborated with the Nazis, she should not be allowed to take part. Moreover, the Basle *Nationalzeitung* began to question Strauss's prosperity under the Third Reich. But there was nowhere else for him to go, and he had to make do with the comfort of his friends and the flattery of his admirers. Unexpectedly, perhaps, one of these was Lionel Barrymore. The wheelchair-bound actor had long admired Strauss and his music, and he invited the composer to stay with him in California, promising easy passage through United States customs; but when Barrymore began to realise the depth of hatred felt by many Americans for Strauss, he was forced to rethink his invitation.

Despite his notoriety Strauss successfully negotiated the first performances of *Metamorphosen* and the Oboe Concerto. *Metamorphosen* was first performed on January 25, 1946, by its dedicatees, Paul Sacher and the Collegium Musicum Zurich. Strauss specifically informed Schuh and Sacher that he would not be attending the première, which points to the work's confessional significance and the pain it evidently caused him. He did ask to attend the final rehearsal on the 24th; Sacher duly met Strauss at his hotel and drove him to the concert hall. En route he asked if he might be allowed to conduct a single performance to the near-empty hall; Willi Schuh recalled Strauss's remarkable recreation of his score: 'Strauss knew above all how to achieve magnificently the great sweep of development through powerful increase of dynamic and tempos, even though it was clear his hearing was failing ... it was an unforgettable experience for the conductor [Sacher], the players ... and the very few listeners present.'

The first performance of the Oboe Concerto followed almost exactly one month later, on February 26, 1946, as part of the eighth concert in the Tonhalle Society Subscription series. Volkmar Andreae conducted the Zurich Tonhalle

Orchestra, and Marcel Saillet played the solo. Strauss wrote to De Lancie and asked him to attend, but he was in America and had to decline. As a measure of Strauss's contemporary standing, the first night saw him consigned to a seat at the back of the hall. The great and the good were happy to hear the music as long as they were not expected to see, or sit near, its composer. As the players began to filter on to the stage a thinking member of the audience sitting in the front row walked to the back of the hall, asked Strauss to stand, marched him to the front and sat him in her chair. She took his seat at the back, and the première followed with the composer in his rightful place.

These public events were a mixed blessing for Strauss, but at least they provided a valuable distraction from the realities of his situation. When Alice arrived for a brief visit she brought with her letters from Franz and the children, as well as news that the house in Jacquingasse had been ransacked by Russian troops; the garages had been used as a slaughterhouse, and the British army were intending to sequester the estate as an officers' mess. Strauss was heartbroken. That evening he wrote out a detailed room-by-room inventory of the entire contents of the house, noting the exact source and location of everything from paintings and *objets d'art* to pianos and wardrobes.

Another Strauss première followed in March, when Hermann Scherchen introduced the Second Sonatina for 16 Wind Instruments to an audience in Winterthur. He dedicated the score 'To the divine Mozart at the end of a life filled with gratitude'. In April, Strauss travelled to Ouchy-Lausanne for minor surgery on his appendix, from which he recovered in Lugano on the Swiss-Italian border and Pontresina, west of St Moritz. Strauss still had to make some money. Aside from the première of new works, his music was not being played and he failed to see why he should be penalised. 'Because I am German?' he wrote to Schuh. 'Wagner is another German. Lehár is Hungarian. The Hungarians also shot at the Russians and two of his operettas are now being performed. The Italians fired on the Allies and they're doing three operas by Verdi. Must all the chauvinistic German-hatred of the entire Swiss nation come down on my head alone?'

Strauss tried to keep his hand in, writing orchestral transcriptions of excerpts from *Die Frau ohne Schatten* and *Josephslegende*, which he pitched to the many conductors with whom he was trying to remain in contact. On June 22, 1947, he wrote, cap in hand, to Erich Kleiber from Pontresina:

My friends tell me that you are working for my music, affectionately and with great success, at that Teatro Colón which I remember with much gratitude . . . I am sitting, ill and unhappy, between the ruins of Berlin, Dresden, Munich and Vienna. Thank God that at least it is only in my sad thoughts that I see them: the sight itself is too dreadful. All I have myself seen are the ruins of the Court

Theatre in Munich ... I'm delighted to hear that you are coming to Europe. If you're in Switzerland don't overlook the lovely Engadine. We've come up here to breathe the air of the chamois for a week; down in the Ticino it was a little too hot for northerly 'barbarians' like us. Is it true that you are going to give *Die Frau ohne Schatten* her American baptism? Has Dr Roth of Boosey's already given you the concert fragments from the *Frosch*? And the *Rosenkavalier* Waltzes? I've at least revised them myself and I feel sure that you and your audiences would have great fun with the brilliant finale.

Always your devoted Richard Strauss

He also badgered a number of his politically suspect colleagues, including the conductor Joseph Keilberth, to perform his music. Presumably sympathetic to more than just Strauss's music, Keilberth staged a production in Dresden of *Die Schweigsame Frau*. Using a bewilderingly tactless analogy, Strauss wrote, in a letter of thanks to the conductor: 'Now, after ten years, the honourable Sir Morosus has been liberated from the concentration camp of the Reichstheaterkammer and has returned to his native town.'

Attending to business helped distract him from his and Pauline's nomadic lifestyle, the blame for which can none the less be placed quite squarely with Pauline. For the first six months of 1947 they travelled between Pontresina, Lugano and Montreux. Pauline hated hotel life, finding the rooms dirty, the food inedible and the service sloppy, and she took her loneliness and homesickness out on anyone foolish enough to cross her path. Moreover, as she complained to Ernst Roth, while Richard had his work, in which he was able to lose himself for hours on end, she had nothing and no one to dispel the boredom of hotel life. Deprived of her intricately cultivated social circle Pauline was just another guest, an itinerant pensioner with a short fuse. Stripped of her status and influence she was a veritable cripple, amusing herself as best as possible by complaining; they rapidly outstayed their welcome and Strauss found himself having to move home every few weeks. As Pauline's reputation frequently arrived before her luggage, Richard was forever having to make excuses for his wife's lack of reason. Fifty years on there are still hotel managers in Switzerland with stories to tell.

In May 1947 Ernst Roth arrived with a proposal. Since the export of sterling was forbidden, Roth (together with Beecham, his newly formed Royal Philharmonic Orchestra and the BBC) would mount a festival of Strauss's music in London in October, enabling the composer to earn respect as a man, and money as a conductor. In September, shortly before his departure for London, Strauss and his wife relocated themselves to the Palace Hotel in Montreux, where they remained until their return to Garmisch in May 1949.[7]

For numerous reasons, Pauline did not accompany her husband to London.[8] She may have been nervous of his plan to make the journey by air –

it was his first trip in an aeroplane[9] – and she was almost certainly deterred by the prospect of renewed anti-German hostility. Strauss left Switzerland on October 4, accompanied by Willi Schuh. For a man approaching his eighty-fourth birthday Strauss's vitality was phenomenal. He visited art galleries, museums and friends, attended numerous dinners and, of course, gave concerts. He did his best to avoid extra-musical attention[10] and kept his dealings with journalists monosyllabic,[11] but he relished the blandishments of music-lovers and he positively purred during the Royal Philharmonic Society's reception and dinner.

The music began on October 5, with a concert at the Theatre Royal, Drury Lane. Thomas Beecham conducted the RPO in performances of the Suite from *Le Bourgeois Gentilhomme*, the final scene from *Feuersnot*, and *Don Quixote*, in which Paul Tortelier played the solo. At the end of the concert a young horn player turned conductor, Norman del Mar, performed the newly completed Fantasia from *Die Frau ohne Schatten*.

The second concert on the 12th included *Macbeth*, an Entr'acte from *Intermezzo*, *Ein Heldenleben*, and the closing scene from *Ariadne* with Maria Cebotari and Karl Friedrich. Seven days later Strauss stepped on to the podium in the Albert Hall to conduct the Philharmonia Orchestra in *Don Juan*, *Burleske* (with Alfred Blumen[12]), the *Rosenkavalier* Waltzes, and the *Sinfonia Domestica*. After the morning's rehearsal Strauss lay down to rest in his changing room. Schuh offered to turn the lights off, but Strauss asked him to leave them on: ' "I don't like being in semi-darkness, I like the light … These afternoons before a concert in a foreign town! Ah well, it won't last much longer." ' Strauss asked that the *Domestica* be scheduled first on the programme; when the BBC's schedules made this impossible the composer flew into a rage. He eventually calmed down, apologised and did as he was asked; as he waited to walk on to the stage he quietly remarked, 'So the old horse ambles out of the stables once more.'

In the audience was Elisabeth Schumann. She and Strauss had not seen each other since 1933, and against her better judgement she was persuaded to introduce herself. The drained composer turned to the soprano and asked, 'Who are you?' Schumann replied 'Elisabeth', and they chatted for a few minutes, but it was strained and she later regretted the meeting.

On October 24 and 26 Strauss attended two broadcast performances of *Elektra*,[13] again conducted by Beecham.[14] On the 29th he was again at the Albert Hall where he made his last professional appearance in England, with the BBC Symphony Orchestra. Adrian Boult conducted Mozart's *Jupiter* Symphony and Holst's *Planets* Suite; Strauss conducted *Till Eulenspiegel*. Two days later, having bade a final farewell to Thomas Beecham, Strauss was driven to the airport from where he flew back to Switzerland. He took with him just over £1,000 in earnings.[15] The reunited couple fell weeping into each other's arms; Strauss was clearly exhausted, and in November there were the first signs of the bladder infection that was to kill him.

Despite the pain, and in defiance of his doctors' constant interference, Strauss returned to work, and at the end of November he completed the short score of an exquisite Duett-Concertino[16] for Radio Lugano, whose orchestra gave the first performance on April 4, 1948.[17] With this gentle work behind him, Strauss appeared to shrink into himself. Aside from drafting some ideas for a short play with music for his grandchildren's school (after Wieland's story *Das Esels Schatten* – *The Donkey's Shadow*) his sketchbooks remained closed. He attempted to counter his mounting depression by rereading Goethe, Wagner and Nietzsche; huge volumes of history and philosophy; Greek drama and Chinese philosophy. But this immersion into 'classical' waters served only to remind him of what had been lost, and his depression spiralled.

Franz did his best to console his father. Almost as an aside he told him to stop brooding and write some songs, suggesting that since many of the country's opera houses had been destroyed there would be an increased demand for concert music. To everyone's surprise, Strauss took the advice to heart. In 1947 he had copied a poem by Joseph von Eichendorff, *Im Abendrot* (In the Sunset), into his diary, beneath a newspaper clipping about the destruction and looting of Dresden. It tells the story of an old couple who, after a lifetime together, look to the sunset and ask, 'Is this perhaps death?' Strauss originally set the poem in 1947, but he returned to the verses at the beginning of 1948 and completed the setting and orchestration in May. He then picked out a book of poetry by Hermann Hesse and chose four poems to make a cycle of five with *Im Abendrot*. He completed only three: *Frühling* (Spring) on July 18, *Beim Schlafengehen* (Going to Sleep) on August 4, and *September* on September 20, 1948.

The *Vier Letzte Lieder*, as these four of his last five songs were published after Strauss's death, are the crowning achievement of a life devoted to composing for the human voice. Each is concerned with death and the fulfilment of old age, and as a group they can be appreciated as not merely the consummation of *Tod und Verklärung* – from which Strauss quotes in *Im Abendrot* – but also his quasi-religious belief in the eternal, defining qualities of melody and musical expression. The retrospective character of the poetry is poignantly developed through Strauss's music which, like so much of his work, wavers between profundity and sentimentality. There are numerous references to music by his idols – such as a direct quotation from the Adagio of Beethoven's String Quartet Op. 59, No. 1, in *Beim Schlafengehen* – and so perfect are the settings, in their mood, style and beauty, that it is difficult not to allow their finality to influence the way in which they are heard. The cycle normally ends with *Im Abendrot* (the exact order remains a matter of continued debate) and, for Strauss's admirers at least, the melancholy of

Eichendorff's verses, allied to the soaring pathos of the music, is almost unbearably sad. His last composition was another song, *Malvern*, completed on November 23. Strauss dedicated it to Maria Jeritza,[18] to whom he sent the manuscript. The soprano put the score in her safe, where it remained until her death on July 10, 1982.[19]

In June 1948, Strauss was cleared by the denazification tribunal in Garmisch. His Austrian citizenship, the highly publicised trip to London, his age, the testimony of friends and admirers and, most importantly, the Allies' wish to demonstrate forbearance and humanity ensured his exoneration. Strauss was an old man, and could not have been expected to endure prison or forced labour, but neither his property nor any of the harvests of his collaboration were seized in reparation. His pardon was typical of the denazification process; while less visible collaborators (those classed as Lesser Offenders, Offenders and Followers) were dragged over the coals, most public figures went unpunished. Of the 947,000 cases tried by June 1949, only 0.15 per cent – less than 1,500 – were tried as Class I; of these few only a handful received anything more than a public admonition.

At the end of the year, on December 5, Strauss underwent a perilous bladder operation, from which his recovery was slow and painful. On the 28th he wrote to Willi Schuh: 'I have actually outlived myself.' To while away the time he studied scores by Mozart (the G minor Quintet[20]), Beethoven (the late quartets and *Fidelio*[21]) and Wagner (*Tristan*) and he began sketching a choral setting of Hesse's *Besinnung*. He also returned to Goethe, whose complete works he knew almost by heart, as well as the theoretical writings of Wagner and huge volumes of Greek philosophy in the original. When not reading he wrote letters and reminisced, mostly to Pauline, who had embarked on her memoirs.

On May 10, 1949, husband and wife returned to Garmisch. Strauss had begun to appear even older than his eighty-four years, and many were shocked to see how seriously he had deteriorated since 1945. His eyes, once described by Zweig as the 'most wide-awake in the world', were huge and watery; his hearing was now seriously impaired (he told Karl Böhm that everything was a semitone higher) and many of the pictures taken at the time show him straining to hear his photographer. For all that, he remained irresistibly handsome and, if the mood took him, his face could still light up with joy. Shortly after their arrival in Garmisch Strauss was informed of the many celebrations being planned for his eighty-fifth birthday, but his health demanded rest and he declined any direct involvement in anything outside the town. But on June 10 he fell to temptation, and asked Martin to drive him to Munich so that he might attend the dress rehearsal of the State Opera's new production of *Rosenkavalier* at the Prince Regent Theatre. He had not conducted since January 1946, but watching Georg Solti from the stalls quickened his spirit and he asked to conduct the finales of Acts II and III. A film crew, whose number included Baldur von Schirach's[22] wife, Henriette, was on hand to capture the moving scenes[23] and they later filmed Strauss conducting the 'Presentation of the Rose' from Act II. As the footage proves, Strauss was as fresh in his responses, and as dry in his technique, as ever.

The following morning Garmisch threw its own modest celebration at the town hall, where performances of the Violin Sonata and the Piano Quintet brought back memories of Strauss's first flush of creative youth. Again, Schirach's wife and the cameras were present. Garmisch made him an honorary citizen; at the University of Munich he was awarded another honorary doctorate (of Law), and the deputy mayor of Munich announced the establishment of a Strauss Foundation. The strain told whenever he was asked to make a speech, but such was the affection of his audiences that there was applause and cheering no matter what came out. In gratitude for Munich's kindness, Strauss donated the score of the original 'München' Waltz to the Bavarian State Library. That evening radio stations around the world broadcast performances of Strauss's music[24] while orchestras and opera houses as far apart as Dresden and Chicago joined in the celebrations.

The Bavarian authorities asked which of his works he would most like to see staged. Unexpectedly, perhaps, Strauss chose *Der Bürger als Edelmann* and on June 13 a new production opened at the Gärtnerplatz Theater. All the time he was shadowed by the film crew of *A Life for Music*. Schirach's wife recalled: 'Strauss enjoyed it hugely. Neither the chaos of cables nor the bright lights disturbed him. He had never seen a sound film in his life.' He was captured at home playing the piano (the finale of *Daphne*)[25] and extensive footage was taken of him walking around the Garmisch villa. Henriette Schirach remembered being 'struck by his silky, tender skin. His blue eyes ... blinked suspiciously as he faced the crowd of people. Suddenly he stopped. It was the spot on which the urn with his ashes was to stand.' Exactly one month later Strauss was driven to Munich by the American Military Governor of Garmisch, a Mr Garlock, to conduct the 'Moonlight' music from *Capriccio* with the Radio Orchestra[26] as background music for Schirach's documentary. He never conducted again.

From Munich, Strauss returned to Garmisch where, from August 13, he was consigned to bed. He was nursed by Franz and Alice, to whom he remarked, 'I hear so much music.' Alice brought him manuscript paper, but he was too tired to write and, as he told Rudolph Hartmann, who paid his last visit on August 29, there was no time left for anything but death.

Of this final visit, Hartmann recalled:

In the room, which seems very bright, stands the white bed, its headboard towards the entrance. Richard Strauss has turned his head a little, stretches his right hand out and greets me ... While I move the chair close to the bed, my eyes fall on the large oxygen tank that stands ready, close at hand, and with anxiety I think of the report I have just heard concerning the course of the illness in recent days . . . His facial expression is not much changed; unusual is only the deep pallor and tiredness of his features. Gradually his thoughts turn to the things that always interest him. He lies there peacefully, propped up quite high; his hands glide over the blankets in brief, emphatic gestures.

I hear the deep, somewhat hoarse voice speaking of the constantly recurring concern for the future of European theatre; and after a short pause he says, 'Imagine a hundred and forty years ago Goethe and Napoleon shook hands in Erfurt! What a development that would have been. Napoleon as the ruler of a united Europe, and Goethe his first Minister of Culture – and the others, Friedrich Wilhelm, Alexander, Franz, could perfectly well have disappeared and the world would have been spared a great deal . . . There is so much I would still like to do – but I believe that some of what I wanted and have begun has fallen on fertile ground.'

He turns his gaze straight ahead in order to pursue his own thoughts. After a while he says, 'I think I did a good job of conducting Wagner's works. A great deal depends on the conductor there; he has to hold it all together and at the decisive moment drive it forward. For example in *Siegfried*, after the Idyll, a powerful animation must begin and continue through to the end; and all the slow tempi must be taken only in a relative sense, but hardly anyone does that. Especially in the great concluding scene with Brünnhilde, where young Siegfried is overcome for the first time by erotic feelings, that is tremendously important.' He becomes very lively, sits up straight. 'You know the passage I mean, after the Idyll?'

Without waiting for an answer, he raises his arms, directs and sings the orchestra melody in a loud voice, demonstrating with his arms. The face is slightly flushed; his shining eyes are gazing far, far beyond the walls of the room. Now he is leaning back into the pillows, his eyes moist with tears. 'You must forgive me,' he says, 'but when you lie here so alone and there is so much to think about you become a little sentimental.' Then he is silent for a long time and follows his thoughts. Quite changed, softly, his voice sounds again after a while, ' "Grüss mir die Welt" – where does that come from?'

I think fleetingly of the similar words from *Die Walküre*, and say so, but he shakes his head: 'No, no, that's not it; this passage occurs somewhere else', and repeats, 'Grüss mir die Welt!' He falls silent again; I see that his face shows signs of fatigue and feel that it is time to leave him. He gives me his hand and thanks me for the visit, in a perceptible attempt to deprive this parting of its all too palpable weight and significance. Then he grasps my right hand once more in both of his and holds me fast: 'Perhaps we will see each other again . . .' A final squeeze, his hands release me, and quickly I leave the room. As I leave, I hear Richard Strauss give a muffled sob and then call loudly for his son . . . The grandson, Richard, brings me home. We do not speak. I look out into the night landscape, all the while listening to the words whose soft, urgent tone does not want to leave me: 'Grüss mir die Welt!' (Greet the world for me!)

The quotation comes from Act I, scene IV of Strauss's most treasured opera, *Tristan und Isolde*. It was no coincidence that Strauss should have thought of Isolde's famous farewell at a time when the future of his music and the sanctity of his reputation were far from assured.

In the following days Strauss dictated his final letters, the last to François-Poncet ('... unfortunately, I am ill ...'), and Alice continued to nurse him, the doctors doing their best to relieve the pain. In spite of his suffering he remained articulate until shortly before the end; Mozart monopolised his imagination (particularly the Clarinet Quintet, the score of which he kept by his bed), but he returned periodically to his own work. He was visited for the last time by Furtwängler, who found Strauss 'in bed and very feeble'. According to the conductor's biographer, Kurt Riess, 'An opened score of *Tristan* rested on his [Strauss's] knees; he was reading the "Liebestod" and said with a smile: "It is quite incredible how marvellously Wagner deals with the bassoon." '

A few days before the end Strauss turned to Alice and whispered: 'It's a funny thing, but dying is exactly like I composed it sixty years ago in *Tod und Verklärung*.' Uraemia, angina and constant pain wore the old man down, and after a series of increasingly severe heart attacks he died at 2.12 p.m. on the afternoon of September 8, 1949. The news was released almost immediately. Casts of his hands and a death mask were taken, preserving the face of a man thirty years younger. That evening Bernard Shaw sat at his upright piano and tearfully played and sang through excerpts from *Ariadne auf Naxos*.

The funeral on September 12 was an extraordinary affair. So many people wanted to attend that the ceremony had to be held in the open air, outside the crematorium at the Ostfriedhof in Munich. According to Strauss's stated wishes, the Funeral March from the *Eroica* was played (by Solti and the orchestra of the Munich State Opera) and after the speeches and service the final Trio from *Rosenkavalier* was performed to an accompaniment of crying and wailing from the crowd. One by one, each of the sopranos broke down although, miraculously, they managed to steady themselves so that the performance ended more or less together. At the end Pauline could take no more and collapsed from her chair sobbing her husband's name. Egon Hilbert, Director of the Vienna Opera, concluded the ceremony with the words: 'Richard Strauss has entered eternity, and his music immortality.'

Pauline returned to Garmisch with her husband's urn, which was placed in the room where he died. On the 18th, a weeping Clemens Krauss managed to get through the Vienna Philharmonic's commemoration concert, where the address was given by an equally tearful Joseph Gregor.

Pauline was inconsolable. The dust against which she had battled all her life began to settle. Alice would find her sitting on the stairs in her nightgown, sobbing into her hands: 'I never realised that a person could weep so much.' In October she returned, as Richard had asked, to the Palace Hotel in Montreux, where she could be looked after in comfort, and avoid constant reminders of her loss. She no longer complained; there was nothing left to fight for. Five months later Alice fetched her back to Garmisch, where she would sit on Richard's deathbed and cry. Eight months after Strauss, Pauline died in Garmisch on May 13, 1950 – nine days before Wilhelm Furtwängler conducted Kirsten Flagstad in the first performance, in London, of the *Four Last Songs*.

In need and in joy
we have travelled hand in hand;
let us now rest from our journey
above the silent land.

Around us the valleys close down,
the air already grows dark,
only two larks still soar
nostalgically into the mist.

Draw near, and let them whirl about,
soon it will be time for sleep,
so that we do not lose our way
in this solitude.

O broad, quiet peace,
so profound in the gloaming!
How weary we are of travelling –
is this perhaps death?

Joseph von Eichendorff, *Im Abendrot*

EPILOGUE: A LIFE TOO LONG

Richard Strauss was the last purely German composer – the ultimate refinement of an evolutionary curve of cultural experience distilled by Mozart, advanced by Beethoven and idealised by Wagner. Like his idols, Strauss's instincts, philosophy and music can be traced through centuries of German history. Had there been no war, the same would have been expected of his successors, but in the rush to deny the Third Reich and its legacy, the baby was jettisoned with the bathwater, and with few exceptions post-war German composers experimented with everything except the German tradition. Reactive movements such as those which grew out of Darmstadt in the 1950s reached for a politicised, left-wing, anti-romantic, denationalised and socially conscious aesthetic that was as hostile to the 'exploitative' bourgeoisie as it was irrelevant to the 'persecuted' majority. But if Strauss's psychology and music were a product of evolution, then he broke with his models through his belief that the composition, performance and propagation of musical art was more important than the people for whom it was written.

Strauss saw in art a conjectural solution, a reflection of personal and national identity, and a hypothetical ideal to which each passing generation might aspire. Art was the reinvention of tradition, a process to which he devoted his life and through which he felt a necessary connection with his forebears. With the exception of *Domestica* and *Intermezzo*, his music circumvented relative social experience. His peers, and the passage of 'real life', provided him with little or no inspiration, and while he may have enjoyed his public admiration, and the wealth it brought him, he was averse to congress with ordinary men and women. Rather, as an antisocial creature he was motivated by a humanistic idealism that precluded compassion and communality. The bitter irony of German music after Strauss's death was that while he had been gifted with a musical language intelligible to, and popular with, the majority, it was at no point used to express anything to which the majority might tenably have related. Conversely, the composer Hans Werner Henze and his contemporaries were animated by ethical questions of social and political relevance which they failed to express in music that the majority might enjoy.

The discord between social reality and the function of art typified Strauss's Lutheran flight into a romantic, irrational, non-European and imagined Germany of the past – from where the ravages of modernism and the decay of tradition could be observed in relative safety. But even with his head buried in the sand, Strauss could still hear the rumblings of progressivism, and his final depression owed much to his concern for the future of German music in the light of the quickening advance of non-tonal aesthetics.

On one occasion after the war he was approached by a young composer with a recently completed work of serialism. After leafing through the score, Strauss asked: 'Why do you compose like this when you have talent?' Though apocryphal, the tale is consistent with Strauss's failure to understand the rejection of tonality. His recognition of the need to look beyond late Romanticism – to which effort he contributed at least four operatic masterpieces – would never dull his hatred of Viennese modernism since tonality, and its representative symbolism, was Man's most civilising achievement.

A comparable divide between ambition and accomplishment haunts Strauss's reputation as a political animal. But it is well to remember that he was born in 1864 and that he lived through the least stable period in modern European history. At his birth Germany did not exist. Like Mozart and Beethoven, he entered life as the subject of a provincial monarchy and lived out his youth by oil-lamp. He left behind an atomic age in which global air travel, electronic telecommunications, television and republican democracy were transforming the order and pace of a world recovering from six years of war. As a child of the 1860s he grew into a man of the 1880s, in which decade he remained until his death in 1949. Those attitudes and beliefs considered acceptable and idealistic during his formative years are today maxims for bigotry and intolerance. In the modern West there is no room for anti-Semitism, racism, isolationism, Aryanism or militarism, and such views are suppressed as the unacceptable face of liberty; but to Strauss's parents, his friends, his teachers, his colleagues and the German society that embraced his music, they were the very oxygen of civilisation.

That he was at liberty to look beyond these values, and that he was sufficiently well-travelled to consider alternatives, disables the rationalisation that he knew no different. It was all a question of priorities. From childhood, Strauss's priorities were repressively aesthetic. Violence, drunkenness, murder and licentiousness were wrong because the law said so, but there was no law protecting Bayreuth from the Jews, no law ensuring the preservation of German theatrical tradition from contamination, no law protecting the purity of German music from modernism. The Third Reich made promises that were simply too good not to believe.

To a limited extent, assertions of naïvety are fair. After becoming aware of the Holocaust, for example, Strauss wrote to his grandson: 'When after thirty years you once more read this melancholy letter I hope you will also remember your grandfather, who for almost seventy years worked for a German culture and the honour and glory of his Fatherland.' But the truth is that Strauss could see what was happening; it would have been impossible for him to do otherwise.

His relationship with the Vienna Philharmonic Orchestra is a valuable case in point. Under the Nazis, Wilhelm Jerger – a double-bass player and lieutenant in the SS – was appointed chairman of the VPO. At the time forty-seven per cent of the orchestra's members belonged to the Nazi Party; many had joined well before 1938 – when it had still been illegal in Austria to do so. Coincidentally, eleven Jewish players – including Mahler's brother-in-law Arnold Rosé – emigrated. The remaining six Jewish players were all transported to concentration camps where they met their deaths. A further nine members were found to be of 'mixed race' or 'contaminated by kinship', for which they were reduced to secondary status within the orchestra.

In total, twenty-six non-Aryans were murdered, exiled or reduced in status and with one or two exceptions Strauss had known them all. His relationship with the VPO was closer than with any other orchestra – a bond that manifested itself not only throughout his time as their director (at the Opera) and the orchestra's loyal promotion of his music, but also by the gift of compositions, the making of recordings, the sharing of tours and an especially close rapport, not least with Jerger, during the Reich, when he and his family lived at Jacquingasse. This familiarity[1] was at no point affected by the VPO board's initiation and implementation of racially-motivated mandates, or its general servility to Hitler, Goebbels, Schirach and the government.

Even if Strauss had not been aware of the VPO's growing, and widely published, list of Nazi members, and had failed to notice the disappearance of every Jewish player, he remained the orchestra's most robust sponsor. As Strauss well knew, the VPO was protected by Goebbels as a valuable propaganda instrument, and he was unlikely to have jeopardised his part in the orchestra's many tours to occupied areas in need of 'Germanization' (such as Krakow, Copenhagen, The Hague, Amsterdam, Paris, and Dijon) in which his music was a prominent feature – frequently as evidence of Austro-German superiority and the merits of ancestral purity.

This obsession was much in evidence during the VPO's centennial in 1942 – to which Strauss made his standard contribution – and the board went so far as to commission from Jerger a celebratory book entitled *Erbe und Sendung* (Inheritance and Mission). It painstakingly documented the ideologies of the orchestra, and reinforced its suitability for appropriation by National Socialism. Genealogies of prominent ancestral generations, with fathers being replaced by sons, were highlighted as evidence of blessed continuity; the name of every 'non-Aryan' was marked with an accusatory asterisk. Jerger validated his anti-Semitism as the manifestation of cultural responsibility:[2] 'It is demonstrated', he wrote, 'that in spite of manifold influences of blood from elsewhere, this Mind continues to implant itself with great toughness through the ancestral lineage, and that it is often very sharply imprinted. It is understandable that such an inheritance must beget outstanding musicians, who in their stylistic education and in their experience of orchestral playing are already extraordinarily schooled. This is Mind from Old Mind, which helps tradition and inheritance, an overcoming investment to a special development and fulfilment.'

Strauss enjoyed friendships with many like Jerger and he was plainly sympathetic to any furtherance of 'tradition and inheritance'; although his actions during the Reich were doctrinal, rather than criminal, the absence of contrition, doubt or regret in his post-war writings, and the failure of his apologists to produce pretextual rationalisation, weigh heavily against his redemption as an historical figure. The unease to which he was prone during his last four years does point towards the existence of a conscience, but it might just as easily be argued that he was fearful for the future of his music in a world hateful to anyone and anything connected with Hitler's Reich.

It would have been a pleasure to have brought this anniversary biography to its close in a major key, but the solemnity of its themes, the seriousness of the historical context and the subject's absolute refusal to account for his contribution to the Nazi regime preclude a happy ending. It has, none the less, long been felt by admirers of Strauss's music that he has suffered excessive criticism for the weaknesses of an unremarkably human personality. Indeed, while Mozart, Beethoven and Wagner have been readily forgiven their eccentricities, simply because they were eccentric to the point of madness, Strauss has provoked extremes of reference. The reasons for this are manifest. The image of an ordinary composer who found success easy and wealth a pleasure but who, even so, appeared to treat his music as work, has consistently provoked animosity from those who like their geniuses to fulfil some unspoken code of difference. As one writer put it: 'Many have found it easier to forgive Wagner his debts, than Strauss his royalties.' Where the nineteenth century bred an anti-pragmatic caricature of the wild and undisciplined virtuoso, Strauss's rigorous and organised approach to composing – to say nothing of his wish to be paid for it – sat at odds with the excitement, daring and eroticism of the finished product.

But as Strauss demonstrated during the 1930s, he was possessed of an extraordinary arrogance, a self-awareness that bordered on the megalomaniac. According to Felix Aprahamian, who met him before and after the war, Strauss simply thought he was superior – above the mire of socio-politics and beyond conventional issues of morality and responsibility. His supreme confidence and self-belief, and his understanding of his significance within Germany's cultural hierarchy, reinforce the cultural pessimism that led him to welcome the Nazis' embrace. Indeed, that he looked to National Socialism as an agent of reform is now irrefutable, and it is to be remembered that, anti-democratic and anti-semitic, Strauss was also intensely superior. As he wrote in a memoir after leaving the RMK: 'We are Aryans and Germans without further being aware of it.' If Strauss has been treated harshly – when Furtwängler, for example, has enjoyed a largely unwarranted renaissance – then it is best to remember that the majority of biographical studies of the composer to date have gone out of their way to find him innocent of all charges.

The issue of Strauss's 'Jewish' family has been wildly exaggerated – much as his son's membership of the Nazi Party has been vigorously suppressed – but it is worth noting that he wrote to the SS in Prague on behalf of his daughter-in-law's grandmother, Paula Neumann, who had been dispatched to the concentration camp in Theresienstadt. This was an isolated gesture – prompted as it was by Franz rather than by compassion – and the old woman remained in Theresienstadt, where she perished. Other members of Alice's maternal family were taken to the camp in Lodz, and a total of twenty-six of her relatives were murdered in the name of the racial purification that Strauss believed central to the deliverance of German culture. Unlike Furtwängler, he saved no one, and risked nothing beyond a solitary letter to save even one of his own family – and so the issue of his Jewish family interests concerns the story of his life only inasmuch as it underlines the balance of his priorities and the consistency of his behaviour.

That he suffered obstruction and political manipulation after 1935 cannot be doubted, any more than can the difficulties suffered by Alice Strauss and her children in Garmisch and Munich. And the issue was undeniably used to keep Strauss on the straight and narrow. But what got Strauss into trouble with the Nazis was the same problem that had dogged him throughout his life: duplicity. Playing for every side took its toll on most of his long-term relationships, and it was no less troublesome during the 1930s when he became embroiled with Goebbels and Rosenberg. To this fairly straight-forward conflict was added the issue of Stefan Zweig, whose services Strauss attempted to retain while making all sorts of oaths and promises to the Nazi State. Zweig did not believe a man could serve two masters, whereas Strauss believed he could serve as many as would pay for the privilege.

There is no doubt that had Strauss not played such a mercurial game, or had he been better at it, his troubles would have been considerably less onerous. As it was, his music continued to be played, and he continued to conduct, until it was no longer possible for anyone to play anything at all. If he became a prisoner in his home, then it was a prison of enviable luxury and comfort, and if it is now possible to see that life during the war was uneven for him and his family, then the same could be said of almost every non-ranking public figure between 1939 and 1945.

None of this matters to devotees of his music, and neither should it. Richard Strauss left behind some of the most beautiful and powerful music ever written, and nothing can or ever will detract from the breadth of this remarkable legacy. His operas remain among the most popular, even compared to those by Mozart, Verdi and Puccini; his tone poetry and the *Four Last Songs* still warrant continual recording at a time when most record companies can barely afford to release their back catalogue, far less add to it.

But for all the popularity and innovation of his finest work Strauss represented an end, not a beginning. Beyond its contained merit, his legacy provided a standard against which later generations have reacted, and even after the passing of the more lunatic abstractions of the avant-garde Strauss's music is still dismissed by most 'serious' composers as sentimental, vulgar and decadent. Outside the concert hall and opera house it is a different story – one that has yet to be written. With the mass Jewish emigrations of the 1930s, many of the Austro-German composers to land in America headed straight for Hollywood to work in the film industry. The majority of this talent had grown up in Strauss's towering shadow, and many imitated his opulent expressionism as the nearest point of stylistic departure. Erich Korngold, Franz Waxman, Max Steiner and Hans Salter – among many others – were all products of Strauss's Vienna, and each brought his chromatically rich and lyrically effulgent theatricality to their film scores. The fashion for such *outré* romanticism died out in the 1950s, but with John Williams's work for Steven Spielberg in the 1970s and 80s Strauss's influence returned to prominence; if Strauss were to hear a contemporary film score by Elliot Goldenthal or Danny Elfman, he might well feel some sense of cultural consummation. That they are both Jewish merely compounds the irony.

While most of Strauss's predictions for the future of music after his death have sadly come true, a few have yet to materialise. Of these, the most hopeful is also the most typical, and it serves as a fitting testament to a man whose greatest tragedy was to have outlived his time:

> Our future lies in art, especially in music. In times when spiritual goods are rarer than material ones, and egoism, hatred and envy govern the world, music will do much to re-establish love among mankind.

Richard Strauss
Diary entry, 1945

NOTES

1 *And Paradise Was All Around Us*

1 'Und um uns ward's Elysium'. The last line of Klopstock's poem *Das Rosenband*, set by Strauss in 1898 and published as one of his three songs, Op. 36.
2 The valveless horn. Precursor to the Viennese horn.
3 Strauss played first horn in Wagner's operatic premières.

2 *'Wach Auf!'*

1 'Wake up!'. A chorus, to words by Hans Sachs, set by Wagner in Act III of *Die Meistersinger von Nürnberg*.
2 August Tombo, a harpist.
3 Benno Walter began teaching Richard the violin in 1871.
4 'Panzenburg' is the Bavarian term for a pile of empty beer barrels.
5 Founded the year of Richard's birth by Joseph Gung'l, a military bandmaster and composer of music in the vein of Johann Strauss I.
6 Thuille would go on to become a leading member of the Munich School, as a composer as well as a theorist. He composed a large body of music, including three operas and, together with Rudolf Louis, he published an important *Harmonielehre* in 1907. In 1903 he succeeded Joseph Rheinberger as professor of composition at the Königliche Akademie der Tonkunst in Munich. He died of a heart attack at the early age of forty-six. He was the dedicatee of, among other works, *Don Juan*.
7 Of texts by Emanuel Geibel.

3 *A Family Affair*

1 Op. 3.
2 Richard the First was Wagner. There could be no second.
3 The scores for both the *Festive Chorus* and the *Elektra Chorus* were destroyed when Munich was bombed by the Allies in 1943.
4 Wihan would give the first performance of Dvorak's B minor Cello Concerto in 1895.
5 After the concert a group of those closest to Richard presented him with his first laurel wreath: 'On the most memorable day of your life, 16 March 1881.' He also received a gold signet ring with his initials carved into a black oval stone which he

wore until November 1, 1945, when he presented it to his grandson Richard on his eighteenth birthday.

6 The symphony did not receive its second performance for another twelve years, until January 5, 1893, when Strauss gave exclusive performing rights to the Wilde Gung'l orchestra.

7 Franz played first horn.

8 In return for Levi's scheduling the D minor Symphony Franz agreed to play first horn for him at the 1882 Bayreuth Festival.

9 In Dresden on November 27 by the Tonkünstlerverein and its conductor Franz Wüllner, in front of an audience that included Hans von Bülow.

10 In Munich on November 28 by Hermann Levi (its dedicatee) at the Odeon. Although the work was played a number of times, it was never published.

11 A Wagnerite, he had premièred *Das Rheingold* and *Die Walküre*, and was then principal conductor of the Meiningen Court Orchestra and Dresden Conservatory.

12 Richard was nineteen, Dora was twenty-three.

13 Strauss had yet to refine his theatrical judgement.

4 *Mentors*

1 Bülow had been Kapellmeister since 1880.

2 It would later drop Society Orchestra from its title.

3 The same Mannstädt who had conducted Strauss's Serenade in Berlin.

4 His description to the Duke of Meiningen.

5 The husband of Elizabeth Nietzsche.

6 Even here Strauss was pandering to Bülow's patriotic isolationism.

7 A small town midway between Frankfurt and Weimar, about eighty-five miles north-west of Bayreuth.

8 Strauss's words.

9 A horn player and orchestral representative.

10 A body of eighty women and, when required, fifty men.

11 Marie Schanzer, originally an actress. They married in 1882.

12 She is referring to *Eight Songs*, Op. 10, after poems by Hermann von Gilm.

13 'I had to practise this not really difficult piece – whose simple scales were nevertheless very tricky for my left hand ...'

14 On October 18, 1885.

15 It was common for violinists to take on percussion parts when funds were low, but this further reduced the already thin string section. Strauss and Bülow were helping bolster this section.

16 Bülow refused even to talk to Brahms, and for over a year they had no contact. Eventually, however, Brahms acknowledged his error and visited Bülow at his hotel in Vienna. Finding the conductor out he left his card, having first written a musical quotation from *The Magic Flute* on the back: the accompanying words, which Bülow would have known, were 'Shall I never see you again, beloved?' Deeply moved, Bülow was forgiveness itself.

17 Originally for string quartet, Op. 133.

18 This was still a modest sum. It had been kept low because, so the court felt, Strauss was already 'in comfortable circumstances'.

19 The Duke was renowned for his brilliantly staged, dramatically faithful productions of Schiller's *Die Jungfrau von Orleans* and Shakespeare's *Julius Caesar*, as well as less well-known and contemporary work.

20 A fascinating woman, Julie Ritter had supported Wagner even though she had five other children to sustain. When an uncle left her a considerable inheritance, she was able to pay the composer rather more, and in doing so enabled Wagner to compose his *Ring* poems. Tragically, since she died in 1865, she never saw the operas.

21 It seems likely that Bülow's support of Alexander Ritter was his way of thanking his mother.

22 Chiefly the essays 'The Music of the Future', 'Opera as Drama' and the infamous racial polemic 'Judaism in Music'.

23 According to George Marek.

24 The real reason, of course, was that Bülow had had a difficult time in Munich, and hated the city with a passion. He was also none too fond of the Jewish Levi.

25 The equivalent of twice Strauss's annual salary at Munich.

5 *The Hero's Adversaries*

1   The second part of Strauss's autobiographical tone poem *Ein Heldenleben*.

2   Music that eschewed extra-musical imagery, the opposite of programme music.

3   Although early Romantics such as Mendelssohn and Berlioz dabbled with picture-painting during the 1820s and 30s, Liszt was the first to create anything worthy of categorisation – *Symphonische Dichtung*. Each of his fourteen tone poems, written during the 1850s and 60s, takes as its inspiration a constituent of romantic imagery – a myth, a play, a painting, a poem, a philosophy, etc. – and each was written with some preconceived extra-musical agenda.

4   In an essay on Liszt.

5   Notably Liszt.

6   Strauss would later poke fun at Italian opera through his own work, notably in *Der Rosenkavalier*, *Die Schweigsame Frau* and *Capriccio*.

7   Although it was Strauss's reverence for the building's architecture and cultural significance, rather than any feeling for its inspiration, that excited his pique.

8   A Chinese pagoda in Munich.

9   The work was not given its first performance until March 1887.

10 Conducting Boieldieu's *Jean de Paris*.

11 Which was none the less still considered amoral and, therefore, some way from the A-list.

12 An expressive effect in which the musical line is stretched backwards and forwards while maintaining a strict metrical time.

13 The Wagnerian tenor Heinrich Vogl.

14 Whom Strauss none the less admired.

15 Perfall composed four operas, all of which were staged, without success, in Munich. The libretto of the first, *Sakuntala* (1853), was later recast and set to music by Weingartner.

16 Liszt had died the day before Strauss began his appointment in Munich, on July 31; his death intensified Ritter's proselytising, just as it swelled Strauss's devotion.

17 Levi was, after all, in charge of the orchestral appointments so Franz considered

the conductor, rather than Perfall, responsible for his departure.

18 By which Strauss meant Levi.

19 *Eine Alpensinfonie.*

20 To the conductor Jan Levoslav Bella.

21 Written in 1880 in honour of the opening of the Naples funicular railway. Strauss was under the misapprehension that it was a genuine folk-song.

22 Bülow was the dedicatee.

23 Strauss's last major work of chamber music, which he dedicated to his friend and cousin Robert Pschorr.

24 About thirty-five kilometres south-west of Munich.

25 The De Ahnas lived opposite the Pschorrs.

26 Pauline's age when she first met Richard.

27 Of Vienna.

28 Strauss's choice of Wagner's names signifies little, for Guntram's character is quite obviously a cross between *Tannhäuser* and *Parsifal*. He must have considered 'Parhäuser' or 'Tannsifal' a little too conspicuous.

29 Sadly, Bülow hated the work, damning it in 1888 as 'an infamous, outmoded concoction'.

30 A bizarre number – running to some eighteen hours – for such a brief programme. Perhaps they were necessary since Strauss spoke no Italian and the orchestra spoke no German. He seems to have made his way using scraps of French and a very articulate stick technique.

6 *Certainty of Victory*

1 When the National Socialists came to power in 1933 Shakespeare was to prove as acceptable to official policy as Goethe and Schiller, particularly as most German plays written after 1890 were banned for their degeneracy, pacifism, left-wing sympathies or, worst of all, Jewish origin. In 1936, for example, there were more productions of Shakespeare's plays in Germany than the rest of the world put together.

2 Beethoven's symphonies.

3 Brahms's symphonies.

4 A reference to the essay 'The Beautiful in Music' by Eduard Hanslick.

5 In 1894 Strauss conducted *Macbeth* in Berlin and, so he claims, Bülow patted him on the back afterwards, saying, 'It's quite a good piece after all.'

6 *Macbeth* was written before *Don Juan*, but it did not reach its definitive form until after *Don Juan* had been published, which is why it has the opus number 23.

7 *Aus Italien.*

8 Had Mahler been Aryan he would have made the greatest of Bayreuth's conductors.

9 March 6, 1890.

10 'Laughter is better than tears!'

11 This was her last letter to Strauss.

12 Nearly sixty.

13 The debt remained extant until Strauss's return to Munich.

14 Lassen and Strauss disagreed over Wagner's music.

15 In a letter to his father.

16 Strauss thought it 'a decent success'.

17 Hermann Wolff, agent and promoter; Siegfried Ochs, conductor; Friedrich E. Koch, conductor.

18 Strauss writing to his father.

19 Liszt premièred *Lohengrin* for Wagner in 1850, two years into his eleven-year reign as Kapellmeister.

20 Meyerbeer, a Jew, was also considered, by Wagnerites at least, to have been a jealous enemy of Wagner.

21 Liszt's orchestra had twenty-one (i.e., 6, 6, 4, 3, 2).

22 As Elisabeth in *Tannhäuser*.

23 A *travesti* role.

24 Strauss sent her for an audition in March 1890 to Kassel, who offered her a five-year contract. She turned it down, hoping for a place in Weimar. Less than two months later she received just such an offer and made her debut at Weimar on May 22 as Pamina in Mozart's *Die Zauberflöte*.

25 *Death and Transfiguration*. He also worked on the libretto of his opera *Guntram*, but he had yet to begin the music.

26 *Der faule Hans*, the more popular of the two, was staged in Riga, Karlsruhe, Dresden, Prague and Frankfurt; *Wem die Krone?* was seen in Leipzig and Brunswick.

7 *The Hero's Battlefield*

1 None of this glory was reflected on to Weimar, as the première was given nearly fifty miles away, in Eisenach, at a meeting of the Allgemeiner Deutscher Musikverein. Bronsart and Lassen failed to secure the première of *Tod und Verklärung*, as the Weimar season did not coincide with the composer's itinerary.

2 'Death and Transfiguration' had always been a provisional title. Ritter had suggested *Seraphic Fantasy*, providing an accompanying motto for the score from Goethe's *Faust*: 'This is powerful to behold / But the place is too sombre / It shakes us with fear and horror . . . / Rise up to a higher level . . . / You who unfold into bliss.' But Strauss eventually retained his own title, rejecting his friend's suggestions. Undaunted, Ritter penned, 'In der ärmlich kleinen Kammer', a turgid poem of homage to the new composition. Strauss suffered the older man's devotion with patience and good humour, and even though Ritter's poem was overcooked, literal and blind to its subject's inner subtleties, Strauss allowed it to be printed alongside his music in the engraved score. He was no less generous when it came to printing the poem in concert programmes, although he withdrew this stipulation after just two performances.

3 Strauss did not, in fact, compose another orchestral work for five-and-a-half years.

4 A reference to the Bayreuth Festival.

5 Music director at Karlsruhe Opera.

6 On November 18, 1890, Strauss conducted a thrilling performance of the *Faust* Symphony during which, according to a letter he wrote to Thuille, he gave himself 'the father and mother of all stitches'.

7 As a guide to her capacity, Pauline later sang Leonora in Beethoven's *Fidelio* for Lassen, who thought the role beyond her.

8 She none the less sang the opera's final scene (the 'Liebestod') on January 26, 1891,

for the fourth of the season's Subscription Concerts, conducted by Strauss.

9 George Pschorr.

10 This seems all the more likely considering the events of the following season.

11 As some of these lasted five hours it is impossible to know how many hours of full orchestral rehearsal Strauss directed, but it must have been in the region of seventy.

12 A work Strauss had yet to conduct.

13 He despised Richter, a conductor with whom he had 'not one artistic point of contact'.

8 *Odyssey*

1 Hamann and Hermand.

2 Felix Dahn, *Ein Kampf um Rom* (1867).

3 *Soll und Haben* (1855). Strauss was fond of Freytag's work and, in 1890, he followed Cosima's advice and read *Bilder der deutschen Vergangenheit*.

4 *Der Hungerpastor* (1864).

5 Whereas there were only 46,000 Jews in England, and 51,000 in France.

6 '... and frequently with an effrontery that was in inverse proportion to the understanding their criticism revealed'.

7 Gordon Craig.

8 Founded in 1817.

9 The poet Heinrich Heine, a Jew.

10 Home-made preserve.

11 The daughter of Cosima Wagner and Hans von Bülow.

9 *The Politics of Ambition*

1 On October 22 Strauss's ire was undimmed. As he wrote to Mahler, 'Germany I can no longer abide, climate and artistic conditions too miserable.'

2 Pauline went on to sing the role on a number of occasions. Most considered her Gretel's true creator, even if she had not actually sung at the first performance. As Strauss wrote to Humperdinck after the last performance of the season, on January 7, 1894: 'Fräulein de Ahna in particular distinguished herself by her high spirits and humour.'

3 Six songs from *Das Knaben Wunderhorn* and the First Symphony in the revised version of 1893, subtitled 'Titan'.

4 Strauss and Mahler had met only once before, in October 1887.

5 This was a less than convincing gesture, since Strauss was merely responding to Mahler's fear that he might not be able to conduct the work himself.

6 In Weimar.

7 Another good reason for Strauss's favouring Behn was Behn's position as chairman of the Hamburg Philharmonic Concerts.

10 *Opera as Expression*

1   Where he died.
2   Which was no less controversial since Bülow turned against Liszt in later life.
3   Although Mahler was so moved by a performance of Klopstock's hymn *Auferstehung* (Resurrection) that he used it to end his Second Symphony.
4   Mahler was trying to persuade the Hamburg Intendant to stage the first production of *Guntram*.
5   Neither Cosima Wagner nor Ludwig Thuille were able to attend, the latter because he was short of money.
6   As in the allusions to *Parsifal* in the Prelude to Act I.
7   Albeit with a twinge of Catholic penance thrown in for good measure.
8   As in Bayreuth.
9   Years later Strauss tried to defend his libretto, claiming that it was 'quite as good as that for Verdi's *Il trovatore!*'

11 *General de Ahna*

1   Pauline was thirty-one when this letter was sent on April 9, 1894.
2   A card game dear to the composer.
3   In this Pauline was wrong. Woyzeck is a private.
4   Pauline continued to sing Lieder until after the turn of the century, although her repertoire was dominated by her husband's compositions.
5   Lehmann maintains that this outburst and the subsequent announcement occurred during a rehearsal for the Weimar production of *Tannhäuser* in which Pauline was singing Elisabeth.
6   Where the De Ahnas had a summer villa.
7   It took place in the parish office of Grassau, a small town sixty miles south-east of Munich.

12 *From Schalk to Superman*

1   *Recollections and Reflections.*
2   He could not have meant this.
3   It was a charge to which Possart happily admitted in a letter to Levi.
4   The Flemish tenor Ernst van Dyck sang the title role, the American soprano Lilian Nordica was Elsa, the Romanian baritone Demeter Popovici was Telramund and the English mezzo Marie Brema was Ortrud.
5   Wiborg was eventually invited to share the role.
6   This was to be Levi's last Bayreuth Festival.
7   It is worth noting, however, the critical opinion of Bernard Shaw, who on July 22 wrote for the *Star*: 'Strauss, the new conductor, seemed a hopeless failure; he kept the band as smooth, but also as inane as a linen collar; and his *tempi*, except for an occasional gallop in the wrong place, were for the most part insufferably slow. After Mottl's handling of *Lohengrin* this sort of thing would not bite on us at all; and we all sat wishing we had not come, and that Strauss had never been born.'

8   Even though Perfall, who retired from his post shortly after Strauss's arrival, had almost nothing to do with his difficulties.

9   With the exception of *Der Ring.*

10 The only work Cosima invited Strauss to conduct.

11 Siegfried begrudged Strauss his conducting fees, and having recently begun composing his own first tone poem he was envious of the financial and critical success enjoyed by Strauss's music. On July 12, 1895, Strauss wrote to his friend Max von Schillings: 'The mountains here rise higher than Humperdinck's royalties (without envy: Master Siegfried!) and are even stranger in "form" than the songs of Richard Strauss.'

12 The other conductors of the season were Franz Richter and Felix Mottl.

13 He conducted the second and fourth of the five cycles, between July 19 and August 19.

14 A park.

15 Arthur Seidl's description, preserved in a letter to Strauss.

16 Strauss and Siegfried's paths crossed more than Strauss would have liked. On one occasion the two met in Berlin at the city's most expensive hotel, the Adlon. Siegfried opened fire by attacking Strauss's supposed avarice: 'Is your business making such good profits, then?' to which Strauss replied, 'Oh yes, and it's my business, not my father's.'

17 Mahler had promised to conduct the Prelude to Act II and the 'Friedenserzählung' scene as well, but they went unplayed.

18 Strauss took Mahler's assurances seriously. When Mahler's ambitions came to nothing he blamed Pollini, with whom he had now 'fallen out completely'. As a result, he claimed to have tendered his resignation, even though he remained in Hamburg, on relatively good terms, until April 1897.

19 The other two being Alexander Zemlinsky's *Zarema*, his first, and Arthur Könnemann's *Der tolle Eberstein.*

20 Pauline was no nearer to being offered a full-time contract.

21 *Les Rougon-Macquart.* Written between 1867 and 1893.

22 Managed by André Antoine between 1887 and 1894.

23 Not without reason did Hofmannsthal turn to Sophocles for inspiration.

24 This is commonly attributed to Dürenberg.

25 Strauss's last opera.

26 Strauss used a modern German version of the 'folk book' by Carl Simrock, published in 1878.

27 One of the episodes features in Chaucer's 'Summoner's Tale'.

28 Munich's only available tenor.

29 *Die Entführung, Don Giovanni* and *Così fan tutte.*

30 *Rienzi, Tannhäuser, Tristan* and *Meistersinger.*

13   *Tilting at Windmills*

1   For example, Strauss's conducting schedule in Munich between August 5 and December 26, 1896, was dominated by Mozart and Wagner: specifically, two performances of *Rienzi*, three of *Die Meistersinger*, three of *Tristan*, five of *Tannhäuser* and eleven of *Don Giovanni*. The only other works he conducted during this four-

month period were single performances of Liszt's *Legend of St Elizabeth* and, bizarrely, Rossini's *Il barbiere di Siviglia*.

2   Composed, to a libretto by Ritter, between 1893 and 1895.

3   In a German translation by Adolph Strodtmann.

4   Wagner's *Tannhäuser* and *Tristan*, and Mozart's *Don Giovanni, Die Entführung* and *Così fan tutte*.

5   A remarkable comment considering that Strauss's mature technique demonstrated nothing but a beat.

6   Rolland was still relatively unknown in 1897, having yet to begin his celebrated four-volume novel *Jean-Christophe* (1904–12, about a German composer curiously reminiscent of one Richard Strauss), but he was increasingly fascinated by Strauss, having first met him at Wahnfried in 1891. Initially suspicious of Strauss's implicit triumphalism, Rolland later came to cherish his contact with the composer, to whom he grew uniquely attached during the first decade of the new century.

7   French soldier, falsely accused of spying for the German army, imprisoned in 1894 and released in 1906, thanks mainly to the work of Zola and Dreyfus's friends and family. The court case polarised the country's anti-militarist and anti-Semitic trends, highlighting the difficulties facing all European Jews.

8   In a letter to his father on February 24, 1898.

9   Strauss's finances were healthier even than Mahler might have guessed. By October 1, 1897, he had amassed a cash holding at the bank of over 30,000 marks.

14   *Protecting the Merchandise*

1   After selling Opuses 39–44 to different firms in Leipzig and Berlin, Strauss finally settled on Adolph Fürstner in 1900.

2   Even more curious, therefore, is Mahler's failure to take an interest in the GDT.

15   *From Hero to Schalk*

1   In fact, Strauss had to wait until October 1900, and a concert in Brussels, before he heard both works played on the same night.

2   Del Mar's claim in his biography of Strauss that Christian Frederik Horneman (1840–1906) composed an *Ein Heldenleben* Overture is, strictly speaking, inaccurate. Composed in 1867, the title of this entirely abstract composition – published in French – is *Overture héroique*, which translates as 'Heroic Overture', not 'A Hero's Life'.

3   Rolland quoted Strauss as saying, 'I do not see why I should not compose a symphony about myself; I find myself quite as interesting as Napoleon or Alexander.'

4   Louis famously dismissed Strauss's work as 'the highest that can possibly be achieved without actual genius'.

5   Which was almost as insolent as it was stale since, like so many others, Louis wrongly considered *Till Eulenspiegel* to be the apogee of Strauss's work as well as the truest expression of his nature.

6   For example, the six movements constitute a grand sonata with 1st subject, transition and 2nd subject Exposition, a Development, a Recapitulation and a Coda – the basic structure of Beethoven's symphony.

7 The one quotation not recognised until now is the appearance of a four-note descending passage, shared by flutes and violins, from Strauss's last tone poem *Ein Alpensinfonie* – a work that he did not actually compose until 1915, some seventeen years after *Heldenleben*. Like *Elektra*'s unplayable violin E's below open G (a note which players are instructed 'to think'), this bold gesture was typical of Strauss, although it is less remarkable than it seems since he first noted the ideas for the *Alpensinfonie* in 1878, after finding himself trapped up a mountain during a storm.

8 Hearing the revision played in 1946 Strauss turned to Willi Schuh and remarked, 'State Funeral.'

9 The first of only two orchestras to receive such a dedication. The other was Dresden's Staatskapelle.

10 A serious dismissal, since Bismarck had, in fact, died.

11 It was not the première, but the third performance in Cologne.

12 In the light of Strauss's concern with copyright, it is worth noting that the composer Gottlieb Noren asked him for permission to quote themes from *Heldenleben* in a work of his own, *Kaleidoskop*. Strauss generously agreed, confident that Noren's interest represented no threat, but his publishers were less compliant and sued for breach of copyright. Amazingly, the case was dragged into the Imperial High Court, where the bench ruled that because the theme representing the Man/Hero 'lacked the integration to make a rounded whole, and the development to form an independent, complete musical structure' there was no breach of copyright. Bizarrely, the court accepted that while Strauss's theme was 'melodic', it was not actually a melody!

13 Who was, after all, Strauss's friend.

14 Mahler conducted it only twice, in New York in 1911.

15 Which Strauss composed for Hitler's 1936 Olympics.

16 *Feuersnot*. It can also be translated as 'sexual famine'.

17 Superplank, founded in 1901. Probably the most powerful artistic/political movement in Berlin, profoundly significant to the development of Brecht, Weill and Schoenberg.

18 Thomas Beecham.

19 The work was dedicated, however, to Strauss's friend and ally Friedrich Rösch.

20 No one can be certain, as the letter is undated.

21 Mengelberg would recommend Strauss as his successor at the Vienna Opera in May 1901.

22 August Freiherr Plappart von Leenheer.

23 Max Graf.

24 His place was taken by George von Hülsen-Haeseler (1855–1922), the son of Hochberg's predecessor, Botho von Hülsen. Strauss had first met, and become friends with, George von Hülsen in 1884, during his first visit to Berlin.

25 Which is odd, considering that *Salome* and *Elektra* are among the most demanding operas ever written.

26 For example, Alma Mahler claims that her husband did not conduct *Feuersnot* because he had 'a horror of the work'. She is wrong in that Mahler conducted every Viennese performance of the work. As to whether or not he hated it, there is no external evidence for his having done so, which is not to say that he didn't privately admit to such feelings.

27 And in doing so, Mahler helped many a musician cope with the pain of anonymity.

16 *Lullaby Before the Storm*

1   Whose number included Steinbach and Lessmann.

2   To Romain Rolland, noted in Rolland's diary for Friday, March 9, 1900.

3   The gloriously overwritten tone poem *Pelléas und Mélisande*. A symbolist play by Maeterlinck, turned by Debussy into an opera between 1892–5 and first performed by Messager on April 30, 1902. It is claimed that Strauss knew nothing of Debussy's work, but this seems unlikely since its existence was well publicised throughout Europe, and Strauss was in Paris when the first performance was announced in 1901.

4   It is significant that Schoenberg referred to Strauss as 'Herr' throughout his letter.

5   Strauss conducted six concerts during the first season.

6   Including Elgar and Charpentier.

7   Not until 1907, when a collapse led to a diagnosis of myocardial weakness, did Strauss begin to curtail his engagements.

8   Taillefer, a servant of William's, sings to the king and his sister, enchanting both. As a reward, he asks to accompany William to England so that he might be the first to fire the first arrow at the English.

9   Including ninety strings, sixty woodwind, eight horns, six trumpets, four trombones and two tubas.

10 For the second year running. *Gerontius* had been premièred the previous year by Buths.

11 Which means that between May 18 and June 10 Strauss conducted seven concerts in twenty-four days and travelled nearly twelve hundred miles by horse-carriage, boat and train.

12 The first movement, at least, had never been played and so this was the first complete performance.

13 The principal conductor of the Gürzenich Orchestra, Franz Wüllner, died in September 1902, aged seventy. He had been one of the first to recognise Strauss's potential as a composer, and premièred a number of his early works. Although Strauss seems to have paid him no direct tribute, he was one of four conductors (the others being Weingartner, D'Albert and Richter) asked to cover Wüllner's itinerary until Fritz Steinbach could take over the post in 1903.

14 The only one of Strauss's tone poems which he labelled a symphony, as opposed to a tone poem.

15 Like many of his countrymen, Strauss venerated awards and medals. After moving to his villa in Garmisch each successive honour was mounted in a prominent glass case.

16 A title blatantly ignored by Strauss's enemies, notably Schoenberg.

17 The official ceremony took place on October 21, 1903.

18 A measure of Strauss's mood may be gleaned from the extraordinary portrait he had taken of himself by the legendary Expressionist photographer Edward Steichen.

17 *The Happy Princess*

1 Strindberg's *Rausch*, Wedekind's *Erdgeist*, Gorky's *Nachtasyl* and Hofmannsthal's *Elektra*.
2 The legendary French actress was nearly fifty at the time, and so hardly looked the part, but this had nothing to do with her unsuitability for the role since Wilde considered her 'the only person in the world' able to do it justice.
3 The first was in Breslau in 1901.
4 More than any other English writer with the exception of Shakespeare.
5 Written by Rolland after the first French performance in 1907.
6 It is possible that this comedy was by a Jewish writer.
7 During which Herod offers Salome everything and anything if she will retract her request for Jochanaan's head.
8 The production to which Adolf Hitler referred was the first in Graz, in 1906. At that first night he was also in the company of Gustav and Alma Mahler.
9 Peter Gay: 'Freud, Jews and other Germans'. Having indulged some of the most hateful propaganda of the Weimar years, Cossmann rejected National Socialism, became a prominent anti-Nazi and died while interned at the concentration camp in Theresienstadt.
10 Wittich complained to Cosima Wagner that the music was far too complicated, and that she could never learn the role in the four weeks remaining to her. Cosima asked Strauss if he would play her something from the opera. He grudgingly obliged, only to have her throw her hands over her ears, and denounce his work as 'absolute madness'. In his memoirs Strauss claims she decided, 'You are for the exotic, Siegfried [her son] for the popular!' After which Strauss wrote 'Clang!'
11 This was an out-and-out lie.
12 The Leipzig première began just fifteen minutes after the Dresden première.
13 Mahler's mind was decided for him after a meeting with Strauss in March 1903, while Strauss was in Vienna conducting the Berlin Tonkünstler Orchestra.
14 A proletarian venue.
15 A London banker, born of German parents. They first met while Strauss was in England in 1899.
16 This directly contradicts Rolland's assertion that Strauss had a terrible voice.
17 To Schuch Strauss wrote: 'It doesn't matter. Voice, Horatio, voice, and once again voice.'
18 Perron would go on to create Orestes and Baron Ochs.
19 Who, according to the Bible, was, by this stage, already an adult. Perhaps the Magi followed Christ throughout his life.
20 For December 26, 1906.

18 *The Elektra Parallax*

1 Munich Opera was not yet ready, or willing, to stage *Salome*.
2 In common with many at the time, Rolland saw something profound in Strauss's physical bearing. He contrasted Strauss's upright Aryanism with Mahler's dark and bruised diminution; this was a popular axis for anti-Semitic metaphor, heightening the lustre of one adjacent to the shadow of the other.

3   Music publisher.
4   Debussy had previously been an admirer of Strauss's music, praising its 'irresistible warmth'.
5   'Absolutely out of the question,' replied Hofmannsthal.
6   A snide reference to Mahler's latest symphony – the Eighth.
7   This was a particularly stressful time for Mahler. His life in Vienna was hellish, with wave after wave of anti-Semitic attacks weakening his resolve to overcome the factions within the Court Opera.
8   Pauline.
9   *Cristinas Heimreise.*
10 Each of these stems from a four-note motif, D-A-F-D, signifying the name of Elektra's murdered father, Agamemnon.

19 *Premature Post-Modernism*

1   *Der Rosenkavalier* (The Knight of the Rose).
2   Count Harry Kessler (1868–1937). Aesthete, pacifist and intellectual, to whom Hofmannsthal dedicated the completed libretto.
3   Alma records that the title role was sung by Maria Labia (1880–1953). It was not. Marazin devoted considerable time and hard work to perfecting the role, going so far as to visit an asylum for the mentally ill for ideas.
4   Zdenka Fassbender was then married to the conductor Felix Mottl.
5   The equivalent in 1999 of £9,400.
6   Not everyone could afford Strauss's enormous fees. In March, Fürstner ran into difficulties with the director of the Prague Opera, Angelo Neumann, who was unwilling to pay the going rate. Fürstner refused to negotiate and offered the Czech première to the National Theatre where, on April 25, it was received with characteristic rapture. In the audience was the 29-year-old conductor Otto Klemperer.
7   Approx. £260,000 in 1999.
8   Approx. £10,340,000 in 1999.
9   Approx. £352,000 in 1999.
10 Strauss later replaced *Feuersnot* with *Salome*, thinking this a less objectionable request.
11 Stage association.
12 In fact some two hundred of the chorus failed to show up.
13 Roller appears to have provided designs for a 1901 *Rienzi*, but whether or not this was commissioned by Mahler is difficult to say. Certainly, they were not used.
14 Strauss saw many of the Meiningen Theatre productions while working alongside Bülow with the Court Orchestra.
15 Mayr later became synonymous with the role. Strauss called him 'the' Ochs and told him, 'I thought of you all the time, Herr Mayr, while I was writing the part.' Mayr replied that he wasn't sure whether this was a compliment or an insult.
16 Hofmannsthal also suggested the Italian bass Antonio Pini-Corsi (1859–1918), creator of Ford in Verdi's *Falstaff.* Strauss did not take the suggestion seriously.
17 Octavian's nickname.
18 Perron nearly didn't make it; a few days before the first public dress rehearsal he

was struck down by a cold, forcing Strauss to apologise to the audience. His performance on the first night was not a success, at least not for the authors. In December 1911 Hofmannsthal, referring to preparations for their next opera, wrote to Strauss: 'A performance like that one in Dresden with Perron made nonsense of one individual character of mine...'

19 At Munich's annual carnival nineteen mounted Knights of the Rose, wearing outfits of silver silk, rode in the procession – followed by the figures of *Salome* and *Elektra* and, above them all, a weeping Richard Wagner.

20 Where the composer conducted the work for the first time.

21 Although Blech was better suited to the new work, the Berlin première was conducted by Karl Muck.

22 William Mann.

23 From the series *Marriage à la Mode*.

24 Puccini tried much the same thing in 1910, with *Fanciulla del West*.

25 A style of writing that comes closer to speech than to music.

20 *Le Bourgeois Gentilhomme*

1 First performed eight years later in 1919. Hofmannsthal had been toying with the idea since 1911 when, on February 26, he wrote in a notebook: 'The woman without a shadow, a fantastic play. The Empress, a fairy's daughter, is childless. She obtains a stranger's child. In the end she gives it back to its real mother. The second pair ... are Harlequin and Esmeralda. She wants to remain pretty. He clumsy and good. She gives up her child to a wicked fairy, disguised as a housewife: the shadow as a bonus.'

2 On April 8, conducted by Franz Schalk.

3 *Der Bürger als Edelmann* in German.

4 Also known as *Ce qu'on entend sur la montagne*. It is worth noting that the leading theme of Strauss's symphony is strikingly reminiscent of the opening of Liszt's greatest work for piano, the Sonata in B minor.

5 Stefan's real name was Dr P. S. Grünfelt.

6 Austria, Germany, Italy, Russia and the United States.

7 Letter to Hofmannsthal, May 20.

8 A view shared by another Bavarian anti-Semite, Max Reger.

9 This was remarkably enlightened. Strauss was one of the first conductors to advocate such authentic practice.

10 Reinhardt would have to move his entire ensemble halfway across Germany.

11 E. M. Forster's phrase in *Where Angels Fear to Tread*.

12 Farrar's and Garden's fees were even greater.

13 Reinhardt's stage designer at the Deutsches Theater.

14 Diaghilev and his Ballets Russes.

15 In his memoirs Strauss mused, 'Was it malice – or chance?'

16 A reinvention of Lully's music for the original Molière play.

17 The first of his operas to be heard in Russia.

18 He 'launched a letter of protest' to the conductor who, in all fairness, appears to have had it in for the composer. Why else would the Music Director of Bavaria's most celebrated opera house have allowed performances of a new production of

an untested work by Germany's most famous composer to be conducted by a répétiteur? To Hofmannsthal, Strauss threatened to withdraw the score. Though no admirer of Walter ('this strange man seems to be constantly in a fever, pro or contra, and never able to weigh anything calmly'), Hofmannsthal urged calm, and told Strauss not to be silly.

19 Because of Nijinsky's marriage.

20 Strauss wrote no testimony and passed no comment.

21 Indeed she did. She was to have danced the role of Potiphar's Wife.

22 Notably by the Ripons, the Speyers, the Woods and the Sitwells.

23 Their fifth and final performance of the work.

21 *Der Mann ohne Schatten*

1 Speyer was none the less interned for his German origin.

2 Either way, judged by 1999 currency values, the Bank of England held on to somewhere between two-and-a-half, and eight million, pounds of Strauss's money.

3 Strauss's savings had been more than sufficient to sustain a small family in a large house, and had the war and sequestration not intervened it is unlikely that he would have conducted much beyond his fiftieth year; without the war, therefore, posterity would have been denied the majority of Strauss's live and studio recordings, to say nothing of the wealth of archive film in which he can be seen and heard on the podium and at the piano.

4 In fact, Hofmannsthal went nowhere near the fighting. Like Rainer Maria Rilke, Stefan Zweig and Franz Werfel, he joined the Military Press Bureau, a safe haven for Austrian writers, whose skills were employed to enhance press reportage of Germany's military progress.

5 He sent his bill, which was never paid.

6 Indeed, the patriotic fervour then sweeping its way through Europe was sufficient to excite none other than Otto Klemperer to join the army. That he rescinded the gesture only a few hours later should not detract from the general atmosphere of exhilaration which must have existed to make someone so ill-adapted to military life enlist in the first place.

7 Twelve horns, two trumpets and two trombones.

8 There were no 'hers' in 1915.

9 The full dedication reads: 'To the Count Seebach and the Royal Orchestra at Dresden, in gratitude'.

10 Hofmannsthal's abbreviation.

11 He 'recorded' selections from *Salome, Feuersnot, Heldenleben* and four songs.

12 Rachmaninov and Busoni were generally considered the greatest pianists of their generation. Strauss was not.

13 This is the first written reference to *Intermezzo*, on which Strauss began working soon afterwards.

14 Strauss was only partly right, for Hofmannsthal's aesthetics were hardly cutting-edge. On May 8, 1916, for example, he reported to Strauss: 'Recently I heard the new opera by K[orngold]. Horrible stuff, *au fond*, like some witchery which reflects only the repulsive realities of the present, and nothing else.'

15 Neither liked the city, but Schuch's successor in Dresden, Fritz Reiner, was an

unknown quantity, and neither wished to take any risks with such a delicate work.
16 Jeritza was then based in Vienna, at the Hofoper.
17 Gutheil-Schoder appears to have borne Strauss no grudge either. She sang the role of the Composer many times, the first on November 13, 1916.
18 The day after the première, Hermann Bahr sent Strauss the first draft of an opera libretto, created in line with the composer's specific requirements for a 'domestic comedy', in which the central protagonist is one Professor Robert Storch – Strauss himself. *Intermezzo* would be Strauss's tenth opera.
19 Strauss to Hofmannsthal.
20 Strauss had known of Furtwängler ever since his 'superior' Mannheim première of the *Alpensinfonie* the previous year. They evidently came to know each other much better relatively quickly since Strauss smoothed the way for Furtwängler to become Music Director of the Berlin Staatsoper Orchestra only three years later, in 1920.
21 Salzburg Festival-House Society.
22 Strauss sent it to Hofmannsthal on August 10. The poet replied: 'shall do my best to read it through, but I must say right away that I am not the public nor, since I lack all sympathy for the genre of realism, a competent judge of the whole thing'.
23 *Don Juan, Till Eulenspiegel* and the Suite from *Der Bürger als Edelmann.*
24 *Edelmann* was given its first performance at Max Reinhardt's Deutsches Theater on April 9, 1918. Einar Nilson conducted.
25 *Salome* was finally given its city première on October 10.
26 He was, of course, partially legitimised since he was, at least, an Austrian Jew.
27 This does not mean that there were not many visitors to the house in Garmisch. It is merely that very few of them were intimates of the composer.
28 Although the coming waves of inflation would make the sum worthless.
29 With the foundation of the Republic all court institutions became State-funded.

22 The Poisoned Chalice

1 Later named after the Thuringian province of Weimar where the Constitution was drawn up.
2 The four most popular composers of opera in Germany in 1918 – Mozart, Wagner, Verdi and Puccini – remained so throughout the 1920s and 30s.
3 Verdi, Verdi, Ambroise Thomas and Gounod respectively.
4 According to his contract Strauss had to conduct fifty opera performances in five months annually, for five years.
5 The Vienna State Opera then boasted a number of Europe's most adored singers, including Jeritza and Piccaver.
6 Between 1,000 and 1,600 kronen a performance for everyone except Jeritza, who asked for, and received, considerably more.
7 High soprano.
8 Dramatic/lyric soprano.
9 Mezzo-soprano.
10 On March 10, 1920, Hofmannsthal wrote to Strauss: 'Roller of course failed me utterly over the magic contrivances. The fact is that he has no sense for the fantastic.'
11 For the scene in Act I when the Nurse tempts the Dyer's Wife with wealth and

luxury Roller conjured a huge glass platform from underneath the stage which he lit from beneath with brilliantly flashing lights.

12 Puccini, who was able to look through the score in Schalk's office during rehearsals, recognised the somewhat forced complexion and remarked, 'It's all logarithms!'

13 *Die Frau ohne Schatten* was scored for 107 players.

14 Letter to Pauline.

15 The concerts might have fared better had Strauss altered the programmes, which included relatively standard fare by Beethoven, Schubert, Weber, Wagner, Debussy and Strauss [Richard].

16 Bekker was a vociferous critic of *Die Frau ohne Schatten*. His vicious assault on the work, written for the *Frankfurter Zeitung* in 1921, did the opera irreparable harm in Germany.

17 Kraus converted to Catholicism as an adult.

18 Based upon an earlier set of piano pieces.

19 Strauss promised to help raise funds for the Opera.

20 Strauss thought that, for German audiences, all operas should be performed in German.

21 *Domestica* had still to win round American audiences.

22 The tour was reputed to have earned Strauss $50,000 (equivalent to £350,000 in 1999). In one of his last reviews of Strauss's tour, the critic Richard Aldrich wrote, 'He also hopes to take back with him $500 for the musicians of Central Europe still suffering from the effects of the war. This he has collected from musicians of the orchestras here and elsewhere that have played under his direction [and therefore not from his own pocket].' With crushing sarcasm, Aldridge continued, 'All will commend the eminent composer's disinterested thoughtfulness in raising this sum...'

23 Before leaving Germany in October Strauss had made his first acoustic recordings as an accompanist – with the tenor Robert Hutt and, famously, the legendary baritone Heinrich Schlusnus.

24 Strauss 'recorded' the piano accompaniments to three of his songs, *Zueignung*, *Alleseelen* and *Traum durch Dämmerung*; each was recorded twice, in different keys, so that different qualities and styles of voice (male and female) could be easily accommodated.

25 Rachmaninov also 'recorded' a number of celebrated rolls for the Ampico Company.

26 The poor attendance can be attributed to anti-German feeling as well as to a genuine dip of interest in Strauss and his music.

27 The limited technology required Strauss to re-orchestrate and cut the score of *Don Juan* (from bars 208 to 232).

28 Julius Korngold.

29 In the August *Musical Times* Bekker wrote: 'Dr Korngold does not ask "How does this or that artist conduct, compose, play or sing?" His question is "What attitude does he or she take towards Erich Wolfgang Korngold?"'

30 The irony of this was that many were genuinely loath to play Erich Korngold's music for fear of provoking his father into personal condemnation.

31 A judgement that was even more spiteful than it appears since Erich Korngold conducted without a fee. Any replacement drained yet more from the house's already exhausted coffers.

32 *Josephslegende* enjoyed an unwarranted run of nineteen performances during Strauss's tenure as director.
33 Except Strauss, who had cars in both Garmisch and Vienna.
34 *Der Ruinen von Athen.*
35 Doubtless due to Reinhardt's being a Jew.
36 Hofmannsthal joined the protest later.
37 Reinhardt owned a magnificent castle, Schloss Leopoldskron, outside Salzburg.
38 In October 1923 Hofmannsthal told Strauss that his quarterly German royalties – from operas, stage plays and books – had brought him the equivalent of two-and-a-half dollars.
39 Argentina, Uruguay and Brazil.
40 The schedule was no less intense – '*Salome* at 4 p.m., followed by *Elektra* at 9 p.m.' – but Strauss enjoyed himself.
41 An admirably contemporary selection.
42 A week earlier, the appointment as Chancellor and Foreign Minister of Gustav Stresemann heralded a process of internal reform and social improvement (as well as foreign reparation); but just three weeks later, after a series of violent confrontations and as a consequence of the worsening social conditions, General Ludendorff and a political activist called Adolf Hitler attempted a putsch in Munich which was violently suppressed, resulting in numerous arrests, including Hitler's.
43 To cultivate publicity, Strauss composed a march especially for the *Rosenkavalier* film.
44 As part of a Viennese 'Strauss Week'.
45 Colette's *L'Enfant et les sortilèges* was turned into an opera by Ravel between 1920 and 1924. It was first performed on March 21, 1925.
46 A reference to unleavened bread.
47 Karpath's attacks against Mahler and Schoenberg (who loathed him) doubtless endeared Karpath to Strauss, who used him as a middleman when his position in Vienna came under threat.
48 Since January 1923, the French were again extremely unpopular in Austro-Germany (in Cologne any French opera set in France was banned) and Rolland was welcomed only by Strauss.
49 Dresden had had a new Intendant, Alfred Reucker, since 1921.
50 Dedicated to 'My dear son Franz'.
51 Some scenes in *Intermezzo* last a mere three-and-a-half minutes.
52 In a letter to Webern on May 3.
53 Generalised interpretation.
54 In the course of *Pages from a Musician's Life* Busch describes Strauss as 'tall', 'lanky', 'stooping', 'insignificant', 'majestic', 'commonplace', 'unimportant', 'simple', 'earthbound', 'worldly' and 'a genius'.
55 Created in Dresden by Ernst von Schuch's granddaughter Liesel.
56 The real Anna was crushed to see herself portrayed in such an unkind light.

23 *Intermezzo*

1 At the time, the score of *Schlagobers* was valued at $10,000, that of *Rosenkavalier* at $25,000.

2 Then valued at $25,000.

3 For which he had borrowed money from his son's in-laws.

4 The equivalent of £300,000 in 1999.

5 He was finally handed the keys on December 11, 1925.

6 Wittgenstein lost his right arm during the First World War.

7 Michael Bohnen played Ochs, Huguette Duflos was the Marschallin.

8 By means of the new electrical (rather than acoustic) process.

9 Which numbered forty.

10 To Strauss, Hofmannsthal claimed this was a reaction to the general fear that everyone would clamour for works by the 'national composer' Hans Pfitzner.

11 Walter also conducted a new production of *Die Fledermaus*.

12 George Szell had conducted the Berlin première of *Intermezzo*, with Maria Hussa as Christine and Theodor Scheidl as Storch, on March 28, 1925.

13 Letter of January 17, 1927.

14 Rolland's diary entry, dated May 20, 1927, written after hearing Fritz Busch and the Dresden company give *Rosenkavalier* for the first time in Geneva.

15 He conducted a performance of the Ninth Symphony in Dresden as part of yet another 'Strauss Week'.

16 At the end of the month, someone very hostile to Strauss and/or his family rang the house in Garmisch to report that Richard had suffered a stroke while in Dresden. The family was deeply upset, especially Pauline.

17 All with the Berlin State Opera Orchestra.

18 Letter dated October 25, 1927.

19 Clemens Krauss and Karl Böhm were the only significant Austro-German conductors of the generation born in the 1880s and 90s to stand resolutely by Strauss throughout their careers.

20 This paranoia was greatly amplified when Schillings was ousted, in 1925, from his Berlin Intendancy by a Hungarian-born Jew – Leo Kestenberg. Schillings had not been successful in the post, and it was a miracle that he lasted six years; but he and the far Right saw things in a different light.

21 While on a train to Paris in 1927 Klemperer and Strauss happened to meet. The conductor told the composer that he intended to mount a production of Stravinsky's Latin-versed opera, to which Strauss sneered 'In Latein!'

22 Equivalent to £280,000 in 1999.

23 The other half went to Fritz Busch. *Helena* was published without dedication, but in 1931 Strauss 'gave' it to the Nazi conductor/administrator Heinz Tietjen.

24 Strauss went out of his way to secure this date: it would be his sixty-fourth birthday.

25 Strauss also played Lehmann and Jeritza off against one another – to such an extent that Lehmann never forgave Strauss his 'treachery'.

26 Approx. £20,000 in 1999.

27 Strauss anticipated this in a radio interview shortly before the first performance: 'There is always the danger that operatic libretti will be criticised before the music which goes with the text has been heard.'

28 Having travelled to Italy to recuperate.

29 This would, of course, seem to contradict Strauss's assertion to Busch that he had no choice but to give 'the general public ... what they want'.

30 A remarkable photograph survives in which Walter, Toscanini, Kleiber, Klemperer

and Furtwängler are captured standing uneasily next to one another.
31 Including *Manon Lescaut, Aida* and *Falstaff.*
32 It is worth noting that of the list of conductor/composers only two, Strauss and Furtwängler, met the racial/aesthetic requirements of the Nazi regime then crossing the threshold of German life. Just six years later Toscanini, Blech, Szell, Kleiber, Busoni, Hindemith, Walter, Ansermet, Klemperer and Stravinsky had all been expelled or escorted from the country.
33 The news of his son's death merely tipped Hofmannsthal over the edge of an illness that had been threatening his life for some time; Gerty had protected him from the prospect of a long and painful end, and he was indeed fortunate to have died so quickly and painlessly.
34 Count Harry Kessler, for example, confessed to his diary that the 'absence of Strauss himself and Max Reinhardt was unexpected'.
35 Hofmannsthal was buried in the Pfarrkirche in Rodaun.
36 Kleiber was an outspoken critic of Nazi racial policy.
37 An admirable plurality that led to Kleiber's exile by the Nazis.
38 Hörth was then Intendant in Berlin.
39 A sarcastic reference to Konradin Kreutzer's pot-boiler.
40 Strauss's relationship with Knappertsbusch also suffered. They had known each other since before the First World War. The composer had influenced the conductor's campaign to replace the 'undesirable' Bruno Walter at the Munich Opera in 1922 – since when Knappertsbusch had repaid his debt by keeping a regular flow of Strauss's operas in repertoire; but when, with negotiations under way for the première of *Arabella*, Strauss extended and then retracted the honour of the first performance to Knappertsbusch, their friendship was brought to an end. Despite the composer's attempts at reconciliation ('Kna – how can you be cross with *me?*' etc.), Knappertsbusch refused to have anything more to do with Strauss.
41 The German Foreign Minister.
42 To Pauline on October 31.
43 By the end of 1930, over 35 per cent of the German work-force was unemployed.
44 *Praktische Kulturarbeit im Dritten Reich.*
45 Arranged by Strauss many years earlier.
46 A character in Mozart's opera.
47 There are live recordings available of Strauss conducting his arrangement in Vienna in 1941.
48 Franz Schalk died on September 3, a day of national mourning in Austria, but which none the less brought no response from Strauss. He did not attend the funeral on the 5th.
49 Zweig was the best-selling biographer of his generation, and Hofmannsthal was so jealous of his young rival's success that Zweig was forced to throw his own parties at the Salzburg Festival so that he and Reinhardt would not be seen by Hofmannsthal to be collaborating *in animus.*
50 Zweig was in the audience, and wrote on August 26: 'Your *Fidelio* was brilliant! We were all entranced.'
51 Upper Bavaria, not far from Garmisch.
52 By the Deutsche Musikbuhne, in which Otto Klemperer's wife Johanna Geissler sang the role of Christine.

53   Klemperer's Krolloper had been closed in July the previous year. It has been sug-
     gested that Strauss spoke up for the venture, but there is no evidence that he did
     anything, either privately or officially.

24 *The Mighty Leverkühn*

1   Hans Pfitzner.
2   Schillings, in a speech to the KfdK in 1933.
3   An argument famously proposed by Richard Wagner in *Das Judentum in der Musik*
    (1851, rev. edn 1869).
4   To Zweig, on February 22, Strauss referred to Busch and Reucker as 'some of my
    most intimate friends and colleagues'.
5   All the more so since the performance had been mounted in honour of the fiftieth
    anniversary of the composer's death.
6   Klemperer conducted only two more performances of the opera, on February 26
    and March 1, before leaving Germany for good on April 5.
7   The petition was signed by the likes of Tino Pattiera and Maria Cebotari and such
    'respected' post-war luminaries as Paul Schöffler, Max Lorenz and Viorica Ursuleac.
8   Reichsverband Deutscher Tonkünstler und Musiklehrer (RDTM).
9   Louise Wolff was Berlin's most influential agent, and a major influence during the
    Weimar Republic. Although her two partners were Jewish, she was born a Christian.
    Her children were Jewish only on their father's side.
10 Then principal conductor of the orchestra.
11 It was really Walter's fee: Strauss would normally have been paid considerably
    more.
12 It was not the last time Goebbels would make this mistake.
13 Both men's dismissals carried Strauss's signature.
14 Mann continued: 'The Jews ... It is no calamity after all that Alfred Kerr's brazen
    and poisonous Jewish-style imitation of Nietzsche is now suppressed, or that the
    domination of the legal system by Jews has been ended ... I am beginning to
    suspect that in spite of everything this process [the persecution of the Jews] is one
    of those that have two sides to them ...'
15 Each of the remaining cast had signed the petition to remove Busch.
16 With Ursuleac, Käte Heidersbach as Zdenka and Jaro Prohaska as Mandryka.
17 *Arabella* also became one of Hitler's five favourite operas.
18 Conducted by Krauss, but with Lehmann in the title role. Toscanini was among
    the audience.
19 There is a recording of excerpts from a performance of this production, made on
    October 22, 1933, with the original cast of Ursuleac, Bokor and Jerger – conducted
    by Krauss – in splendid form.
20 Friedelind Wagner recalled that, having arrived, this petrol-guzzling monster was
    garaged. Thereafter, Strauss requested the use of one of Bayreuth's cars – for which
    he paid nothing, not even for the fuel.
21 They were later photographed together, smiling and shaking hands at a reception
    in Wahnfried.
22 Contrary to his reputation for speed and vitality, the Italian conductor's Bayreuth

performances of *Parsifal* in 1931 were the slowest on record – 4 hours, 48 minutes, not including intervals.

23 Having attended the first performance of the opera in 1882, Strauss believed he was reproducing Levi's original tempi – as validated by Wagner himself.

24 During Strauss's visits to Dresden and Bayreuth the Nazis had been hard at work restructuring German musical life (on June 20, Jewish concert/artist agencies were banned from taking any part in it; on August 17, the German Singing Association was 'cleansed' of all Jewish members) – a process that continued throughout what was left of the summer – when Strauss divided his time between taking the waters (September) in Bad Wiessee, and *Die Schweigsame Frau*.

25 In a letter to Pauline, Strauss reported meetings with Hitler and Goebbels, as part of their 'most intimate circle'.

26 When news of this was broadcast in America Toscanini reputedly announced, 'To Strauss the composer, I take off my hat. To Strauss the man, I put it on again.'

27 Gustav Havemann, Fritz Stein, Paul Graener, Gerd Kernbach and Heinz Ihlert.

28 Strauss, none the less, wrote to Zweig on January 21 that the post 'produces a lot of extra work'.

29 Whom Strauss gave power of attorney for, among other tasks, the removal of 'non-Aryans'.

30 With Jews occupying many of the more important positions of authority in concert management, publishing and broadcasting, their expulsion from German life left many significant vacancies – all of which had to be filled by 'true' Germans.

31 Fürstner emigrated to London in 1933.

32 As a young man, Strauss had on many occasions enjoyed lunch in the Wolffs' house on Rankestrasse, Berlin and was counted among friends of the family.

33 Vedder was dismissed on July 5, 1935 – again for embezzlement.

34 Vedder's first official action was to remove all Jews from musical positions in the provinces.

35 After leaving the RMK Vedder formed another agency, where he handled the careers of the young Herbert von Karajan, Clemens Krauss, Eugen Jochum, Wilhelm Mengelberg, Hans Swarovsky, Claudio Arrau, Benedetti Michelangeli, Franz Fischer and Georg Kulenkampff.

36 One of the edicts by which Strauss was determined to stand was his proposal that, in accordance with the stated wishes of the Wagner family, Bayreuth's exclusive right to perform *Parsifal* should be restored. A petition was raised, and Strauss made a personal request to Hitler while they were together in Bayreuth, but as more American musicians articulated their disgust at Nazi racial policy, and in view of Germany's departure from the ISCM (International Society for Contemporary Music), it would have been impossible to police such a measure outside Germany. To Strauss's great disappointment, his proposal was rejected.

37 The one unexpected, if short-lived, exception was the modernist Paul Hindemith.

38 Membership of the Association was compulsory – a law that was self-enforcing since, without membership, no German composer could be accepted by a German publisher. Application for membership had to be sent in writing to Strauss.

39 The president of the RTK (Reich Theatre Chamber).

40 To Otto Laubinger.

41 On June 11, 1935.

42 During the operatic season 1927–8, sixty new operas were performed in Germany's forty-seven most important theatres. In 1932–3 nine received their première.

43 In his memoirs Böhm denied any complicity, writing: 'I believe, in the course of my work in Dresden, as in Vienna later, I had always proved on which side I stood.'

44 At Hitler's expressed wish.

45 Famously during the 1936 Olympic Games.

46 This first night was attended by Zweig, who wrote to Strauss that the performance was 'extraordinary'. The British critics did not agree; but then, according to the writer, *Fidelio* had recently been dismissed as a 'novelty ... dull and tedious' – so what did they know!

47 See Chapter 25.

48 None the less, German radio constantly bracketed Strauss's name with those of Mozart, Beethoven and Wagner as if they, and he, provided confirmation of the continuing line of German creative excellence.

49 Which, none the less, only came because Toscanini had again refused to conduct in Germany while Hitler (who phoned him personally to ask him to change his mind) was in power.

50 The news was brought to Hitler by Goebbels while the Führer was in Bayreuth listening to Strauss conduct *Parsifal.*

51 Strauss also composed a delightful work for eight-part *a capella* chorus called *Die Göttin im Putzzimmer,* in which a woman tidying her bedroom manages to produce beauty and order from chaos and contortion!

52 Strauss was the most played living composer on German radio between 1933 and 1945.

53 These proposals were officially approved on January 29, 1935.

54 Like Strauss, Raabe was passionately idealistic in his views of German culture and the future of German music, but he took his anti-Semitism more seriously, and after July 1935 the RMK anti-Jewish proclamations increased in both vehemence and number.

55 A reference to the music, not the man.

56 The extravagance of the wedding provoked a great deal of private resentment: Goering gave his wife a piece of diamond jewellery costing 70,000 RM, she gave him a luxury yacht (with a 'people's cabin', that could be hired for 1600 RM), and Lufthansa made the couple a present of a private plane, costing 100,000 RM. The ceremony itself was said to have cost over 150,000 RM.

57 Strauss's description of Walter as a 'lousy scoundrel' has been the source of remarkable contention over the years. Most of the composer's biographers leave it out, as does Max Knight, the translator of the Strauss–Zweig correspondence into English. Kurt Wilhelm deliberately misquoted the words as 'greasy rascal', believing such terms less inflammatory.

58 While condemning Strauss as 'politically totally lacking in character', Goebbels's anger was directed at Rosenberg. They had been at each other's throats, mainly over cultural policy, since the early 1920s. When, in August 1934, Rosenberg publicly attacked Strauss for working with 'the artistic adviser to a Jewish emigré theatre' in Switzerland, Goebbels delighted in informing Rosenberg on the 25th that he was mistaking Stefan Zweig 'an Austrian Jew ... [for] the emigré Arnold Zweig'. This soured their relationship even further, and while Goebbels actually tried to defend

Strauss and his opera against attack – not least since Strauss was the president of Goebbels's RMK – Goebbels found himself in an unusually compromised situation. Strauss's letter to Zweig gave Rosenberg all the ammunition he needed to belittle the RMK and the Minister of Propaganda, who must have feared a resurgence of Rosenberg's earlier accusations in the *Völkischer Beobachter* (November 14, 1925) of 'pro-Bolshevist' tendencies and 'modernist' sympathies.

59 Instead of Zweig's name, it read 'Adapted from the English of Ben Jonson'.
60 Leading to his dismissal from Dresden.
61 As was each of Strauss's remaining operas.
62 But not Zweig, who was 'unable' to attend.

25 *The Unpolitical German I*

1 It is worth noting a few facts and figures: in a survey of orchestral performance trends between 1933 and 1945 Strauss was, by a huge margin, the most performed living composer in Germany. In the Reich's opera houses he was also the leading German figure, but between 1925 and 1933 his star had fallen so dramatically that not even *Rosenkavalier* could make it into a list of the twenty-five most performed operas in Germany. In the 1938–9 season, however, *Rosenkavalier* received a staggering 230 performances. The work of only one living composer (Mascagni's *Cavalleria rusticana*) was performed more often.
2 Norman del Mar: 'On 6th July 1935 he was expelled from the Reichsmusikkammer and thereafter treated with ostentatious disfavour.'
3 As evidence of which is the incredible statistic that *Rosenkavalier* received 123 performances in Germany during the 1935–6 season, making him by far the most performed living composer in Germany.
4 This being the common interpretation among Strauss's biographers.
5 The stone is a metaphor for the Weimar Republic.
6 Eugen Rostock-Huessey.
7 *Hymne an die Liebe* (Hymn to Love), *Rückkehr in die Heimat* (Return to the Homeland), and *Die Liebe* (Love).
8 Strauss's apologists invariably excuse his attitude by highlighting its ubiquity.
9 Strauss's vice-president at the RMK.

26 *The Unpolitical German II*

1 And also of burlesque. At the beginning of December he was sent a questionnaire by the RMK. In answer to the request 'Provide the names of two composers who would attest to your professionalism.' Strauss wrote, 'Mozart and Rich. Wagner.'
2 He none the less continued to work through the RMK until the war's end, holding his tongue and paying his annual subscription (one per cent of his income).
3 Sir Henry Morosus, a character in *Die Schweigsame Frau*.
4 His character in *Intermezzo*.
5 The situation at the opera was extremely tense. Knappertsbusch had been reported for making derogatory remarks about Hitler and, after refusing to join the Party, he had been threatened with dismissal. This threat became a reality on the 19th. He was succeeded by Clemens Krauss.

6   February 5–7, 11–12 and 17.
7   At a time when a middle-ranking civil servant could expect an annual salary of 3,600 RM.
8   August 1, 1936. The winter Olympic Games had been held in Garmisch.
9   Towards the end of the performance thirty-six doves were released into the air.
10 The fourth award went to an Italian, Liviabella.
11 On November 2 and 10.
12 After the interval Sir Adrian Boult conducted a performance of *Also Sprach Zarathustra*.
13 Which he reciprocated with an autograph of the first page of *Macbeth*.
14 He later changed these plans, and travelled 'direct, round-trip, by sleeping coach'.
15 Since 1936 Strauss had started composing during the winter as well as the summer – a change of routine that many attribute to the aimless character of *Friedenstag* and *Danae*.
16 As part of the summer festival.
17 Indeed, Toscanini conducted 40 per cent of the events.
18 Lehmann sang *Befreit* and *Freundliche Vision* at the first concert on August 1, and *Befreit*, *Freundliche Vision*, *Mainacht*, *Therese* and *O liebliche Wangen* at the second on August 20.
19 In his memoirs Böhm claimed that the postcard was of the Bernini statue of Daphne.
20 Böhm had revived Strauss's arrangement of Gluck's opera in Dresden.
21 This could easily be mistaken for a memoir of Mozart's working practices.
22 This might also be mistaken for a description of Saint-Saëns who, legend has it, could write music with his left hand, and script with his right.
23 In which capacity he was wildly successful. In January 1933 the Hitler Youth numbered 107,956. In January 1939, just six years later, it numbered 8,870,000.
24 NS-Kulturgemeinde (NS Cultural Community).
25 The inspiration for 'Entartete Musik' was the 'Entartete Kunst' (Degenerate Art') exhibition, held in Munich the previous year.
26 The exhibition included photographs and portraits, as well as music examples, with captions beneath each item. These were invariably designed to draw attention to questions of race rather than talent, so that Blanche's painting of Stravinsky was accompanied by the question, 'Who has spun the fairy-tale that Stravinsky is of Russian nobility?'
27 When Bartók heard of the exhibition he demanded to know why he and his music had been overlooked.
28 Furtwängler, like most of the country's leading musical talent, refused to have anything to do with the Reich Music Festival. A few months later, on December 11, he registered his disgust by conducting the German première of the Suite from Stravinsky's ballet *The Fairy's Kiss*. He repeated the work on December 12 and 13.
29 A few days later Strauss was given permission to attend the Lucerne Festival.
30 A few weeks earlier Strauss began work on the score of *Die Liebe der Danae*.
31 Who was keen for Strauss to benefit from the talents of his producer Rudolph Hartmann.
32 Ursuleac took the role so seriously that she would sing it through in its entirety immediately before going on stage for the performance.

33 It is surprising that Strauss did not suggest his own arrangement with Hofmannsthal.

34 Which argued the up-side of the Nazi mythologising of Austrian baroque theatricality.

35 After 1940 the apparently pacifist message of *Friedenstag* was considered incompatible with world events, and it fell from the repertoire. It has never recovered.

36 Böhm's now legendary company prevailed, however, and the first night was a musical and critical triumph (Gregor again did not attend), with the unfortunate exception of the title role, sung by Margarete Teschemacher, whom Strauss considered 'too Wagnerian' and over-loud. He informed Böhm of his preference for Maria Cebotari, who duly sang the role at the Berlin première in March the following year. Otherwise, the Dresden cast was matchless: Torsten Ralf sang the punishingly difficult, but heroically rewarding, tenor role of Apollo, Martin Kremer (Henry in the first *Schweigsame Frau*) soared above the comparably demanding tenor role of Leukippos, and Helene Jung glowed in the fleeting mezzo role of Gaea. Fanto's stage designs were said to be exquisite, with the final transformation of Daphne into a tree effortlessly beautiful. Strauss was delighted, even if – due to illness – Pauline had missed the first night. On their way to visit her after the performance Strauss turned to Böhm and remarked, 'Believe me, I really, really needed my wife. I actually have a lethargic temperament, and if it were not for Pauline, I shouldn't have done it all.'

37 Another explanation for its obscurity is that the final scene requires the producer to transform Daphne into a tree.

38 November 9 was the anniversary of the Munich Beerhall Putsch of 1923.

39 This was a private showing for those who had taken part. Strauss did not attend.

40 Fritz Stein gave a speech on February 9 in which he predicted a 'potential catastrophe', ostensibly because Nazi education policies were failing to take into account the needs of German musical life (resulting in a dramatic decline in the number of emerging instrumentalists), but also because of the vast Jewish artistic emigration.

41 This constituted the grandest Strauss Festival ever mounted in Germany.

42 Strauss attended the rehearsals and invited Karajan to breakfast to discuss the work. Typically, however, all the composer could manage was, 'You are much closer to it than I am, for whom it's so far in the past.'

43 Fritz H. Landshoff, of the publishers Querido Verlag.

44 Attended by Pauline, Franz, Alice and the grandchildren, Richard and Christian.

45 Wilhelm Jerger, manager of the Philharmonic Orchestra.

46 It is also possible that Hitler informed Strauss personally of his wish to withdraw *Friedenstag* from the repertoire – despite his own attraction to the work – since the opera's ostensible message was now almost comically at odds with governmental foreign policy. Either way, it was withdrawn after the first performance.

27 *Orpheus in the Underworld*

1 Memories of the confiscation of his savings in 1914 must also have resurfaced, although Strauss had learned from this painful lesson not to invest outside Germany.

2 Henceforth known by its published title, *Capriccio*.

3 Gregor hated Krauss not only for squeezing him out as Strauss's librettist, but also because of a number of Krauss's quite public allegations about him.

4 One of Strauss's last wartime journeys beyond the Austrian/German border.

5 Strauss's last work for a large orchestra.

6 As much is suggested by the headings of the five movements: Seascape, Cherry Blossom Festival, Volcanic Eruption, Attack of the Samurai and Hymn of the Emperor.

7 At the Japanese Embassy in Berlin.

8 *Capriccio* was given its Austrian première in January 1942, in Vienna, conducted by Strauss's nephew Rudolph Moralt.

9 Strauss dedicated the opera to Heinz Tietjen. This was Tietjen's second dedication.

10 Although he enjoyed a prominent post-war career as a conductor, it was as a translator, chiefly of Verdi's libretti, that Swarovsky was 'officially' engaged by Krauss.

11 Taken from one of Ronsard's *Amours*.

12 For string sextet.

13 Considering the weight of Krauss's responsibilities in Munich, to say nothing of his many guest engagements, it is a wonder that the text was completed as soon as it was.

14 Of *Capriccio* Norman del Mar wrote that Strauss's 'psychological rejuvenation could not have been more fortunate for it impacted directly upon his creative powers, opening up springs of a freshness which had not risen to the surface in years ... With the beautiful string sextet ... Strauss's marvellous Indian Summer period was triumphantly launched.'

15 Like *Falstaff*, *Capriccio* also centres around a mighty, cumulative fugue.

16 Verdi's last opera, widely considered to be his finest.

17 Nostalgia and denial clearly had a hand in Strauss's revision, in 1940, of *Guntram*.

18 Staged at the Weimar Nationaltheater, conducted by Paul Sixt, the musical consultant for the 'Entartete Musik' exhibition at the 1938 Reichsmusiktage.

19 Strauss dedicated *Capriccio* to 'My friend and colleague Clemens Krauss'.

20 Hans Hotter, none the less, told of one occasion when he and his wife visited Garmisch for a meal: Pauline had made soup, of which everyone had a bowl. After watching Pauline serve a second helping to the Hotters, Strauss timidly said, 'I'd like some more, too, please' to which Pauline snapped, 'You're not having any – there's a war on!'

21 Pauline.

22 In 1938 – and for much of the war – Funk was Hitler's Minister of Economics and general plenipotentiary for the war economy. During the war he hoarded and exploited bounty stolen from the Jews and occupied countries. At Nuremberg he denied any such actions. The tribunal did not believe him and sentenced him to life imprisonment.

23 As things turned out, it was the last performance.

24 March 9, 1942; Weinheber killed himself in 1945.

25 With a dedication to the baritone Alfred Poell and the soprano Viorica Ursuleac.

26 Their bodies were discovered on February 23.

27 Despite his assurances that there would be a 'dawn after the long night', Zweig patently did not believe this.

28 When, seven years later, the orchestra sent Strauss their congratulations on his eighty-fifth birthday, he presented them with a page of the sketches for his unfinished homage with the inscription: 'A few drops from the dried-up source of the Danube.'

29 At the Krolloper.

30 With Ursuleac singing and Krauss conducting the Berlin Philharmonic.

31 Heavily revised and conducted by Krauss.

32 He was being modest. Musically, *Capriccio* is an exquisite work, stuffed to overflowing with indelible melody and invention.

33 The Propaganda Minister's blessing was a prerequisite for any major festival and/or première.

34 Shortly before the première, on October 20, Strauss conducted a performance of *Daphne* (with Ursuleac) in Munich. It was to be his last ever performance at the National Theatre.

35 A heartthrob, created the 'Italian Tenor' in *Capriccio*.

36 Hans Hotter, bass-baritone.

37 With Ursuleac as the Countess, Horst Taubmann as Flamand, and Hotter as Olivier.

38 Strauss's concern for his income had been heightened since December 1941 when the attack by the Japanese on Pearl Harbor, and Germany's declaration of war against America, led to the freezing of royalty payments to all resident German composers.

39 Böhm moved to Vienna where he was appointed Director of the State Opera.

40 The first performance of *An den Baum Daphne* was given on January 5, 1947, in Vienna.

41 Frank was responsible for the murder of tens of thousands of Polish Jews. For his crimes he was executed in 1946.

42 Strauss also dedicated it to the Governor-General.

43 An air raid on October 31 reduced what was left of the National Theatre to rubble.

44 Dated January 13.

45 At which he invited Strauss to conduct.

46 In fact, Vienna's commemoration of Strauss continued throughout June, during which most of his operas and all his tone poems were performed.

47 Strauss recorded on to tape almost all of his symphonic poems with the Vienna Philharmonic Orchestra, a priceless collection that was all but completely destroyed by bombs in 1945.

48 Not least the destruction of the sets.

49 This was Strauss's last opera première; it was also the last opera première mounted under the auspices of the Third Reich.

50 The cast included Ursuleac (Danae), Horst Taubmann (Midas) and Hans Hotter (Jupiter).

51 Anna Glossner hardly 'upped and left'. She was suffering the advanced stages of cancer and wanted to die with her family, which she duly did in November.

52 Remarkably, these (sensational) performances survived the war and can now be heard on CD.

53 This is not to suggest that Hitler had no opposition. In 1939 German law upheld three capital offences. Three years later there were forty-two. It is also well to remember that over 1,000,000 'pure-blood' Germans were imprisoned in concentration camps.

54 Numerologists note: 12.3.45.

55 In whose works he buried himself throughout the last eight months of the war.

56 It is significant that, having devoted his life to the portrayal of extra-musical imagery, Strauss settled on Absolute music for the profoundest utterance of his life.

57 Both theories are buttressed by Strauss's refusal to attend the first performance in January 1946.

58 The second verse of *Niemand wird sich Selber kennen* ends with the line 'It's gone all right till now, so it may well go on to the end.'

28 *Im Abendrot*

1 Whose 'hero' was based upon the actor and Nazi collaborator Gustav Gründgens.

2 De Lancie was then with the Pittsburgh Symphony Orchestra.

3 Franz, Alice and the children had to remain in Germany.

4 Theodor Martin continued to work for the Strausses.

5 In his diary Strauss wrote, 'They deserved them.'

6 Roth later recalled: 'Strauss met me in the corridor, a little bent but still very tall, his face a little more wrinkled than I remembered it but otherwise hardly changed.'

7 Among their many visitors was Karl Böhm, who recalled the endurance of Strauss's defining obsession: 'He feared that German theatrical culture would never recover from the almost total destruction of the opera houses and felt himself to be rejected and superfluous.'

8 Strauss had become an Austrian citizen on January 31, 1947, which helped smooth his passage through Customs.

9 'From here the world looks like a patched-up coat.'

10 In the United States Strauss's visit to London provoked scorn. In an article headed 'Music lives on – the man forgotten', the *New York Herald Tribune* announced: 'At 83 Richard Strauss, the composer who thinks that music is all that counts, has gone to London to earn money. He needs it to pay his rent. If the world had kept a steady course, he might have been able to dream in some pleasant chimney corner. But as it worked out, there is no placid corner for him . . .'

11 Asked what he planned to do in the future Strauss replied, 'Well, to die.'

12 It is significant that, in their attempt to regenerate Strauss in the eyes of the British public, Roth and Beecham engaged a Jew to play the piano solo.

13 With Erna Schlüter and Elizabeth Höngen.

14 One of which has survived in a primitive recording.

15 The equivalent of £22,000 in 1999.

16 For clarinet, bassoon, strings and harp.

17 The Duett-Concertino was none the less dedicated to its inspiration, the bassoonist Hugo Burghauser, to whom Strauss wrote on December 16, 1946: 'I am busy with an idea for a double concerto for clarinet and bassoon, thinking especially of your beautiful tone.'

18 'To beloved Maria this last rose.'

19 It was first performed in January 1985.

20 To Willi Schuh, Strauss remarked that it came 'directly from above!'

21 Beethoven's utopian message of brotherhood and universal love had grown in significance for many of Europe's musicians since the end of the war.

22 Schirach was in prison.
23 This was part of a documentary on Strauss, *A Life for Music.*
24 In Paris a performance of *Friedenstag* was relayed from the Opera in honour of a Peace Conference due to begin the following morning.
25 The last time Strauss played the instrument.
26 At the Prinzregenten Theater.

Epilogue: A Life too Long

1   According to legend, Strauss was one of only two conductors – the other being Furtwängler – never to have been criticised by the Vienna Philharmonic's players.
2   Which is hysterically manifested whenever Jerger discusses the 'over-bred' Mahler. Jerger makes much of comparing the 'Golden Hun' Hans Richter to the 'dark ... gangly' and 'neurotic' Jew.

SOURCES

Allgemeine Musikzeitung, Berlin and Leipzig (various)
Bank of England, London
Bayerische Staatsbibliothek, Munich
Bayerische Staatsoper, Munich
Bayreuther Festspielbuch (various)
Berliner Tageblatt (various)
Boosey & Hawkes, London
British Library, London
Bulletins and Blätter of the International Richard Strauss Gesellschaft (various)
Colindale Newspaper Library, London
Daily Telegraph Archive, London
Decca Record Co., London
Deutsche Grammophon Ltd, London
Die Musik (various)
Encounter 31 (various)
Die Fackel (various)
German Historical Society, London
Gesellschaft der Musikfreunde, Vienna
Goethe Institute, London
History Today (various)
Imperial War Museum, London
Jewish Chronicle, London
Journal of the American Musicological Society
Journal of Contemporary History (various)
Koch International, London
Die Kunst (various)
La Monnaie/De Munt, Archive, Brussels
Landesarchiv, Bibliothek, Berlin
Logos (various)
London School of Economics, London
London Symphony Orchestra, London

Melos (various)
Musical Times (various)
Musik im Zeitbewustssein (various)
Neue Freie Presse (various)
Neues Wiener Journal
New York Metropolitan Opera, New York
New York Times, New York
Oper den Linden, Berlin
Opéra National de Paris, Archive, Paris
Österreichische National Bibliotechek, Vienna
Richard Strauss Society, London
Royal College of Music, London
Royal Opera House, Covent Garden, Archive, London
Royal Philharmonic Orchestra, London
Staadtsarchiv, Düsseldorf
Staadtsarchiv, Leipzig
The Times, Archive, London
Universal Edition, London
Zeitschrift für deutsche Bildung (various)
Zeitschrift fur Musik, Regensburg (various)

BIBLIOGRAPHY

Abendroth, Walter: *Hans Pfitzner*, Langen-Müller, 1935

Adami, Giuseppe (ed.): *Letters of Giacomo Puccini*, J. B Lippincott, 1931

Allday, Elizabeth: *Stefan Zweig, A Critical Biography*, W. H. Allen, 1972

Amory, Mark: *Lord Berners, The Last Eccentric*, Chatto & Windus, 1998

Anderson, Robert: *Elgar*, J. M. Dent, 1993

Antongini, Tom: *D'Annunzio*, William Heinemann, 1938

Austin, William W.: *Music in the 20th Century*, W. W. Norton, 1966

Avis, Styra: *Johannes Brahms, Life and Letters*, Oxford University Press, 1997

Bahr, Hermann: *Essays*, Insel, 1912

Bazzana, Kevin: *Glenn Gould, The Performance in the Work*, Oxford University Press, 1997

Bekker, Heinz and Gudrun: *Giacomo Meyerbeer, A Life in Letters*, Christopher Helm, 1989

Blackbourn, David and Eley, Geoff: *The Peculiarities of German History*, Oxford University Press, 1984

Blaukopf, Herta (ed.): *Gustav Mahler and Richard Strauss, Correspondence, 1888–1911*, Faber and Faber, 1984

Böhm, Karl: *A Life Remembered, Memoirs*, Marion Boyars, 1992

Boyden, Matthew: *The Rough Guide to Opera*, Rough Guides, 1997

Burleigh, Michael (ed.): *Confronting the Nazi Past, New Debates on Modern German History*, Collins & Brown, 1996

Busch, Fritz: *Pages From a Musician's Life*, Hogarth Press, 1953

Cardus, Neville: *Sir Thomas Beecham*, Collins, 1961

Carr, Jonathan: *The Real Mahler*, Constable, 1997

Clare, George: *Last Waltz in Vienna*, Macmillan, 1981

Coole, W. W. and Potter, M. F. (eds): *Thus Spake Germany*, Routledge, 1941

Craig, Gordon A.: *Germany, 1866–1945*, Oxford University Press, 1984

Crew, David F. (ed.): *Nazism and German Society, 1933–1945*, Routledge, 1997

Dallapiccola, Luigi: *Selected Writings*, Toccata Press, 1987

de la Grange, Henry-Louis: *Gustav Mahler, Vienna: The Years of Challenge*, Oxford University Press, 1995 de la Grange, Henry-Louis: *Gustav Mahler, vol. I*, Oxford University Press, 1974

del Mar, Norman: *Richard Strauss, A Critical Commentary on his Life and Works*, 3 vols, Barrie & Jenkins, 1978

Dizikes, John: *Opera in America, A Cultural History*, Yale University Press, 1993

Duchen, Jessica: *Erich Wolfgang Korngold*, Phaidon, 1996

Einstein, Alfred: *Essays on Music*, Faber and Faber, 1958

Eliot, T. S.: *Notes Towards the Definition of Culture*, Faber and Faber, 1918

Erhardt, Otto: *Richard Strauss, Leben, Wirken, Schaffen*, Otto Walter, 1953

Fifield, Christopher: *True Artist and True Friend, A Biography of Hans Richter*, Clarendon Press, 1993

Fischer, Klaus P.: *Nazi Germany, A New History*, Constable, 1995

Friedländer, Saul: *Nazi Germany and the Jews, vol. I: 1933–39*, Weidenfeld & Nicolson, 1997

Friedman, Richard Elliott: *The Disappearance of God, A Divine Mystery*, Little, Brown, 1997

Fröhlich, Elke (ed.): *Die Tagebücher von Joseph Goebbels, 1924–1941*, K. G. Saur, 1987

Furtwängler, Wilhelm: *Notebooks, 1924–54*, Quartet Books, 1989

Gardiner, Patrick: *Schopenhauer*, Penguin, 1963

Gay, Peter: *Freud, Jews and Other Germans*, Oxford University Press, 1979

Gay, Peter: *Weimar Culture, The Outsider as Insider*, Harper & Row 1968

Geissmar, Bertha: *The Baton and the Jackboot, Recollections of Musical Life*, Hamish Hamilton, 1946

Gilliam, Bryan: *Music and Performance During the Weimar Republic*, Cambridge University Press, 1994

Gilliam, Bryan: *Richard Strauss and His World*, Princeton University Press, 1992

Gilman, Sander L.: *Jewish Self-Hatred, Anti-Semitism and the Hidden Language of the Jews*, Baltimore, 1986

Gilman, Sander L.: *Difference and Pathology, Stereotypes of Sexuality, Race and Madness*, Ithaca, 1986

Goléa, Antoine: *Richard Strauss*, Flammarion, 1965

Gollancz, Victor: *Journey Towards Music*, Victor Gollancz, 1964

Grace, Helen: *The Legend of Salome and the Principle of Art for Art's Sake*, London, 1960

Gray, Cecil: *The History of Music*, Alfred Knopf, 1931

Gregor, Joseph: *Richard Strauss, Der Meister der Oper*, Piper, 1939

Groos, Arthur and Parker, Roger (eds): *Reading Opera*, Princeton University Press, 1988

Grunberger, Richard: *A Social History of the Third Reich*, Penguin, 1994

Hamm, Charles: *Music in the New World*, W. W. Norton, 1983

Heyman, Ronald: *Nietzsche, A Critical Life*, London, 1978

Heyman, Ronald: *Thomas Mann*, Bloomsbury, 1987

Heyworth, Peter: *Conversations with Klemperer*, Faber and Faber, 1985

Heyworth, Peter: *Otto Klemperer, His Life and Times, vol. I: 1885–1933*, Cambridge
  University Press, 1983
Hiden, John: *Germany and Europe, 1919–1939*, Longman, 1993
Hiden, John: *Republican and Fascist Germany, Themes and Variations*, Longman,
  1996
Hiden, John: *The Weimar Republic*, Longman, 1987
Hobsbawm, Eric: *The Age of Capital, 1848–1875*, Weidenfeld & Nicolson, 1995
Hobsbawm, Eric: *The Age of Empire, 1875–1914*, Weidenfeld & Nicolson, 1995
Hughes, Spike: *Opening Bars*, Pilot Press, 1946
Jefferson, Alan: *Elizabeth Schwarzkopf*, Victor Gollancz, 1996
Jefferson, Alan: *Lotte Lehmann, A Centenary Biography 1888–1976*, Julia MacRae,
  1988
Jefferson, Alan: *The Lieder of Richard Strauss*, Cassell, 1971
Jefferson, Alan: *The Life of Richard Strauss*, David & Charles, 1973
Jefferson, Alan: *The Operas of Richard Strauss in Great Britain, 1910–1963*, Putnam,
  1963
Jerger, Wilhelm, *Erbe und Sendung*, Wiener Verlag, Ernst Sopper & Karl Bauer, 1942
Jullien, Adolphe: *Richard Wagner, His Life and Works*, Paganiniana Publications,
  1981
Jungk, Peter Stephan: *A Life Torn by History, Franz Werfel, 1890–1945*, Weidenfeld &
  Nicolson, 1990
Kaminiarz, Irina: *Richard Strauss Briefe aus dem Archiv des Allgemeinen Deutschen
  Musikvereins 1888–1909*, Weimar, 1995
Kamper, D.: *Richard Strauss und Franz Wülner in Briefwechsel*, Cologne, 1963
Kapp, Julius: *Richard Strauss und die Berliner Oper*, Berlin 1925
Kennedy, Michael: *Mahler*, J. M. Dent, 1993
Kennedy, Michael: *Richard Strauss*, J. M. Dent, 1995
Kerman, Joseph: *Opera as Drama*, Faber and Faber, 1989
Kesten, Hermann (ed.): *Thomas Mann, Diaries, 1918–1921, 1933–1939*, André Deutsch,
  1983
Knight, Max (ed.): *A Confidential Matter, The Letters of Richard Strauss and Stefan
  Zweig, 1931–1933*, University of California Press, 1977
Korngold, Julius: *Child Prodigy – Erich Wolfgang Korngold's Years of Childhood*,
  Willard, 1945
Korngold, Luzi: *Erich Wolfgang Korngold*, Lafite-Verlag, 1967
Krause, Ernst: *Richard Strauss, The Man and His Work*, Collet's, 1964
Lambert, Constant: *Music Ho!, A Study of Music in Decline*, Faber and Faber, 1937
Laqueur, Walter: *Weimar, A Cultural History, 1918–1933*, Putnam, 1974
Laurence, Dan H. (ed.): *Shaw's Music: The Complete Musical Criticism of Bernard
  Shaw*, vol. I: 1876–1890; vol. II: 1890–1893; vol. III The Bodley Head, 1981
Lazare, Bernard: *Antisemitism*, Britons, 1967
Lee, Stephen J.: *Aspects of European History, 1789–1980*, Methuen, 1985
Lehmann, Lotte: *Singing with Richard Strauss*, Hamish Hamilton, 1964

Leiser, Clara: *Jean de Reszke*, Gerald Howe, 1933

Levi, Erik: *Music in the Third Reich*, Macmillan, 1994

Littlejohn, David: *The Ultimate Art, Essays Around and About Opera*, University of California Press, 1994

Magee, Bryan: *Confessions of a Philosopher*, Weidenfeld & Nicolson, 1997

Magee, Bryan: *The Philosophy of Schopenhauer*, Oxford University Press, 1983

Mahler, Alma and Mitchell, Donald (eds): *Gustav Mahler, Memories and Letters*, John Murray, 1973

Mahler-Werfel, Alma: *Mein Leben*, Fischer, 1960

Mann, William: *Richard Strauss, A Critical Study of the Operas*, Cassell, 1964

Marek, George R.: *Cosima Wagner*, Julia MacRae, 1981

Marek, George R.: *Richard Strauss, The Life of a Non-Hero*, Simon & Schuster, 1967

Martner, Knud (ed.): *Selected Letters of Gustav Mahler*, Farrar, Straus & Giroux, 1979

Messmer, Franzpeter: *Richard Strauss, Biographie eines Klangsauberers*, Zurich, 1994

Millington, Barry and Spencer, Stewart (eds): *Wagner in Performance*, Yale University Press, 1992

Murray, Isabel (ed.): *The Writings of Oscar Wilde*, Oxford University Press, 1989

Myer, Michael: *The Politics of Music in the Third Reich*, Peter Lang, 1993

Myers, Rollo (ed.): *Richard Strauss and Romain Rolland, Correspondence, Diary and Essays*, Calder & Boyars, 1968

Nattiez, Jean Jacques (ed.): *Orientation, Collected Writings, Pierre Boulez*, Faber and Faber, 1986

Newman, Ernest, *Richard Strauss*, The Bodley Head, 1908

Newman, Ernest: *Essays From the World of Music*, (2 vols), John Calder, 1976

Nice, David: *Richard Strauss*, London, 1993

Nietzsche, Friedrich: *Der Antichrist*, Ayer, 1974

Nietzsche, Friedrich: *Beyond Good and Evil*, Prometheus, 1989

Nietzsche, Friedrich: *The Birth of Tragedy*, Penguin, 1976

Nietzsche, Friedrich: *Thus Spake Zarathustra*, Penguin, 1961

O'Connor, Gary: *The Pursuit of Perfection, A Life of Maggie Teyte*, Gollancz, 1979

Osborne, Charles: *The Complete Operas of Richard Strauss*, Grange Books, 1988

Panofsky, Walter: *Richard Strauss, Partitur eines Lebens*, Piper, 1965

Parkinson, David: *The History of Film*, Thames & Hudson, 1995

Part, Philip: *Fritz Reiner, A Biography*, North-Western University Press, 1996

Potter, Pamela M.: *Most German of the Arts, Musicology and Society from the Weimar Republic to the end of Hitler's Reich*, Yale University Press, 1998

Prater, Donald: *Thomas Mann, A Life*, Oxford University Press, 1995

Prawy, Marcel: *The Vienna Opera*, Weidenfeld & Nicolson, 1969

Prieberg, Fred K.: *Musik im NS-Staat*, Fischer, 1982

Prieberg, Fred K.: *Trial of Strength, Wilhelm Furtwängler and the Third Reich*, Quartet Books, 1991

Reinhardt, G.: *The Genius: A Memoir of Max Reinhardt*, Knopf, 1979

Reuth, Ralf Georg: *Goebbels*, Constable, 1993

Riess, Kurt: *Wilhelm Furtwängler, A Biography*, Frederick Muller, 1955

Russell, John: *Erich Kleiber, A Memoir*, Seven Arts Book Club, 1958

Sachs, Harvey: *Arthur Rubinstein, A Life*, Weidenfeld & Nicolson, 1996

Sachs, Harvey: *Toscanini*, Robson Books, 1993

Sadie, Stanley (ed.): *The New Grove Dictionary of Music and Musicians, vols 1–20*, Macmillan, 1980

Safranski, Rüdiger: *Martin Heidegger, Between Good and Evil*, Harvard University Press, 1998

Said, Edward W.: *Musical Elaborations*, Chatto & Windus, 1991

Samson, Jim: *Music in Transition, A Study of Tonal Expression and Atonality, 1900–1920*, J. M. Dent, 1993

Schirach, Henriette: *The Price of Glory*, Frederick Muller, 1960

Schmisgall, Gary: *Literature as Opera*, Oxford University Press, 1977

Schopenhauer, Arthur: *The World as Will and Idea*, J. M. Dent, 1995

Schuch, Friedrich von: *Richard Strauss, Ernst von Schuch und Dresdens Oper*, Leipzig, 1953

Schuh, Willi and Trenner, Franz (eds): *Hans von Bülow and Richard Strauss, Correspondence*, Boosey & Hawkes, 1955

Schuh, Willi (ed.): *Richard Strauss, Recollections and Reflections*, Boosey & Hawkes, 1953

Schuh, Willi (ed.): *The Correspondence between Richard Strauss and Hugo von Hofmannsthal*, Collins, 1952

Schuh, Willi: *Richard Strauss, A Chronicle of the Early Years, 1864–1898*, Cambridge University Press, 1982

Scruton, Roger: *The Aesthetics of Music*, Clarendon Press, 1997

Sereny, Gitta: *Albert Speer, His Battle With Truth*, Macmillan, 1995

Sheehan, James J.: *German History, 1770–1866*, Oxford University Press, 1989

Shirakawa, Sam H.: *The Devil's Music Master, The Controversial Life and Career of Wilhelm Furtwängler*, Oxford University Press, 1992

Silvester, Christopher (ed.): *The Penguin Book of Interviews*, Viking, 1993

Solti, Sir Georg: *Solti on Solti, A Memoir*, Chatto & Windus, 1997

Specht, Richard: *Richard Strauss und sein Werk*, Leipzig, 1921

Splitt, Gerhard: *Richard Strauss 1933–35, Äesthetik und Musikpolitik zu Beginn der nationalsozialistischen Herrschaft*, Centaurus, 1987

Spotts, Frederic: *Bayreuth, A History of the Wagner Festival*, Yale University Press, 1994

Stachura, Peter D.: *The Shaping of the Nazi State*, Barnes & Noble, 1978

Stein, Erwin (ed.): *Arnold Schoenberg, Letters*, Faber and Faber, 1964

Steinberg, Michael P.: *The Meaning of the Salzburg Festival, Austria as Theater and Ideology, 1890–1938*, Ithaca, Cornell University Press, 1990

Steinitzer, Max: *Richard Strauss*, Schuster und Loeffler, 1911

Strauss, Richard: *Richard Strauss Edition* (18 vols), Boosey & Hawkes, 1996

Stravinsky, Igor and Craft, Robert: *Conversations with Igor Stravinsky*, Faber and Faber, 1959

Stuckenschmidt, H. H.: *Schoenberg, His Life, Work and World*, Schirmer, 1978

Stuckenschmidt, H. H.: *Arnold Schoenberg*, Calder Books, 1951

Taruskin, Richard: *Text and Act*, Oxford University Press, 1995

Taylor, Ronald (ed.): *Furtwängler on Music*, Scolar Press, 1991

Tenschert, Roland (ed.): *Richard Strauss–Joseph Gregor: Briefwechsel*, Otto Müller, 1955

Tenschert, Roland: *Richard Strauss und Wien*, Vienna 1949

Trenner, Franz (ed.): *Richard Strauss–Ludwig Thuille, Ein Briefwechsel*, Schneider, 1980

Trenner, Franz: *Richard Strauss, Dokumente seines Lebens und Schaffens*, Beck, 1943

Tuchman, Barbara W.: *The Proud Tower*, London, 1966

Wagner, Friedelind: *The Royal Family of Bayreuth*, Eyre & Spottiswoode, 1948

Wagner, Richard, *Wagner on Conducting*, Dover Publications, 1989

Wagner, Richard: *My Life*, Da Capo Press, 1992

Wagner, Wolfgang: *Acts, The Autobiography of Wolfgang Wagner*, Weidenfeld & Nicolson, 1994

Walter, Bruno: *Gustav Mahler*, Quartet Books, 1990

Walter, Bruno: *Theme and Variations*, Knopf, 1948

Warrack, John: *The Oxford Dictionary of Opera*, Oxford University Press, 1992

Weingartner, Felix: *Buffets and Rewards, A Musician's Reminiscences*, Hutchinson, 1937

Wilhelm, Kurt: *Richard Strauss, An Intimate Portrait*, Thames & Hudson, 1889

Williamson, John: *The Music of Hans Pfitzner*, Clarendon Press, 1992

Wood, Henry J.: *My Life of Music*, Victor Gollancz, 1946

Woodhouse, John: *Gabriele D'Annunzio, Defiant Archangel*, Clarendon Press, 1998

Wulf, Joseph: *Musik im Dritten Reich*, Ullstein, 1983

Zweig, Stefan: *The World of Yesterday*, Cassell, 1943

ACKNOWLEDGEMENTS

Hundreds of people have played a part in the genesis of this book. Most are staff at the associations, organisations and societies recognised on pp. 406–7. I apologise in advance to anyone who finds themselves unjustly omitted.

To begin with, I owe a debt of appreciation to Ion Trewin and Rebecca Wilson at Weidenfeld & Nicolson, for giving me the opportunity to satisfy my life's ambition. I would also like to thank my agent and oracle Mandy Little for her support, faith and continuing encouragement. For their judgement, intelligence, kindness and holistic contributions to my thesis and its development in this book I would like to thank Angelo Villani, one of the finest musicians it has been my privilege to know; Keith Burstein, possibly England's most gifted young composer; and Alan Jefferson, the doyen of British Strauss scholars and a man of peerless wisdom, learning and generosity. The manuscript would have been much the poorer and considerably less cogent without Elsbeth Lindner, for whose intuition and intelligence as editor I am deeply grateful. For his company and friendship, and for our many tireless hours at the piano, I would like to salute the memory of Neil Vint.

I would not have been able to write this book – literally and practically – without my parents, John and Bette, and not one of the photographs would have found their way between the covers had not my mother devoted so many hours to her work as picture researcher-cum-detective.

The following also made valuable individual contributions, many of which opened more doors than I was able to walk through: Malcom Smith, Janis Süsskind, Lloyd More, and everyone at Boosey & Hawkes. Libby Rice (London), John Heidrich (London), Francesca Franchi (London), Anna Charin (London), Jane Birkett (London), Jo Nicholson (London), Rachel Leyshon (London), Professor Richard Overy (London), Professor David Welch (London), Professor Mary Fulbrook (London), Mike Coleman (London), Richard Goldsmith (London), Carlos Kleiber (Munich), Gilles Lebrund (Brussels), Janik Vermiersch (Brussels), Marcus Poyet (Paris), Robert Schwartz (New York), Anthony Holden (London), David Morley (Munich), Dr Irene Kohl (Vienna), Amy Turner (Oxford), Felix Aprahamian

(London), Bette Gilbert (London), Dettef Eberhard (Munich), Joanna Ste-ichen (New York), George Burr (Fife), Ursula Niebergall (Marburg), Dr Christian Strauss (Garmisch), Elbe Lebrecht (London), Bettina Buckholz (Berlin), Sandy Hulton (London), Tom Norden (Canterbury), Susanne Hillen (London), Angelo Villani (Melbourne), Maurus Pacher (Geertruidenberg), Neil Black (London), Roger Kabin-Boye (Alfriston).

For their friendship, and for keeping me and my work afloat during its two-year gestation, I would like to thank Jo Littlefair, Jo Ince, Dixie Stewart, Girish, Punam and Saga Waze, Tahnee Wade, Joanna Price, Brian and Kath Watterson, Jo Smart (and all the little Smarties), Rosemary and Ernest Brad-shaw, Anne Wallace, Gareth Edwards and Ruth Summerfield.

Finally, three people made contributions to this book that serve as a pale reminder of their wider benefit to my life: Jonathan Buckley, whose heart may almost be as grand as his talent, and whose intellect serves as an enduring inspiration, David Summerfield, the godfather of this book and its spiritual and academic guide from start to finish, and Lorraine Bradshaw, for whom Strauss might have written his most beautiful music.

INDEX